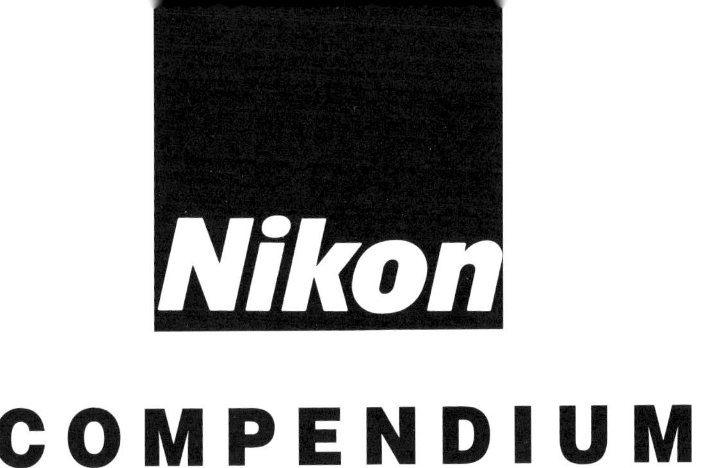

COMPENDIUM

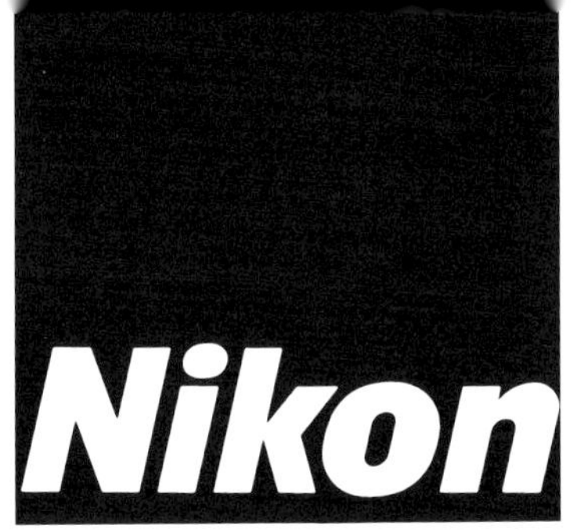

COMPENDIUM

Handbook of the Nikon System

HOVE
BOOKS

Nikon Compendium

by Rudolf Hillebrand and Hans-Joachim Hauschild

First English Edition April 1993

Hove Books
34 Church Road, Hove
East Sussex BN3 2GJ

English translation and additional text: *Rolf Krueger*

Editor: *Dennis Laney*

Design and typesetting: *Facing Pages*

Cover photo: *Erwin Stegmann*

Printed in Wales by Macdermott & Chant Ltd., Welshpool

British Library Cataloguing-in-Publication Data
A catalogue record for this book is available from the British Library

ISBN 1 897802 02 1

U.K. trade distribution
Fountain Press Ltd.
Queensborough House
2 Claremont Road
Surbiton
Surrey, KT6 4QU

Distribution in U.S.A.
The Saunders Group
21 Jet View Drive
Rochester, N.Y. 14624-4996
Fax: (716)328-5078

Distribution in Canada
Amplis Foto Inc.
22 Telson Road
Markham, Ontario L3R 1ES
Fax: (416)477-2502

Acknowledgements

This Nikon Compendium is the result of extensive research on the basis of the material made available to us. We would like to express our gratitude to a number of people who have contributed to the realisation of this book: Dietrich Exner, Rolf Krueger, and especially Daniela Glauerdt from Nikon Germany in Düsseldorf who were a great help in gathering data and information, as well as Renato Gerussi and Marco Rosenfelder from Nikon Switzerland in Ksnacht. Jochen Beyss and Peter Braczko readily allowed us to photograph parts of their collections. We owe special thanks to Rosmarie and Adrian Bircher for their creative assistance and much more.

Publisher's Note

The publisher would like to specifically thank Rolf Krueger for his English translation and for his help in supplying the additional material which brings this book right up to date.

Contents

Introduction

The Nikon SLR-system is and always has been unique. This short and simple statement sums up a camera system and its manufacturer's philosophy which for the professional and commited amateur has provided access to a system of limitless possibilities and features. No photographic situation or task, however difficult, could not be accomplished with the flexible, not to say adaptable Nikon equipment. The Nikon SLR-system stood and stands for reliability in any situation without exemption – in professional photography, for example in tough on-the-spot reporting that might best be described as a form of "infighting", in fast-moving sports photography with the longest telephoto lenses, in severe cold that tends to put the photographer out of action before his equipment, as well as in scientific applications with their own special demands. For the professional who must master his daily assignments to the satisfaction of his clients, his Nikon is an indispensable neccessity.

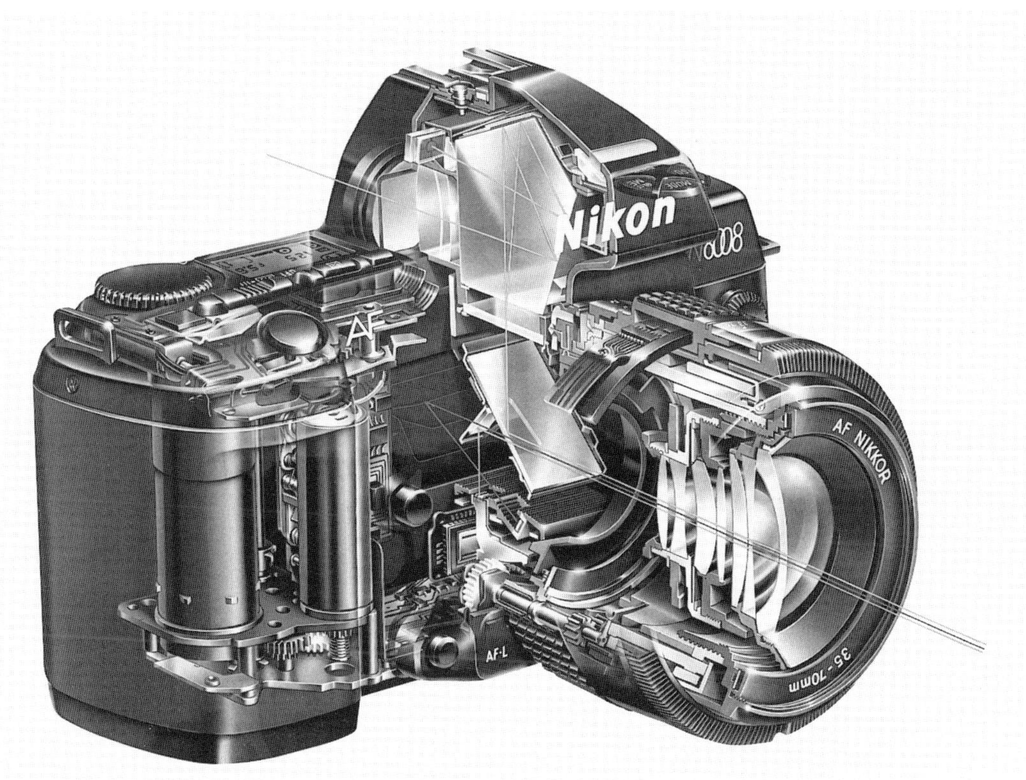

Demonstrating tradition as well as innovation: the Nikon bayonet has ensured compatibility throughout the decades right into the autofocus era.

If a professional takes this approach why shouldn't the ambitious amateur photographer, and also take advantage of the proverbial Nikon quality, the technical advantages, and the much-praised robustness for his purposes? Especially since his position differs only in one basic point from that of the pro: the latter has to earn his living with his camera while the amateur photographer can work free of the pressures of assignments without having to justify himself to anybody. That does not mean that he should be satisfied with anything less than his professionally orientated colleague. The dedicated pursuit of photography as a hobby in one's spare time is just as demanding of a modern camera system's features and possibilities which must ensure easy and reliable operation in every respect.High-sounding phrases? Admittedly, yes – but they represent reality and need not be proven here. Countless photographers around the world, from the professional side as well as from the army of hobbyists are living proof of this.

What could be a clearer confirmation for a supplier like Nikon than the customers' decision in favour of Nikon products? The Nikon system, of which the foundation was laid in 1959 with the legendary and trend-setting Nikon F – numerous examples of which continue to stand up to their daily tasks even today – has been refined and advanced throughout the more than three decades that have passed since then.

Always being aimed at the needs of its users and constantly being adapted to the latest possibilities offered by technology, a large family of cameras has emerged which have one thing in common besides their individual qualities. This is an unsurpassed consistency in terms of compatibility of the whole system to this very day. Even the advent of automatic focusing, which wasn't invented by Nikon in its

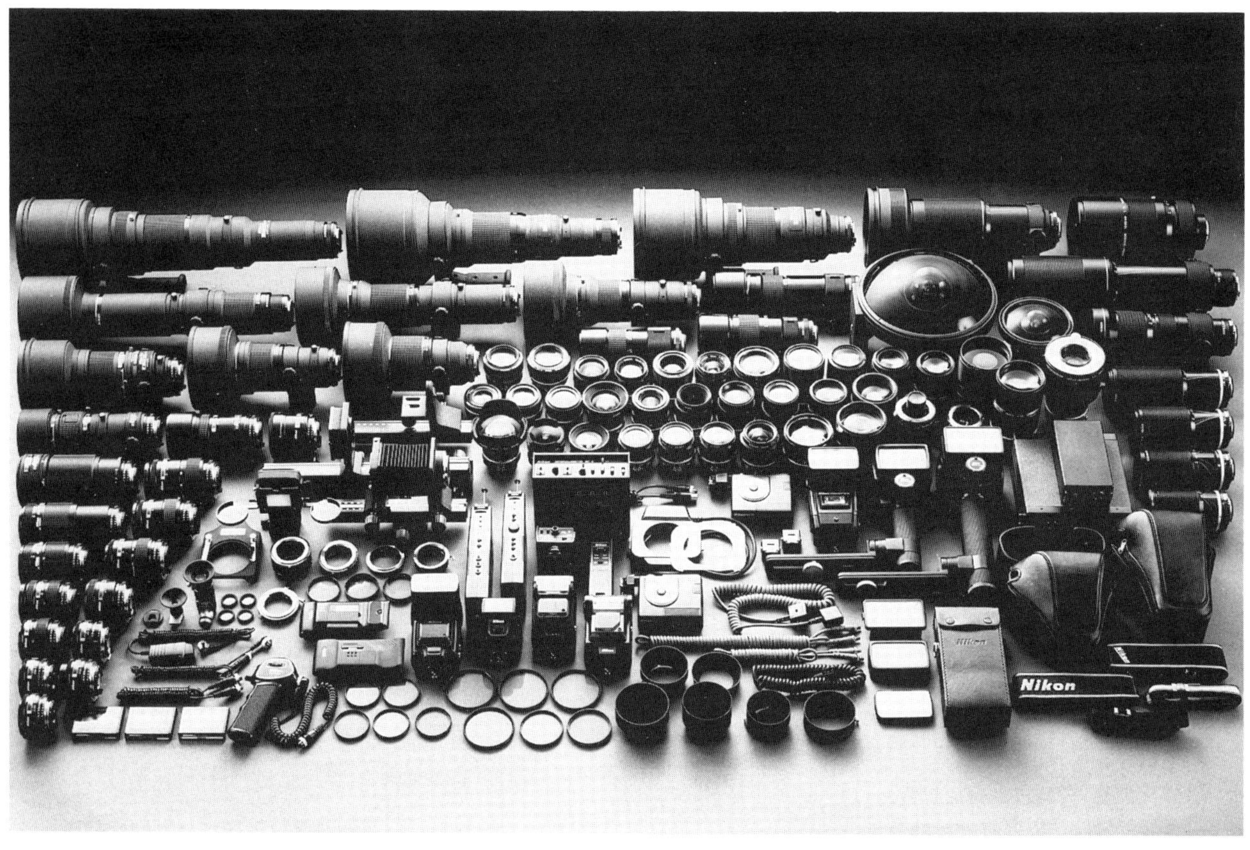

Nikon offers the most extensive professional camera system in the world. Appropriate accessories are available even for unusual tasks.

presently realised form although they contributed decisively to its development, propagation and constant improvement, did not break this chain of compatability. It was precisely this technical development that led almost all the other camera makers, except Nikon, to abandon their more or less consistently pursued idea of compatibility. The modern F4 with its fascinating technical possibilities allows even the oldest F-type lenses to be used – with a few exemptions; and vice-versa. So it`s no wonder that Nikon products are as popular as ever.

It cannot have come as a surprise either that the Nikon system – due to its openness to even the most extraordinary accessories – is second to none in terms of intricacy and versatility. In addition, whereas the array of products was initially mainly aimed at professionals, the program has long since been expanded to include camera models and further equipment of widespread popularity. It is obvious that such a system can only be fully understood and utilised by those completely informed about every part as well as all the possible combinations.

This book`s goal is to supply you with just this information – a general account of every single Nikon product within its scope from the very beginning to the present. We intend this to be a description of the individual camera models, lenses, and accessories as well as an outline of the countless combinations possible between them. We have included within the Compendium many detailed tables to illustrate this. In addition to the individual descriptions, the tables will quickly supply you with reliable answers to even the unusual questions which neccessarily arise in the face of such a number of combinations. This precise information will put you in the position to rule out any uncertainty in the event of future acquisitions and enable you to make use of every one of the features of your Nikon equipment. It would indeed be too bad if you were only able to take advantage of just a fraction of its fascinating possibilities.

CHAPTER 1

The Early Years 1917–1958

The Nikon story began in the year 1917 when three small companies involved in the optical industry – Tokyo Keiki Seisaku Sho, Iwaki Glass Manufacturing and Fujii Lens Seizo Sho – merged to form Nippon Kogaku K.K. The deal was accomplished through the existing Mitsubishi Trust, which still owns Nikon today. Translated, "Nippon Kogaku" from which the brand name "Nikon" was formed, means simply "Japanese Optical Company". The Ohi plant was established in 1918 in Tokyo and is still Nikon's headquarters and is where the F3, for example, is assembled and the research and development department is situated. To start with, staff numbered 200, including, in 1921, eight German technicians. However, Nikon was not initially a camera manufacturer but, like Zeiss and Leitz, primarily a producer of optical instruments. Its first large customer was the Japanese army to which it supplied sights, binoculars, and periscopes.

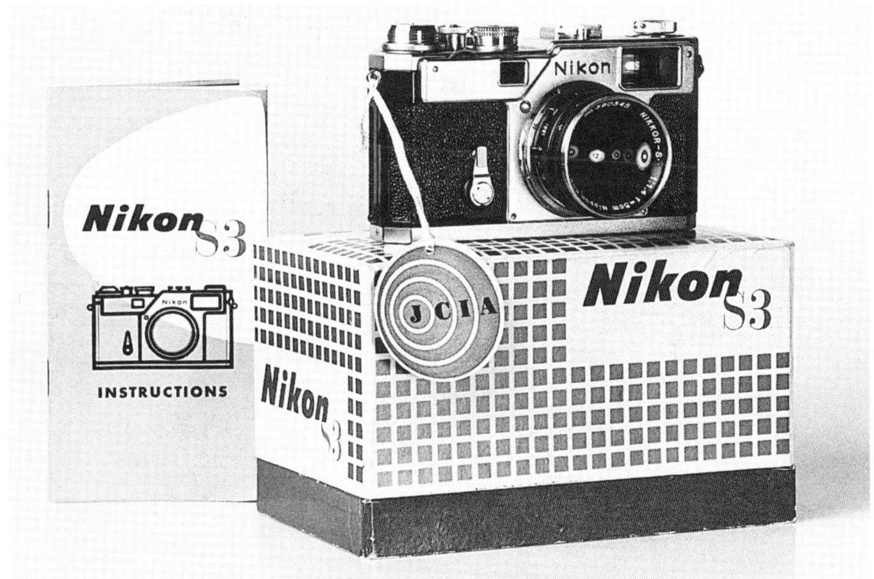

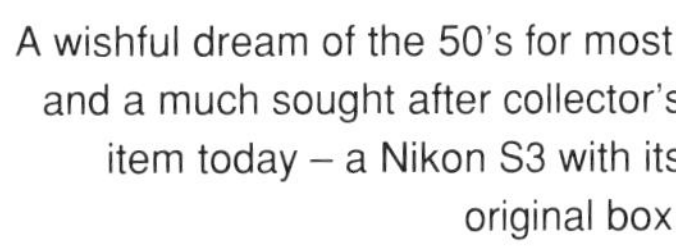

A wishful dream of the 50's for most, and a much sought after collector's item today – a Nikon S3 with its original box.

The Way It All Began

The first non-military products, three telescopes with effective diameters of 5, 7,5, and 10cm, were introduced in 1921. In 1923 it was decided to set up a glass research laboratory in order to ensure technological independence. The first microscopes were sold under the brand name "Nikko". In 1932 production of the first camera lenses began, named "Nikkor" as now. They were supplied to camera manufacturers in focal lengths between 50mm and 700mm and included quite fast ones for those days, such as the 500mm,f/4,8 for plate cameras. A number of 50mm lenses with maximum apertures between f/4,5 and f/2,0 for the 35mm-format were developed in 1937. The order came from another young company, the "Seiki Kogaku Precision Optical Research Institute" which was looking for top-quality lenses for its "Hansa Kwanon" camera. Today this company's name "Canon" is also a synonym for first-class advanced cameras. In the same year the first enlarging lens called "Hermes" was introduced.

During the ensuing years leading up to and during the Second World War production was almost entirely devoted to the needs of the arms industry. In the aftermath of the war Nikon had to close down all but one of its factories – its headquarters in Ohi. After the war it was decided to manufacture cameras as well as lenses. A twin-lens 6x6cm or a 35mm model were the disputed alternatives. As we all know, the latter option luckily turned out to be the winner. Nikon's subsequent contribution to 35mm photography cannot be underestimated.

The Rangefinder Cameras

In 1948 the Nikon I was introduced with a film-format of 24x32mm. Even then there were attempts to get away from the not very advantageous aspect ratio we still have today.

The outer appearance of the Nikon I is strongly reminiscent of the Zeiss Contax II, in fact it even has the same bayonet lens mount. But on the inside Nikon's firstborn bears far more resemblance to the Leica IIIa, especially the shutter mechanism. It came equipped with a standard Nikkor 50mm lens,

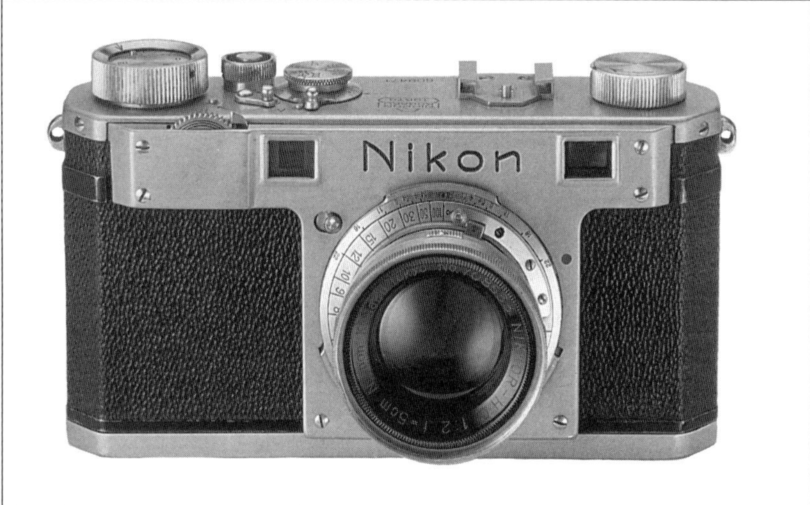

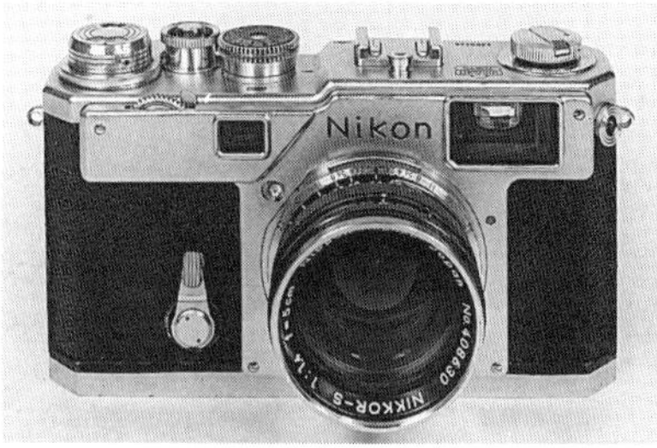

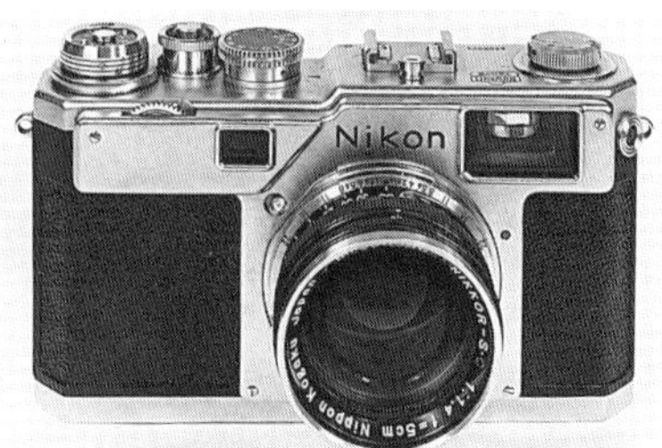

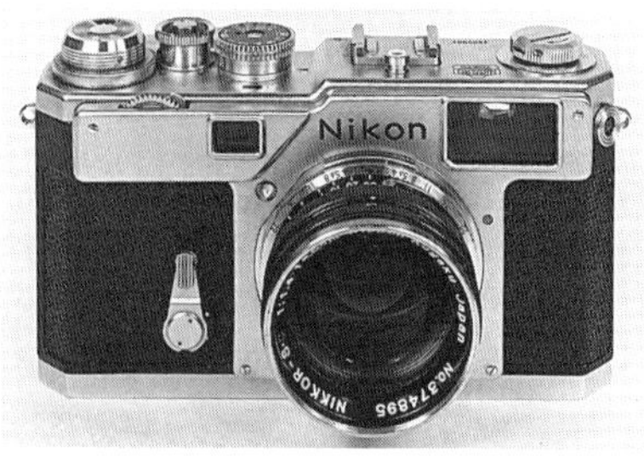

Four of the rangefinder classics that laid the foundation for Nikon's world fame and also represent the starting point for the successful SLR models. The German Contax cameras served as models for the Nikon rangefinders which at least equalled them in quality. At the top the very first, the Nikon I which served as the basis for the following models. Below are the Nikon S3 and S4,and at the bottom the S3M with its 24x34mm format.

either f/2 or f/3.5, and a split-image rangefinder and fell into place as the first in a long line of top-notch cameras. It should be mentioned that the rangefinder is incorporated into the viewfinder – so you do not have to focus first before determining your final framing through a separate finder, as was usually the case at the time.

Shutter speeds from 1/500 to 1 sec. can be set on two dials, one located on top of the other. A knob advanced the film; a rapid-wind lever was only devised later. There was no self-timer or flash socket.

According to Nikon experts, a mere 739 specimens of the model No.1 were produced. Thus it is a true rarity commanding high prices from collectors.

Nikon M – Two More Millimeters

In 1949 Nikon's second model was introduced – but rather than carrying the number "II" as might have been expected, it was named Nikon M. Since the 24x32mm-format had not met with any mentionable degree of acceptance, it was at first stretched to 24x34mm. As this dimension was half-way between that of the first model and the usual 35mm-format of 24x36mm they confusingly called it "medium format", which led to the "M" in the name. Except for a few details, its features are the same as those of the Nikon I. In the 50's Nikon became an insider's tip among professional and demanding amateur photographers, but due to the quality of its lenses rather than its cameras.

Besides the 50mm lenses, two more focal lengths became available for the Nikon I, a four-element 35mm,f/3.5 and a 135mm,f/4. Then, along with the Nikon M, a 85mm,f/2 was introduced which became one of the reasons leading to Nikon's world fame. The following story explains why.

In the early 50's the Korean war was raging and Tokyo was the starting-point for the reporters covering it for the big news magazines. Almost all of them used Leicas or Contaxes. Nikon offered their lenses with both mounts – the Nikon/Contax bayonet or the 39mm screw thread. David Douglas Duncan, probably one of the best known photojournalists of his time, was working for *Life* magazine. He happened to be confronted with a 85mm,f/2 Nikkor, put it to a test and was enthusiastic about its excellent image quality. Within a very short time all the staff photographers from *Life* were equipped with Nikkor lenses: the foundation of a legend was laid. The first 50mm,f/1.4 appeared that same year, opening up areas of photography not feasible before, thanks to its extremely fast maximum aperture.

After the production of only 3200 Nikon M's it was replaced in 1951 by the Nikon S – "S" possibly standing for the flash "sync" terminal included this time. This is not the standard DIN-terminal we are familiar with today but a special one with two sockets. It was designed for flash bulbs because electronic flash units were not yet available. The Nikon S was Nikon's first best-seller. In 1953 Nippon Kogaku (U.S.A.), the first subsidiary, was founded in New York. In the same year new optical delicacies appeared, a 28mm,f/3,5 and a 85mm,f/1,5. Within only three years more than 35,000 S-models were manufactured – Nikon was well on the way to becoming a mass-producer.

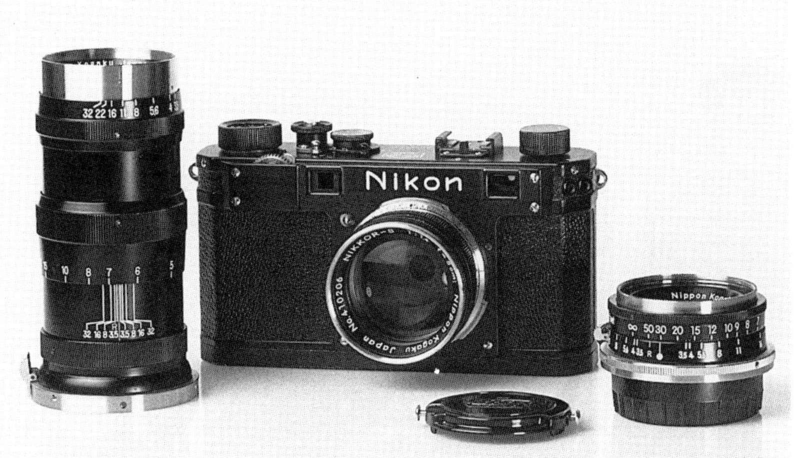

A bestseller from 1951: The Nikon S along with the interchangeable lenses 135mm,f/3.5 and 35mm,f/3.5.

In 1954 the time had come for Nikon to bow to the popularity of the 24x36 format with the introduction of the Nikon S2, which also featured some changes in details. The most obvious as well as most practical is the film winding lever that put an end to the tedious turning of a knob. Rewindiong is quicker too, with a folding rewind crank providing faster and easier film changing situated on the opposite side of the body.

The shutter speed range was extended to 1/1000 sec. and thanks to the new flash terminal it became possible to use electronic flash units. Speeds up to 1/60 sec. are synchronized and marked with an "X" on the shutter speed scale.

The viewfinder system was also improved. An extremely large eyepiece ensures pleasant viewing and at the same time the split-image rangefinder can be controlled much better. As a matter of taste the Nikon S2 offered a choice between chrome and black versions for the first time. Alogether some 50,000 were built, which makes it the Nikon rangefinder camera with the highest production numbers. The lens programme also continued to grow. In addition to a 105mm,f/2.5, a wide-angle with a focal length of 25mm was added to the family, while things were happening in the telephoto range too. Two longer lenses, a 180mm,f/2.5 and a 500mm,f/5 were introduced. Naturally the camera's viewfinder cannot be used with these long focal lengths and a mirror-box mounted between lens and camera becomes neccessary in order to control framing and focusing. Even though the lens programme available by then hardly left room for any wishes compared to other makes, Nikon was constantly anxious to enlarge it. Progress was also constantly being made in terms of maximum aperture and in 1956 two really superfast lenses appeared; a 35mm,f/1.8 and a 50mm,f/1.1. In addition the macro range was made accessible with the first Micro-Nikkor 55mm,f/3.5 which covered the distances between 0,45m and infinity. At that time it was a real sensation since the distance range of the lenses available then usually ended at about one meter. The rarest lens is without question the Stereo-Nikkor 35mm,f/3.5 which yields two 17x24mm pictures on one 24x36mm frame. Of course a special viewfinder was available as well as a stereo viewing gadget.

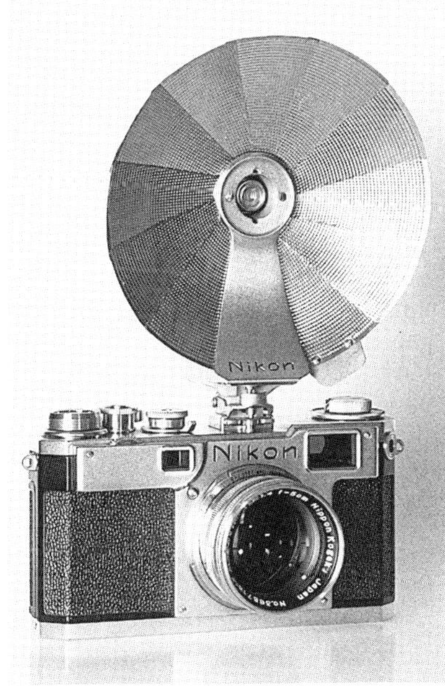

The S2 – the first Nikon with the 24x36mm picture format.

Nikon SP – Preparing For The F

The Nikon SP, the new supercamera, was introduced in 1957. The "P" most likely stands for the "professional" at whom the camera was aimed. To many, the Nikon F appearing two years later is nothing more than an SP with a built-in mirror-box. This point of view cannot be completely ruled out – after all the controls on the top right of both cameras are nearly identical.

There is only one dial for all the shutter speeds from 1/1000 to 1 sec. The exposure counter resets to zero automatically whenever the camera back is opened, making operation easier by eliminating a source of error which can always happen during hectic work.

For the first time shutter blinds made from titanium foil were employed, just as in the later F-models. No doubt, though, the most exiting new feature was the first battery-powered motor drive which enables the SP to advance the film continuously up to a rate of 3 frames per second. Its code is S 36, later changed to F 36 for the Nikon F. A bulk-film camera back for up to 250 exposures is supposed to have existed for the SP, but strangely enough, this cannot be verified today. A selenium exposure-meter, to be mounted on the top of the camera and connecting with the shutter speed dial, was also new. The viewfinder system was equipped

Nikon Rangefinder Cameras

Camera-model	Frame size (mm)	Date of introduction	Product. figs. (approx.)	Shutter speeds	View-finder magnif.	Finder frames for:	Film advance	Synch. terminal	Self-timer	Motor-drive coupling
Nikon I	24 x 32	1948	739	1/20 - 1/500; 1 - 1/8	0.6x	50 mm	Rotating knob	—	—	—
Nikon M	24 x 34	1949	3200	1/20 - 1/500; 1 - 1/8	0.6x	50 mm	Rotating knob	— *	—	—
Nikon S	24 x 34	1951	35200	1/20 - 1/500; 1 - 1/8	0.6x	50 mm	Rotating knob	M	—	—
Nikon S2	24 x 36	1954	56715	1/30 - 1/1000; 1 - 1/15	1.0x	50 mm	Rotating knob	M + X 1/60	+	S 36
Nikon SP	24 x 36	1957	22350	1 - 1/1000	1.0x	28/35; 50; 85; 105; 135 mm	Advance lever	M + X 1/60	+	S 36
Nikon S3	24 x 36	1958	14310	1 - 1/1000	1.0x	35; 50; 105 mm	Advance lever	M + X 1/60	+	S 36
Nikon S4	24 x 36	1959	5900	1 - 1/1000	1.0x	50; 135 mm	Advance lever	M + X 1/60	—	—
Nikon S3M	17 x 24	1960	195	1 - 1/1000	1.0x	35; 50; 135 mm	Advance lever	M + X 1/60	+	S 72

* Sometimes fitted later

with frames for focal lengths between 28mm and 135mm as a standard feature. The finder frames for 50mm, 85mm, 105mm and 135mm can be selected by means of a dial located beneath the rewind crank. A separate optical finder displays the frames for 35mm and 28mm, but in addition also conveys a wideangle perspective. A finder illuminator was also available as an accessory so that the photographer can stay in control even in poor lighting conditions. The sync-speed was raised slightly from 1/50 to 1/60 sec. and the SP was also equipped with a self-timer.

A lower priced version for the amateur, the Nikon S3, was introduced in 1958, succeeding the S2. The expensive switchable finder frames were sacrificed in favour of fixed frames for 35mm, 50mm and 105mm. Otherwise the features remained the same as those of the SP.

Despite these advances, the high time of rangefinder cameras was inevitably coming to an end, the market called for a single lens reflex. The legendary Nikon F finally appeared in 1959 and at the same time a less expensive alternative in the form of the Nikon S4 was offered which was developed by further simplifying the S3. It was not to become a success, perhaps because the American subsidiary did not include it in its

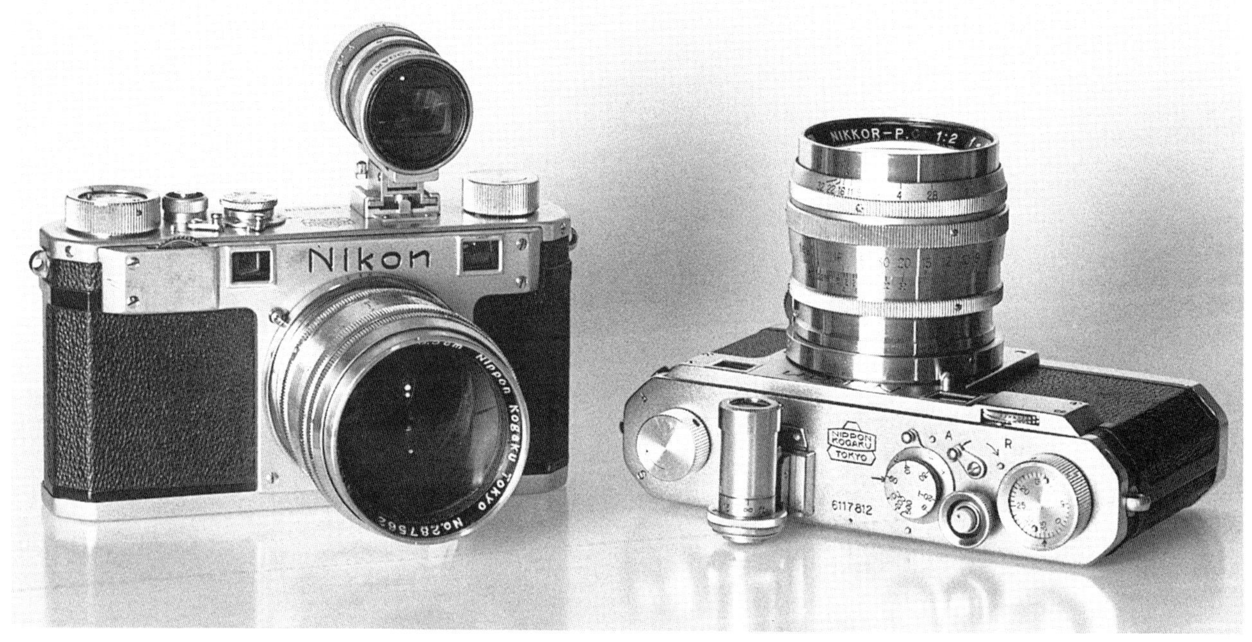

Two cameras with an obsolete picture format – the Nikon M and the Nikon S with their 24x34mm frames.

catalogue. A mere 6000 customers chose an S4 instead of saving for an F or an SP. The only features missing in the S4 are the self-timer, the motor drive coupling, and the automatic resetting of the frame counter back to zero.

Nikon's last rangefinder camera is also the rarest. Just 200 examples of the Nikon S3M left the assembly lines in 1960. This is a 17x24mm half-frame model based on the S3. Delivered only in black finish, it achieved the then extremely high continuous film advance speed of up to 4.5 frames per second with the assistance of the S-72 motor drive derived from the S-36.

The lens program by then consisted of twenty focal lengths from 25mm to 500mm and was finalized with the last four models for rangefinder cameras. These were a 21mm,f/4 super wide-angle, a 105mm,f/4, a telephoto 350mm,f/4.5 and a 1000mm,f/6.3 mirror lens, initially devised for the SLR camera. In the twelve years of production over 140,000 rangefinder cameras had been produced.

Besides the versatile lens programme, the mirror-box and the motor drive, Nikon was already offering an extensive list of accessories, including different viewfinders, a bellows attachment, a reproduction stand, a microscope adapter, close-up lenses, and lots more.

Technologically of course there is a world of difference between the present Nikon highlights and those of 30 years ago, so naturally Nikon

Lenses for Nikon Rangefinder Cameras

Type	Bayonet/ Thread	Date introduced	Smallest aperture	Closest focusing distance	Elements/ groups	Filter thread	Weight (g)
21/4.0	B	1959	16	0.90	8/4	43	140
25/4.0	B/T	1953	22	0.90	4/4	—	140
28/3.5	B/T	1952	22	0.90	6/4	43	155
35/3.5	B/T	1948	22	0.90	4/3	43	200
35/3.5 Stereo	B	1956	16	0.90	4/3	40.5	185
35/2.5	B/T	1952	22	0.90	6/4	43	220
35/1.8	B/T	1956	22	0.90	7/5	43	170
50/3.5 Micro	B/T	1956	22	0.45	5/4	34.5	145
50/3.5	B/T	1945	16	0.90	4/3	—	170
50/2.0	B/T	1946	16	0.90	6/3	40.5	185
50/1.5	B/T	1950	11	0.90	7/5	40.5	205
50/1.4	B/T	1950	16	0.90	7/3	43	210
50/1.1	B/T	1956	22	0.90	9/6	62	435
85/2.0	B/T	1948	16	1.00	5/3	48	465
85/1.5	B/T	1951	32	1.00	7/3	60	600
105/4.0	B	1959	22	1.20	3/3	34.5	280
105/2.5	B/T	1953	32	1.20	5/3	52	570
135/4.0	B/T	1947	16	1.50	4/3	40.5	560
135/3.5	B/T	1950	16	1.50	4/3	43	520
180/2.5 *	B/T	1953	32	2.10	6/4	82	1860
250/4.0 *	B/T	1951	32	3.00	4/3	68	1240
350/4.5 *	B	1959	22	4.00	3/3	82	1830
500/5.0 *	B/T	1952	45	7.50	3/3	110	8600
1000/6.3 *	B	1959	6.3	30.0	3/2	52	9980

* usable only with mirror box

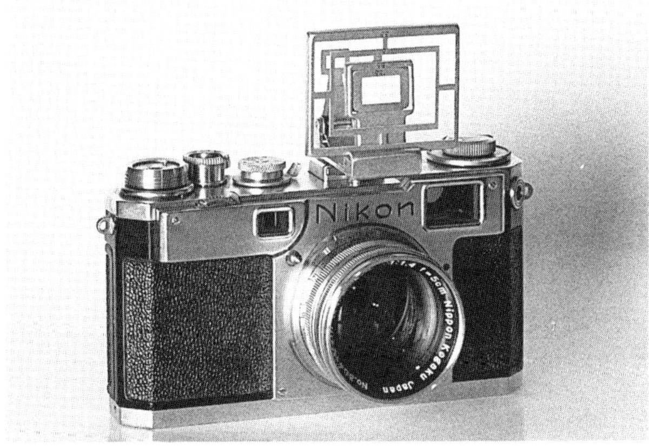

The name says it all: the Sportsfinder, making it easy to follow movement.

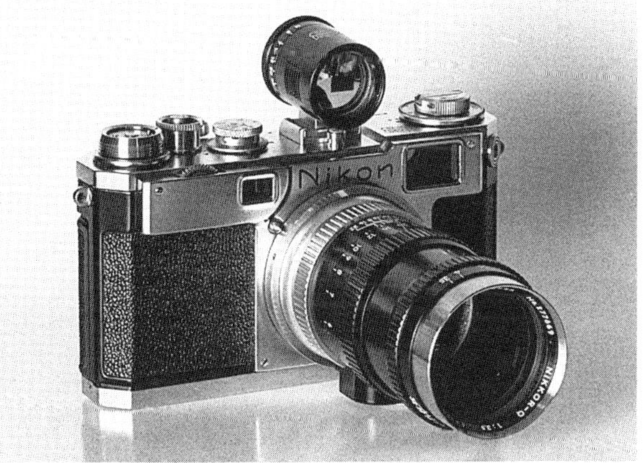

Easy viewing: A Nikon S equipped with the universal viewfinder for a number of focal lengths.

rangefinder cameras are of less interest to present users. On the other hand they are becoming increasingly popular with collectors. From today's point of view it is fascinating to see what Nikon was capable of achieving in technical terms from the very beginning. Anybody who is fond of precision mechanical costruction will find collecting these early viewfinder cameras very rewarding.

We would like to recommend two competent author's books on the subject to those interested in further information concerning the different features of individual models: Robert Rotoloni's "Nikon Rangefinder Cameras", published by Hove Books, and Peter Braczko's "Nikon Faszination" and "Nikon Handbuch" published by Wittig in Hückelhoven, Germany.

Nikkorex – The Unknown Nikon

The Nikkorex cameras are an unknown part of Nikon history. They prove that models like the EM and the F-301 were not Nikon's first attempt at a mass market product. Just as the rangefinder models S3 and S4 were intended as less expensive alternatives to the SP, they wanted to place a cheaper camera next to the professional Nikon F. Still, the question remains why the Nikkorex series never appears on any official Nikon family tree. Apparently Nikon prefers not to be reminded of these models, the main reason perhaps being the fact that the Nikkorex models were the result of a cooperation with Mamiya and not of pure Nikon design and manufacture as in every other case. Also it probably does not fit into Nikon's present attitude as a professionally orientated company to once have included cameras of such relatively poor quality in its list. The idea behind the Nikkorex design was that of an inexpensive SLR with a built-in lens. In 1960 the first Nikkorex 35 appeared with the 50mm,f/2.5 Nikkor. It featured a lens shutter by Citizen, a company known more as a supplier of watches and office machines.

A window with a honeycomb structure revealing the built-in exposure meter is located immediately above the lens of the Nikkorex 35. The metering range stretches from EV 6,5 to 18 and a needle on the top plate indicates the proper shutter speed/aperture-combination. All of the exposure controls are situated on the lens along with the focusing ring and the film speed settings, possible between ISO 100/21° and 1600/33°. Shutter speeds are available from 1/500 to 1 sec., while apertures can be set from f/2.5 to f/22. The finder eyepiece is located slightly off-centre to the left and the rather dim focusing screen makes the split-image range-finder a real necessity. The Porro-type finder design used in this camera, which does not employ a reflective prism as usual to deliver an upright and true-to-side image, is partly responsible for the poor viewing quality. Nikon compensated for the disadvantage of the non-interchangeable lens somewhat by offering supplementary lenses as accessories. The wide-angle attachment increases the angle of view to 60°, corresponding to a focal length of 35mm, but this reduces the maximum aperture to f/5.6. The use of the telephoto-attachment, which increases the focal length to 90mm, results in the same loss of speed. Image quality also deteriorates considerably with these attachments. In addition, a supplementary lens of 1.5 dioptres reduces the closest focusing distance from 60cm to 35cm. The Nikkorex 35 was modified one year later with a shutter supplied by Seikosha and an enlarged film-advance lever.

Another addition to the Nikkorex range was far more important – a model offering the possibility of changing lenses, logically by means of the F-type bayonet. This represented an especially economical access to the universal Nikon system. The camera is named Nikkorex F and is the first Nikon having a vertical-travel focal-plane shutter with metal leaves supplied by Copal. Once again we find the classical shutter speed dial on the top, but not an integrated exposure meter.

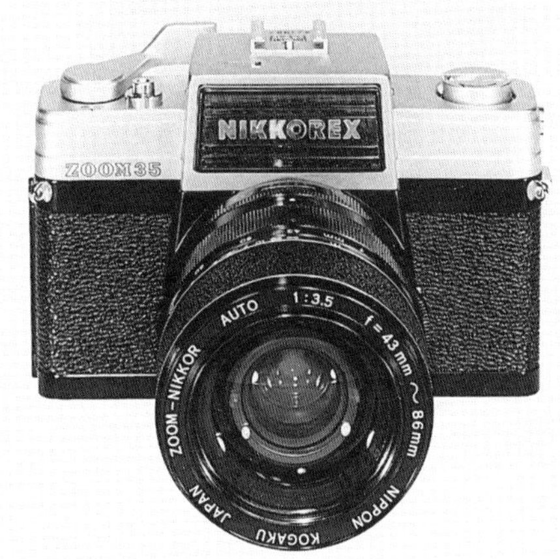

The unknown Nikon: The Nikkorex Zoom with its built-in zoom lens from 43mm to 86mm.

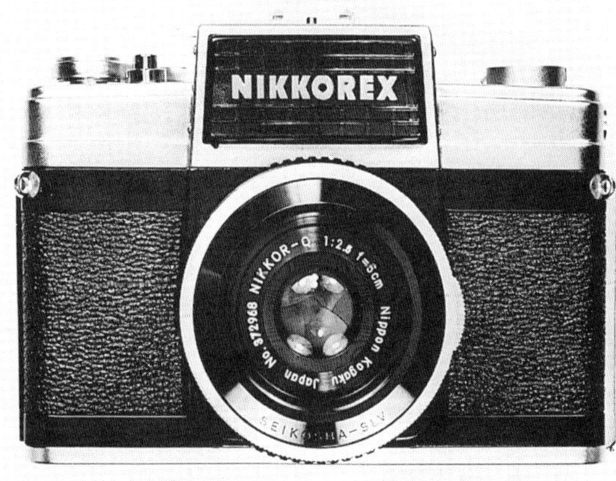

A Nikon with a lens shutter: The Nikkorex from 1960 with its 50mm,f/2.5 lens.

If needed, a selenium-type unit can be mounted which couples with the shutter speed dial as well as the meter coupling pin of the lens. The Nikkorex F's features are comparable to those of the Nikkormat FS developed later, but in common with the other Nikkorex models it does not convey that customary feeling of a robust, everlasting design and sound workmanship.

The next Nikkorex, the Nikkorex Zoom 35, displays a real novelty – an integrated zoom lens with a focal length range from 43mm to 86mm. The shutter remained unchanged, resembling the Nikkorex 35-2 in this respect. The zoom lens is, in fact, the same design as the Zoom Nikkor 43-86mm,f/3,5 available from the early 80's .

The last Nikkorex is also Nikon's first camera with an automatic exposure mode. Equipped with a Seikosha lens shutter again, it features a shutter-priority AE mode within the range of f/2.0 to f/16 since the built-in 48mm lens has a maximium aperture of f/2. In the viewfinder a needle displays the aperture selected by the camera. In the manual mode a second needle must be brought to coincide with the first to ensure a correct exposure.

On the outside the body was smoothed with rounded edges, corresponding to the prevailing trend. It also has one unmistakable feature in having the shutter release button not located on the top of the camera but, like the Praktica, slanted on the front next to the lens. This Nikkorex is the only one of the series which, in the case of a few specimens, carries the well-known Nikon logo.

CHAPTER 2

The F-Series

Cameras equipped with a reflex mirror in order to facilitate easy viewing of the focusing screen were known before the turn of the century. The large formats used at the time made them correspondingly clumsy and heavy. The Kine-Exakta from Ihagee of Dresden, introduced in 1936, pioneered the SLR principle in the 35mm format. Further innovations came from Japan. In 1954 Pentax presented the Asahiflex IIB, the first SLR with an instant-return mirror. This means that the mirror swings upwards after the shutter is released in order to allow the light to pass through to the film, and then back again into its initial position as soon as the shutter blinds have completed their travel. Prior to that improvement the viewfinder was blacked out until the shutter was cocked; an action which also returned the mirror to its viewing position. In 1958 the lens manufacturer Zunow introduced an SLR equipped with an automatic diaphragm so that the lens was only stopped down to working aperture when the shutter was released.

1959 was the decisive year in which Nikon introduced the Nikon F and laid the foundation for their present position. It was in fact a double first because, along with their first SLR, Nikon brought out their F-type bayonet which has remained principally unchanged until today in spite of the incorporation of autofocus.

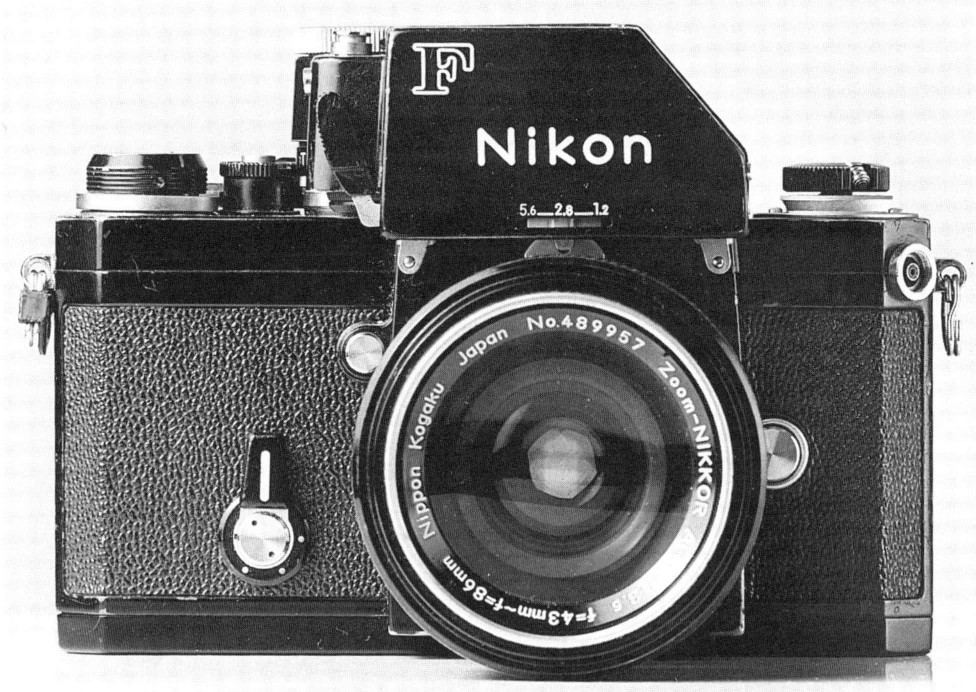

A Nikon F with the Photomic FTN and the Zoom-Nikkor 43-86mm,f/3.5.

Nikon F

Try to call to mind the situation. At a time when most of manufacturers were still equipping their SLR cameras with the clumsy M42 thread-mount, the Nikon engineers conceived the F-type bayonet which provided an unprecedentedly easy and safe changing of lenses. The continuity of the system and the consistency with which the compatibility throughout the series has been upheld until today cannot be found with any other company. So it comes as no surprise that you can use a modern autofocus lens with no drawbacks whatsoever on the old Nikon F. The other way around works too: mounting the oldest F-lens on a modern F4.

If you look at the Nikon F from above, apart from the prism finder it shows a strong resemblence to the rangefinder models SP or S3. The film counter is located concentric with the advance lever. Right next to it is the shutter release button which is situated quite a bit back compared to later models. The reason for this is the fixed connection with the take-up spool. The release button is encircled by a collar with two positions marked "A" and "R". In order to rewind the film the collar has to be lifted slightly and turned to "R", which unlocks the take-up spool. This collar also serves as the mount for a cable release with the female-threaded "Leica bell".

To the left of the release button you will find the shutter speed dial with settings from 1/1000 to 1 sec., as well as B and T. The position "T" which is not very common now has its advantages whenever a cable release is not available and you need time exposures. When set to "T" the shutter opens after being released: it remains open even if the button is not pressed again until the exposure is terminated by setting the dial to another position. A pin rises above the surface of the dial for connection to the shutter speed dial of the Photomic head when it is mounted. In the centre a black dot indicates whether or not the shutter is cocked. Another window in front of the dial displays the type of synchronization chosen. The collar of the dial must be lifted and turned to switch from one to the other. In the case of flash bulbs, one of the three coloured dots should be chosen according to the desired shutter speed. The corresponding speeds are marked with the respective colors. The FX-position is neccessary when using electronic flash units. The shutter speeds click-stop at every position, but they can also be set to intermediate values within the range of 1/1000 to 1/125 sec.

The standard prism finder is removeable and can be replaced by a Photomic-, a waist-level-, or an action-finder. In order to do so the locking button next to the finder eyepiece must be pressed firmly. A second pressing will then unlock the focusing screen, and if you turn the camera upside down it will fall out (onto a soft surface or your hand). When first introduced there were just four types of finder screen available for the F, by the end of its production run this had risen to 15.

The Nikon F was the very first SLR to display a viewfinder image showing the full 100% of the actual frame size. Most other cameras still force you to settle for much less: 96%, 95%, or even only 93%, so that the negatives and slides show a lot more than you see in the viewfinder at the time of taking the picture. Every model in the F-series features this 100% finder image. The rewind crank is situated in the usual place to the left, and beneath it the special accessory-shoe with its central contact designed for the flash units BC-7 and SB-2/7. The additional viewfinder for the fisheye lenses and the then remarkable super-wide-angle with a focal length of 21mm can also be mounted here since these lenses could not be focused with the reflex mirror. The serial number which also indicates the film plane is also engraved on this side.

The Serial Number Reveals The Manufacturing Date

Collectors will be interested to know that the first two digits of the serial number indicate the date of manufacture. Care must be taken though, because they really only say when the top-plate was produced. Since it is quite possible that the top-plate is a replacement resulting from a repair, an F dating from 1965 may well be fitted with a top-plate carrying a 73 as its first two digits.

The logo on the right side of the top-plate is another feature which helps identification. "Nippon-Kogaku-Tokyo" stood there until 1966, and after that the lens denomination "Nikkor". At the time Zeiss-Ikon had prevented the use of the name Nikon. According to them the similarity between the two brand-names was too great. As a result only the last series of F-models is marked with the Nikon logo.

The eyelets for the carrying strap on the left and right sides of the body are not really worth mentioning except for the fact that they tend to wear out in the course of time when put to extensive use. This was only remedied in the final series with the help of steel inserts.

The bayonet dominates the front view with its inner diameter of 44mm, designed to provide a passage to the film free of vignetting even with the faster lenses. The lenses are secured by the three inward-pointing claws positioned every 120°. A 60° turn is sufficient to lock the lens into place.

The mirror-lockup function is somewhat complicated and was designed in a more practical manner in the later F2. First a knob next to the bayonet has to be rotated through 45°, then after the following shutter release the mirror swings up and remains in that position. This method results in one frame being lost every time. It can be avoided by pressing the release button just halfway instead of all the way so that the mirror swings up without tripping the shutter.

The Nikon F has a depth-of-field button as well as a self-timer. The latter is not activated by the shutter release button, but with a separate

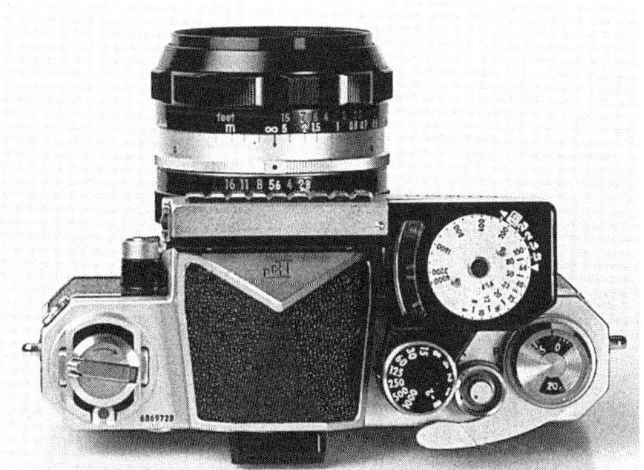

LEFT: The predecessor of the Photomic. An F-"Eyelevel" with a selenium exposure meter attached.

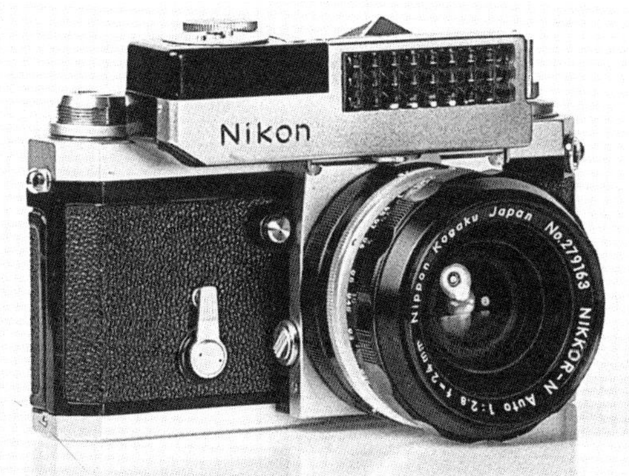

RIGHT: The attachable selenium exposure meter from the front. The large metering-cell dominates this aspect.

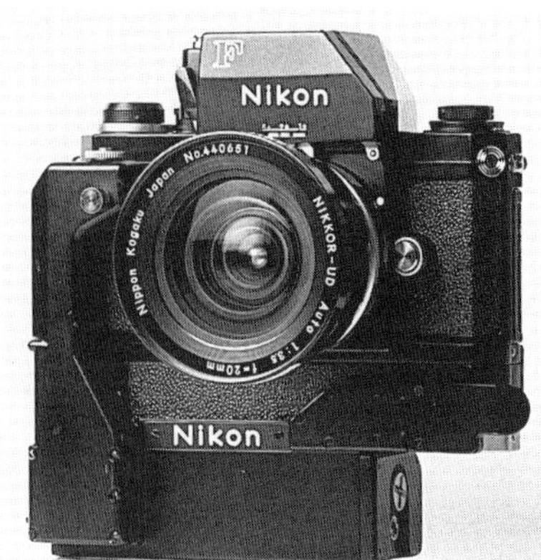

An F Photomic with the motor drive F36 and the first super wideangle UD 20mm,f/3.5.

little button which is unlocked whenever the delay lever is set to a value between three and ten seconds. If you choose the "B" position on the shutter speed dial an exposure of two seconds can be achieved rather precisely in combination with the self-timer.

Unlike the backs on present-day cameras, the back of the F is not hinged but is removed completely by pulling it down off the camera. A small catch in the base-plate of the back serves as a lock. When removing the back you have to be careful not to damage the leading-rails on the body by pulling it at an angle. This is especially dangerous in the case of the motor drive F 36 where the back is an integral part. Which brings us to one of the most important features of the F that helped to establish this camera's overwhelming success: the first electrical motor drive for a standard 35mm SLR camera. It was capable of achieving a maximum firing rate of up to 4 frames/sec. – remarkable considering the fact that even the modern models MD-12 and MD-15 cannot compete with it. An extremely rare special version of the F, unknown to most people, was even capable of up to 7 frames/sec. But, unlike today where the motor drive can be attached to the camera easily and safely, the combination of the F with the F36 requires a modification first at a Nikon service workshop. Both units have to be matched to each other by replacing the camera's internal base-plate with a motor drive version drilled for the release-pin. This plate also carries the tripod mount.

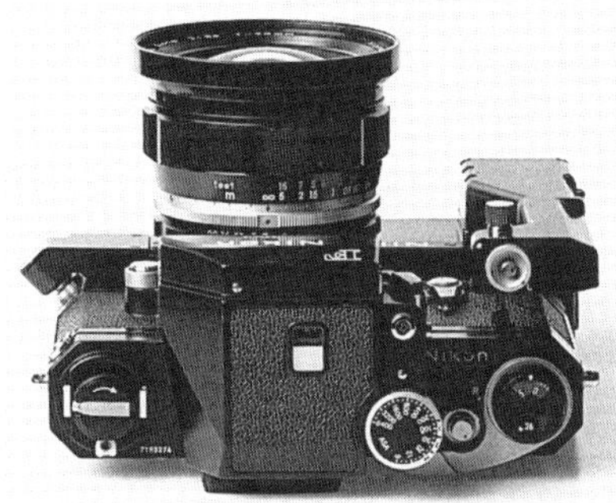

The same equipment from the top: Motor drive F36 along with the directly connected battery compartment.

The Nikon F shutter blinds are made of the same titanium foil already found in the rangefinder model SP. They take some 12ms to cross the film

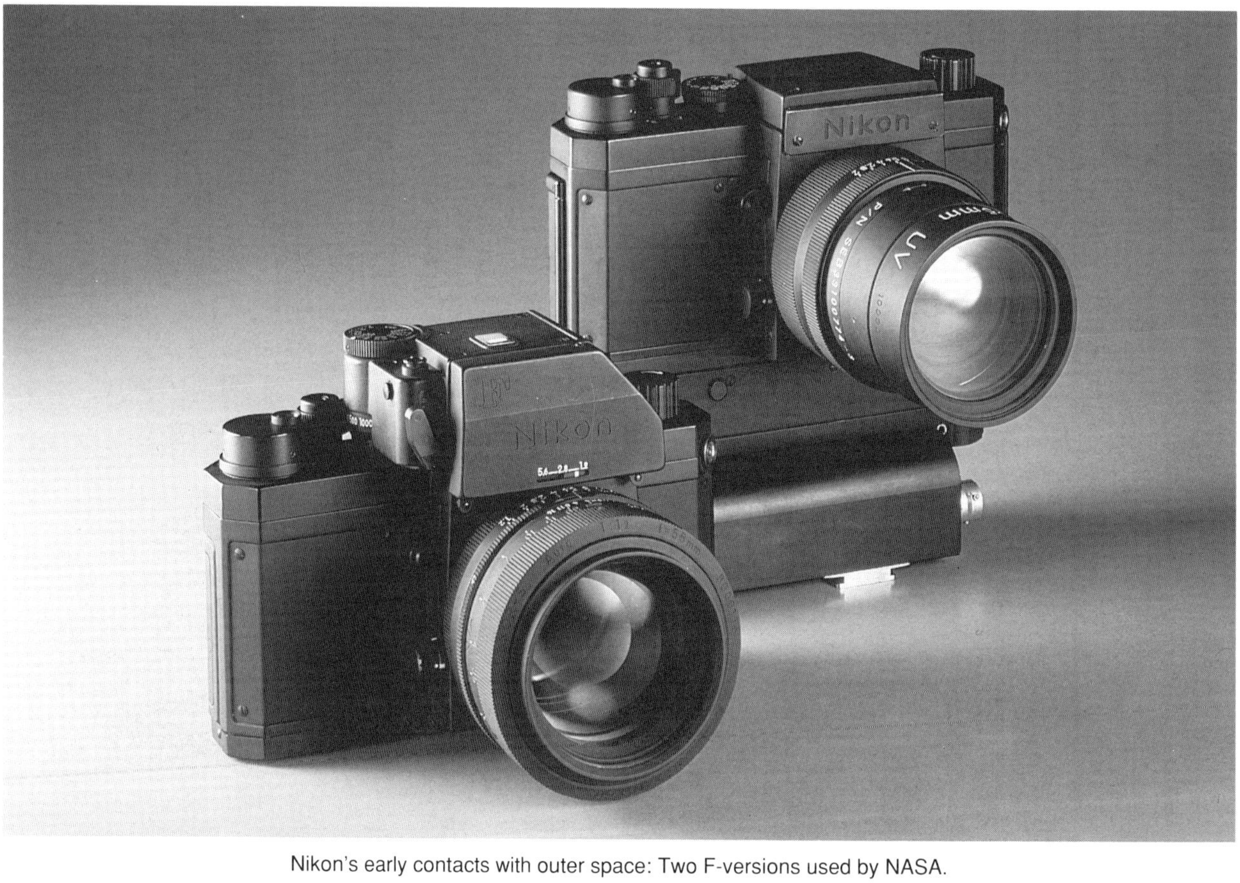

Nikon's early contacts with outer space: Two F-versions used by NASA.

plane from right to left, which results in a synchronization speed of 1/60 sec.

Bit by bit during the 11 years of its production the Nikon F became the centre of one the most professional camera systems in every respect. In addition to the lenses one can choose between four different finder systems, fifteen focusing screens, and two motor drives for either 36 or 250 frames. F-type cameras are still in daily use all over the world in spite of the fact that they have long deserved their place of honour in a cabinet. Can there be a more convincing proof for a camera's strength and reliability? And whoever likes to work with his F for understandable reasons can fall back on a number of accessories from the F2 system. The fully compatible focusing screens and finders, with the exception of the Photomic prism models, are surely the most important, but in order to attach an F2 finder the name-plate must be removed first. The F2 flash adaptors are also usable with the F.

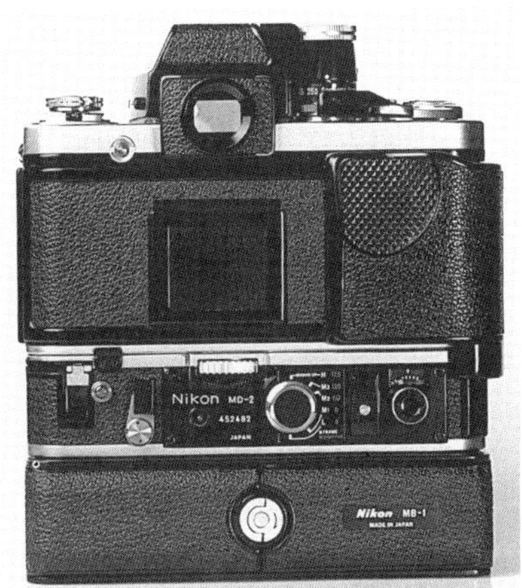

The F2 with the Motor drive MD-2, directly connecting battery compartment MB-1, and the stop-back MF-3.

Nikon F2

During the 60's, especially in the USA, the Nikon F slowly developed from an insider's tip to the number one professional camera. In Europe, though, the F remained rather unknown until the end of the 60's. It was the F's successor, the Nikon F2, that achieved the breakthrough in Europe. Introduced in 1971, it was in general a further developed F. The body has rounded edges and fits into the hand even more snugly. The basic construction remained almost identical to that of the F, but some design details were changed and improved. The film advance lever operates with a single 120° stroke and switches on the exposure meters in the new Photomics at the 20° position. The shutter release button was moved further towards the front edge of the camera allowing easier control, but the collar located around it has different functions compared to the Nikon F. Turned to the right to "L", the shutter can be secured against accidental release, in the opposite direction to "T", time exposures can be made in combination with the B-setting of the shutter speed dial. This function comes in handy when, for example, no cable release is available. Pressing the release button trips the shutter and setting the collar back to the normal position terminates the exposure.

The F2 has a fastest shutter speed of 1/2000 sec. This was achieved by reducing the running time of the blinds to 10 ms as well as reducing the width of the slit. This also resulted in a faster synchronization speed of 1/80 sec.

The attachment system for the finder remained the same as in the F, so that focusing screens and finders, with the exception of the Photomics, are compatible. Another major difference between the two series of metering finders should be mentioned. Whereas the power supply for the F-type Photomics is situated within the finders themselves, in the case of the F2 it was moved to the bottom of the camera. Two contacts to the left and right

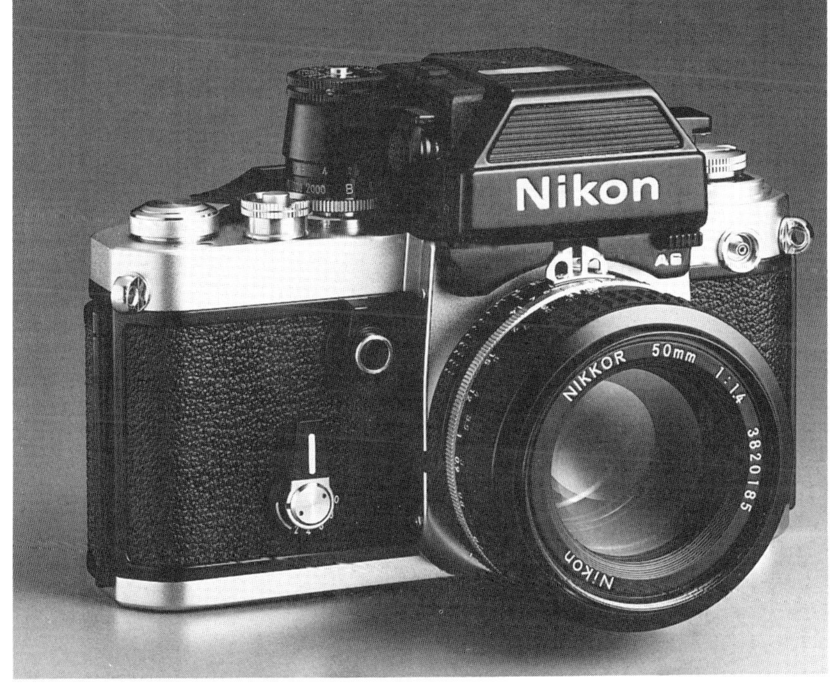

The classic F of the 70's: the Nikon F2A with a Nikkor 50mm,f/1.4.

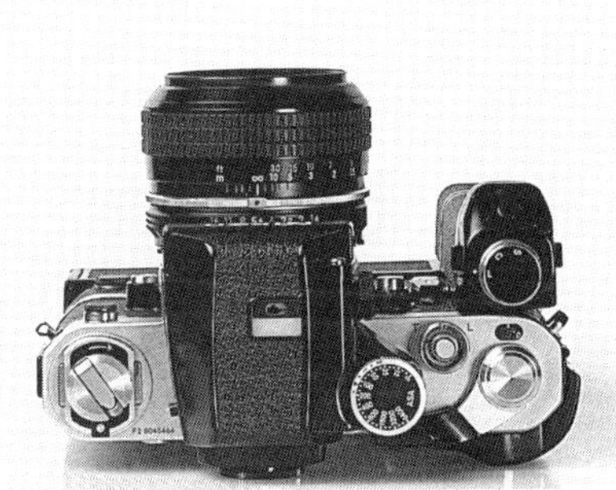
The F2 motor offers a number of convenient features such as power rewinding.

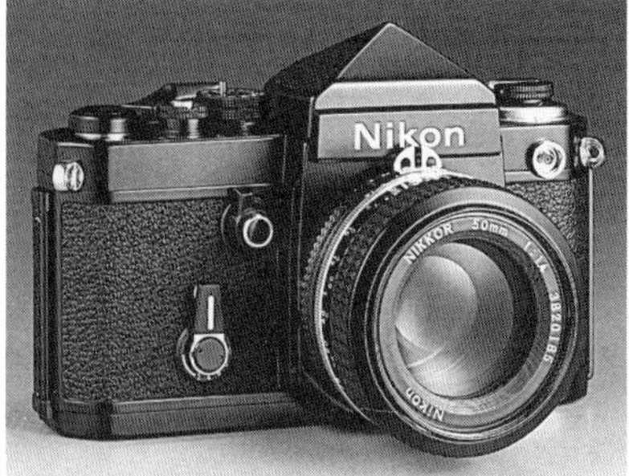

The F2 with the finder DE-1.

of the F2-Photomics facilitate the neccessary connection to the two batteries in the camera.

The F2's rewind crank can be pulled up out of the body by about 6mm so that the film can be wound back much faster and easier, while the accessory shoe beneath the crank is identical to that of the F. The first two digits of the serial number are the date of manufacture.

In order to improve durability for everyday professional work the bayonet and the shutter parts subject to heavy strain are made of a chrome-nickel-steel alloy. In addition, tiny ball-bearings within the shutter mechanism contribute to its precise functioning. Compared to the F, the mirror is longer, to avoid vignetting in the viewfinder when using very long telephoto lenses or lens extensions such as bellows attachments. The depth-of-field preview button is located in the same place as on the F, concentric with it is the mirror lockup lever which now works independently of the shutter function and therefore without the cost of one frame, unlike the F.

The self-timer has its own release button similar to the F. The T-position, however, opens up additional possibilities: if the shutter speed dial is simultaneously set to "B", long exposures from 2 to 10 seconds can be controlled with it.

The camera back is hinged in what is now the usual manner. Even so, it can be removed so that the bulk film

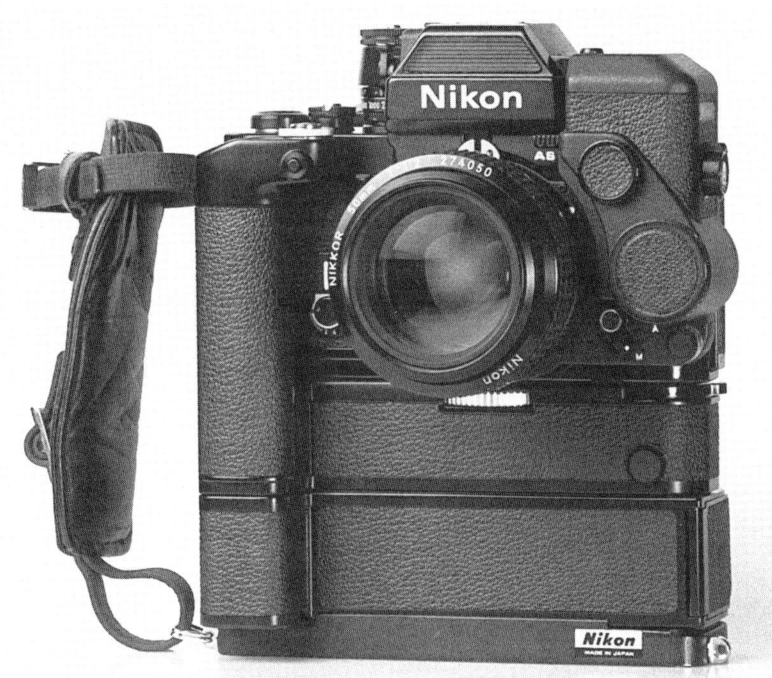

A rare combination: the F2 AS with a 50mm,f/1.2 Nikkor, motor drive MD-3/MB-2, DS-12, and the grip strap AH-1.

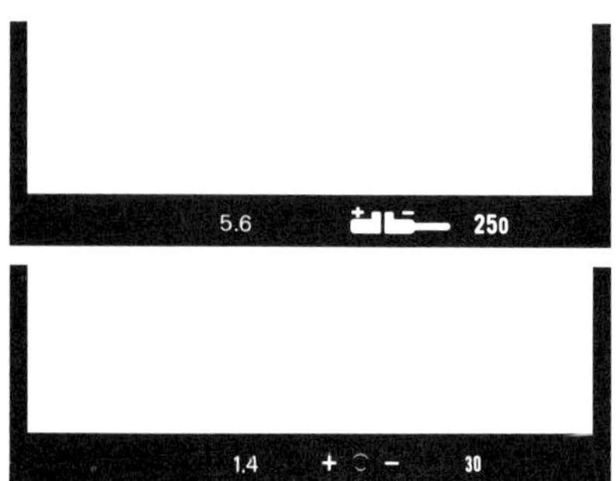

DP-11 and DP-12 in comparison: above, exposure meter indication by needle; below, with LEDs.

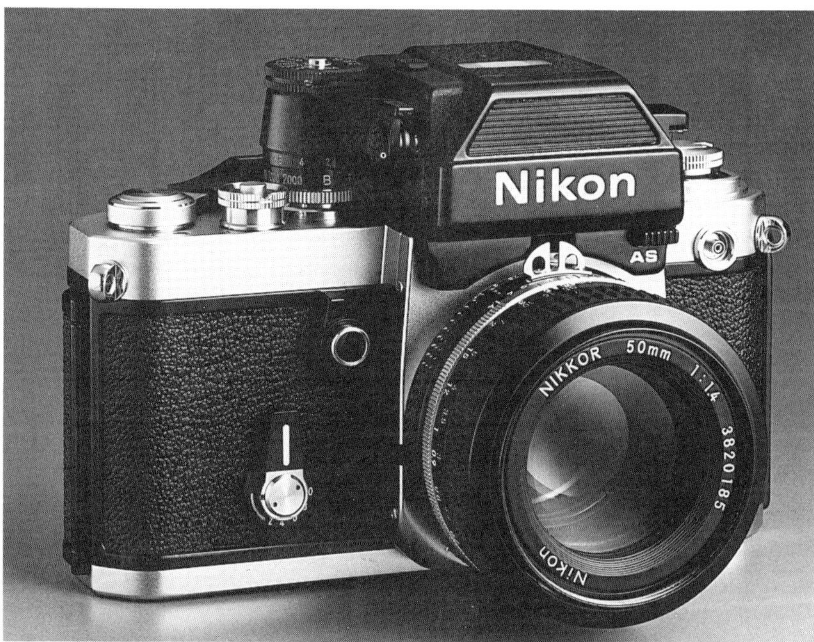

The F2 AS with a 50mm,f/1.4 Nikkor: the mechanical model in the F-series.

backs for 250 or 750 exposures can be mounted. The special MF-3 model was available with a back which prevents the film leader from disappearing into the cartridge when the motor drive MD-2 is employed to rewind the film.

In continuous mode the MD-1 and MD-2 motor drives are capable of accelerating the F2 to speeds of 4 and even 5 frames/sec. if the mirror is locked in the up position. The motor's performance in reverse is also remarkable; it can rewind a 36-exposure film completely into the cartridge in a mere 7 seconds, a feature much appreciated by press photographers.

The back of the camera is opened by turning a catch recessed into the base-plate, which has to be removed when a motor drive MD-1 or MD-2 is mounted in order to allow the rewind-spindle access to the cartridge. Since such a small part could be easily lost, a place to store this O/C-key was provided in the grip section of the motor. Because of this need to unscrew the catch, a motor should only be mounted or removed in subdued light, or when there is no film in the camera because of the possibility of light entering the cartridge compartment through this hole. The motor drive coupling is located on the opposite side of the base-plate together with the rewind release button and the motor drive release coupling.

In spite of the different versions and except for internal detail modifications, the body of the F2 remained practically unchanged throughout its production life. The exposure metering finders, the Photomics, on the other hand were updated as technical developments allowed. It was this system as a whole, consisting of viewfinders, motor drives, focusing screens, camera backs and of course the lenses that made Nikon a synonym for professional 35mm-photography. If the versatility and adaptability of the standard F2 to the widest range of tasks was still not enough, one of the special versions will have done the job.

Nikon F2 Titan

Introduced in 1978, this was the special version of the F2 that demonstrates quite clearly Nikon's determination to produce the most durable cameras that will work perfectly, even in extremely adverse conditions. Unlike most cameras, this model did not allow a choice between black or chrome finish. Previously Nikon had only used titanium for the shutter blinds of the F and F2 models. In cameras intended for hard professional use the parts subject to knocks, like the the base-plate, the back, the bayonet mount cover, and the prism cover, were made of matte black titanium. The first series was marked with the conspicuous gold-coloured logo "Titan" on the front, afterwards they were content with a discreet "T" to the left of the serial number. The chrome-coloured "Titan" version, belonging to the last F2's ever produced, is virtually unknown in Europe. Technically the F2 Titan is identical to the normal F2, but it is 5 grams lighter.

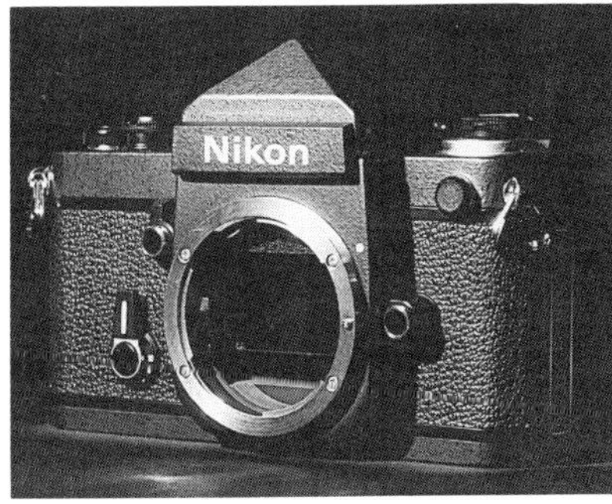

The super durable F2 Titan is easily recognized by its textured surface.

Nikon F2 Data

Whereas a databack is available as an accessory for many cameras today, and even some modern compact cameras can be purchased with the option to imprint data, this was certainly not

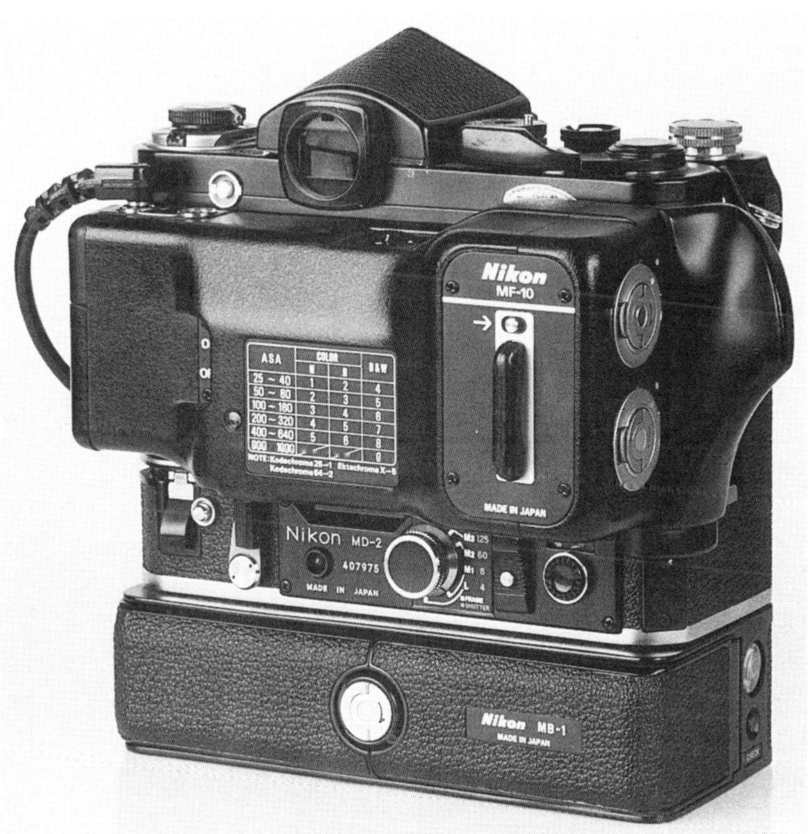

The archetype of all databacks and an outstanding example of precision mechanical workmanship: the F2 Data.

the case in the days of the F2: then a special version was neccessary. The F2 Data is equipped with a special back that can imprint various kinds of data onto the lower left corner of the frame, simultaneously with the exposure, by means of a tiny built-in electronic flash unit. Besides the time and the date, individual hand-written information can also be imprinted by noting it on a 3,5x10mm data-card. In order to prevent this area of the negative or the slide film from being exposed normally, a small masking-plate is situated directly in front of the film at the edge of the picture frame. The special S-type focusing screen was provided with the databack, with a mark denoting the imprinting area. The F2 Data was available either with the model MF-10 databack for 36, or the MF-11 for 250 exposures. If the masking-plate is removed in the picture frame and you attach the standard camera back belonging to the equipment provided when purchased, you can turn the F2 Data into a normal F2. It can then only be identified by the logo "Data" above the serial number. The databack is still available today as a part of the MF-17 back for the F3 for bulk film up to 250 exposures.

Nikon F2 H

As mentioned before, the F2 is capable of a maximum firing rate of 5 frames/sec. with the motor drive MD-1/2. But for some professionals faced with special assignments even this speed was not enough. Based on the F2 body, Nikon designed an extremely fast, special version for this purpose that really makes things move. The F2 H ("H" stands for High Speed) manages up to 10 frames/sec. No mechanical construction in the world is capable of controlling a mirror swinging at that rate. For this reason the F2 H employs a fixed and partially transparent mirror that allows 65% of the light to pass through to the film and reflects the remaining 35% upwards into the viewfinder. The film transport system was also modified and changed in a few details. The fastest speed available is 1/1000 sec. and in the second series the B-setting, which would not have been used very often in such a special camera, was sacrificed. The depth-of-field preview button actually stops down the aperture since stop-down metering is standard procedure in this case: a mechanism capable of opening and closing the diaphragm at a frequency of 10 frames/sec. was not feasible then.

The high-speed F2 is driven by a modified MD-2, the MD-100. The considerable power demand is provided by two coupled MB-1-type battery packs called MB-100. This provides the motor with 30 volts enabling it to transport a 36-exposure film in just 3.6 seconds. Even though the standard F2 High Speed was only equipped with the normal prism finder (with a titanium cover) it can easily be used with one of the Photomic finders as long as the film speed is reduced by 1EV in order to compensate for the loss of light through the partially transparent mirror.

What type of user actually needed such a high firing rate of 10 frames/sec.? Apart from technical applications such as in the analysis of motion, sports photography is probably the main application and several possibilities are feasible. One sports

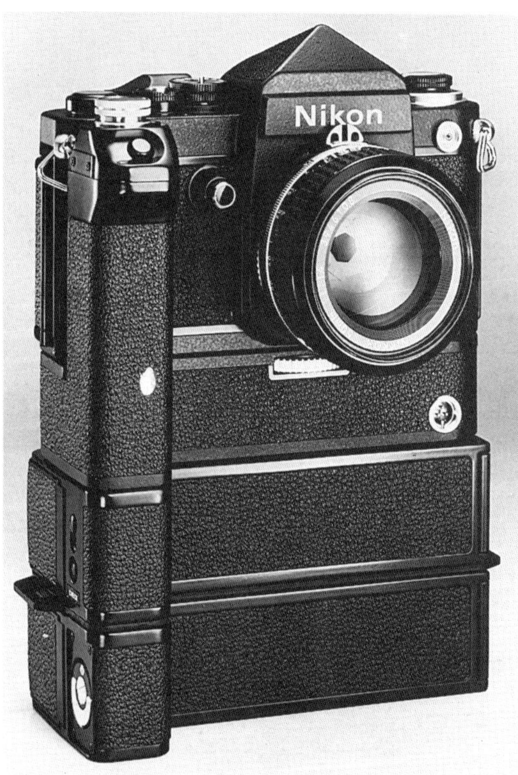

LEFT: A really fast combination: the F2 H with its motor drive MD-100. "H" as in High Speed = 10 frames/sec.

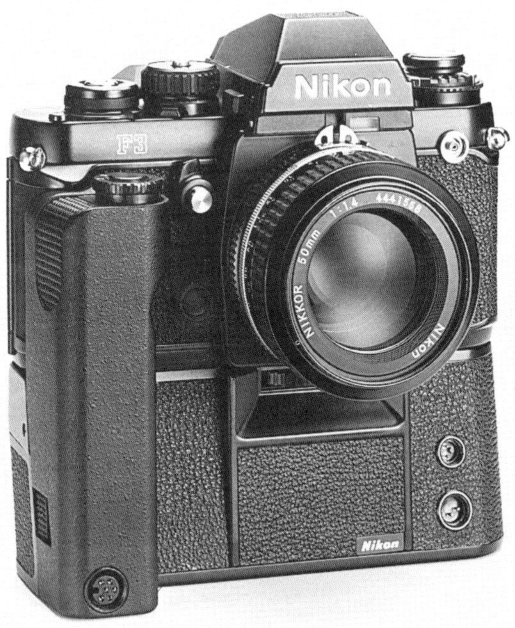

RIGHT: The F3 with its motor drive MD-4.

photographer described it as follows: "If I happen to be working for different clients I can offer each of them a picture of the decisive moment – and none of them will be exactly the same. Actually I do not need 10 frames/sec. but rather 3 in ⅓ sec. In return, I am willing to carry the 2 kilos around."

When the F2 was discontinued in 1980 to make room for its successor an outcry could be heard throughout the ranks of Nikon enthusiasts. No, they were not willing to trust an electronically controlled camera like the new Nikon F3 and all of them could tell a story about the F2's ruggedness and longevity. One should never say never. Many F2 owners who originally desperately resisted electronic progress went on to employ its worthy successor the F3 for years on end, and indeed until the present day.

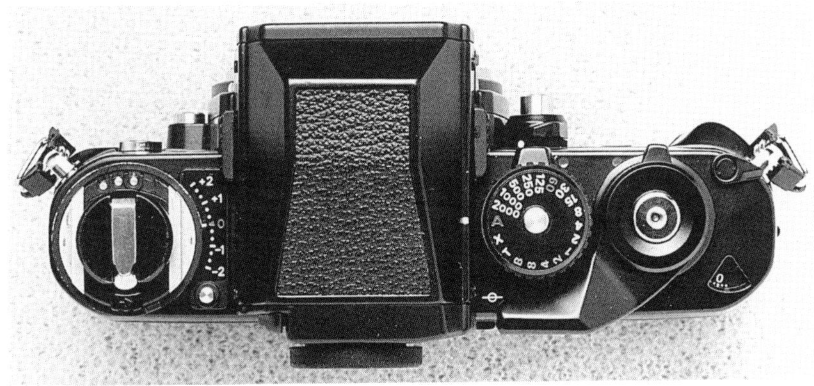

Not very many things in common with its predecessor: The F3 seen from above.

Nikon F3

From a technical point of view a purely mechanical camera has obvious shortcomings compared to an electronic model. However, on taking a closer look only some of the Nikon F3 mechanical units were actually replaced by electronics; the film transport and mirror-box, for example, are still mechanically operated, only the shutter speeds are electronically controlled. It is precisely these units with their numerous geartrains, control levers, and pawls which are subject to abrasion and wear and quite sensitive to dust and grime. Their reaction times and running speeds change with differing temperatures and their space requirements determine the location of the controls as well as design. So it was only logical to introduce electronics to the F2's successor. At the time Nikon had already gathered experience with the Nikkormat EL, the Nikon EL-2, and the Nikon FE, so the know-how resulting from building these cameras could be applied to the coming new top model. Many users, especially among amateur photographers, had expected a multi-mode model but the camera introduced in 1980 exhibited only the aperture-priority mode and did not have much more in common with the F2 than the bayonet.

The outside appearance of the F3 was the work of the Italien industrial designer Giorgetto Giugiaro who had already proven his abilities on the Nikon EM body. Some Nikon fans will consider this reference with mixed emotions but you cannot but agree

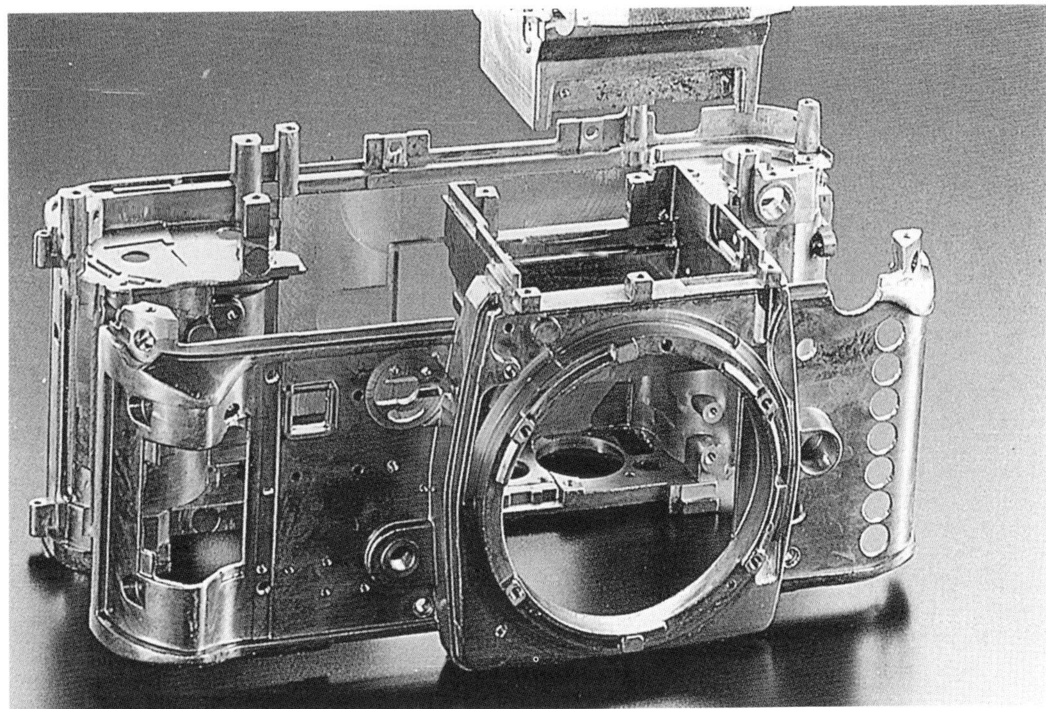

The naked F3 during assembly. The basis is a durable die-cast chassis.

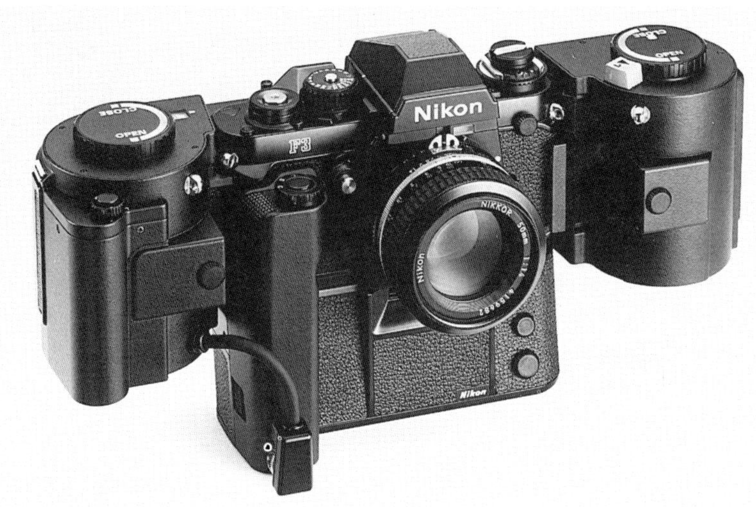

Designed for remote control and long series of exposures: The F3 with the MD-4 and the bulk film back MF-17.

that the F3's exterior is quite elegant. Its die-cast body is made of a copper-silumin alloy which is more resistent to corrosion than the previously used material. The thickness of the casting wall varies between 1.4mm and 2mm, another sign of the consistent dedication to stability. The outside covers and the back of the camera, though, are still made of brass.

The F3 comes alive with the help of a switch beneath the film advance lever; lightly pressing the release button activates the meter for 16 seconds, but only if the film counter is standing at least at "1" – before that all exposures are controlled at 1/80 sec. The release button which is situated on the film advance axis for the first time works as a two-step switch. The first step activates the exposure meter when lightly pressed, the second step temporarily neutralizes a magnet inside the mirror-box – and the mirror trips the shutter. The result is a very soft shutter release that greatly reduces the danger of camera shake. A thread within the release button allows the use of standard ISO-type cable releases – the good old Leica-bell finally belonged to the past.

The film advance lever is made of plastic and shows plenty of play: A point of criticism for some users which proved to be completely negligible in practical application. Even more so as the F3's mechanical film transport system had received special attention and was designed employing several ball-bearings which drastically reduced the torque neccessary to cock the shutter. You hardly notice the difference between an empty camera or one loaded with film when you operate the advance lever. Naturally this also makes it easier for the motor drive MD-4, designed especially for the F3, to accelerate the camera up to 6 frames/sec.

A small lever located next to the advance lever allows multiple exposures. It features a click-stop position and returns to its initial setting after the shutter is released and cocked the second time. So if a multiple exposure is planned to consist of more than two shots the lever must be reset to the appropriate position every time.

Located next to the prism is the shutter speed dial with its 18 click-stop settings from 1/2000 to 8 sec., B- and T-positions, an X-position for flash synchronization at 1/80 sec., and an A-position for aperture priority automatic exposure mode. After pressing the lock button on top of the shutter speed dial any of the manual speeds can be set. They are precisely controlled by a quartz oscillator resonating at a frequency of exactly 32,768 hertz (that is, per second) as long as the camera is loaded with the neccessary batteries. This quartz control circuit is 100% reliable and does its calculations precisely. If you set 1/2 sec. the shutter gets the signal to close again after exactly 16,384 oscillations, and in the case of 1/2000 sec. it monotonously counts down from 16. This facilitates a precision far beyond that achieveable with a mechanical construction. The T-setting is also released electronically, but is arrested mechanically – in order to keep power consumption down to a minimum during extremely long exposures. The X-setting on the shutter speed dial is meant for those electronic flash units not capable of setting the synchronization speed on the F3 automatically, mostly for the frequent occasions when a grip-type flash gun is to be connected via a syncro cable. Another lever beneath the shutter speed dial activates the electronically controlled self-timer. After starting it with the release button a red LED blinks every 1/2 sec. for 8 seconds as a reminder. The frequency is raised to 8 hz during the last two seconds. The function can be deactivated at any time by setting back the lever.

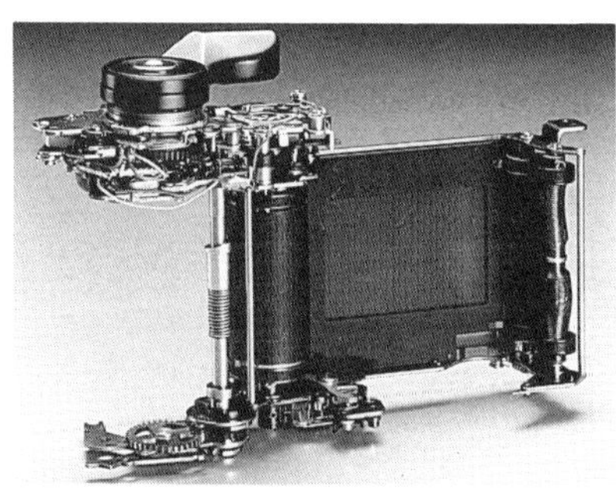
Separated from the rest of the camera: The shutter of the F3 along with the release and transport units.

Incorporating The Electronics Into The Body

Whereas with the F and the F2, depending on the model, the metering system and/or the complete power supply was integrated in the Photomics metering prism finders, in the case of the F3 everything is built into the camera body. Along with the standard prism finder DE-3, a waist-level finder DW-3, an action finder DE-2, and a 6x magnifying finder DW-4 were introduced with the F3. This design eliminated what was probably the weakest point of the F2: the mechanical construction of the metering and display systems made the F2 Photomics rather sensitive to knocks.

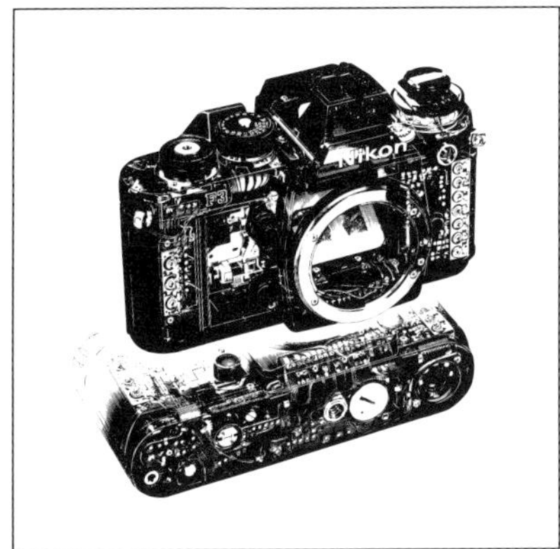

A cross-section through the F3: Electronics have replaced large parts of the mechanical construction.

The F3 on the other hand features an LCD located on the front edge of the mirror-box to inform about the exposure data. It is reflected into every finder above the image frame by a system of mirrors. The F3 was, in fact, Nikon's first camera employing an LC-display. Its advantages are a low power consumption rate and the ease of viewing even over a long period of time. There are, of course, some disadvantages too. Since LCDs do not emit light themselves they have to be equipped with separate illumination for dim conditions. The F3 features a small red button on the outside of the prism for this purpose which is difficult to find every time without some practice. A number of professionals had their illuminators modified by Nikon sevice so that it was activated along with the metering system. Another shortcoming of LCD's is their sensitivity to temperature change: they becomes sluggish below 0° and turns black above 60°, but recover again in normal temperatures. In addition, the contrast of LCD's deteriorates after about 7 to 10 years and should be replaced by then.

Viewfinder information provided by the F3: When set to automatic exposure, the display information about the shutter speed is in whole increments, so a display of 1/250 sec. may well stand for 1/217 sec. Overexposures are indicated by "+2000", underexposures by "-8". In manual mode a plus-sign in addition to the small "M" in front of the speed display informs of overexposures, a minus of underexposures, when + and – are displayed simultaneously this indicates a correct exposure within a tolerance of +/- 1/5 EV. The viewfinder display also serves as a battery check: when the display disappears again immediately after pressing the shutter release it is about time to think of replacing the batteries.

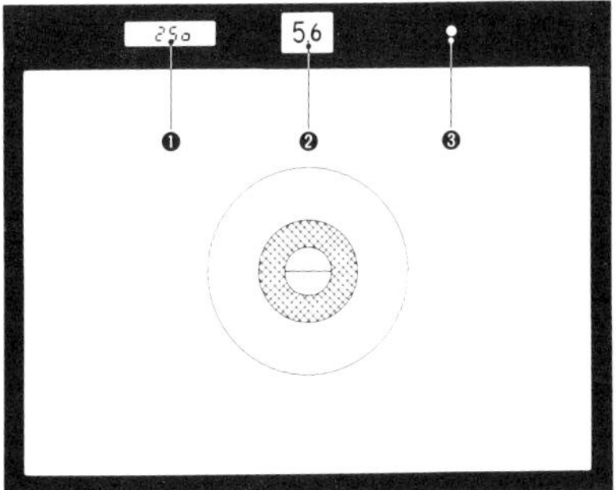

The F3 offers a clearly arranged and informative viewfinder image.

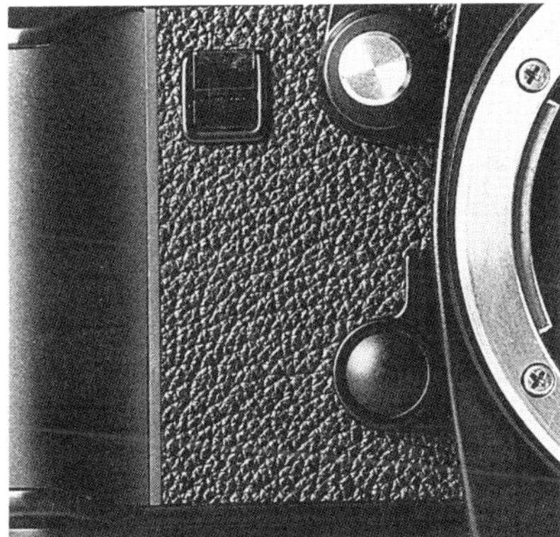

Works even without battery power: The F3's mechanical "emergency" release button.

The aperture set on the lens is visible in the centre above the image, but only in connection with AI-type lenses. The small scale on the aperture ring is absent on other versions so that the display window remains blank when they are in use. A red LED in the left of the viewfinder serves as a flash-ready signal.

The effective inside dimensions of the focusing screens are identical to those of the F and F2 so that the F3 also posesses a 100% viewfinder image. However, the F3 screens deliver an image about 1/3 EV brighter and are mounted in a different type of frame with a gripping strip. So it is not neccessary to turn the camera over in order to remove them. There are 22 different versions available, and even the special versions do not call for the use of correction factors anymore because the exposure is not metered on the focusing screen but down in the mirror box. That is where the SPD-photocell is located. It is also responsible for flash metering which will be described later. This is how the exposure metering of the F3 works: the centre of the reflex mirror is perforated, allowing about 8% of the light to pass through and be reflected down by a secondary mirror, hinged to the main one, onto the metering cell in the base of the camera. This location means the F3 is all but immune to stray light and it allowed the metering's centre-weighted characteristic to be concentrated further. The F3

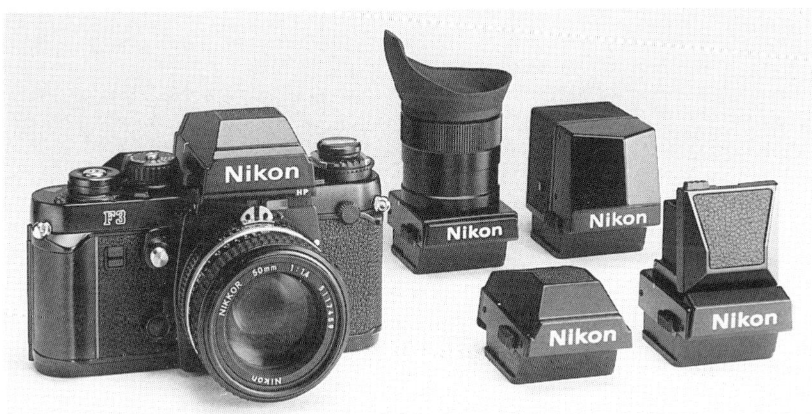

A feature of all F-models: Interchangeable viewfinders for different tasks.

metering features an 80%:20% characteristic for the first time as opposed to the 60%:40% usual up to then. The stronger concentration makes it possible to meter a certain portion of the subject more precisely, but on the other side there is a danger of coming to completely useless results if it is pointed in any old direction. The perforation of the mirror avoids the problems that come with partly reflective systems: On the one hand it allows the complete spectral range of the light to pass through evenly, and on the other hand the angle of the light entering is irrelevant. This system also allows the use of a normal linear polarizing filter instead of a circular version.

The film speed dial is situated on the left side of the top plate, a range of ISO 12/12° to 6400/39° can be set by pulling up the outer collar. Next to it there is an exposure correction scale marked in increments of ⅓ EV. Additionally, the special accessory shoe was integrated there in order to secure a secure mount for the F3's Speedlights. A small cam on the ISO-ring conveys the film speed to the flash unit mechanically. This is the reason why the F3's TTL-metering – the first one in a Nikon camera – does not work with flash guns with ISO-type hot shoes. The metering cell in the bottom of the camera is employed for this. Mounting the flash next to the prism – as it had already been in the case of the Nikon F and F2 – is a disadvantage insofar as the rewind crank and the lock for the camera back are covered. So whenever the film is to be changed the flash must be removed. Later, the special flash adapter AS-7 was designed which allows the film to be rewound and the back to be opened even with a flash attached.

A normal sync-terminal is located on the front of the body beneath this "multi-function tower", but of course at the cost of TTL-flash control. Situated around the bayonet is the meter coupling lever which can be turned up in order to allow the use of lenses without this coupling.

To the left of the bayonet where the self-timer is usually found, the F3 has a small lever with which the camera can be released in case the batteries are missing or exhausted. The exposure-lock button is placed right in the middle on its axis. This was a weak spot of the otherwise really perfect F3, perhaps one of our readers may have had an unpleasant experience with it: this button had the nasty habit of dropping off once in a while. It took several years until Nikon managed to solve this little problem for good. Tiny details often prove to be the most difficult.

To improve its handling without the motor drive attached the Italian designer Giugiaro supplied the F3 with a bulge on the front of the body

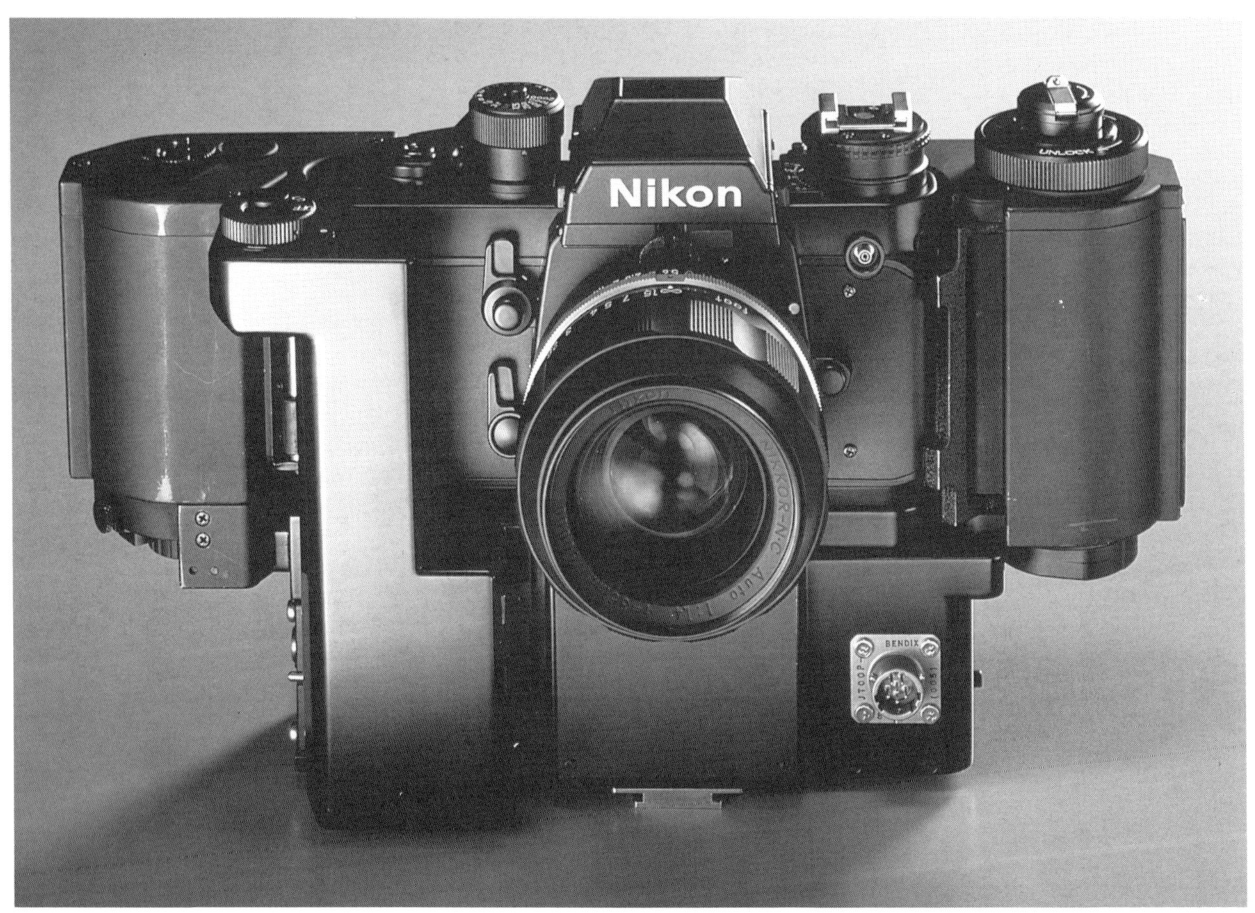

The F3 can also look back at experience in space: A special NASA version.

to secure a better grip. A first step towards ergonomical camera design. Further improvements of details in construction can be recognised from behind when the camera back is removed. The take-up spool is equipped with six slots to allow faster film loading. A roller next to the cartridge is responsible for a better film guidance, ensuring an optimal flatness even when using the motor drive.

Two gold contacts below the film guide rails serve as a wireless connection between the camera and an attached databack. In order to mount the motor drive MD-4 the black threaded cover must be removed from the base-plate to allow the rewind spindle free access to the film cartridge. Similarly consistent as in the case of the F2 and its motor drive MD-1/2 the battery compartment provides a place for this cap, thereby preventing it from getting lost. Whenever the motor is removed the cap can be replaced immediately.

Seven contacts are situated round the rewind spindle. The MD-4 is controlled by the F3 and only begins to transport the film when the camera gives the signal. This is a major difference to its predecessor: in the case of the F2 the motor frequency had to be synchronized with the shutter speed first. Also, the motor takes over the power supply for the camera electronics, avoiding almost completely the problems of low temperature operating conditions.

In spite of the obvious advantages of electronics compared to mechanical designs mentioned and described before, and its enormous popularity among the Nikon "freaks", the F3 never acquired the image of an F2, even though, all in all, it proved to be more durable. Anyway, the F3 is undisputedly the embodiment of "the photographic tool". Even after the introduction of the F4 it is still being employed daily all over the world and it will continue to do so for quite some time to come. At the time of writing it was still being produced.

Nikon F3 HP

Those who wear glasses often have problems with viewfinders because

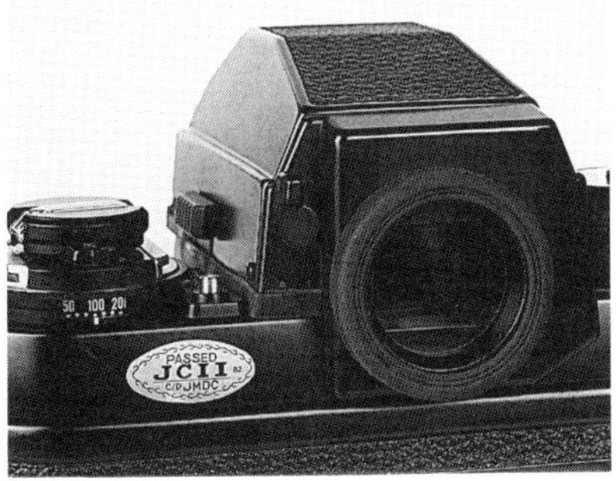

Relief for those who have to use glasses: The F3 HP finder delivers a complete view of the image.

they cannot position their eyes close enough to the eyepiece. As a result they are not able to see the complete finder image all the way into the edges without "looking round the corner". Normal viewfinders are designed for a distance of about 17mm between eyepiece and eye. When this distance gets larger the corners of the finder image begin to disappear out of the field of vision. In order to solve this problem Nikon developed a special F3-finder with the additional denotation "HP" (high eyepoint). It has the invaluable advantage of allowing a complete view of the finder image from up to a distance of 25mm between eye and eyepiece, and that suffices for most persons with glasses.

The HP-viewfinder with the code-name DE-3 turns every normal F3 into an F3 HP, in doing so the total weight rises from 700 to 745 grams. It is not just those with glasses who have come to treasure the HP-version of the F3; photographers with normal vision also enjoy the more comfortable viewing achieved with this finder. So it comes as no surprise that the F3 has been sold mostly as the F3 HP during the last years.

Nikon F3 T

Following the precedent set by the F2 Titan, Nikon introduced a titanium bodied version of the F3, emphasising its professional status. All the vulnerable casings of the F3 T are made of titanium and it has only been available with the HP-type finder. The first series have the original silver finish of the titanium metal, while the later F3 T's have a black finish. The camera can be identified by the addition of a T after the F3-logo and its textured surface.

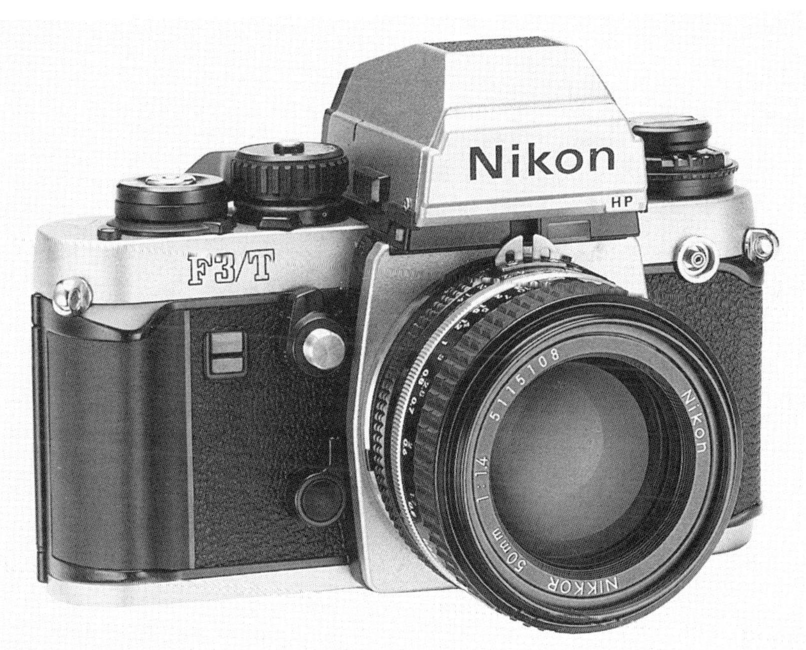

Elegant and sturdy: The F3 Titan in the first version with the bright metal finish and HP-type finder.

Nikon F3 P

A professional version of a professional camera? This may seem to be a paradox, but even professionals' needs differ. A fashion photographer has different priorities than one working for the press and this is exactly the group the F3 P was made for: "P" as in press. The user profile of the F3 P was developed together with the Japanese press agency Kyodo. The following points distinguish it from the normal F3. One of the most conspicuous outer features is the additional ISO-type hot shoe attached to the standard HP-finder with its titanium housing. The shutter speed dial and the release button are built higher and the latter has a silicone rubber cover to protect it from the rain, but lacks the cable release thread. Inside the F3 P are a number of rubber seals to ensure that the camera works perfectly even in drenching rain. Certain details that are seldom required, or even undesirable in everyday press work, were omitted, including the self-timer, the eyepiece shutter, the lever for multiple exposures, and the security-catch for the camera back lock.

Further differences are the enlarged film counter window for easier viewing, and the automatic exposure mode is always being active instead just from frame no.1. The bayonet of the F3 P is made of stainless steel and the camera is delivered with the B-type focusing screen as well as the rewind-stop back MF-6B.

As mentioned before, these features are based on the ideas and wishes of Japanese press photographers. Perhaps they might have been different if sports photographers or photo-journalists from America or Europe had been consulted. In order to ensure that the F3 P is really only available to professional photographers, in Germany at least a valid press identity card has to be presented, which is only issued to those who can prove they work mainly as a photojournalist.

Nikon F3 AF

Automatic focusing is now a reality. The Minolta 7000 Introduced in 1985 created a trend that could not be ignored. But why did Nikon present its first autofocus model as early as 1983 in the form of a professional version? It is more usual for manufacturers to introduce automatic functions first in their amateur cameras before trusting them to a professional model. The reason Nikon did it this way is understandable. The unit construction of the F3 was suited to the development of an autofocus version of the existing camera without having to start from scratch. So the F3 AF body, except for the finder, is almost identical to the normal F3. The only differences are an additional row of contacts on the

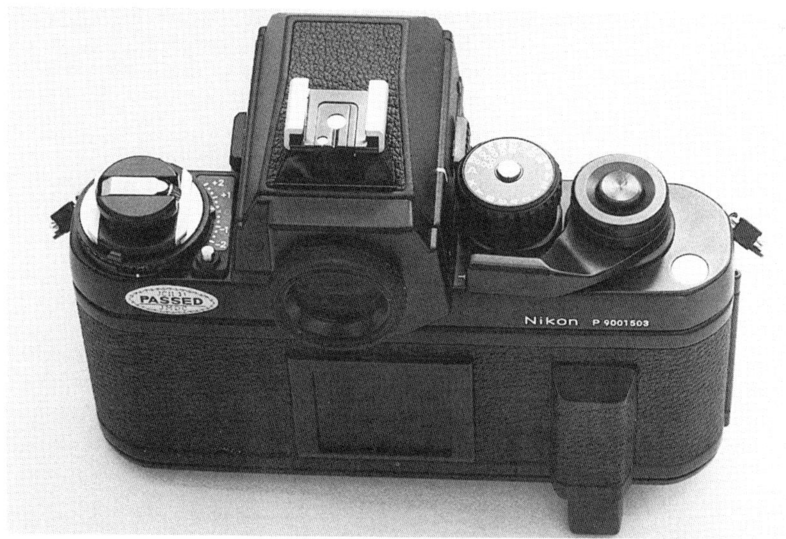

P as in press and designed for toughest use even in torrential rain: The F3 P.

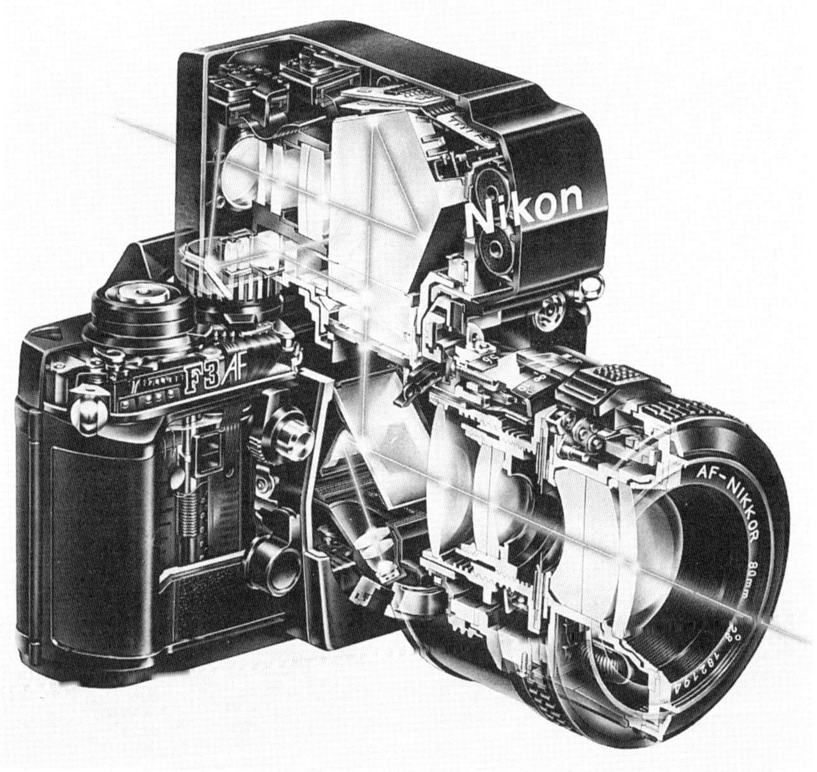

The cross-section illustrates the complex construction of the F3 AF.

finder mount and bayonet which serve to relay the signals from the AF-finder to the AF-lenses. The actual automatic focus evaluation is done in the autofocus prism finder DX-1. It is a self-contained system with a fixed focusing screen and its own power supply.

Within the finder two portions of the light rays entering in the middle are singled out and directed at two silicon photo cells. Similar to a split-image rangefinder, the system recognises whether or not the parts of the subject centered in the focusing zone are in or out of focus. Depending on whether the subject is in front of or behind the correct focus plane the system sends the autofocus lens different signals telling the built-in motor which way to turn it in order to achieve correct focus. The focus indicators in the viewfinder inform about the turning direction of the lens with the help of two red arrows. When both light up simultaneously, focusing is correct. A red "X" on the other hand indicates that the system is not capable of focusing correctly; for example when there is insufficient contrast within the focusing zone.

The AF-finder DX-1 can be attached to any normal F3, with the exemption of the F3 P, and serve as a focusing aid with the normal Nikkor lenses. There is one restriction in that the AF-finder works only with lenses at least as fast as f/3.5. Two autofocus lenses were introduced with the F3 AF, a 80mm,f/2,8 and a 200mm,f/3.5 IF-ED. The teleconverter TC-16A, appearing later, remained the only supplement to the system. The converter's motor drives its own optical system, turning a normal lens into an autofocus lens. Since the converter causes a loss of light of ⅓ EV, the attached lens must have a maximum aperture of at least f/2. In addition the shorter focusing range, especially of telephoto lenses, becomes inaccessible. The present AF-lenses cannot be used with the F3 AF except if the battery in the AF-finder is removed.

The F3 AF did not turn into a sales hit, but Nikon can hardly have expected it to. They had intended to test the market and gather experience for the models to come.

Nikon F4

During the 1980's SLR-technology was being developed at an ever quicker pace. At the time the F3 appeared a programmed automatic exposure mode was an extremely advanced feature, today it is considered as a standard. Multi-pattern metering was introduced in 1983 with the Nikon FA and then in 1985 the Minolta 7000 represented the breakthrough in autofocus technology in SLR cameras. By incorporating more and more microelectronics nothing seemed to be impossible, but there are two sides to every coin, in this case the coin stands for compatibility. Almost all manufacturers' new autofocus cameras forced their customers to purchase a whole new set of lenses as well. This may be acceptable for amateurs, but for the pro it meant not being able to use his expensive lenses. For Nikon, "supplier to professionals", this meant the camera had to be designed combining the F-bayonet which had existed since 1959 with the most advanced technology – an extremely difficult task that Nikon mastered brilliantly. The result is the Nikon F4. To mention every possible combination and feature of this fascinating camera would exceed this book's volume. Therefore we will limit ourselves to the most important features in their relation to the system as a whole. After all, the F4 posesses features described in other Nikon models, for example the Nikon F-801's autofocus system or the Nikon FA's multi-pattern metering.

Let us begin with its weight for a change: 1,100 grams for the body is something that cannot be ignored. But this is compensated – especially when the camera is used with long and heavy telephoto lenses – by its comfortable and secure handling. The external design is once again a result of the cooperation with the Italian Giorgetto Giugiaro and the priority given to ergonomic handling. The release button is located on the slanted top of the protruding grip. The film-advance mode dial is built around the release button. In addition to a single mode, two continuous modes are available. The position CH allows firing rates of up to 4 frames/sec. when the F4 is equipped with the battery pack MB-20, the F4S with the more powerful battery pack MB-21 and the

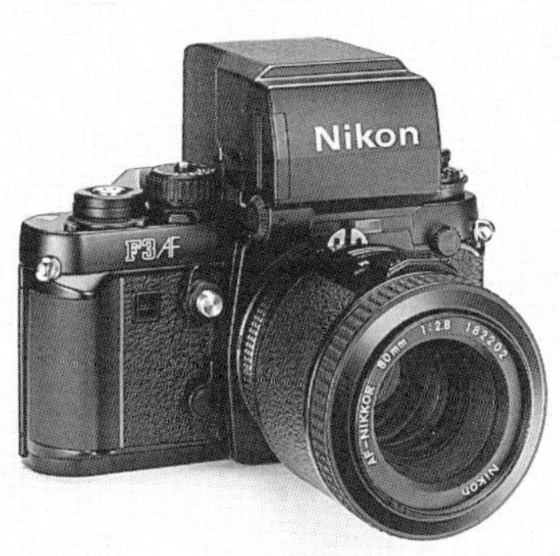

Nikon's first autofocus camera, the F3 AF with its DX-1.

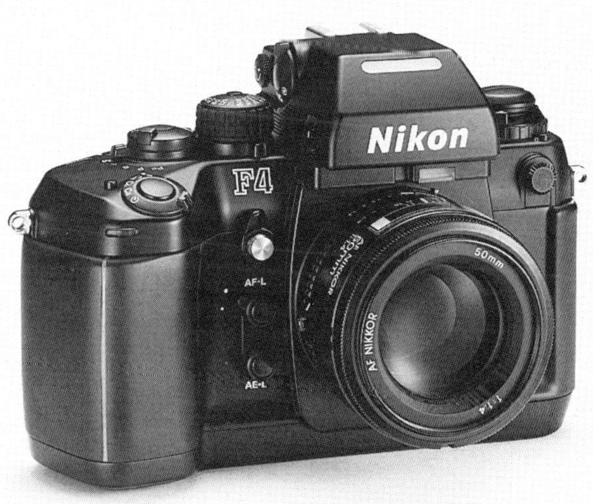

The F4 with the "smaller" battery pack MB-20.

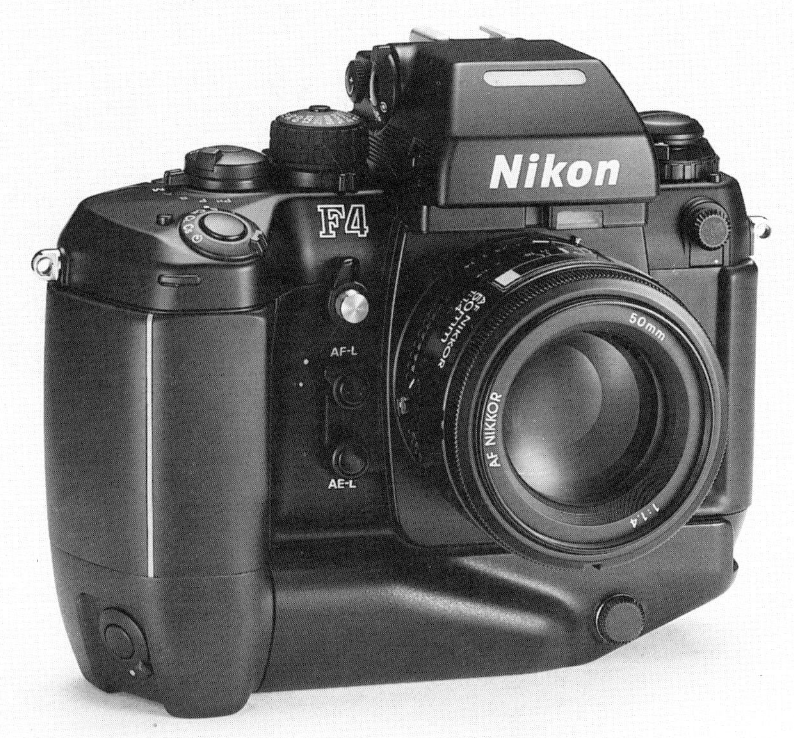

Would you prefer a little more? The battery pack MB-21 offers plenty of power reserves and converts the camera to the F4S.

F4E with the MB-23 pack are capable of an amazing 5.7 frames/sec. The body of the F4 had to be equipped with four internal motors in order to realize such extreme speeds. One is in charge of transporting the film only, the next solely responsible for cocking the shutter and the mirror-box mechanics, the third for rewinding. The fourth motor is for driving the lens focusing mechanism.

The position CL represents a firing rate of "only" 3.4 frames/sec. The setting CS is something really special: in this position the film is only transported at a rate of one picture a second but because the motor is switched to intermittent operation it works extremely quietly. This was meant for situations in which the photographer cannot afford to make himself unpleasantly conspicuous with the motor's whining noise. The last position on the dial activates the electronically controlled self-timer.

A dial to set exposure correction factors sits right next to the classical shutter speed dial instead of in its usual place concentric with the film speed setting. A lever below this dial serves as a switch for the different exposure modes: two program versions (normal and high-speed), aperture and shutter priority modes, as well as manual. In this context the restriction should be mentioned that the program and shutter priority modes are only available with AF-lenses equipped with an integrated CPU.

The multiple-exposure control as well as the rewind lever are also situated in this main operational area. The shutter speed dial is built especially high so that it can be handled easily even with gloves on – once again a proof of how well this camera is adapted to the reality of everyday work. The shutter speed dial offers 19 click-stops for speeds between 1/8000 and 4 sec., B, T, and the X-synchronization speed of 1/250 sec. Obviously the realization of such extremely fast speeds

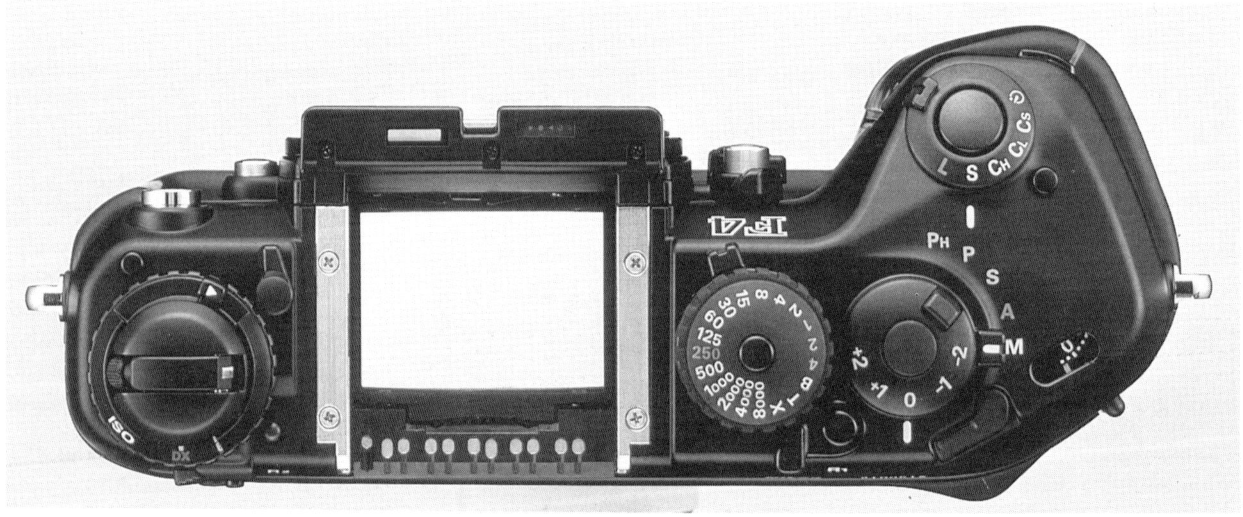

The F4 seen from above. A cockpit with well tested and classical controls.

would not be possible with the well tried horizontally travelling shutter of the F, F2 and F3. For this reason the F4 received a vertical-travel, multi-bladed shutter similar to those in other Nikons. The blades consist of carbon-reinforced epoxy material only 1/10mm thick.

Since the mirror of the F4 can be locked in the upper position there could be a danger of light finding its way past the edges of the individual blades. In order to prevent this the second blind with its epoxy blades normally rests directly behind the first with its aluminum blades. Additionally, a tungsten alloy balancer is included to minimize vibration caused by the shutter. As in every model of the F-series the shutter of the F4 is designed to withstand at least 150,000 cycles.

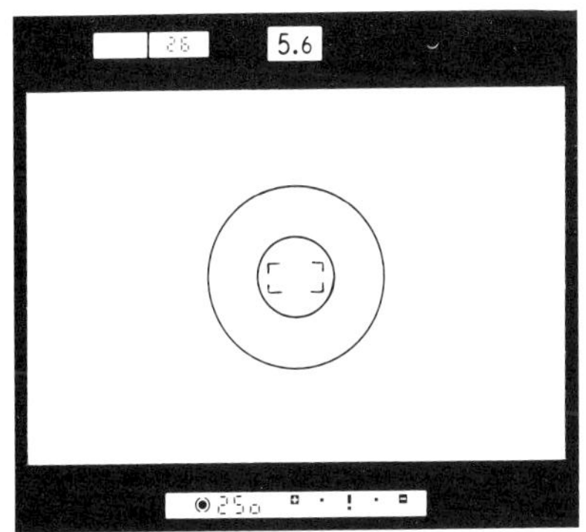

The F4 viewfinder image: The AF-focusing zone is marked within the usual 12mm-circle.

The standard DP-20 finder is detachable, and as with the other F-models a waist-level finder (DW-20), a 6x magnifying finder (DW-21), and an action finder (DA-20) are also available. Some of the electronics had to be built into into the finder in order to create space for the F4's over 1700 separate parts, including its 4- and 8-bit microcomputers and the controlling ICs. Normally the prism finder DP-20 would be used. It offers the same matrix metering as the Nikon F-801, which in turn was developed from the multi-pattern metering of the Nikon FA. The F4 has a very clever little addition however. Two tiny mercury switches register whether the camera is being held vertically or horizontally so that the electronics can change the segment orientation appropriately. Furthermore the finder DP-20 features a built-in dioptre correction and a compensation scale for the F4's different fiocusing screens.

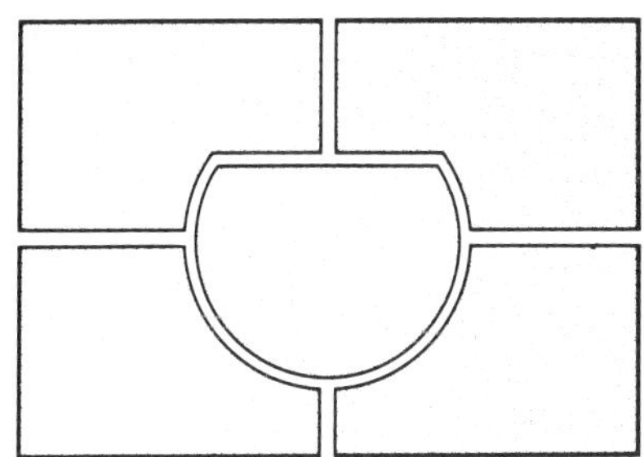

The advanced matrix metering mode divides the image frame into five separate segments.

The dial for the three metering modes is located on the right side of the finder housing. In addition to the matrix mode mentioned before, the classic 60:40% centre-weighted mode is provided as well as – for the first time in a Nikon – a spot-metering mode. The neccessary sensor is situated on top of the AF-module in the bottom of the camera and covers an area represented by the 5mm circle in the centre of the finder screen. Spot metering is possible with any finder and even without, but matrix metering only with the prism finder DP-20, the 60:40% metering characteristic with the DP-20 as well as the action finder DA-20. The complete viewfinder information is also only available with the standard prism finder DP-20. The information provided includes a display of both the aperture and shutter speed, the metering mode, the exposure mode, a possible exposure correction factor, and the frame counter. The finders are mounted by sliding them onto the guide rails and are connected to the camera's electronics by a row of contacts behind the focusing screen. A separate lever under the shutter speed dial allows the finder illumination to be activated – along with the exposure meter.

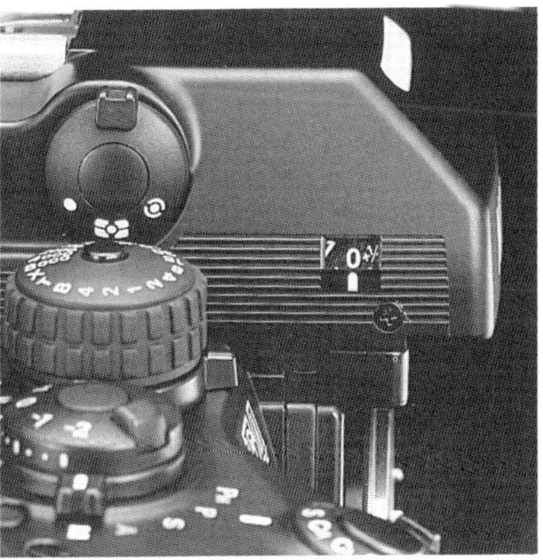

A dial on the finder DP-20 serves as a switch for the three metering modes.

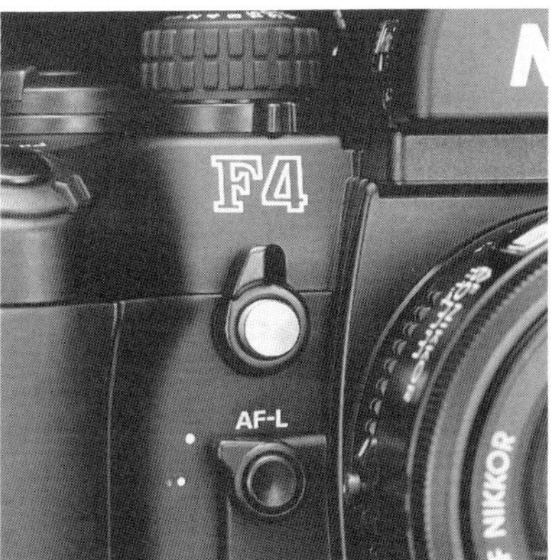

The difference can be felt: The autofocus and exposure-lock buttons.

An ISO-type hot-shoe is mounted on both the DP-20 and DA-20, which in the case of the DP-20 means you can perform matrix balanced fill-flash, as known from the F-801. In order to protect the camera's electronics from flash units using too high trigger voltages a special semiconductor-switch is incorporated.

Besides the standard super-bright B-type focusing screen twelve further versions are available for the F4, but unlike with the former models featuring interchangeable screens, they will probably not find frequent use because of the autofocus.

The First F-Model With Autofocus

Which brings us to one of the F4's main features – autofocus. It should be pointed out, though, that in the case of the F4 autofocus is just one out of the multitude of features – something one can say of only very few other cameras.

The AF-module used is the AM-200 with its 200 CCDs, also known from the F-401x and F-801s. Its metering range stretches from EV -1 to +18.

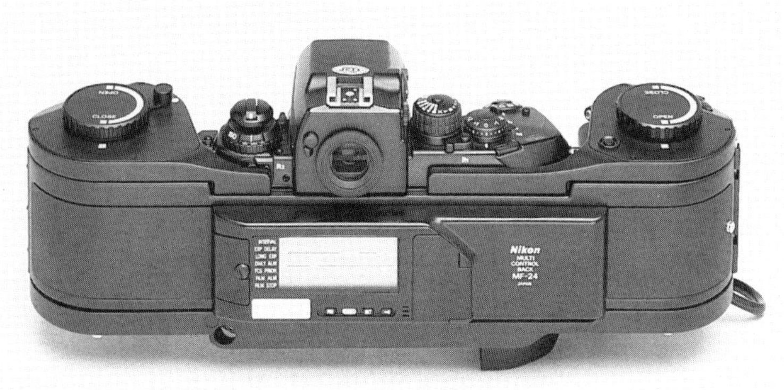

More than just lots of pictures: The Multi-Control Bulk Film Back MF-24 for the F4.

In combination with a coreless motor the autofocus system achieves a response speed that well deserves the attribute "professional". Additionally, the system offers a focus tracking mode for moving subjects. This technology was introduced first in the Minolta 7000i and works by focus being determined at least twice before shutter release. The electronics compute the difference between the values determined and thus the distance the subject will have moved up to the actual moment of exposure. Focus is then preset to the position that will guarantee sharpness at the instant the picture is taken.

A filter is situated in front of the AF-module to remove infrared. When an AF-Speedlight is attached which has an AF-illuminator using infrared light, a second filter is switched in that only lets such light pass. To top it off, any dust is automatically removed from the surfaces of the filters. It remains to be mentioned that the autofocus system only functions with lens speeds of at least f/5.6, or in combination with the AF-teleconverter TC-16A of at least f/3.5. The "Freeze Focus"- mode becomes available together with the Multi-Control Backs MF-23 and MF-24. In this mode the focus is preset manually to a certain distance and as soon as a subject comes into this position the camera releases the shutter automatically.

An warning LED is located to the left of the finder which lights up when the film has been transported completely. It's up to the photographer whether he prefers to have the film rewound by motor within 8 sec. or save energy and reduce the operational noise by employing the good old crank. This warning LED also comes into action when the film speed has been set to DX but a film without this type of code has been loaded. In this case a film speed range from ISO 6/9° to 6400/39° is available.

The autofocus mode selector is situated below the lens release button. Inside the bayonet you will find the electronic contacts for the AF-lenses and the complete set of control pins and levers which ensure compatibility with almost all types of lenses. Program and shutter priority automatic exposure modes are, as stated earlier, only accessible with AF-lenses but aperture priority and manual modes will work with any type of lens.

Matrix metering is also dependent upon AF- or Ai/CPU-type lenses, centre-weighted metering is usable with almost all types of lenses, and spot metering is possible with all but the mirror- and PC-lenses.

The depth-of-field preview button and mirror lockup-lever are situated to the right of the bayonet, below it the AF-lock button which can also work as exposure lock simultaneously if preferred. A bit lower down another button serves only as exposure lock.

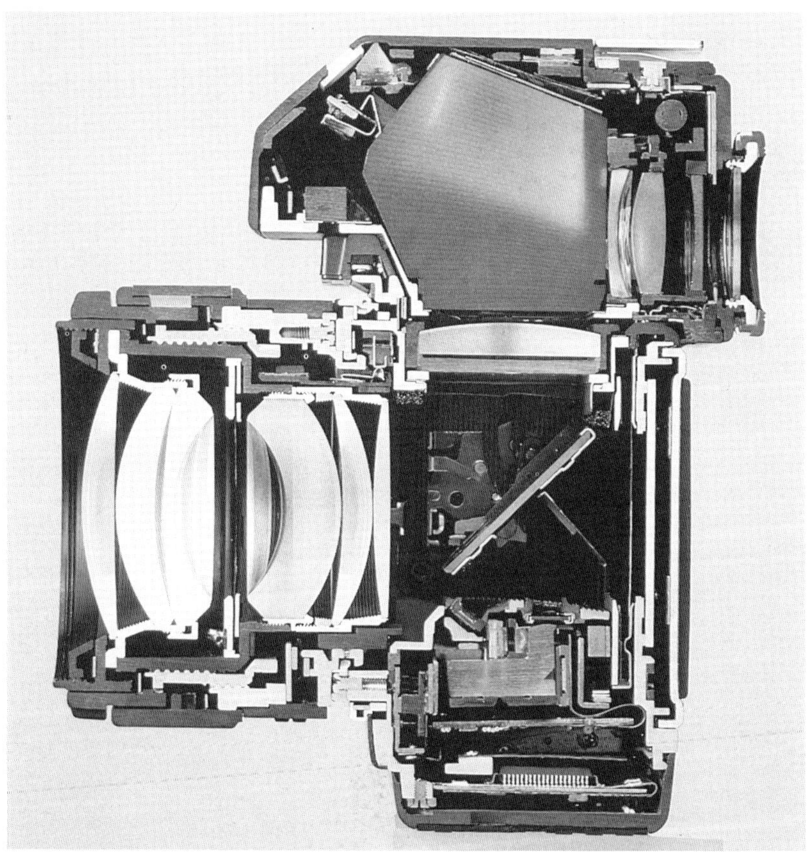

A perfect cooperation between optics, electronics, and mechanics: A cross-section through a Nikon F4.

Nikon F4S and F4E

The power supply of the F4 – a vital subject in the case of a camera so dependent on electrical energy – can be provided from different sources. Four AA-size 1.5v batteries fit into the grip of the smallest battery compartment MB-20. The next largest, MB-21 takes six batteries or rechargeables of the same size. This pack also has an additional release button for more comfortable vertical operation as well as a terminal for remote control equipment. The camera equipped with the MB-21 becomes the F4S. The MB-22 consists of a grip section shaped exactly like that of the MB-21 and is neccessary when external power supplies are employed. The MB-23 is a one-piece battery pack that can be loaded with either AA-size units or the Nikon rechargeable battery MN-20. The camera with the MB-23 pack becomes the F4E. The capacities of these battery packs vary between 30 films with the MB-20 and 150 films with the MB-23 equipped with the MN-20. If somebody purchases the camera with the small battery pack MB-20 which does not have an electric remote control terminal, he can still use the F4 with a conventional mechanical cable-release. The socket is hidden away on the base-plate.

One of the Nikon engineers once stated in an interview that he was astonished himself how they managed to incorporate all these features and possibilities into such a body. Not one millimetre inside has been wasted. Success has proved the Nikon designers to be right, never before had there been such an interest for a new camera model. Immediately after the introduction of this dream camera Nikon was literally overwhelmed by the demand, such a success simply could not be forseen. For a long time deliveries were very slow; customers of camera stores had to be recorded on waiting-lists.

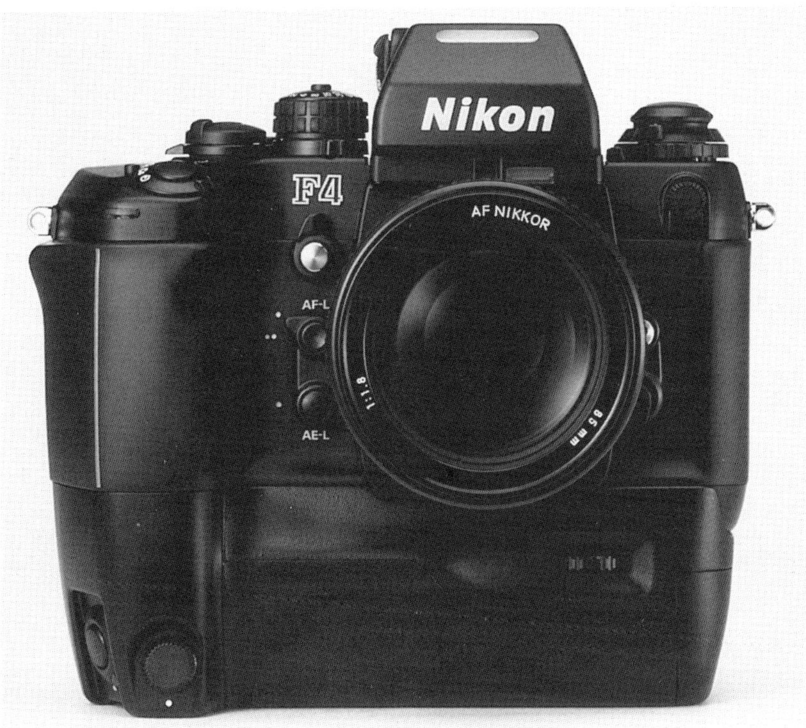

The Nikon F4E with its MB-23 battery pack has the biggest power reserves of the F4 models.

CHAPTER 3

The Nikkormat Models

1965 – the Nikon F was well on its way to becoming the professional`s first choice. Even so, many pros as well as demanding amateur photographers felt the need for a simpler second body. They were willing to go without the less needed features in return for a more moderate price. In photojournalism particularly two bodies were perfectly normal, either to exploit different types of film or simply to increase one's shooting capacity without the need to change films in critical situations. The Nikkorex F could not satisfy these needs since it had the reputation of being a "snap-shooter's camera".

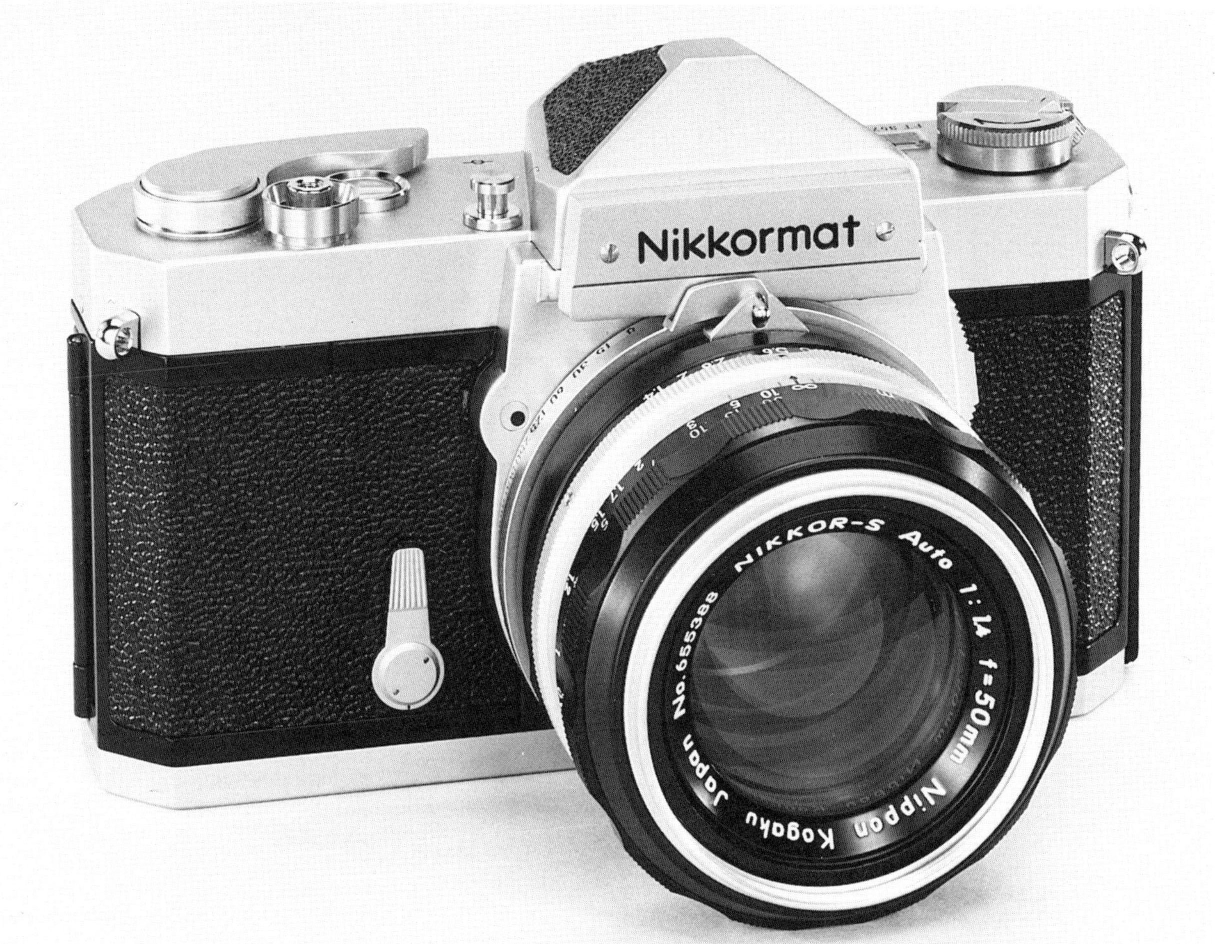

The Nikkormat, a more modestly priced alternative to the F-models; here the Nikkormat FTN, the most popular Nikkormat with the 60:40% metering configuration typical of Nikon.

Nikkormat FT

The Nikkormat FT closed this gap. It was equipped with a TTL-exposure meter, a fast shutter with speeds ranging from 1 to 1/1000 sec. and 1/125 sec. X-sync speed, and of course it accepted all the lenses, including the specialist ones, thus meeting the most important requirements. It was more compact and lighter in weight than its "big sister", the F, and was intended to allow the critical amateur access to the Nikon family.

The Nikkormat FT features a fixed prism finder along with a fixed viewfinder screen. Turning the film advance lever 20° switches on the exposure meter. A full stroke of 135° cocks the shutter and transports the film to the next frame; contrary to the F or F2, it is not possible to do this with several half-strokes. The film counter and depth-of-field preview button are situated next to the release button with its normal as well as Leica-bell-type threads for cable releases.

The shutter speed dial is not on the top of the camera, but is located around the lens bayonet. The set

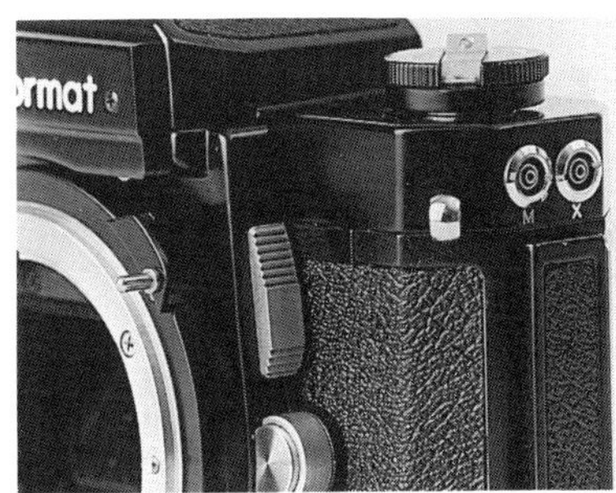

One of the Nikkormat's characteristic features: the mirror lockup-slider.

speed can be seen on the ring that is operated with a lever located on its opposite side. The meter coupling prong is also found around the bayonet. The camera's exposure meter must be informed about the preset as well as the lens's maximum aperture. In order to ensure this the ISO-film speed has to be turned to the mark corresponding to the latter – a chore which proved to be quite a troublesome and annoying procedure.

The mirror lockup-slider – the use of which I consider to be a bit too difficult – is situated immediately above the lens release button. In any case it is a very helpful feature in everyday use that unfortunately more and more cameras no longer have. Of course, the Nikkormat FT also has the obligatory self-timer with a running time of about eight seconds. The fixed screen in the viewfinder, which we would describe as dim by today's standards, has a microprism area. The exposure meter needle is displayed to the right outside the finder image. Whenever the needle is centred within the bracketing frame the resulting exposure will be correct. In addition the exposure setting can be monitored from outside the camera. On the top-plate, located between the prism and the rewind crank, is a small window with its own needle, so that the exposure can be controlled without having to look through the viewfinder. This feature comes in handy, for example, when you want to take some shots unnoticed.

The FT metering system incorporating two CDS-cells to the left and right of the eyepiece still covered the whole frame without favouring any area and worked within the range of EV 3 to17 at ISO 100/21°. Just like the Nikon F, the Nikkormat also uses a single 1.35v button-size battery that has its place in the bottom of the camera. The Nikkormat FT has two different sync-terminals: labelled "X" for electronic units and "M" for flashbulbs.

Besides the fixed finder there is another important difference to the Nikon F: the missing motor coupling. Nikon sacrificed these two features, mainly demanded by professionals, in favour of a more modest price. As an extra, a separate accessory shoe was available which could be mounted on the eyepiece protection-lens. This shoe also allowed the attachment of special viewfinders for fisheye lenses. A hot-shoe contact was not provided on this accessory shoe though.

The FT, available in chrome or black finish, formed the starting point of the little "Nikon tanks" series of Nikkormats. All of the following models, the FTN, the FT-2, and the FT-3 were more or less thorough modifications, so together they represent a production time of 12 years between 1965 and 1977. In this respect the Nikkormat exceeded one or two of the F-models.

Nikkormat FS

A sister model to the Nikkormat FT, the FS was introduced at the same time. Its features are nearly identical to those of the FT except that the exposure meter and the mirror lockup-slider were omitted. Whereas, at least in Germany, the Nikkormat FT is not exactly a common camera, the FS may be considered an outright rarity.

Nikkormat FTN

The best known Nikkormat model, the FTN, was introduced in 1967 as the successor to the FT and was popular for many years. It remained successful for quite a while until it was replaced by the FT-2 in 1975. Compared to the FT it was improved in several points that were very useful in everyday work. Its exposure meter is centre-weighted 60:40%, a characteristic that was to remain a standard in Nikon cameras for many years. The viewfinder image was brightened somewhat and the Nikkormat FTN could be supplied with one of two different focusing screens – the A-type with a split-image rangefinder or the J-type with microprisms – but you did have to decide before purchase because the screen was fixed in the factory and could not be removed by the photographer. The last series of FTN-models was furnished with K-type screens, with a combination of the A- and J-features.

The display of the shutter speeds in the viewfinder was new and a real help in general practice. There are always three speeds visible simultaneously: the preset speed is displayed in the middle, with the next faster and slower speeds to the left and right. The bracket for the metering needle was equipped with plus and minus symbols to make it easier to discern between over- or underexposure.

The FTN was the first model to be equipped with the semi-automatic maximum aperture indexing of the mounted lens as a coupling between the exposure meter and the lens. To do this, the meter coupling prong must be turned to the left in the direction of the rewind crank and the lens set to f/5.6. The lens is then attached, and after it clicks into its proper position the aperture ring must be turned once all the way to the left and once to the right. This procedure, which may seem tedious at first and was often criticised by the users of other makes, is soon something the photographer does almost automatically. The fact that long-time Nikon users still unnecessarily turn their lenses back and forth even after the change to the AI-standard, goes to show how much of a habit it had become. This technology was only modified in 1977 with the advent of the AI-system.

A scale for the maximum aperture of the mounted lens is included in the aperture ring at about the height of the mirror lockup-slider. As a routine a casual look from time to time was advisable since the very sensitive mechanics, consisting of three metal rings running within each other, are sometimes hampered by moisture and dust. The result of these occasional defects were overexposures that could not be explained at first – especially since they only occurred once in a while and only with certain lenses that otherwise worked perfectly. The film speed setting of the FTN was a real source of vexation, though. Setting was by means of a tiny metal frame in the lower part of the shutter speed dial that was rather difficult to handle and must have cost countless fingernails through the years. Nevertheless, this is the only point the Nikkormat can be criticized for in terms of handling.

Nikormat FT-2

After a production period of eight years the Nikkormat FTN deserved a number of modifications, it was time for the FT-2. At first sight it can be distinguished from its predecessor by its accessory shoe, with sync-contact in the centre, on the prism. The plastic-covered film advance lever had become more comfortable to handle and further improvements enhanced the FT-2's looks as well as its operation. For example, with a new leather surface, a plastic-coated self-timer

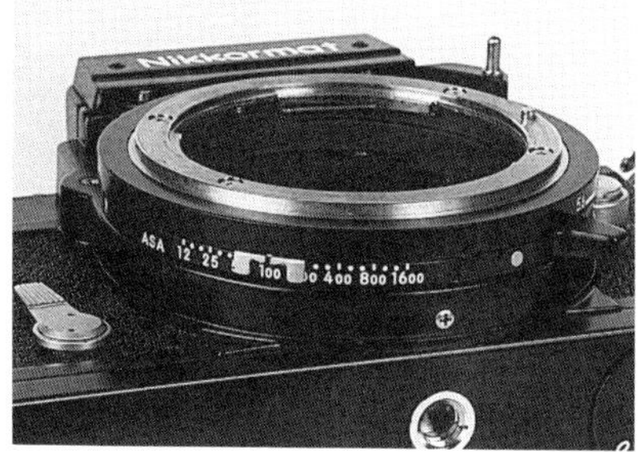

The film speed setting below the shutter speed scale

lever, and small plastic inlets in the depth-of-field button and lens release buttons. The ISO setting had become decisively easier and was equipped with a lock for the shutter speed lever, so Nikkormat users had no need to complain about broken fingernails anymore. The proven "Copal Square" shutter construction was modified by including an automatically switching sync-contact, so that the FT-2 only needed one sync-terminal, another distinctive feature. Plus and minus symbols were added to the exposure meter window on the top of the

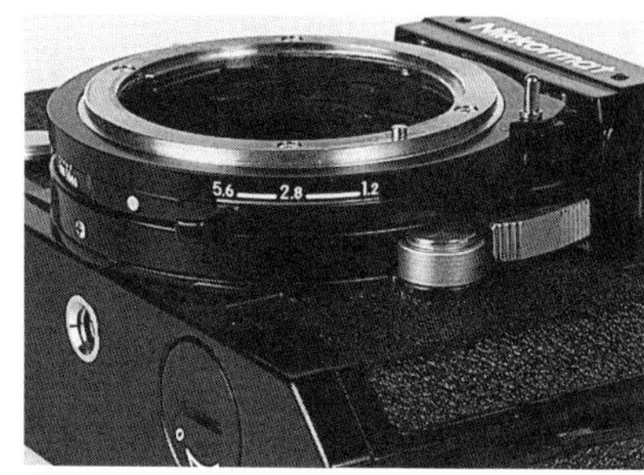

Situated on the opposite side to the shutter speed scale is the maximum aperture scale.

camera as signs for over- and underexposure and the power was now supplied by a 1.5v battery.

Nikkormat FT-3

In 1977 Nikon introduced the AI-control system for the automatic conveyance of the len's maximum aperture to the exposure metering system, so the FT-2 was updated to the FT-3. The only difference between the two models is the AI-aperture coupling. But the high time of Nikkormats was over, the market called for a more modern camera.

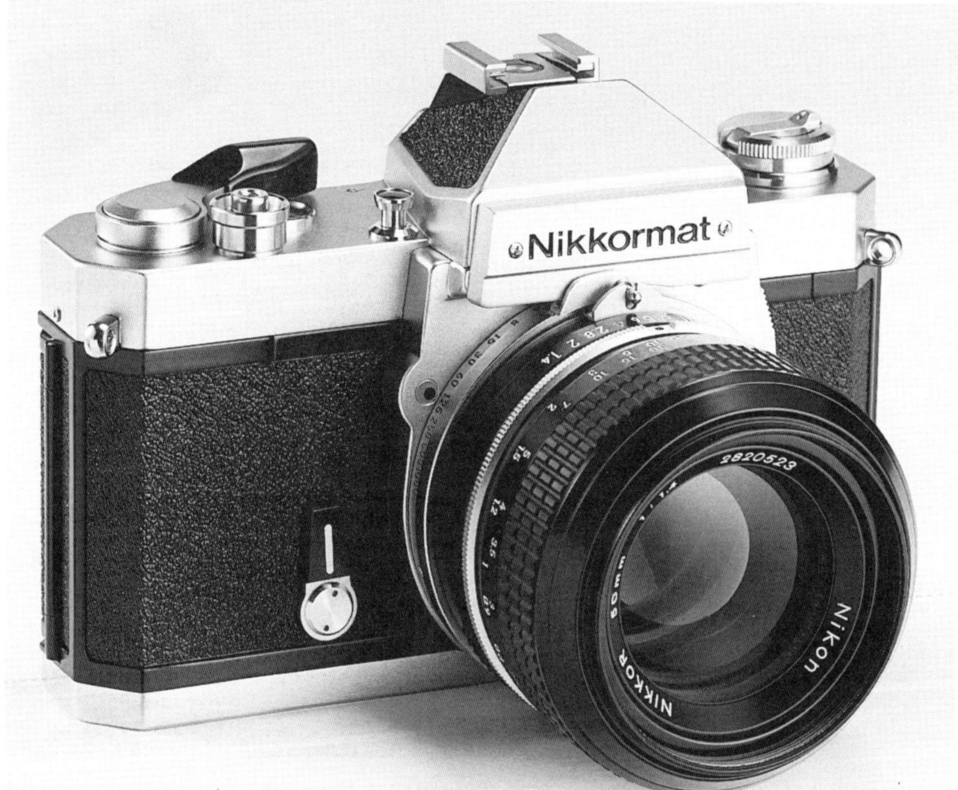

The Nikkormat FT-2 can be recognized immediately by its built-in accessory shoe.

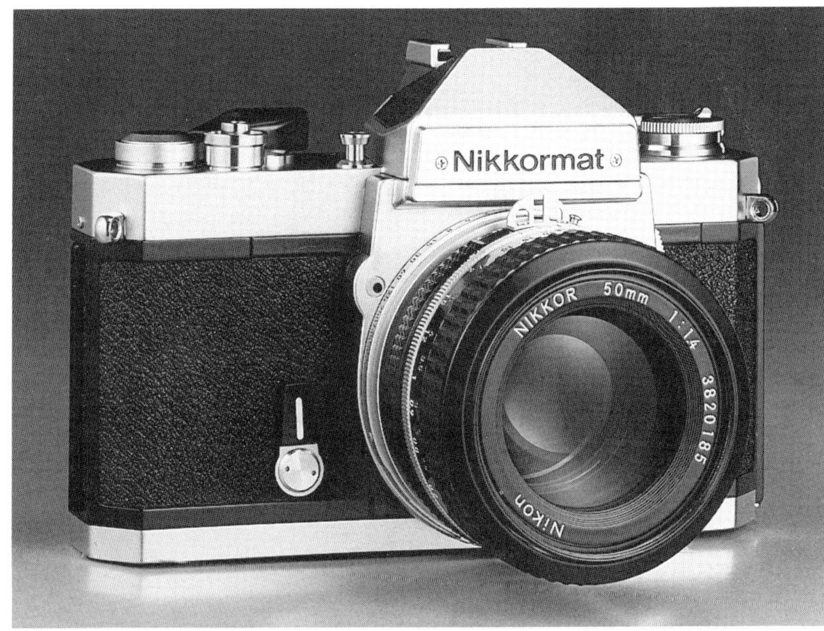

The last Nikkormat before the advent of the FM-era: the FT-3 with its AI-coupling.

Nikon discontinued the Nikkormat series in the very same year the FT-3 appeared and replaced them with the more compact and efficient FM. Even so, countless Nikon photographers, professionals as well as amateurs, had learned to treasure their Nikkormats as reliable and rugged photographic tools and many are still doing their daily job without a problem.

Nikkormat EL

This was not Nikon's first camera with an automatic exposure mode, the Nikkorex Auto 35 takes the honours for this. But the latter, a little known exotic camera from the Nikon stable, had neither TTL-metering nor interchangeable lenses. Nikon's first system camera with aperture priority automatic exposure mode, the Nikkormat EL appeared on the market in 1972. A somewhat late arrival, considering that Konica had introduced an automatic system SLR four years before with the Autoreflex T (although it was a shutter priority model).

The EL falls between the Nikkormat FTN and the F2. In terms of design, though, it is a completely different camera, which actually had no more in common with the mechanical Nikkormat models made up to that date than the name. It was equipped with the proven 60:40% centre-weighted metering system and the Copal shutter was electronically controlled by a single IC – something revolutionary then. Two CDS-cells serve as metering sensors whose sluggishness in dim light was very apparent. When pointed to a dark subject immediately after a bright one it takes 1 to 2 seconds for the metering needle to settle at the exact exposure value. This so-called memory-effect is more or less typical of all CDS-metering systems and not peculiar to the EL.

Which brings us to the viewfinder display. Within the EL's fixed prism finder a shutter speed scale is located on the left with a range from 1/1000 to 4 sec. A black needle moves over this scale and indicates the shutter speed chosen by the automatic exposure system. When set to manual mode a green needle marks the preset shutter speed while the black one still indicates the meter's selection as a comparison. A very practical method which enables you to meter the brightest and the darkest subject details in order to evaluate the degree of contrast. When set to automatic mode the green needle moves to the "A" at the top of the speed scale. In order to influence the automatic mode quickly, the Nikkormat EL is equipped with an exposure lock function which is activated with the self-timer lever. As long as it is pressed in the direction of the bayonet the value displayed will remain locked.

The viewfinder had either the A-type (only a split-image rangefinder) or the J-type (with only microprisms) focusing screen built in. They are not interchangeable. The last models

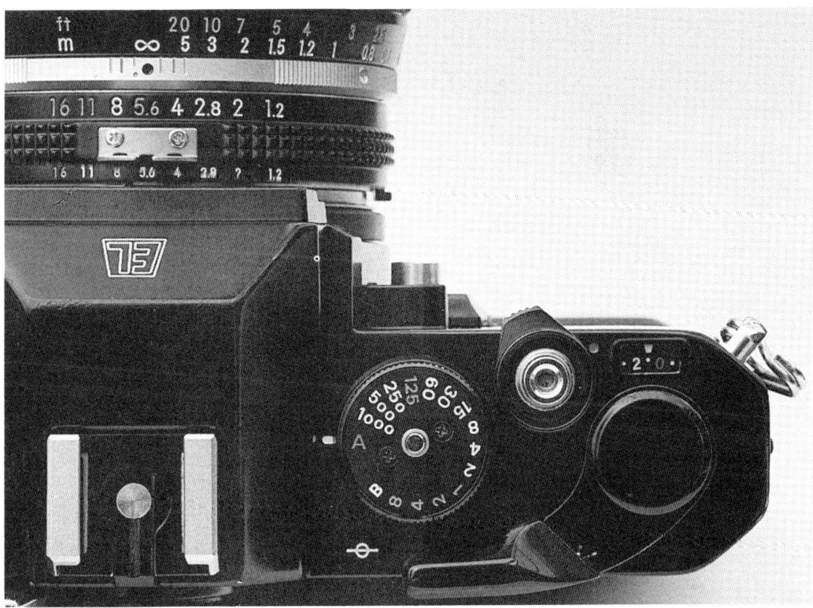

The electronic shutter control on the Nikkormat EL, "A" as in "aperture priority".

(1976) were equipped with the K-type screen combining both features.

A 6v silver-oxide battery serves as the power supply, and Nikon gave it a very peculiar place in the camera's body. You will find it in the mirror-box where the mirror has to be locked in its upper position and the battery compartment's cover unlocked before it can be exchanged – almost a game of skill. A button to the left of the eye-piece operates a battery test with an LED. If the battery output falls below 4,5v the shutter will revert to its mechanical speed of 1/90 sec. The B-position on the other hand does indeed call for sufficient battery power.

The exposure meter is activated when the film advance lever is turned, which also unlocks the release button. The switch for the type of synchronization is located within the shutter speed dial: a red arrow for X (electronic flash units), a white bulb symbol for the M-type synchronization of flash bulbs. Because of its built-in accessory shoe it is Nikon's first model that was equipped with a hot-shoe contact as a standard.

A typical example of Nikon striving to achieve the best possible solutions even for the smallest details is the switch located in the accessory shoe that only activates the central X-contact when a flash gun is attached. This prevents the photographer from getting an electric shock when a flash gun with a higher triggering current is released. The procedure of opening the EL's back also represents a first for Nikon – it was the first camera that is not opened with a key in the base-plate, but instead by pulling up the rewind crank. The film speed dial (also something new) with a range from ISO 25/15° to ISO 1600/33° is now located beneath the crank as well.

In the case of the EL the information about the chosen film speed and aperture set on the lens is relayed to the camera's electronics by means of a

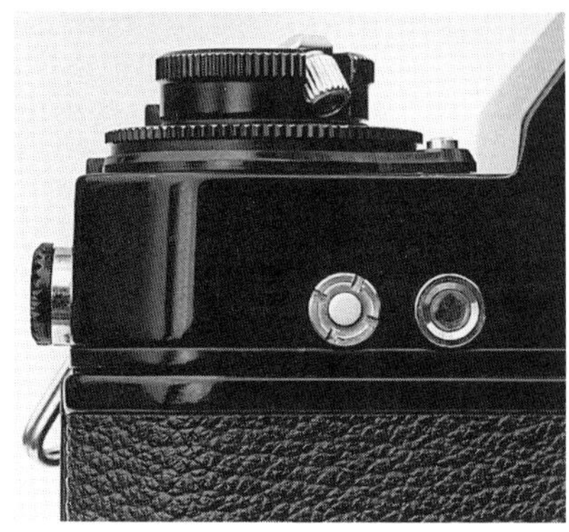

The battery-check button alongside its LED.

resistor plate. Depending on the ISO and aperture values a tracing brush touches a certain section of the plate. These resistor elements used to be made of graphite with the disadvantage that dust or moisture could lead to contact problems. This can be recognized by a jumpy meter needle. In the EL an FRE (functional resistance element) was employed which uses a hard glass baseplate onto which

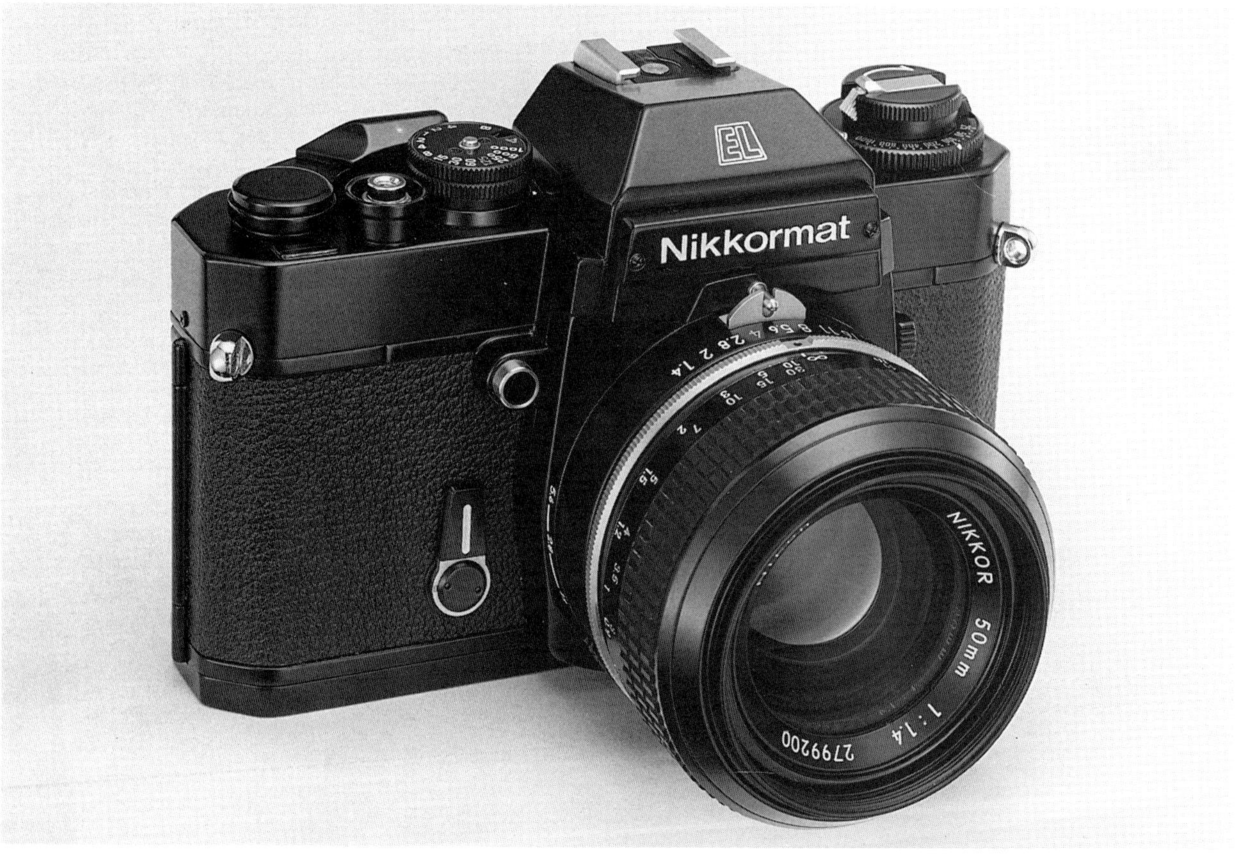

Speedy exposure control: the Nikkormat EL with aperture priority mode.

the resistors are fastened so that outside influences cannot lead to defects.

An advantage of the EL visible in the viewfinder is that by means of an asymmetrical rotation axis the mirror could be designed a bit longer, leading to less vignetting with long telephoto lenses and in extreme close-up situations.

Nikon ELW

Soon after the appearance of the EL the demands for a motorized film transport system became louder, indeed as a practical supplement to the automatic exposure mode. The EL was not originally designed for the attachment of such an accessory, so an appropriately modified successor had to be developed, the Nikkormat ELW – W as in winder. It was introduced in 1976 and only available in black finish. It is practically an EL with additional electrical contacts as well as a mechanical coupling in the camera base-plate for the motor drive. The accompanying motor is called AW-1, its dimensions are almost equal to those of the camera base-plate and is a mere 4cm high. The winder is controlled by the camera release button and runs at about 0.5 sec. per frame. A continuous mode may not be available, but the winder does make a quick second shot possible without having to take the eye from the viewfinder. The ELW was equipped with a separate switch situated around the release button so

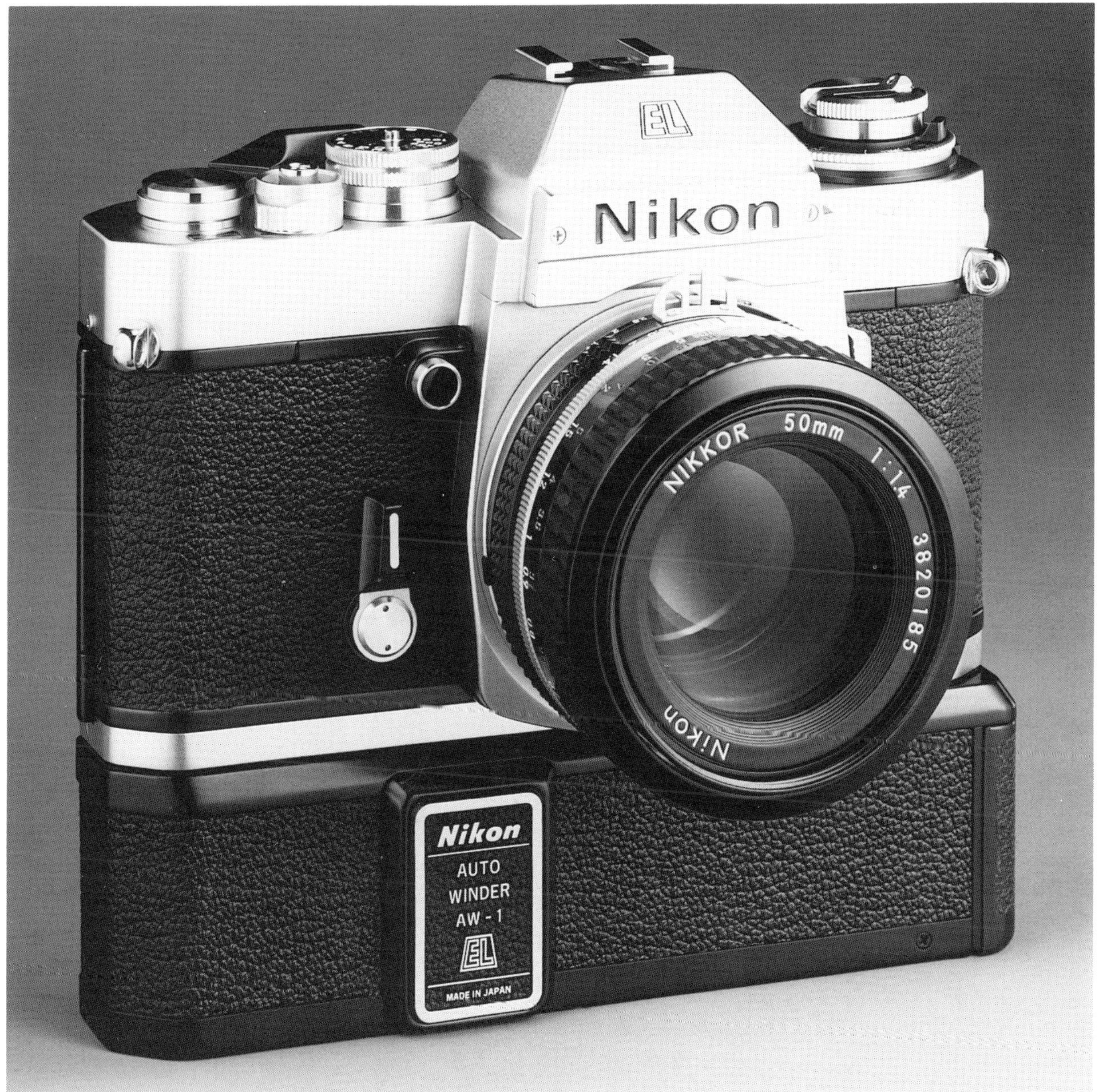

The Nikkormat with the Nikon logo: the EL-2 together with the winder AW-1.

that the film transport lever does not have to stay at the stand-off position constantly to activate the exposure meter. It should not be forgotten, though, to turn the collar back to its basic position when the camera is not being used because the battery would otherwise be drained within two or three days. By the way, the EL cannot be turned into an ELW. Only a small number of ELW's were produced, since its successor, the EL-2 was ready to be marketed just one year later.

Nikon EL-2

In comparison to the EL, two major differences stand out on the EL-2 which was the first in this series of cameras to carry the name Nikon instead of Nikkormat. In 1977 all Nikon cameras and lenses were equipped with the AI-system for automatic maximum aperture indexing. The times were over when you had to set the aperture ring to f/5.6 before mounting a lens, the prong to its normal position, and after securing the lens turn the aperture ring back and forth once. The AI-system reduces it all to one single, simple operation with the help of the lens's meter coupling ridge that automatically brings the body's prong into the proper position. A very welcome relief, supporting a quick lens change.

Background Information: The Light Meter

Light metering cells have certain upper and lower limits to their abilities to evaluate incident light precisely. Above, and especially below these limits their precision deteriorates more than is tolerable. The metering range is represented in EVs, that is exposure values. Most cameras possess metering ranges from EV 1 to 18 at ISO 100/21°. The basis EV 0 represents a correct exposure with a shutter speed of 1 sec. and an aperture setting of f/1. According to the rule of reciprocity this is valid regardless of whether a film is exposed with a fast shutter speed and a large aperture or vice versa, presupposing the same brightness. So, EV 0 also represents an exposure with a shutter speed of 2 sec. and an aperture of f/1.4 or 4 sec. and f/2. The exposure value always depends on the film speed.

At a certain brightness an ISO 100/21° film may need an exposure of EV 10 (1/60 sec. at f/4 or 1/15 sec. at f/8 and so on). In comparison an ISO 400/27° film will need an aperture/speed combination of EV 12 (1/250 sec. at f/4 or 1/60 sec. at f/8 and so on). This shows how the EV-range changes according to the film speed, so that a range of EV 1 to 18 with an ISO 100/21° film corresponds to EV -1 to 16 with an ISO 25/15° film or EV 3 to 20 with an ISO 400/27° film. Of course this does not mean that the metering cell's sensitivity increases or decreases, but only that the usable range of shutter speed/aperture value combinations changes.

As a result there is always a longest exposure time with the metering system still working, for example in the case of the FM it is 1 sec. at ISO 100/21° or 1/4 sec. at ISO 400/27° or 1/30 sec. at ISO 3200/36°. When a slower shutter speed is employed correct metering becomes impossible. Modern cameras like the FA or the F-801 indicate this by signalling "Hi" or "Lo". Older cameras such as the Nikkormat models react by erratically jumping between over- and underexposure displays.

The second major modification concerns the electronics. Instead of the relatively sluggish CDS-cells, the EL-2 works with the new and very much more responsive silicon (SPD)-cells. The complete electronics are integrated into one flexible printed circuit with far fewer soldered connections. This markedly reduces the electronic system's sensitivity to outside influences. But there are also improvements to details in the EL-2. The standard K-type focusing screen (split-image rangefinder and microprisms) is still fixed. The shutter speed range is extended to 8 sec on the long exposure end and the film speed range is expanded from ISO 12/12° to 3200/36°.

The new possibility of setting exposure correction factors from +2 EV to -1 EV in increments of 1/2 EV is quite practical. The self-timer lever which also serves as exposure-lock was shaped to prevent the finger from slipping off. Of course, as the immediate successor to the ELW the EL-2 was also designed to have the film transported by the winder AW-1. The EL-2 was available either in chrome or black finish but, only for a short while. In 1978 the compact FE followed for which the EL-2 had tested the electronics.

Exposure value: Shutter speed/Aperture combinations

Shutter speed (sec.)	Aperture value										
	1	1.4	2	2.8	4	5.6	8	11	16	22	32
4	-2	-1	0	1	2	3	4	5	6	7	8
2	-1	0	1	2	3	4	5	6	7	8	9
1	0	1	2	3	4	5	6	7	8	9	10
1/2	1	2	3	4	5	6	7	8	9	10	11
1/4	2	3	4	5	6	7	8	9	10	11	12
1/8	3	4	5	6	7	8	9	10	11	12	13
1/15	4	5	6	7	8	9	10	11	12	13	14
1/30	5	6	7	8	9	10	11	12	13	14	15
1/60	6	7	8	9	10	11	12	13	14	15	16
1/125	7	8	9	10	11	12	13	14	15	16	17
1/250	8	9	10	11	12	13	14	15	16	17	18
1/500	9	10	11	12	13	14	15	16	17	18	19
1/1000	10	11	12	13	14	15	16	17	18	19	20

CHAPTER 4

The Modern Classics

From 1965 Nikon had offered the Nikkormat models to amateur photographers as well as to professionals looking for a second body. Their rapid growth in popularity made it clear that they could very well be compared to the F and F2 in terms of reliability and ruggedness. However, in spite of constant improvements – from the first FT to the FTN, FT-2, and finally the FT-3 with the AI-coupling – in 1977 the time was ripe for a new type of camera. The length of time during which this new model, the Nikon FM, was to be manufactured goes to show how well Nikon had anticipated the future when this series was introduced. With the same body dimensions as the FE, FM-2, and FE-2 and the same system accessories, for example the motor drives MD-11 and MD-12 fitting all models, along with its compact dimensions and light weight, the FM became popular with Nikon enthusiasts, both amateur and professional.

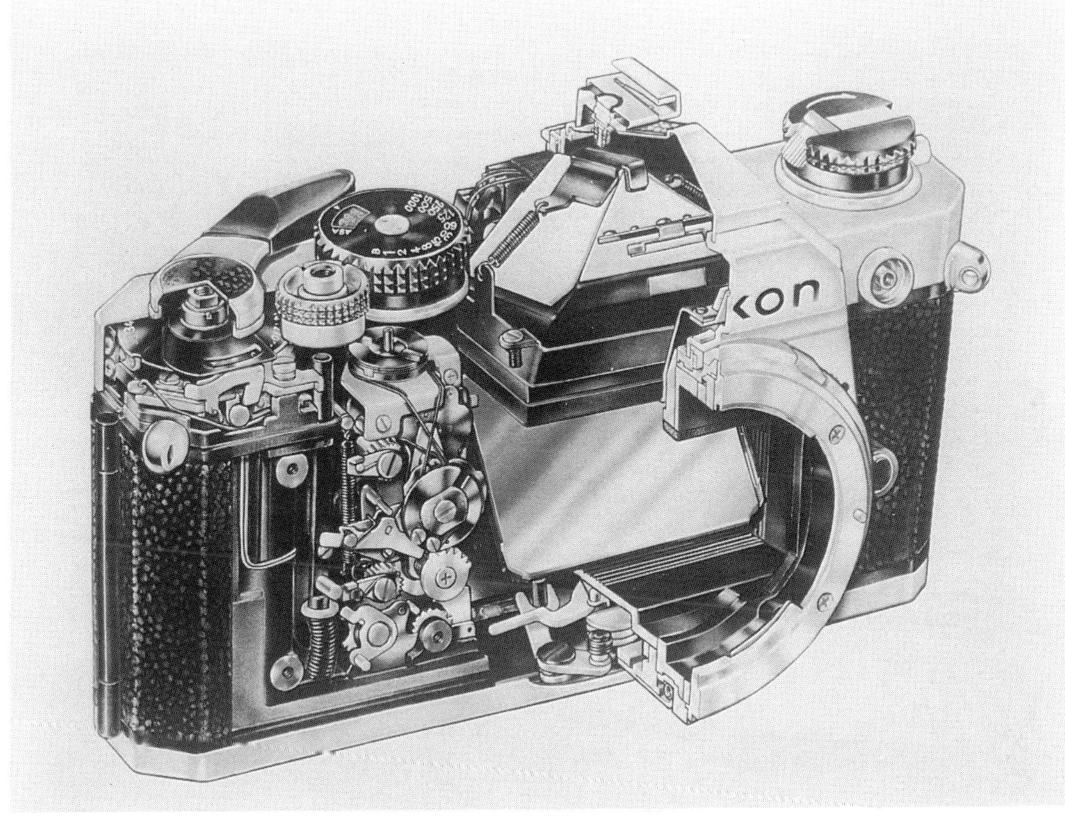

The last of the mechanical models: the Nikon FM. In the form of the FM-2 the oldest model still being produced today.

Nikon FM

Nikon introduced a completely new design of camera with the FM. Even though its dimensions are almost identical it weighs about 200 grams less than the good old Nikkormat. From the very first use of the film advance lever, which works extremely smoothly, you will realize that this camera has only one thing in common with an FTN or its successors – the bayonet. One look through the viewfinder shows that the era of metering displays with needles had come to an end. Three LEDs indicate the result of the proven 60:40% centre-weighted metering. The circle in the centre indicates a correct exposure with a maximum deviation of +/- 1/5 EV. If the + or – LEDs light up additionally, this indicates over- or underexposures of up to 1 EV. If only + or – light up the difference from a correct exposure amounts to 1 EV or more.

The extremely responsive gallium arsenide photo diodes were chosen as light metering cells. Their sensitivity and speed becomes particularly apparent when, pointed at monitors or tv-screens all three LEDs light up simultaneously. They react even to the CRT's image transmitting frequency of 25 pictures/sec. The metering range reaches from EV 1 (1 sec. at f/1.4) to EV 18 (1/1000 sec. at f/16) with ISO 100/21°. The film speed is set inside the shutter speed dial and covers an impressive range from ISO 12/12° to 3200/36°. Besides the shutter speed, the preset aperture is also displayed in the viewfinder. AI-type lenses and those modified to this standard are furnished with a second aperture scale for this purpose.

The FM viewfinder image. In addition to the shutter speed the aperture is also visible.

The FM is equipped with a fixed K-type focusing screen as standard. In order to avoid vignetting when using extremely long telephoto lenses or in close-up photography the FM was given a larger mirror. Vibration resulting from its operation is reduced by a kind of pneumatic damper built into the mirror-box. Because of this a lockup function was omitted, but a depth-of-field preview lever is placed so it can be used easily. The AI-coupling lever can be turned out of the way so that the use of non-AI lenses does not cause any problems.

The internal mechanical construction was greatly improved. Hardly any of the usual lubricating oils and greases have to be used. This means that this completely mechanical camera can be employed throughout the enormous temperature range from -40° to +50° without a problem. The FM was the first Nikon to be equipped as standard with a multiple exposure facility. The first FM-models had to be prepared for the use of the motor drives MD-11/12 by turning the collar round the release button to the red position in order to allow metering without the advance lever in the stand-by position when the motor was switched on. The motor MD-11 as well as the later version MD-12 can accelerate an FM up to a frequency of nearly 3.5 frames/sec. Since this compact unit weighs a considerable 500 grams less than a motorized F2 it quickly won the hearts of many sports and press photographers. The shutter is a Copal CCS with a sync-speed of 1/125 sec. which represented the state of the art at the time. The mechanical, resettable self-timer was also new. The FM's back is removable and can be replaced by the databack MF-12. The memo holder, a clip for the film box flap as a reminder of the type of film loaded, was a practical and novel little detail.

In addition to the chrome and black versions Nikon introduced a limited edition in 1977 with a body and a 50mm,f/1.4 Nikkor in gold finish in honour of the 60th anniversary of Nippon Kogaku K.K. The FM has turned into a classic model in the form of its successor, the FM-2 which is still being produced today.

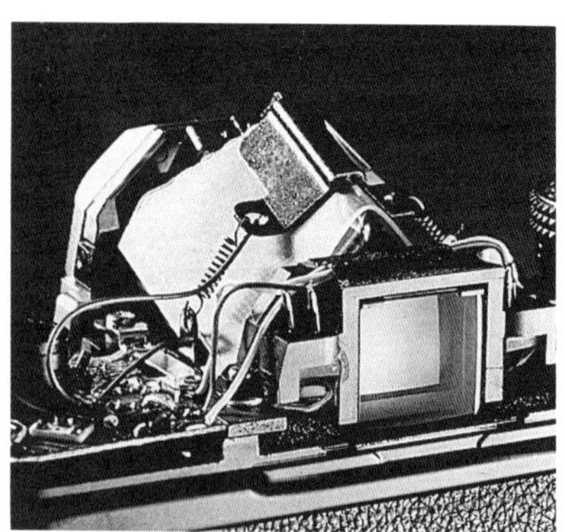
A detailed view into the FM with its prism housing removed. The printed circuits are also folded over the prism.

Nikon FE

If you take the mechanics of the FM and combine them with the electronics of the EL-2, what you get is the Nikon FE. That is exactly what happened in 1978 as an answer to the demand for a sister model to the newly introduced FM. Nikon did not take it quite so lightly though. First of all the electronic system was converted to work with 3v in order to allow the choice between two 1.5v silver oxide batteries or one 3v lithium battery.

Many users were also grateful for the option to change the focusing screen themselves – which was not possible with the FM. Due to the non-detachable prism they have to be changed through the bayonet opening. Besides the standard K-type screen with split-image rangefinder

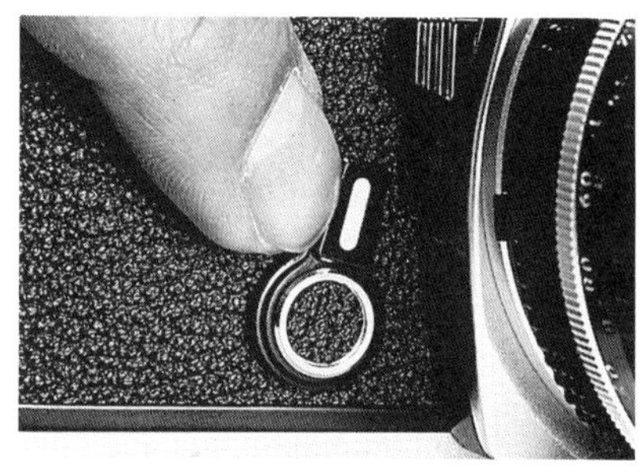
A double function – auto exposure lock with the help of the self-timer lever.

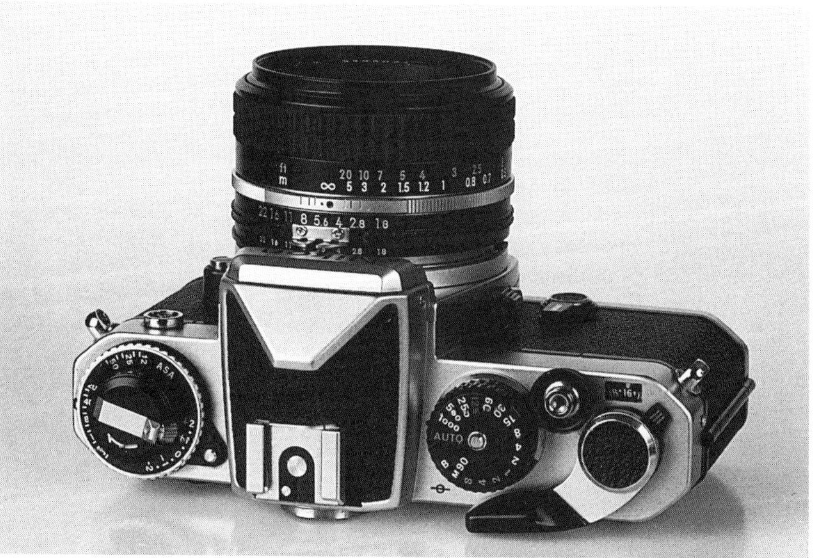

Thanks to its aperture priority automatic exposure mode and compact dimensions the Nikon FE was a very successful model.

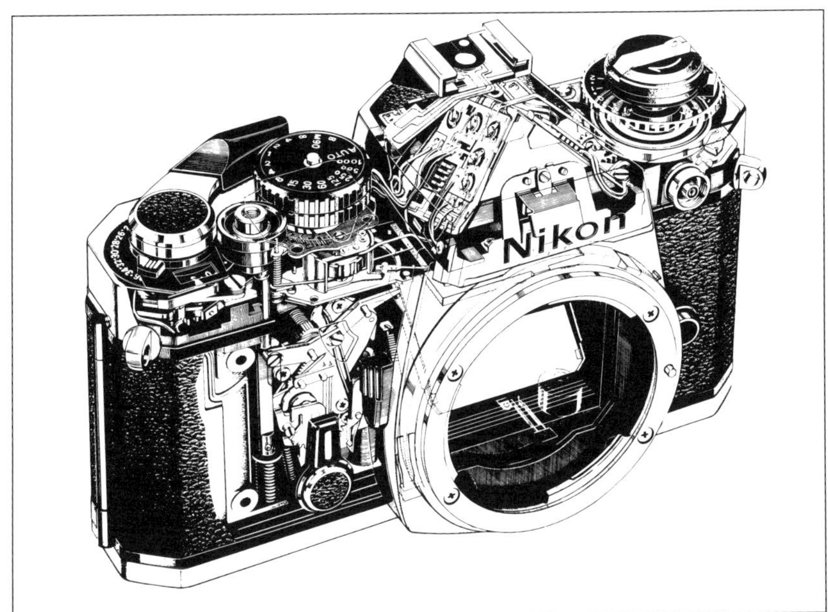

The FE has the same dimensions as the FM, but with aperture priority mode in addition to manual control.

and microprism ring, the B- and E-types were also available (the latter with horizontal and vertical grid lines, very helpful for multiple exposures and architectural photography). Nikon supplies a pair of tweezers with these screens in order to make it easier to remove and replace them without damaging them or the mirror. Users need to practise this procedure, but changing screens is not often necessary. Those who prefer the matte screen, with or without the grid, to the standard version will have their reasons and stick to their alternative. By the way, the FE-2/FA's brighter screens K2, B2, and E2 can also be used in the FE so that the camera can be updated in this respect. You must remember to correct the film speed accordingly, though, because the metering cells also have an image brighter by 1/3 EV. So an ISO 100/21° film should be set to ISO 80/20°.

Further modifications in the FE are a flash-ready signal in the viewfinder and the automatic switch to the sync-speed of 1/125 sec. whenever a flash unit is attached. An additional contact in the accessory shoe next to the one in the centre allows Nikon Speedlights, as of the SB-10, as well as compatible units of other brands to do this by supplying the ready-light in the viewfinder with power. Also by attachment of a flash unit the shortest possible sync-speed of 1/90 sec. is set automatically if aperture priority mode has been chosen. But the conspicuously flashing LED in the FE is also a reminder of manually set faster speeds.

The exposure metering display in the viewfinder was taken over from the EL, with the addition of the position "M" for the mechanically controlled 1/90 sec. This serves as a stopgap for situations in which the batteries have gone flat. If the camera is released in this condition the mirror swings up and can only be returned to its initial position by setting the shutter speed dial to the mechanical 1/90 sec.

The film speed range was also extended up to ISO 4000/37° in the FE. The multiple exposure lever was placed directly beneath the film advance lever in order to facilitate easier handling together with the motor drive. It remains to be said that the FE was equipped with a rubber-coated eyepiece so as not to scratch spectacles with the edges. Due to their design it may happen that the aperture ring is blocked when the FE and FM are screwed tightly to a tripod head with a large surface. That is the reason for the black plastic disc supplied with every FE from the start.

Nikon FM-2

In 1982 Nikon caused a sensation: the FM was modified and received a shutter with a fastest speed of 1/4000 sec. – the FM-2 became the world record holder. But that was not enough: as a spin-off – although many consider it to be the main argument for the

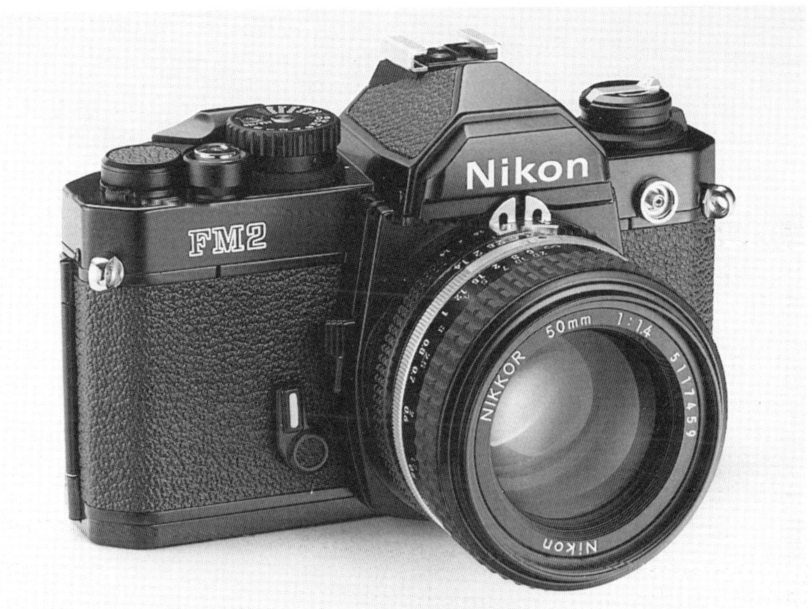

The FM-2: in spite of its high-performance shutter the body dimensions remained unchanged.

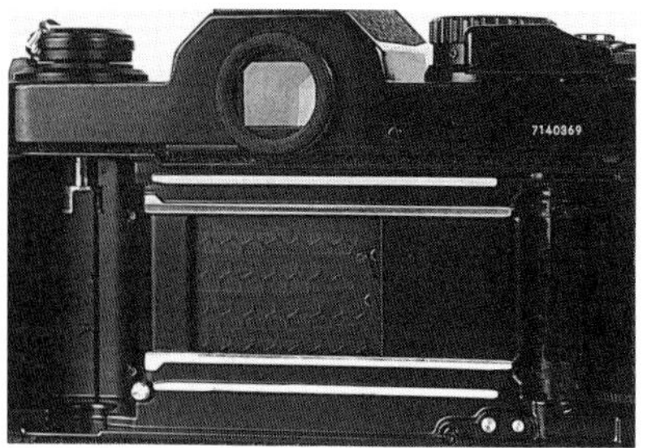

A world record at the time: 1/4000 sec. with the FM-2.

camera – this shutter is capable of a fastest sync-speed of 1/200 sec., and later, in the FM-2n of a 1/250 sec. Shutter speeds can be increased to a certain degree by reducing the width of the slit between the two blinds, but a faster sync-speed can only be achieved by increasing the shutter's running speed because it must stay completely open for about 1/1000 sec. when an electronic flash is employed. Nikon managed to realize both demands in cooperation with Copal, the manufacturer of the shutter. To do so, this advanced mechanical construction accelerates the shutter blinds to an average speed of about 25 km/h. This becomes especially impressive when you realize that the start, the acceleration phase, and the retardation take place within a mere 24mm. Nikon developed shutter blades made of extremely light and mechanically sturdy titanium foil into which a honeycomb pattern was etched in order to further decrease their weight and increase their stiffness. This allowed the weight of the blades to be reduced by nearly 60%. The mass of a normal shutter blind accelerated at this rate would have caused vibrations that would probably have prevented any sharp picture.

Since 1989 the FM-2 has been equipped with the F-801 shutter blinds. Many other things have also been modified in the FM-2, keeping in mind the more conservative photographers who still miss the purely mechanical F2. At last the FM-2 also allows the focusing screens to be changed, first those of the FE were used, later the FE-2 brighter versions. The mirror mount, now made of titanium, and its retarder were also

Background information: The Shutter

The shutter has the job of allowing the film to be exposed for a certain time that can be reproduced repeatedly. In the early days of photography this was done by removing and replacing the lens cap, since the plates employed then demanded exposures of at least several minutes. As film materials became more sensitive exposure times were reduced to seconds and towards the end of the last century they reached fractions of a second. Of course, this could no longer be controlled with the lens cap. The first shutters for photographic cameras appeared in the 1890's and mass-produced shutters at the beginning of this century. These were lens shutters, the most common construction having curved leaves (the shutter blades) cover the shutter port. When released these blades are rotated around a fixed axis by the power of a spring so that the port is opened from the centre. Lens shutters uncover the complete frame at every speed so that they can be flash synchronized at any speed. However, due to their inertia, speeds are only possible up to 1/500 sec. Another disadvantage for system cameras with interchangeable lenses is that such shutters have to be integrated into the lenses. This restricts the maximum aperture, and also means that if you have five lenses you also have five shutters.

An advanced type of lens shutter which is mainly employed in medium and large format lenses today can be found in modern AF-viewfinder cameras, where the blades do not always open completely and so also take over the diaphragm's function. In 35mm SLR cameras focal plane shutters within the body are employed without exception. The main parts of these shutters consist either of two roller blinds of rubberized fabric (Nikon I, S and M), or especially in Nikon's case, of titanium foil (Nikon SP, F – F3). As of the Nikkormat series jointed metal strips (blades) were employed instead of the roller blinds (FT – FT-3, EL/EL-2, FM – FA, EM – FG, F-301 – F-801s, F4) which occupy much less room in the body than roller blind shutters.

During the exposure these blinds or blades travel across the film window at a constant speed. The exposure duration is determined by the width of the slit between the blinds. A narrow slit of only a few millimetres represents a short exposure, the longer the exposure, the wider the slit. The exposure takes place in strips, so to say.

In the F3 a blind takes about 10ms (1/100 sec.) to travel from one end to the other. At a shutter speed of 1/2000 sec. the slit is just under 2mm wide. In the Nikon F the shutter travels across the film window's 36mm at almost 11km/h. An impressive achievement at that time considering that the complete operation, starting in the initial position through acceleration to retardation and back again, takes place over a distance of less than four centimetres. But in the FE-2 the blades whizz across the shorter stretch of 24mm at more than 28 km/h from top to bottom. There are several reasons behind the engineers' efforts to increase the shutter's operating speed:

1. The sync-speed. Modern electronic flash units, with the exception of studio systems, cannot achieve a light output longer than about 1/1000 sec. even at full power. When used together with focal plane shutters a flash unit can only be triggered after the first blind has completely travelled across the film window and the second has not yet moved. For example, the Nikon F's blind takes 12ms to do so. If you add 0,5ms margin and a flash duration of 1ms, the result is about 14ms between the beginning of the exposure and the earliest possible starting time for the second blind. So, the shortest X-sync-speed has to be longer than 14ms. At 1/60 sec. (equalling 16,6ms) this is the case. Anyone can imagine how precise the shutter must work at a sync-speed of 1/250 sec..

2. The width of the slit. In the course of the exposure the entering light is subject to diffraction at the shutter blind edges, which may cause the same kind of degradation in image quality as the diaphragm blades. The narrower the slit, the higher the degree of diffraction. In the FE-2 the slit is

2mm wide at a shutter speed of 1/4000 sec. which only results in a tolerable amount of diffraction. If the slit in the F were to be narrowed down in order to achieve a shutter speed of 1/4000 sec. it could be no wider than 0,75mm. The degree of diffraction would be so high that the negative would turn out unsharp in spite of the extremely short exposure.

3. Image distortion. If you photograph a moving subject, it will travel a certain distance during the exposure. For example; if a motorcycle travelling at a speed of 100 km/h is photographed from the side with a Nikon F and a shutter speed of 1/1000 sec., it will cover a good 30cm during the shutter's 12ms operating time. Not much at first sight, but in certain situations, for example a football flying past being captured with a long telephoto lens, this effect can become evident. Subjects moving in the opposite direction to the travel of the shutter blinds will be compressed, subjects moving in the same direction will be stretched.

What will the future bring us in terms of shutter design? Much higher speeds do not seem to be possible with mechanical designs. Constructions employing liquid crystal technology are feasible. In such a shutter the blinds would be replaced by a liquid crystal plate which, reacting to electrical signals, can turn from translucent to transparent within fractions of a second and so expose the film.

FM-2 also allowed the use of the 1/250 sec. in combination with a flash unit. Some photographers may have been stopped or at least irritated by the winking flash-ready light that seemed to indicate a malfunction.

The metering symbols are LEDs now. Metering is activated for about 30 seconds by pressing the release button. The multiple exposure lever is situated directly beneath the advance lever as in the FE. The release button itself was enlarged so that only cable releases with an ISO-type thread can be employed. A fundamental restriction is that because its AI-coupling lever cannot be folded away, non-AI standard lenses cannot be used on the FM-2. Two gold-plated contacts are located under the FM-2 film guide rails in order to control the databack MF-16.

Nikon FE-2

One year after the FM-2, the FE was updated into the FE-2, naturally with the new super shutter with the 1/4000 sec. and 1/250 sec. sync-speed. Along with the FE-2 the new focusing screen versions K2, B2, and E2 appeared that are about 1/3 EV brighter than before. In order to further reduce the

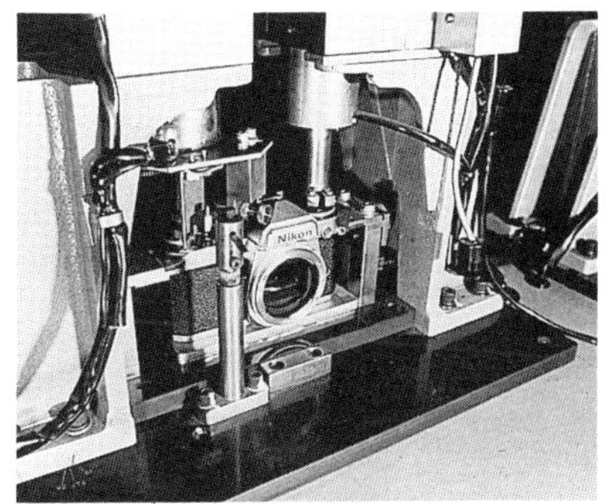

An extremely tough laboratory test: Nikon considers quality checks to be very important.

changed. The film transportation mechanism is now mounted in five ball-bearings. The film speed dial was enlarged and the film speed setting range extended up to ISO 6400/39°. The metering cells employed are SPD-photodiodes that work three times as fast as the type formerly used. The first special click-stop X-position of the FE-2 was a slight mishap because the metering system is switched off in this position. This was a handicap especially in fill-in flash situations when a fast sync-speed is really necessary. Luckily this shortcoming was eliminated in the FM-2n. Known only to few and no problem in everyday use, the first

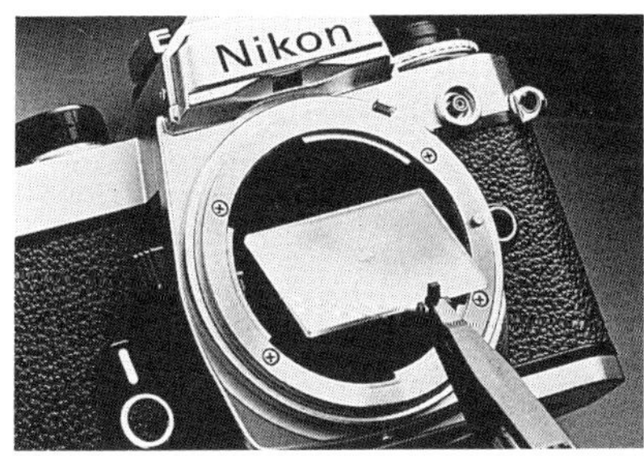

Changing the focusing screen through the bayonet with the help of the special tweezers.

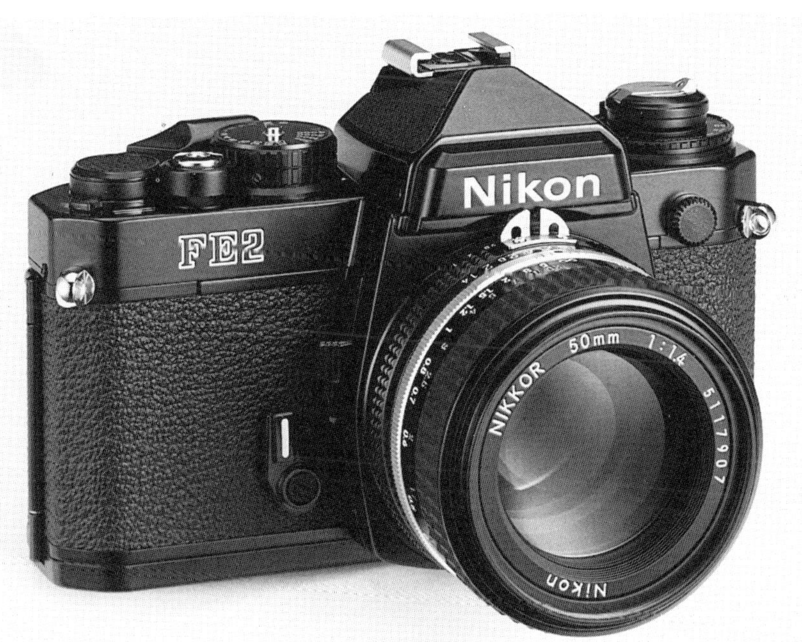

Compared to the FE, the FE-2 was modified – among other things – by including TTL-flash metering.

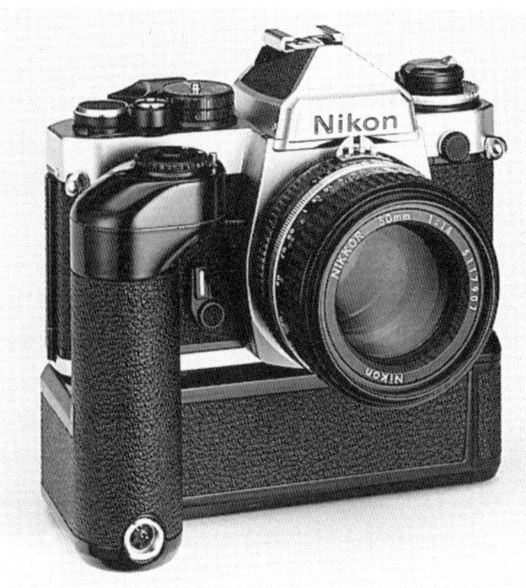

A fast combination: the FE-2 with the motor drive MD-12.

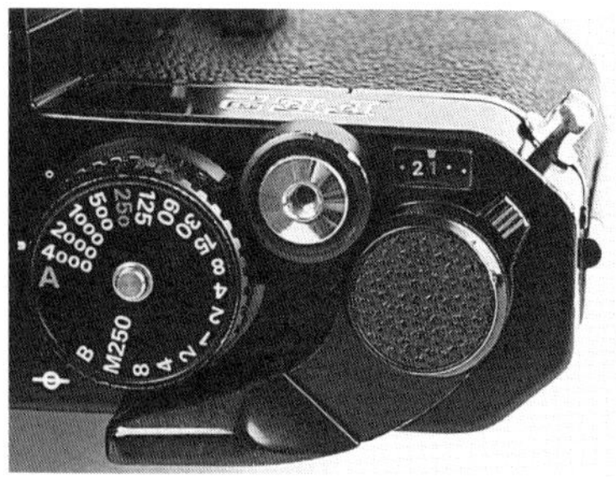

In the case of the FE-2 the light meter is only activated when the film counter has reached "1".

vibrations caused by the reflex mirror a counter-rotating plate was incorporated.

Of course the FE-2 also possesses TTL-flash control circuitry, which is effective within a range of ISO 25/15° to 400/27°. If the film speed is below or above this range, the FE-2's flash-ready light flashes as an indication. When a shutter speed higher than 1/250 sec. has been set manually, the electronic system automatically reduces it to 1/250 sec. The metering system remains activated even if a flash unit is attached which proves to be quite practical in daylight fill-in flash situations since it allows incident light and flashlight to be balanced perfectly. The same two SPD-cells that had already proven themselves in the EL-2 and FE were employed in the metering system. The information brochures at the time included some very technical jargon: "A well-tested bi-MOS IC and highly sensitive metering cells make up the

Background information: Metering Systems

"f/8 when the sun is shining" or "f/4 is always right indoors" – everybody has probably heard phrases like these. They are the result of the attempt to find the correct exposure for the prevailing subject in photography. In the past one had to be satisfied when the film was close to being dark enough to be duplicated, the rest was up to the laboratories. The early photographers usually had exposure tables if they did not have enough experience. They could look up the correct exposure for every month, the time of day, and all sorts of cloud conditions.

The first exposure meters were based on a photochemical principle. A piece of paper was coated with silver chloride, rolled into a tube and held towards the light. The time it took for the paper to turn grey was considered to correspond approximately to the appropriate exposure "speed". A fairly complicated and time-consuming procedure which was also not very precise. Optical exposure meters were used until the middle of this century which employed a transparent stepped grey-scale marked with figures. The last number that could be recognized indicated the correct exposure. All these systems had the disadvantage that they depended on the photographer's subjective judgement.

In 1932 the American Weston company introduced the first selenium photo-electric exposure meter. The semiconductor selenium converts the incident light into electrical energy which causes a needle to react. The first exposure meters with cadmium sulphide photo-resistors appeared on the market in the middle of the 60's. These CdS-cells were small enough to be built into cameras, but they needed a battery as a power supply. Nikon's first camera with a built-in exposure meter was the Nikon F Photomic from 1962. The CDS-cell was still placed on the outside but a connection between the shutter speed dial and the aperture ring had already been made. The first Nikon with a TTL – (through the lens) – metering system arrived three years later in the form of the Nikon F Photomic T which evaluated the light on the focusing screen unbiased across the whole frame.

The first cameras with the 60:40% – centre weighted – metering system were the Nikon F Photomic FT and the Nikkormat FTN. The centre-weighted configuration was devised because most subjects are placed in or near the centre of the picture. So the metering cell was modified to concentrate 60% of its sensitivity on the inner 12mm-circle of the focusing screen even though it only makes up ⅓ of the whole surface. The remaining ⅔ just influenced the result to 40%. This made it possible to evaluate the specific subject details considered to be the most important. The next improvement followed in the F2 SB in 1976. The CDS cells which reacted relatively sluggishly in poor light were replaced in this case for the first time by the Nikon SPD – (silicon photo diodes) – cells that are extremely responsive. In the FM Nikon tried out GAPs (gallium arsenide photodiodes) that were faster still but they were not satisfied with their spectral sensitivity.

In the EM the centre-weighted characteristics were moderated by switching to 40:60%: now the 12mm-circle received 40% "attention" and the surroundings 60%. This made it easier for the EM-users who most likely will never have remembered to direct the meter at the important parts of the scenery. In the F3 the metering cell migrated to the bottom of the mirror box and was supplied with light through the main mirror, that was perforated in the middle, and then with the help of a smaller secondary mirror. The centre-weighted characteristics were concentrated to a proportion of 80:20%, so you can almost compare it to selective metering. With this metering method only a certain part of the focusing screen's surface is taken into account.

The big advance came in 1983 in the form of the FA's AMP- (Automatic multi pattern) metering. A really "automatic" metering system was available for the first time. Integral, centre-weighted, selective, or spot metering systems all work according to an inflexible scheme. The smaller the metering area, the more precisely subject details can be evaluated, but the number of hits also decreases if it is not used very carefully for every picture. In the case of matrix metering the frame is divided into five almost equally large segments which are simultaneously, individually, and automatically evaluated. The resulting five exposure values are fed into an exposure program software that analyses the prevailing incident light. The subject's contrast is decisive, the location of extremely bright or dark parts of the subject or the brightness of such extremely bright subject details as the sun, lamps, or snow, for example. Along with this information the exposure values are compared to a master matrix and as a result a final exposure value is computed. This leads to a far higher number of acceptable pictures even in very difficult lighting situations.

In a simplified form – with only three segments – this multi-pattern-metering system was also employed in the first version of the F-401. In the F-801 it was improved further. Additionally, the F-801 was equipped with the 75:25% centre-weighted metering system. The F4 was given two mercury switches in order to change the orientation of the segments according to how the camera is being held. This flagship also received the good old 60:40% centre-weighted metering system, as well as the first spot metering mode in a Nikon camera. In the F4 only the tiny spot in the centre of the frame marked by the 5mm ring is covered.

metering system. An LSI in I2L-configuration controls the shutter speeds steplessly..." Did you get it? If the LSI in I2L-configuration cannot operate for a change due to failing battery power the photographer still has the mechanical stop-gap shutter speed and the B-position at his disposal. The FE-2 uses the 1/250 sec. until the film counter reaches "1". Unlike the FE, it is not equipped with an extra battery check.

Exposure correction factors can be set in increments of 1/3 EV now and an LED in the viewfinder informs the photographer when they are being used. In spite of the many modifications and improvements the FE-2 is so similar to the 11 year-old EL that it causes no problems in switching from one to the other. When the FE-2 was discontinued in 1987 an outcry went up from Nikon fans and the prices of used FE-2's soared; sometimes the camera secondhand was more expensive than when new. After all, it belonged to the ever dwindling group of classic SLRs without built-in motor drives, multi-mode automatic exposure modes, and autofocus.

Nikon FA

In the middle of 1983 the FM/FE-series was expanded by a sensational new top-of-the-line model, the FA. A completely new type of exposure metering system was incorporated into a body practically identical to that of the FE-2. This was the AMP – (automatic multi- pattern) metering system. At last a metering system that did not evaluate the incident light

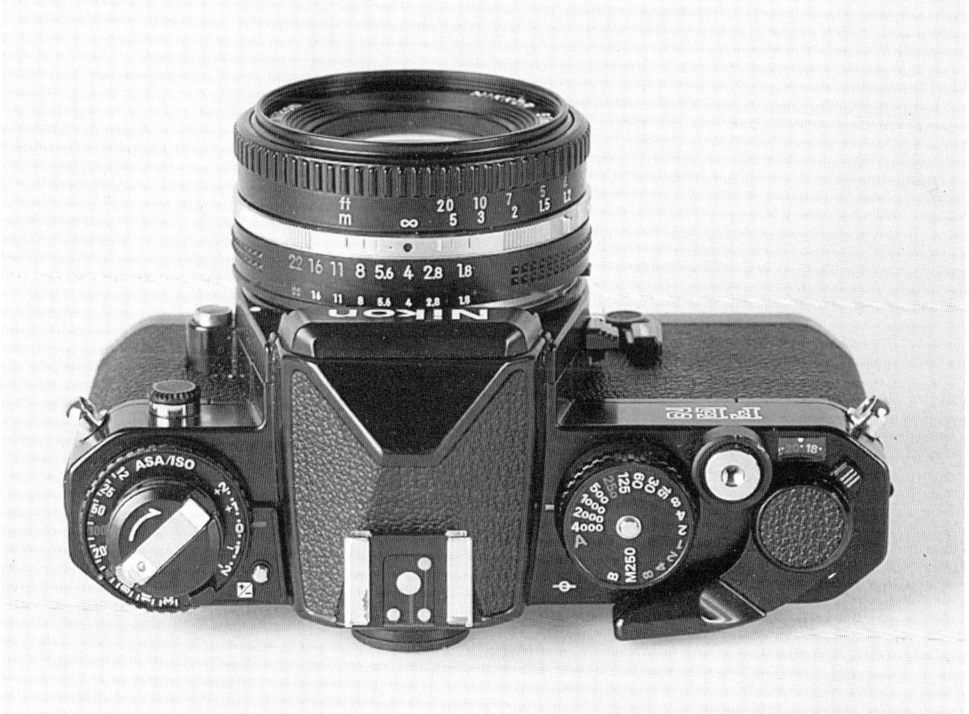

The FE-2 from above; easy to handle thanks to clearly arranged controls.

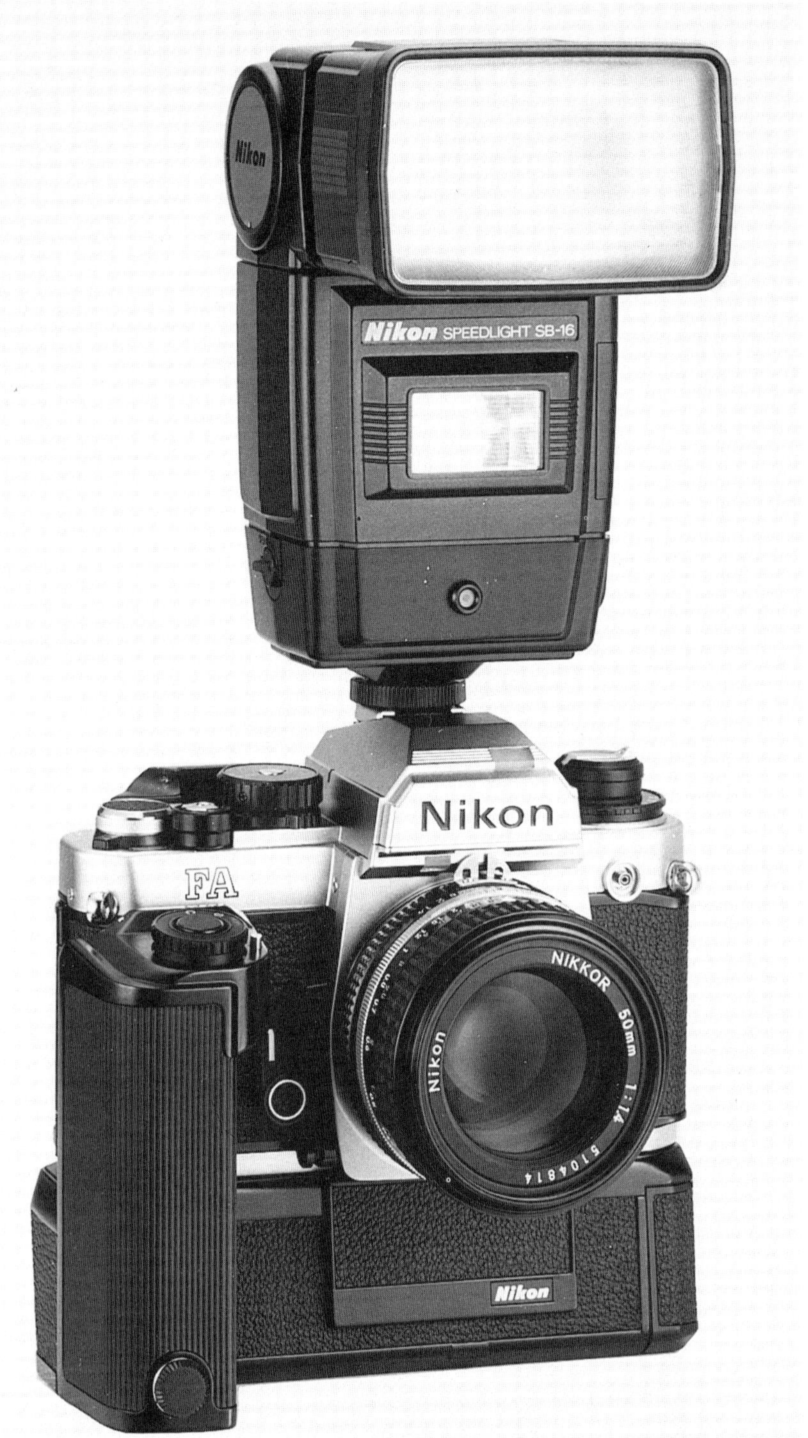

A powerful combination: the FA with the fast motor drive MD-15 and the Speedlight SB-16B.

indiscriminately over the scene, but divided the scene visible in the viewfinder into five segments and surveyed them separately.

Depending on the brightness distribution in the frame an evaluation system computes the correct exposure in several steps. Multi pattern metering is clearly superior to any other system even in situations with strong contrast, when shooting against the light and similarly extreme lighting situations. At last we had a nearly foolproof automatic metering mode. The FA was provided with all the exposure control systems: program, aperture priority, and shutter priority automatic modes. This made the FA Nikon's first multi-mode camera.

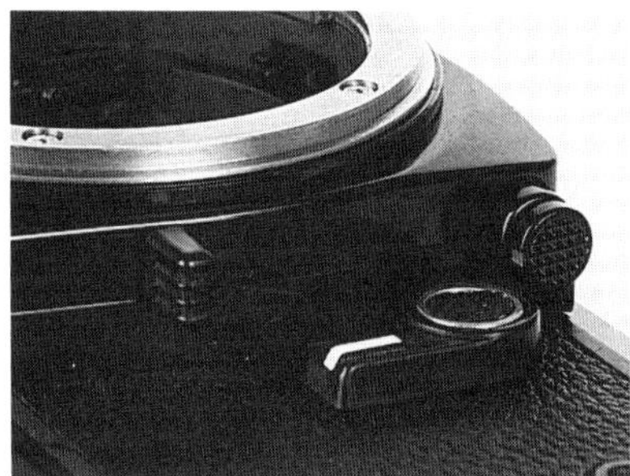

The button for changing the metering mode.

The program mode is available in a normal and a faster version which is biased in favour of faster shutter speeds at the expense of the aperture by 1½ EV. The program variations are chosen automatically by the focal length of the lens in use. All lenses from 135mm and the zooms with ranges beyond 135mm are equipped with an indexing ridge, situated in the black rear lens protection ring, that triggers a switch in the mirror box called the focal length indexing pin. All AI-S-type-, the E-series-, and the AF-Nikkors have this focal length ridge. The shutter priority mode also reveals a new feature, an automatic switchover at the ends of the range (cybernetic override). In practical use this function has the following effect. Whenever the aperture range does not suffice for a correct exposure in combination with the preset shutter speed, the camera changes it automatically.

This feature can also be used to create a personal kind of program mode. Let us suppose you would like to photograph portraits with a 105mm lens. The shutter speed should be at least 1/125 sec. and the aperture should not become smaller than f/5.6. When you set the camera to the 1/125 sec. and f/5.6, then normally the aperture will

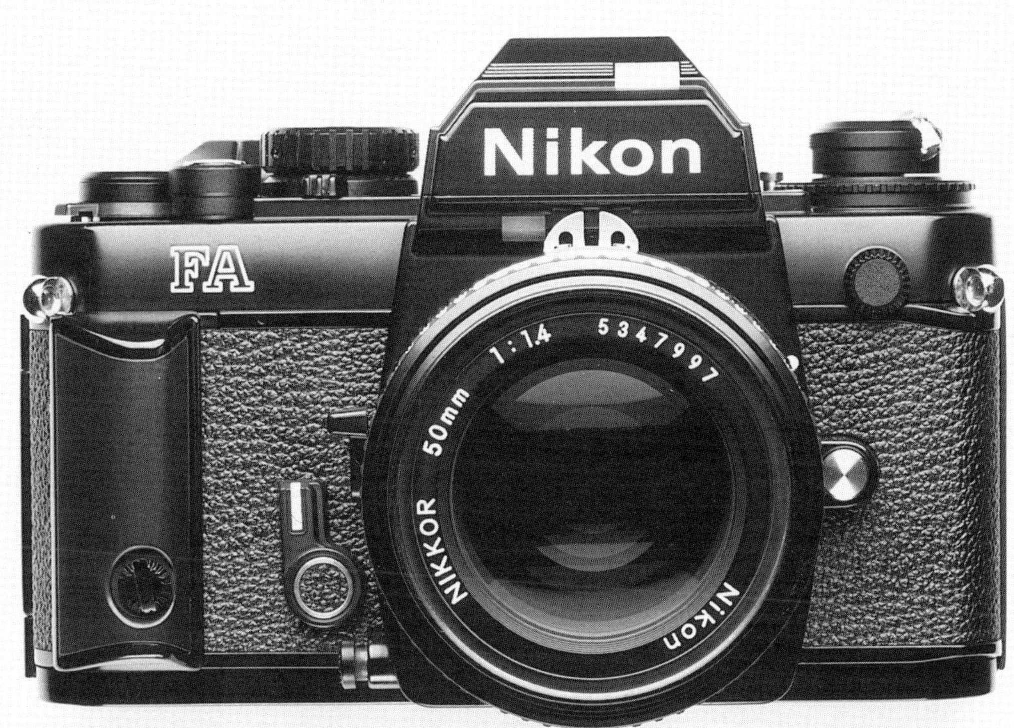

The FA with its prominent, rectangular body and the typical viewfinder illumination window in the prism housing.

be set according to the 1/125 sec. If the light deteriorates, slower shutter speeds will be set as soon as the maximum aperture has been reached. But if the brightness increases the aperture will only be stopped down to f/5.6 and after that faster shutter speeds will be set. The way I see it, this method of operation is superior even to a program shift in terms of working speed.

It does not need to be mentioned that the FA also possesses aperture priority and manual exposure modes. Just like the FG, the FA also has a removable grip. The top-plate is made of a plastic as opposed to metal on the FM/FE-2 and is a lot wider above the prism than these in order to make room for the comprehensive electronics for the AMP-metering and the complex mechanics for the finder displays.

The main display in the finder is an LCD in the top left corner. Depending on the chosen exposure mode, the shutter speed, the aperture, or warning signals are displayed. As in the FE/FM the preset aperture is visible in the centre, but only when employing manual and aperture priority exposure modes. When shutter priority mode is being used the preset speed appears on the left side. If set, a signal reminding of the correction factor is also displayed here and the flash-ready light is located here too. The focusing screens are the same as in the FE-2/FM-2n. The FA meters the light on the screen with two SPD-sensors placed right and left of the viewfinder eyepiece, but these were

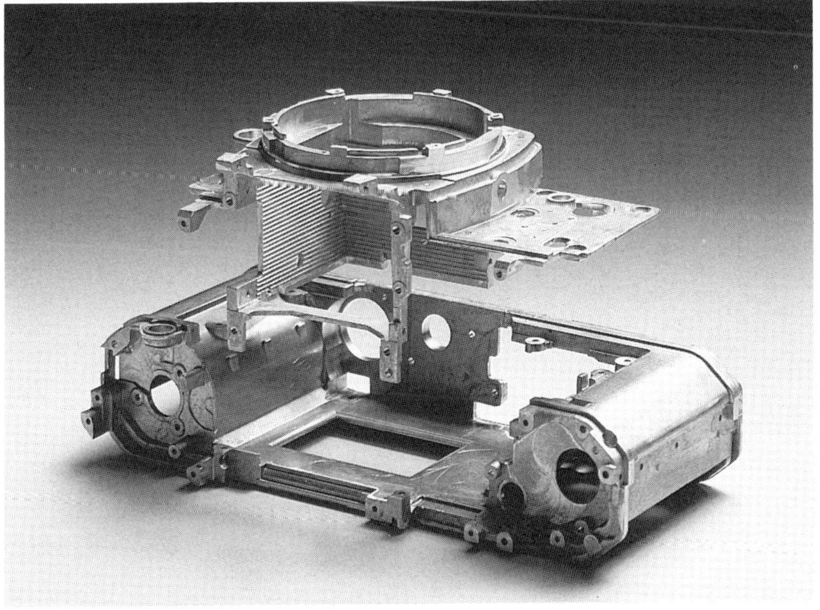

The Nikon FA's backbone is a sturdy and resistant die-cast aluminium chassis.

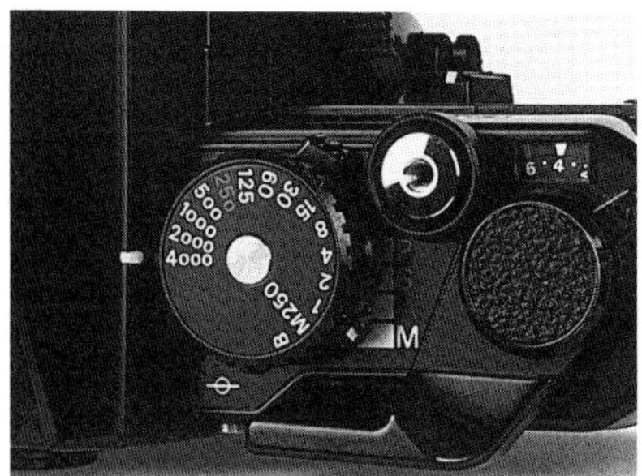

Situated beneath the shutter speed dial is the switch for the exposure modes.

divided into three segments each. As a result, the centre of the frame is the only part that is covered by two segments. Besides the AMP-metering the FA also has the classic 60:40% centre-weighted metering mode. If desired this mode can be switched on with the button below the self-timer lever. The FA switches to this metering system automatically in manual mode and when a lens is used that has been modified to the AI-standard, since the cam is still missing which transmits the maximum f/stop.

Besides the above-mentioned focal length indexing switch, a small pin situated slightly above the lens release pin was also new and identifies the lens type being used. In the case of AI-S-, Series E-, and AF-Nikkors this switch remains inactivated due to a recess in the bayonet flange. Older lenses without this recess activate the switch telling the FA that it is operating with a non-linear diaphragm mechanism and must take more time (about 20ms) to control the actual size of the aperture. In order to be capable of coping with this amount of information and the combinations a microprocessor is necessary, while for example the EL only needed one IC and a couple of transistors.

The FA was the first Nikon which computed all of the information such as the lens speed, the focal length in use, the preset aperture and film speed digitally, thus preventing faults such as the metering results becoming distorted by dust lodged on a resistor plate. In spite of all these high-tech features the FA looks like a classic camera. But the FA also has some mechanical treats. In addition to the 1/4000 sec. and the mirror mechanism with a damper it has an electromechanical shutter release button that allows extremely smooth and vibration-free operation. The eyepiece shutter should not be forgotten either.

The new MD-15 was introduced as the motor-drive especially designed for the FA. It also took over the camera's power supply. The MD-11 and MD-12-models could be employed just as well, although only with a highest shooting rate of 2.7 frames/sec. since these motors could only release the camera mechanically with a tappet protruding into its baseplate. The two older motor models, of course, could not supply the camera's electronics with power.

All in all the FA could be considered to be a dream camera, not only by the standards of the time, but even so it did not become a big sales success. Several reasons will have been responsible for this. One of the main ones was probably that when the FA could finally be delivered in quantity another dream camera had appeared on the scene, the Minolta 7000 AF. Technically the FA is a complete success since it was the first camera with a multi-pattern metering system and set new standards at the time. The 45 members of the "Grand Prix Executive Committee" jury came to the same opinion in Japan and voted the FA to be the best new camera of the year. Nikon issued a limited edition in gold and crocodile leather finish to celebrate this.

CHAPTER 5

Nikons For Everyone

For decades now the brand name Nikon has stood for the incarnation of professional 35mm photography. In the 60's it may still have been little known, but by the appearance of the F2 Nikon was recognized as offering the most comprehensive professional camera system. Myths came into being about the reliability of these cameras, summed up in comments such as "You can drive nails into the wall with it". Go ahead and try! The service facilities can tell plenty of stories about Nikon bodies in horrific condition being brought in by professionals.

In 1979 a shock went through the ranks of Nikon enthusiasts. They had expected a successor for the F2. Instead, a beginner's camera for less than £200 complete with lens appeared, and what is more with a plastic body and without a manual mode. A world collapsed for Nikon-freaks. Was that the ruin of a glorious make? The production of such an amateur's camera should have been left to the competitors – this was the opinion of many a Nikon photographer. They would have expected only the best of the best from the company that had established itself as a supplier of high-class cameras – and now this?

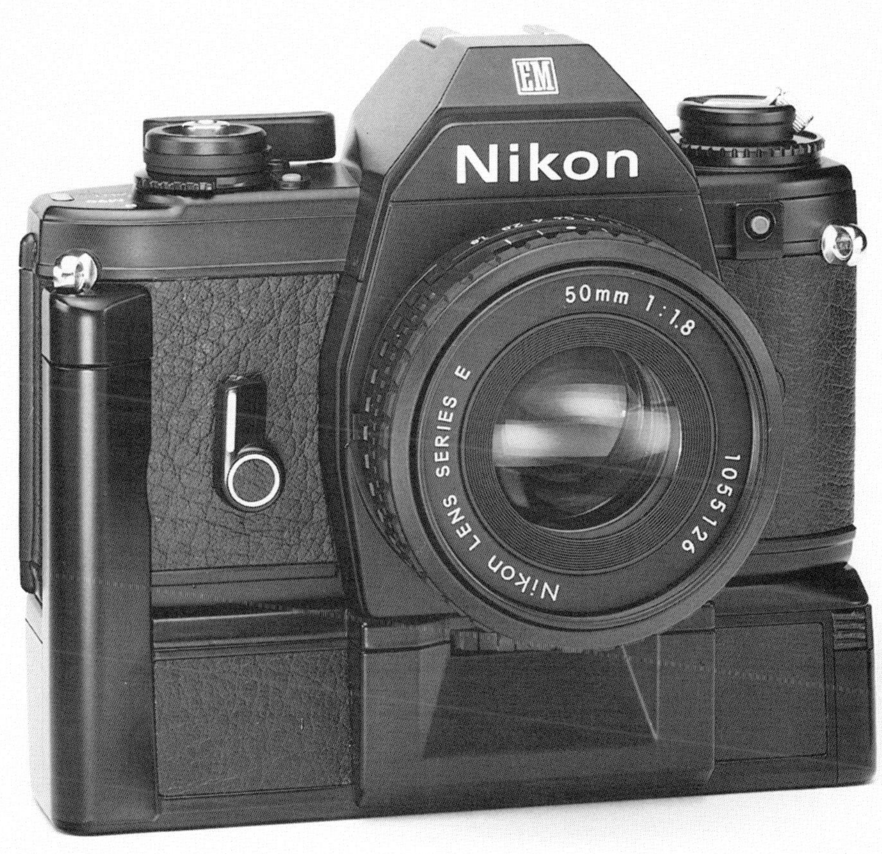

Small, light, but even so – fast: the Nikon EM with the motor drive MD-E.

During the 70's cameras had become more and more electronic in operation and the life-spans of the individual models ever shorter. Manufacturers who wanted to stay in the lead were forced to invest heavily in new camera designs in order to keep up with technical developments, especially in the area of microelectronics. Efforts on this scale are only worthwhile when high volumes can be sold. This was impossible with an F2 or even with an FE-2. So a camera was needed in the amateur sector that offered good value for money. This in turn was only possible by reducing the specification by sacrificing features only really needed by professional or advanced amateur users. The family photographer, interested in holiday pictures and records of the children does not need a motor drive with 5 frames/sec., interchangeable viewfinders, or a depth-of-field preview button.

Nikon had always had more moderately priced amateur models in their range, the S3 and S4 in the 50's, the Nikkorex series and the Nikkormat models in the 60's, but the EM was the first camera that was not a cheaper version of a better equipped one. It was designed from the start as an independent model to meet the needs of average amateur photographers. Let us take a closer look at the "people's Nikon".

Nikon EM

The Italian star-designer Giorgetto Giugiario made his Nikon début with this elegantly rounded body – weighing a mere 460 grams and as compact as an AF-viewfinder camera. To begin with we must refute any prejudice concerning this "plastic job". Only the top-plate, the base-plate, and the bayonet surround are made of this material. The chassis is of the same die-cast aluminium as other Nikon SLRs.

One look in the viewfinder shows the fixed K-type screen as well as the shutter speed scale known from the Nikkormat EL and FE. An aperture display in the finder was omitted for cost reasons. Whenever the prevailing brightness would lead to overexposure with even the fastest shutter speed of 1/1000 sec., or to lower speeds than 1/30 sec. which might cause blurred photos, the EM warns by beeping quietly but firmly.

A blue button is located next to the film advance lever to test the condition of the batteries. The shutter release button and the operating mode switch with its three positions – "Auto" for aperture priority exposure mode, "M90" for the mechanically controlled sync-speed of 1/90 sec., and "B" for long exposures without power consumption – are placed concentric to the advance lever. Nikon introduced a new feature with the EM whereby the exposure metering is only switched on when the film counter has reached the "1"; before that, a fixed speed is used to release the shutter. This is meant to prevent the automatic exposure mode from using too slow a shutter speed which would result in an unnecessarily long time for the film to be transported to the first frame.

After the release button is pressed the exposure meter will stay activated for about 20 seconds. The film speed setting is located on the other side of the prism and has a range of ISO 25/15° to 1600/33°. Below, the backlight switch can be found which biases the automatic exposure by 2 EV towards slower speeds – sadly there is no exposure-lock feature.

This sums up most of the EM's controls except for the self-timer with the usual running time. A practical tip: in order to minimize the vibration caused by the mirror swinging up during long exposures the self-timer should always be used. This helps, since the mirror swings up immedi-

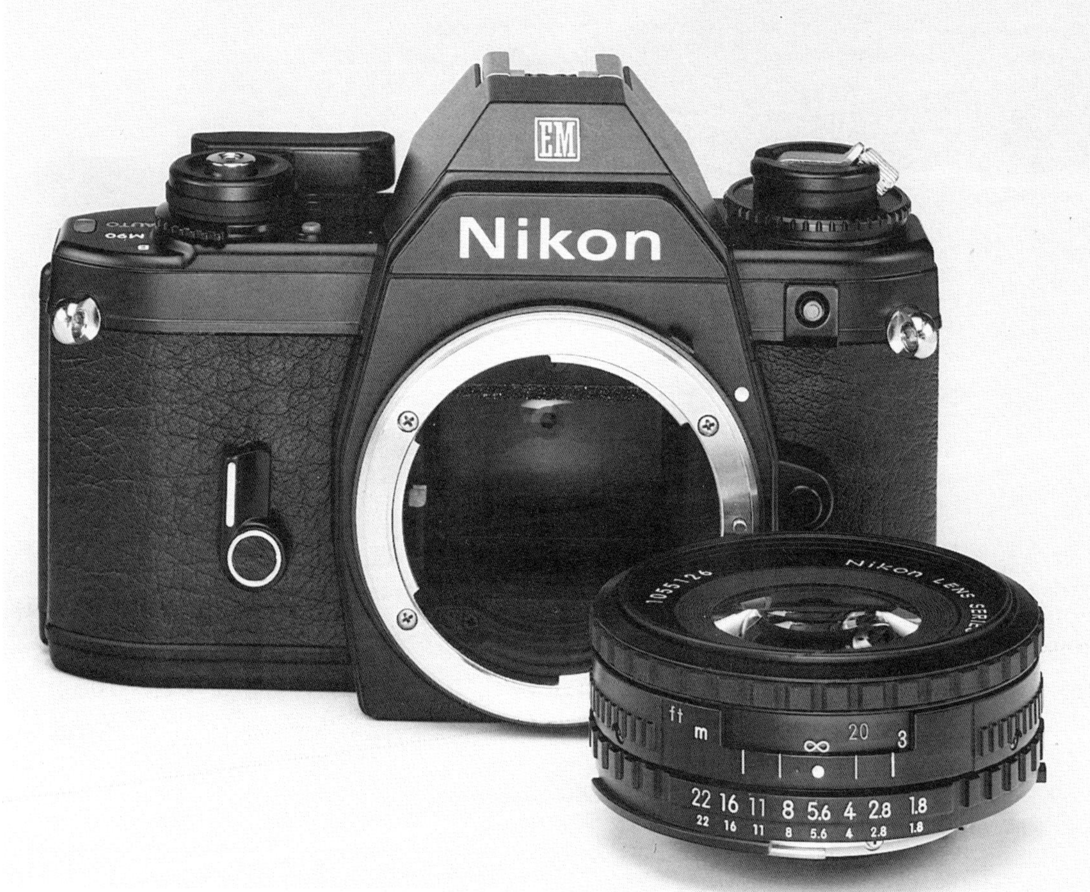

Nikon's most economical SLR: the EM with a 50mm,f/1.8 lens.

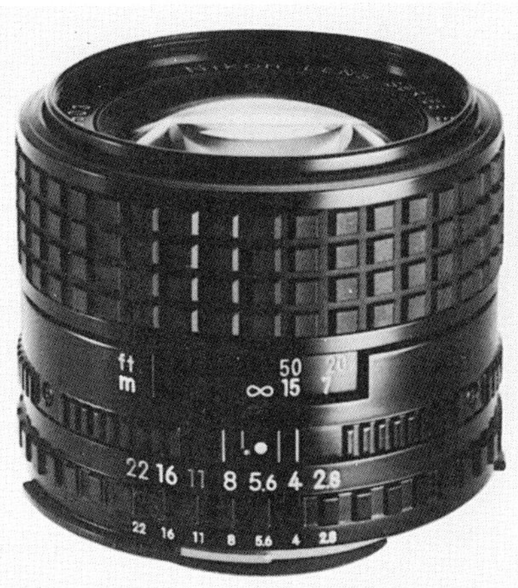

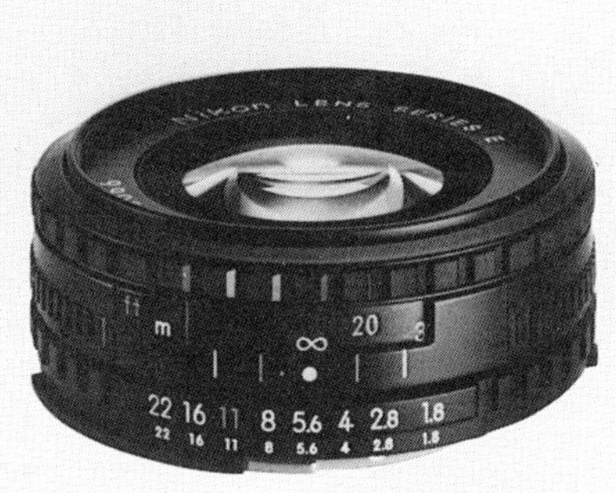

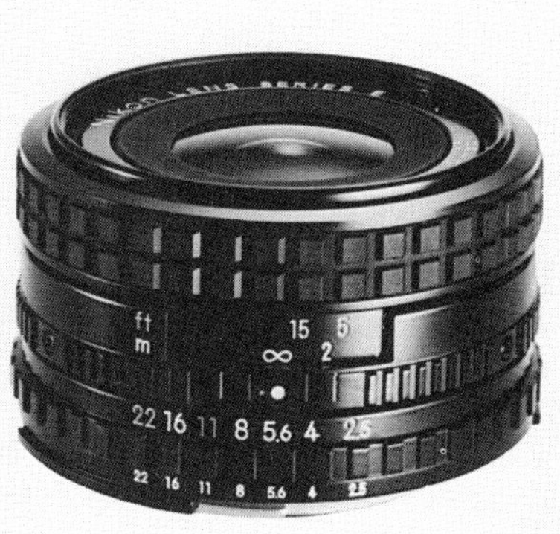

Three of the E-series lenses – 100mm, 50mm and 35mm – very light and optically quite acceptable.

Background Information: Automatic functions

"Automatic" – a term which often causes irritation among ambitious amateur photographers. Every new surge of innovation brings us new automatic functions, and every one will raise the arguments anew for and against the current technology. In the 60's it was the automatic diaphragm, in the 70's aperture and shutter priority automatic exposure modes, in the beginning of the 80's program mode, and since the middle of the 80's autofocus. Every new automatic function sparks off the joke about the little bell in the camera that rings to tell us what to photograph. In fact we do not seem to be too far away from that, especially when you consider that automatic modes do have their advantages but can also lead to uncritical shooting instead of serving to enhance creativity. Camera manufacturers boldly claim in their advertisements "Now, all you have to do is...", but the practical results soon show that it is still necessary to do your share of thinking. A badly exposed picture is always blamed on the camera's automatic modes whereas nobody would blame a car's automatic gearbox in the case of the driver's misjudgement.

Even though we speak about an automatic exposure we should distinguish between the metering and the automatic setting of the exposure value as a result. An automatic exposure mode works just as well or badly as a manually operated camera – provided the same metering system is employed – it simply achieves the settings a bit quicker and, without a doubt much more conveniently

ately after the shutter is released and before the self-timer starts to run. Officially Nikon stated the EM's slowest shutter speed as 1 sec., but in reality up to five minutes proved to be possible without a problem. Of course, reciprocity failure must be taken into account in such cases and compensated by changing the film speed.

An SPD-sensor situated above the viewfinder eyepiece is responsible for the exposure metering. The metering is centre-weighted, but not as strongly as in the FE or the F2. In the EM the inner 12mm circle on the focusing screen defines the area where 40% of the measurement is concentrated, the rest of the frame accounts for the remaining 60% – traditionally it was the other way around in Nikons.

The vertically travelling Seiko metal leaf shutter was never unreliable, even when it was accelerated up to more than 3 frames/sec. by the motor-drive MD-14. Both motor-drives MD-E and MD-14 are controlled by the release button. The MD-14 is the perfect fit for the EM; with it the camera handles even better.

A Speedlight, the SB-E, also belongs to the system. In combination with the EM and an AI- or E-series lens it offers three automatic shooting ranges which can be set directly on the lens. If any aperture other than the three is chosen the ready-light in the viewfinder will start flashing. Of course the sync-speed of 1/90 sec. is set automatically by the SB-E.

It is a sign of Nikon's consistency that this inexpensive camera was sup-

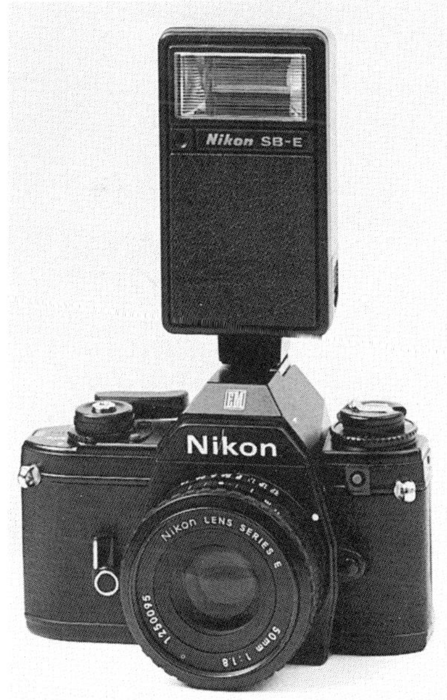

A perfect match for the camera: the Speedlight SB-E with three computer-controlled automatic shooting ranges.

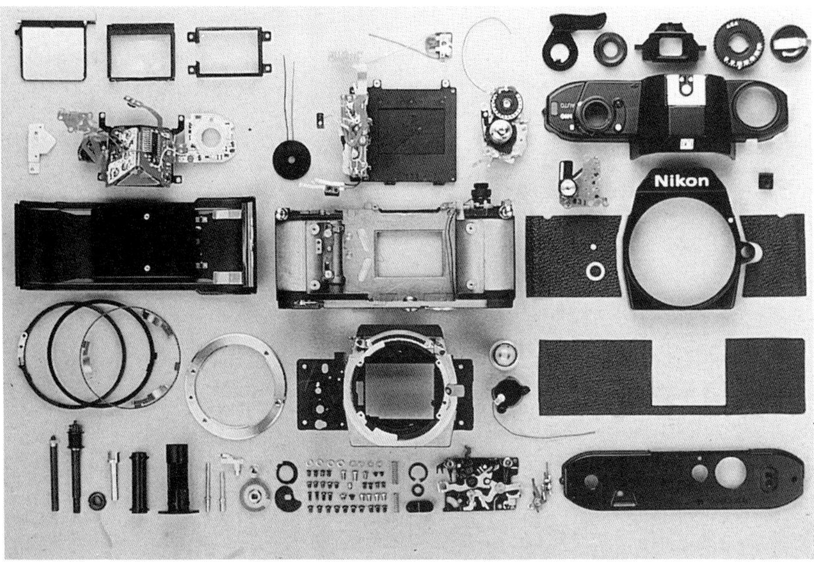

The completely disassembled EM reveals a fairly complex internal construction.

plied with equally priceworthy accessories, such as the motor drive MD-E and the flash unit SB-E, and most importantly a corresponding lens programme – the E-series. As well as the 50mm,f/1.8E the fast wide-angle 35mm,f/2.5E and the portrait telephoto 100mm,f/2.8E were immediately available. No, the lenses are not made of plastic and they were not produced in Korea or Taiwan, they are of original Nikon manufacture. Only the lens body and the helicoid are made of plastic and in the case of the fixed focal lengths the complex and expensive multi-coating was omitted. The AI-coupling lever on the EM body cannot be turned out of the way, so that it may be damaged by trying to mount a non-AI lens with force. Later Nikon completed the E-series with a 135mm,f/2.8E, a 28mm,f/2.8E, and three zooms – 36-72mm,f/3.5E, 75-150mm,f/3.5E, and 70-210mm,f/4E.

The E-series lenses could never shake off the image of being cheap and poor performers – even though Nikon tried very hard to inform its customers, so the whole series was later discontinued. Instead, Nikon began to introduce less expensive alternatives to the Nikkor range. Those who sneer at the EM with its modest features is forgetting that from today's point of view Nikon's entrance into the mass-market was exactly the right thing to do. It was the only way the company could achieve the economic foundation necessary to be able to afford to develop an FA or an F-801.

Nikon FG

In 1982 the top model in the compact class appeared in the form of the FG. This is an EM body with more features. The improvements compared to the EM are a manual exposure mode, TTL-flash metering, and a program mode. The FG was Nikon's first SLR with such a program mode. Up to then an automatic exposure mode in a Nikon had been synonymous with aperture priority, with the exception of the DS-aperture control attachments for the F2. It proved to be difficult to construct a precisely operating aperture control device that works with the diaphragm stop-down lever. At the time the F-bayonet and the mechanics of the lenses were designed – towards the end of the 50's – nobody had thought about a program mode. The aim was to achieve a fast firing rate with a motor drive and so the stop-down lever was designed with a high leverage. It only moves a mere 5mm between the maximum and the smallest (f/16) aperture. In the course of this movement it covers a range of six f/stops. In other words, when the stop-down

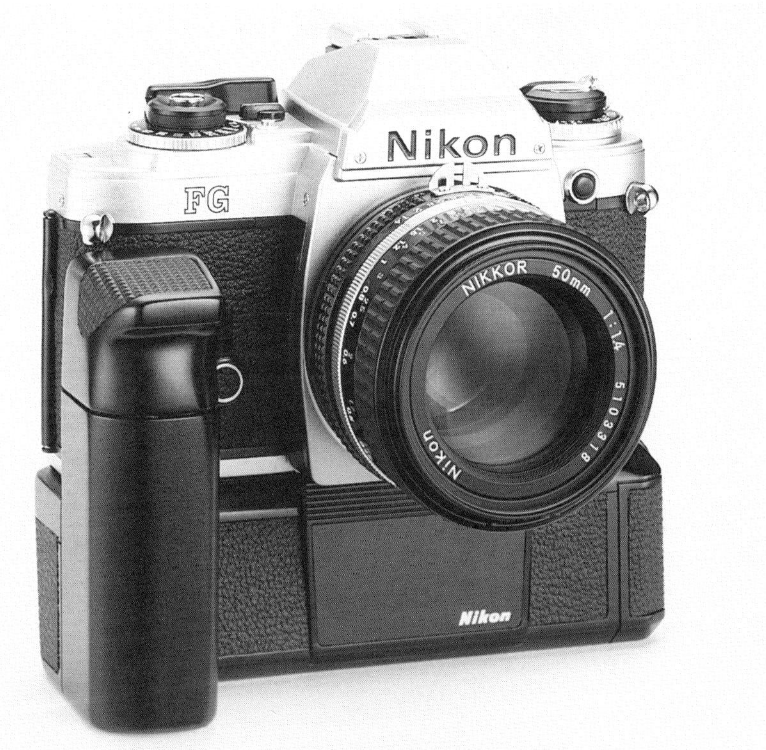

The FG with several improvements compared to the EM, especially in the case of the program mode.

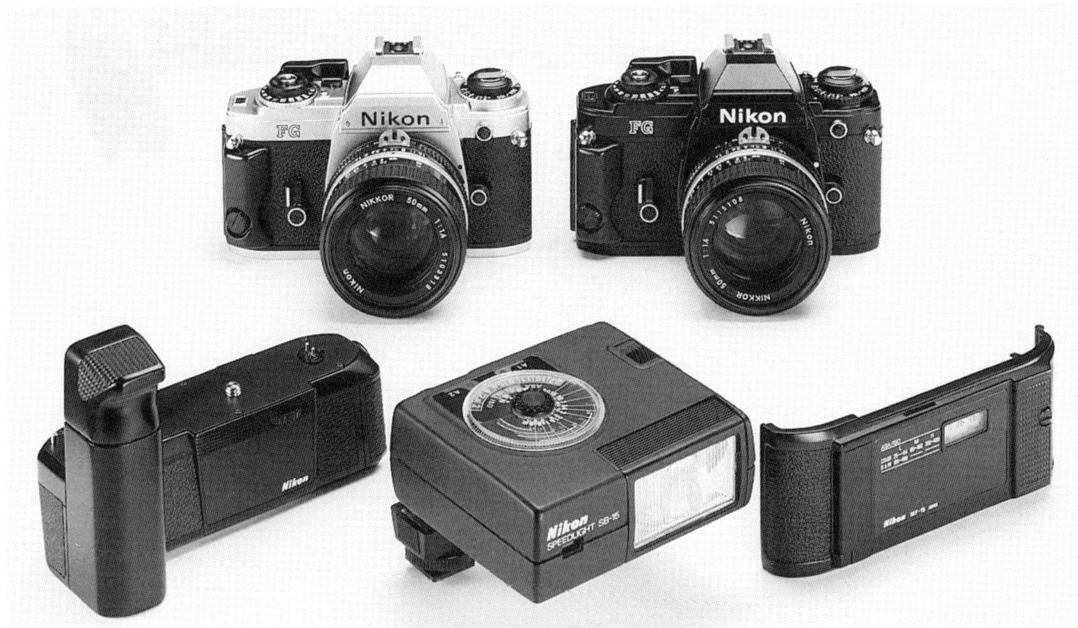

The most important accessories for the FG were the motor-drive, Speedlight, and databack.

lever moves 3/10mm this can make a difference of 1/3 EV. No mechanical construction is capable of working that precisely, especially since it has to operate with almost all system lenses as well as those types modified to the AI-standard. So a trick was conceived. Suppose the program chooses a shutter speed/aperture combination for the prevailing light of 1/125 sec. at f/5.6. When released, the diaphragm is first stopped down to the calculated value, then just before the mirror swings up to clear the way for the exposure, the FG measures the stopped-down diaphragm's actual port dimension and, if necessary, corrects the shutter speed accordingly.

For example, if the camera should discover that the effective aperture value is not f/5.6, as in the above mentioned case, but f/6 instead, then the second metering would lead to an appropriately slower shutter speed. This trick allowed the program mode to be included in the Nikon system without jeopardizing its compatibility. Not even a malfunctioning stop-down lever would necessarily lead to a bad exposure. The program mode was designed to change shutter speeds and aperture values evenly, supposing the photographer is shooting a static subject and prefers an average depth-of-field.

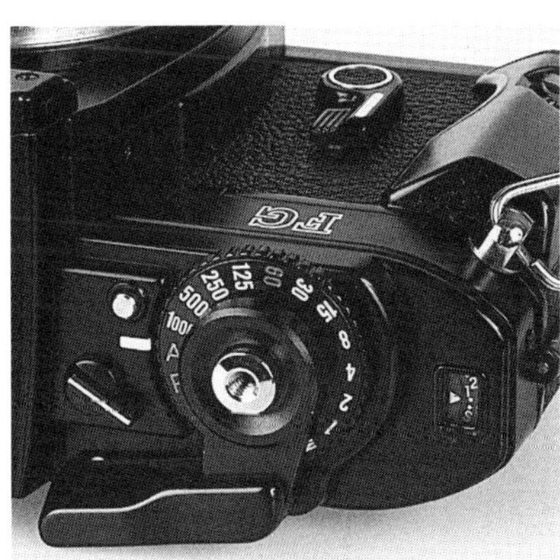

Shutter speeds can be set manually on the FG, as opposed to the EM.

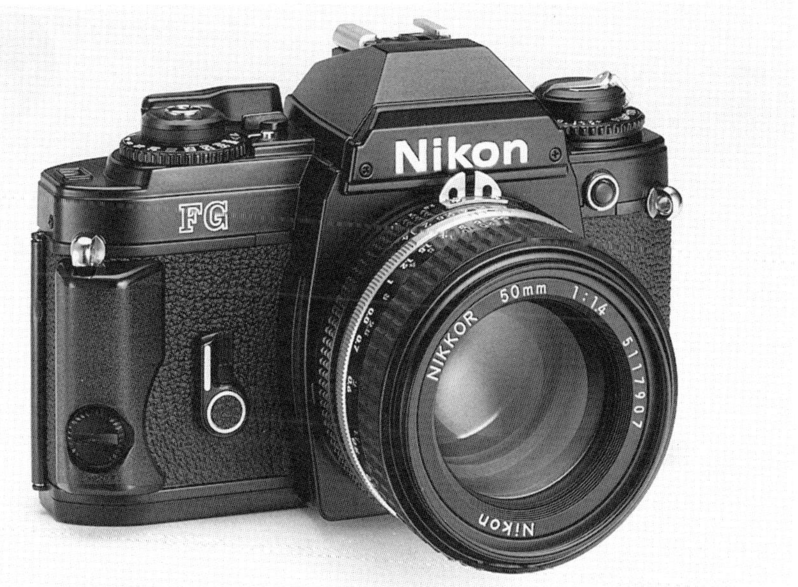

Not exactly a pro's choice but nevertheless available in "professional" black finish: the FG.

Background Information: Shutter Priority Automatic Exposure Mode

Nikon indicate this mode with an S = shutter priority. The very first Nikon with any kind of automatic exposure was the Nikkorex Auto 35 in 1965 with its shutter priority mode. Nikon prefers not to be reminded of this model since it was only partly a Nikon, manufactured in cooperation with Mamiya, and did not compare in quality with their other products.

The second example of a shutter priority mode in a Nikon were the already mentioned DS-aperture control units for the F2. Together with the Photomic viewfinders DP-2 (F2 S), DP-3 (F2 SB), and DP-12 (F2 AS) they allowed the F2 to be operated with a shutter priority automatic exposure mode. This accessory is mounted on the front of the camera and, controlled by the Photomic viewfinder, rotates the complete aperture ring. A system which was more suitable for "unmanned" photography than for normal use.

The first shutter priority mode incorporated within a body can be found in the Nikon FA. During the operation of the shutter priority mode the camera's stop-down lever is restricted in its downward movement by a peripheral lug. If the metering system computes a large aperture such as f/4, following the release the lever is stopped after only a few millimetres, while it would travel through almost the complete range in the case of a small aperture value such as f/22.

During the late 70's it was hotly disputed which of the automatic modes was superior. Whereas, for example, Canon and Konica preferred the shutter priority mode, Nikon and Minolta placed their bets on aperture priority. Without a doubt the shutter priority mode has its advantages for the casual snapshooter. He chooses a speed he expects will prevent any camera shake, perhaps 1/125 sec., and leaves the rest to the automatic aperture setting. The ambitious amateur photographer would rather employ the aperture priority mode though. He will preset the aperture to determine the depth-of-field, that is the distribution of sharp and unsharp areas, and keep an eye on the shutter speed in the viewfinder. The shutter priority mode is useless for long exposures as well as for close-up and macro-photography. It is advantageous for panning shots for which a certain shutter speed is necessary. Thus each mode has its justification and can make sense according to the task.

The exposure-lock function is an important additional accessory for every automatic mode. Pressing a button or lever can "memorize" the metered value for a specific scene while it is recomposed and the shutter released. An automatic camera does not become a practical instrument until an exposure-lock is included to allow the exposure to be biased quickly and individually if desired.

In comparison to the EM, the only thing noticeable, besides the 30 grams extra weight, is the grip fastened with a screw which provides the small camera with improved handling. It must be removed though when the motor drive MD-14, introduced with the FG, or the MD-E is to be attached.

In addition to the program mode the FG also possesses an aperture priority mode with quartz-controlled shutter speeds from 1/1000 to 1 sec., as well as the two settings B and 1/90 sec. that are not in need of battery power. The beeping can be switched off and exposure correction factors of +/-2 EV are incorporated in the film speed dial (ISO 12/12° to 3200/36°). A chain of red LEDs to the right of the image frame in the viewfinder, with its fixed K-type focusing screen, indicates the shutter speed chosen in the automatic exposure modes. In manual mode one LED identifies the preset speed while one or two flashing LEDs inform of the exposure meter's suggested values. Under- or overexposures are signalled by LEDs below the 1 sec. and above the 1/1000 sec. marks respectively. If both of them flash, the FG is signalling that the lens's smallest aperture has not been preset in program mode. This warning operates whenever the lens is set to larger apertures than f/11.

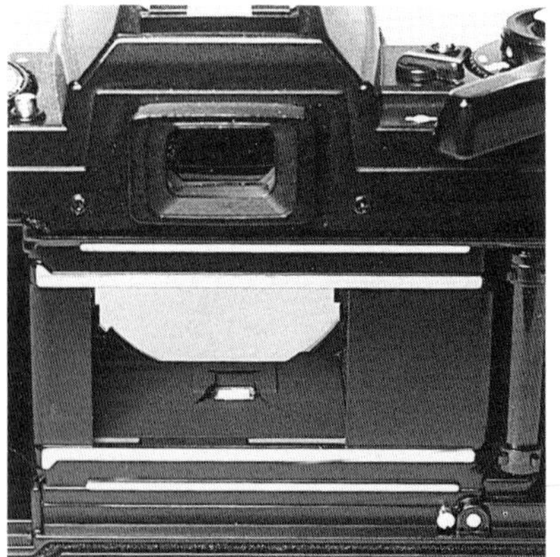

A look at a detail in the FG's mirror-box: the sensor for TTL-metering.

Just like the EM, the FG has a backlight button instead of an exposure-lock function, and a depth-of-field control and aperture display were sacrificed in favour of a lower price. The camera back can be removed and replaced by the databack MF-15 – an accessory which was becoming quite trendy at the time of the introduction of the FG.

Nothing was left out though in terms of flash technology. The FG was equipped with a sensor in the bottom of the camera for TTL-metering. These are the features with which the FG had to compete for the amateur photographer's favour. It was not easy though, since the SLR-market was declining at the time and it could not match the image of a Canon AE-1 or Minolta XD-7 due to its similarity to the EM.

Nikon FG-20

In 1984 the EM was succeeded by the FG-20. Actually it should have been named EM-20 because it looked more like the EM than the FG. Whereas its outer appearance had not necessarily been improved, it has more technical features than the EM. The most important modification was the possibility of setting shutter speeds manually from 1/1000 to 1 sec.

Background Information: Aperture Priority Automatic Exposure Mode

This mode is often denoted on cameras by an "A" on the shutter speed dial standing for "aperture priority". In aperture priority mode the camera's shutter is controlled steplessly and automatically. To facilitate this the shutter is equipped with an electromagnet in series with a capacitor. Depending on the subject brightness, the film speed set, and the preset aperture this capacitor is charged to a greater or lesser extent. When the camera is released the last metered value immediately before the mirror swings up is stored and simultaneously determines the capacitor's degree of charge. As soon as the mirror is up the first shutter blind is released and the exposure begins.

The magnet retains the second blind for a certain time depending on the capacitor's charge. It is not before its holding power has almost completely diminished that the second blind can be started by the power of a spring. A lowly charged capacitor would result in a fast shutter speed, a high charge in a slower speed. According to Nikon's information, the slowest shutter speed almost always coincided with the slowest manual setting available. In reality even much longer exposures did not pose any problems. For example, the slowest speed officially available in the FE is 8 sec. Presupposing fresh batteries, exposures of up to an hour and more are possible; a theoretical value maybe which takes no account of reciprocity failure with such long exposures but impressive just the same.

Exposures lasting around one minute are much commoner and allow many kinds of experiments. You should remember to cover the eyepiece though, since more light could enter the camera through the viewfinder than the lens, depending on the shooting situation. In order to compensate for reciprocity failure within an automatic mode the film speed can be changed or the exposure-lock can be used. It is advisable to bracket the exposure in steps of ½ EV

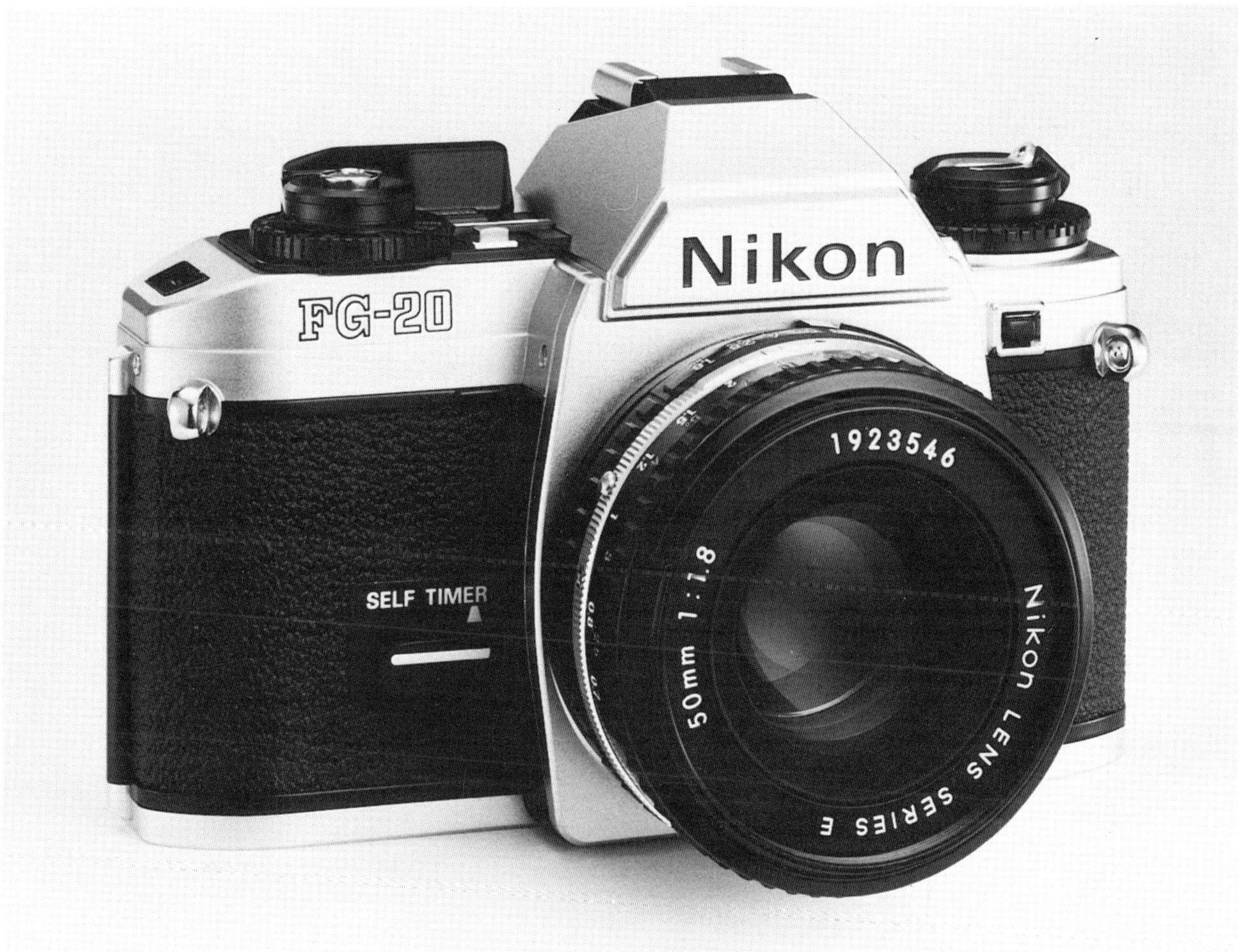

The immediate successor to the EM was the FG-20 with aperture priority and manual mode.

Background Information: Programmed Automatic Exposure Mode

It was only a question of time before camera technology would knock the bottom out of the arguments for and against the best type of automatic exposure mode. In this mode, indicated by a "P", the camera chooses a combination of both shutter speed and aperture itself depending on the prevailing light. The decisive thing in this case is the shape of the program line, that is which aperture is combined with which shutter speed. A shutter speed/aperture combination of 1/1000 sec. at f/2, for example, will deliver the same exposure as 1/4 sec. at f/32 – as well as every combination in between. The basic idea behind the most common program curve is that most amateur photographers will confine themselves to certain types of situation or motif, such as landscapes or family.

In the example mentioned above, the FG will set 1/125 sec. and f/5.6, not an unusual combination. If the light gets brighter by 1 EV the shutter speed will be set faster – and the aperture smaller – both by half a step to 1/60 sec. and f/ 6.7. If it darkens the shutter speed will be set slower and the aperture larger. When the maximum aperture has been reached, that is the diaphragm cannot be opened further, increasingly deteriorating light will be compensated by appropriately slower speeds as if it were an aperture priority mode.

Such a program curve is unsuitable for telephoto shots or in sports photography where fast shutter speeds are necessary, so designers began to improve the normal program mode. The FA was the first Nikon to switch automatically between two programs with different curves. In this camera the so-called high-speed program, denoted as "P Hi", is activated automatically by the focal length indexing ridge of all lenses 135mm or longer. If, for example, an exposure combination of 1/125 sec. at f/5.6 was set with a 50mm lens it would be shifted to 1/370 sec. at f/3.5 with a 135mm-lens. From the F-301 onwards the high-speed program could even be chosen manually: P = normal program, P Hi = high-speed program.

This makes it possible to employ the designer's original intention for "wrong" purposes, like using the faster program with a wide-angle lens instead of the normal mode the camera would otherwise have chosen. The F-801 even has a program shift function which allows the user to choose any shutter speed/aperture combination appropriate for the subject's brightness. This improvement liberated the program mode from being considered merely an uncreative snapshooter's automatic mode.

They are quartz-controlled but are not displayed in the viewfinder. So when working with the manual mode you have to remember your preset speed. A kind of handling that does not exactly help in avoiding mistakes. Another difference to the EM is the beeping signal which can be switched off. The fixed focusing screen has become brighter and the split-image rangefinder only darkens with apertures of f/5.6 or smaller. In a way this was a kind of predecessor to the "Brite-View" screens introduced later in the F-301.

In addition to the shutter speed display in the viewfinder, another LED indicates with an "M" when the automatic mode is switched off. The film speed range has been extended to ISO 3200/36°, in comparison to the proven EM everything else remained technically unchanged internally – with one exception: in the EM the aperture value was transmitted by the meter coupling lever to an unprotected resistor track. Even the tiniest dust particles could interrupt the contact resulting in the needle trembling or jumping erratically whenever the aperture ring was rotated. In the FG-20 this problem was solved by the use of a FRE = functional resistance element. The FG-20 was not to have a very bright future though, since after less than one year of production it was discontinued. Many deep-rooted Nikon fans will neither shed a tear for the EM nor for the FG-20. But in the end their automatic exposure modes will produce the same pictures as that of the F-801.

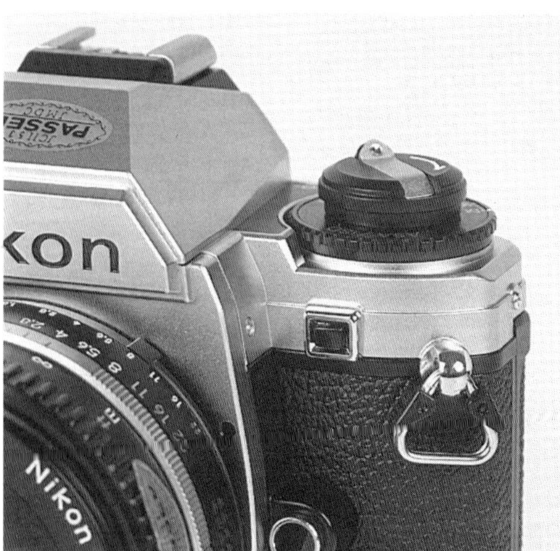

The backlight-button is located on the front of the FG-20 beneath the rewind crank.

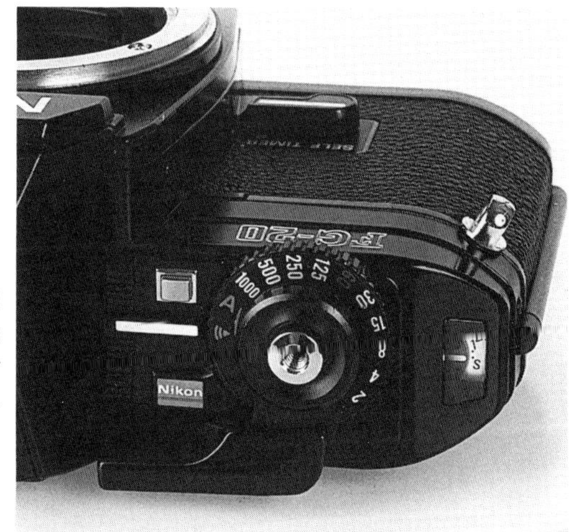

The shutter speed dial of the FG-20 with the conspicuous symbol for the acoustic warning.

CHAPTER 6

The New Generation

Throughout the first forty years of Nikon production a camera's character was mainly determined by its mechanical design – for Nikon as well as all the others. Everything feasible was built into the top model and then later might appear in the less expensive ones. The EM marked the step into the amateur mass market. The target group for such a camera was carefully evaluated and ease of handling became more important. In 1985, after only 3 years of production, the FG was discontinued in order to replace it with the Nikon F-301.

Its integrated motor drive suddenly put the Nikon photographer's right thumb out of work. Later, in spite of the F-301's compact dimensions, Nikon engineers managed to incorporate an autofocus system into the same body in the form of the F-501. Looking back today, a very remarkable achievement.

Nikon Model Names

The new generation of cameras also heralded another departure for Nikon. They started the practice of giving a camera model a different name in North America to that in the rest of the world. Other manufacturers such as Canon, Pentax and Minolta did the same. In a few cases with cameras from other makers there might also be a slight difference in specification. The equivalent Nikon names are as follows:-

N2000	*in U.S.A. and Canada*	*= F-301*
N2020	*in U.S.A. and Canada*	*= F-501*
N4004	*in U.S.A. and Canada*	*= F-401*
N4004s	*in U.S.A. and Canada*	*= F-401s*
N5005	*in U.S.A. and Canada*	*= F-401x*
N6000	*in U.S.A. and Canada*	*= F-601M*
N6006	*in U.S.A. and Canada*	*= F-601*
N8008	*in U.S.A. and Canada*	*= F-801*
N8008s	*in U.S.A. and Canada*	*= F-801s*
N90	*in U.S.A. only*	*= F-90*

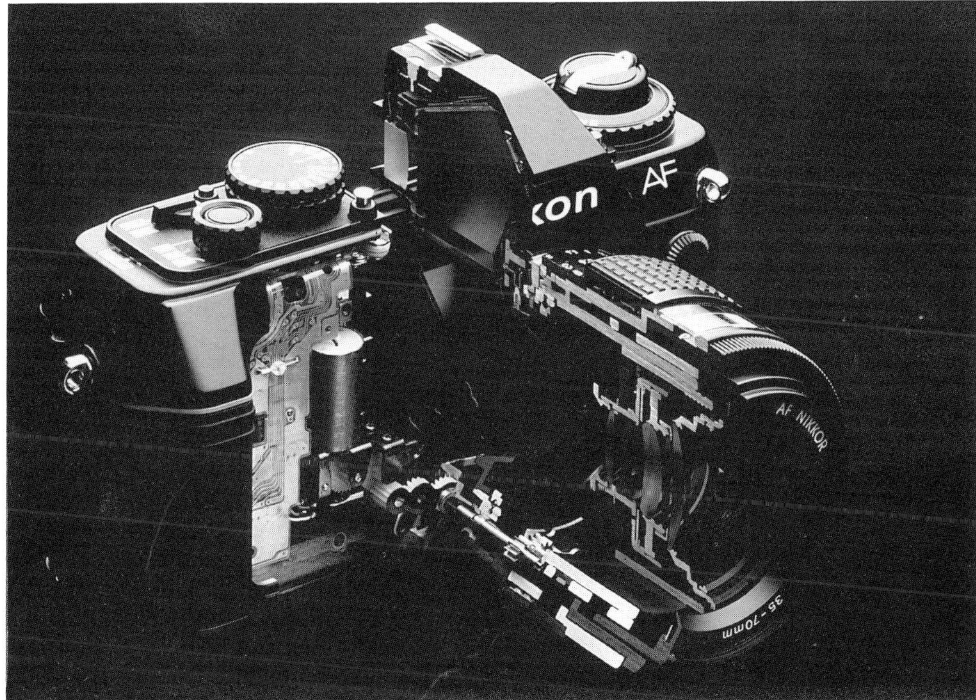

A cut-away of the F-501/N2020. The mechanism for automatic focusing can be seen quite clearly.

Nikon F-301/N2000

This model was introduced as the start of a "new generation", and as we know today it was really the first of a completely new class of camera, culminating in the F-90. The F-301 was the first Nikon SLR with a built-in motor drive. Critics pointed out that it was no faster than an FG in combination with its motor drive, and when only the technical features are examined they were right. But the real advantages are in its easy handling which allows an inexperienced amateur to enjoy SLR photography. The F-301 is a fully-fledged Nikon that can be used with almost all AI-type lenses as well as those modified to this standard. Because of the film transport motor, which allows up to 2.5 frames/sec., the F-301 depends on battery power. The base-plate must be removed to insert the 4 AAA-size, 1.5v batteries – enough for about 50 rolls of

36-exposure film, which should last a long time, especially for users in the target group. If you want to be on the safe side, or if you are forced to work in extremely low temperatures, you can employ the optional and larger base-plate MB-3 which includes a clamp. This takes AA-size batteries with three times the capacity and which are much more common in Europe. It is also possible to use rechargeable batteries in this compartment.

When the film is to be loaded the leader only has to be pulled to a red mark after the camera back has been opened. As soon as the back is closed a spring-suspended roller presses the film against the take-up spool. The first press of the release button results in the film advancing and three blank exposures – leading to frame no.1 – and the F-301 is ready to shoot.

In order for the user to check that the film is advancing properly, an indicator on the camera back rotates as long as it is running correctly. This feature, taken over from the AF-compact cameras, prevents any faulty operation. The distinct bulge on the front of the F-301 aids its excellent handling, even long and heavy telephoto lenses can be held securely and without fatigue.

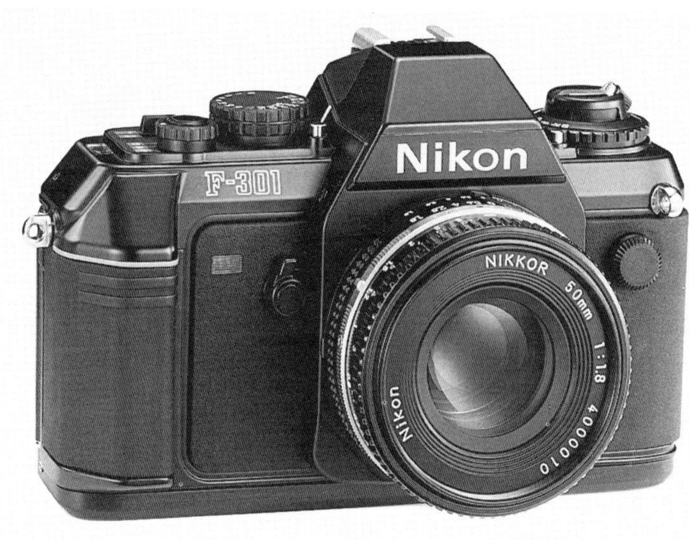

The integrated motor of the F-301/N2000 is hidden underneath the ergonomically styled grip section.

New Features, New Design

The top-plate is well arranged: the release button is ergonomically located directly behind the front edge, together with the dial for single or continuous mode. The switch for the acoustic signal is immediately behind it. This signal warns of shutter speeds above 1/2000 sec. or below 1/30 sec., of when the self-timer is activated, or when a non-DX-coded film is loaded.

The exposure mode switch is conservative dial instead of the LCD's and multiple button operation that was very fashionable at the time. Besides the manual shutter speeds from 1/2000 to 1 sec. and B, the F-301 has a normal aperture priority mode as well as the two program modes P and P Hi. When it is set to the most frequently used P-position the camera selects a shutter speed/aperture combination which is designed for static subjects. "P Hi", on the other hand (the "Hi" stands for "high speed") presupposes moving subjects or snapshot situations and therefore prefers the fastest possible speeds. Compared to P, the shutter speed with P Hi is about one stop faster and the aperture accordingly one stop larger. The manual shutter speeds are controlled by a quartz oscillator. The locking button for the exposure mode dial is situated in front of it. The safety catch and button to release the film for rewind, which still has to be done with the conventional crank, is immediately behind it.

The view through the finder is a delight: a newly developed, fixed focusing screen gives a brilliant image with scarcely visible grain. The decisive advantage of this "Brite View" focusing screen is that the split-image rangefinder does not darken with lenses slower than f/4 as before, but only from f/11. This makes it possible to use it with zoom lenses and even with a 500mm mirror lens.

A row of LEDs on the right side of the finder indicates the shutter speed chosen by the camera. In manual mode the preset speed lights up and the flashing LED indicates the

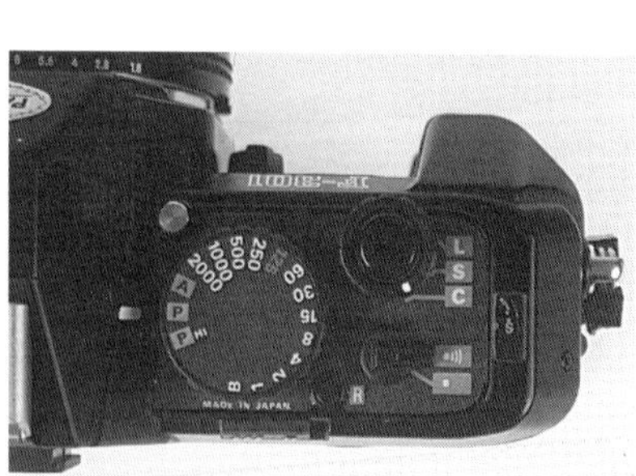
Despite the change of generation, it still has classic controls instead of buttons.

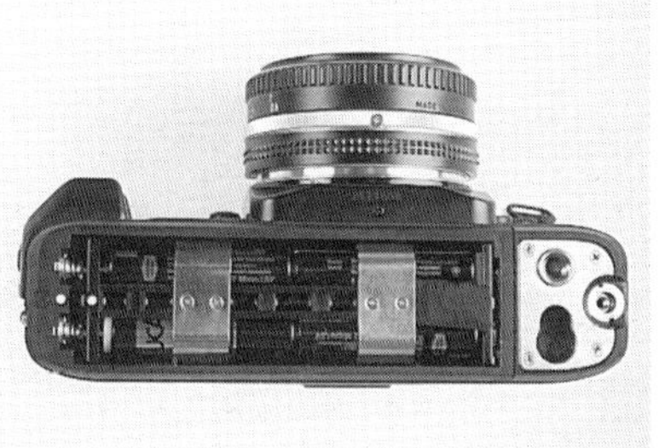
The power supply occupies the whole width of the camera.

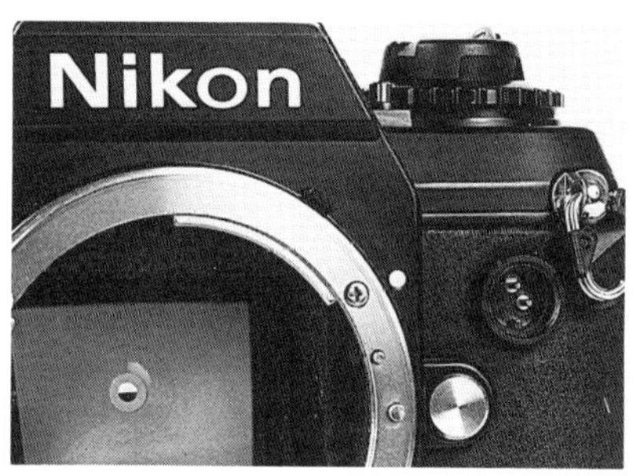

No cable release socket but a terminal for electric remote-control accessories.

camera's suggested speed. Two flashing triangles above the 1/2000 sec. and below the 1 sec. markings indicate lighting situations that exceed the metering range. Since the F-301 is designed mainly to be used with one of the program modes the preset aperture is not displayed in the viewfinder. An SPD-sensor is responsible for the centre-weighted metering with the typical Nikon 40:60% split. A second SPD-sensor in the bottom of the camera serves the TTL-flash metering circuit, which operates within a range from ISO 25/15° to 1000/31°.

The flash program mode is also new. When the camera is set to P or P Hi the appropriate aperture for flash operation is chosen automatically. In the case of ISO 100/21° the aperture is fixed at f/5.6; with a faster film correspondingly smaller and with a slower film larger. This is based on the idea that most amateur flash photographs are made with smaller flash units mounted on the camera and with guide numbers between 25 and 30, and that the subject distances will vary between two and five metres on average. If the photographer wishes to choose the flash aperture himself he can employ both aperture priority and manual modes. The camera will then display the shutter speed that would be correct without the use of flash by means of a flashing LED: a big help for fill-in flash photography. This flash program mode is only accessible together with AI-S-standard lenses.

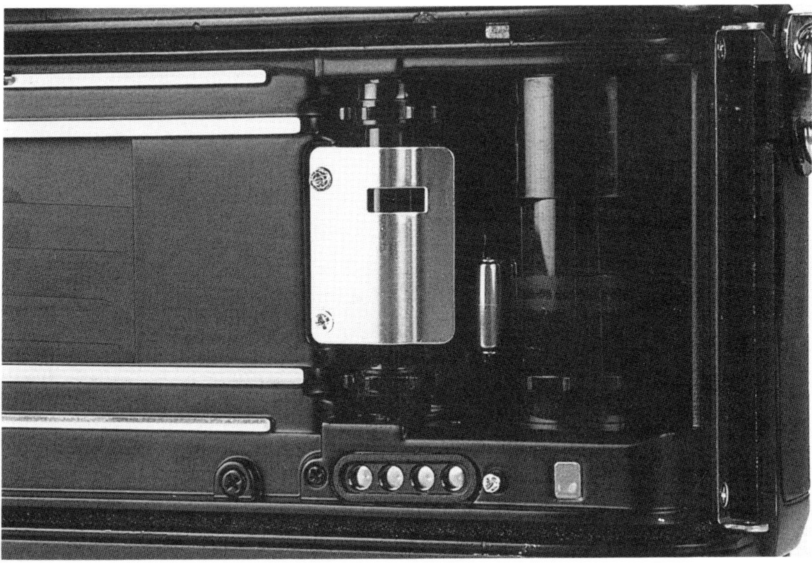

The F-301/N2000 with the back removed. The take-up spool for automatic film loading can be seen on the right.

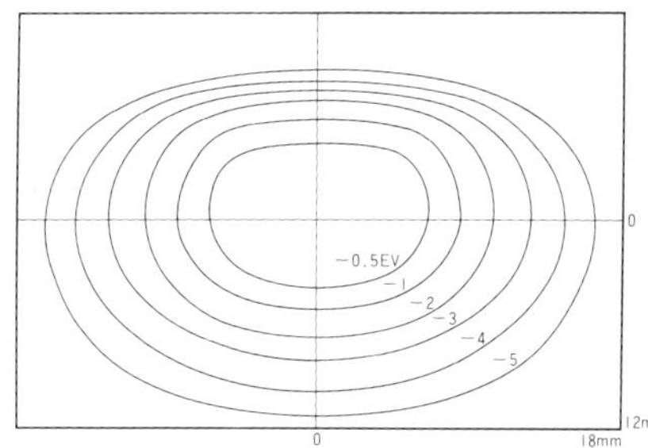

The diagram illustrates the distribution of metering sensitivity in the F-301/N2000.

In order to prevent stray light from entering through the eyepiece during tripod shots the eyepiece cover (DK-5) is delivered with the camera. It is necessary to use an eyepiece adapter when the right-angle viewing attachment or the eyepiece magnifier are to be attached. A red LED, situated next to the prism housing, lights up when the film reaches the end of the roll. If it blinks, this indicates that an uncoded film has been loaded even though the film speed dial is set to DX-identification.

Because people often forget to reset the film speed on their meters when changing from one type of film to another, Kodak developed the DX-code system and introduced it at the beginning of the 1980's and it has now become a worldwide standard. The metal film cassette is not enamelled in certain places, depending on the film speed, leaving a pattern of bare metal which conducts electricity. A row of contacts is located in the film chamber of the camera where the cassette is placed when a film is loaded. Depending on the film's speed, different combinations of the contacts are short-circuited and the resulting ISO-value relayed to the camera's electronic controls. This code enables speeds from ISO 25/15° to 5000/38° to be scanned. The F-301 has a DX-range from ISO 25/15° to 4000/37°. Speeds from ISO 12/12° to 3200/36° can be set manually. When the dial is rotated beyond the ISO 12/12° position the DX-mark appears on a red background. The exposure compensation factors are also incorporated in the film speed dial.

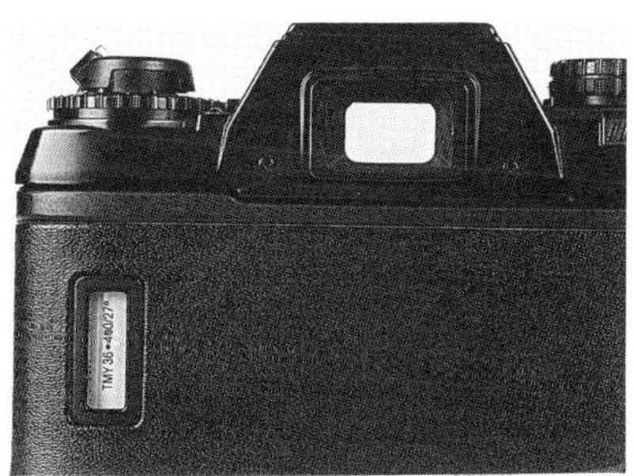

A reminder of the loaded film is provided by a window instead of a memo clip.

The F-301 has a terminal for electric remote-control accessories but no cable release socket. Any photographer who insists on using a cable release can fall back on the terminal release MR-3 or the more convenient release cord MC-12A.

A second pin which identifies whether or not the lens in use is an AI-S- standard type is situated just above the lens release pin as on the FA. If it isn't, the stop-down mechanism is given some more time to set the correct aperture during program mode.

The self-timer, controlled electronically, is located to the left of the bayonet and its activity is indicated by an LED situated next to it. The exposure-lock lever, which allows the most important part of the subject to be metered, is located round the self-timer button. A depth-of-field preview button and a mirror lockup were omitted from the F-301 but will only be missed by a few of its owners. By and by the F-301 became popular with amateurs, and even press photographers, because of its many features, light weight, and easy handling. It won itself countless fans even at a time when autofocus cameras were becoming more and more predominant.

A tip for the user: those who are annoyed by the off-centre tripod bush will find a solution to their problems in the tripod adaptor AH-3. Anyone missing additional features can attach the Multi-Control Back MF-19. Besides the option to imprint the date, the time, or a random number, it also allows interval and timer operation and includes an alarm clock.

Nikon F-501/N2020

In 1985 Minolta introduced the "7000", the first mass-produced autofocus SLR, and started a new chapter in the story of SLR-photography. The Nikon F3 AF had appeared two years earlier, but it was more a special version within the F3-system than an independent autofocus camera since there were only two telephoto lenses for it. It was also expensive. Nikon's very first autofocus lens was introduced in 1972 as a prototype that never went into production. It weighed almost 3 kilos, was a good 30cm long, had a modest maximum aperture of f/4.5 for its 80mm focal length and barely managed to focus slowly between one metre and infinity. Canon and Ricoh offered one AF-lens each for their manual bodies which possessed integrated active AF-systems similar to those in the compact cameras. But these were all just learning steps on the way to the body-integrated system which Nikon introduced shortly after the Minolta 7000 appeared.

At first sight you might believe you were dealing with another F-301 since the F-301 and the F-501 have the same body, except for a few minor details. Compared to the F-301, the shutter speed dial has another program position: "P Dual". It stands for the automatic switch-over between the normal and the high speed programs, depending on the focal length in use, similar to the principle employed in the Nikon FA. A pin protruding from the bayonet flange for this purpose is pressed in by AI-S- and AF-lenses of at least 135mm focal length in order to activate the high speed program.

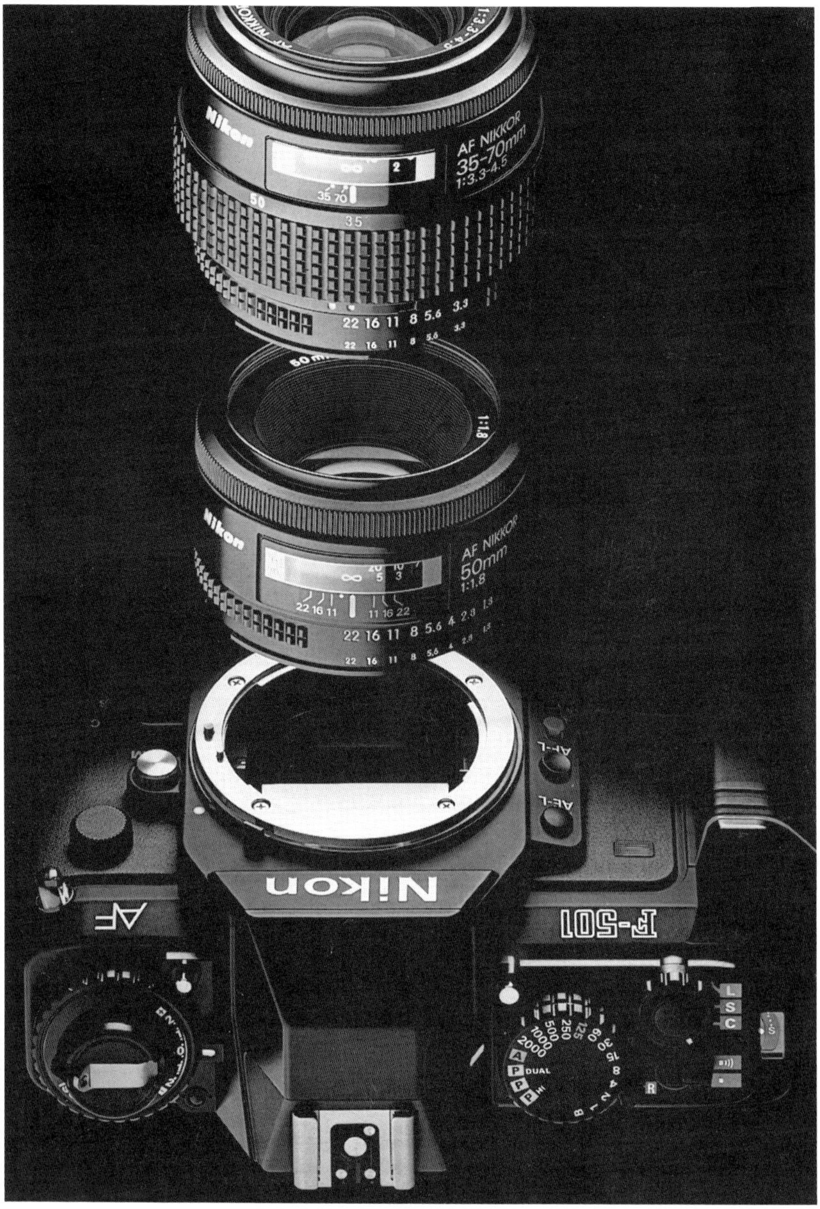

The age of autofocus begins for Nikon: the F-501 with a 50mm,f/1.8 and the compact zoom 35-70mm,f/3.5-4.5.

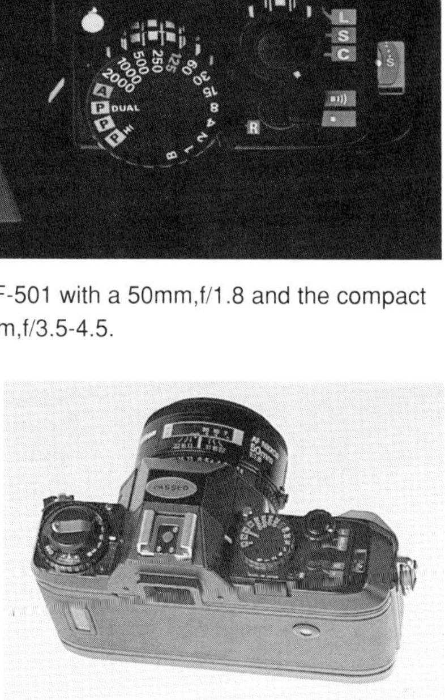

Provision for interchangeable focusing screens is the second difference to the F-301. Next to the standard B-type screen, the E-type with an etched grid and the J-type for manual

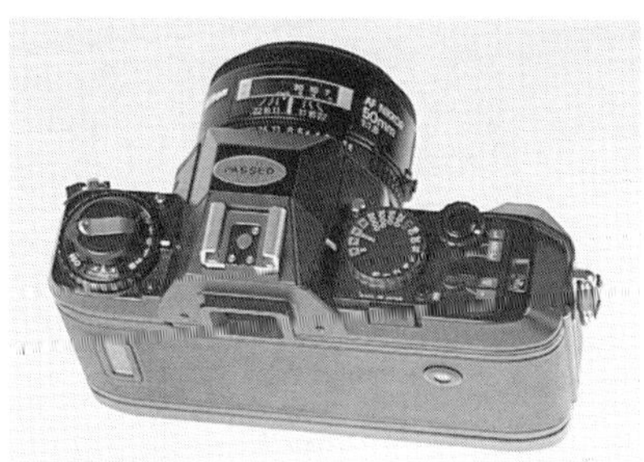

The F-501/N2020 seen from above. Differences from the F-301/N2000 are only apparent on closer inspection.

focusing with microprisms were also available. The range of the automatic DX-coding was extended from ISO 25/15° to 5000/38°. The exposure-lock button was slightly changed too.

It's obvious that the major differences are hidden inside – the AF-coupler in the bayonet that can be seen when the lens is removed is an outer sign of this. It is fascinating in this respect that Nikon succeeded in maintaining the original bayonet, which had remained generally unchanged since 1959, even in the face of such a far-reaching development as autofocus. As a result every AI-, and F-lens modified to that standard can be used on the F-501.

When the release button is pressed the AF-system is also automatically activated. A switch marked with the positions "S", "C", and "M" is located below the lens release button. In the S-position the release button is locked until the lens has been set to the correct focus.

The AF-system works continuously in the C-position and if the subject moves it will correct the focus setting. In this mode it is possible to release the shutter at any time, even if the subject is not correctly focused. In everyday use the S-position should be employed for static subjects while C is more appropriate for sports, journalistic, and snapshot photography.

When the M-position is activated, the coupler spindle is retracted to allow manual focusing with AF-lenses. But the AF-system is also helpful with non-AF lenses because the focus status indications are displayed below the image in the viewfinder. The green circle in the centre signals proper focus, while the red arrows to the left and right inform about which direction to rotate the lens. If a red "X" appears the camera is not able to identify the correct focus. This can happen, for example, when there is insufficient contrast or when the AF-metering area is aimed at items showing a high degree of reflectivity. But in spite of all the automatic modes one still has to do some thinking because the metering only takes place within the brackets marked in the centre of the finder image. Whenever the main part of the subject is not located in the centre of the picture focus must be locked just like the exposure. Focus is locked automatically in the S-mode, whereas an intervention is necessary in the continuously active C-mode. The appropriate button is situated beneath the exposure-lock button. This makes it possible to measure on a subject which is not in the centre, lock the focus by pressing the button,

Background Information: Passive Autofocus

As in all other comparable SLRs, the Nikon autofocus system works according to the so-called passive principle. Unlike autofocus compact cameras which emit a beam of light, it uses the light entering through the lens to measure the distance. The reason is that this system functions with interchangeable lenses. The reflex mirror is partially transparent in its centre so that, similar to the F3 design, a proportion of the light can be directed to the bottom of the camera. A semiconductor image converter with 2x24 individual elements (CCDs) is located there, which converts the incoming light energy into electricity. Special lens elements in front of the CCDs direct the focal point onto only one pair of them when the focusing is correct. If the focusing is not correct, then two separate CCDs are "hit". With this information – the distance between the activated CCDs and depending on whether the upper or lower half of the CCD is addressed – the electronics calculate the degree of defocus as well as its direction, that is if the lens is set too near or too far.

The F-501 has two rows of these (96) CCD-sensors. One for maximum apertures up to f/2.8 and a second for those up to f/4.5. This makes a more precise measurement possible for the faster lenses which have smaller tolerance at large apertures. As soon as the degree of defocus is determined, the microprocessor (CPU) of the AF-lens is questioned how many of the AF-motor's revolutions are necessary to move the optical system into focus. Naturally, a wide-angle lens will not have to be moved as far as a telephoto lens. The motor then starts to operate in order to focus the lens accordingly. Nikon as well as most of the other makers place their AF-motor in the camera body which then drives the lens through a gear-train. In the F-501, for example, the AF-system takes a good 2 seconds to drive the 70-210mm zoom all the way from infinity to its shortest distance of 1.1 metres. This time was reduced in the following models and the system's precision in the case of very small subjects was also improved considerably. This is one of the weak spots of passive autofocus systems, as well as the fact that the subject must have a certain minimum brightness. In the F-501 this minimum is defined as EV 3, which is the equivalent of an exposure of 1 sec. at f/2.8 with ISO 100/21°. A certain minimum degree of contrast is another prerequisite the autofocus sensors need to discern between sharp and unsharp. Improvements have been made since in all of these areas so now there is virtually no photographic application in which autofocus cannot be employed.

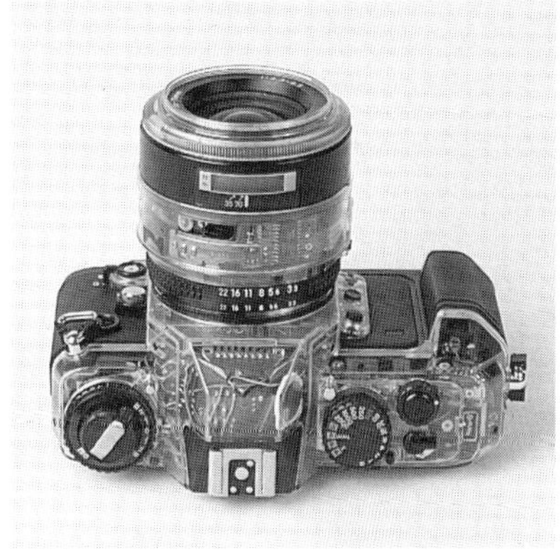

Transparent Nikon technology – a demonstration model of the F-501/N2000.

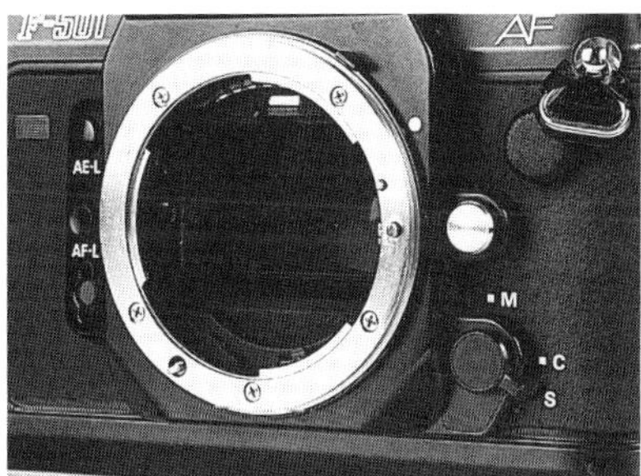

Some of the F-501/N2020 controls are grouped around the bayonet.

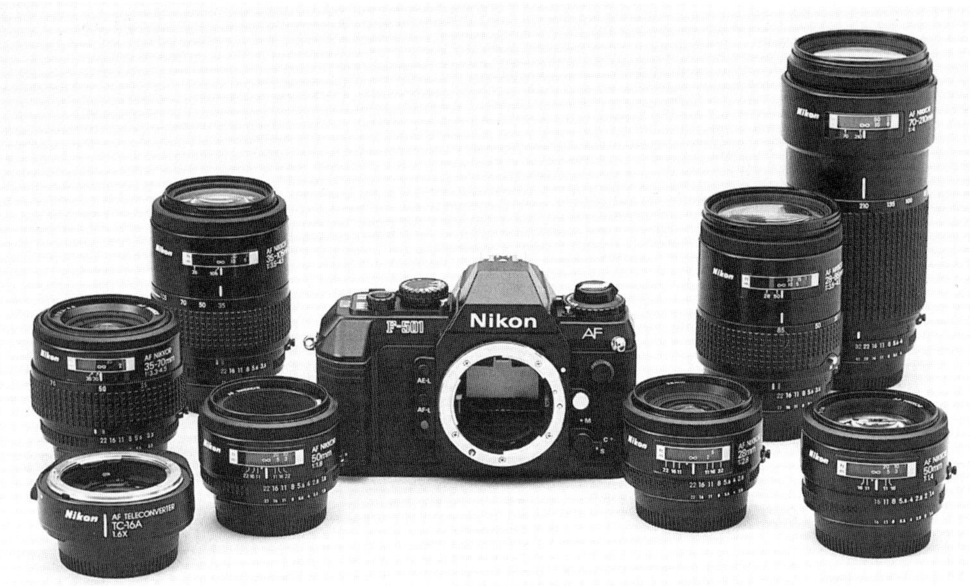

The F-501/N2020 together with the original AF-lens line-up, which has been extended considerably since then.

recompose and shoot, even when the C-mode has been chosen for action subjects.

When the F-501 appeared at the beginning of 1986 only three autofocus lenses were offered. In order to provide a good start for Nikon photographers in the autofocus era an AF-teleconverter was offered, as it had been in the case of the F3 AF. The optical system of the TC-16A converter is driven by the AF-motor in the body through the coupling spindle. This allows over 30 conventional Nikkor lenses to be converted into autofocus ones – from the fisheye 6mm,f/2.8 to the 400mm,f/2.8, with the restrictions that the maximum aperture must be at least f/2.8. The focal length is increased by 1.6x by the converter but a decrease of the effective aperture by 1 1/3 EV must be taken into account. With longer focal length lenses it is also necessary to preset the distance manually if they are to be employed at short range.

Maintaining the bayonet was a remarkable achievement on Nikon's part, and a highly valued advantage to countless Nikon photographers who have been able to change smoothly to the new technology without making their existing equipment worthless. No other company has shown such consistency in their dedication to a system and it has paid off for Nikon. The F-501 became one of the biggest selling Nikon-SLRs.

Nikon F-401/N4004

One year after the F-501 it was expected that Nikon would present another autofocus model with faster focusing, faster film transport, and further professional features. But it turned out differently. Since the EM, no other model has caused such confusion among Nikon fans than the F-401. Was Nikon going to change from being the professional's manufacturer to the provider for the amateur snapshooter? The F-401 does have the F-bayonet, but with non-AF lenses not even exposure-metering is possible. For whom was the F-401 conceived? Since the beginning of the 80's AF-compact cameras had enjoyed a boom. They were becoming technically ever more comprehensive, equipped with two focal lengths or even zooms, and so becoming more and more attractive for hitherto SLR users. Such photographers, tempted by automation, were the group the F-401 aimed at – a single lens reflex with the operating ease of a viewfinder camera.

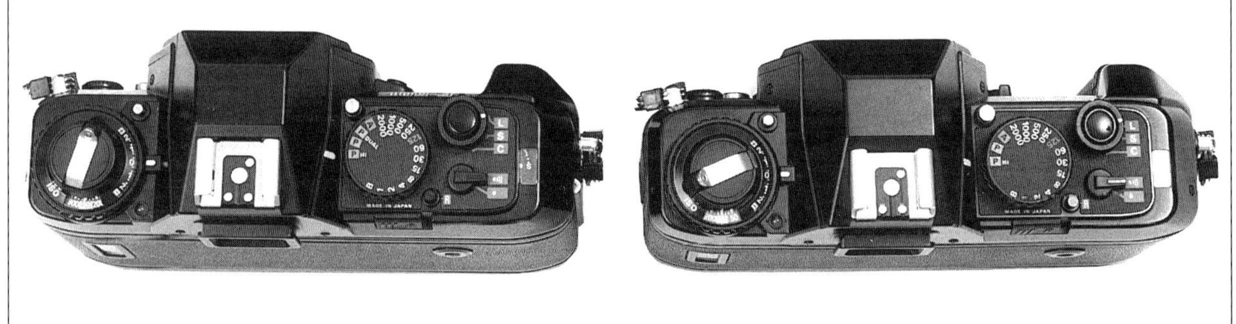

The F-501/N2020 and the F-301/N2000 in direct comparison. The only difference to be found is on the shutter speed dial.

The flash incorporated in the prism is the unmistakeable feature of the F-401/N4004.

The body is conspicuous because of the very large grip, its rounded corners and edges, and a tiny flash unit built into the viewfinder prism. The release button is recessed into the slanted top of the grip. The camera reflects Nikon's conservative attitude towards controls – setting dials and scales dominate instead of LCDs on the F-401. Not only is there the usual one for the shutter speeds but also a second for aperture values. Only the edges of these dials are accessible under the dark grey plastic cover, an equally elegant and practical solution.

Turning the shutter speed dial from the L-position activates the F-401, when it is set to "A" and the aperture dial to "S" the program mode is switched on. The camera possesses a normal and a high-speed program, the latter is activated when AF-lenses of 135mm or longer focal length are mounted or a zoom is used beyond this range. If aperture priority is employed the desired value is set on the dial and not on the aperture ring of the lens. This ring must be set to the largest value and locked in this position. In shutter priority mode it is exactly the other way around. The speed is set while the aperture dial is standing at "S". If anybody really wants to use the F-401 manually, it can be done with the help of both dials.

The rewind button along with its security latch is situated next to the aperture dial, when both are operated, motorized rewinding starts – which takes about 25 seconds.

A brilliant, fixed focusing screen, without any rangefinder aids, just like the B-type, can be seen in the viewfinder. Only the most necessary information is displayed, no shutter speed or aperture values appear. Similar to the FM-2, the indications are limited to + and – signs and a circle for the correct exposure setting. When the circle blinks it signals the danger of camera shake since the shutter speed has fallen below 1/30 sec. If one of the other symbols blink it indicates over- or underexposure. If the + and – symbols blink alternately this signals that the aperture ring has not been set to the largest value. A green LED next to these lights up in the viewfinder when the focus setting is correct and of course the flash-ready light is there too, which also has another function in the F-401. Normally the camera evaluates the exposure with a three-segment multi-metering mode. This only changes to the 40/60% configu-

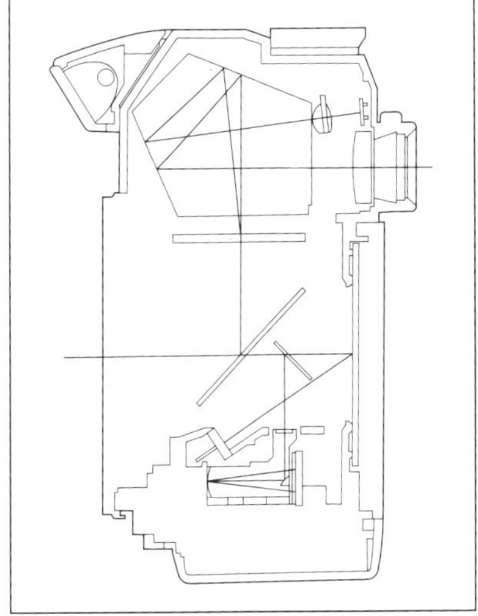
The light path inside the F-401/N4004.

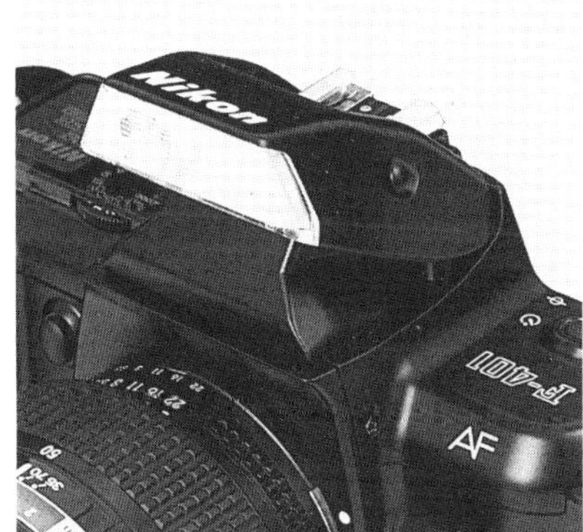

If it's built-in it can't be forgotten. The built-in flash in its operating position.

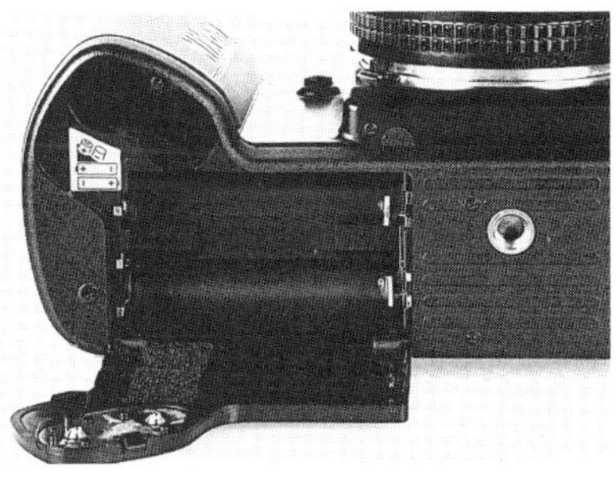
The batteries are stored upright as well as horizontally.

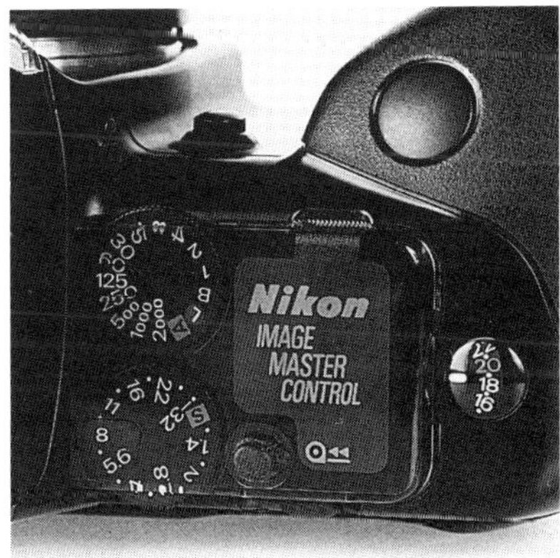

The transparent cover serves as a protection.

ration in manual mode and when the exposure-lock button is pressed. Whenever the multi-metering mode registers high subject contrast, for example in backlit situations, the camera's electronics suggest switching on the built-in flash with the blinking flash-ready signal. If the suggestion is followed the result will be a balanced fill-flash picture. The built-in flash is switched on by pressing the locking buttons on the left and the right of the prism housing, when the reflector will pop up. Normally the modest guide number of 12 will be perfectly adequate. Because of its closeness to the axis of the lens there is a strong probability of the red-eye effect showing up in pictures of people. Anyone who wants to avoid this and also wants to have greater power at his disposal can employ the F-401's advanced flash controls with more powerful units mounted on the camera.

Except for the button to activate the self-timer there is absolutely nothing else to the left of the viewfinder. The focus mode switch on the front has only two positions: one for autofocus mode according to the single servo focus priority principle (S), and "M" for manual focusing. In practical use one eccentricity of the F-401 proves to be quite annoying: in spite of the indication for correct focus lighting up, it sometimes takes up to 1 sec. for the shutter to actually be released, and this even though the camera is equipped with the brand-new AM-200 module that is also employed in the F-801 and F4. In this respect the F-401 was certainly not Spartan, 200 CCDs compared to the 96 of the F-501 ensure that the AF-system registers sufficient "material" for perfect automatic focusing, even on finely textured surfaces such as a carpet. In addition the sensors are arranged diagonally so that horizontal structures or round objects are recognized more surely. Compared to the F-501, the system's sensitivity was expanded by 2 EV at the low end, and in the later models even further to -1 EV (F-801/s, F-401s/x, F-601, F-90, and F4).

The F-401 does not possess any other mechanical links in its bayonet besides the stop-down lever. The complete communication between the body and the lens takes place through the microchip (CPU) incorporated into the AF-lenses. This is the reason why non-AF lenses can be attached but pose problems in practical use. Only the focusing works the usual way along with the setting of the shutter speeds. The use of the AF-teleconverter TC-16A is not possible either. In order to ensure that the AF-lens's aperture ring is set to the highest value a switch is placed just outside of the bayonet.

The exposure-lock button is situated all by itself next to the grip. The battery compartment is accessible after opening a flap in the camera's baseplate. Four 1.5V AA-size batteries are responsible for the complete power supply; they have enough capacity for about 20 films, presupposing about 50% of the shots are made with flash.

The F-401 could also be purchased in the form of the F-401 QD with a permanently attached databack. It allows either the date or the time to be imprinted.

Although unjustified, the F-401 had a hard time defending its position in the market throughout its existence, and especially among traditional Nikon owners. When the F3 appeared there were also protests from deep-rooted Nikon users, who later were to proudly employ the camera they had originally rated as an electronic toy.

Nikon F-401s/N4004s

In 1989,less than two years after the F-401, a modified model identified by an "s" was introduced. The external appearance differs by the larger Nikon logo on the grip, and of course the name on the front. The numerals for the shutter speeds and aperture values on the dials are larger, while the plastic cover above them is now completely transparent, instead of being tinted. The A-, S-, A+S- (=P), and L-

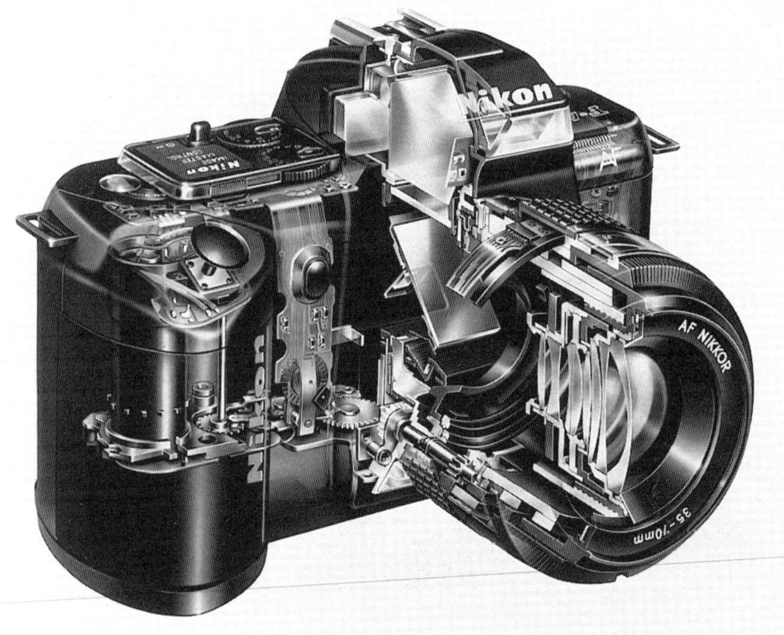

A cut-away of the F-401/N4004. The built-in flash adds to the complex internal construction.

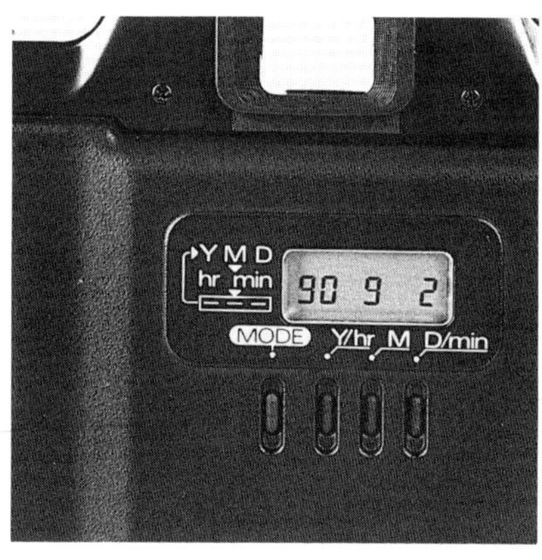

The F-401s/N4004s was also available in a data-version as the model F-401s QD.

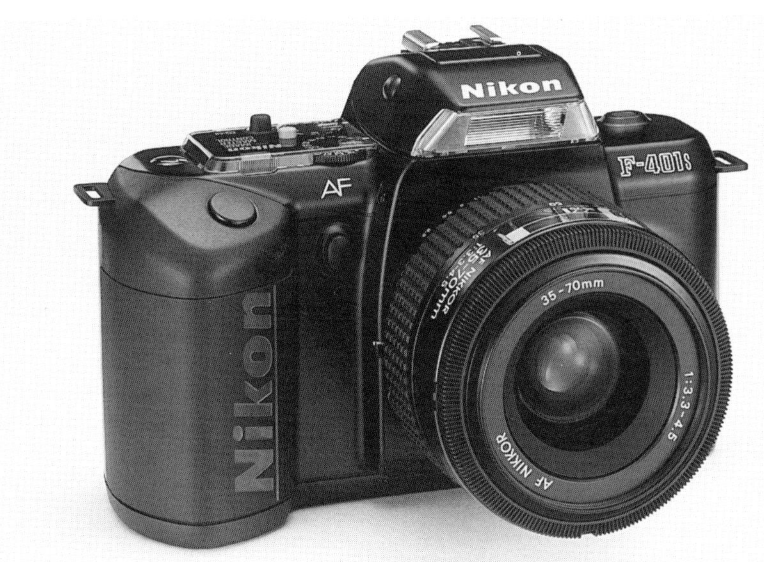

The F-401s/N4004s had improvements to details such as the enlarged dials.

positions can be locked and only changed by pressing an extra button so as to prevent any accidental miss-setting. The shutter release button rises somewhat higher and the operating range of the AF-system begins at -1 EV. In addition the AF-motor has a higher torque resulting in faster and more powerful focusing. A data-version named F-401 QD was also available.

Nikon F-401X/N5005

The F-401 was updated once again in 1991 to match the standards of the later Nikon models, particularly in regard to the AF- and metering systems. Besides including the Focus-Tracking mode known from the F4, the sensitivity of the AF-module was extended by 2EV to 19EV at the "bright" end. Probably as much a matter of rationalizing the production as increasing the model's attraction, the Nikon F-401x received the same Matrix exposure metering and control circuitry as the other AF-SLRs, based on five instead of just three segments and with an expanded range down to 0EV instead of just 1EV.

The F-401x shutter allows speeds down to 8 and 30 sec. in programmed and aperture priority automatic modes respectively instead of 1 second only. While the previous program modes of the earlier models were only dual, automatically switching to faster speeds, and larger apertures, to reduce the danger of camera-shake as of 135mm focal length, the F-401x is equipped with an Auto Multi-Program. This means the camera will not set slower speeds than 1/focal length of any lens being used until the lens diaphragm is fully opened, thus making full use of hand-held possibilities.

The additional "T"-position on the F-401x makes up for the missing cable release socket in earlier models when making long exposures. This is because once the dial is set to T (in manual mode), the shutter is only activated 0,5 sec. after the finger is removed from the release button and then remains open until pressed again.

The sync-speed was also improved slightly to 1/125 sec., which brings us to the F-401x flash exposure control system that really benefits from the enhanced electronics. First of all the built-in unit, looking unchanged, now covers picture angles down to a 28mm-lens – at the same guide number of 12. Film speeds up to ISO 800 and 1000 are accessible for TTL-control with the internal or external units respectively, as opposed to the former models' limited range of only ISO 25 to 400. These features lead us to the much acclaimed Matrix Balanced Fill-Flash mode now also available in the F-401x. Centre-weighted fill-flash operation is also possible. The triggering contrast for the flash signal in the viewfinder is a centre segment at least 2EV darker than the other four, themselves being at least 10EV (former models reacted at 1EV difference). The normal exposure information is also displayed so as to allow precise control and manual override if desired.

The double self-timer may be one of the less important spin-offs from the new electronics but their major bene-

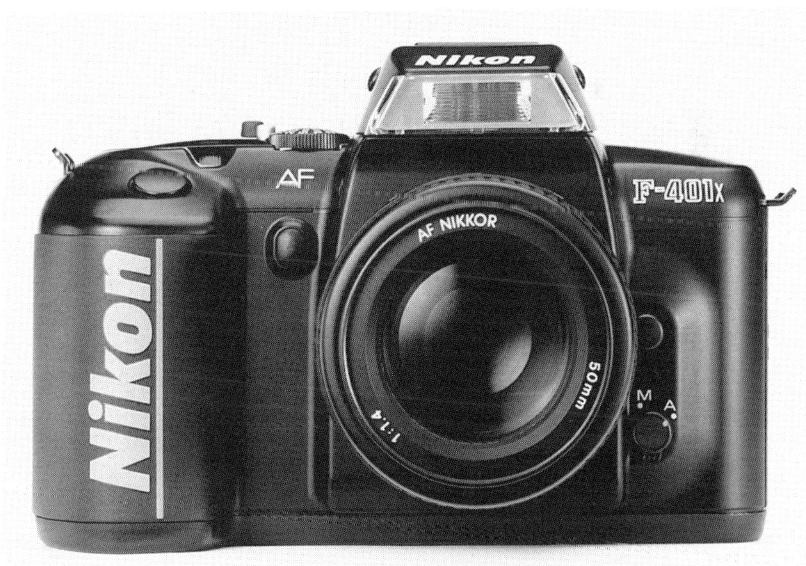

The F-401x/N4004x is characterised by the more rounded grip section and no cover over the shutter speed and aperture dials.

fit is in greater efficiency since, according to the specification, the F-401x manages up to 50% more films per battery-set.

This third generation F-401 is easily recognized by its rounder grip and no cover over the shutter speed and aperture dials. A QD-model with an integrated data-back is also available.

Nikon F-801/N8008

In 1988 the top AF-model for advanced amateur photographers finally appeared and was soon adopted by professionals too. It was a camera in the same category as the FE-2, discontinued in 1987. The F-801 came with an abundance of technical refinements and retained its popularity and attraction even after the advent of the F4. It is clear that Nikon took much care with details to ensure convenient operation of the many manual modes as well as the automatic focusing and exposure functions.

The F-801 was the first SLR-camera with the sensationally fast shutter speed of 1/8000 sec., and it also had the fastest integrated motor-drive at the time with its 3.3 frames/sec. For Nikon it was also their first SLR with LC-display and functional buttons instead of conventional controls. One dial survived though in a slightly different form as the command input control dial. The information may be shown in an LCD, but the settings are changed with this dial on the right edge and can be operated easily with the right thumb. In fact this is where every setting is controlled, after the function – there are seven in all – is chosen by pressing the appropriate button.

The F-801 is activated by a sliding switch above the release button which is on the large grip, as on the F-401. The slippery surface of the camera back does not contribute to secure handling because the thumb cannot find any hold on it. But that is just about the only thing hampering handling.

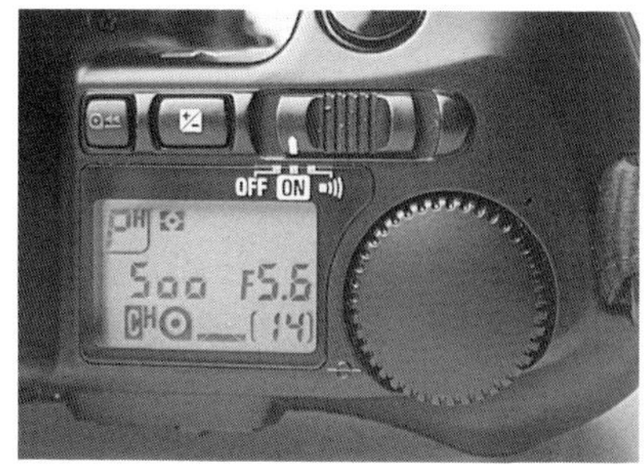

It is easy to stay in complete control thanks to the LCD.

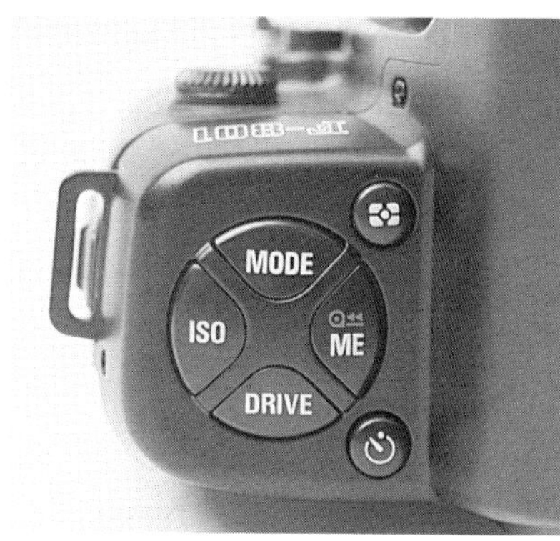

The control buttons for the basic operations are one of the characteristic features of the F-801/N8008.

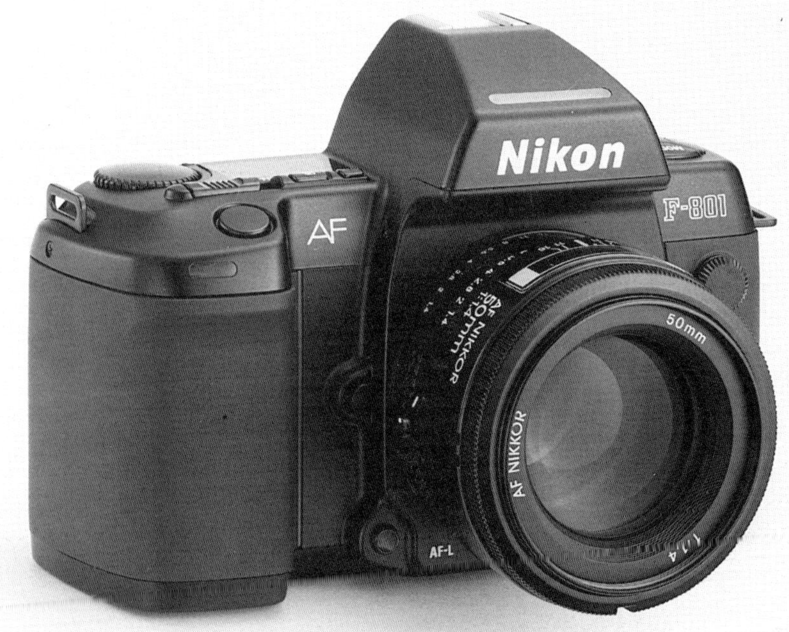

Pure high-tech: the F-801/N8008 offers a number of fascinating features.

The F-801 always proves to be quite communicative, the LCD provides total information about the camera's operational state. The exposure and exposure metering modes and any compensation factor set are displayed in the top row. The film speed, the shutter speed, and the aperture value can be seen in the central row, and at the bottom are the film-advance control symbol, any multiple exposures set, and the frame counter. These are not all displayed simultaneously, that would lead to total confusion. When it is switched on only the exposure and exposure metering modes, the film advance control symbol, and the frame counter are visible, whereas the shutter speed and aperture values don't appear until the release button is pressed.

In terms of exposure control the F-801 offers everything the heart could wish for: shutter and aperture priority modes, three program modes – normal, high-speed, and dual – including automatic switching from one program line to another depending on the focal length in use, as in the F-501. The program-shift function is new: the shutter speed/aperture combination chosen by the camera can be changed any time to fit personal needs with the command dial. The P-signal blinks for information in such cases. In shutter priority mode the speed is set with the command dial. If this leads to an aperture value not available with the lens in use, "HI" or "Lo" appear instead of the aperture value. How many steps the speed should be corrected by is then also displayed there.

As usual, the aperture ring on the lens is used in aperture priority mode and the command dial has no function for once. Settings exceeding the available range are indicated in the same manner as in shutter priority mode. In manual mode the aperture is set with the lens aperture ring and the speed with the command dial.

Without a doubt the Nikon technicians deserve an extra pat on the back for this LC-display. In addition to the shutter speed and aperture, the F-801 also shows any deviations from the preset combination of values precisely, in increments of ⅓ EV. This proves to be just as informative in practical use as the meter-needle displays in the EL and FE/FE-2. The available shutter speeds range from 1/8000 sec. to 30 seconds. One of the metering methods available in the F-801 is the AMP multi-pattern-metering known from the FA, which was modified from experience with that model and is now called Matrix Metering. The alternative is a centre-weighted mode which is concentrated almost as strongly as in the F3 with 75% within the 12mm-circle on the focusing screen and 25% for the rest. If an exposure compensation is desired it can be set in the enormous range of +/- 5 EV which hardly ever proves to be necessary in practice. If the compensation factors are used in combination with the film speed range from ISO 6/9° to 6400/39°, which is very extensive in the first place, it leads to almost unusable extreme values.

The shutter speed and aperture are displayed in whole steps with an "f" in front of the aperture value. If "FEE" appears instead of the aperture value in the program and shutter priority modes, it means the aperture ring on the lens is not set to its smallest value and the F-801 will lock the release button.

When you don't need the fastest speed of 3.3 frames/sec. offered at the CH-position you can choose the alternative CL with its 2 frames/sec., which is usually sufficient, or the S-position, standing for single mode. Multiple exposures up to nine per frame can be programmed by pressing the ME-button. Of course the necessary compensation must be set manually since it will vary from subject to subject.

The self-timer also offers different options. Its duration can be set between 2 and 30 seconds, but that is not all: in the 2F-position the camera will be released twice. The first time after 10 seconds, and the second after another 5 seconds. This allows you to take the "second shot", even for self-portraits.

The sliding exposure-lock lever and the button to switch on the finder illumination, which turns on automatically whenever the ambient light falls below EV 6, are placed conveniently on the back. This viewfinder deserves to be lit because it displays almost all the information visible on the outer LCD: shutter speed, aperture value, exposure mode, any compensation value, flash-ready signal, and the AF-indications are shown beneath the finder image. Even the film speed can be controlled in the finder by pressing the ISO-button.

The standard focusing screen can be replaced by the B-,E-, or J-type, all allowing about 92% of the effective frame to be seen. The finder is the same high-eyepoint type known from the F3 HP which allows people wearing glasses to see the complete viewfinder image.

The ISO hot-shoe is located on top of the prism housing. It connects far more than just the TTL-metering cell in the camera with the flash unit – the F-801 is a flashing genius. The fill-flash technique already available in the F-401 was improved further by adding "cybernetic synchronization". This describes the camera's ability to change not only the aperture but also the sync-speeds between 1/60 and 1/250 sec., depending on the existing light, in order to achieve well-balanced shots by including as much of the ambient light as possible. As a result the pictures do not look like typical

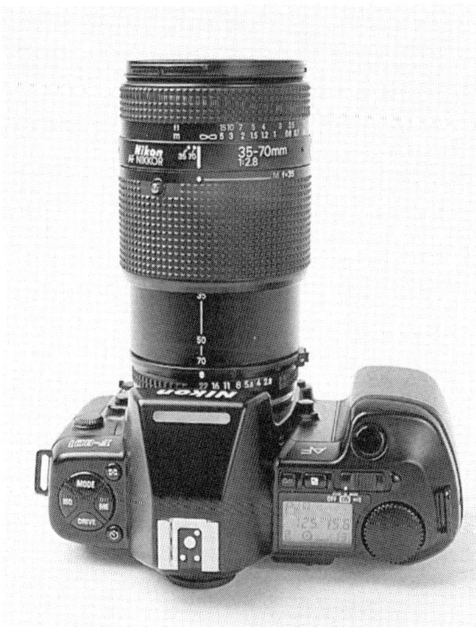

A very versatile combination: the F-801/N8008 with the fast AF-zoom 35-70mm,f/2.8.

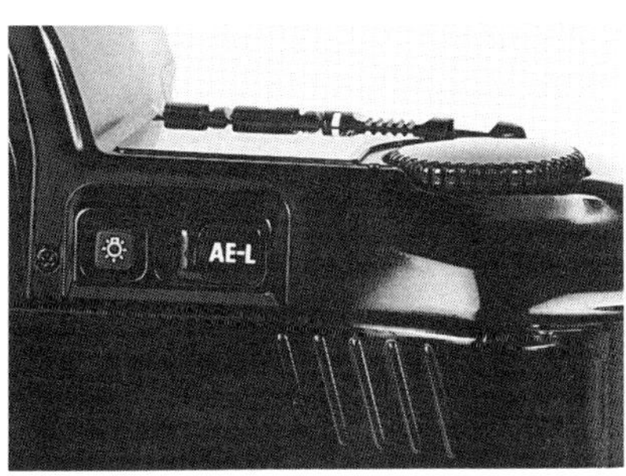

The exposure-lock and viewfinder illumination buttons.

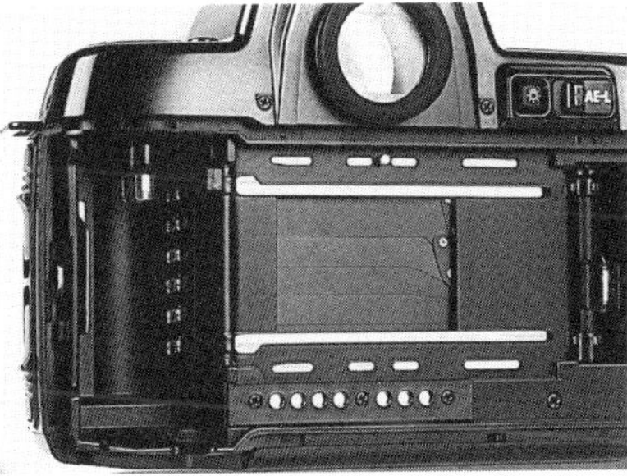

Communicative contacts for the attachable Multi-control- and databacks as well as for reading the DX-code.

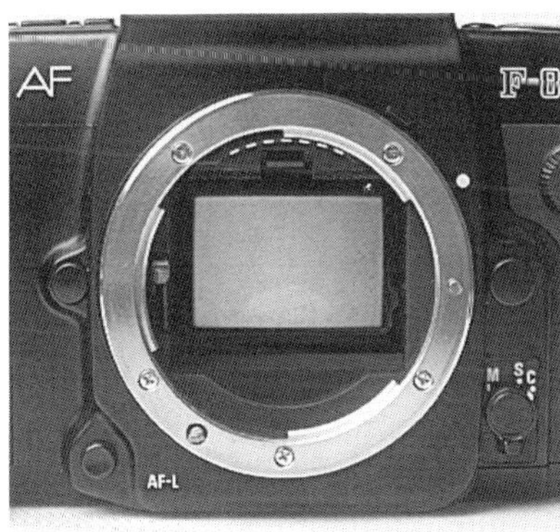

Just as in the F-301/N2000 and F-501/N2020, some of the controls are to be found around the bayonet.

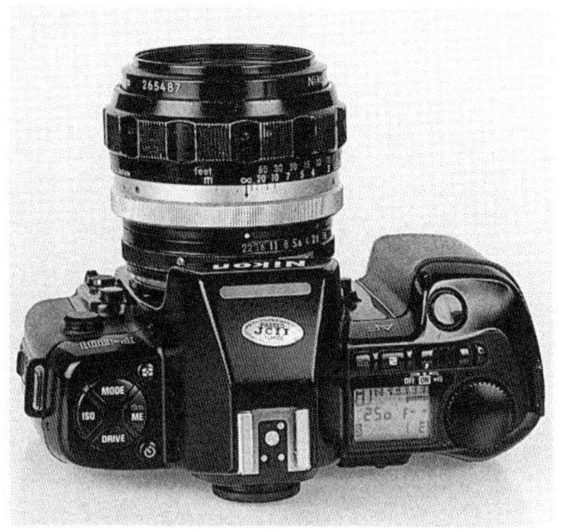

Continuity in the Nikon system 1: A new body with an old lens.

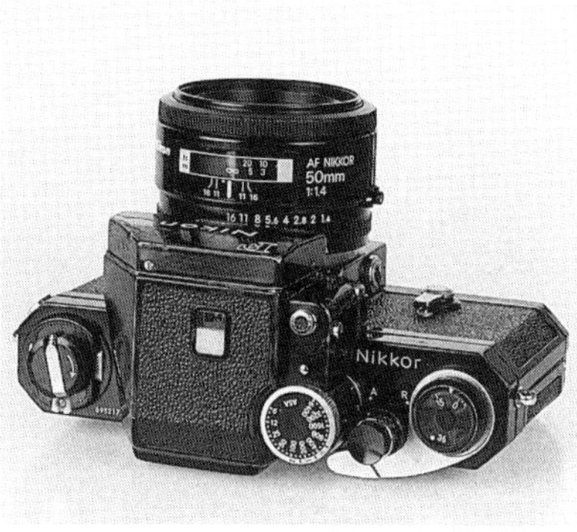

Continuity in the Nikon system 2: An old body with a new lens.

flash shots with milky-white faces against a pitch-black background. It would be a great loss to employ flash lighting only with the F-801 when it gets too dark for hand-held photography. On the contrary, it reveals its advantages when most amateur photographers would never think of using a flash: in the daytime, when bright sunlight leads to high contrast which often exceeds the latitude of the film. With the Matrix-metering mode, flash output is controlled so that it contributes up to 1 EV less to the total exposure. In combination with the centre-weighted mode it is reduced by exactly ⅔ EV. When the Nikon Speedlight SB-24 is used together with the F-801 the output can be controlled as desired on the flash unit within a range of +1 to-3 EV. The SB-24 also allows synchronization to be switched to the second shutter blind, so that the flash is fired at the end of longer exposures for example. It remains to be said that this automatic fill-flash mode is available with any compatible unit and thus also for other makes in the SCA-system.

In a camera offering such a multitude of features and controls it is easy to loose track of the last settings. The F-801 possesses a kind of "panic switch": when both the Mode and Drive buttons are pressed simultaneously the camera returns to its basic, totally automatic modes: P-Dual and Matrix-metering, any compensation factor will be defaulted, and film transport will be set to single mode. With the exception of the exposure compensation button, all the other controls are grouped on the top left next to the prism where traditionally the rewind crank was situated. The F-801 no longer has such a thing, one of its built-in motors rewinds the exposed film within 15 seconds.

Until the F-801, cameras were constructed so that the operation of all the functional systems such as the film transport mechanism and the shutter and mirror units were linked to each other. This resulted in the mirror always being cocked by the film transport system. The F-801 was freed of such connections and received two additional motors besides the one for AF-operation. One is responsible for winding and rewinding the film, the other cocks the shutter and the mirror mechanism. You can hear this motor starting whenever the camera is switched on and the release button pressed. The camera's electronics take over co-ordinating all three motors' functions.

As usual with Nikon the vital parts of the body are made of die-cast aluminium. The working speed of the shutter blinds was increased further compared to the cameras with a maximum of 1/4000 sec. The blade material was changed from titanium to aluminium. The result was a fastest shutter speed of 1/8000 sec. and a wider slit during longer exposures, but the sync-speed of 1/250 sec. remained unchanged. In the case of the AF-system the same proven AM-200 module as in the F-401 was put in the F-801, but its sensitivity was modified. By improving the data processing it is capable of working all the way down to EV -1, and a new coreless motor of the same size providing a higher torque and with quicker acceleration provides the necessary drive power.

The good old mechanical aperture coupling can be found around the bayonet. This makes non-AF lenses usable, too, although not with all of the camera's modes. Generally speaking, with non-AF lenses the F-801 works in a similar manner to the FE-2. This means aperture priority and manual modes, along with centre-weighted metering. The operation of the camera calls for four AA-size batteries, or rechargeables of the same size, which are located in a compartment inside the grip section. The external battery-pack DB-5 with a 6V lithium battery should be connected if the camera is to be exposed to severe cold.

A databack is also available for the F-801 (MF-20) as well as the Multi-Control Back MF-21, which can match the camera in terms of versatile functions. Together with this accessory the camera even allows the use of the "Freeze Focus"-mode. This is done by first setting the lens manually to the desired distance and as soon as your subject crosses the focused plane the camera will be released automatically. This function is especially helpful in sports, action, and animal photography where the electronics prove to be superior, even to the photographer with the fastest reactions. In this mode he doesn't't even have to be on the spot to release the shutter.

The F-801 became an immediate best-seller. Old Nikon hands can have an advanced photographic instrument that can fit into their existing system and, most importantly, allows the use of all their lenses. If you compare closely, you will realize that the F4 offers only a few more functional possibilities – if you disregard the latter's more professional stature and its interchangeable viewfinders.

Nikon F-801s/N8008s

In spite of its versatility and widespread acceptance the F-801 was confronted with growing criticism by 1990. This was not because of the temporary "blackouts" it sometimes suffered due to excess static charge, a problem that was soon greatly reduced by modification to the electronics. What customers actually found annoy-

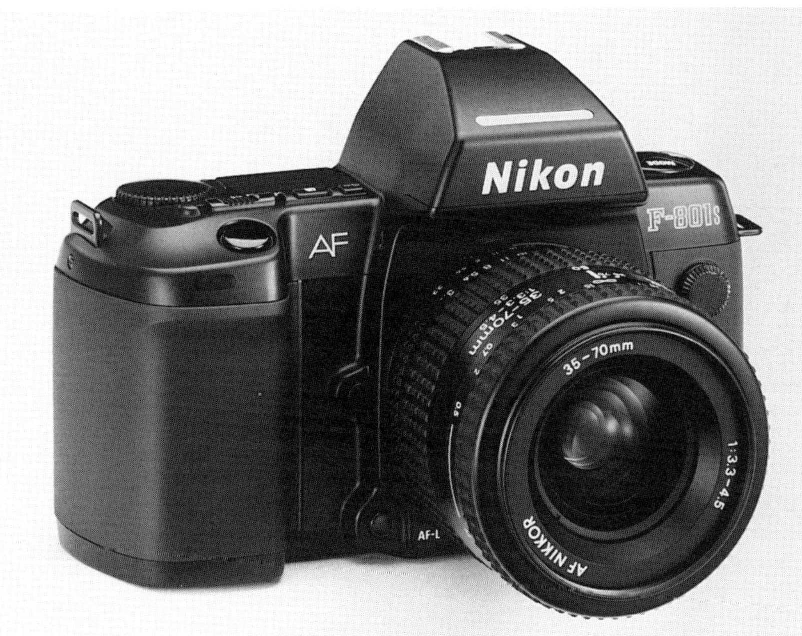

The F-801s/n8008s brings this very versatile camera into line with the latest features and technology pioneered in the F-601/N6006.

ing was a seemingly confused hierarchy in the range of Nikon cameras. They could not understand why the F-601, described below, was a cheaper model but offered very desirable features not available in the more professionally orientated F-801.

Nikon had expected this and was already working on an update. In 1991 the F-801s settled the matter. Its AF-system was improved so that operation is slightly faster, and focus tracking is accessible together with the C-type AF-mode and the slower continuous CL film transportation mode. Most critics were quite satisfied when their main request for spot metering as a third exposure evaluation method was granted. Dare we ask how many of them are expert enough to make successful use of this feature and how many secretly turn back to the reliable Matrix mode? In any case, the Nikon F-801s is still a deservedly very popular model within its price class.

Nikon F-601/N6006

The design of the F-601, introduced in 1990, as well as the arrangement of its controls, resembles the F-801 so much that changing from one model to the other will cause no problems whatsoever. It marks another step away from the tradition of mechanical cameras, but does not depart from Nikon's tradition of compatibility, which means that all of the AF-Nikkors available before can be used with the new camera without any restrictions, and the older lenses within the described limitations depending on the type.

The most conspicuous novelty on the F-601 is its integrated flash unit with a guide number of 13, naturally TTL-controlled and usable for matrix as well as centre-weighted metering. As the successor to the discontinued F-501 it represents a synthesis, as it were, between the F-401 and the F-801. New in terms of flash technology is the camera's ability to control the shutter speed during flash operation within the remarkable range of 1/125 all the way to 30 sec. Slow-sync. is another available mode, and rear-blind

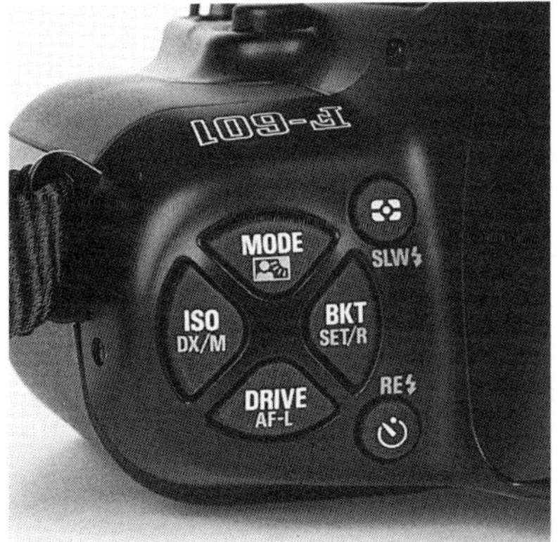

Developed on the model of the F-801/N8008 is the four-part array of buttons for different functions.

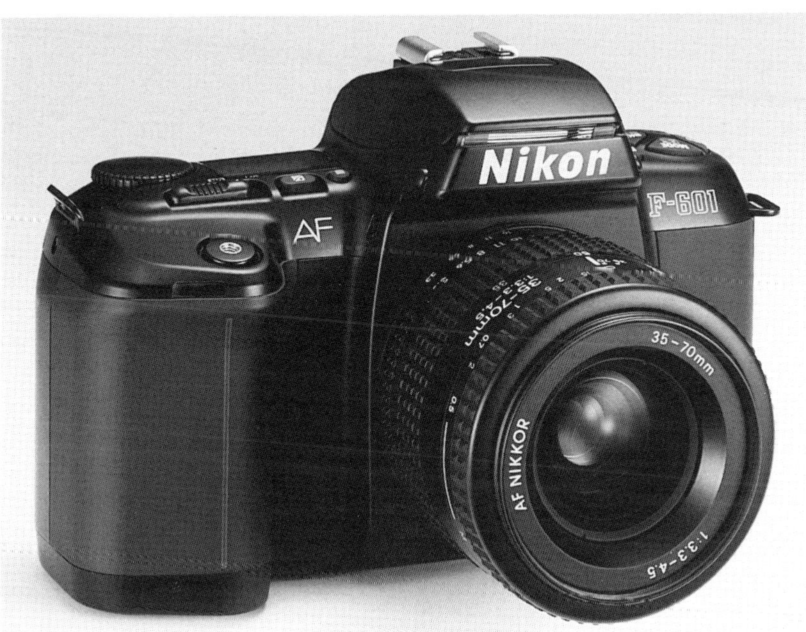

Together with the AF-Zoom 35-70mm, the Nikon F-601/N6006 is a fast and powerful unit.

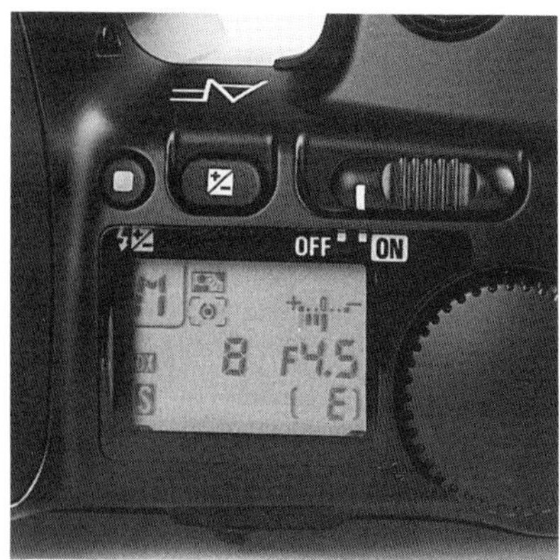

The clearly legible LC-display.

sync. makes it possible to depict moving subjects in flash photography much more realistically. The Flash Output Level Compensation mode allows ambient and flash light to be finely balanced within the range of +1 to -3 EV in increments of ⅓ EV, and compatible flash guns, especially those of independent brands within the SCA-system, can also take advantage of the comprehensive flash techniques. The flash reflector is elegantly incorporated into the prism housing just as in the F-401; it is switched on by pressing the two lock-release buttons which let it swing up into its ready-position.

When it comes to exposure metering and control, which are definitely the most important functions in modern SLR-cameras, the F-601 offers a choice between three different modes. First is Matrix Metering as in the F-801. It should be employed whenever the user desires to have the metering done quickly, surely, and automatically. As an alternative the centre-weighted mode, known from the F-401, with its sensitivity concentration of 75:25% is available. Finally, the F-601 also offers spot-metering, which may not be the fastest way to work but in the hands of the experienced photographer is the most precise.

Not only exposure metering, but also exposure control is becoming more and more important in advanced cameras and the techniques are getting ever more sophisticated. The F-601 offers a choice between a normal and the Auto Multi-program mode for quick and uncomplicated operation as well as for simpler functions. In Multi-program mode the camera registers the data stored in the AF-lens's electronics concerning focal length and maximum aperture and alters the program curve accordingly in order to avoid slow shutter speeds which bring the danger of camera-shake. In addition, Program-shift allows the photographer to change the camera's automatic shutter speed/aperture combination in steps of 1 EV any time. It is hardly worth mentioning that three more exposure modes are also available with aperture and exposure priority and manual control.

Anybody who does not wish to rely on the automatic matrix metering in every instance can employ the exposure-lock feature in the other two metering modes to influence the exposure manually. The necessary operation of the sliding lever on the rear can be done with the right thumb and without taking one's eye from the finder. The available range is also very generous and compensation can be set in increments of ⅓ EV up to five EV-steps up or down. Last but not least, the F-601 is capable of Automatic Exposure Bracketing with a choice of either three or five shots in a row, and the possibility to vary the steps between ⅓, ⅔, or whole EV-steps.

First on the F-601 is a focusing mode which thinks ahead called "Focus Tracking". In both AF-modes – "S" standing for Single- and "Cf" for Continuous Focusing – the camera switches to this function automatically whenever it registers a moving subject. Cameras without this feature lock the focused distance the moment the release button is pressed, resulting in blur when the subject continues to move unseen during the "blackout" phase.

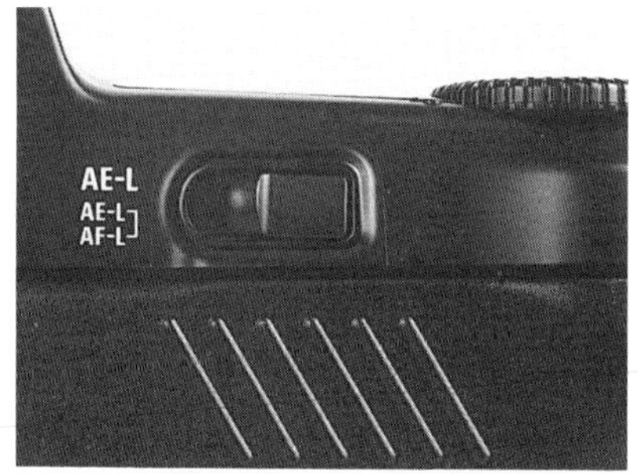

Easy to operate with your thumb – the sliding lever for exposure-lock and focus-lock.

Besides these basic features the F-601 also demonstrates ultra-modern technology in other areas. The camera possesses an integrated motor responsible for winding and rewinding the film, as well as loading and transporting it to frame no.1. A single or a continuous mode with 2 frames/sec. can be chosen.

The viewfinder is particularly brilliant and informative. Thanks to its high-eyepoint characteristics, similar to the F3, F4, and F-801, people who have to wear glasses can see its whole finder image. The Brite-view focusing screen, which had become a standard for Nikon since the F-301, provides convenient control of the subject. The aperture value, shutter speed, film speed (in case of manual setting), the number of frames in Auto Bracketing mode, the electronic analogue display, the exposure mode, any compensation factor, and the focus indicators are visible in the viewfinder.

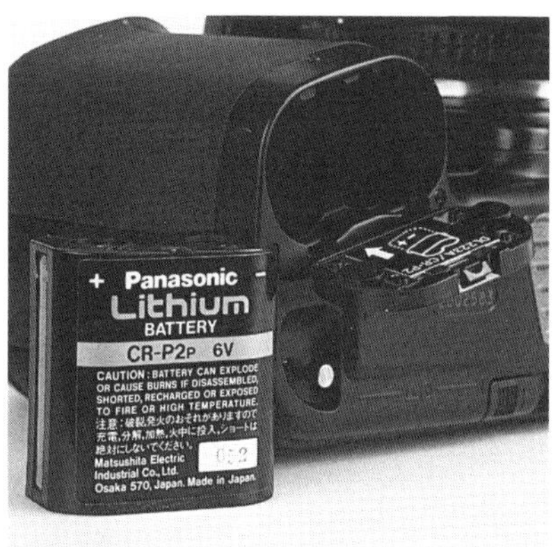

A powerful lithium battery supplies the energy for all electrical functions.

The self-timer with its programmable duration from 2 to 30 seconds is another one of the features modern electronics offer. If set to 10 sec. you can choose to get a second shot shortly after the first. This increases the probability of all of the members of a group, including the photographer, being satisfied with their facial expressions. The DX-system is usable within the usual range from ISO 25/15° to 5000/38°, manual setting is possible from ISO 6/9° to 6400/39°.

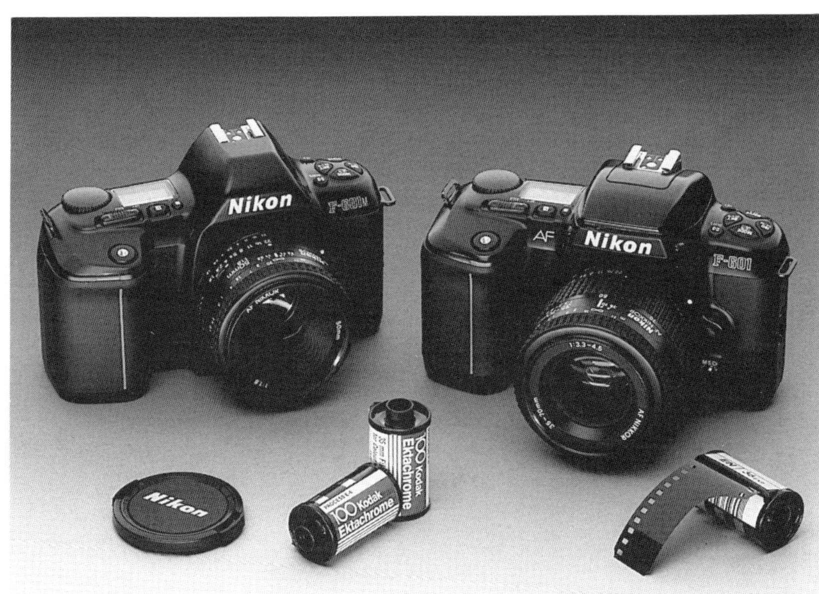

The "AF"-logo next to the prism identifies the twin sisters: the F-601M/N6000 and the F-601/N6006.

I regard the F-601 as a well-designed camera that aims at ambitious and advanced amateur photographers with its complete set of features. However, this otherwise outstanding impression is marred considerably for me by the fact that this of all target groups was not supplied with such an important feature as a depth-of-field button.

Nikon F-601M/N6000

Nikon entered unknown territory with the introduction of a second new camera at the same time as the F-601, aimed at photographers who did not (yet) wish to work with autofocus. At the time the market shares of both systems were about equal, though the AF-sector was obviously growing since it had taken the amateur market by storm.

The F-601M is equipped with almost all the F-601 features, except for its automatic focusing mode and its built-in flash unit. The spot metering method is also absent, although this is due to a design necessity: in order to facilitate easy focusing the F-601M has a screen with a split-image rangefinder which makes it impossible for a metering cell located in the finder to offer such a mode. On the other hand, the advantage of the Brite-view focusing screen becomes even more obvious in this camera than in the F-601. The viewfinder image is bright and clear so that focusing can be done quickly and comfortably even with slower zoom-lenses. One drawback of the camera is the mandatory use of AF-lenses if one wishes to employ all of the camera's exposure controls. When using non-AF lenses one has to do without matrix metering as well as shutter priority and program modes.

Nikon F-90/N90

By 1991 Nikon had achieved a feat unparalleled by any competitor. Without sacrificing the proven F-bayonet they had developed an equally complete and impressive line-up of multi-mode automatic AF-cameras ranging from the F-401x to the sophisticated F-801s and the professional F4.

It was clear that further modifications of existing technology and simply adding features at random would not lead to another decisive step in camera development so the question was asked what systems needed to be improved.

After more than six years of experience with its first two generations of autofocus cameras Nikon was well aware of the weaknesses of the system. These were its dependency on the subject's surface texture, expanse, position in the frame, etc. Ten years after the world's first multi-pattern metering system was introduced in the Nikon FA, the difficulties involved in backlit subjects, determining what the main part of the subject is in the first

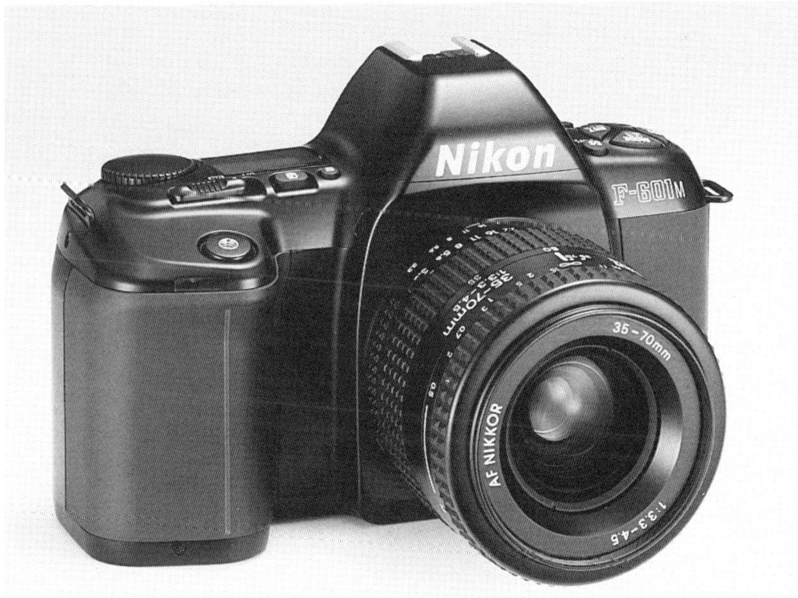

The F-601M/N6000 only offers all its automatic exposure controls when it is used together with AF-lenses.

place, specially when using slide film, were well known.

Finally, even though the F-801 had opened up a hitherto unknown world of fully automatic flash exposure in 1988 with its Matrix Balanced Fill-flash mode, certain lighting situations still resisted automatic perfection.

In 1992 Nikon presented their answer to these problems. The F90 was positioned between the F-801s and the F4 and packed to the brim with very useful new features and offering a new level of performance. Even though it strongly resembles the F-801 in every respect, its designation clearly indicates that this model marks the beginning of a completely new generation of cameras to come, capable of superior performance in automatic shooting situations.

The AF-system of the F90 is different from that in previous Nikon models. The AM 200-module was replaced by a unit called CAM 246: this Cross-type Autofocus Module covers a horizontal detection area of 7mm with 172 CCDs while 74 further elements are arranged across a vertical area of 3mm. Both the hard- and software responsible for processing the incoming data were refined so that level line patterns like the horizon, slightly off-centre, and moving subjects are all detected more securely than before. Spot autofocus limiting the sensor module to an area 3 mm in diameter is available as an alternative when the subject is too small to be metered precisely with the normal Wide-Area mode (in which the closest and/or brightest of the detected objects usually determines focusing). A 4x more powerful microcomputer than in previous models, as well as the Overlap-Servo technique (meaning that the lens already begins to be driven while the final setting is still being calculated), adds up to an around 30% faster autofocus operation.

Focus tracking is automatically activated in both AF- modes and regardless of the set motor drive speed, and of course the F90 is also able to work with the new AF-I-type Nikkors driven by their own built-in AF-motors. Normally, the system's single servo mode is linked to focus priority and continuous servo to release priority, but this can be changed with the multi-function databack MF-26 or one of the electronic organizers – but that is another story.

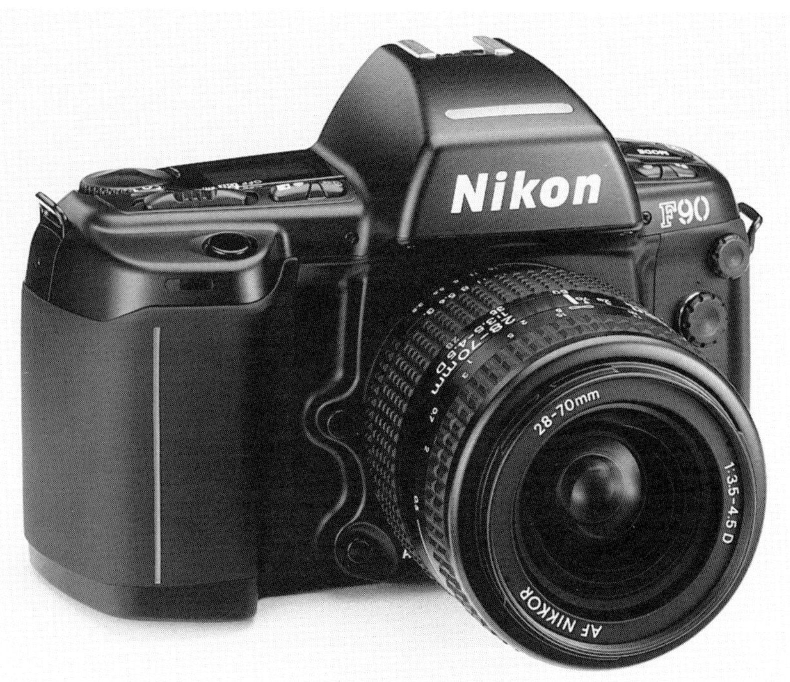

The F90/N90 represents the first of a new generation of advanced Nikon cameras.

The so-called 3D Matrix exposure metering system of the F90 represents both a refinement of the original and an equally logical and surprising connection to the focusing unit. Instead of the five segments used before, this sensor subdivides the central one into three separate areas – so there are eight in all – allowing distant subjects in backlit situations to be analyzed more individually. At closer ranges the segmentation is switched back to five, so as not to confuse exposure calculation due to large magnification ratios. The necessary distance information is provided by the new D-type AF-Nikkors' modified CPUs. So,"normal" AF-lenses can also take advantage of this feature, the only drawback being possibly slightly less perfect exposures in certain close-up situations.

The second part of the"third dimension"new to the F90's matrix metering system is the use of the focus data, which had always been gathered anyway, to help decide upon the main subject within the frame, i.e. which metering segment is most relevant for the exposure. The additional information is based on a quite simple assumption. If the AF-sensor registers only a very little amount of defocus after the composition has been completed, it is fair to say the main subject will be situated in the centre. Whereas larger defocus values will almost certainly indicate an off-centre main subject – except if the focus-lock function is used and the matrix sensor simultaneously detects strong contrast, most likely harsh backlight. In this case the clever electronics will base the exposure on the scene encountered before the final composition!

Further refinements in the matrix-software, in this case a fuzzy-logic algorithm, serve to prevent sudden drastically changing exposures as a result of only minute differences in lighting or composition. The system also includes automatic consideration of vertical shots without the need for expensive switches as in the F4. Since these computation methods are all internal to the camera they are available regardless of the attached type of CPU-equipped lens.

Besides the 75/25% centre-weighted method identical to the

F-401x/601/ 801/s, the F90 also offers the narrowest spot-metering mode of any Nikon camera. By activating only the sensor's tiny central segment it covers an area representing just 1% of the frame, described by the 3mm-circle in the viewfinder.

The innovations concerning the F90's flash exposure system are definitely the most spectacular. The F90 is the first camera in the world equipped with a multi-segment TTL-flash metering sensor. Its five areas are arranged very much like the matrix sensor and serve as the missing link in flash exposure control, so to speak. Together with the distance information supplied by the D-type AF-Nikkors they secure correct flash output when even the F-801s' otherwise excellent system cannot cope with the situation. No camera other than the F90 is able to recognize when less important parts within the frame displaying an untypically high or low degree of reflectivity would lead to under- or overexposed main subject areas. This is how it works. When the release button is pressed and the mirror has reached its upper position, the dedicated new Nikon Speedlight SB-25 emits imperceptible, low-power monitor pre-flashes – 1 to 16 depending on the distance and the aperture set. After being reflected back by the subject and passing through the lens the light is reflected by the 18%-grey first shutter blind onto the TTL multi sensor. The camera's computer then compares the pre-flash brightness metered by each of the TTL multi-sensor's five segments with the theoretical calculation based on the lens' distance information, the guide number, and aperture in use. This double-checking permits extremely bright or dark segments to be sorted out for the final output control. Of course, these proceedings will not lead to any noticeable delay in releasing the shutter. The resulting 3D Multi-Sensor Balanced Fill-Flash is without a doubt the most advanced – and reliable system available today. Even if "normal" AF-lenses are attached, the F90 still produces flash pictures superior to the other Nikons by basing the output on the ambient light reading. Even if other units without the pre-flash option are employed, the F90 still offers advantages thanks to the use of the AF-sensor's information on the amount of defocus. So much for Nikon's idea of system compatibility even in the face of almost revolutionary technological developments.

Among the many other useful functions such as slow- and rear blind sync, the F90's flash control system also allows manual high-speed sync from 1/250 to 1/4000 sec. and flash bracketing (with MF-26 or electronic organizers) – modes which can further increase the percentage of successful flash pictures.

Next to the features known from the previous Nikon cameras, the F90 is equipped with a Vary-Program – a system of seven program modes customized (and fixed) for different types of subjects. They were designed to add to the ease of operation for snap-shooting: silhouette, hyperfocal, landscape, sport, close-up, portrait, and portrait with red-eye reduction pre-flashes (with SB-25).

Many F-801s and F-601 owners will surely envy the F90 for its LCD-illumination facility as well as its additional film counter in the viewfinder display, while only a few will probably ever make full use of its new 10-pin remote socket. Appropriately designated data-link system, this terminal allows the attachment of Sharp electronic organizers with the MC-27 cord, resulting in a multitude of remote control- as well as customized operations as soon as the Nikon Data-Link card AC-1E is inserted. Briefly, beyond the functions available with the MF-26, the connection can also memorize shooting data, serve as a remote display, and develop and store up to five individual program curves. Without the cord connection, the organizers can serve as a concise instruction manual, as a short photographic handbook, and a data file.

The ten-pin terminal called for a new set of remote accessories as well, and naturally Nikon not only presented them along with the camera but also the two adaptors necessary to secure compatibility backwards and forwards. MC-20 is the new 80cm cord with handgrip, fitted with an illuminated LCD of its own and allowing remote setting of long exposures. MC-21 is a 3m extension cord for MC-20. The 1m long MC-22 is the equivalent of the MC-4a. MC-23, 40cm long, connects two ten-pin cameras for simultaneous or intermittent release. MC-25 permits the use of conventional two-pin remote-control accessories with ten-pin cameras, while MC-26 works exactly the other way – connecting the new equipment with older cameras.

Since the F90 will most certainly also meet the needs of a number of professional photographers, the external battery-pack DB-6 taking six D-size cells introduced for the F4 and connected to it with the MC-28 was also made accessible by supplying the MC-29. Its terminal plugs straight into the F90 battery holder.

All in all the Nikon F90 represents a really big step towards the goal of the perfect – and perfectly simple – picture taking machine. It combines all the automatic functions resulting in a handling speed that can make the difference between a successful shot or no shot at all, state-of-the-art performance in all crucial technical areas, supportive and/or alternative modes, and the option to set almost everything as manually as desired or considered necessary.

CHAPTER 7

The Accessory System

SLR-cameras, especially those with the 24x36mm format which offers such a wide range of applications, are often referred to as system-cameras. We can regard the body as representing the centre of a system which can then be equipped with all sorts of lenses and many different accessories to meet the needs of most photographic tasks. Difficult photographic situations reveal the limits or the flexibility of a camera system, and from the very beginning Nikon has striven to maximise the flexibility and reduce the limitations of their SLR system. Besides the numerous lenses which are covered in the next chapter, Nikon has always offered a broad array of accessories for every single camera.

Most of them can be used in combination with each other, but it is obvious that this will not always be possible due to the continuous technical developments. This is especially true of the metering finders of the F-models which are not interchangeable.

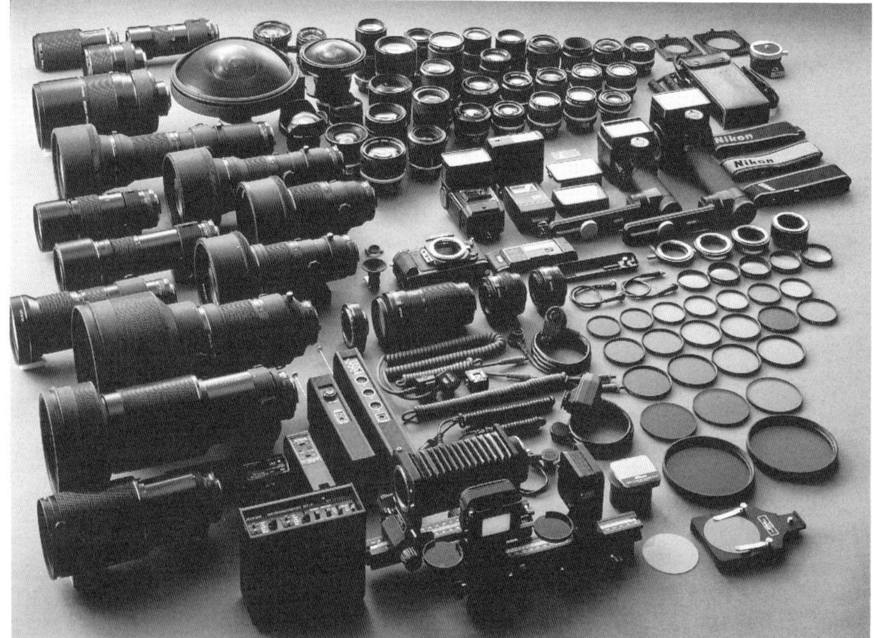

The solution to every photographic task – the incomparably versatile Nikon system.

Viewfinders and Viewfinder Systems

The viewfinder of a camera keeps the photographer in touch with the subject. This is where the picture is composed, and, depending on the particular camera model, information concerning the status of the camera's functions and that of the exposure meter are displayed.

In principle the viewfinder of an SLR camera consists in its simplest form of the reflex mirror and the focusing screen. The mirror deflects the light projected through the lens upwards by 45° in onto the focusing screen. In such a simple system the image on the screen is viewed at waist-level and some sort of hood is provided to shield it from the light, a flip-up magnifier to aid focusing is usually provided. This simple viewfinder design has two drawbacks: the image appears upright but reversed left to right, and it forces the user to look down from above – which can be an advantage in some situations but is awkward in most.

For these reasons a pentaprism is usually placed above the focusing screen to divert the light into an eyepiece to supply a right-way-round image and allow it to be viewed at eye level and to give a natural "point of view". In the vast majority of SLR cameras this prism is fixed, although some allow the focusing screen to be changed.

There are several reasons why photographers may want to work with other types of finder instead of the prism model, and this is why the finders of the Nikon F-series are interchangeable. Most manufacturers avoid the complications and the number of competitor models that attempt to match the Nikon F professional outfit can be counted on the fingers of one hand.

Exposure Meters For The Nikon F

The first exposure meter for the Nikon F was an attachable selenium-type. Its advantages compared to hand-held meters were that it was coupled to both the shutter speed dial

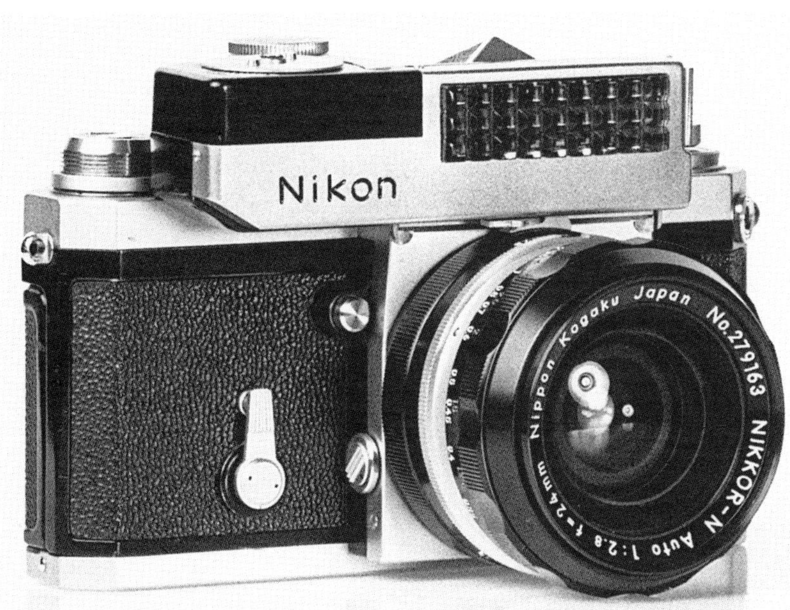

The first exposure-meter attachment for the Nikon F. The selenium cell did not require batteries.

and the lens aperture ring, thus always reacting to changes of the shutter speed/aperture combination. This finder was simply called "Model 1"; it had a film speed range from ISO 6/9° to 4000/37°. It was followed by the improved Models 2 and 3, the latter with an increased sensitivity in low-light, thanks to an amplifier-cell. These early finders were quite large and unwieldy and impaired the handling of the camera.

The First Photomic

In 1962 the first finder with an integrated exposure meter appeared, named "Photomic". With one of these a plain Nikon F was converted into a Nikon F Photomic. This first Photomic model has a CdS-metering cell built into the top right corner of the finder body. The camera's shutter speed dial is rotated together with that of the Photomic, and a second coupling on the front conveys the aperture setting to the exposure meter. The preset aperture value is displayed on the back, above the eyepiece. This not only makes for comfortable operation but also has another reason: the Photomic's protruding front makes it impossible to see the lens aperture ring. An ISO-scale with values from 6/9° to 6400/39° is situated within the shutter speed dial – a range hardly surpassed even by current top-models. The film speed must be set on the inner dial so that the value in use is opposite the black triangular index.

Two converters were provided along with the Photomic which allowed the characteristics of the metering cell to be modified. This was because the first Photomic did not measure the light on the camera focusing screen. A black cylindrical tube which narrows the metering-angle is meant to be screwed to the metering-cell whenever telephoto-lenses beyond 105mm are used. The second converter is an opal plate that disperses the light falling on the cell and thus allows for incident light metering. Both converters can be screwed to the battery compartment lid on the side when they are not needed. The exposure meter is switched on by flipping up a hinged shield that covers the metering-cell when it is not in use. Later, "On" and "Off" switches were added to the right and above the meter's "eye" respectively.

In 1965 the era of TTL-metering began for Nikon. Two CdS-cells located inside the viewfinder next to the eyepiece measure the light from the subject on the focusing screen. The advantage of this is obvious: only the light that actually exposes the film is evaluated, and the angle of view of the lens is taken into account automatically, as are any factors necessary when employing filters or close-up accessories. Complicated calculations are no longer required and metering is easier and more reliable. The name of this metering prism is "Photomic T", and it was introduced at the same time as the

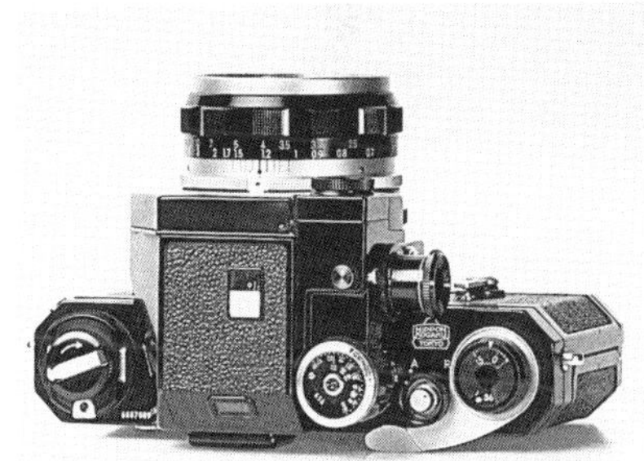

A respectable film speed range for those times: from ISO 6/9° to 6400/39°.

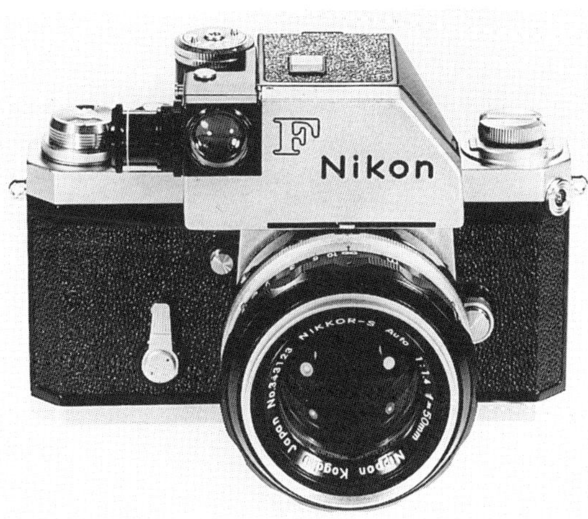

It still had outside metering: the first Photomic with the more sensitive CdS-cell.

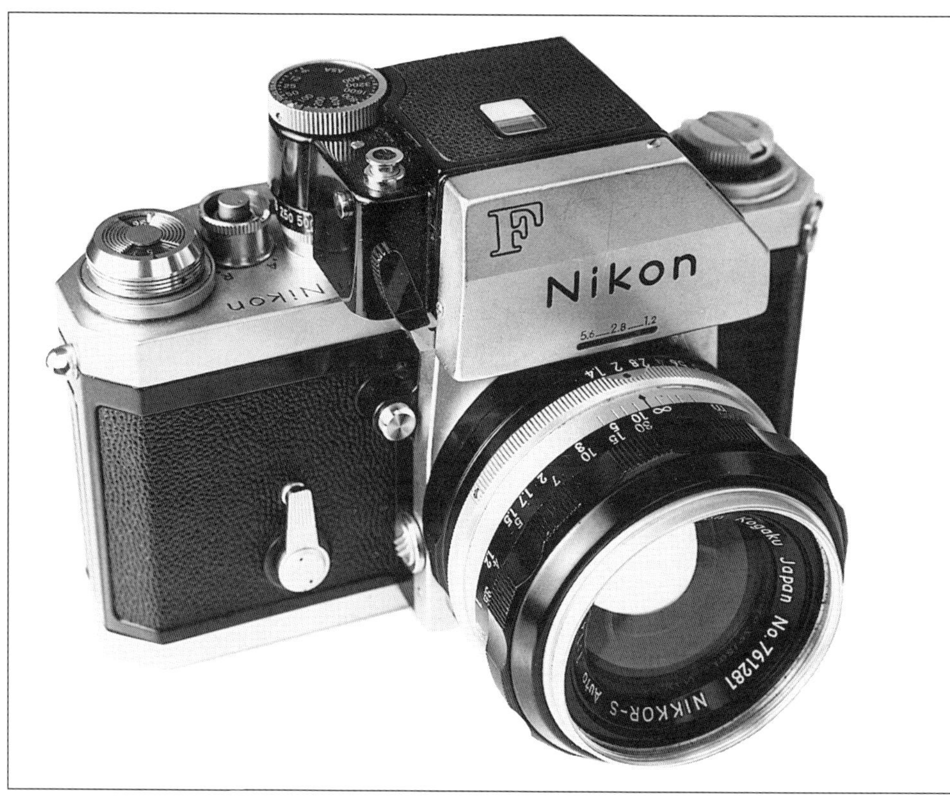

The origin of the 60:40% metering configuration typical for Nikon: an F with the Photomic TN.

Nikkormat FT. Two button-size cells of 1.35v each are needed for the power supply and metering is possible from EV 2 to 17.

Two years later this version was succeeded by another. The most important difference was that the new model had aspheric lenses placed in front of the metering cells to modify their measuring characteristics. While the Photomic T evaluates the light integrally, meaning evenly across the whole of the focusing screen, the Photomic TN employs the metering configuration that was to become Nikon's typical method for many years. The area within the 12mm-circle on the focusing screen is responsible for 60% of the meter reading and the rest for 40%. This makes it easier to meter details within the scenery and so come to precise results. The Photomic TN can be positively identified by an "N" engraved beneath the power-off switch, and a small white battery-check button. Sufficient battery power is indicated when the meter needle in the finder moves to the left. The meter needle can be seen below the finder image in all of the Photomics. When this needle is exactly centred on the notch, the exposure setting is correct. The shutter speed setting is displayed next to the needle. A second display is placed on top of the Photomic in a small window, which is quite helpful during tripod shots when one is not looking through the viewfinder.

In 1969 the last metering-finder for the Nikon F was introduced, the Photomic FTN. Its biggest advantage is that it automatically indexes the maximum aperture of the lens in use. Until then it had been necessary to change the ISO-value opposite the maximum aperture mark on the Photomic every time a different lens was attached. A very clumsy procedure that was often forgotten and led to false exposures. With the new FTN-version the aperture ring is rotated all the way to the left once and then to the right after the lens has been attached, thus indexing the maximum aperture. The correct setting can be controlled easily: a moving pin in the slit on the front underneath the Nikon logo indicates the maximum aperture

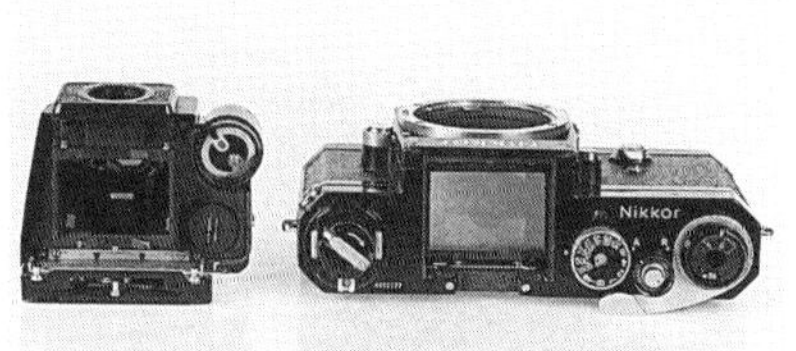

A characteristic feature of the F-series: interchangeable viewfinders, here the F with the Photomic.

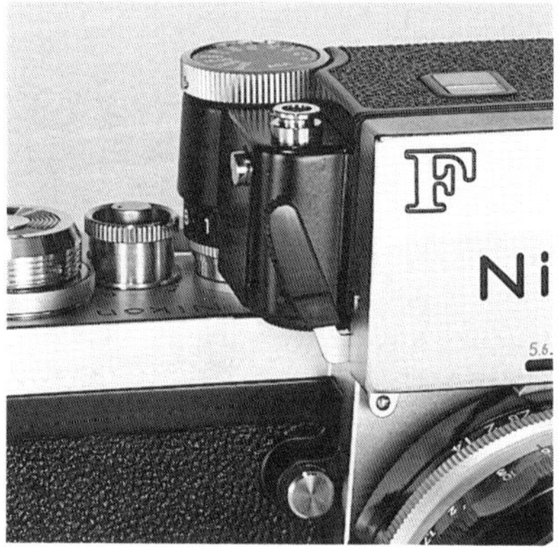

The power-on switch on the side and the finder-lock lever are typical for the Photomic F.

of the lens between f/5,6 and f/11. The expanded film speed range from ISO 6/9° to 6400/39°, another improvement, should be mentioned too.

The Photomic FTN can also be recognized by its battery chamber which is located in the bottom, only allowing battery replacement after the finder is removed from the camera. The silver button on the side of the finder is the power-on switch. When the power-off switch on the top is pressed, it lets the former pop out again. It also serves as a battery check: when it is pressed and held down the meter needle should move to the small central circle. The Photomic FTN is the finder most likely to be found with a Nikon F.

Photomics For The F2

The perfected internal technical design of the Photomic FTN for the Nikon F was taken over in the first metering finder for the Nikon F2. It was called DP-1 and turns an F2 without a metering device into an F2 Photomic. Compared to the F-Photomics, the preset aperture is visible in the viewfinder – a considerable improvement in ease of handling. A plus/minus mark indicates whether the preset shutter speed/aperture combination will result in an over- or underexposure.

Whereas the F-Photomics were available with front plates in either chrome or black finish, those for the F2 were uniformly black. A small silver button on the front is the battery check and rubber seals between the finder and the camera body prevent dust and moisture from entering. Inside the eyepiece a red LED serves as a flash-ready signal: it is linked to the Nikon Speedlights SB-2/7E through the terminal on the outside of the prism body via the adaptor cord SC-4. The power supply is secured through the two contacts to the left and right of the camera's focusing screen frame, since in the F2 the batteries are located in the bottom of the camera. Turning the film advance lever 30° to its stand-off position switches on the exposure meter. Due to the different position of the power supply the F2-Photomics could be more compact and smaller than the bulky F-versions. But alas, because of this the F- and F2-Photomics are not interchangeable.

When the AI (aperture indexing) system was introduced the Photomic DP-1 mutated into the DP-11, turning the F2 Photomic into the F2 A Photomic. The maximum aperture indexing was changed and the preset aperture is visible in the finder thanks to a second, smaller scale on the aperture ring. A small viewfinder illuminator – DL-1 – was available as an accessory for low-light conditions. It can also be employed for the F-Photomic by fastening it on the finder eyepiece, and the little LED powered

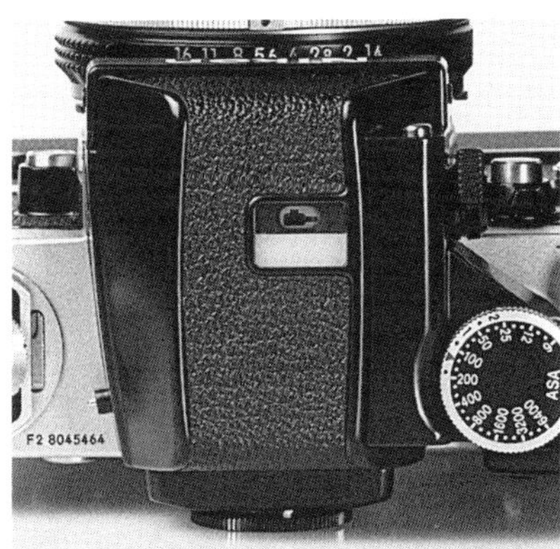

As in the F-series finders, the meter needle is also visible on the top of the DP-1 and DP-11 versions for the F2.

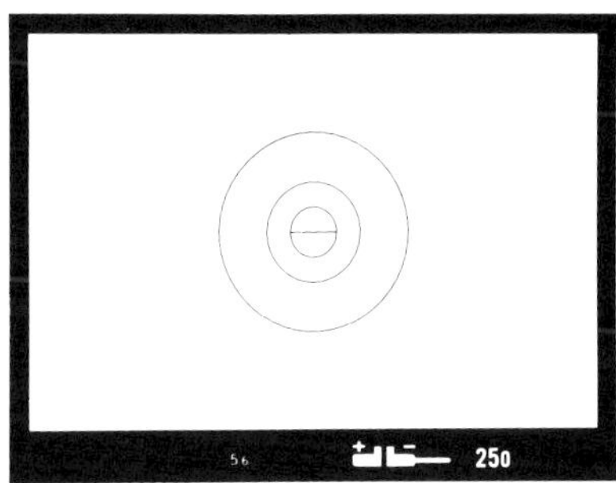

The viewfinder image in the DP-1 and DP-11; a meter-needle display instead of LEDs.

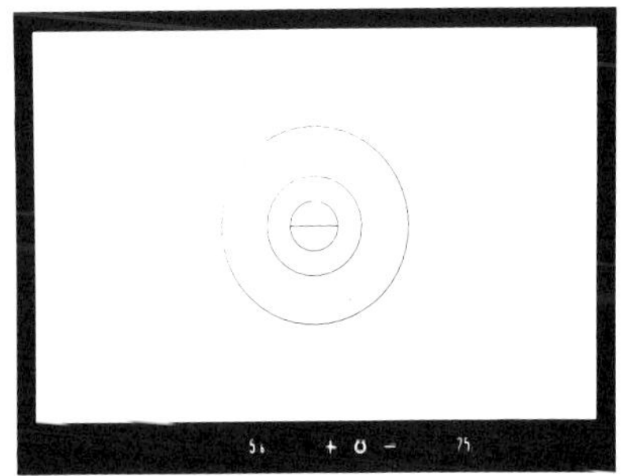
The viewfinder image of the most advanced F2-finder: red LEDs in the F2 AS.

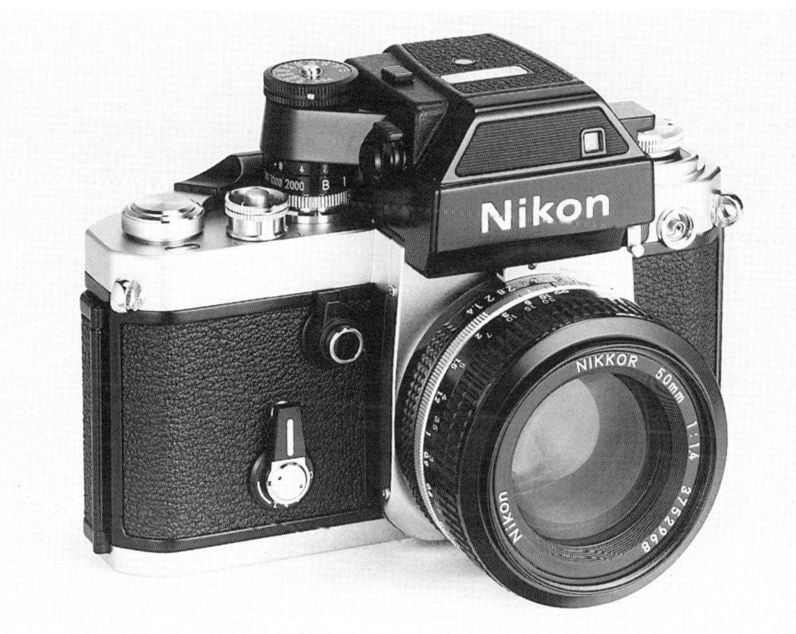

The successor takes over in 1976: the F2 with the third Photomic, DP-3, and a 50mm/f/1.4.

by a button-size battery then illuminates the meter-needle.

Such an accessory was no longer necessary for the DP-2 viewfinder introduced in 1973 which turns the F2 into an F2 S Photomic. An LED-display replaced the needle in this metering finder. Two red plus and minus symbols inform the photographer about the correct exposure setting. The system's sensitivity in low-light conditions was also enhanced. The metering range begins at EV -2, representing f/1.4 and 8 sec. at ISO 100/21°. Shutter speeds slower than one second which are not available directly on the dial can be set on a smaller scale below. When the dial is rotated as far as it goes to "B", the second scale can be employed by pressing the central button which releases a lock. The contacts for the aperture control attachment DS-1, which supply the F2 with a shutter priority mode even though it operates mechanically, are another one of the improvements brought about by the DP-2.

The F2 S Photomic was replaced by an intermediate model in 1976 named F2 SB Photomic. Its DP-3 finder was the first Nikon model to employ the super-sensitive silicon cells and could be built just as flat as the normal DP-11, thanks to a new internal construction. Three LEDs indicate the correct exposure in this version: if only the central circle lights up the correct exposure has been set with a margin of +/- ⅕ EV at the most. If the plus or minus symbols also appear, the deviation can range from ⅕ to 1 EV. These plus and minus symbols only light up alone if the deviation is larger than 1 EV. The indication on the top of the finder was reduced to a single red LED. When the integrated eyepiece shutter is used, this diode lights up along with the circular symbol. Its second function is to indicate sufficient battery power when the sliding lever on the top is used to illuminate the shutter speed display in the viewfinder.

In the AI-version the DP-3 was modified into the finder model DP-12

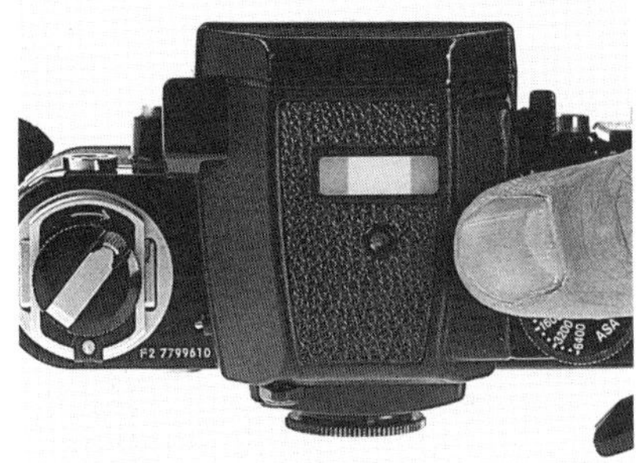

The Photomic DP-12. The switch which activates the illumination of the shutter speed display.

which changes the F2 into its most advanced and also last version – the Nikon F2 AS.

Viewfinders For The F3

Unlike the mechanical F and F2 models, the F3 has its metering system built into the camera body, so that the finders only have the job of supplying an unimpaired view of the subject. In the F3-series a new kind of finder was introduced in 1982, the HP-model. Photographers who wear glasses had only two choices up to then: either to keep their glasses on when looking through the finder or to replace their glasses with matching correction lenses screwed to the eyepiece. Their main disadvantage is that they can only correct simple short or long sightedness but offer no remedy for complex eye defects. In addition they are only available from the manufacturers in rather large steps of 1 dioptre, from +3 to 15 dioptres. It is also inconvenient to have to take one's

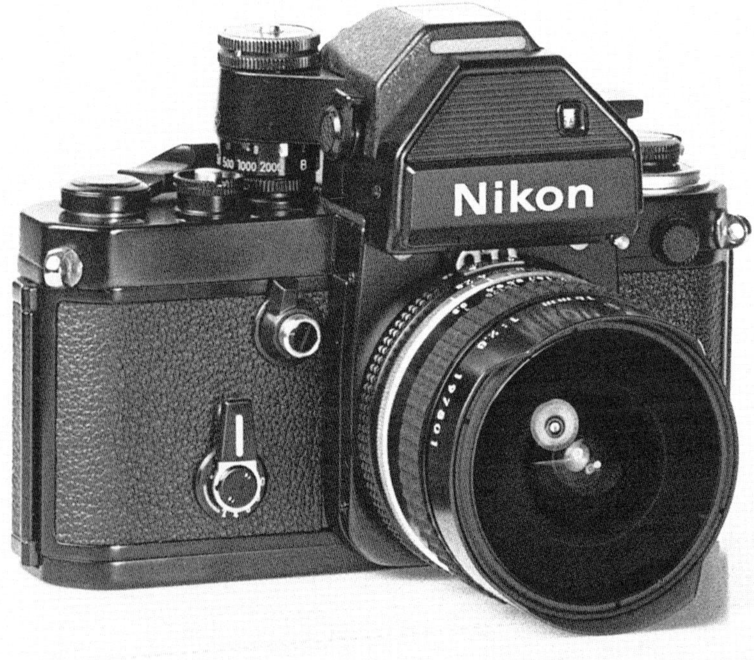

The F2 S Photomic with a Fisheye-Nikkor 16mm,f/3.5.

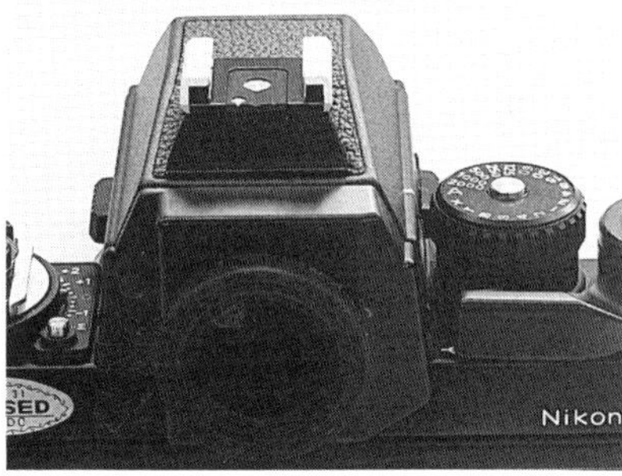

The F3P can be recognized immediately by its ISO-type hot-shoe.

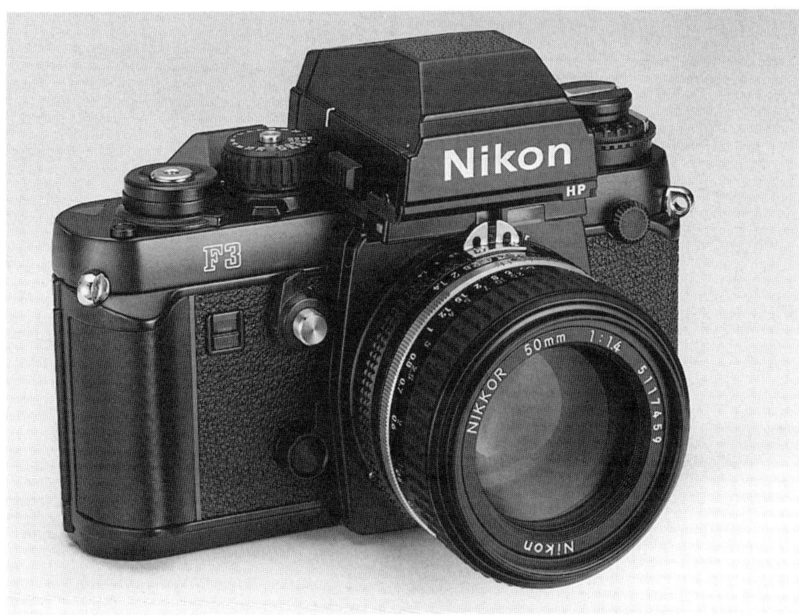

The F3 HP with its High-Eyepoint viewfinder is ideal for those who have to wear glasses. The whole of the focusing screen can be viewed very comfortably.

glasses off or push them to the forehead for every view through the finder. On the other hand, doing without a correction lens and keeping one's glasses on makes it impossible to see the complete finder image because the eye is too far from the eyepiece. The normal finders in all other cameras are designed so that the eye can keep a distance of about 18mm from the eyepiece. In the case of the HP (high-eyepoint) finder the eyepiece has a larger diameter so that it is not necessary to come closer than 25mm to see the whole image at one look.

One metering finder is also available in the F3-system. This is the Autofocus-finder DX-1. Its main purpose is not exposure metering, but the evaluation of distance. It can be used with any F3 and supplies an optical symbol for correct focus. It is only with the F3 AF that the DX-1 finder is able to relay the control signals to the F3 AF-lenses.

Viewfinders For The F4

With the F4-system Nikon returned to former tradition by incorporating the exposure metering in the viewfinder once more. This was necessary for several reasons. Firstly the F4 offers three different metering methods and secondly, due to its many functions, they were simply faced with space problems in the body. Therefore the F4 can only provide spot-metering without a viewfinder attached, the metering cells responsible for the Matrix- and centre-weighted modes are located inside the finder next to the eyepiece. The DP-20 is standard equipment. It has an HP-type eyepiece with an integrated shutter and the three available metering methods can be chosen by rotating the dial on the right side. This viewfinder possesses a real technical novelty, two tiny mercury switches not only inform the Matrix-system if the camera is being held horizontally or vertically, but also in which direction. This is because the positions of the metering segments in the upright and landscape formats lead to them evaluating different parts of the subject and the exposure control system must be informed about this. The liquid mercury in the switches makes

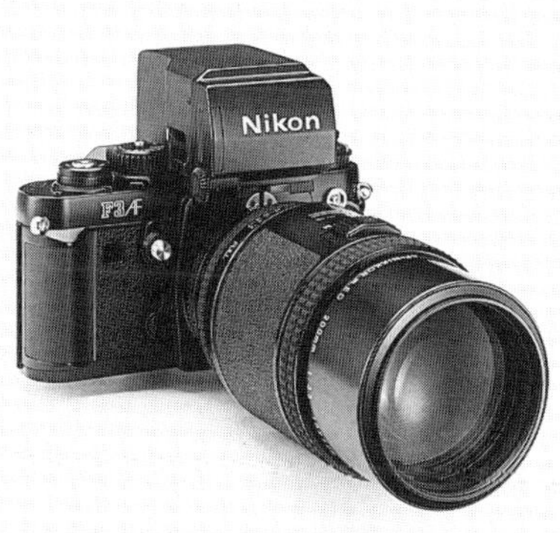

Nikon's early autofocus solution: the F3 AF with the finder DX-1 and the AF 200mm,f/3.5 IF-ED.

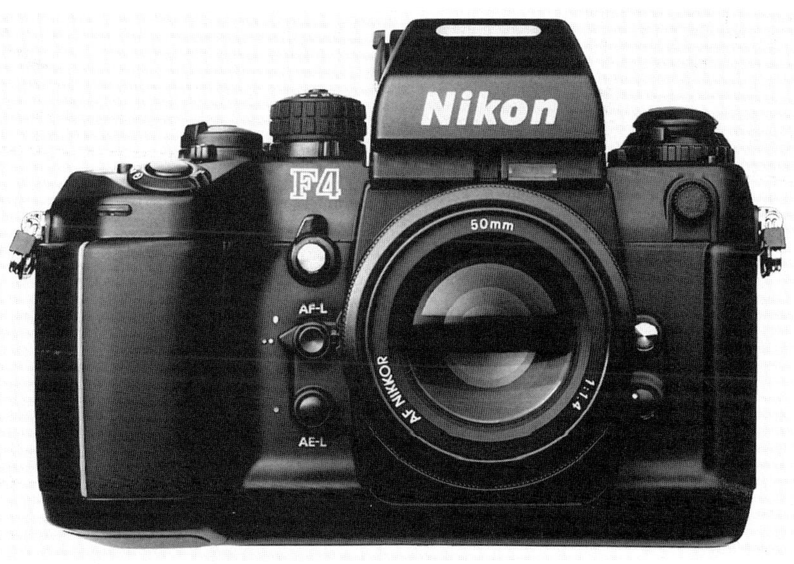

The DP-20 offers a choice of three metering modes: Matrix, spot, and centre-weighted.

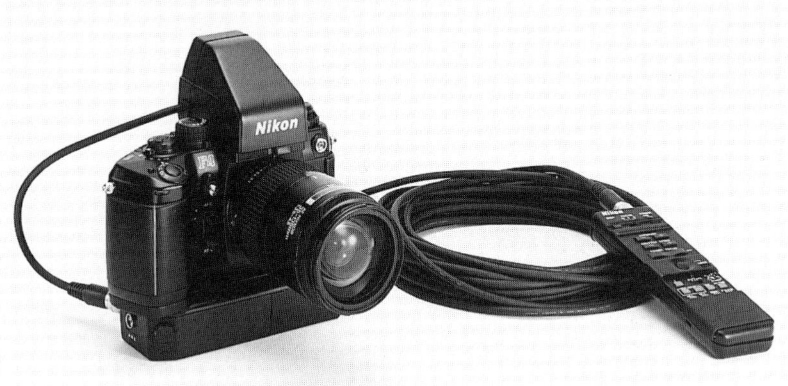

Not (yet) in serial production: the F4 with a video-finder and complete remote-control.

and breaks the necessary electrical contacts: ingeniously simple, but effective.

Since the metering-cells are situated in the viewfinder, compensation factors have to be set when certain special focusing screens are employed. Values within a range of -2 to +0.5 EV can be set with the help of the screw-like dial on the bottom of the finder body and controlled in a window on the its lower right side. The finder itself offers a multitude of information above and below the image, even the film counter is displayed. The necessary links are made via eleven contacts located at the bottom rear edge of the finder. No correction lenses are needed in the case of the DP-20, it has its own built-in dioptre correction adjustment with a range of +1 to -3 dioptres which can be set with the small knob on the right side.

The viewfinder is protected by a double-reinforced plastic cover against the blows and knocks of hard daily professional work. Even though professional photographers usually prefer the more powerful grip type flashguns, a normal ISO hot-shoe is available on top of the finder which allows access to all of the F4's flash-techniques.

The Action-Finder DA-20, available as an accessory, could almost be called a super-HP version. It does not offer Matrix-metering – apparently there was no room left next to the enormous hunk of glass. The second row of displays below the finder image was also sacrificed. Only the shutter speeds in the P- and A-modes, or the aperture values in the S-mode and the exposure modes, are visible in the upper row.

The 6x Magnifying Finder DW-21 and the Waist-Level Finder DW-20 allow only spot-metering, but they do have a terminal for the adaptor cable SC-24 which secures all of the flash facilities.

Special Viewfinders For The F-Models

The interchangeable viewfinder system is without doubt the most obvious difference between the Nikon F and other Nikon models. Besides a pentaprism finder bare of any metering system, only a waist-level model was available in the very beginning. With it the image is viewed directly

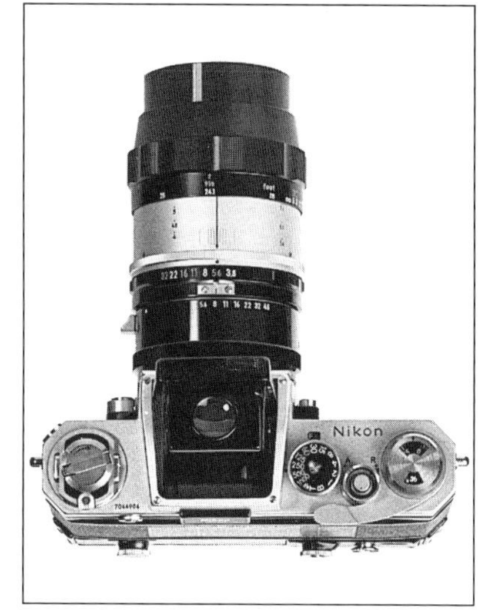

The waist-level finder on an F – ideal for reproductions and macro-photography.

on the focusing screen. When its folding hood is opened it shields the focusing screen from side light which would impair the image quality. A small magnifier can be flipped up which enlarges the centre of the image 5x to aid focusing.

The waist-level finders for the different models of the F-series are: F2 = DW-1, F3 = DW-3, and F4 = DW-20. The version for the Nikon F had no code-name.

Action Finders

The Action Finders, which are often referred to as TV-finders, provide the possibility to see the com-

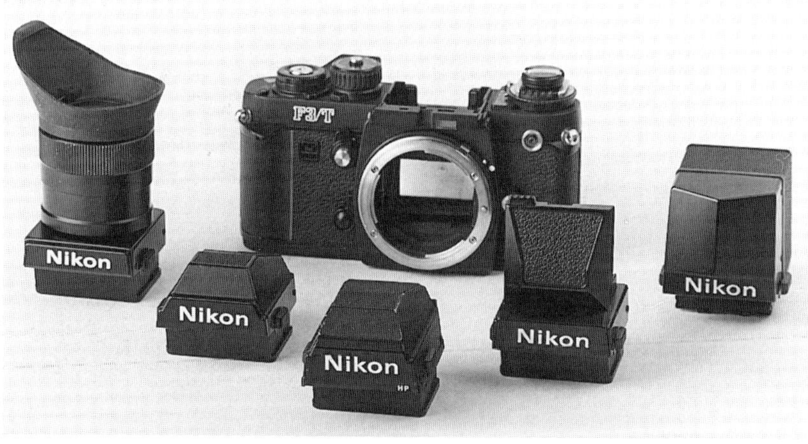

The F3 with the four interchangeable viewfinders.

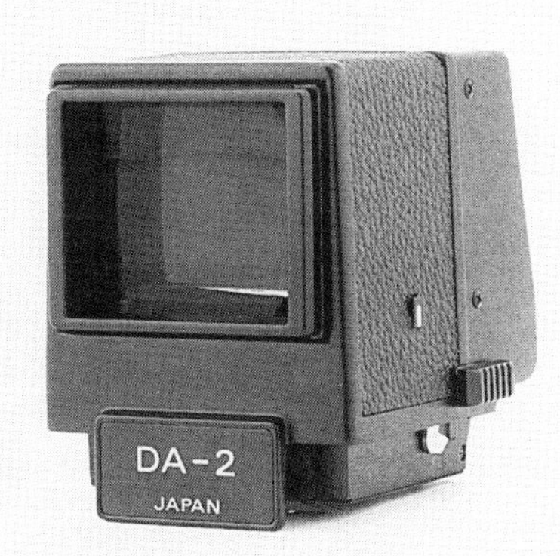

The Action Finder offers a total overview from a greater distance, in this case the DA-2.

plete image without having to hold the camera as close to one's eye as normally. This not only allows for quick reactions in sports photography but also unusual applications, for example when the photographer is forced to wear a helmet or goggles in aerial shots. An Action Finder is also essential when the camera is in an underwater housing. It is designed to be used with a viewing distance of about six to eight centimetres between eye and eyepiece. The names of the Action Finders are: F = Action Finder, F2 = DA-1, F3 = DA-2, and F4 = DA-20.

Magnifying Finders

The 6x High-magnification Finder is designed for difficult work in the macro area or, for example, in reproductions. It enlarges the complete viewfinder image by a factor of 6 and possesses a built-in eyesight correction adjustment from +3 to -5 dioptres. The names of the magnification finders are: F2 = DW-2, F3 = DW-4, and F4 = DW-21.

A finder of this type was not available for the Nikon F, but the DW-2 version for the F2 can be mounted after unscrewing the Nikon name-plate on its front. For this purpose two Philips-type screws are situated on the back of the plate. This design also makes it possible to employ all of the F2's finders, except for the Photomics, on the Nikon F. It works the other way around, too, that is using the F-type finders on the F2. The F3's and F4's

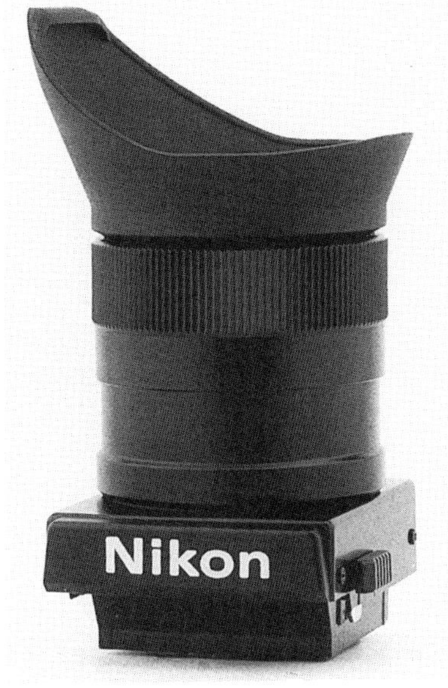

The complete viewfinder image is enlarged 6x by the magnification finders.

viewfinders cannot be mounted on the two older models though.

Viewfinder Accessories

As well as the obligatory eyecup for the different types of finder which prevent false metering results due to stray light entering the eyepiece, the already mentioned eyepiece correction lenses are also available for those with eyesight deficiencies. The eyepieces themselves are designed with a correction of -1 dioptre, which most users with 20:20-vision never notice. This construction was chosen to give a comfortable view of the image by simulating a distance of one metre from the focusing screen, even though the eye is actually only a few centimetres away. The dioptre designation on the frame, however, describes the complete system effect. So a lens with the designation "0" is actually a +1 dioptre lens. Those who wear glasses must keep in mind the need to subtract 1 dioptre from their prescription value when ordering correction lenses. These lenses are available for all Nikon models, slip-on versions for the rectangular eyepieces of the EM, FG, FG-20, F-301/401/s/x/501, and screw-in types for all the others. Special versions are also available for the HP-type finders.

The Eyepiece Magnifier DG-2 which enlarges the centre of the image by a factor of 2 can be employed in certain cases for critical focusing. It is screwed into the eyepiece and a hinge allows it to be swung out of the way when it is necessary to see the complete finder image. It has a dioptre correction facility from +1 to -5 and an eyecup. In order to allow the owners of camera models without interchangeable finders to view the image from above the Right-Angle Viewing Attachment DR-3 can be screwed into the eyepiece instead of the magnifier. It allows the complete frame to be seen but, unlike the waist-level finder, the image is right way round. It has an eyecup, as well as a dioptre-correction with a range of +3 to -5. In order to use these viewfinder accessories on cameras with rectangular eyepieces an adaptor must be mounted between

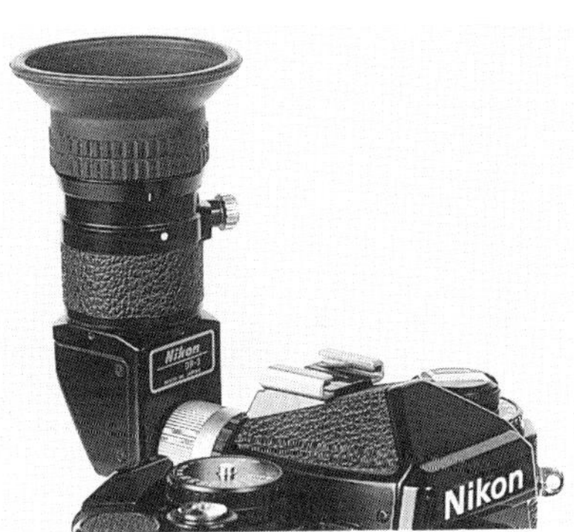

The hinged Eyepiece Magnifier DG-2 doubles the size of the centre of the image.

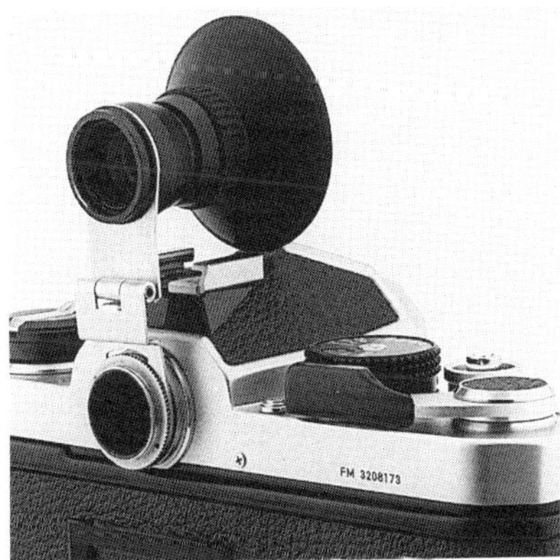
An alternative to the waist-level finder for models with fixed viewfinders is the Right-Angle Viewing Attachment DR-3.

them. The adaptor DK-1 is necessary with the HP-type finders.

To set the continuous dioptre correction look through the camera's finder without a lens mounted. The setting is correct when you can see the grain of the matte focusing screen and the other rangefinder aids clearly and completely sharp.

Interchangeable Focusing Screens

The purpose of the focusing screen is to make the image created by the lens visible in an exactly defined plane. This is the plane corresponding to the plane of the film which becomes accessible whenever the 45°-mirror swings up and out of the way. The first focusing screens, not only Nikon's, were rightly called "matte screens". Due to the production method employed to achieve the matte surface – sandblasting – they provided a very dark and grainy image. Nowadays the focusing screens are the result of laser treatment. They offer a fine and hardly visible grain and a degree of light transmission coming close to the theoretically possible.

Nikon offers a multitude of focusing screens for their cameras which provide optimum viewing of the subject in almost every feasible situation and for any photographic task. The possibility of changing them quickly and easily allows the photographer to adjust the viewfinder image to his personal needs and preferences. Not everybody considers the split-image and microprism ring focusing aids to be the best solutions, and often these devices not only prove unnecessary but also annoying – for example with slower lenses or longer focal lengths.

Type A: F/F2; F3; FTN; EL

This was the first standard screen, with a split-image rangefinder and Fresnel lens. The latter enhances overall brightness and prevents the otherwise unavoidable darkening of the image edges. The split-image rangefinder consists of two prisms arranged at an angle of 20° to the screen plane, one surface slanted to the left, the other to the right. In the centre they meet exactly at the screen surface. If focusing is not correct, edges within the subject will not coincide in the split-image area. In many cases this screen ensures very precise focusing, but it does have the drawback that a distinct edge or line within the subject is necessary. In addition, with

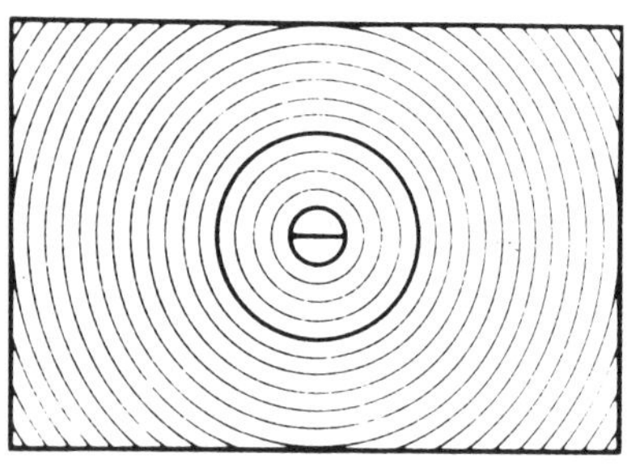

Focusing screen Type A.

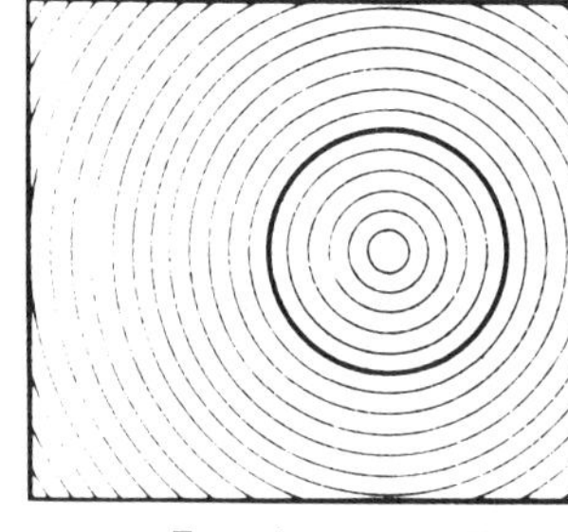

Focusing screen Type B.

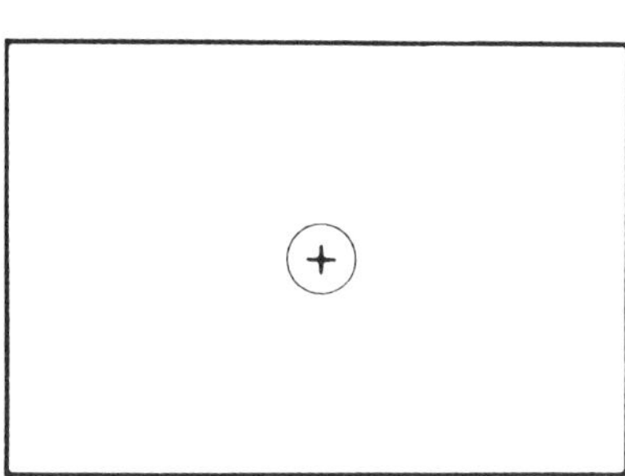

Focusing screen Type C.

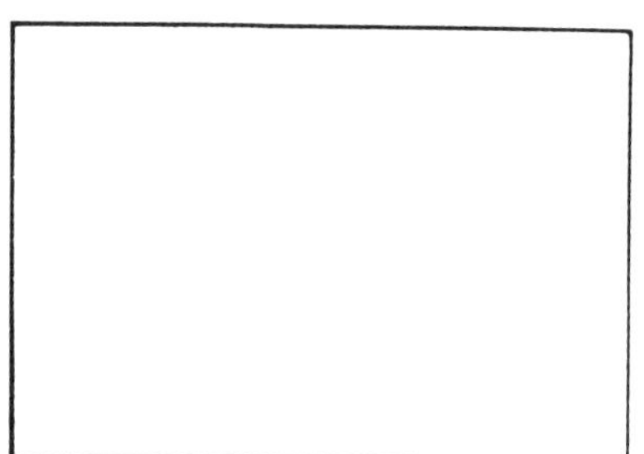

Focusing screen Type D.

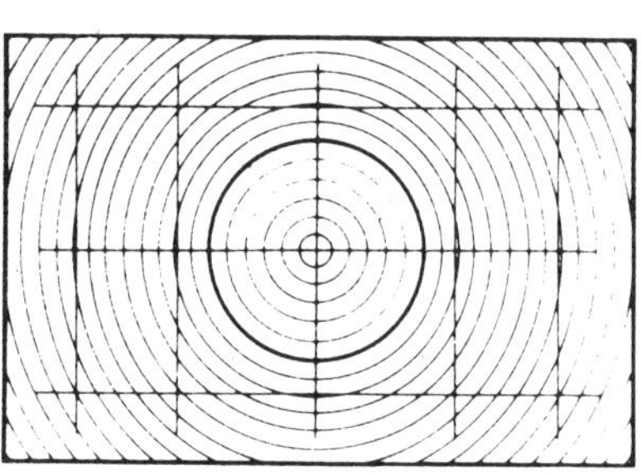

Focusing screen Type E.

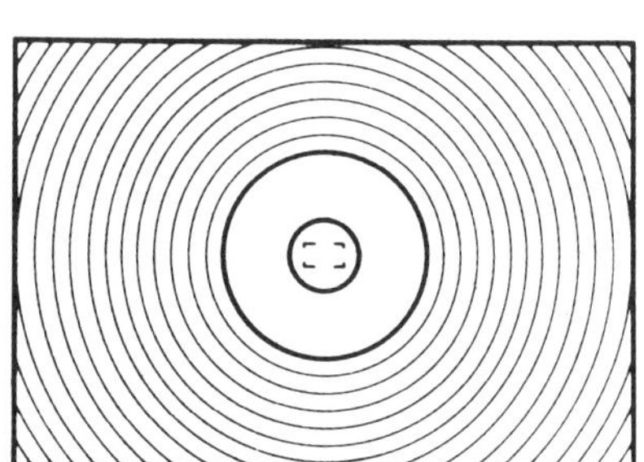

Focusing screen Type F.

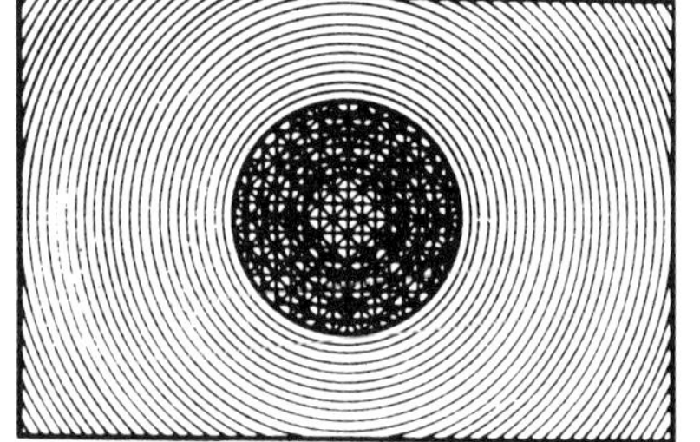

Focusing screen Type G.

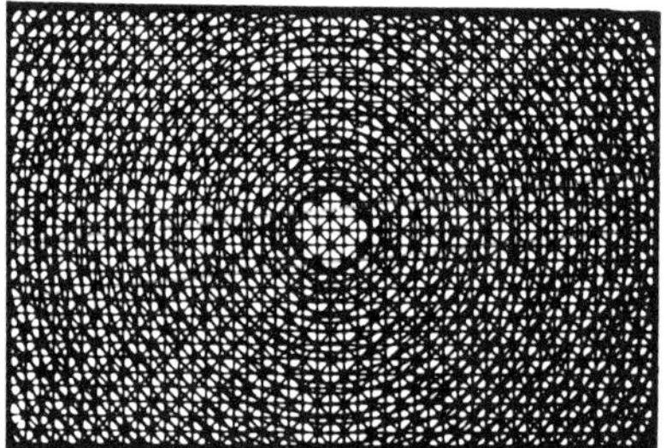

Focusing screen Type H.

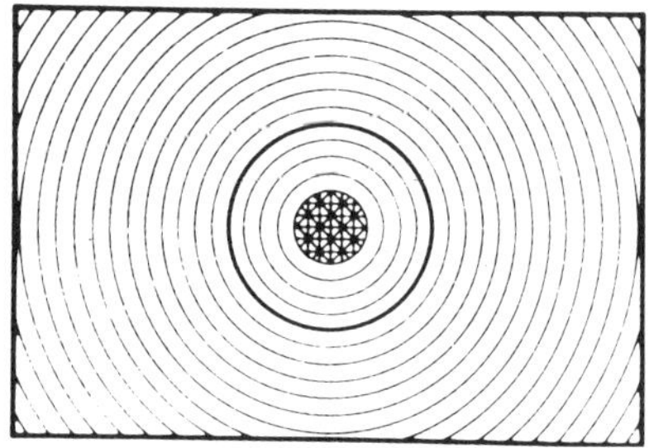

Focusing screen Type J.

this type of focusing aid one of the prism halves may darken if lenses with maximum apertures smaller than f/4 are used. So this type of focusing screen is not suitable for lenses with longer focal lengths and small maximum apertures, and it is also only of limited acceptability with zoom-lenses.

Type B: F/F2; F3; F4; FM/FE/FA; F-501/401/s/x/801/s; F90

This is the standard screen for all the AF-cameras and does not have any focusing aids. It is ideal for fast lenses, and for close-up and telephoto shots when shallow depth-of-field renders such aids unnecessary.

Type C: F / F2; F3; F4

A special screen supplied with a cross-hair reticle for astro-photography, this was designed to enable aerial-image focusing that is necessary for the extreme reproduction ratios when photographing through telescopes. In macrophotograhpy this screen is also very efficient.

Type D: F/F2; F3

This focusing screen is completely matte, a relic from the early days of the F and F2 and meant to be used with simple long focal length lenses. Since these have been replaced by the faster ED-versions with their modern telephoto-designs, this type of screen is only interesting today in combination with fisheye-lenses.

Type E: F/F2; F3; F4; FM/FE/FA; F-501/801/s; F90

Resembles type B but includes a grid of horizontal and vertical lines dividing the image every 7.5mm. Ideal for architectural photography and reproduction work when precise alignment of the camera is absolutely mandatory.

Type F: F4

A new focusing screen similar to type B, designed especially for focusing with mirror lenses.

Type G: F/F2; F3; F4

This super-bright screen supplies an incomparably brilliant viewfinder image. Its big disadvantage is that the depth-of-field cannot be controlled with this clear Fresnel lens. A 12mm microprism spot is located in the centre for this purpose. A screen designed for special applications and therefore available in four different versions corresponding to certain focal lengths: G1 for fish-eyes only; G2 for fixed focal lengths from 24mm to 200mm; G3 for focal lengths of 300 and 400mm, and G4 for super-telephoto lenses of 600mm and longer.

Type H: F/F2: F3

The H-types have a microprism pattern over the entire screen area, not only in the central 12mm spot. This makes the complete image shimmer as long as focusing is not perfect: a clear image only appears when the setting is correct. This is meant mainly for sports photography, and like the G-screen it is available in four versions for the different focal lengths. It has the same drawback as the G-model – it does not allow visual control of the depth-of-field, limiting its applications.

Type J: F/F2; F3; F4; FTN/EL; F-501/801/s

A screen with a 5mm microprism spot. In this case the microprisms consist of tiny split-image units that provide a clear image only when the exact focus is set. Compared to a normal

Focusing screen Type K.

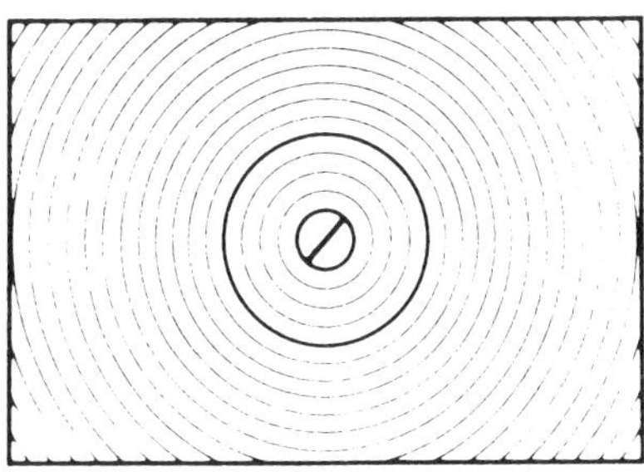

Focusing screen Type L.

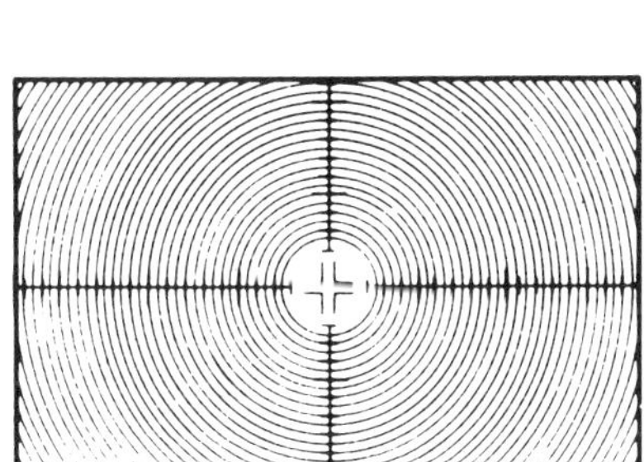

Focusing screen Type M.

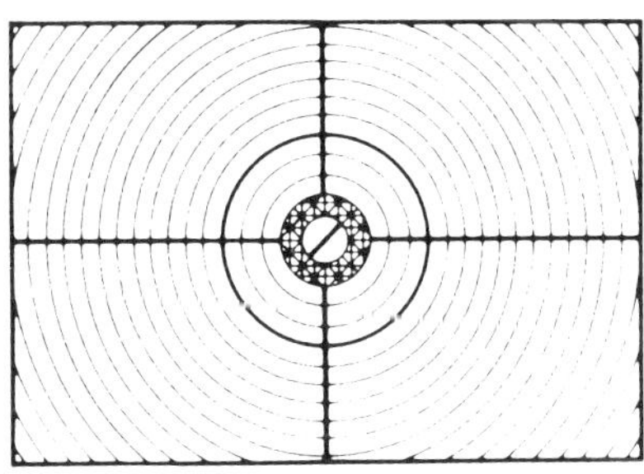

Focusing screen Type P.

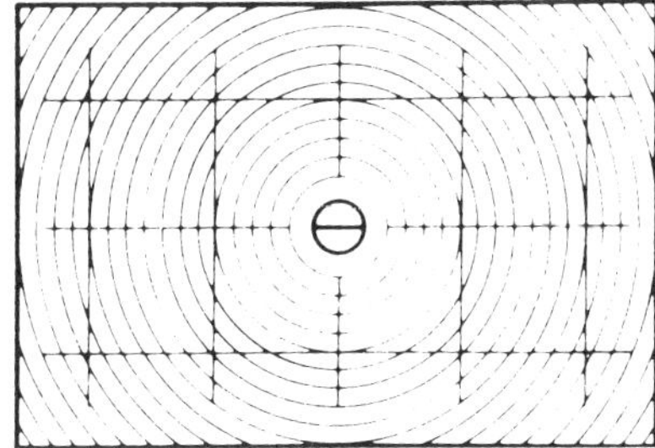

Focusing screen Type R.

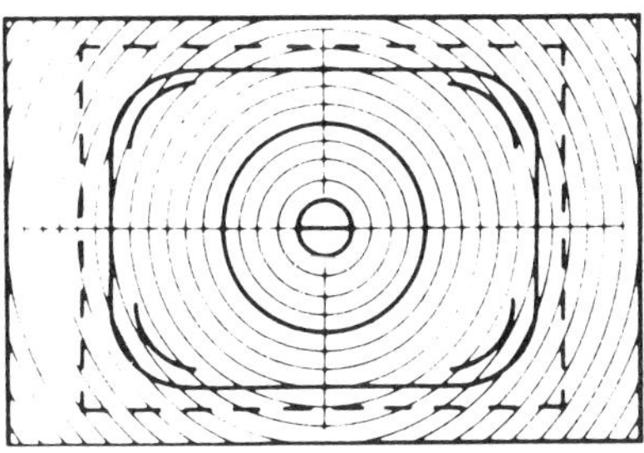

Focusing screen Type T.

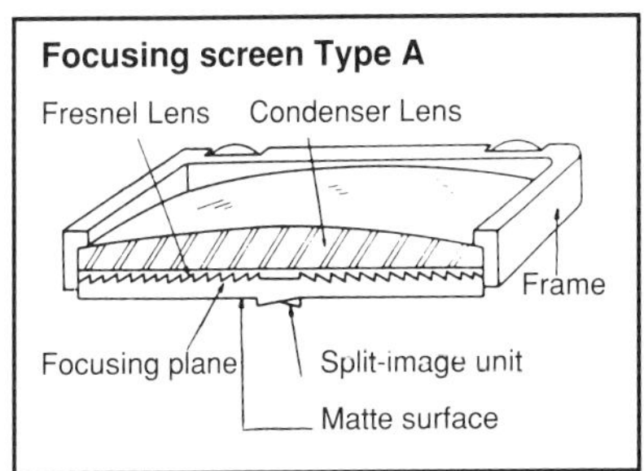

Focusing screen with split-image rangefinder

split-image focusing aid it can also be used with slower zoom-lenses. One must get accustomed to this screen in practical use though. Nikon cameras were equipped with the J-screen as well as the A-type as a standard until the middle of the 70's.

Type K: F/F2; F3; F4; FT-2/EL-2; FM/FE/FA; EM/FG

Since the middle of the 70's the K-version, a combination of the A- and J-models, has been the standard screen for all of the non-AF cameras. A microprism collar is situated around the split-image rangefinder, so that the photographer has two methods of focusing at his disposal. In the course of time the brightness of this screen has been improved again and again. The latest achievement in this respect is the "Brite View" K-type screen which was introduced together with the F-301. Its split-image prisms are ground in such a way that the halves only darken with apertures of f/11 and smaller; a noticeable advantage especially in macrophotograhpy.

Type L: F/F2; F3

This screen is almost the same as the A-version except for the fact that the split-image prisms are arranged diagonally instead of horizontally. The advantage is that the subject need not necessarily have a vertical edge or line as an orientation. This type is also well-suited for use as a standard screen.

Type M: F/F2; F3; F4

A Fresnel lens with a clear central area, especially fitting for macrophotography beyond reproduction ratios of 1:1. It is equipped with double cross-hairs and scales calibrated in mm, and also delivers an exceptionally bright image.

Type P: F/F2; F3; F4

Resembles the P-type screen with a diagonally instead of horizontally arranged split-image unit and etched vertical and horizontal lines to aid the parallel alignment of the camera.

Type R: F3

A combination of the A-type screen and the grid from the E-version. Its speciality is a split-image unit particularly designed for lenses with maximum apertures of f/3.5 to f/4.5, which makes it suitable for zoom lenses.

Type S: F/F2; F3

Resembles the A-type, but has an engraved marking on the left side outlining the area where data is imposed when the data-backs MF-1, MF-11, and MF-17 are used.

Type T: F3

A TV-screen, also principally an A-version, but with additional crossed lines and a marked area corresponding to the aspect ratio of a TV-screen.

Type U: F3; F4

Resembles the B-type, but is designed especially for telephotography with fixed focal lengths from 135mm.

Motor Drives

From the very beginning of 35mm photography many wished to have the film transported and the shutter cocked by a motor, be it in order to expose a series of shots or to get a second shot without having to take the camera from the eye.

In the first half of the century this was done with a strong spring-powered clockwork motor built-in or attached to the camera. It was wound like a clock, worked completely mechanically and, depending on the picture format, transported approximately 15 frames at a fastest rate of about 4 frames/sec.

Clockwork has obvious disadvantages, including the stress the necessarily strong spring puts on the mechanism. Nikon did not approve of this construction so they designed a battery powered motor. In 1957 a motor-drive was introduced as a prototype with the Nikon S2, but it did not go into serial production until later that year as the S-36, together with the Nikon SP. It was connected to its external battery compartment containing six 1.5v AA-size cells by a cable and was capable of propelling the SP at a remarkable rate of three frames/sec.

This motor-drive was sensational at the time, as the very first battery-powered motor-drive it constituted another one of the cornerstones to Nikon's professional reputation. Slightly modified it was later also

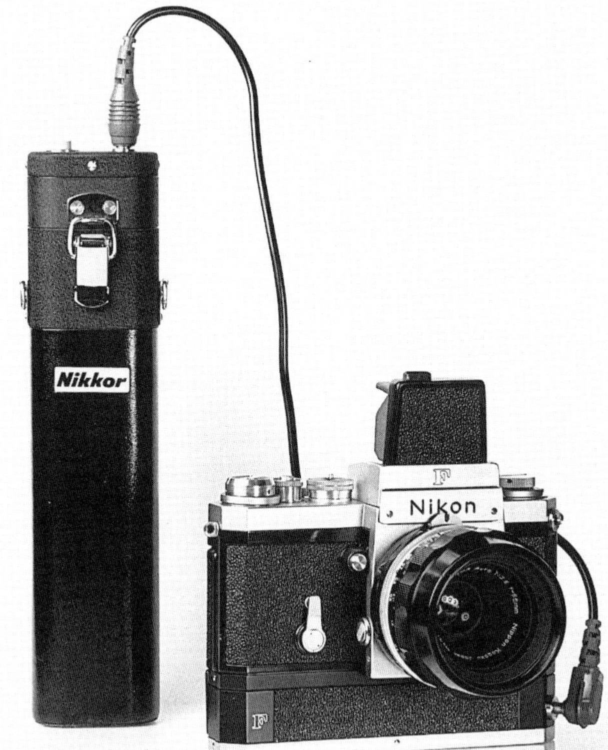

The F with the Motor-Drive F-36 and the external battery compartment for eight baby-size cells.

available as the model S-250 with a bulk-film magazine attached for 250 exposures and as the model S-72 for the half-format camera S3-M. Together with the last it was even able to achieve 4,5 frames/sec.

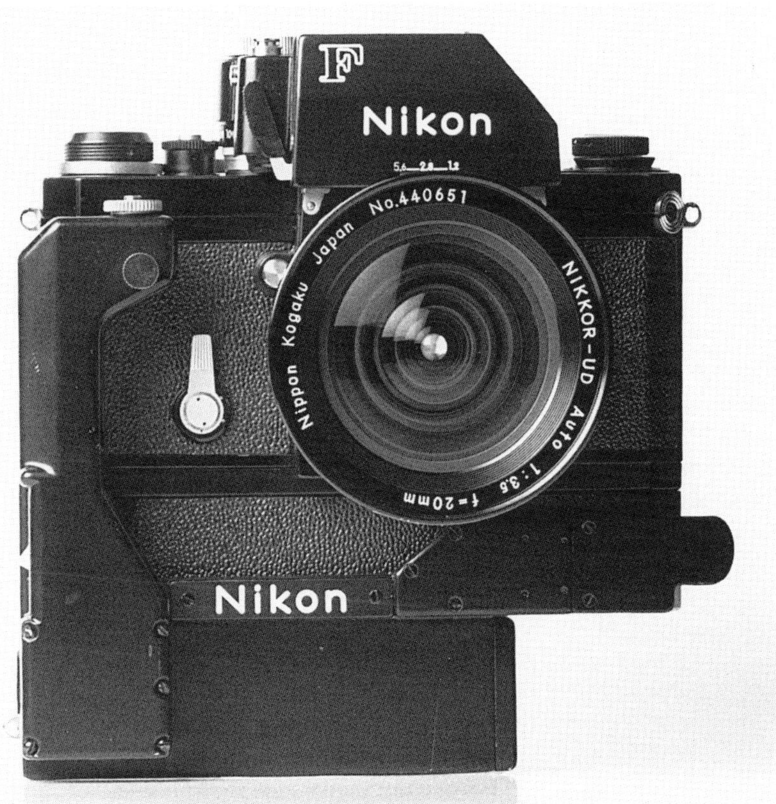

A classic Nikon outfit: Nikon F together with F-36 and the cordless battery compartment.

F Motor-drives

Based on the S-36, the F-36 was developed for the Nikon F, and even though the two versions may look exactly alike they cannot be interchanged. The F-36 is capable of 4 frames/sec. but only when the mirror is locked in the upper position. With the mirror in operation, which no doubt is the normal usage, it can still achieve 3 frames/sec. The firing rate can be set to four frequencies: 2, 2,5, 3, and 4 frames/sec. The release button is located on the back of the motor-drive and concentrically round it the dial for the single and continuous modes. An integrated film counter allows the desired number of exposures to be preset after which film transport is stopped automatically. At first the power was supplied by an external battery pack as in the case of the S-36, later a cordless version became available which could be screwed under the motor-drive and had an additional grip. This of course allows the camera to be released with the button on the grip. Understandably this combination was the most popular since camera, motor-drive, and battery supply make up a compact and easy-to-handle unit. So, together with its attachable battery compartment, the F-36 can be considered to be the ancestor of all the Nikon motor-drives to come. Even a remote-control terminal was already available.

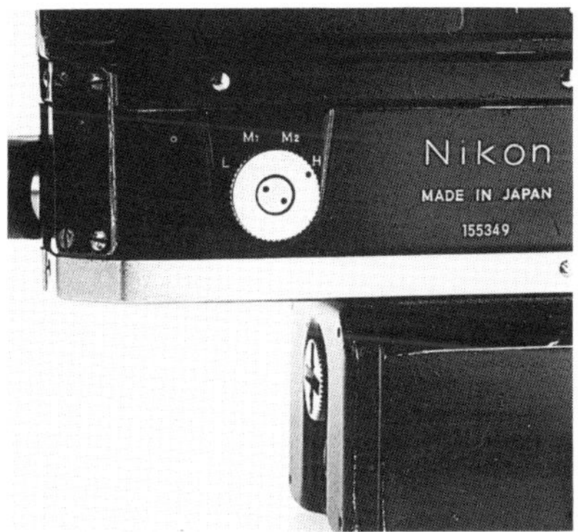

Four firing-rates can be set on the F-36 motor-drive.

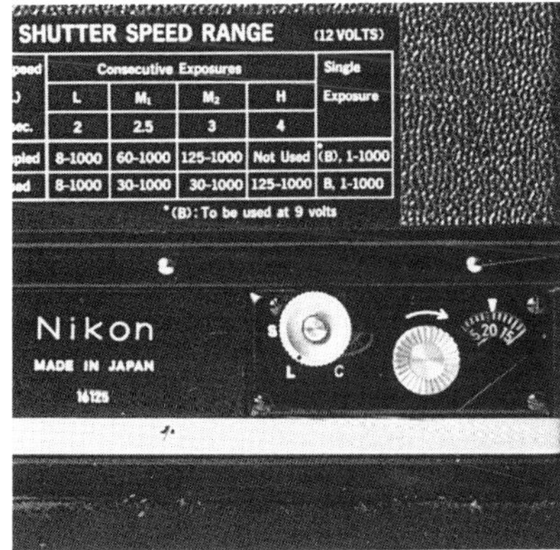

The F-36 seen from the rear with the additional film-counter and its second release-button.

One of the unique features of the F-motor was that each camera/motor-drive combination had to be matched in a Nikon service facility. Anybody trying to avoid this modification risked damaging the mechanism of both camera and motor. The camera back is an integral part of the motor. This feature was utilized when a bulk-film magazine, F-250, for 250 exposures was constructed which could be loaded with 10m of film and was driven by its own motor. Its performance is identical to that of the F-36.

A Nikon F that has been used together with a motor-drive can often be recognized by damaged guide-rails for the camera back. When they are broken – the typical result of attaching the motor-drive carelessly – light may enter the camera.

F2 Motor-drives

The new top-model that succeeded the classic Nikon F in 1971 was supplied with a completely new motor-drive, the MD-1, which was different from the F-36 in several ways. It can be mounted on any F2 without special modification, has an integral grip,

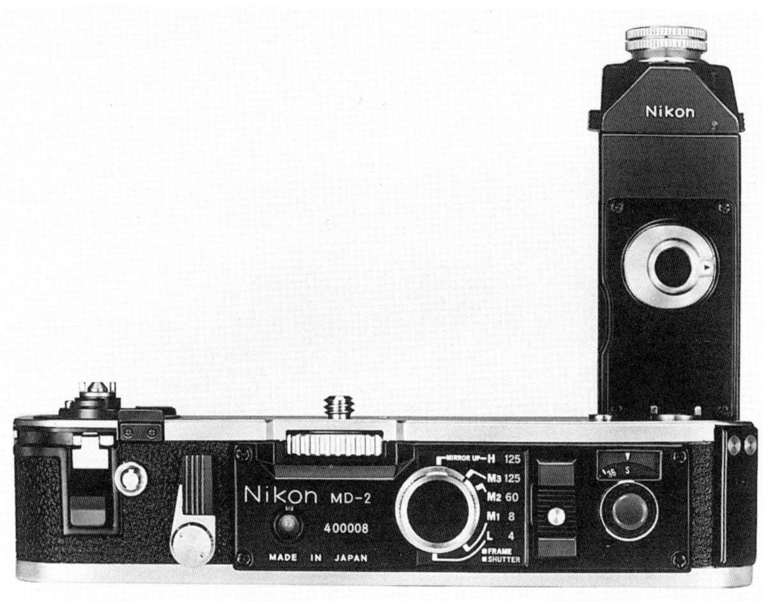

A mechanical masterpiece: the fast and powerful MD-2 for the F2.

and is capable of a maximum firing-rate of 5 frames/sec. with the mirror locked up and 4.3 frames/sec. in normal mode. In order to attach the motor the locking-catch for the camera back, the so-called O/C key, must be removed because the spindle for the film rewind enters through this opening – another one of the MD-1's major advantages compared to the F-36. If desired the exposed film can be returned to its cassette within seven seconds. When the O/C key is removed from the bottom of the camera it can be stored in a specially designed terminal in the grip-section of the motor to prevent it from getting lost.

The motor-drive is attached to the camera by screwing it to the camera's tripod bush and therefore it has its own tripod bush. All the controls are located on the back where the photographer can keep his eye on them: the film-counter with its resetting lever, the firing speed selector knob with its five steps (1.3; 2.5; 3.8; 4.3; and 5 frames/sec.), the lever for power rewind, and the O/C lever for opening the camera back.

The firing-rate must be chosen in accordance with the preset shutter speed since the motor-drive cannot "know" when the camera will be ready to transport the film again due to the wholly mechanical functions of both the camera and the motor. If one were to try to use the maximum firing-rate with a preset shutter speed of 1/15 sec., for example, the camera would react with a suspicious clattering noise.

The release button has three positions: S (single), C (continuous), and L (lock). This release button can be removed and used as a remote-control unit via the Extension Cord MC-1. Later this method was dropped and replaced by using the terminal on the front of the motor. This terminal, which is employed by Nikon even today, has a double function. It either serves as a remote-control connection for the cord MC-10 or for an external power supply with the MC-2 cord and the AC/DC Converter MA-4.

Normally the motor-drive is supplied with power by the attached battery compartment MB-1. It contains two battery holders which are loaded with five AA-size cells each, or the corresponding rechargeables. When the motor-drive is used professionally and a large amount of energy is needed over a long period of time the battery compartment MB-1 can be loaded with two of the powerful NC-units MN-1 which can be recharged to full capacity with the separate Quick Charger MB-1. The power status of the battery and or the NC's can be checked by a gauge underneath the grip. The Motor-Drive MD-1 was later replaced by the almost identical MD-2. The difference between the two is a modified release-button and a double contact located at the motor's right rear corner. The Stop-Back MF-3 uses these to relay a signal to the motor not to wind the film back completely into the cassette in motorized operation.

The Motor-Drive MD-3 was a less expensive option for anyone who did not consider operating ease so important. It has no motorized rewind and is only capable of a firing rate of 2.5 frames/sec. with the battery compartment MB-2 which is powered by 8 AA-size cells. But it is also possible to use the bigger F2 motor-drive's battery compartment MB-1 which

A popular combination: the F2A with the MD-2 and the battery compartment MB-1.

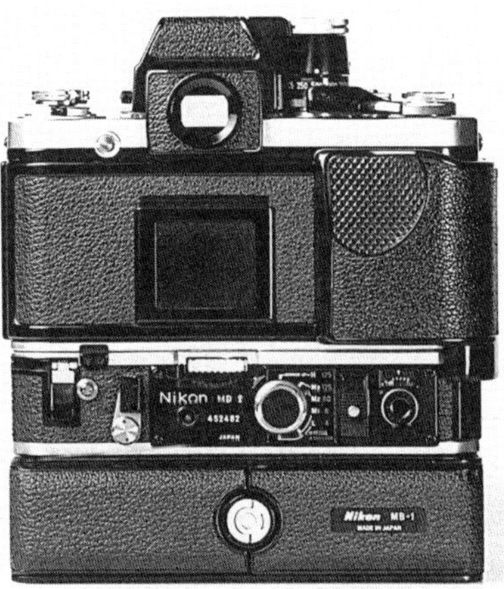

Automatic cut-off with motorized rewinding. The MD-2 with the Stop-Back MF-3.

improves the frequency to 3.5 frames/sec. with its 15 volt-system. The speed cannot be changed though, the only choice is between single or continuous modes.

The MD-3 also has a terminal for remote control and external power supply. The Stop-Back MF-3 cannot be employed because the necessary contacts are absent. When the motor is attached the O/C key does not have to be removed from the camera base-plate, it is just folded out vertically so that it fits into the corresponding slot in the motor. In doing so, care should be taken to fit the motor drive shaft coupling exactly to the camera's counterpart, otherwise the motor may be blocked after only half of a film transport step.

Besides the motor-drives described above there was the MD-100 designed specially for the F2 H and only delivered with that camera, since both components had to be precisely matched to each other at production stage. Everything must work absolutely flawlessly and without play at a maximum firing-rate of 10 frames/sec. The MD-100 is a modified MD-2 equipped with two Battery Packs MB-1 below, making 30 volts available. The use of batteries does not make very much sense with this combination; four MN-1 NC-units are employed instead.

F3 Motor-Drive

In the case of the mechanically controlled Nikon F and F2 models the corresponding motors are not released by the camera but begin to operate as soon as the motor's release-button is pressed. As a result the camera and motor mechanisms can confuse each other when an incompatible shutter speed/firing-rate combination is set. The gear-box will generate crackling and crunching noises. Not so with the F3's MD-4. It is controlled by the camera through six contacts situated around the rewind port and it only transports the film after the camera gives the "order" to do so. This interdependency allows up to 6 frames/sec. when the mirror is locked up, only reduced slightly to 5.5 frames/sec. in normal operation.

The motor-drive section and the battery compartment form a single unit in the case of the MD-4, with 8 AA-size cells or the rechargeable NC-battery MN-2 providing the power supply. When the MD-4 is attached, its batteries also provide the camera's power supply with their considerably larger capacity, rendering the button-size cells in the camera unnecessary. This is an additional safeguard in extremely cold conditions. This total communication logically also leads to the camera's metering system being activated when the motor release button is pressed. The AC/DC Converter MA-4 can be employed too

An impressive tower: the F2 H with its motor-drive MD-100 in a side view showing the battery test-button.

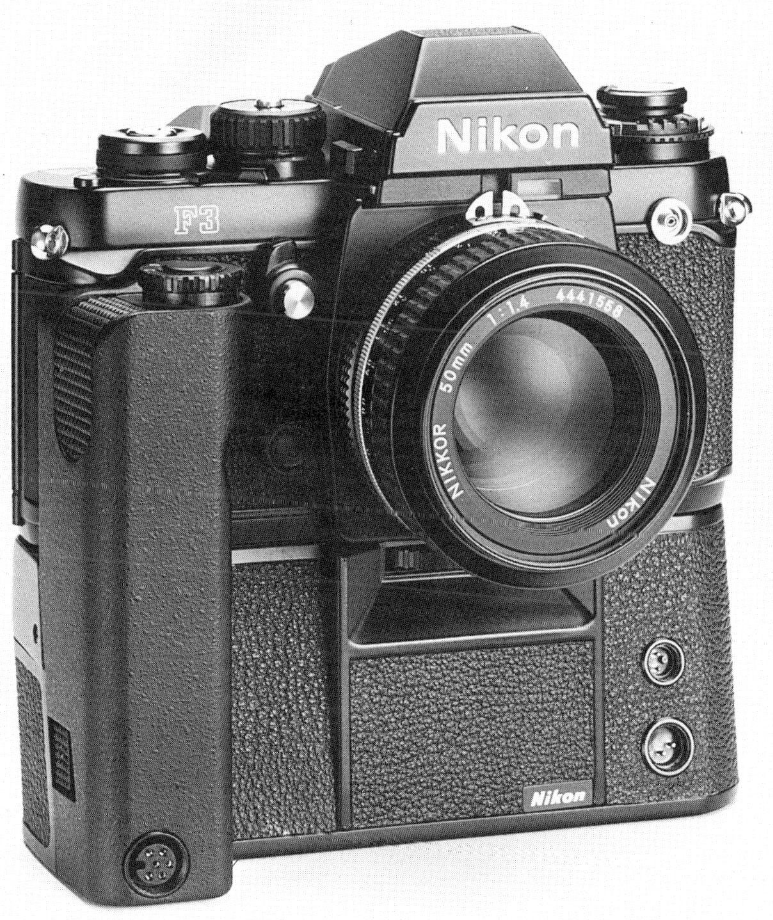

The motorized F of the 80's: the F3 with the robust and fast MD-4.

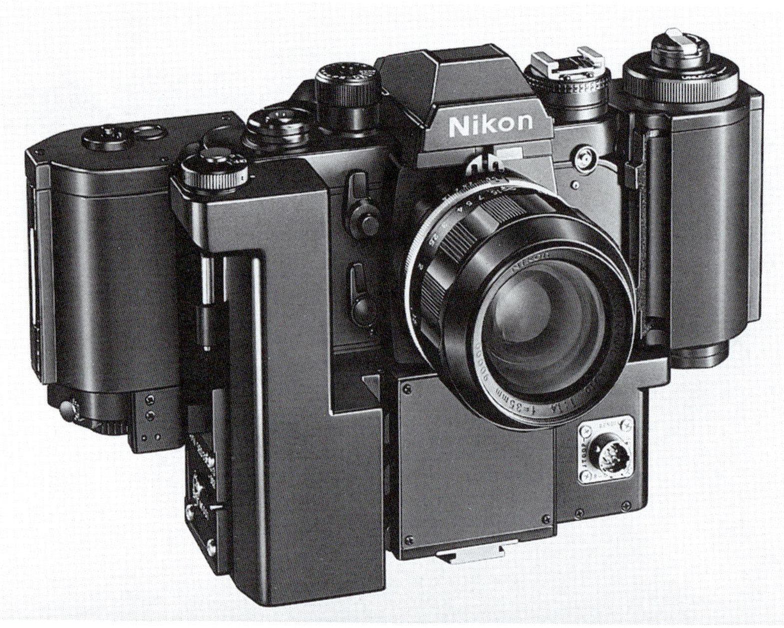

Modified for outer space: the F3 in an impressive NASA version.

since a second socket is accessible above the remote terminal. A third socket in the grip serves as a connection for the Bulk-Film Magazine MF-4 or to release a second motorized camera simultaneously by means of the cord MC-17.

A stop-back, the MF-6B, is available for the MD-4 just as with the MD-2, and the missing ability to set different frequencies is made up by an accessory, the Firing Rate Converter MK-1. Anybody who does not need the 5.5 frames/sec. available in continuous mode can use it to reduce the frequency to 1, 2, or 3 frames/sec., and this unit also possesses a second release-button for vertical shots. Another advantage of the mounted MK-1 is its tripod bush located exactly below the lens axis. That of the MD-4 had to be placed off-centre because most of the room in the lower part of the motor is occupied by the battery holder.

It may be a point of interest that the MD-4's drive spindle rotates with three times the speed of that of the MD-2 in order to reduce its operational noise and the stress the on the camera mechanism.

Two LEDs provide a means of checking the batteries. When the motor is attached to the F3 the motor drive coupling cover in the camera base-plate must be removed. A small compartment for it in the battery holder prevents it from being lost. The combination of the F3 and the MD-4 was designed so that their centre of gravity is very low. This ensures secure handling without the danger of camera shake even when using long focal lengths.

Aperture Control Attachments

There was another motor in addition to the film transport units in the F2-system, but this one was capable of controlling the aperture setting. It allowed the F2 to be updated subsequently into a camera with shutter speed priority automatic exposure. This was only possible though together with the LED-Photomics DP-2, DP-3, and DP-12. A good 500g of extra weight had to be taken into consideration which made the rather troublesome unit more suitable for static applications.

The DS-type aperture control attachments are screwed into the sync-terminal of the F2 and automatically connect to the two outside contacts of the metering finder. It is important to mount the parts in the right order: first the Photomic, then the DS-unit, and lastly the lens. The ring with which the attachment sets the aperture is situated around the bayonet mount. Since the F2 is a mechanical camera the lens aperture ring also has to be set manually. The motor needs a power supply of its own to do this, either the 3.6v rechargeable battery DN-1 must be inserted in the lower part of the body or the external battery compartment DB-1 or the AC/DC Converter MA-4

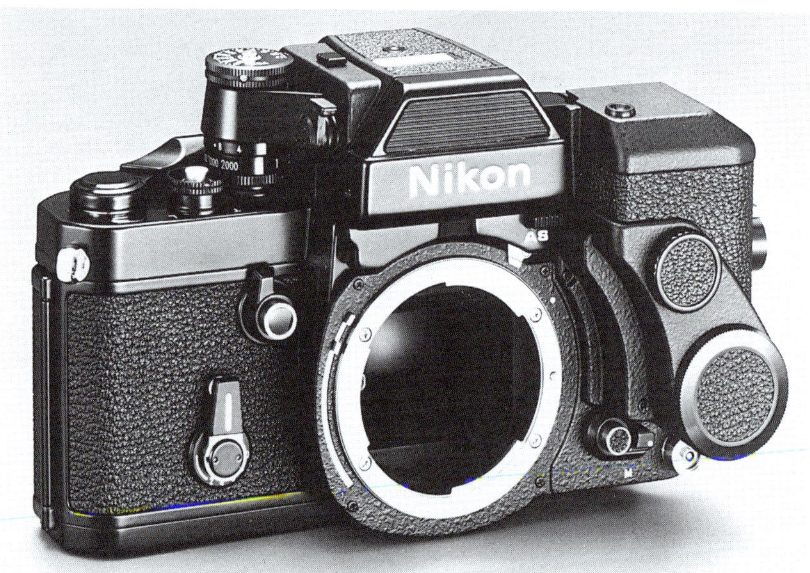

The F2 AS with the DS-12 motor for automatic aperture control attached.

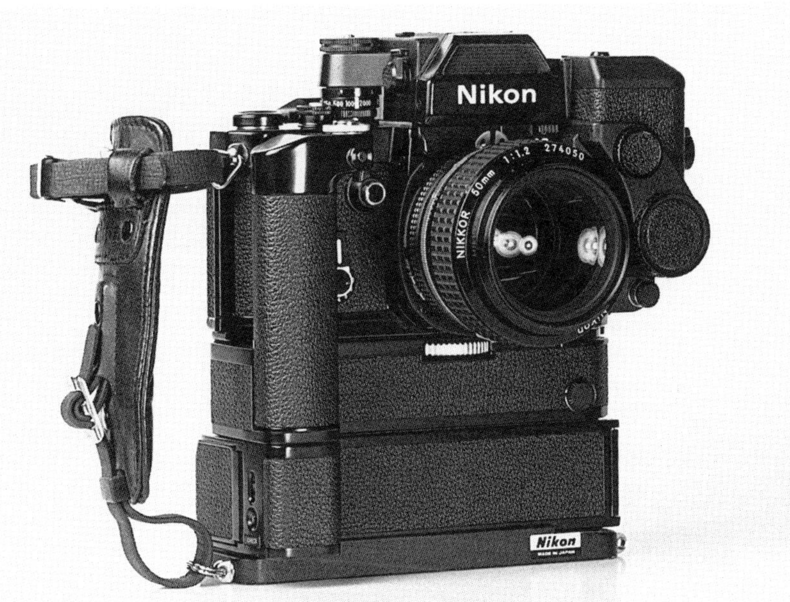

Motorized in every respect: the F2 AS with the MD-3, MB-1, DS-12, and the Grip Strap AH-1.

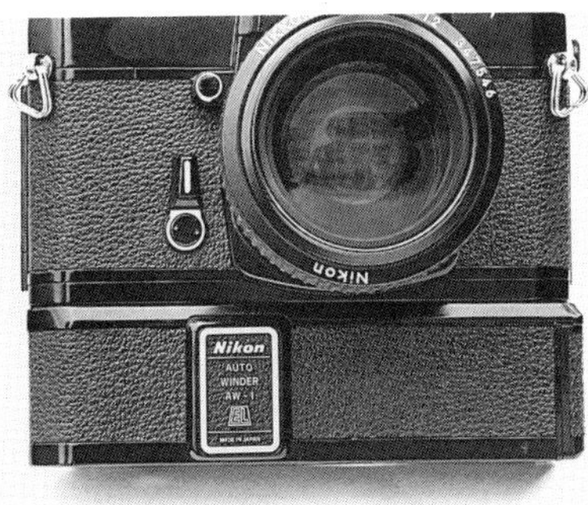

The Autowinder AW-1 provides motorized film transport for the Nikkormat ELW and Nikon EL-2.

have to be connected. The attachment takes about 3 seconds to run through its available aperture range from f/1.2 to f/32. Of course this is far slower than shutter speed priority automatic modes incorporated in camera bodies, but bear in mind when this unit was introduced.

When the lens is mounted special care must be taken to secure perfect coupling of the meter pins of both the camera and the aperture control attachment. Three different versions were made. The DS-1 and DS-2 versions can only be told apart by the latter's additional sync-terminal, which became necessary because that on the camera is used to fasten the attachment itself. The DS-12 is the version designed for AI-type lenses, so it can only be combined with the F2 AS. The first two DS-versions control the lens aperture ring with the help of its coupling fork. In the case of the AI-type lenses the DS-12 uses the AI-type aperture ring ridge. In order to mount the lens, or when manual aperture operation is preferred, the attachment motor can be switched off. Two modes are available: either set the desired shutter speed and press the on/off button when the automatic aperture control will subsequently set the metered value; or move the on/off switch to "On" and the unit will set the appropriate aperture continuously.

These operations do consume considerable energy, and in just under one hour the NC-battery will be drained and have to be recharged for a good three hours. Commenting on this, Nikon say they did not conceive the aperture control unit to relieve the photographer from having to do the setting himself. The DS-attachments were mainly intended to be employed in remote-controlled applications, such as in scientific and technical photography for time-lapse series.

Motor Winder AW-1

A motor-drive has other uses than when a series of shots in a short space of time is the aim, as sports photographers demand. Another aspect is the ability to take two shots immediately one after the other without taking the camera from one's eye. This is especially useful with an automatic camera, and most of all in portrait photography – the quick second shot will often deliver the better picture.

Nikon developed the winder AW-1 in 1976 which can be combined with the two Nikkormat models ELW and EL-2. This winder has neither an integrated grip nor any controls apart from its on/off switch and a battery-check LED. The power is supplied by six AA-size batteries and the motor's functioning is indicated very clearly by a whining sound. It is activated through the camera release button. Neither continuous operation nor remote controlled operation are available. The camera informs the winder through two contacts when it has completed its shutter operation and can be cocked again. This takes about 0.5 seconds which corresponds to a firing-rate of 2 frames/sec. Not enough for sports-photographers, but usually sufficient for on-the-spot shots. The AW-1 was the first motor drive unit for Nikon cameras outside the professional range.

Motor-drives for the FM, FE and FA

The successor generation of the Nikkormat models was designed for motorized operation right from the start. The first representative of this series is the MD-11. Its capability of up to 3.5 frames/sec. and the possibility to choose between single and continuous modes are its most remarkable features. It was developed from the AW-1, but it has a hand-grip and takes eight AA-size batteries to achieve its relatively high frequency. It was this motor that made numerous professionals consider buying two FM-bodies along with MD-11s instead of one F2 with a motor.

Four contacts facilitate the communication between the motor and the body – which means electronic instead of mechanical controls. Two of the contacts convey the signal which starts the film transport after the shutter operation, while the other two activate the metering system when the motor is switched on. A terminal for remote control accessories is included in the front of the ergonomically rounded grip section, but an external power supply cannot be employed.

The MD-11 was later succeeded by the MD-12. Both models appear to be identical on the outside, only details differ. In the case of the MD-12 the camera's exposure meter is activated by pressing the motor drive's release button. About a minute after the last release the power supply is cut off automatically – an important advantage of the MD-12, since users often forgot to switch off the previous model which also led to the camera's button-size cells also being drained. The second difference is hidden in the circuitry. The MD-11 only transports the film after the photographer removes his finger from the release button. In comparison, the MD-12 starts immediately after the shutter operation.

Camera/Motor-drive combinations

Camera	Frames per second												
	F-36	F-250	MD-1	MD-2	MD-3	MD-4	MD-11	MD-12	MD-15	MD-100	AW-1	MD-14	MD-E
F	4	4	—	—	—	—	—	—	—	—	—	—	—
F2	—	—	4-5	4-5	2.5-4	—	—	—	—	—	—	—	—
F3	—	—	—	—	—	3.8-6	—	—	—	—	—	—	—
ELW/EL-2	—	—	—	—	—	—	—	—	—	—	0.5	—	—
FM/FE	—	—	—	—	—	—	3.5	3.5	—	—	—	—	—
FM-2/FE-2	—	—	—	—	—	—	3.5	3.5	—	—	—	—	—
FA	—	—	—	—	—	—	2.7	2.7	3.2	—	—	—	—
EM	—	—	—	—	—	—	—	—	—	—	—	3.2	2
FG-20	—	—	—	—	—	—	—	—	—	—	—	3.2	2
FG	—	—	—	—	—	—	—	—	—	—	—	3.2	1.5
F2 H	—	—	4-5	4-5	2.5-4	—	—	—	—	10	—	—	—

Together with the Nikon FA, another member of this family of motor drives was introduced. It can easily be recognized from the two models mentioned before by its sharply cornered grip and was designed specially for the FA.

When used with the MD-11 and MD-12 the camera is released mechanically by a pin which springs upwards, whereas in the case of the MD-15/FA combination this is done electronically. That is the reason why this unit is capable of a maximum firing-rate of up to 3.2 frames/sec., whereas with the MD-11/MD-12 motor-drives the FA only manages 2.7 frames/sec. Another feature of the MD-15 is that it also supplies the camera with the necessary power. If the FA is used always with the motor mounted the batteries in the camera body become redundant. Although

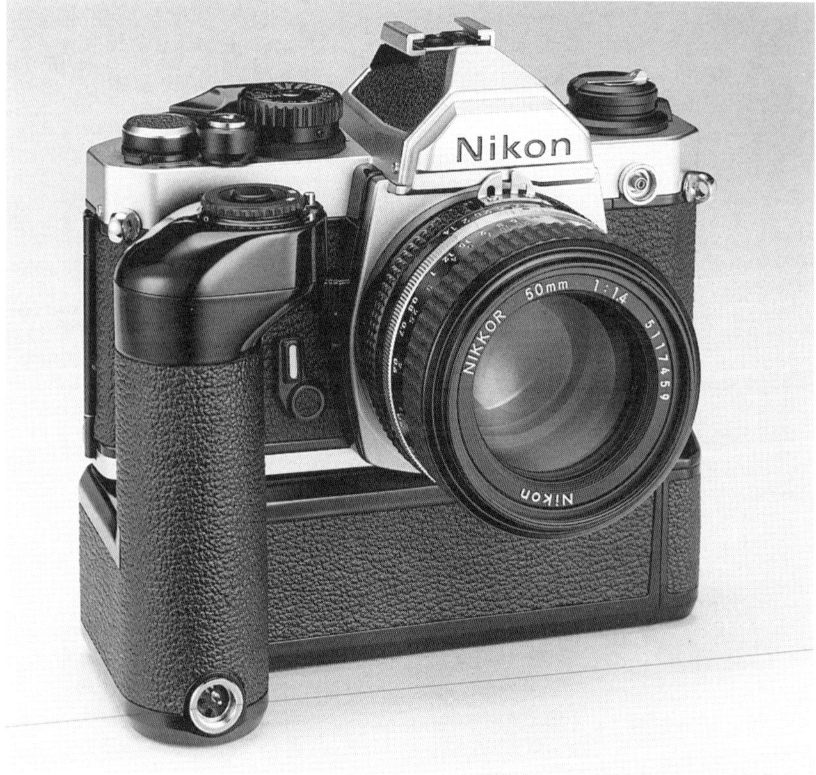

The FM-2 with the nimble MD-12 was also very popular with photojournalists.

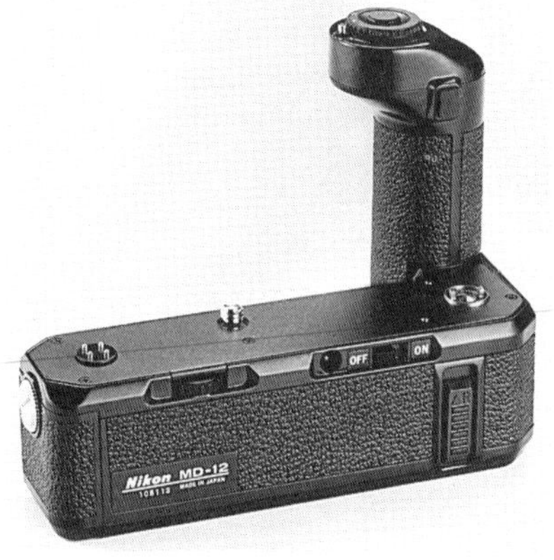

The MD-12, capable of 3.5 f.p.s.

Nikon Motor-drives

Motor-drive/ camera	Operating modes[1]	Firing rates (frames/sec.)	Battery compartment	Battery holder	Type of recharge-able battery	AC/DC converter	Rewind time (Sec.)	Capacity (No. of films)	Remote cord	MT[2] MW[2]	Film counter	Weight (g)	Dimensions in mm (BxHxT)
F-36	S/C	4/3/2.5/2	kabellos	—	—	MA-2/4	—	15	+	–	+		147x127x65
F-36	S/C	4/3/2.5/2	Standard	—	—	MA-2/4	—	20	+	–	+		147x80x38
MD-1	S/C	5/4.3/3.8 2.5/1.3	MB-1	MS-1	2x MN-1	MA-2/4	7	50	MC-1/10	+	+	710	147x148x78
MD-1	S/C	4/3.5/3/2/1	MB-2	MS-2	—	MA-2/4	7	30	MC-1/10	+	+	710	147x148x78
MD-2	S/C	5/4.3/3.8/ 2.5/1.3	MB-1	MS-1	2x MN-1	MA-2/4	7	50	MC-1/10	+	+	710	147x148x78
MD-2	S/C	4/3.5/3/2/1	MB-2	MS-2	—	MA-2/4	7	30	MC-1/10	+	+	710	147x148x78
MD-3	S/C	4	MB-1	MS-1	2x MN-1	MA-2/4	—	100	MC-10	+	+	595	147x148x72
MD-3	S/C	2.5	MB-2	MS-2	—	MA-2/4	—	80	MC-10	+	+	595	147x148x72
MD-100	S/C	10/7.5/6/ 3.5/3	MB-100	4x MS-1	4x MN-1	—	6	80	MC-10	+	+	960	147x185x77
MD-4	S/C	3/2/1 (with MK-1)	—	MS-3	MN-2	MA-2/4	4.5-8	60-140	MC-12A	+	+	480	146.5x115x71
AW-1	S	—	—	—	6xMN-1	—	—	150	—	–	–	280	145x40x35
MD-11	S/C	3.5	—	+	8xMN-1	—	—	100	MC-10	+	–	410	144x109x68
MD-12	S/C	3.5	—	+	8xMN-1	—	—	100	MC-10/12	+	–	410	144x109x68
MD-15	S/C	3.5	—	MS-4	8xMN-1	—	—	70	MC-12A	+	–	390	147x99x73
MD-E	C	2	—	—	—	—	—	50	—	–	–	185	132x32(82)x46
MD-14	C	3.2/2	—	MS-4	8xMN-1	—	—	50	—	–	–	350	140x92x64
F-301	S/C	2.5	MB-3/4	—	—	—	—	60 MB-4/ 180 MB-3	MC-12A	+	+	3)	—
F-401 (S)	S	—	—	—	—	—	25	50	—	–		3)	—
F-501	S/C	2.5	MB-3/4	—	—	—	—	30 MB-4/ 120 MB-3	MC-12A	+	+	3)	—
F-601 F-601 M	S; CL; CH	2/1.2	—	—	—	—	26	75	AR-3	–	–	–	—
F-801	S/C	3.3/2	—	MS-7	—	—	15	120	MC-12A	+	+	3)	—
F-90	S;CL;CH	3.6/2	DB-6	MS-8	4xMN-1	—	15	75	MC-20	+	+	–	—
F4	S; CL; CH; CS	4/3.3/0.8	MB-20	—	—	—	8	30	AR-3	–	+	–	—
F4 S	S; CL; CH; CS	5.7/3.4/1	MB-21	—	—	—	8	90	MC-12A	+	+	–	—
F4 E	S; CL; CH; CS	5.7/3.4/1	MB-23 (DB-6)	MS-23	MN-20	MA-4	8	150	MC-12A	+	+	–	—

[1] S = single; C = continuous; CL = continuous low; CH = continuous high; CS = continuous silent

[2] MT = Intervalometer; MW = Wireless remote control set

[3] One AA-Battery weighs approx. 20g.

the MD-11/MD-12 motors can be fitted to the FA, the other way around – a combination of the MD-15 with the FM or FE – will not work.

Motor-drives for EM, FG and FG-20

The EM family also includes a small motor drive, the MD-E. This midget weighs a mere 185g and is reminiscent of the Nikkormat winder AW-1 and has a permanent continuous mode at 2 frames/sec. The MD-E does not have grip, but instead a ridge which offers acceptable handling for the camera/motor combination. The small MD-E can also be used on the FG and FG-20, even though another motor drive was introduced for the FG, the MD-14. That is capable of driving all three bodies of this camera series up to a rate of 3.2 frames/sec., which means that it is not surpassed by its bigger brothers MD-11, 12, and 15 in any respect, it can also be set to 2 frames/sec. The higher speed has to be paid for in terms of weight – twice that of the MD-E. Although it is equipped with a grip it does not

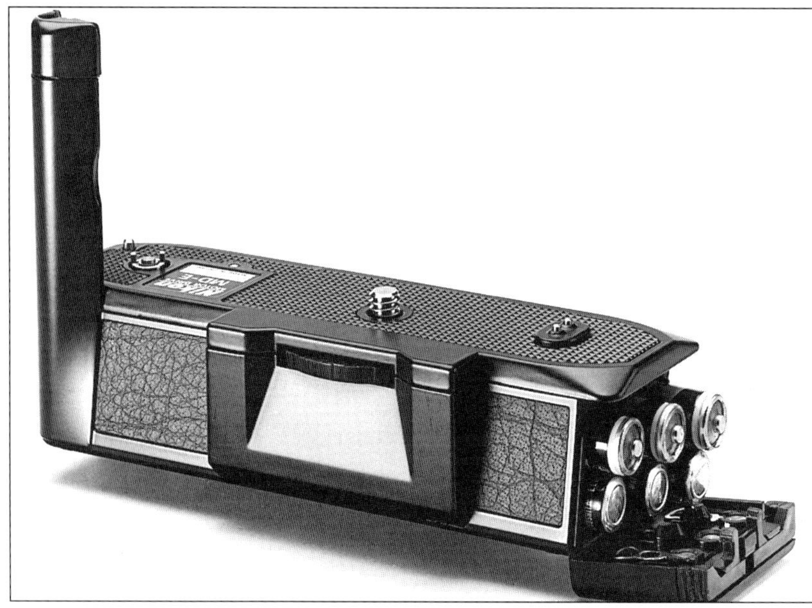

The "people's Nikon" can also offer motorized film winding: the MD-E for the EM.

possess a release button, so one must get accustomed to the handling of the combination. As in the case of the MD-E, no remote control accessories can be attached.

Motor Drive Accessories

Both the F and F2 motor drives and their corresponding power supplies were separate units. For later cameras they were all in one body. In the F4 there was a return to the original concept. With the F-36 for the Nikon F, the photographer can choose between an external or a cordless attachable battery pack with an integrated grip section. The 15 Volt battery pack MB-1 and the 12 Volt unit MB-2 are available for the F2 motor drives.

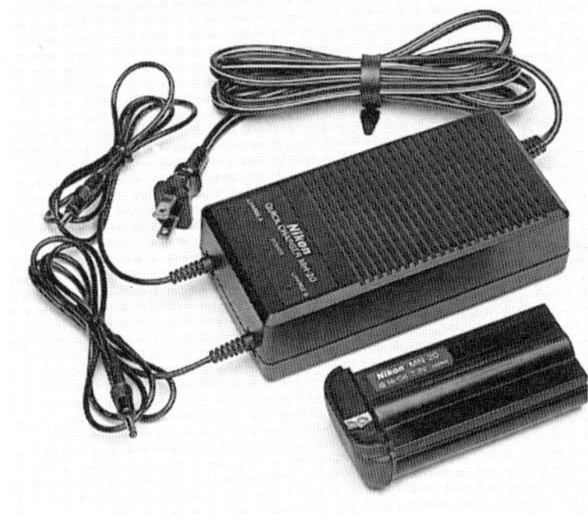

The Quick Charger MH-20 and the NC-battery MN-20 as a high-power energy supply for the F4.

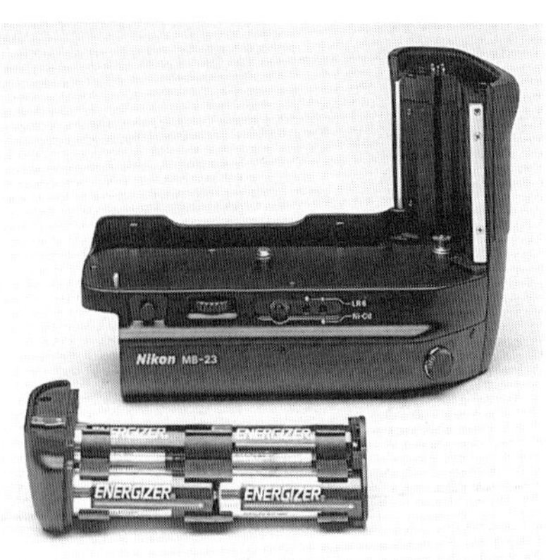

Quick exchange of the power supply thanks to the Battery Pack MB-23.

The more powerful MB-1 can be loaded with two of the rechargeable NC-batteries MN-1 of 7.5v each, which in turn makes the Quick Charger MH-1 necessary. For extreme low temperatures the Battery Pack Jacket MA-3 can help. It takes the battery compartment MB-1 which is connected to the motor by a cord.

The F3 motor drive MD-4 is loaded with the NC-unit MN-2 which can be recharged with the MH-2. In the case of the F4 the photographer can choose between four different power supply sources. The battery grip MB-20 with its four AA-size cells is standard equipment. The F4S is equipped with the two-piece battery compartment MB-21 that can be loaded with six batteries or rechargeable units of the same size. Unlike the MB-20, it has an additional remote control terminal and a second release button for vertical shots. The third unit, MB-22, serves as a terminal for external power sources such as the AC/DC Converter MA-4 and possesses an additional socket for the magazine back MF-24. The battery pack introduced last is called MB-23. Its one-piece body was designed for quick changes in professional applications. It can be operated with the high-power rechargeable NC-battery MN-20, two of which can be loaded simultaneously with the MH-20.

The AC/DC Converter MA-4 is available for static operation of the F-models. It supplies the camera with a steady 15 volts and possesses an additional terminal for the DS-type aperture control attachments.

Remote Control Units

Over the years several different remote control accessories for motorised cameras have been offered by Nikon. The most important of these are described below.

MC-12A. A 3m-long remote control cord with a handgrip and a two-step switch that activates the exposure meter when pressed halfway. It can be

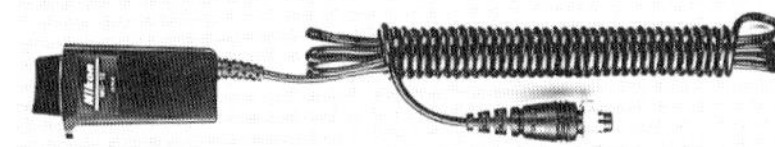

The Remote Control Cord MC-12A.

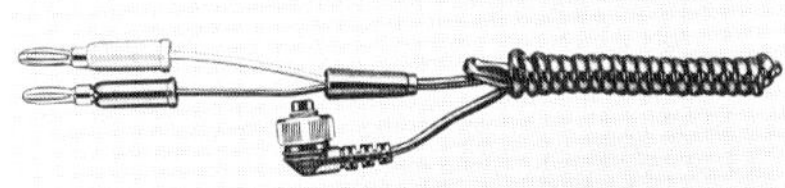

The Remote Control Cord MC-4A.

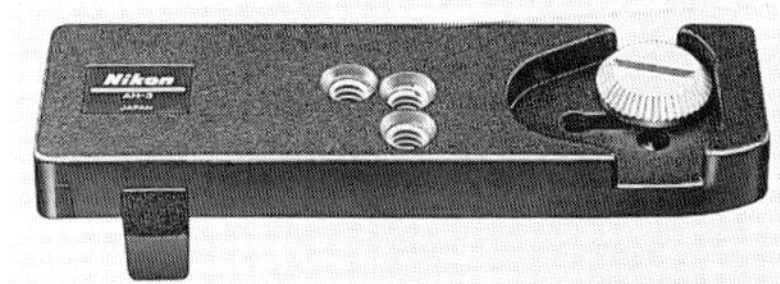

The Tripod Adaptor AH-3.

used with all modern cameras and motor drives as of the MD-12 (1980). The previous model MC-10 is necessary for the motor-drives MD-2/3/11.

MC-4A. A 1m-long remote control cord with banana-type plugs for individually constructed release mechanisms, for example with several cameras or with automatic triggering devices. The camera is released by shorting the two pins.

MR-3. A release button that allows the use of a cable-type release with the motor drive. The new ten-pin remote-control accessories introduced with the F90 are described in the appropriate section of the book.

AH-3. An adaptor which places the tripod thread directly beneath the lens axis, useful because in the case of most motors and cameras such as the F-501/301 their tripod bush is situated on the far right side. The AH-3 brings the camera into a central position when shooting from a tripod or a reproduction stand and so results in better balance.

Besides the direct connection it is also possible to release a camera without a cord connection. Nikon offers two accessories for this purpose. The most popular method was represented by the two-channel ML-1, a remote control set which works with a modulated light output signal and can cover a distance of up to 60m. Due to this method of operation with light no radio licensing authorities are involved. The ML-1 system consists of a receiver that can be mounted in the accessory shoe and connected to the camera's remote control terminal, and a transmitter. Single as well as continuous modes are possible. It was replaced by the ML-2 set in 1990 which operates with infra-red, has a range of up to 100m, and offers three instead of the ML-1's two channels. The ML-3 set was introduced with the F90 in 1992. It includes a feature many users had always missed: auto triggering, whereby the camera is automatically released whenever an object interrupts the – then continuously emitted – infrared light. Both components of the set are considerably smaller than the ML-2 parts because the ten-pin terminal of the F90 supplies the power for the receiver and two AA-size batteries suffice for the transmitter's reduced range of 8m.

The operation of the Radio Control Set MW-1/2 is not permitted in some countries. Depending on the weather conditions and the line of sight this unit can cover a distance between 150 and 700m and control up to three cameras individually or simultaneously.

Before multi-function backs were available, interval or time-lapse photography was only possible with the control units MT-1 and MT-2. Intervals between 0.5 seconds and 27 hours can be set with them, and the release signal duration can be set between 0.1 and 30 minutes.

Camera Backs

There are situations in which the normal 36 exposures allowed by a 35mm film are insufficient, for example in the case of surveillance or nature observation. The Leica Reporter which appeared in 1934 and was capable of 250 exposures was one of the first cameras to be equipped with a bulk film magazine. It had special cassettes, holding up to 10 motres of film, which had to be loaded by the user. The present-day bulk film backs still work on this principle.

Camera Backs For Bulk Film

Nikon reacted to calls for this kind of accessory very early in the days of the Nikon F, for which a combination of motor drive and bulk film back was provided. In the case of the F2 this led to the development of the MF-1. One of the motors MD-1 or MD-2 also have to be attached to the camera because they are needed as a power supply to turn the heavy film spools. Nikon offers a special bulk film loader for these MZ-1 cassettes. The MF-2, a second magazine back, was also available for the F2 which had a capacity of 750 exposures from a 30m film roll. In order to remove exposed sections of film a film cutter was built in.

A magazine back for 250 exposures called MF-4 is available for the F3. That for the F4 is named MF-24 and is still loaded with the MZ-1 film cassettes. The MF-24 is capable of more than just providing 250 exposures though: it is fitted with a multi-function unit with options exceeding by far those of a normal databack.

Databacks

The F2 Data, a special model within the F2-series, was the first Nikon which enabled the photographer to imprint the date, the time, and additional information onto the negative or the slide. A tiny flash unit lights up the display as well as the analogue clock, and a small mirror reflects this data into the picture frame. Small memo plates allow written information to be imprinted. This databack unit MF-10 was also available as an integral part of the magazine back which converted the unit

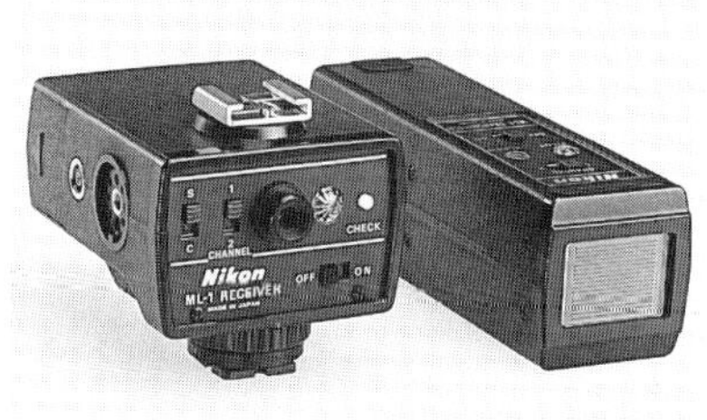

Shutter release up to 60m with near-infrared light: the Remote Control Set ML-1.

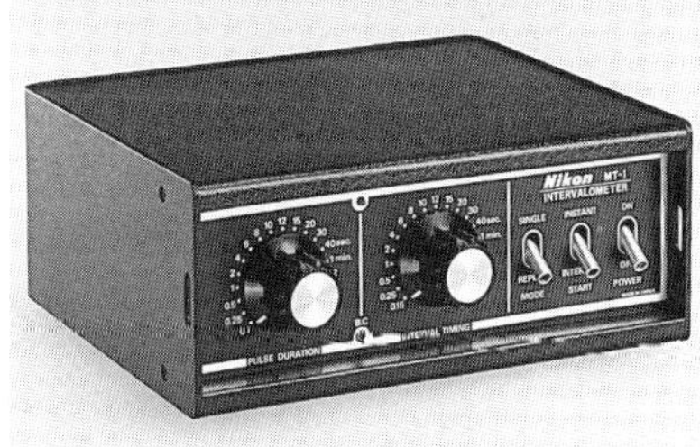

Shutter release within preset intervals of up to 27 hours: the Intervalometer MT-1/2.

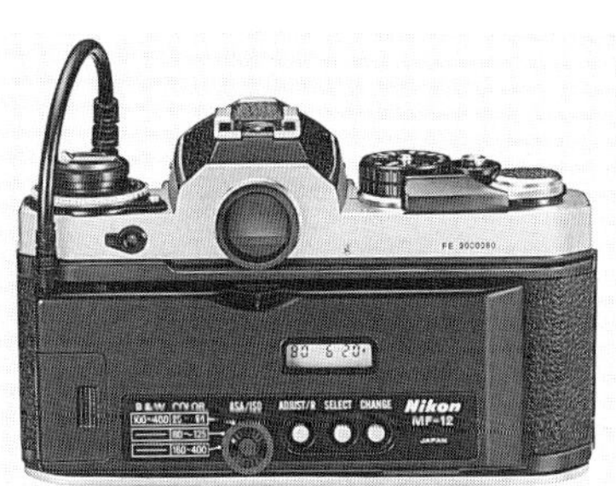

The first databack in the new, flat design: the MF-12 attached to an FE.

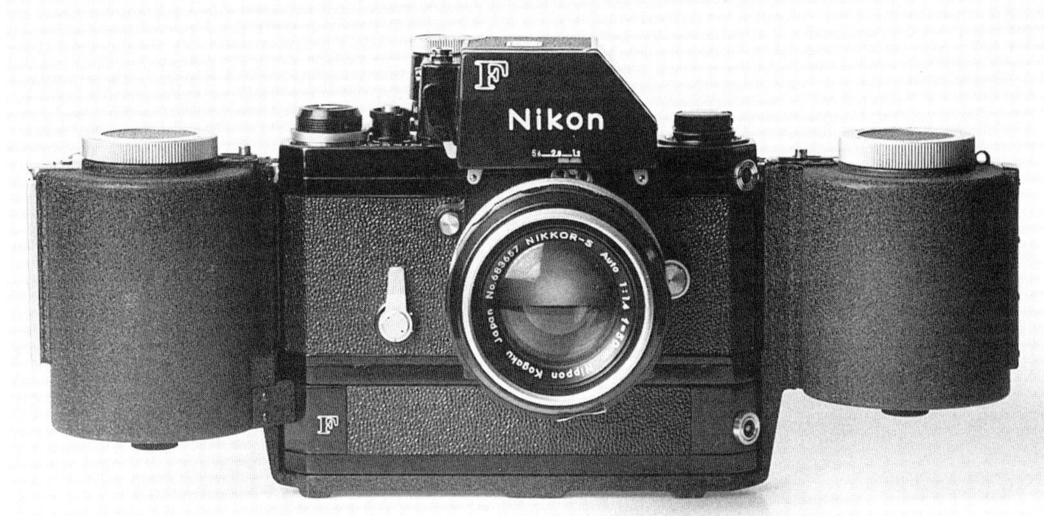

The first magazine back combined with a motor-drive: the F-250, an accessory for the Nikon F for 250 exposures.

into the MF-11. The corresponding model for the F3 is called MF-17.

Whereas these versions are quite large and heavy, the present databacks are only a few millimetres thicker than the camera back, in spite of their similar or even more numerous possibilities. This flat type of databack first appeared in 1981 in the form of the MF-12 for the Nikon FM and FE. The imprinting is facilitated by tiny LEDs situated in the pressure plate which expose the film from behind in an area 7mm wide and 0.5mm high. In order to ensure the synchronization of the shutter with the imprinting the cord from the back has to be connected to the camera's sync-terminal. Either year/month/day, or day/hour/minute, or a two-digit number can be imprinted in the picture. Two 1.5v mercury batteries of the same type used in the camera provide the power. The sensitivity of the film in use must be preset within the range of ISO 25/15° to 400/27° with the small dial,

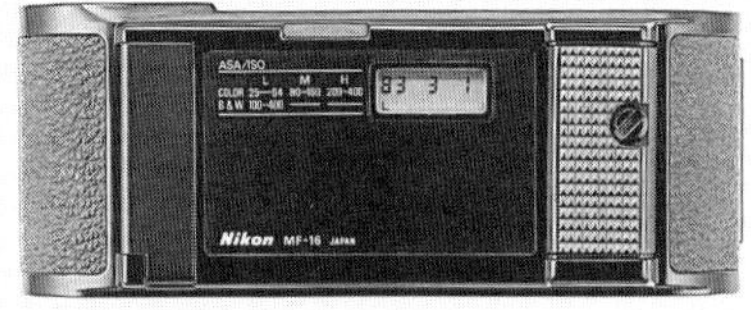

The MF-16 which operates without a sync-cord on the camera models FM-2, FE-2 and FA.

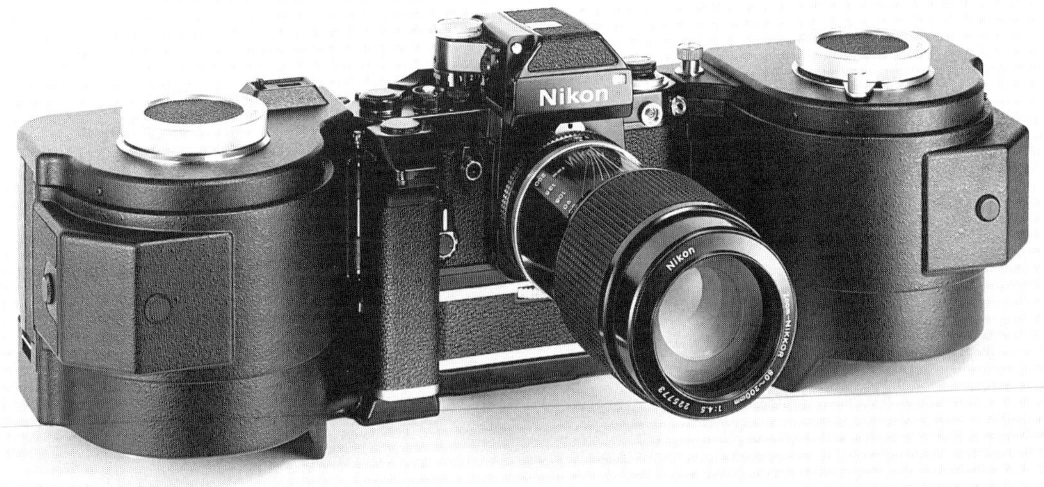

The awesome magazine back MF-2 for 750 exposures developed for the F2. It can be loaded with up to 30m of film.

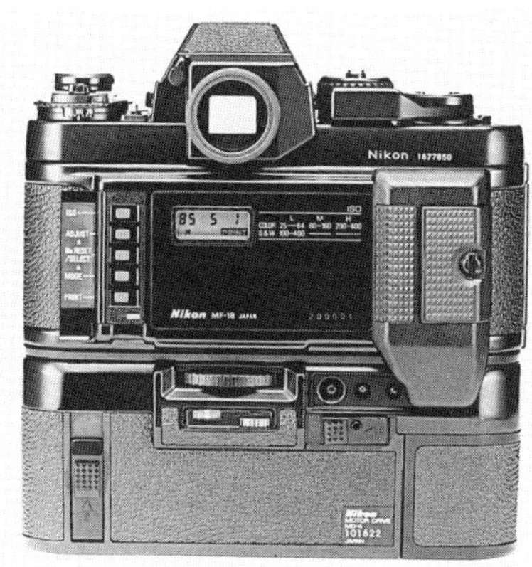
The databack attached to the F3.

Nikon Magazine Backs						
Model	Usable with	Maximum no. of frames	Firing rate	Dimensions (mm)	Weight (g)	Special features
F-250	F	250	4 B/Sec.	303x108x67	1250	Built-in motor-drive
MF-1	F2	250	5 B/Sec.	302x127x73	1250	
MF-2	F2	750	3.7 B/Sec.	425x144x129	4200	
MF-4	F3	250	6 B/Sec.	303x98x84	1100	
MF-24	F4	250	5.7 B/Sec.	303x89x91	1400	Integral data-back

since the imprinting level should neither be too strong nor too weak.

Nikon's next databack, the MF-14 for the F3, does not need a sync-cord because two gold contacts beneath the film guide rails connect the back to the body. This version also allows a sequential four-digit number to be imprinted while the integrated clock can even serve as an alarm-clock. Similar databacks were also available in the form of the MF-15 for the Nikon FG and the MF-16 for the FM-2, FE-2, and FA-models. The MF-18 for the F3 offers an additional function: although it is equipped with the same basic features and options as the MF-14, it imprints the data between the frames. Since this logically calls for absolutely steady transport of the film, this back can only be employed together with the motor-drive MD-4. The MF-18 also replaces the stop back MF-6B's function when the film is being rewound by the motor.

Multi-Control Backs

The MF-19 for the F-301/501 represented the beginning of a new chapter in the history of databacks. It is not only able to imprint data but can also control the camera's operation in several ways. For one thing, intervals between two exposures of up to almost 100 hours can be set, on the other hand it can be programmed to release the shutter once or more often, for example every day, month, or year. Before that, the five-times as expensive intervalometer MT-1 had been necessary to do this.

These first multi-function backs were only the beginning. There are

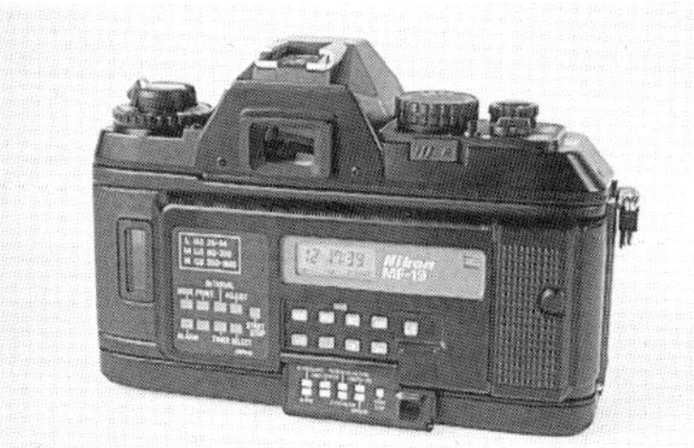
The very first multi-function back: the MF-19.

two different backs for the F-801 models. While the MF-20 only allows the time or the date to be imprinted, the MF-21 is really versatile. It is capable of anything the MF-19 can do, but also automatic exposure bracketing is available with up to 19 frames and compensation increments of ⅓ or ½ EV. The MF-21 also allows long exposures between one second and 100 hours to be programmed. But its main attraction is probably the freeze-focus mode. When the distance is preset manually with the F-801/s the shutter will be released automatically the moment the subject comes into the focused position.

The F4 can be fitted either with the MF-22 – corresponding to the MF-20 – or the MF-23 which is almost identical to the MF-21 for the F-801/s. The difference is that the MF-23 can also imprint the data between the frames. In addition it allows the centre frame of the bracketed exposures to be positioned freely.

The multitude of functions multi-function backs such as the MF-21 and MF-23 provide means their operational complexity is not far off that of home computer, yet it had all begun

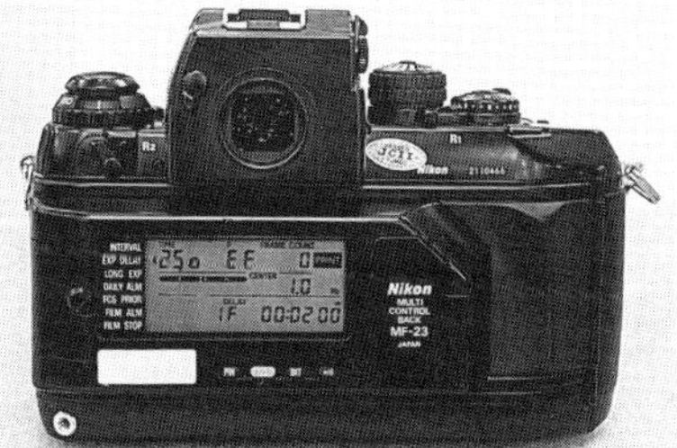
The F4 can be combined with several databacks. The MF-23 is shown here.

so simply – with the desire to imprint the date for the sake of memory. But if anyone had thought there were no more functions that could be added to these units they were proved wrong at the advent of the F90. The MF-25 is merely a world time data back whereas the MF-26 hosts even more unprecedented features such as flash exposure bracketing in addition to the normal mode, flash output compensation, and custom resetting. These controls extend further the photographer's scope to influence the picture according his imagination. In order to prevent the camera's top deck from becoming cluttered the multiple-exposure function was exiled to the MF-26. Since the F90, we must con-

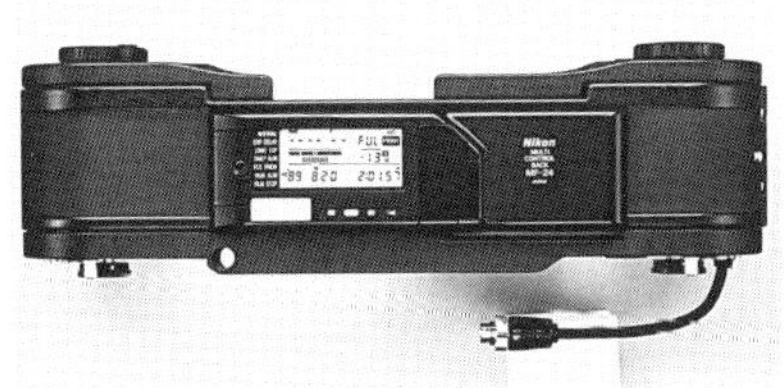
A multi-function back built into a bulk film magazine: the MF-24 for the F4.

Nikon Camera Data- and Multifunction-backs										
Model	Usable with	Type of display	ISO-range	Displayed data	Alarm clock	Internal timer	Battery capacity	Dimensions (mm)	Weight (g)	Special features
MF-10	F2	ANA	32-1600	YY/MM/DD; H/M/S; HS	–	–	3000 frames	176x60x69	400	Special data-back for the F-2 Data
MF-11	F2 + MF-1	ANA	32-1600	YY/MM/DD; H/M/S; HS	–	–	3000 frames	302x	650	Data-back unit for MF-1
MF-12	FM; FE	LED	25-400	YY/MM/DD H/M; Nr.	–	–	ca. 2 years	118x46x7	75	external battery pack DB-3 available
MF-14	F3	LED	25-400	YY/MM/DD; H/M; Nr.	+	–	ca. 1 year	148x53.5x26	85	
MF-15	FG	LED	25-400	YY/MM/DD; H/M; Nr.	+	–	ca. 1 year	136x53.5x26	85	
MF-16	FM-2 FE-2; FA	LED	25-400	YY/MM/DD; H/M; Nr.	+	–	ca. 1 year	142x53x26	90	
MF-17	F3 + MD-4	ANA	32-1600	YY/MM/DD; H/M/2; HS	–	–	3000 frames	299x69x78	650	Data-back unit for MF-4
MF-18	F3 + MD-4	LED	25-400	YY/MM/DD; H/M; Nr.	–	–	ca. 1 year	148x69x30	100	Data is imprinted between the frames
MF-19	F-301; F-501	LED	25-1600	YY/MM/DD; H/M; Nr.	+	+	ca. 1 year	147x53x24	90	
MF-20	F-801	LED	32-1000	YY/MM/DD; DD/H/M	–	–	ca. 1 year	140x61x26	70	
MF-21	F-801	LED	25-3200	YY/MM/DD; DD/H/M; Nr.; Shutter/aper.	–	+	ca. 1 year	140x61x29	90	Further functions: automatic exposure bracketing; long exposures; freeze focus
MF-22	F4; F4 S	LED	32-3200	YY/MM/DD; DD/H/M	–	–	ca. 1 year	160x56x22	100	Data can be imprinted between the frames and/or into the picture; shutter speed/aperture or compensation factor can be imprinted
MF-23	F4; F4 S	LED	25-3200	YY/MM/DD; DD/H/M; Nr.; Shutter/aper. comp. factor	+	+	ca. 1 year	160x56x30	120	Data can be imprinted between the frames and/or into the picture; exposure delay; automatic exposure bracketing; film stop; long exposure; freeze focus; alarm function
MF-24	F4; F4 S	LED	25-3200	YY/MM/DD; DD/H/M; Nr.: Shutter/aper.; comp. factor	+	+	ca. 1 year	330x98x91	1400	Same as MF-23
MF-25	F-90(D)	LCD	25-3200	YY/MM/DD; DD/H/M; (world time) Nr; Shutter/aper.	+	–	ca. 1 year	140x61x29	80	
MF-26	F-90(S)	LCD	25-3200	YY/MM/DD; DD/H/M; Nr; Shutter/aper. comp. factor Flash exp. comp.; Flash bktg.	–	+	ca. 1 year	140x63x29	90	

sider a kind of "external multi-function back" as well: the Data-Link system with the Nikon Data Card and with an electronic organizer offers an almost infinite number of additional functions, the most important of which have been mentioned in the description of the F90.

Nikon Close-Up Accessories

For many enthusiasts close-up or macrophotography is one of the most interesting subject areas of all. The 35mm SLR is particularly well suited for it because the numerous accessories which are necessary remain reasonably priced, whereas larger formats call for considerable investment.

The decisive factor in macrophotography is the reproduction ratio, which in turn determines several further values. It defines the size at which a subject will be recorded on

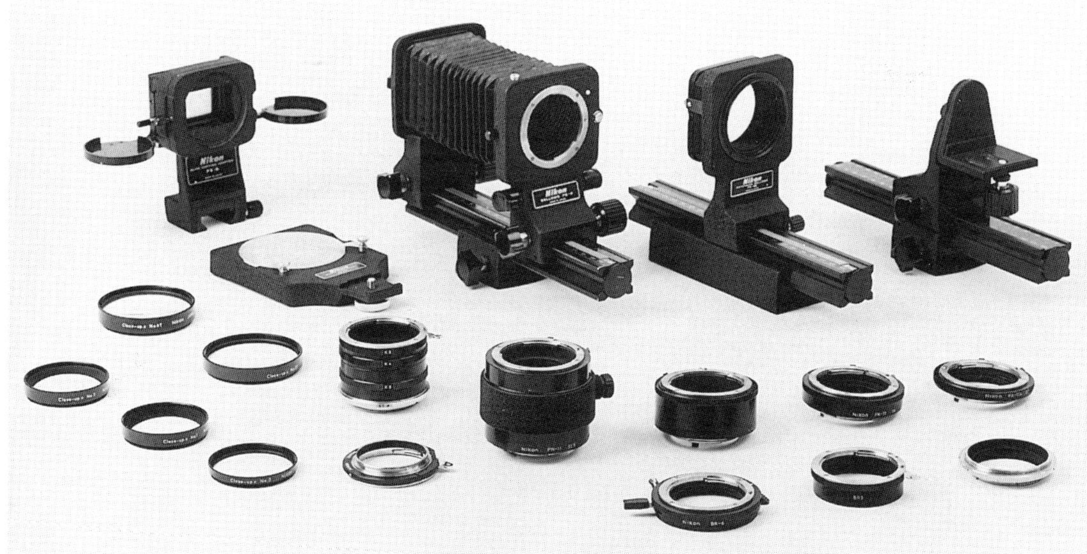

Close-up accessories ranging from the simple to the complex; from a close-up lens to the bellows attachment.

the film in relation to the original. Therefore the reproduction ratio is always related to a given format, 24x36mm in the case of Nikon. For example, a reproduction ratio of 1:10 means the subject is actually 24x36cm large, 1:5 reduces it accordingly to only 12x18cm. The ratio 1:1 corresponds to life size. A helpful tip: if you cannot remember whether 2:1 represents half or twice the natural size, just replace the colon by a slash making it look like a fraction – and immediately everything becomes perfectly clear.

Extension rings of different lengths allow a choice of several close-up distances .

Almost all fixed focal length lenses can be set to reproduction ratios between 1:8 and 1:10 with no further accessories. Modern zoom lenses can achieve ratios up to 1:4 or 1:5 and sometimes even 1:3 with their so-called macro positions. Only the Micro-Nikkors, with optical designs optimized for macrophotography, are able to exceed them. The shortest focusing distance of all three results in a maximum ratio of 1:2 (half natural-size). With the PN- and PK-type automatic extension rings 1:1 becomes accessible. The 55mm, 60mm, and 105mm AF Micro-Nikkors are capable of achieving 1:1 without any extension rings. But let us enter the world of close-up photography with the least complicated type of accessory.

Close-Up Lenses

Close-up lenses, also known as supplementary lenses, are generally the least expensive, lightweight, and convenient means to reduce the closest focusing distance of the lens in use. They screw into the filter thread of the lens and have an effect similar to that of a far-sighted person's reading glasses. Low weight and moderate price however have to be paid for. Close-up lenses will not have been

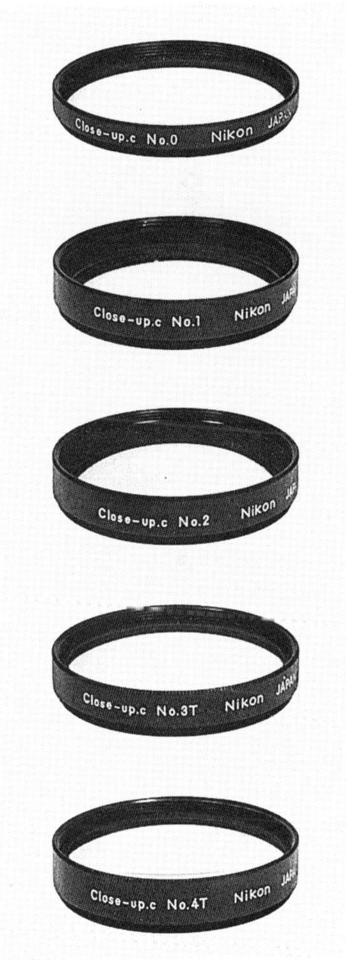

Close-up lenses available in different strengths are the cheapest entry to macrophotography.

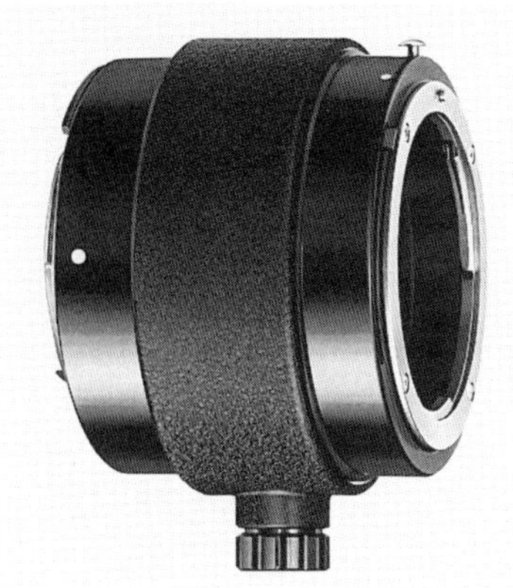

The automatic extension ring PN-11 which also serves as a 1:1 adaptor for the Micro-Nikkor 105mm.

taken into account in the optical design of the lenses to which they might be fitted, and so they do lead to a certain degree of deterioration in image quality. This is particularly noticeable at the corners of the frame where distortion and curvature of field are apparent. Often such reduction in image quality does not matter with natural subjects such as flowers, for example. One should never consider employing close-up lenses for reproductions though.

In the range of close-up lenses available from Nikon the model No.0 has the least dioptre power of 0,7. In combination with the 50mm lens the reproduction ratio can be improved from 1:9.6 to 1:7. The No.1 of 1.5 dioptres is next in the line and allows a ratio of 1:5.7. It is followed by No.2, whose 3 dioptres lead to a ratio of 1:4. Special two-element achromats give a better performance and are available for lenses with focal lengths from 50mm: the No.3T of 1.5 dioptres and No.4T of 2.9 dioptres. The possible ratios are the same as with the simpler versions but the resulting image quality is considerably better.

All of the close-up lenses mentioned up to now are designed for the 52mm-thread common to many Nikkors. Zooms with their filter thread size of 62mm can be fitted with two models corresponding to the Nos. 3T and 4T. As a rule of thumb: the longer the focal length, the stronger the magnification. Close-up lenses can also be used in combination with each other, but it is advisable only to do so with the T-models. Of course all the close-up lenses are NIC-multicoated just like the lenses themselves.

Extension Rings

Reproduction ratios larger than those possible with close-up lenses can be reached with extension rings mounted between the camera body and the lens. These are available in several different lengths and substantially reduce the closest focusing distance of the lens in use. They can be purchased separately or as a set. As a rule the effect becomes stronger the shorter the focal length of the lens in use.

Nikon presently offers four automatic extension rings of differing lengths: PK-11A at 8mm, PK-12 at 14mm, PK-13 at 27.5mm, and PN-11. at 52.5mm. The latter is also the 1:1. adaptor for the Micro-Nikkor 105mm. Since, depending on the lens mounted, the combination may become somewhat unstable, the relatively long PN-11 has its own tripod bush. All Nikon extension rings preserve the automatic diaphragm function as well as full aperture metering within the AI-system, while the previous models, PK-1/2/3 and PN-1, were equipped for the non-AI pin and prong system used until 1977.

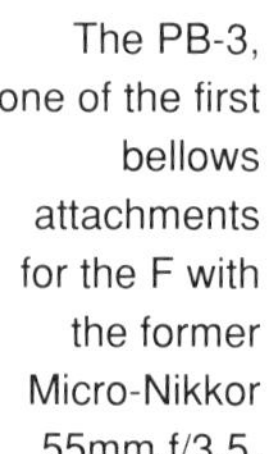

The PB-3, one of the first bellows attachments for the F with the former Micro-Nikkor 55mm,f/3.5.

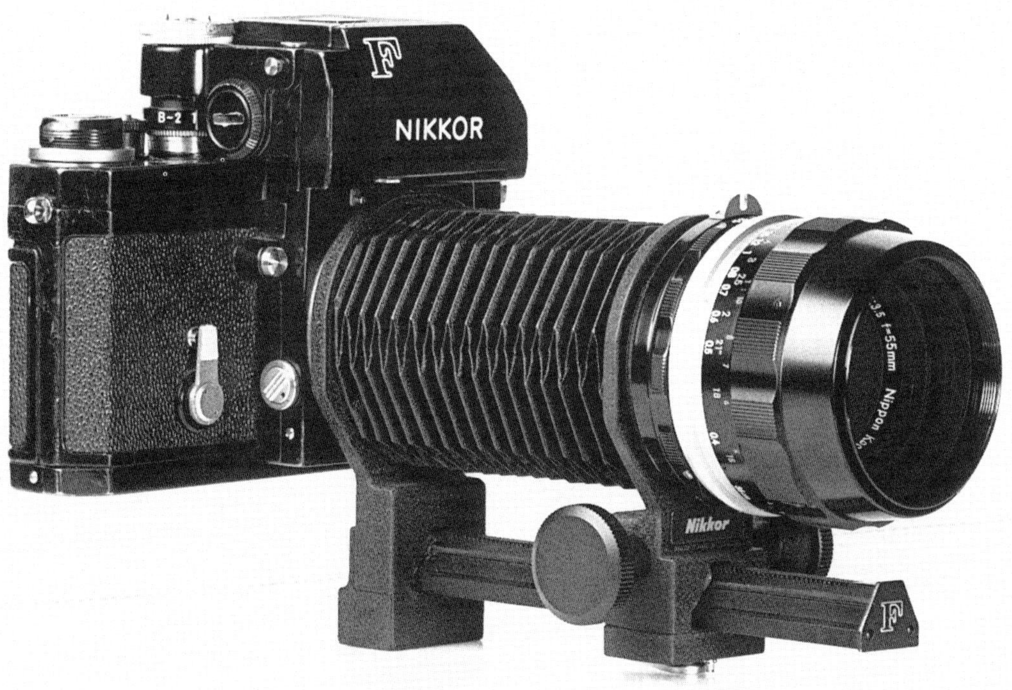

Autofocus extension rings are not available yet and probably cannot be expected in the near future. A modified ring called PK-11A which succeeded the model PK-11 was introduced shortly after the beginning of the autofocus era. It avoids the danger of damaging the autofocus electrical contacts, but otherwise is similar to the others.

Before the age of the PK-rings only two models were available, without an automatic diaphragm function – instead the PK-2's predecessor, the smaller E2-ring, had to be operated with a cable release to do this. Prior to the longer model PK-3, an M2-ring was available. Nikon also offered the K-type extension ring set until the beginning of the 80's. It consisted of a camera bayonet ring, plus three extension tubes with no mechanical transmission elements between the body and lens. Extensions between 5.8 and 46.6mm can be created with these rings.

Here are some examples of the reproduction ratios possible with the automatic extension rings in combination with a 50mm-lens which is capable of up to 1:7 on its own: 1:3.3 with PK-11A, 1:2.4 with the pk-12, 1:1.5 with PK-13, and 1.1:1 with PN-11.

One of the general advantages of extension rings is that the image quality remains virtually unchanged, but on the other hand there is a loss of light depending on the amount of extension – approximately one stop in the case of the PK-13. Another disadvantage is that they reduce the standard of the lenses used to that of the AI-system. This naturally limits their possibilities in connection with modern Nikon cameras such as the F4 and F90. Matrix Metering would come in quite handy in the case of moderate reproduction ratios.

Bellows Attachments

Bellows units offer applications beyond what is possible with rigid extension rings. Longer extensions are possible and there is the advantage of continuously variable reproduction ratios. Nikon's first bellows unit was introduced in 1958 for the rangefinder cameras and was only usable with a reflex-mirror box.

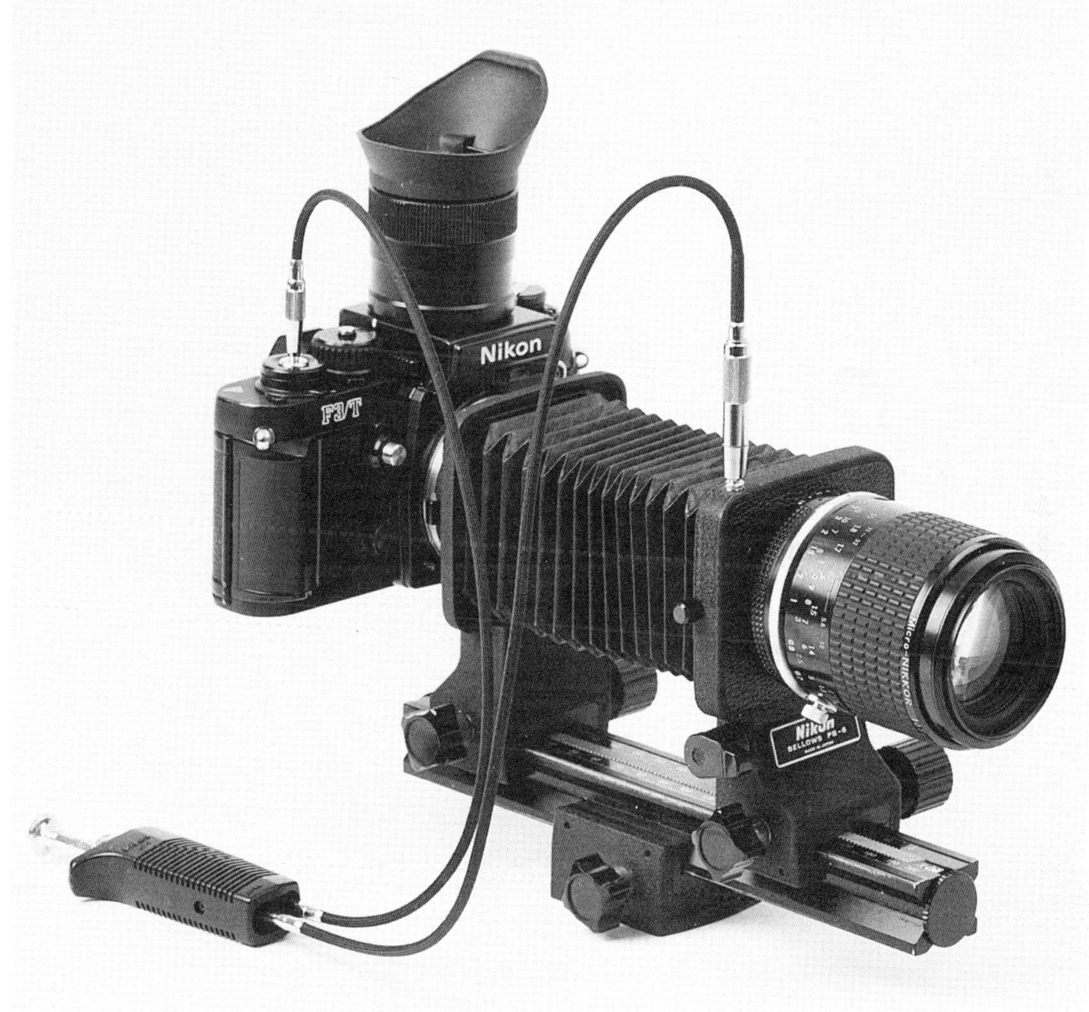

F3 T with the 6x Magnification Finder DW-4, the Bellows Attachment PB-6, and the Micro-Nikkor 105mm,f/2.8.

Versions for the Nikon F were introduced at the same time as the camera. The first was the Model II with a variable extension from 52mm to 132mm. The successor was designated PB-3 and offered a range of 33mm to 142mm as well as an improved tripod mount. By the time the PB-4 had arrived it was legitimate to speak of a bellows system, which included slide copying adaptor PS-4. Duplicates can be made with this from framed slides as well as from uncut strips of film. The bellows unit itself is a precision instrument. Not only can the front lens panel be adjusted but also the independently movable camera panel along with the mounted body. All this within the remarkable range of 43mm to 185mm giving impressive magnifications. The twin-rail design is fitted with a tripod bush on its bottom section. This allows the complete bellows unit to be moved back and forth even if it is mounted on a tripod – a very important feature that greatly reduces the difficulty of changing the composition, because otherwise the whole assembly, including the tripod, would have to be moved. That is still not all though: the front panel can be shifted just as with large format cameras – horizontally as well as vertically up to 10mm and even a vertical swing up to 25° is possible. But understandably this unit does have its price, which is why an "economy" version was added in the form of the PB-5, which is technically similar to the PB-3 but retains the PB-4's 43mm to 185mm extension range. A mixture of the PB-3 and PB-4, so to speak, which allowed the slide copying adaptor PS-5 for framed 35mm slides to be attached.

The currently available bellows unit is called PB-6. With the exception of the tilt and shift of the front panel, it offers the same facilities as the PB-4. Its panels are mounted on a double dovetail rail within an extension range of 48mm to 208mm. In case that is not sufficient, this range can be enlarged to 83mm to 438mm with the help of the Extension Unit PB-6E which will lead from macro- to microphotography. Together with a 20mm-lens this amount of extension allows a maximum reproduction ratio of 23:1. For users of bellows unit/camera/motor-drive combinations a spacer-piece PB-6D is available in order to raise the panels.

The Copy Stand PB-6M can be attached to the double dovetail rail for small subjects and two clips hold the subject securely in place. Either a white opaque acrylic or a grey-painted aluminium plate with a reflectivity of 18% can serve as a baseplate. The matching slide copying adaptor for the PB-6 is designated PS-6. It can be shifted up to 6mm in any direction, thus permitting slight corrections to composition.

None of the Nikon bellows attachments possess the couplings necessary for automatic diaphragm function and full aperture metering. If you prefer to preserve this convenience a double cable release will

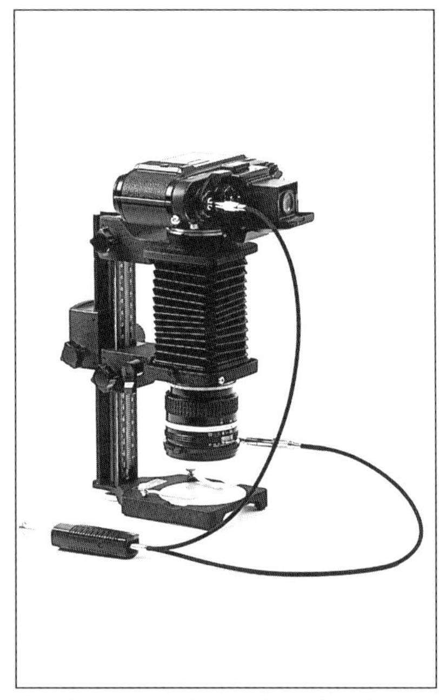

The PB-6M Macro Copy Stand.

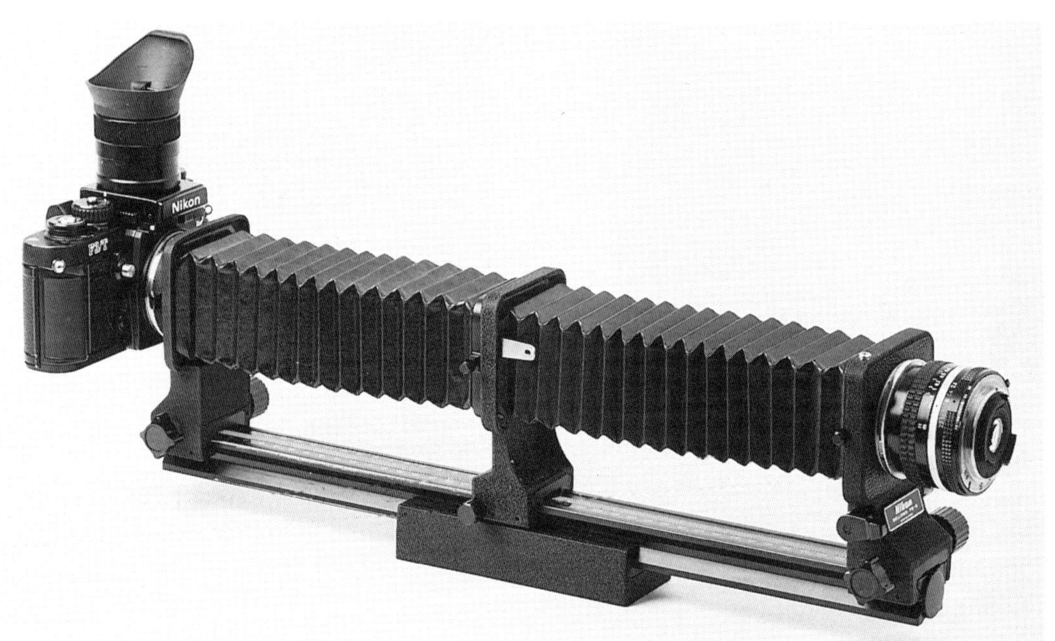

A venture into the realm of extreme micro-photography: the Bellows Unit PB-6 with the Extension Unit PB-6E attached.

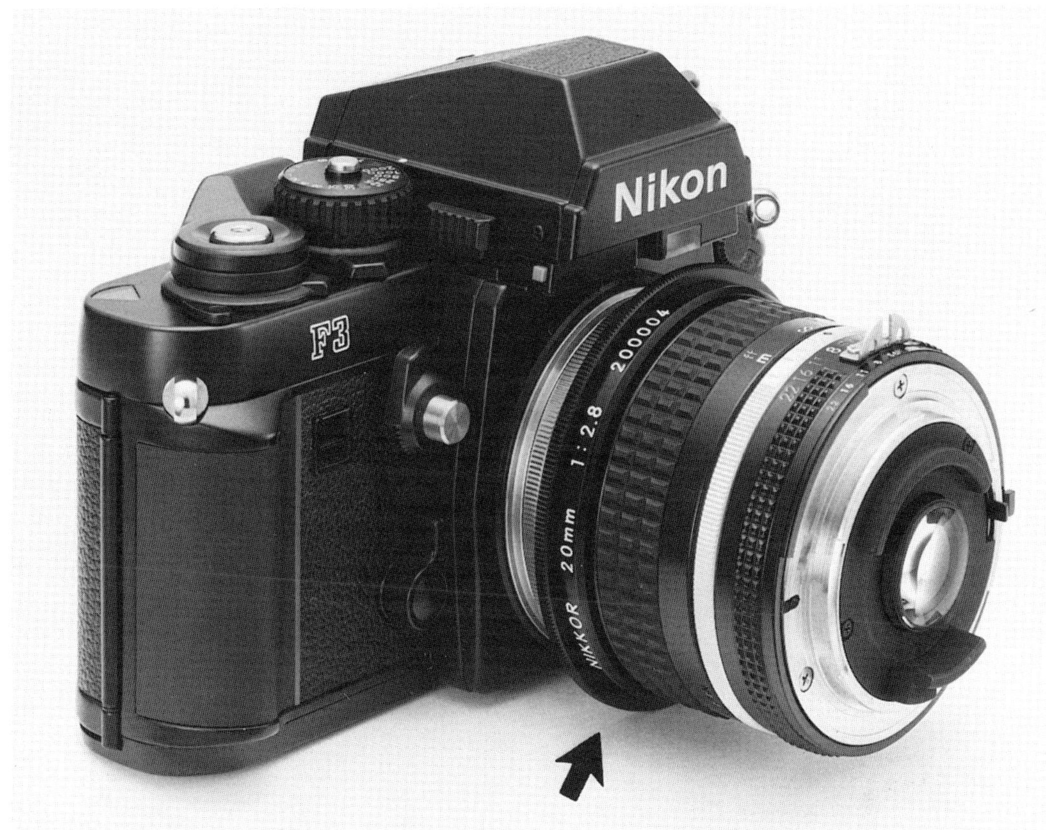

Together with the retro-ring BR-5, the 20mm,f/2.8 wide-angle permits extremely short focusing distances.

have to be employed in order to secure simultaneous operation. The AR-4 version is available for Nikon cameras whose shutter release button is fitted with the Leica-type male thread, the AR-7 for those with the ISO-type female thread, while the AR-10 is needed for motorized cameras. The first cable must be screwed into the camera while the second, marked by a red ring, is connected to the front panel of the PB-6 bellows unit. In the case of the older bellows units this also calls for the Auto Ring BR-4. The moment the plunger of the double cable release is pushed, the lens diaphragm is stopped down to the preset value and then the shutter is released. For optimum image quality at reproduction ratios larger than 1:1 it is advisable to reverse the lens to the retro-position, that is with its rear element pointing towards the subject. Due to their extremely short free working distances wide-angle lenses do not allow any other way. The Macro Adaptor Ring BR-2A is necessary to mount the lens to the front panel with its 52mm filter thread and the newer 20mm,f/2.8 super wide-angle demands the Auto Adaptor Ring BR-5 in addition. In order not to sacrifice the handling ease of the automatic diaphragm the Adaptor Ring BR-6 should also be mounted.

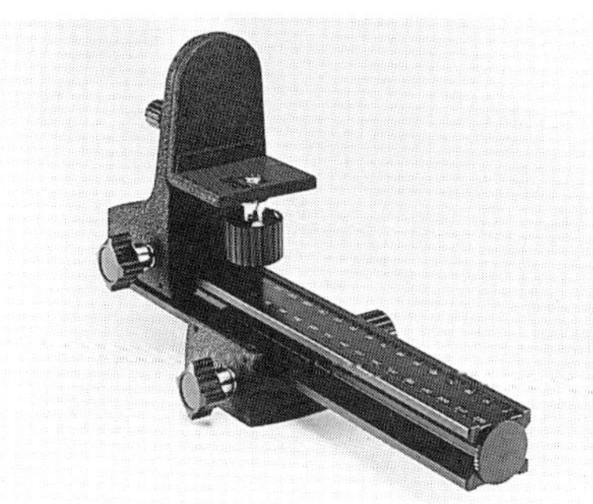
The independent focusing stage PG-2 allows quick adjustments to the focusing distance.

The normal Nikkors are not the only ones which can be employed in close-up photography. Thanks to their optical design, enlarging lenses are well-suited for the task too. In order to attach these with their usual 39mm-thread the special adaptor BR-15 becomes necessary. Even microscope lenses with their RMA-thread can be combined with the Nikon bellows units. They call for the use of both the

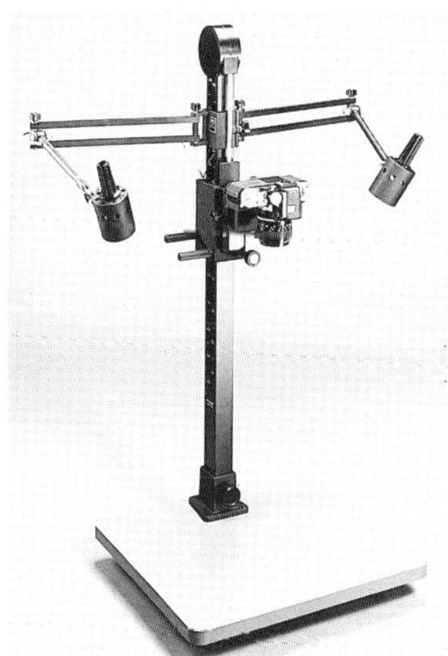
The Reproduction Stand PF-4 with a counterweight for the head is ideal for copying work.

Achievable reproduction ratios with different close-up accessories

Focal length	Lens alone		With supplementary lenses								With extension rings								With Reversing Ring BR-2A		With Bellows Unit			
			No. 0		No. 1/3/5		No. 2/4/6		No. 3/4		PK-11		PK-12		PK-13		PN-11				PB-6		+ PB-6E	
	A	E	A	E	A	E	A	E	A	E	A	E	A	E	A	E	A	E	A	E	A	E	A	E
20mm	1:11	20	1:70 – 1:9.5	150 – 18	1:33 – 1:8.5	67 – 15	1:17 – 1:7	34 – 12	—	—	1:2.6 – 1:2.1	3.3 – 2.5	1:1.5 – 1:1.3	1.1 – 1	—	—	—	—	3.2:1	4.4	4.5:1 – 11:1	3.8 – 3.5	5:1 – 23:1	3.8 – 3.4
24mm	1:8.7	20	1:60 – 1:8	150 – 18	1:27 – 1:7	68 – 16	1:14 – 1:5.5	34 – 13	—	—	1:3 – 1:2.3	6 – 4.4	1:1.7 – 1:1.3	2.8 – 2.4	1:1 – 1.2:1	0.8 – 0.7	—	—	2.5:1	4.6	3.6:1 – 9:1	4 – 3.6	3.6:1 – 19:1	4 – 3.5
28mm	1:7	20	1:50 – 1:6.5	150 – 18	1:23.5 – 1:6	68 – 16	1:12 – 1:4.7	34 – 13	—	—	1:3.6 – 1:2.4	10 – 7.2	1:2.1 – 1:1.6	6 – 5	1:1 – 1.1:1	3	1.7:1 – 1.9:1	1.5	2.2:1	5	3.2:1 – 7.5:1	4.2 – 3.7	3.2:1 – 15:1	4.2 – 3.5
35mm	1:5.5	20	1:40 – 1:5	150 – 18	1:19 – 1:4.5	68 – 16	1:9.5 – 1:3.7	35 – 14	—	—	1:4.5 – 1:2.5	16 – 9.5	1:2.6 – 1:1.8	9 – 6.5	1:1.3 – 1:1.1	4.5 – 4	1.4:1 – 1.6:1	2.2 – 2	1.6:1	6.2	2.1:1 – 5.8:1	4.7 – 4	2.1:1 – 12:1	4.7 – 3.6
50mm	1:6.7	35	1:6 – 1:2.7	150 – 42	1:5.7 – 1:13	68 – 23	1:6.5 – 1:3.5	33 – 18	1:4.4 – 1:2.7	30 – 15	1:6.4 – 1:3.3	34 – 19	1:3.7 – 1:2.4	20 – 14	1:1.9 – 1:1.5	10.5 – 9	1:1 – 1.1:1	6.2	1.1:1	10	1.5:1 – 4:1	7 – 4.6	1.5:1 – 8.6:1	7 – 4
85mm	1:8.1	75	1:5.3 – 1:16	150 – 60	1:8 – 1:4	68 – 47	1:4 – 1:2.5	45 – 35	1:2.7 – 1:1.9	34 – 30	1:10.5 – 1:4.5	95 – 45	1:6.3 – 1:3.5	56 – 35	1:3.1 – 1:2.2	31 – 25	1:1.7 – 1:1.4	19 – 17.5	—	—	1:2 – 2.5:1	21 – 9	1:1 – 5.2:1	14 – 7.1
105mm	1:8.3	88	1:5 – 1:13	153 – 70	1:6.4 – 1:3.5	80 – 53	1:3.2 – 1:2.2	46 – 40	1:2.2 – 1:1.6	35 – 32	1:13 – 1:5	144 – 60	1:7.5 – 1:4	85 – 48	1:3.8 – 1:2.6	46 – 35	1:2.1 – 1:1.7	28 – 25	—	—	1:2.5 – 2:1	30 – 12	1:1.2 – 4.3:1	20 – 9.2
135mm	1:7.5	115	1:10 – 1:4.6	155 – 85	1:5 – 1:3	80 – 60	1:2.5 – 1:1.7	50 – 45	1:1.7 – 1:1.2	37 – 35	1:17 – 1:5	240 – 85	1:9.6 – 1:4.5	145 – 73	1:5 – 1:3	80 – 56	1:2.7 – 1:2	51 – 43	—	—	1:3 – 1.5:1	52 – 23	1:1.5 – 3.8:1	35 – 19
180mm	1:8.2	163	—	—	—	—	—	—	—	—	1:22 – 1:6	420 – 125	1:13 – 1:5	250 – 108	1:6.5 – 1:3.5	135 – 84	1:3.5 – 1:2.5	80 – 63	—	—	1:3.7 – 1.2:1	83 – 31	1:2 – 2.5:1	51 – 23
200mm	1:7.4	185	1:7 – 1:3.2	160 – 102	1:3.3 – 1:2	83 – 64	1:1.7 – 1:1.2	51 – 48	1:1.1 – 1.2:1	40	1:25 – 1:6	530 – 150	1:14 – 1:5	320 – 130	1:7 – 1:3.7	180 – 110	1:4 – 1:2.6	115 – 88	—	—	1:4.3 – 1:1	120 – 52	1:2.4 – 2.4:1	80 – 42
300mm	1:10	300	—	—	—	—	—	—	—	—	1:37 – 1:8	1180 – 305	1:21 – 1:7	700 – 270	1:11 – 1:5.3	385 – 220	1:6 – 1:3.8	240 – 175	—	—	—	—	—	—
55mm Micro	1:2	10	1:26 – 1:1.9	141 – 10.5	1:12 – 1:1.7	70 – 9	1:6.2 – 1:1.5	35 – 9	—	—	1:7 – 1:1.5	38 – 5.1	1:4 – 1:1.3	22 – 7.8	1:2 – 1:1	11.5 – 6.1	1:1.1 – 1.4:1	6.1 – 4.3	1.1:1	10	1:1.4 – 3.8:1	6.5 – 1.6	1.3:1 – 8:1	4.3 – 0.8
105mm Micro	1:2	28	1:13 – 1:1.7	142 – 21	1:6.4 – 1:1.5	69 – 17	1:3.2 – 1:1.2	35 – 13	—	—	1:13 – 1:1.7	144 – 26	1:7.5 – 1:1.6	86 – 24	1:3.8 – 1:1.3	47 – 19	1:2 – 1:1	29 – 18	—	—	1:2.5 – 2:1	30 – 12	1:1.2 – 4.3:1	20 – 9.2
200mm Micro	1:2	49	1:7.1 – 1:1.5	142 – 37	1:3.4 – 1:1.2	68 – 29	1:1.7 – 1.2:1	35 – 21	—	—	1:25 – 1:1.8	510 – 46	1:14 – 1:1.7	300 – 45	1:7.3 – 1:1.5	160 – 40	1:4 – 1:1.2	96 – 37	—	—	1:4.3 – 1:1	120 – 52	1:2.4 – 2.4:1	80 – 42

A = maximum reproduction ratio E = shortest focusing distance (in cm)

mentioned BR-15 and the adaptor ring BR-16.

The bellows models PB-4 and PB-6 are equipped with integrated focusing stages so as to facilitate easier adjustment during difficult close-ups. Since this convenience is also desirable when working without a bellows unit, for example with extension rings, a separate focusing stage, the PG-2 is available.

Finally, the last Nikon accessory to be mentioned here opens up further close-up applications. The Slide Copy Lens attachment ES-1 can be screwed directly onto the 55mm Micro-Nikkor filter thread and enables you to produce 1:1 duplicates. In the case of the non-autofocus Micro-Nikkor the extension ring PK-13 is also necessary for this, while the 55mm,f/2.8 AF calls for the BR-5 adaptor ring.

General Accessories

Any SLR camera can only be as good as its system, and the Nikon system is one of unsurpassed comprehensiveness and adaptability. The value of a camera outfit can often be greatly enhanced by simple, but efficient accessories.

Neck Straps

Let us begin with a practical little thing, the indispensable neck strap. Whenever you come across the letters "AN" you will know they refer to a neck strap, while the following numerals describe the width and the material – leather or nylon mesh.

Cases

The neck straps are followed by the cases which are meant to protect the valuable equipment. Some critics have coined the expression "never-ready" case, and the use of such an accessory is indeed a matter of personal taste. It is difficult to see any special advantage in them. They can accommodate no accessories, only the body and a single lens.

Nikon offers various camera cases for every model with different front flaps for different focal lengths, and the occasional opening for the data-backs. Those designed especially for the camera bodies are designated "CF-xx" and are made of semi-soft leatherette material. All of the cases are black with the exception of those for the F3 and F4 which only come in a Bordeaux-red colour. In the days of the Nikon F and F2 hard cases called "CH-xx" were on offer too.

The CS-versions can be regarded as simple dust-protection accessories and are available for all the cameras

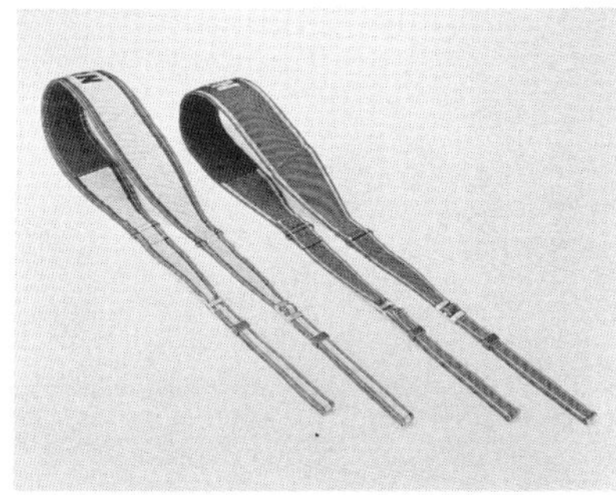

Nikon offers neckstraps with the prominent logo in different versions.

from the Nikkormat to the F3. They differ according to the focal lengths they can house. Two special ones deserve to be mentioned. The Speed Case CF-34 allows the camera to be carried face-down in a kind of holster like a pistol. Even lenses up to the 100-300mm zoom on the camera will fit. The other is the CS-13 which looks somewhat like an oversized boxing glove and is employed to reduce the motor's penetrating whining noise that can be very annoying in certain situations – an accessory for discrete photographers.

A number of compartment cases designated "FB-xx" which can accommodate complete outfits of different sizes are also available from Nikon. We will describe just one, the FB-8. This case has a metal baseplate onto which three bayonet lens mounts are attached. When its front side is swung open, it provides quick access to the lenses and also protects them well when being carried around. Too bad that except for the FM-2 and F3, none of the other current models fit into its camera compartment.

Pistol Grip

This is a very rarely used accessory. When it is screwed to the tripod thread the camera can be held safely with one hand. A trigger in the grip section serves as a release button that can either operate one of the special cables or short the contact for the MC-3A.

Cable Releases

Compatible cable releases are also available from Nikon. It is often a false economy to buy cheaper releases from other makers because the workmanship and the durability of the Nikon releases are superior. The AR-3 is the version with a conical thread, and the AR-2 the Nikon cable release with the male thread for the F and F2.

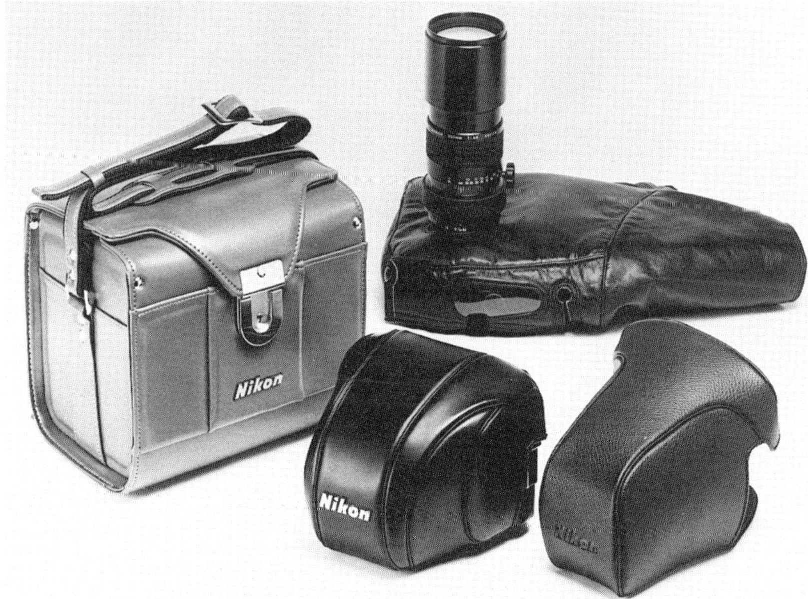

Camera and compartment cases for any purpose ensure safe storage as well as secure transportation.

Panorama Head

The Panorama Head AP-2 should not be forgotten. It is mounted on a tripod and permits slightly overlapping shots through 360°. It has click-stop settings for focal lengths from 28mm to 105mm.

Battery Holders

Since the introduction of the Nikkormat EL all of the succeeding cameras, except the FM and FM-2, have depended on battery power for almost all their functions. Therefore it always wise to have a set of fresh batteries to hand. Up until the F-301 with its built-in motor, the exposure metering systems were supplied with two 1.5v silver oxide or one 3v lithium cell to power their electronic shutters. These are especially vulnerable to extremely low temperatures. Even brand-new cells can be exhausted after only one film at a temperature of -10°C. Lithium batteries are less sensitive to cold, but this does not completely rule out worries as to their total breakdown.

Nikon offers external battery holders for certain camera models to overcome this problem. The DB-1 for the DS-type aperture control attachments was the first battery holder. It prolonged operation time by a factor of four with its four D-size cells. The battery holder DB-2 is intended for camera models EM to FG, F3, and FM to FA. It holds two AA-size batteries that can easily be kept warm underneath a coat or in a pocket and the terminal of its 50cm-long cord is screwed into the camera's battery compartment. The DB 3 was designed

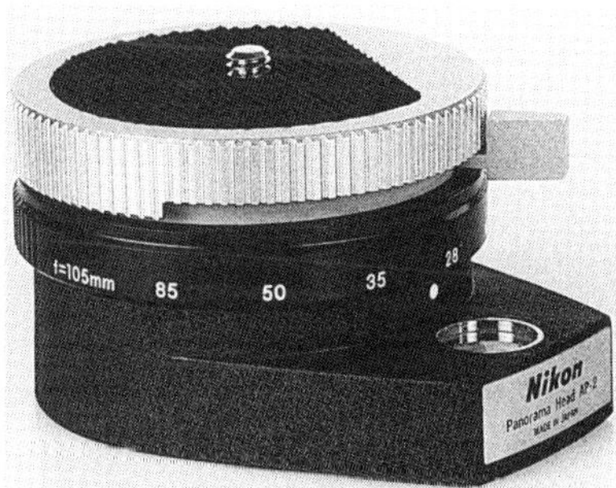

The Panorama Head AP-2 with its click-stops for different focal lengths provides a complete 360° view.

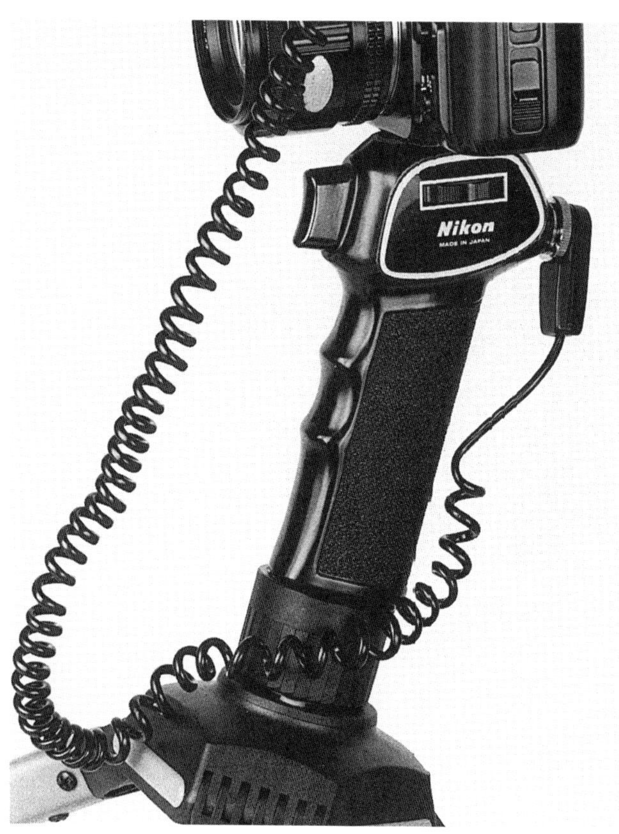

The Pistol Grip Model 2 with its trigger and the Connecting Cord MC-3A makes it easy to hold long focal lengths steady.

for the databack MF-12 and provides power from two AAA-size cells. The DX-1 finder of the F3 AF can be supplied from the DB-4 taking the same two AA-size batteries as the DB-2 to power the autofocus motor. The DB-5 substitutes the four AA-size cells in the F-801/s with one 6v lithium battery which can easily be kept warm close to one's body.

The much larger DB-6, introduced for the F4E but can also be used with the F90, ensures much longer operation thanks to its six D-size cells.

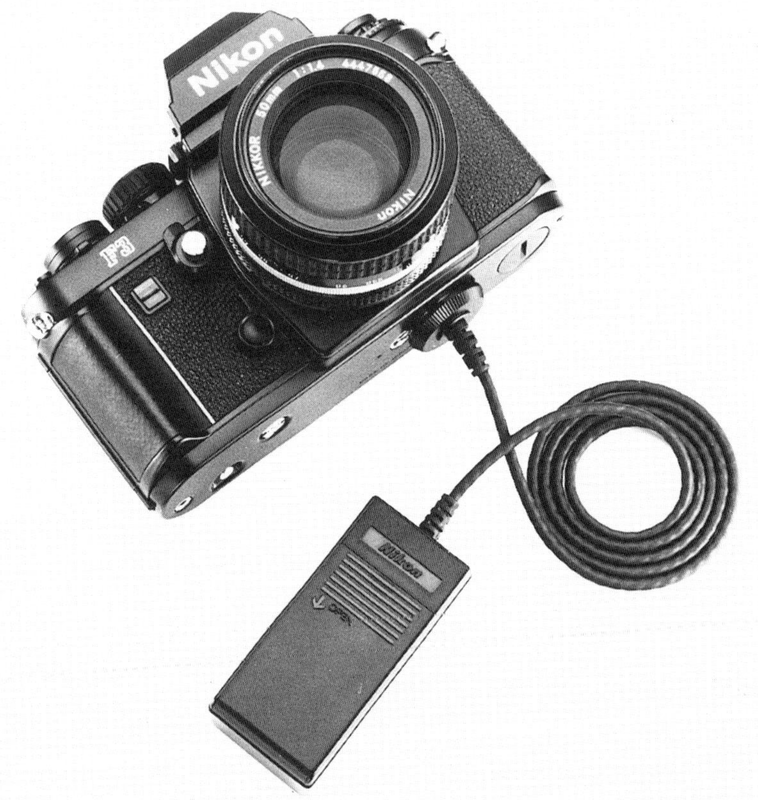

The external Battery Holder DB-2 ensures reliable operation even in extremely cold environments.

CHAPTER 8

The Speedlights

The desire to have an artificial source of illumination as an alternative to daylight is as old as photography itself. But it has to be a source that is intense enough to permit blur-free action shots. It started with devices in which a mixture of potassium nitrate and sulphur was ignited to produce a very bright flash of light. From about 1860 magnesium powder or strips were used: a quite dangerous practice which cost some photographers more than just their hair. The first commercially successful flash bulb, a magnesium strip sealed in a glass bulb filled with oxygen and ignited electrically, did not appear until 1929.

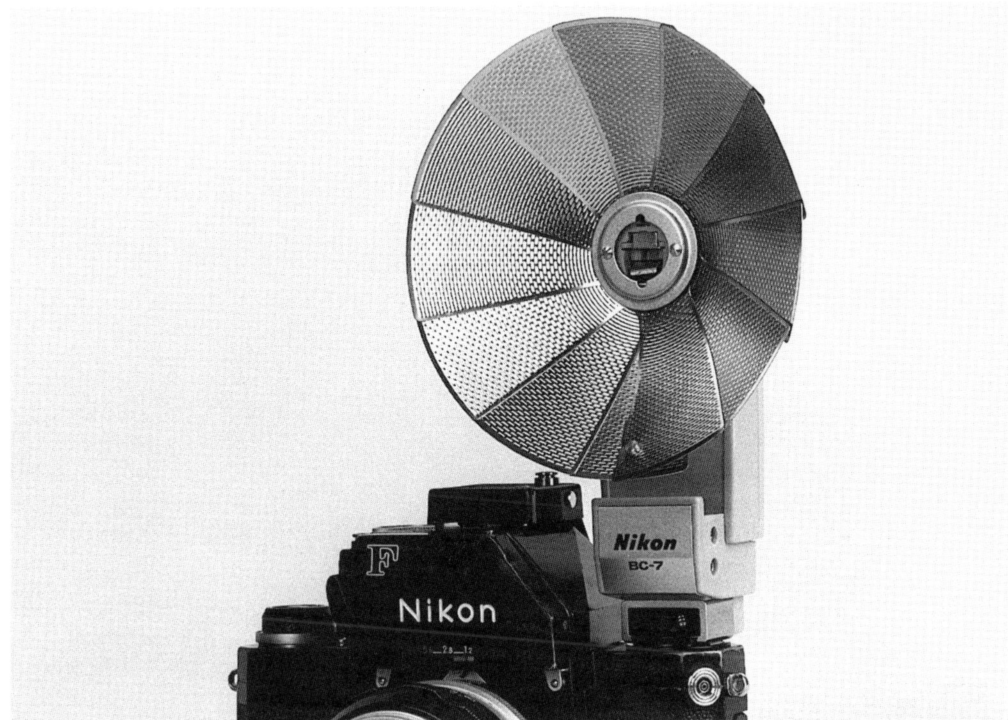

The ancestor of all Nikon's electronic flash units: the flashbulb unit BC-7.

From Flashbulbs to Electronic Flash

The first practical electronic flash apparatus was produced by the American, Harold Edgerton, in 1940. Early electronic flash units had very modest outputs by today's standards, perhaps a guide number of about 20 at the then normal ISO 50/18°, for a weight measured in kilograms.

Sometime in the middle of the 1960's the Honeywell company developed a flash unit with a metering sensor that measured the light reflected by the subject and switched off the flash as soon as the sensor registered sufficient for a correct exposure. This made it possible to preset an aperture on the lens and leave the exposure control to the flash unit's "computer". Naturally this called for a metering sensor capable of reacting extremely quickly, since a modern electronic flash can emit light bursts that only last between 1/1000 and 1/50,000 sec. Such metering technology was euphorically termed "computer-control".

Towards the end of the seventies it was perfected to the extent that the metering sensor was built into the camera instead of the flash unit: the birth of TTL-flash control. In the case of Nikon the highly sensitive metering sensor is located in the mirror box of the camera. It registers the light reflected from the film surface and cuts off the flash tube's output instantaneously – precisely when the flash exposure is correct. Should the power be insufficient for an appropriate exposure, perhaps because the preset aperture was too small or the distance to the subject too large, the TTL-flash unit's ready-light will blink for about two seconds after the exposure to indicate this. Just to be on the safe side though, this warning will actually appear about one EV-step earlier, thus informing the photographer that he is working close to the system's limits. In addition, this facility also indicates whenever the range of usable ISO film speeds for TTL-operation is exceeded.

Nowadays flash-lighting is not used exclusively to brighten up dark interiors. Years ago it had already been recognized that much more could be achieved with supplementary light. Fill-in flash in daylight is a very practical technique used by far too few hobby-photographers. In principle it has always been possible within the acceptable sync-speed range but the photographer depended very much on experience and intuition to get it right. Today, modern microproccessor controls take care of it automatically without the need for complicated calculations – in Nikon's case in the models F-401/s/x, F-601/601M, F-801/s, and the F90 and F4.

Flash Units In The Nikon System

Nikon's involvement in flash technology began with the rangefinder model S – the first Nikon to be equipped with an M-type sync-terminal for flashbulbs. At the same time the first Nikon flash unit, the BC-1 was introduced. Six further versions followed. The last of these, the BC-7 for the SLR-models F and F2, mounts in the accessory shoe and is released without a cord. Three types of bulbs can be used, FP, M, and MF. The most powerful have an enormous guide number of up to 60 at 1/30 sec. At 1/30 sec.? The explanation is that flashbulbs have a relatively long burn time of about 1/20 sec., and only part of the resulting light can be effective during fast shutter speeds – a more or less significant amount is cut off. The aperture setting scale on the back of the BC-7 takes this relationship into account. The reflector has a diameter of 120mm and can be folded in order to save space during storage. It can be tilted upwards up to an angle of 120° for indirect flash operation and was designed to cover the angle of view of a 35mm lens. It takes a 15v battery.

From the SB-1 to the SB-10

From the S2 onwards all Nikon cameras were equipped with an X-type sync-terminal for electronic flash. Nikon's first electronic flash appeared in 1971 – it was a hammer-head type with a guide number of 28 at ISO 100/21°. It was powered by a rechargeable battery in the grip section that could deliver just under 80 flashes. After that, the SB-1 had to be connected to its recharging unit for about 15 hours. If greater capacity was required the external battery pack SD-2 was available. Its six D-size cells could deliver more than 1000 flashes. The 510v high-power battery unit SD-3 was a speciality not available everywhere. It could store energy for about 700 flashes and had a recycling time of 1.5 sec., not the 4 sec. usual in the case of the other power supplies. The SB-1 covered the angle of view of a 35mm lens, had a fixed reflector and no output-reducing facility. Together with the battery and the connecting bracket, the SB-1 weighed almost a kilo.

At the time its terminal for connecting to the ringlights SM-1 and SR-1, which drew their power from the SB-1, really was a special feature. When used in this way the flash tube in the SB-1 was automatically switched off. The flash-ready signal was on the flash unit itself, but with

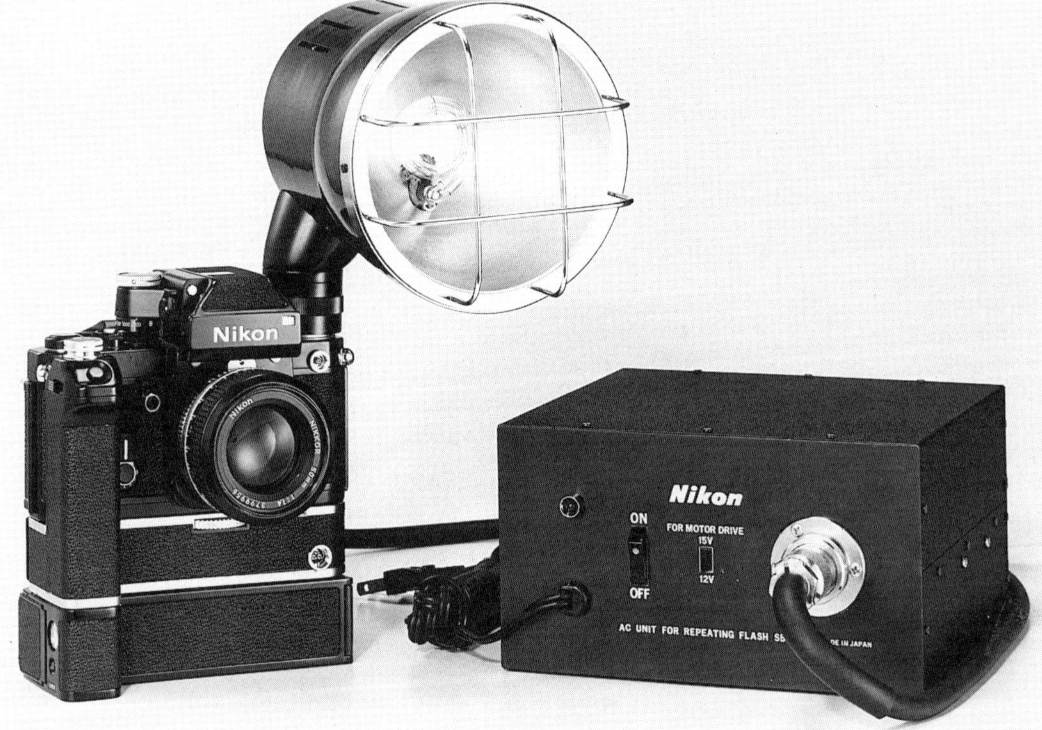

The appropriate flash equipment for a motorized camera: the repeating flash unit SB-6.

the help of the adaptor SC-4 for the F2 and the SF-1 for the other cameras it could be transferred to the viewfinder. Later, the ringlights SM-2 and SR-2, identical in other respects to the SM-1 and SR-1, were self powered.

Nikon's first compact electronic flash units which could be mounted on the camera were the SB-2 and SB-3. The only difference is that the SB-2 is equipped with a mounting foot for the F and F2, in the latter's case this connection includes the connection for the ready-light in the viewfinder. The SB-3 on the other hand has the usual ISO-type foot for the Nikkormat cameras with the hot-shoe contact for cordless operation. The guide number for both was 25 at ISO 100/21° and 35mm coverage. Three automatic stops were available – f/4, f/5.6 and f/8 at this film speed. Four AA-size batteries served as the power supply – sufficient for just short of five films with 36 exposures each. At full output the recycling time was about eight seconds. An external power supply was not provided. The thyristor circuitry was an interesting new feature, which retains excess energy in the capacitor in the automatic modes, thereby saving it for the following shot. This feature has two welcome side-effects. Not only is the recycling time shortened, but the number of flashes per battery or rechargeable set is also increased considerably. The reflector of the SB-2/3 cannot be tilted upwards but an additional wide-angle flash adaptor matched to the angle of view of a 28mm lens was available.

At the same time as the Nikkormat EL Nikon introduced the small SB-4, a light unit with a guide number of 18 and weighing a mere 180 gr. It is equipped with one automatic setting at f/4, is capable of a recycling time of 10 to 12 sec., and was conceived for simple snapshot photography. The SB-4 was powered by two AA-size batteries and neither a sync terminal nor a wide-angle adaptor were provided.

The next in the line, the pro-flash SB-5 was a completely different story. This is a powerful unit with a guide number of 32 with a coverage matching a 28mm lens. Three automatic shooting ranges can be chosen – at f/4, f/5.6 and f/8 – as well as three output levels – "Full" = GN 32, "1/4" = GN 16, and "MD" (motor drive) = GN 11. The last two settings enable

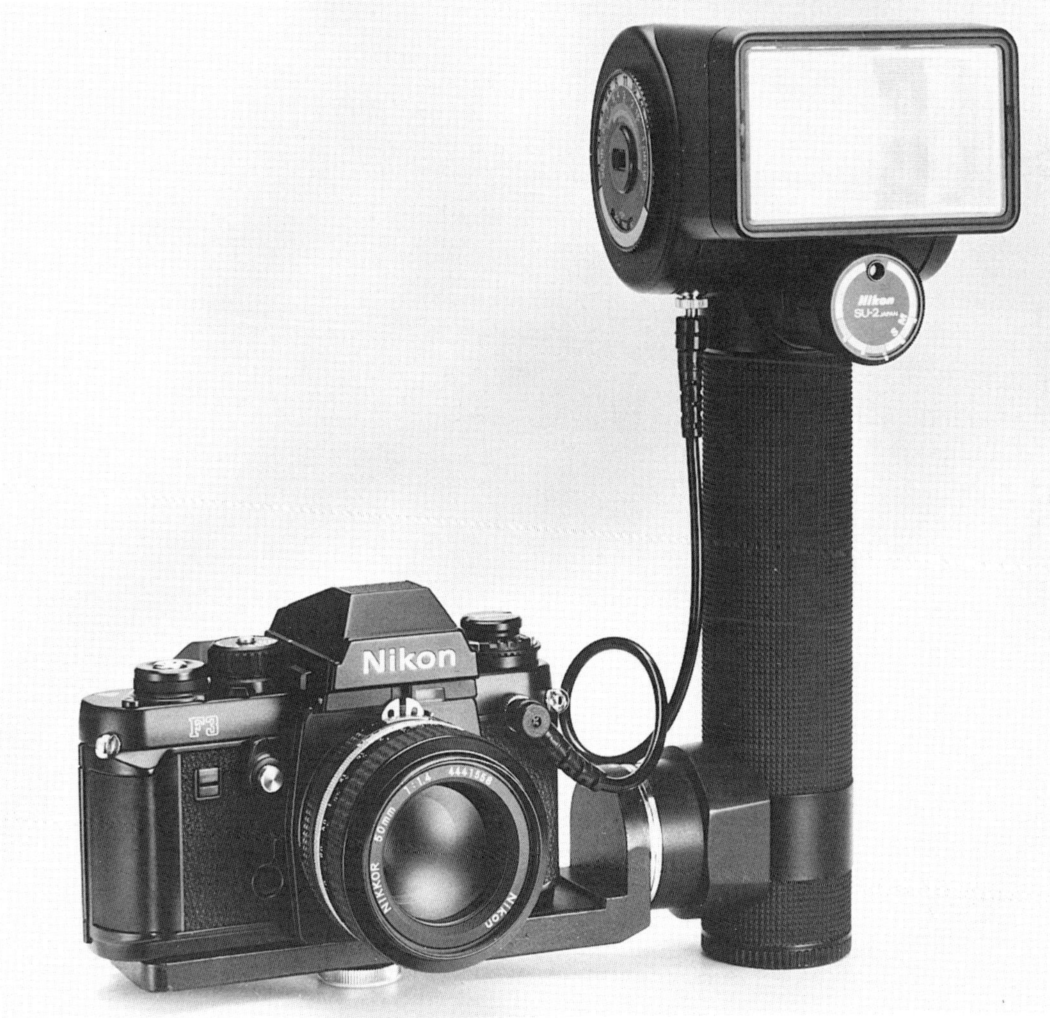

Nikon's first TTL-controlled flash unit: the "hammer-head" type SB-11 attached to the F3.

the SB-5 to produce up to 2.5 and 3.8 light pulses per second respectively. The necessary energy is supplied either by the special rechargeable NC-unit housed in the grip section, or by the external power pack SD-4 which operates with two customized 240v batteries. The accessory sensor unit SU-1, normally plugged into the side of the flash, can also be attached directly to the hot-shoe of the F and F2 with the extension cord SC-9. The whole unit can be tilted in 30° steps for bounce-flash operation and its recycling time is less than 3 seconds, even in the "Full"-position. The extension cord SE-2 permits the simultaneous release of several flash units, and with the special sensor SU-3 the SB-5 can be triggered by the radio-control set ML-1 from distances of up to 60 metres. This true mammoth of a light production machine weighs in at 1200 grams.

The SB-6 is the oldest electronic flash unit still available. This is not due to its powerful guide number of 45 but because of its ability to fire up to 40 flashes per second for stroboscopic shots. With its large 13cm reflector it is an imposing sight. Six output levels can be chosen: "Full", 1/2, 1/4, 1/8, 1/16, and 1/32. The last positions permit a firing rate of up to 3.8 frames/sec. just like the SB-5 for shooting together with motor-driven cameras. Whenever the additional sensor unit SU-1 is attached three automatic settings also become available. Its size and weight mean it will mainly be used in static set-ups, even though the AC-unit SA-3 is available as well as the NC-unit SN-3 for the battery pack SD-5. But even with the lightest of these power supplies the outfit still weighs 6 kilos.

The flash unit SB-7 is a modified version of the SB-2 with modern thyristor circuitry replacing the less precisely operating rectifiers usually employed until then. Its weight was reduced by 100 grams and the choice of automatic settings was limited to f/4 and f/8. The wide adaptor SW-2 was available as an accessory.

The SB-3 was succeeded by the SB-8E offering the same features as the SB-7E.

The SB-9 replaced the SB-4, only 24mm thick and weighing a mere 90 grams, superflat and also a flyweight. Two automatic settings can be chosen (f/2.8 and f/4 at ISO 100/21°), and the guide number of 14 is accordingly low. A handy little unit that can always be stashed away even in a case seemingly packed to the limit.

After just a short production period the SB-8E was replaced by the SB-10, the only difference being a second contact in the mounting foot which, in connection with the Nikon FE and the following models, was responsible for the transmission of the ready-signal to the viewfinder.

The TTL-Era

The age of TTL-controlled flash units began for Nikon with the introduction of the F3 and the SB-11 as the first of a number of compatible flash units. It has a guide number of 36 and eight AA-size cells housed in the grip section provide the necessary energy. In spite of their quantity they only result in a capacity of 150 flashes and a recycling time of 8 seconds. Later the optional external battery pack SD-7 became available with an additional six C-size cells allowing up to 270 flashes. The reflector can be tilted for bounce flash operation, and together with the wide adaptor SW-2 the coverage is adequate for a 28mm lens. Located beneath the reflector is its sensor SU-2 which offers an "M"-position for manual full output besides the three automatic settings for f/4, f/5.6 and f/8, plus the position "S" which takes over the transmitter's function when working with the remote control set ML-1. The sensor is removable and can be mounted on the camera accessory shoe with the help of the connecting cord SC-13. If the TTL-control facility is to be employed with the F3 the sensor-

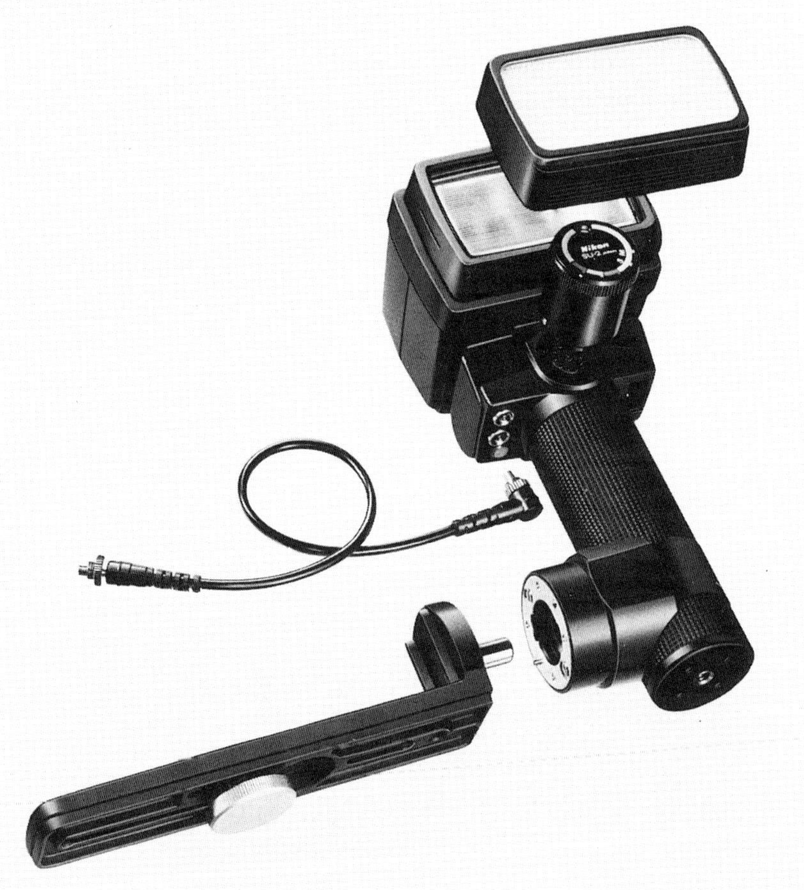

The SB-14 operates only with the external battery pack SD-7.

cord SC-12 will be necessary, only then does the SB-11 operate as a TTL-flash unit. TTL-control with a camera equipped with an ISO-type hot-shoe calls for the sensor cord SC-23 instead. Due to its limitations the SB-11 never became accepted by professionals – it is simply not powerful enough in terms of recycling time and capacity per set of batteries.

Nikon's smallest TTL-controlled electronic flash used to be the SB-18 with a guide number of 20. Its four AA-size batteries allow a recycling time of 6 seconds, surely adequate for such a compact model. The only other mode is manual full output, and understandably it lacks a multi-flash terminal.

The SB-E, with a guide number of only 17, was made for the amateur models EM and FG-20. When mounted on these two cameras it offers a choice of three automatic shooting ranges – f/2.8, f/4 and f/5.6 at ISO 100/21° which are set directly on the lens. This results in convenient operation comparable to that of the TTL-controlled units, even though the light is measured by a sensor in the flash. Four 1.5v AAA-size batteries suffice for two films with 36 exposures. On any other camera only one automatic setting – f/5.6 – is available.

The SB-E was succeeded by the SB-19, which has a fixed reflector with a coverage adequate for a 35mm lens. Its guide number is 20, and in combination with the EM and FG-20 six automatic settings between f/2 and f/11 at a film speed of ISO 100/21° are available.

The SB-20 is the first TTL-controlled flash unit with an integrated AF-illuminator. This device projects narrow stripes of light onto the subject whenever the ambient light is insufficient for normal autofocus-type distance metering. The facility has an operating range from about 0.5 to 10 metres depending on the sensitivity of the camera's AF-system. The rest of its specification is not bad either for such a compact unit; it has a guide number of 30 at its N-position for 35mm. The round diffuser can be rotated in order to change the coverage angle to T = 85mm and W = 28mm. The reflector can be tilted up and down with a knob by 7° for close-ups. Besides its 5 automatic settings (f/2 to f/8 at ISO 100/21°) in TTL-mode, the SB-20 also has 5 manual positions ranging

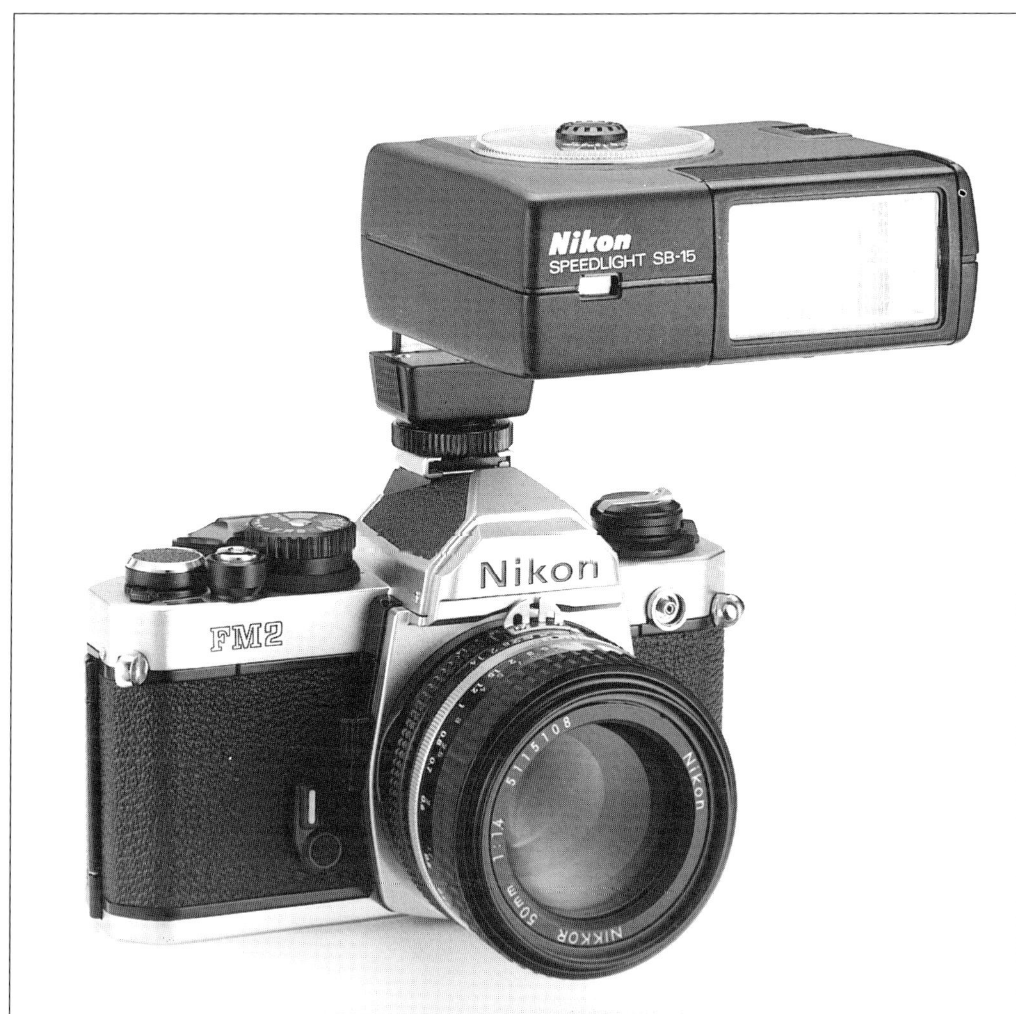

The SB-15, the first flash unit with an ISO-standard foot, was introduced at the same time as the FG: here mounted on an FM-2.

from "Full" to 1/16. The latter permits high-speed operation for up to 8 flashes per second for motorized cameras. If the external battery pack SD-7 is employed, 10 flashes per second become possible even at 1/8 output. The stand-by mode is a new feature in this model. This third click-stop for the main switch results in the flash unit shutting itself down automatically about one or two minutes after the last shot. All you have to do then is to press the shutter release button lightly to activate the unit once again.

The SB-21 is a specialist for flash photography at close range and replaced the two ringlights SR-2 and SM-2. Unlike these two it does not have a single ring-shaped flashtube but two separate tubes, left and right in the reflector, that can be used individually or together. The whole unit can be attached to both 52 and 62mm filter threads with adaptor rings. As well as the TTL-controlled mode, the SB-21 can also be used with full manual output or 1/4 or 1/16 power. The guide number is only 13 at ISO 100/21° which may appear rather low at first sight, but at the extremely short distances for which it is intended it is sufficient. The additional wide adaptor SW-8 for a more uniform illumination at distances shorter than 40mm is provided with the set. In order to make focusing easier in critical close-ups, a small lamp to illuminate the subject is located in the reflector, but although the intention may have been good, this dim little light is not much help. A cord connects the SB-21 to its power supply and control unit which looks like an SB-15 or SB-17 without a reflector. Two of these, differing in their mounting feet, are available: together with the AS-12 it becomes an SB-21A for the F3, with the AS-14 an SB-21B for ISO-type hot-shoes. TTL and manual modes are set on these controllers. Further features include the ready-signal and a second yellow LED meant to warn of overexposures if too large an aperture is set at short distances. The SB-21 can be powered by three sources: four AA-size batteries, the external battery pack LD-2 known from the Medical Nikkor 120mm/f/4, or the AC Unit LA-2. The AS-12 controller is equipped with an additional multiflash terminal. If the SB-21 is to be attached to a lens mounted on the camera in the retro-position, the Auto Adaptor BR-6 is necessary.

The SB-20's little brother is the SB-22 with a reduced guide number of 25. When the built-in wide adaptor for 28mm lenses is in use, a guide number of 18 remains. Its technical features are similar to those of the SB-15, that is TTL-mode as well as M, standing for full manual output, two automatic settings (f/4 and f/8 at ISO 100/21°), and the Motor Drive mode with a guide number of 8. The reflector can be tilted 90° up as well as down by 7° in order to achieve more evenly lit close-ups, and when this facility is used the LED on the rear marked "Bounce" will light up. Even at full discharge the four AA-size batteries take a mere 4 seconds to recharge the capacitor between two flashes. The SB-22 can be made to react even quicker with the additional power of the external battery pack SD-7. Just right for a long series

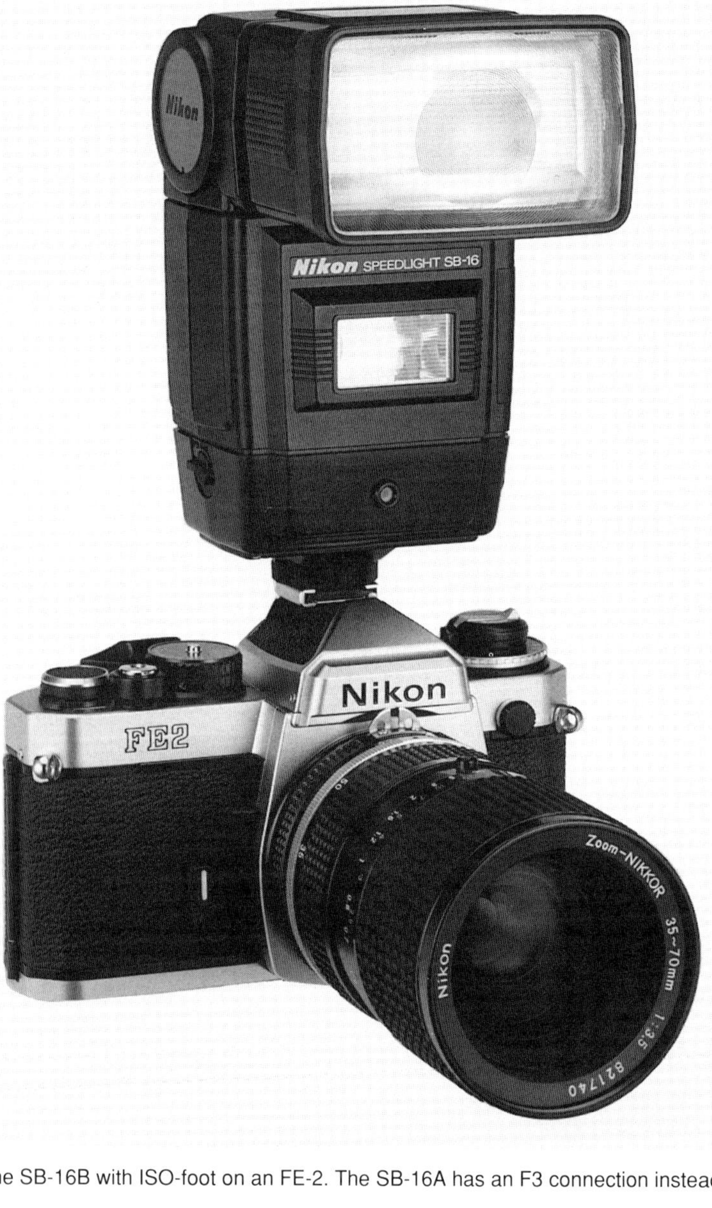

The SB-16B with ISO-foot on an FE-2. The SB-16A has an F3 connection instead.

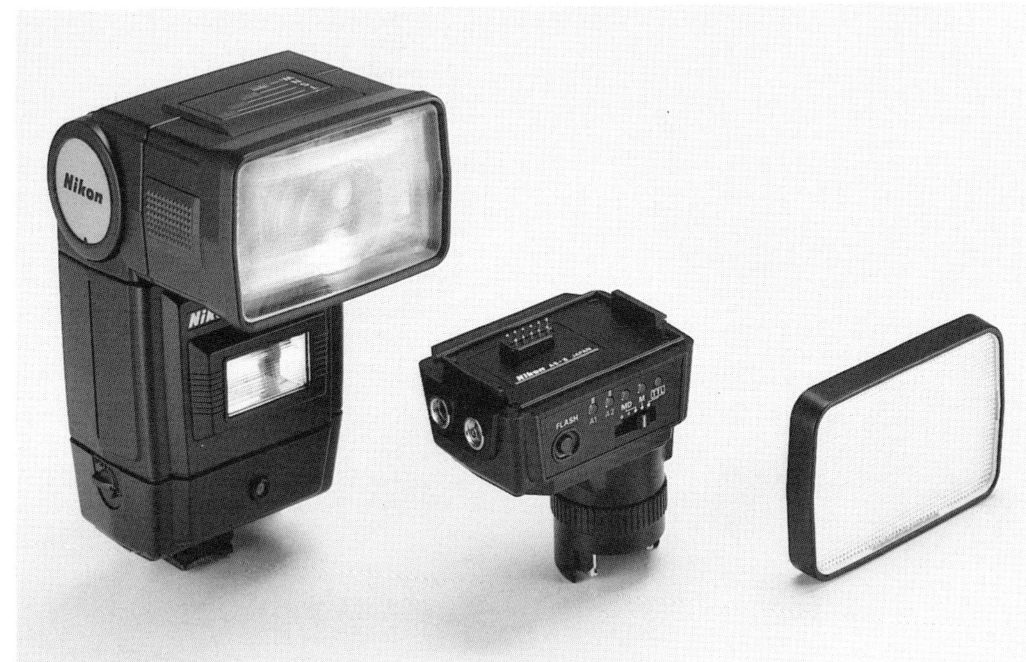

The SB-16B is converted to a SB-16A by interchanging the lower part for one with the F3 foot (middle).

of shots and short recycling times – the ready-light hardly ever seems to appear. Care should be taken though since there is a danger of damaging the flashtube due to overheating if more than 40 flashes are fired at such a rate.

The SB-18 equivalent for autofocus cameras is the SB-23. It provides a guide number of 20, a fixed reflector and the choice between TTL and manual modes. It's an ideal secondary flash unit that can always be taken along, thanks to its compact dimensions, and will always be handy to utilize the fill-flash facilities of the F4 and F90. The features the SB-23 lacks are compensated for by other very favourable advantages: its weight of a mere 140 grams, a recycling time of 2 seconds, and a capacity of 400 flashes per set of batteries.

The SB-24 was the flagship of the AF range before the advent of the SB-25, possessing many more features than the SB-16 it replaced – its

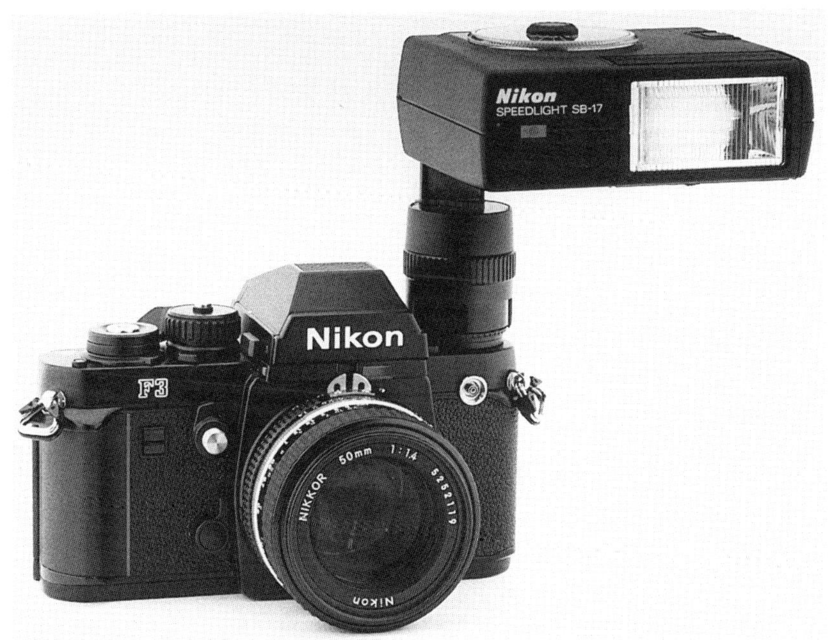

Equipped with a foot for the F3 and a multiflash-terminal: the SB-17.

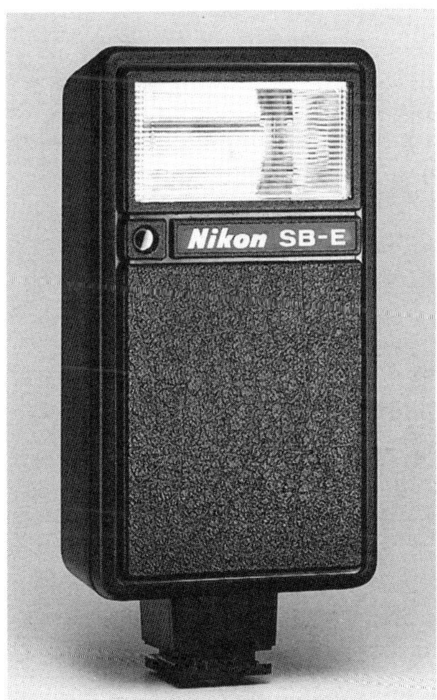

Designed equally small and light for the EM and the FG-20: the SB-E.

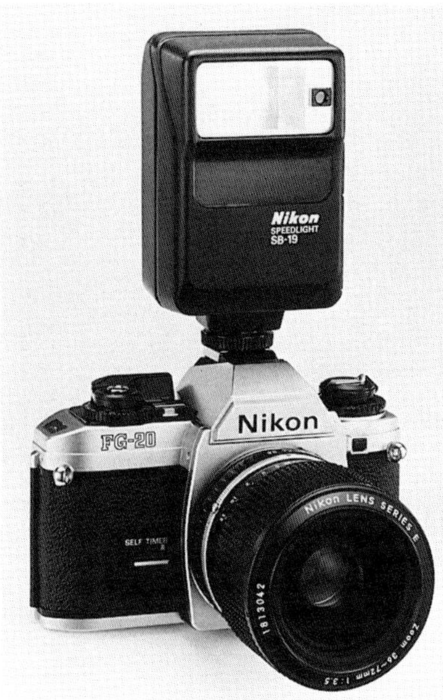

The Speedlight SB-19 attached to an FG-20.

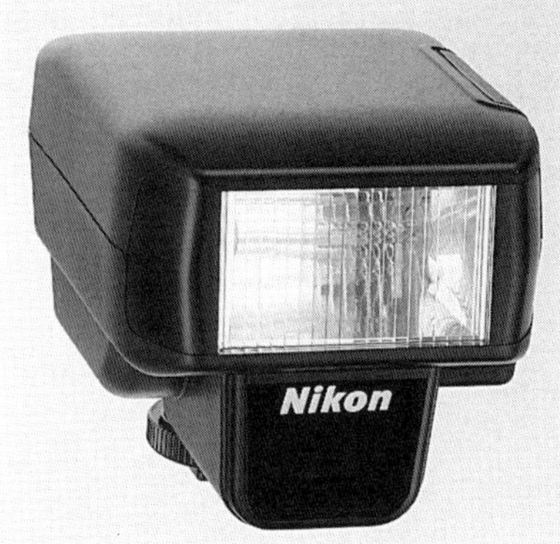

The SB-23 is ideal as a second unit which can always be taken along thanks to its compact build.

automatic zoom head positioning between 24 and 85mm, for example. Its basic guide number is 36, but this varies from 30 to 50 depending on the focal length. The reflector can be tilted upwards by 90°, downwards by 7°, and rotated by 180°. The standard recycling time is around 7 seconds, about 6 with the external battery pack SD-7, and with the new SD-8 loaded with rechargeable NC-batteries reduced further to just short of 2 seconds. Together with the F4 and the F-801/s the SB-24 permits rear blind sync. operation, an interesting function whenever you want to add artificial light during long exposures. The LCD-panel, which can be illuminated if you wish, is really necessary to display the multitude of functions. Besides the TTL-controlled mode, including fill-flash, the unit permits the flash output to be overridden manually within the range of +1 to -3 EV in order to balance the artificial light in favour of the ambient light. While doing so the LCD-panel continues to indicate the resulting shooting range. Additionally the SB-24 offers 6 automatic settings from f/2 to f/11 at ISO 100/21° and 5 manual positions from full output to 1/16. At 1/8 and 1/16 output stroboscopic operation is available with up to 8 flashes at a frequency of up to 10 hertz. To list all the options offered by this flash miracle, let alone to describe them, seems impossible. Even the 80-page instruction manual restricts itself to

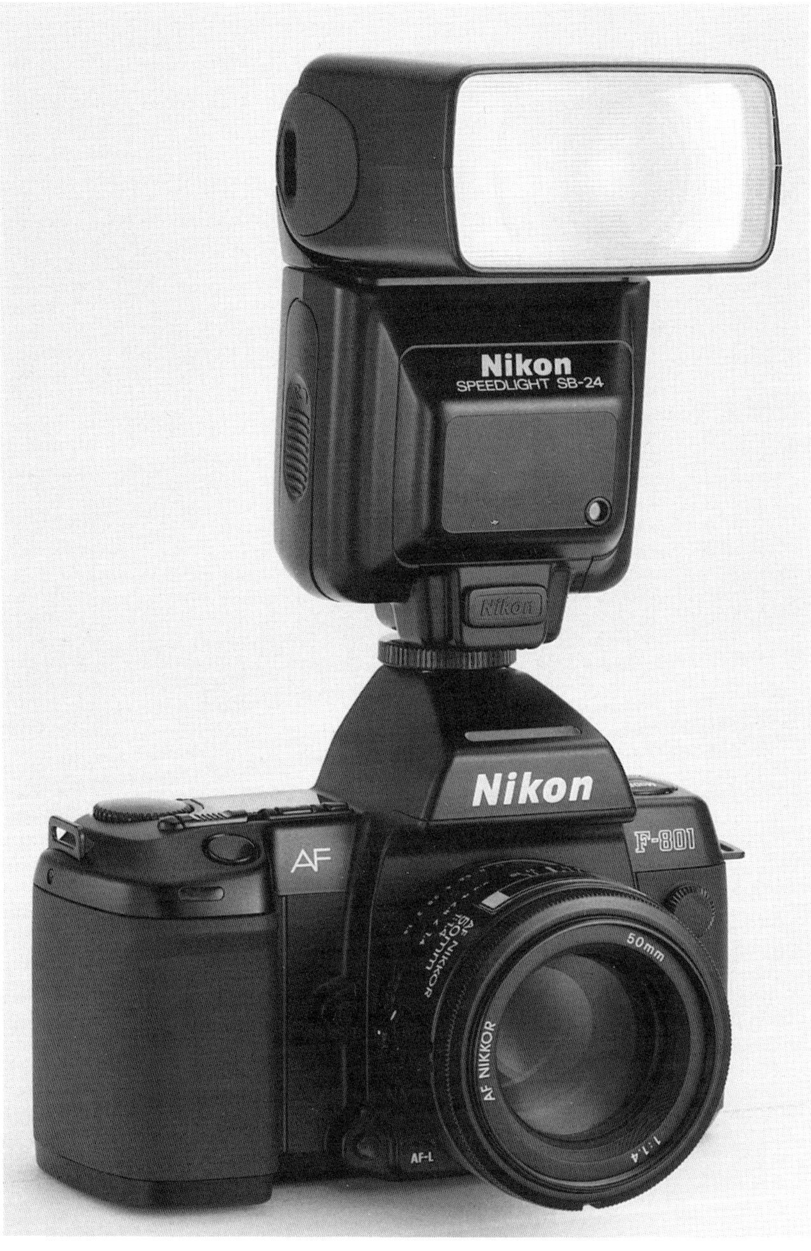

The SB-24 offers flash convenience with all the tricks in the book, and together with the F-801/F-801s it turns into a universal genius.

Nikon Flash Units

Model	Type of unit	External battery pack	Type of rechargeable battery	Mains connection unit	Manual aperture settings	Automatic aperture settings	TTL mode	Viewfinder flash-ready light	Reflector tiltable	Wide-angle adaptor	Battery clip	Guide number @ 24mm	Guide number @ 28mm	Guide number @ 35mm	Guide number @ 50mm	Guide number @ 85mm	Guide number in MD-posit.	Synch. terminal for sec. unit	Multiflash terminal	Recycling time (sec.)	Max. flash duration (sec.)	No. of flashes per battery set	Weight (without battery) g.	Dimensions (mm)	AF-illuminator	Min. flash duration (sec.)
SB-1	S	SD-2	SN-1	SM-1	+	—	—	SF-1	—	—	—	—	—	28			–	+	–	4	1/2000	1000	670	80x238x50	–	
SB-2	K	+	—	SA-2	+	3	—	SF-1	—	SW-1	MS-2	—	18	25			–	+	–	8	1/1200	140	430	110x40x104	–	
SB-3	K	+	—	SA-2	+	3	—	SF-1	—	SW-1	MS-2	—	18	25			–	+	–	8	1/1200	140	430	110x40x104	–	
SB-4	K	+	—	—	+	1	—	—	—	—	—	—	—	16			–	–	–	12	1/800	140	180	75x70x40	–	
SB-5	S	SD-4	SN-2	—	3	3	—	SC-4 SF-1	↑	—	—	—	32	—	—	—	11	+	–	2.6	1/1000	75	900	93x252x125	–	MD 1/6500
SB-6	K	—	SN-3	SA-2	6	SU-3	—	SC-4 SC-1	—	—	—	—	—	45	—	—	16	+	–	—	1/440	—	1100	128x128x190	–	1/32; 1/3800
SB-7E	K	+	—	—	+	2	—	SF-1	—	SW-2	MS-2	—	18	25	—	—	–	+	–	8	1/1200	160	300	110x37x79	–	
SB-8E	K	+	—	—	+	2	—	SF-1	—	SW-2	MS-2	—	18	25	—	—	–	+	–	8	1/1200	160	270	110x37x39	–	
SB-9	K	+	—	—	–	2	—	—	—	—	—	—	—	14	—	—	–	–	–	9	1/6600	200	90	56x99x24	–	
SB-10	K	+	—	—	+	2	—	+	—	SW-2	MS-2	—	18	25	—	—	–	+	–	8	1/2000	160	270	110x37x79	–	
SB-11	S	SD-7 SD-8	—	—	+	3	+	+	↑	SW-3	+	—	25	36	—	—	–	+	–	8	1/800	150	860	104x276x118	–	
SB-12	K	+	—	—	+	–	+	+	—	SW-4	—	—	18	25	—	—	–	+	–	8	1/1000	160	350	105x40x85	–	
SB-14/ 140	S	SD-7 SD-8	—	—	+	3	+	+	↑↔	SW-5[2]		22	32	—	—	—	–	+	–	8	1/800	270	515	94x217x91	–	
SB-15	K	+	—	—	2	2	+	+	↑	SW-6	MS-6	—	18	25	—	—	7	+	–	8	1/1400	160	270	101x42x90	–	MD; 1/1000
SB-16	K	+	—	—	2	2	+	+	↑↔	SW-7	MS-5	19	27	32	38	42	8	+	+	11	1/1250	100	485/ 445	82x155x100	–	MD; 1/8000
SB-17	K	+	—	—	2	2	+	+	↑	SW-6	MS-6	—	18	25	—	—	7	+	+	8	1/1400	160	300	101x42x90	–	MD; 1/10000
SB-18	K	+	—	—	+	–	+	+	—	—	—	—	—	20	—	—	–	–	–	6	1/2200	250	150	66x113x42	–	
SB-19	K	+	—	—	–	6[3]	–	+	—	—	—	—	—	20	—	—	–	–	–	7	1/2200	250	170	66x116x46	–	
SB-E	K	+	—	—	–	3[3]	–	+	—	—	—	—	—	17	—	—	–	–	–	9	1/2000	80	80	55x110x33	–	
SB-20	K	SD-7 SD-8	—	—	5	5	+	+	↑	—	—	—	22	30	—	36	–	+	–	7	1/1200	160	260	71x110x70	+	1:16 1/15000
SB-21	K	LD-2	—	—	3	–	+	+	—	SW-8	MS-6	—	13-15	–	—	—	–	+	+[5]	8	1/1600	200	410	130x120x21	–	1:16 1/25000
SB-22	K	SD-7 SD-8	—	—	2	2	+	+	↑	—	—	—	18	25	—	—	8	+	–	4	1/1700	200	250	80x105x68	+	MD: 1/8000
SB-23	K	+	—	—	+	–	+	+	—	—	—	—	—	20	—	—	–	–	–	2	1/2000	400	140	64x67x84	+	
SB-24	K	SD-7 SD-8	—	—	5	6	+	+	↑↔	—	—	30	32	36	42	50	–	+	+	7	1/1000	100	390	80x131x100	+	1:16 1/11000
SB-25[7]	K	SD-7 SD-8		—	6	6	+	+	↑↔	—[6]	—	30	32	36	42	50	–	+	+	7	1/1000	100	380	79x135x101	+	1:64 1/23000
SR-2	—	LD-1	—	LA-1	2	–	–	SF-1	—	—		—	16	–	—	—	–	–	–	8	1/500	110	200	106x140x24	–	
SM-2	—	LD-1	—	LA-1	2	–	–	SF-1	—	—	—	—	v[4]	v[4]	v[4]	v[4]	–	–	–	8	1/500	110	185	70x100x35	–	
Med. 120/4	—	LD-2	–	LA-2	+	–	–	+	—	—	—	—	—	—	—	16	–	–	–	9	1/500	90	—	—	–	
Med. 200/5.6	—	LD-1	–	LD-2	+	–	–	–	—	—	—	—	—	—	—	11	–	–	–	9	1/500	600	—	—	–	

1 S = grip-type unit; K = compact unit (for hot-shoe mounting)

2 for SB-140: SW-5 IR (for infra-red photography); SW-5 UV (for ultra-violet photography); SW-5V (for visible light photography

3 only with camera models EM and FG-20, otherwise only 1

4 V = variable

5 only SB-21

6 Built-in for 20mm at guide number 20

7 Also FP high-speed sync. up to 1/4000 sec; red-eye reduction pre-flash; 3-D sensor fill-flash with pre-flashes for subject analysis; reflector for simultaneous direct/indirect operation

the basic operation. The user simply has to gain his own experience with the SB-24; it will be an almost endless story revealing completely new sides of flash photography.

This is even more true in the case of the SB-25 which succeeded the SB-24 in 1992 for the F90. Besides offering every feature the SB-24 had made available for the different camera models, the SB-25 includes still more options – without having to change the accustomed manner of operation in any combination. Thanks to its built-in wide-flash adaptor, the SB-25 reflector allows even the picture angle of a 20mm lens to be covered completely. A built-in diffuser card can be used in bounce-flash photography to deflect a smaller – and softer – part of the

Camera/Speedlight Combinations

Camera	SB-1		SB-2/7		SB-3/8		SB-4/9		SB-5		SB-6		SB-10		SB-11/14/140	
	Accessory	F	Accessory	F	Accessory	F	Accessory	F	Accessory	F	Accessory	F	Accessory	F	Accessory	F
F	SF-1	R	+	X	AS-1	X	AS-1	X	SC-9	X	SC-9	X	AS-1	X	SC-11	X
	SC-5/6/7	X							SC-5/6/7	X	SC-5/6/7	X				
F2	SC-4	R	+	R	AS-1	X	AS-1	X	SC-9	R	SC-9	R	AS-1	X	SC-11	X
	SC-5/6/7	X							SC-5/6/7	X	SC-5/6/7	X				
F3	SF-1	R	AS-3	X	AS-4	X	AS-4	X	SC-9 + AS-3	X	SC-9 + AS-3	X	AS-4	X	SC-12	TTL
	SC-5/6/7	X													SC-11	X
F3 P	SF-1	R	AS-3	X	+	X	+	X	SC-9 + AS-2/3	X	SC-9 + AS-2/3	X	+	R	SC-12	TTL
	SC-5/6/7	X	AS-2	X											SC-11	X
F4	SF-1	R	AS-2	X	+	X	+	X	SC-9 + AS-2	X	SC-9 + AS-2/3	X	+	R	SC-23	TTL
	SC-5/6/7	X													SC-11	X
Nikkormat FS; FT; FTN	SF-1	R	SF-1	R	SF-1	R	SC-10	X	SC-5/6/7	X	SC-5/6/7	X	SC-10	X	SC-11	X
	SC-5/6/7	X	SC-5/6/7	X	SC-5/6/7	X	SC-8	X					SC-5/6/7	X		
FT-2/3;EL/ ELW/ EL-2; FM	SF-1	R	AS-2	X	+	X	+	X	SC-9 + AS-2	X	SC-9 + AS-2	X	+	X	SC-11	X
	SC-5/6/7	X														
FE/FM-2	SF-1	R	AS-2	X	+	X	+	X	SC-9 + AS-2	X	SC-9 + AS-2	X	+	R	SC-13	R
	SC-5/6/7	X													SC-11	X
FE-2; FA	SF-1	R	AS-2	X	+	X	+	X	SC-9 + AS-2	X	SC-9 + AS-2	X	+	R	SC-23	TTL
	SC-5/6/7	X													SC-11	X
FG	SC-5/6 + AS-15	X	AS-2	X	+	X	+	X	SC-9 + AS-2	X	SC-9 + AS-2	X	+	R	SC-23	TTL
															SC-13	R
EM; FG-20	SC-5/6 + AS-15	X	AS-2	X	+	X	+	X	SC-9 + AS-2	X	SC-9 + AS-2	X	+	R	SC-13	R
F-301; F-501	SC-5/6 + AS-15	X	AS-2	X	+	X	+	X	SC-9 + AS-2	X	SC-9 + AS-2	X	+	R	SC-23	TTL
															SC-13	R
F-401; F-401 S/X	SC-5/6 + AS-15	X	AS-2	X	+	X	+	X	SC-9 + AS-2	X	SC-9 + AS-2	X	+	R	SC-13	R
F-601 (M); F-801/S; F-90	SC-5/6 + AS-15	X	AS-2	X	+	X	+	X	SC-9 + AS-2	X	SC-9 + AS-2	X	+	R	SC-23	TTL
															SC-13	R

F = function possible with the accessories listed
X = Speedlight is only triggered

light directly towards the main subject.

Although its guide number is the same as the SB-24, the SB-25 permits both a higher flash frequency as well as a higher total amount of flash bursts in its Repeating mode: up to 90 at 50 Hz (up to 160 with an SD-8 attached). Its manual output power can also be reduced further and in smaller increments: down to 1/64 in 1/3 EV-steps.

While the above mentioned features are accessible with all camera models, the following are exclusively available for those with F90-standard electronics. Next to the functions described in the section concerning the F90, the SB-25 is able to display the exact amount of (flash) underexposure in 1/3 EV-steps after each shot, and in the FP High Speed mode it allows shutter speeds from 1/250 to 1/4000 sec. to be utilized for flash photography. This is realized by emitting a very fast series of low-power bursts having almost the same effect as a continuously glowing source throughout the duration of the exposure. It must be taken into consideration though that the guide number is determined by the shutter speed in this manual mode. Both features further increase the photographer's control of flash exposure and also allow him to use fast films and shutter speeds to stop action, together with wide apertures to isolate the main subject. One last feature of the SB-25 should not be overlooked since it eliminates a problem many have suffered from. An additional mounting pin automatically locks the flash unit into its proper position in the hot-shoe of F90-standard bodies as soon as the wheel around its foot is tightened. Thus, Posi-Mount prevents the flash from accidentally slipping off the camera and at the same time secures correct contact between both parts of the outfit.

The Multiflash System

SB-12		SB-15/16B/21B		SB-16A/17/21A		SB-18/23		SB-E/19		SB-20/22/24/25		SR-2; SM-2; Medical 200/5.6		Medical 120/4	
Accessory	F	Accessory	F	Accessory	F	Accessory	F	Accessory	F	Accessory	F	Accessory	F	Accessory	F
AS-5	X	AS-1	X	AS-5	X	AS-1	X	AS-1	X	AS-1	X	SF-1 SC-5/6/7	R X	SC-20	X
AS-5	X	AS-1	X	AS-5	X	AS-1	X	AS-1	X	AS-1	X	SF-1 SC-5/6/7	R X	SC-20	X
+	TTL	AS-4	R	+	TTL	AS-4	R	AS-4	R	AS-4	R	SF-1 SC-5/6/7	R X	SC-22 + AS-4	R
+	TTL	+	R	+	TTL	+	R	+	R	+	R	SF-1 SC-5/6/7	R X	SC-22	R
AS-6	R	+	TTL	AS-6	R	+	TTL	+	R	+	TTL	SF-1 SC-5/6/7	R X	SC-20	R
SC-11	X	SC-11/15	X	SC-11	X	SC-10	X	SC-10	X	SC-10	X	SF-1 SC-5/6/7	R X	SC-20	X
AS-6	R	+	X	AS-6	R	+	X	+	X	+	X	SF-1 SC-5/6/7	R X	SC-20	X
AS-6	R	+	R	AS-6	R	+	R	+	R	+	R	SF-1 SC-5/6/7	R X	SC-22	R
AS-6	R	+	TTL	AS-6	R	+	TTL	+	R	+	TTL	SF-1 SC-5/6/7	R X	SC-22	R
AS-6	R	+	TTL	AS-6	R	+	TTL	+	R	+	TTL	AS-15 + SC-5/6/7	X	SC-22	R
AS-6	R	+	R	AS-6	R	+	R	+	R	+	TTL	AS-15 + SC-5/6/7	X	SC-22	R
AS-6	R	+	TTL	AS-6	R	+	TTL	+	R	+	TTL	AS-15 + SC-5/6/7	X	SC-22	R
AS-6	R	+	TTL	AS-6	R	+	TTL	+	R	+	TTL	AS-15 + SC-5/6/7	X	SC-22	R
AS-6	R	+	TTL	AS-6	R	+	TTL	+	R	+	TTL	AS-15 + SC-5/6/7	X	SC-22	R

R = flash-ready light in the viewfinder and automatic switchover to the synch. speed (in the case of automatic cameras)
TTL = TTL-type flash exposure control (includes X and R)

What amateur does not wish to achieve the same kind of flash illumination as a professional? A single unit is rarely sufficient to create that perfect lighting and those subtle effects. Only the use of several units allows the lighting to be well-balanced, with a main source as well as one illuminating the background and/or another for special effects. The combined use of more than one flash unit was not Nikon's invention. The simultaneous triggering with the help of multiple flash adaptors or cordless operation with photocells was a well-known practice, but the calculation of the appropriate aperture setting was a problematic task, especially if the units had different guide numbers.

Since the introduction of the TTL-controlled multiflash system this problem has been largely overcome. The flash sensor in the camera switches off all connected units simultaneously as soon as their output secures a correct exposure – regardless of how powerful the different units may be and whether or not they are pointed directly at the subject. The distance to the subject of the individual units determines how they affect the lighting as a whole. The guide number only plays a role as long as the flash units are employed at full manual output. If, for example, two flash units are used in multiflash mode, one at a distance of 1 metre and the other at 1.4 metres, the latter will contribute 1EV-step less to the exposure.

Up to 5 flash units can be employed within the Nikon multiflash system. If more are connected the resulting exposure may vary. There is a certain restriction though concerning the combination of the different flash units with autofocus cameras. It may not be possible to release the shutter a second time if the electric current in the synchro-circuit exceeds a certain level. The combined total of the coefficients (shown in parentheses) of the Speedlights listed below should not amount to more than 20:

SB-18 (16), SB-20 (9), SB-22 (6), SB-15/ 6/17/21/23 (4), SB-19 (2), SB-11/12/14/ 24/25 (1).

With the exception of the SB-12, all the Speedlights can operate as part of a multi-flash system, and the following Nikon flash units have an appropriate terminal: SB-15/1/ 21A/24/25. The others need the TTL Remote Cord SC-17. Its hot-shoe base is fitted with two of the three-pin multi-flash terminals. The first Speedlight connected to the camera – whether directly or via the SC-17 cord – is the master flash unit. All the others, the slaves, are controlled by this first one. Every additional unit is connected to the main one with the Multi-Flash Sync Cord SC-18 (1.5 metres long) or the SC-19 (3 metres long). In order to mount these secondary units securely and to ensure their proper function, adaptors are necessary – either the TTL Multi-Flash Adaptor AS-10 for ISO-type mounting feet or the AS-11 for the F3-type foot. Both these adaptors are equipped with tripod sockets in their base. The AS-10 is also fitted with three additional multi-flash terminals, so the game can be continued. The main unit does not have to be mounted on the camera to ensure the necessary contacts when using the F3 if the TTL Remote Cord SC-14 is attached. If more that one unit is to be connected to the F3 an AS-10 adaptor becomes necessary to serve as a junction.

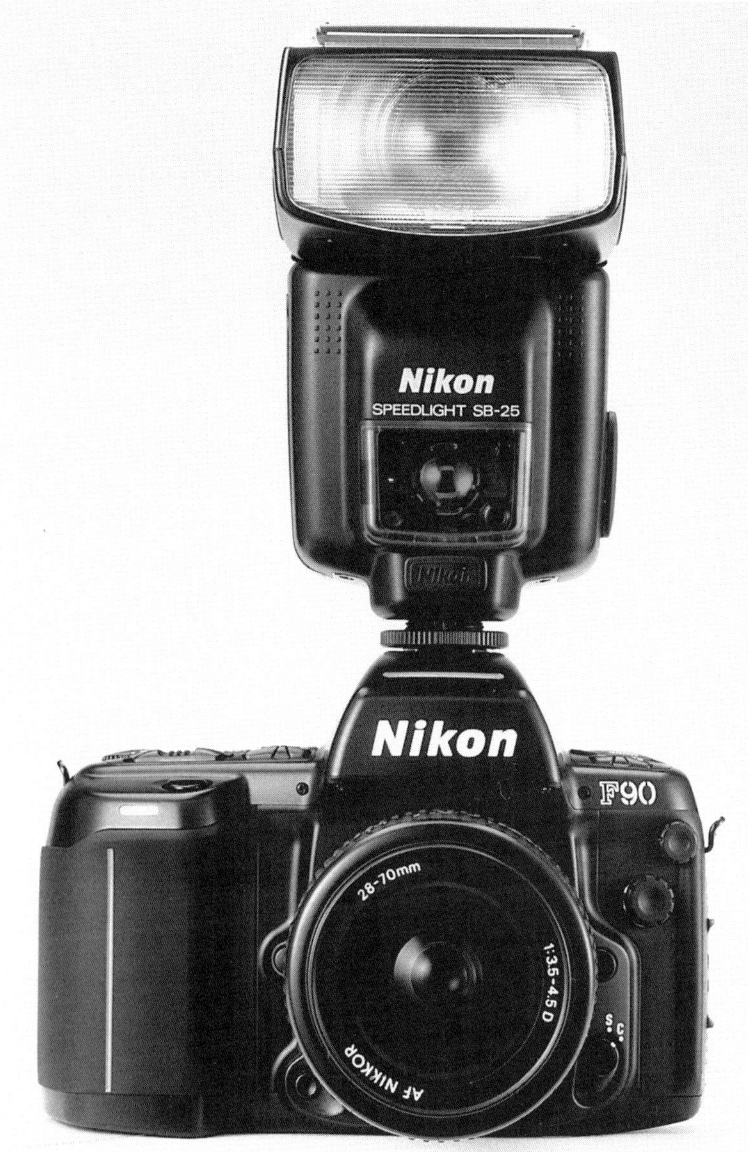

Introduced with the F-90, the SB-25 offers even more options than the SB-24.

Adaptors for every possible combination

Flash photography is very limited without the appropriate connecting cords. Mounting the Speedlight directly on the camera rules out a number of interesting applications. Each of the cords – in Nikon's case they can be identified by the two letters "SC" – has its own special purpose for certain connections. A selection of the most important and most common connecting cords in the Nikon system are as follows:-

SC-11 and SC-15 are simple connecting cords with normal PC-type terminals. SC-11 is 35cm long, SC-15 is a 1m long spiral version.

The SC-12 is designed to connect the F3 with the SB-11, SB-14, and SB-140, including TTL-control.

SC-14 and SC-17 are intended for off-camera use in TTL-mode, the SC-14 has a hot-shoe and a foot for the F3, while the SC-17 is for cameras with ISO-type accessory shoes.

SC-18 and SC-19 are connecting cords for TTL multi-flash operation differing only in length.

The SC-23 is a TTL cord for connection of SB-11, SB-14, and SB-140 with cameras fitted with ISO-type hot shoes.

SC-24 becomes necessary for TTL-operation when the F4 is used with the finders DW-20 and DW-21.

Due to the different camera systems Nikon offers three types of flash mounts: for the F/F2 system, for the F3, and for the other models with conventional accessory shoes. Flash units for the F, F2, and F3 were mounted on a special shoe situated round the rewind crank. This was done because it used to be considered impossible to achieve acceptable rigidity for a hot-shoe built onto an interchangeable viewfinder. Since it would have contradicted the ideal of compatibility not to be able to attach, say a flash unit with an ISO-type foot on an F2, Nikon offers a number of coupling adaptors (designated AS-xx) for making the necessary connections. The most important are:-

AS-1 permits the use of ISO-type flash units on the F and F2, but it does not transmit the ready-light signal.

AS-4 allows the same for the F3 except that it does convey the ready-light signal.

AS-7 has a special task. It is attached to the F3 in order to be able to rewind the film and open the camera back even though the flash unit remains mounted. Because it has both shoes it also permits TTL-controlled operation with the Speedlights for the F3, as well as the ready-light with ISO-footed flash units.

AS-10 and AS-11 are multi-flash adaptors: AS-10 for ISO-flashes, and AS-11 for the F3.

AS-15 is meant to provide a PC-type sync-terminal for cameras that do not have one of their own: EM, FG, FG-20, F-301/401/401s/401x /501/601/601M/801.

Foreign brand flash units

In the days of the F2 no such problem existed, it did not matter one bit to the camera which flash it was triggering – but of course Nikon preferred and still prefers to see its own Speedlights mounted on its cameras. From a technical point of view things began to get complicated when further contacts were added to the original single one in the centre of the hot-shoe in order to enable the ready-signal to light up in the viewfinder, for example, or to permit TTL-controlled flash operation. These contacts lead straight to the camera's heart.

All Nikon Speedlights possess the central hot-shoe contact that touches nothing but its counterpart when they are mounted on the camera. In cheap models this contact is often nothing but a simple broad metal strip. If such a unit is mounted on, or removed from the shoe while it is switched on, its central contact may touch one of the others in the hot-shoe, sending a current direct to the camera's "central switchboard", which might destroy it. This is why no flash unit should ever be mounted or removed unless it is switched off.

The second problem is that some cheaper flashes use a high triggering voltage, causing too much corrosion in the camera's sync-contact. As a result the connection to the camera's circuitry may be interrupted or its precise function impaired. Additionally this high voltage may adversely influence the camera's metering electronics, leading to varying exposures.

These warnings are directed mainly at cheap "bargains" and "oldies". When flash units designed by well-known reputable makers are used there will probably be nothing to worry about. Some companies joined forces in the development of the equally comprehensive and widespread SCA-system which allows many different flash units to be employed for all sorts of cameras while securing the present degree of flash control and automation. But in spite of this, functional disturbances do occur with units of other makes, mainly during multi-flash operation. In any case: you will have to try to find out for yourself. Logically Nikon cannot be made liable for damage clearly due to using flash equipment without the Nikon-logo.

CHAPTER 9

The Lenses

A photograph does not reveal the type of camera it was taken with, but it does tell us a lot about the kind of lens that was used. In respect of the angle of view particularly, the dynamic impression created by an ultrawide-angle lens is as easily distinguishable as the more or less compressed perspective of a telephoto. The decision to go for the Nikon system gives a photographer access to an extremely versatile and high quality series of lenses, making possible the realization of even the most extraordinary ideas and desires concerning composition, effect, perspective, lighting conditions, etc.

Nikon is one of the few manufacturers who produce their lenses entirely in their own factories, beginning with the melting of the glasses, continuing through computation and design, and culminating in the assembly. Even though rumours arise every now and then alleging that Nikon has some lenses produced by other companies – not a word is true. In fact the opposite is the case: Nikon manufactures lenses for certain other firms.

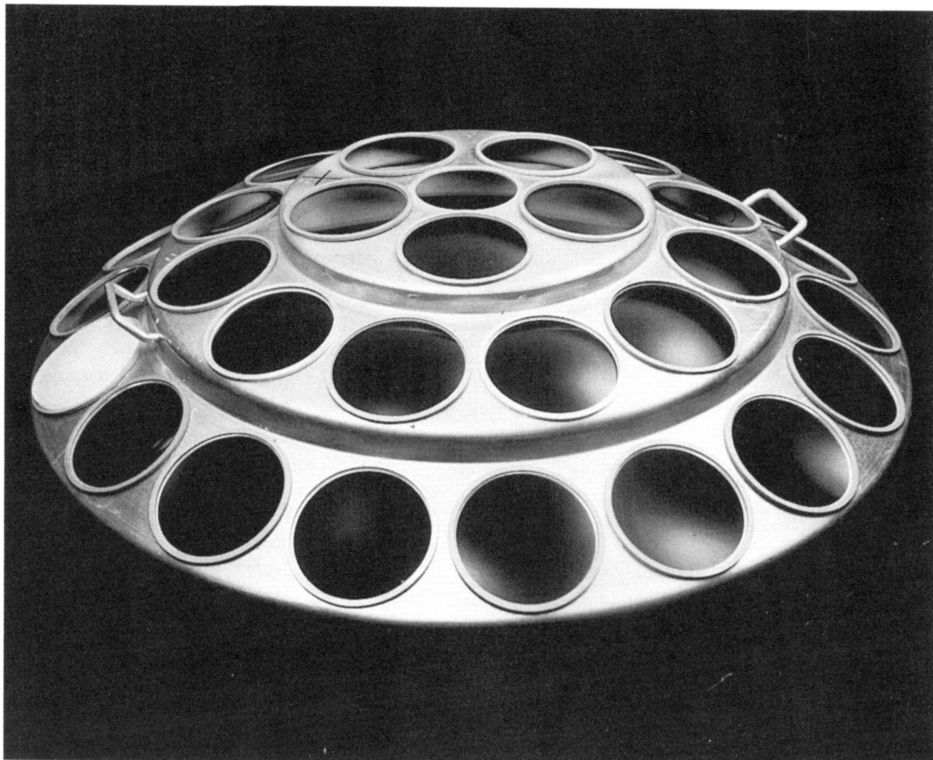

Nikon insist on manufacturing their own high-quality lenses from start to finish. Polished lens elements immediately after the coating process.

Since 1932, lenses made by Nikon have carried the name Nikkor. The first lens for 35mm format was produced in 1934 for the Hansa Kwanon, it was a 35mm,f/3.5. Even after Nikon had begun to sell their own cameras they continued to supply other camera manufacturers with lenses. For example, 39mm-thread mount versions during the age of rangefinder cameras for the then dominant Leica, and also for the Contax, whose bayonet was adopted for the first Nikon rangefinder cameras. A 135mm,f/3.5 for the Exakta also existed. Even today customers still call Nikon asking if and why the Nikkors for the Zenza Bronica are not available anymore, after all Nikon supplied the first lens series for this medium-format camera – eight focal lengths from 40mm to 200mm. When Plaubel introduced their "Makina", a 6x7 rangefinder camera, it had a built-in Nikkor 80mm,f/2.8, and the sister model equipped with a wide-angle lens, the W67, was also adorned by the Nikon logo. Even Hasselblad was interested in Nikon lenses for some time.

The Nikon Bayonet

A bayonet lens fitting was adopted for Nikon's first SLR camera, the Nikon F, in 1959. This bayonet has remained unchanged in its basic features to the present day. As a

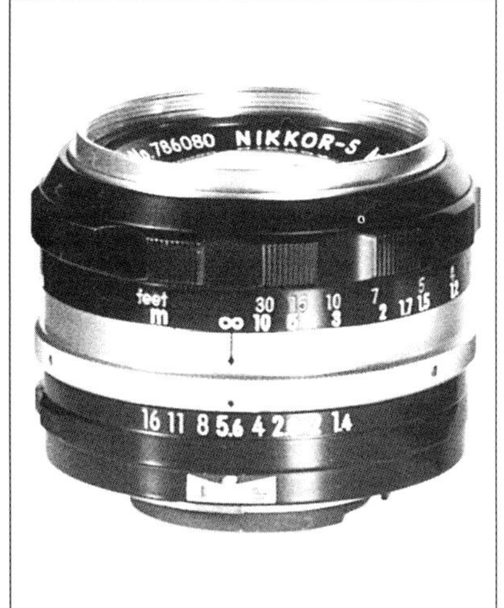

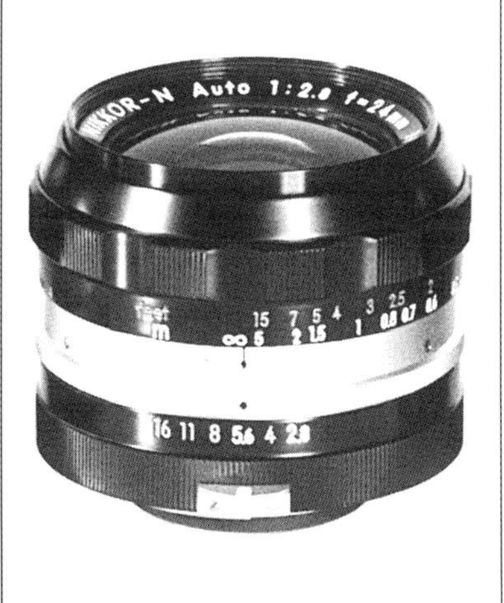
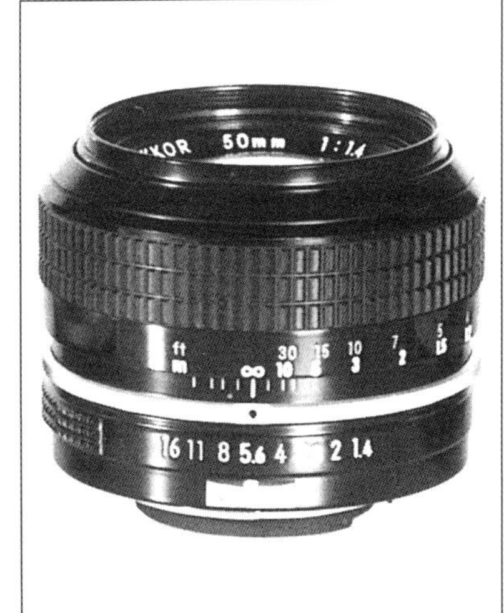
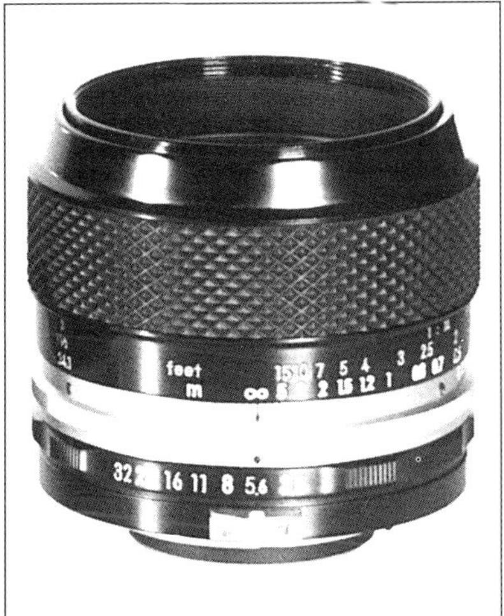
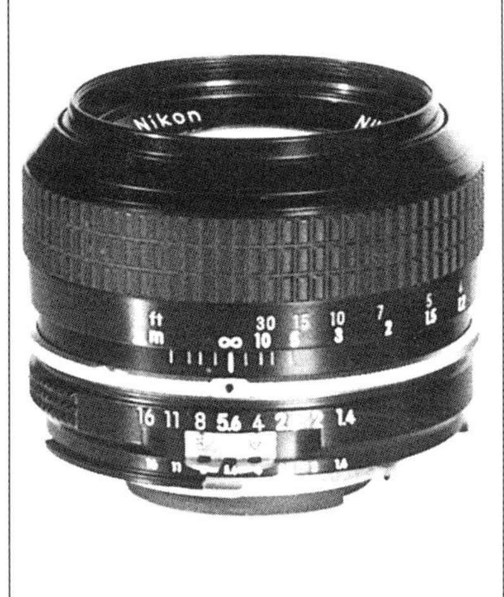

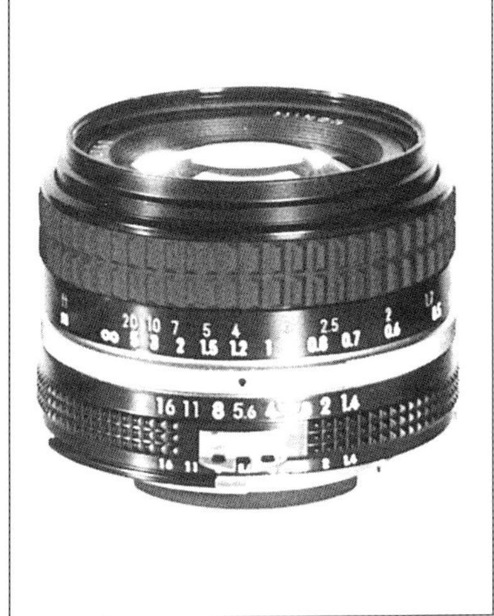
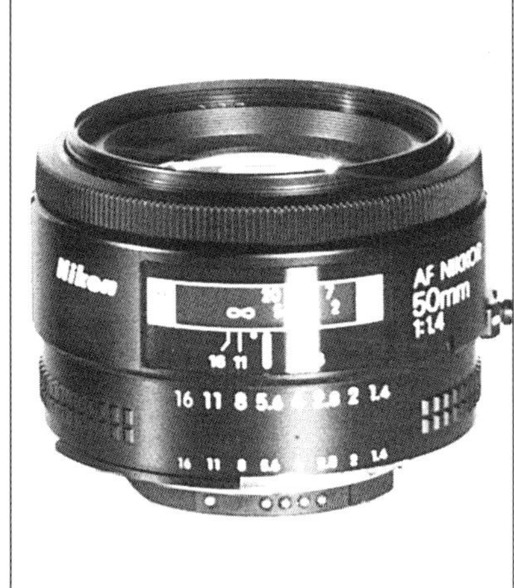

From A to AF, all the lens versions at a glance. From left to right and top to bottom: the A-type with its chrome filter ring, the C-type with a black filter ring, followed by the K-, N-, and the first AI-S- type, and finally an AF-Nikkor 50mm,f/1.4.

result of this continuity the newest lenses with autofocus coupling and contacts can be mounted on the oldest body, and it works the other way around too. In principle the combination of an early Nikkor and a modern autofocus body poses no problem. The only thing to be considered in this case is that certain functions are not available because the neccessary notches, ridges, pins, etc., are missing on the lens – but that seems to be a small sacrifice for complete compatibility.

In the tables at the back of this book, *All Nikon Lenses At A Glance*, and *Lens/Camera Combinations* at the back of this chapter, classifications are used referring to different series of lenses. Every Nikon photographer should be aware of the differences between these versions if he works with cameras and lenses from different generations, or if he is not sure whether an older Nikkor he is thinking of buying will operate on a present-day body. Basically, Nikon lenses can be classified into six different versions: these are the A-, C-, K-, N-, AI-S-, AI-E-, and AF-series. This may confuse or even disconcert someone used to mounting his lenses on his body without a thought. But it is not difficult to memorize their features and how to identify them. The different versions are described in the following paragraphs, including the possibilities and restrictions

Background Information: Lenses and their features

What is a good lens? All photographers would like their lenses to excel in every respect: lenses with the best possible resolution, with extremely large apertures, not to say compact, lightweight and moderately priced. But one cannot have everything combined in one lens. A lens is always designed and built to achieve the best possible compromise with respect to all the desirable performance factors for a certain area of application.

Thus it would not make any sense to employ a wide-angle lens for reproductions, since it would display an unavoidable amount of light fall-off towards the corners as well as a degree of distortion unacceptable in this field of photography. Micro-Nikkors on the other hand are ideal for reproductions because their design is optimized specifically for large magnifications. These, in turn, pay for this ability with relatively small apertures, making them less suitable for available-light photography. So, every would-be customer should consider very carefully what he is intending to do with the desired lens before going out to buy it.

The primary quality demanded in a lens is to produce the best possible sharpness. But what exactly does that mean? Technically speaking, sharpness is the ability to reproduce contrast and resolution – to put it simply. A more brilliant picture will always be considered to be sharper than a less contrasty one. But that is not all. In a 35mm camera the picture information is compressed into a space of 864 square millemetres. The developed negative is only an intermediate result, its information has to be printed onto photographic paper in the processing lab. This poses no problem for the widespread standard 9x13cm-format, it represents a magnification of just 3.7x. But if, say, an enlargement of 30x40cm is to be made, it calls for a formidable magnification of 12x, and this will clearly show whether or not the resolving power of the lens was high enough to reveal the minutest details. We will disregard here the resolution of the film and the

concerning their compatibility with the various cameras.

The A-type

The very first lenses for the Nikon F and the Nikkormat FT/FTN belong to the A-type. During these early years no screws were used in the bayonet and the distance scale was only marked in feet. The filter-ring was chromed and the ring carrying the designation was engraved with the maximum aperture, the focal length, and the name "Nikkor". A letter after the name indicated the number of elements. Nikon used the initial letter of the Greek word for the appropriate number as the code:

U	= Uns	=	1 element
B	= Bini	=	2 elements
T	= Tres	=	3 elements
Q	= Quatuor	=	4 elements
P	= Pente	=	5 elements
H	= Hex	=	6 elements
S	= Septem	=	7 elements
O	= Octo	=	8 elements
N	= Novem	=	9 elements
D	= Decem	=	10 elements

Thus, the 135mm,f/3.5 with its four elements carries the name Nikkor-Q, while the 15mm,f/5.6 with its 15 elements is a Nikkor-PD. There was a general belief among camera buyers at the time that many elements packed into one lens was indicative of especially high quality. A myth, but Nikon knew very well how to take advantage of the situation.

Originally the term "Auto" was also included, indicating the automatic diaphragm. A good 20 lenses from 21mm to 1000mm were available during the 60's in the A-version. Several A-type lenses mutated to C-types due to their NIC-multicoating, but without further changes in design.

The C-type

The C-Nikkors resemble the A-versions, but they are all multi-coated. By this process several ultra-thin layers of special substances are applied to every single lens surface, resulting in two advantages. It reduces the reflection of the incident light from about 2% in the case of a single-coated surface (4% if uncoated) to less than 0.2%. Even more important than the higher light transmission is the reduction of flare caused by reflections. Flare is the reason for pictures showing poor contrast – seemingly having been taken in hazy conditions.

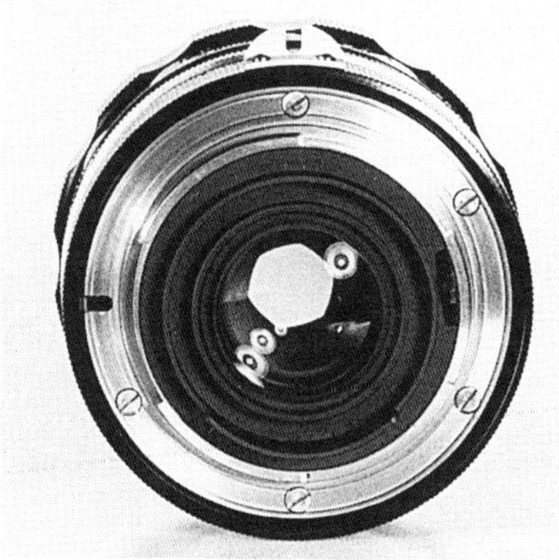

Recognized by its metal distance setting ring: a C-type Nikkor.

Not every element is coated with the seven layers though: "NIC" stands for Nikon Integrated Coating – meaning the coating is an integral part of the lens construction. The designer decides which elements are to receive how many layers of coating. This also permits the lens to be colour corrected, so that all the lenses in the system have the same color rendition. In a normal photographer's daily work the multi-coated surface is usually immune to abrasion. So there is hardly any danger of damaging it when the front and rear elements are cleaned, but do not use any solvents other than approved Nikon lens cleaners. Besides its conspicuous shimmering coating, the C-type can also be recognized by its black filter ring and the additional "C" after the code letter for the number of elements. The C-versions succeeded the A-types between 1967 and 1970.

unavoidable losses caused by the enlarging lens as well as other influential factors easily forgotten or underestimated, such as slight vibrations even in the case of tripod shots due to the operation of the mirror, slight malfocusing, low subject contrast, marred front and rear lens surfaces, a filter that is not 100% plane-parallel, a missing lens hood, etc., etc.

Depending on the circumstances, two other optical faults may be even more annoying than the lack of super sharpness. These are light fall-off towards the corners (vignetting) and distortion. In every lens the passing light is reduced towards the corners. The difference between the centre and the corners depends on the lens design and angle of view. In the case of the highly corrected Micro-Nikkors both values are so small they can only be established with the help of extremely sensitive measuring instruments. These two aberrations are considerably more serious in zooms, wide-angle and especially fast lenses.

Vignetting can be reduced to a degree by stopping down the lens, whereas there is no optical remedy against distortion. Vignetting becomes particularly obvious in pictures with uniformly coloured or bright backgrounds, such as a cloudless sky, snow, or a blank wall. Distortion is due to the inability of the lens to render straight lines perfectly straight, an aberration not very bothersome except in critical applications such as reproductions and architectural photography. Depending on the lens design, the straight lines can be bent inwards at the corners (barrel-shaped distortion) or outwards (pincushion distorsion)

As indicated before, the more complex the optical design of a lens becomes, and the more individual elements are involved, the higher the probability of certain aberrations. Designers and the powerful computers serving them are at best capable of achieving the best possible compromise – regardless of how nearly perfect the resulting product may seem to be.

The K-type

This series of lenses can be identified at first sight by the rubber-covered distance ring fitted to most of them, as well as their black depth-of-field rings. The mechanics inside are the same as the C-type. At the time the K-versions prevailed the total number of different lenses in the programme had risen to 50. The K-series after a relatively short time were replaced by the new N-versions from 1977. Some lenses were never available in a K-version.

The N-type

The N-type was introduced in 1977, equipped with the new AI-system. AI stands for Automatic Maximum Aperture Indexing. Before this the value had to be conveyed to the camera's exposure meter by the pin-and-prong coupling on the lens and body. In order to do so, the aperture ring had to be rotated once completely to the right and once to the left after the lens was attached. The AI-versions were still fitted with the prong, but it was only neccessary for "pre-AI" cameras. In the new AI-standard bodies a cam on the aperture ring informs the camera directly about the maximum as well as the preset aperture. Depending on the lens speed, this cam is situated at slightly different angles on the ring. In addition to the usual aperture values, these lenses also have a second and smaller scale on the aperture ring which can be read inside most AI-standard cameras; Nikon calls this system ADR = Aperture Direct Readout. A second pin on the

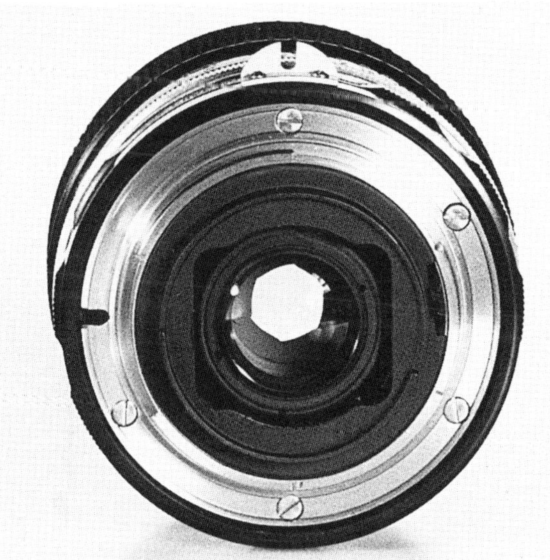

A K-type lens, easily identified by its rubberized focusing ring.

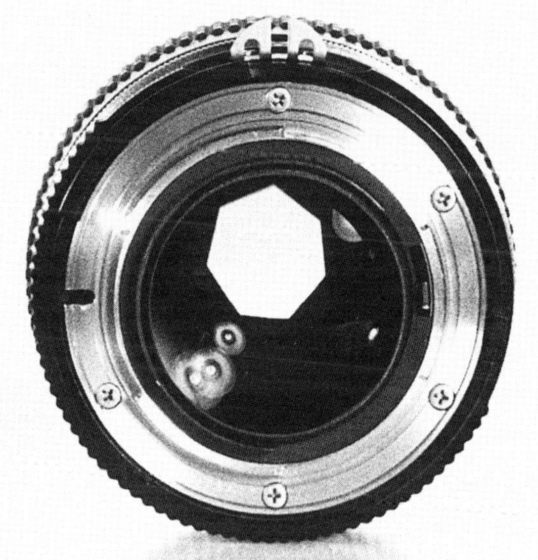

An N-type lens with AI-coupling system and the cut-out prong.

aperture ring serves as a coupling for the AI-version of the F2 DS-12 aperture control unit.

Nikon offered a service to convert older C- and K-type lenses to the new AI-system standard. The original intention had been to continue this modification service for five years, but even today it is still possible in principle. Only in principle because the modification sets are no longer being manufactured. The sets for popular lenses have been sold out for some time now, so Nikon can only offer the service for a few of the less common models. Nevertheless, two authorized service stations have devised a way to achieve the same effect: they cut out the old, wider aperture ring precisely at a predefined position.

The difference between an original AI-lens and a version modified to that standard can easily be identified. An additional lens speed indexing post is located right next to the rear lens element which has the function of informing the electronics of those modern cameras with a programmed automatic exposure mode. At the same time the mechanics of the lens were improved. A double helix moves the optical system away from the film plane when focusing at close quarters. In the former versions the focusing ring was also moved forwards a bit. The different pitches of the two helixes in the N-series lenses avoid this disadvantage. While the optical system is moved forward, the focusing ring only moves away from its original position by less than a millimetre. The depth-of-field scale is now located on the chrome ring between the focusing and aperture rings, and the N-versions also have a small advantage in terms of size and weight, being generally a little shorter and lighter.

The AI-S-type

This lens series was introduced in 1982. From the outside they can be distinguished by their orange-coloured maximum aperture value and a milled semi-circular notch in the bayonet flange. This was initially designed to inform Nikon cameras with exposure modes involving mechanical automatic aperture control, such as the FA, that a lens with a linear aperture mechanism is attached. Linear means that every millimetre the aperture coupling lever moves corresponds to an equal amount of stop-down operation. In a non-AI-S-type lens a movement of one millimetre results in a change of a mere ⅓ step at first, but more than one whole step at the end. Thanks to this internal modification, which does not show on the outside, AI-S lenses make it easier for the camera to control the diaphragm automatically in the various modes.

The E-series

The E-series was introduced together with the Nikon EM so that less expensive lenses could be offered with this beginner's camera. Their bayonet corresponds to the AI-S-types except that the aperture prong for older cameras is missing. The focusing ring and the helixes were made of plastic. With the exception of the 35m, 50mm, and 100mm lenses, which only had single coatings, all the individual elements of the others were multi-coated.

The AF-type

Nikon's first lenses designed for automatic focusing were the 80mm and 200mm, introduced with the F3 AF, that had focus motors of their own. Although they can be used with the F-501, F-801/F-801s, F90 and F4, their autofocus technology lags behind that of the present lenses.

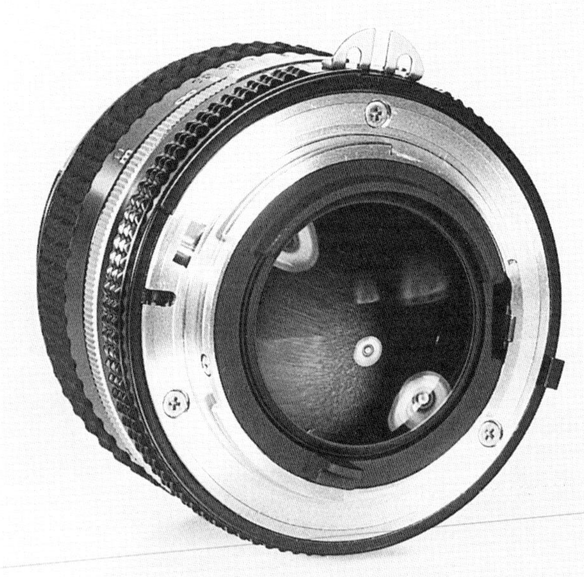

The milled, semi-circular notch distinguishes the AI-S-lenses.

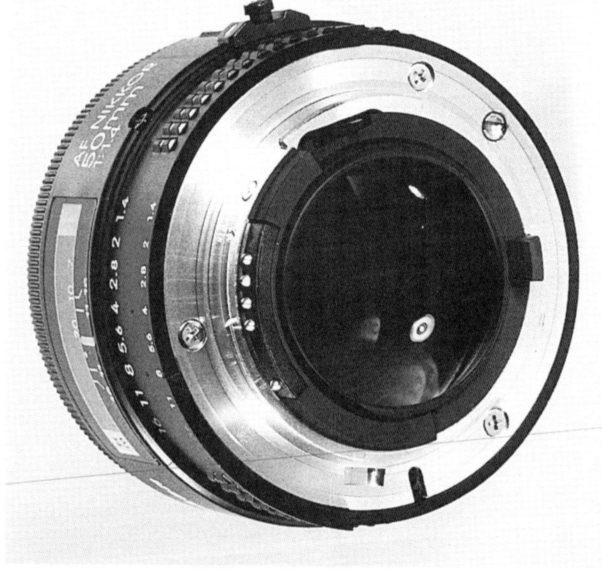

An AF-Nikkor 50mm,f/1.4, immediately identifiable by the electrical contacts.

The current line of AF-Nikkors was introduced in 1986 with the F-501. Their bayonet standard is comparable with the AI-S-type, but without the prong. A CPU (central processing unit) is built-in. It signals the specific lens data to the camera's autofocus drive and exposure metering systems through five contacts situated above the rear element. The aperture ring can be locked in its smallest position to rule out any accidental miss-setting.

The helixes were replaced by a cam construction similar to that employed in zoom lenses to change the focal length. The advanced standard of exposure and autofocus technology introduced with the Nikon F90, as well as the sports photographers' demands for faster focusing, called for minor changes within the lenses, for modifications of the lenses' CPUs and drive-mechanics to be precise. Two different developments serve to meet these needs. The first was the incorporation of the AF-drive motor and gear-train into the lens itself. This is only necessary and sensible in the case of lenses in which the focusing elements must travel a considerable distance between the infinity and closest settings – taking decisively longer than in other, mostly shorter focal length lenses. So the first three AF-I lenses (I as in integrated) appearing early in 1992 and late in 1993 were fast, super-telephoto types. It was clearly stated by Nikon that not all AF-Nikkors will be converted to this standard even in the long run (as in the case of one prominent competitor), but only certain, otherwise too slow models.

Users of these AF-I Nikkors should be aware of the fact that only cameras of F4 and F90 standard are equipped with the electronics to communicate with these lenses, i.e. only they allow autofocus operation. On the other hand these lenses offer very convenient additional features. A third focus-setting permits manual override of the autofocus operation at any time and four AF-lock buttons are situated around the front barrels – making them the perfect instrument for fast action-photography.

As has been described before, the F90-standard cameras make additional use of the distance information to determine the whereabouts of the main subject and thus further improve automatic exposure. In order to do so they depend on the attached lens delivering the neccessary data. When the F90 as the first model of the new generation appeared, it was along with AF-D Nikkors whose CPUs had been modified to provide the "3D-Matrix Metering"-system with the lens distance setting.

Although Nikon was not prepared to state whether or not all AF-Nikkors would be replaced by AF-D types at the time, it now seems to be the case that at least every newly introduced lens will be of the D-standard. This was done because the autofocus motor would be overstrained if it had to move the greased helices found in normal lenses.

The motor's power is transferred to the gearing in the AF-lens by means of a coupling resembling a screwdriver in a slot.

In 1987 Nikon announced their intention to replace all non-AF lenses by AF-versions step by step. This caused a wave of shock and anger among Nikon photographers who did not wish to work with an AF-camera. The main reason for all the disturbance was the very slim focusing ring which was not very convenient for manual operation. Nikon was well-advised to go back on this decision and find a far better solution instead. Since 1988 all AF-lenses have been fitted with a broader focusing ring to improve the manual handling.

Special Features In Nikon Lenses

Besides the listed versions there are some lenses which differ due to special features independent of the various generations. First to be

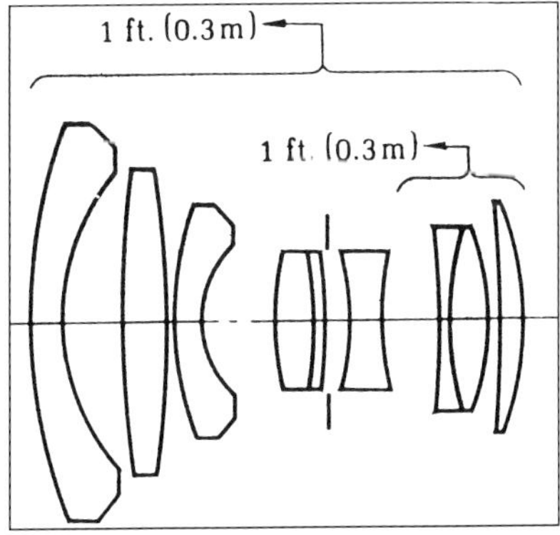

A technique ensuring high image quality even in the case of close-ups. Nikon's CRC-system shifts the individual groups within the lens seperately so that they change their relative distances.

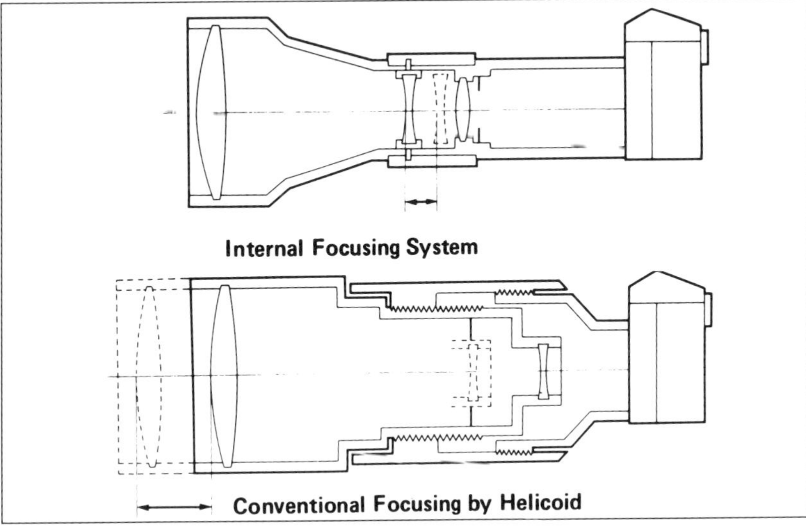

A schematic illustration of a conventional helical construction as opposed to internal focusing which avoids any change in the length of the lens during focusing.

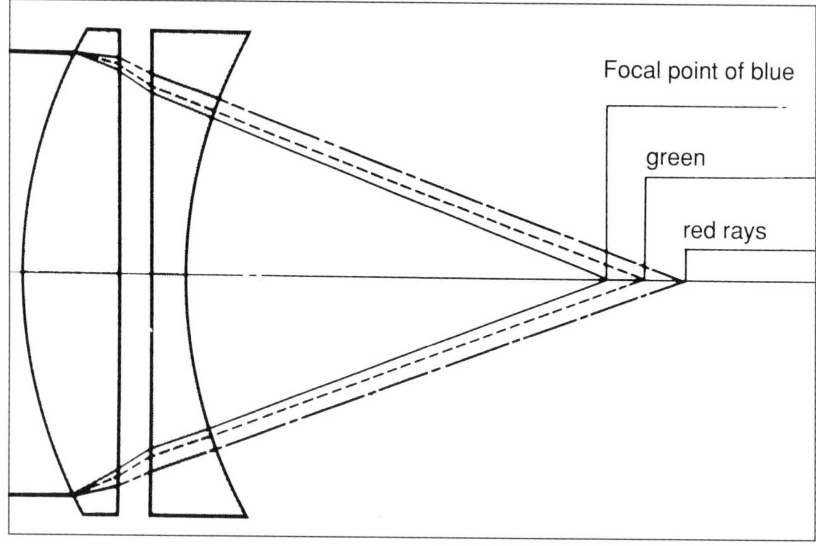

The use of ED-glass unites the focal points of all parts of the spectrum.

mentioned is a technique designated "CRC". The letters stand for Close Range Correction. In the cases of extreme wide-angle lenses and large aperture lenses a marked image fall-off can be observed if the lenses are used at close range. In order to diminish this problem the CRC-design – also called "floating elements" – is employed in certain lenses. Depending on the focus setting, the front and rear elements within these lenses change their distances relative to each other. This keeps the image quality on a high level even at short ranges. The same technique is employed in the Micro-Nikkors 55mm,f/2.8 and 105mm,f/2.8 as well as the 85mm, f/1.4.

IF stands for Internal Focusing and is used in telephoto lenses. Normally the whole optical system is moved forward out of the infinity position by the helical construction. This calls for a considerable effort in the case of fast telephoto lenses, and also makes the units rather weighty. At short ranges, i.e. when its extension is fairly long, the centre of gravity of the lens is shifted forwards too. Internal focusing eliminates these drawbacks by moving only one small lens group inside the lens. This makes it easy to use long focal lengths for hand-held shots even if they also happen to have a large maximum aperture. Even at close range, the lens will not change its length or its centre of gravity during focusing, and the image quality is also comparable to the CRC-equipped lenses.

ED stands for Extra Low Dispersion and distinguishes Nikon's lenses with extraordinary image quality. This measure acts against a problem particularly bothering with longer focal lengths. White light consists of a mixture of the complete spectrum of visible light. Beginning with the short-wave radiation in the ultraviolet range all the way to the long-wave infrared sector. These constituent parts of the spectrum come to focus at slightly different points though. Visually based focusing works with the blue-green wavelengths of the light. When the focal length and the lens speed increase, the focal points diverge so much that they sometimes exceed the maximum aperture's depth-of-field, which results in visible colour fringing and generally a reduced sharpness. Thanks to ED-glass, the focal points converge so closely that crisp sharpness and brilliant contrast can be expected even when the diaphragm is fully open. The ED-models can be identified by the gold ring on the lens barrel signalling their exceptional image quality. Of course, the unusually high manufacturing costs are reflected in the significantly higher prices of ED-lenses.

Standard Lenses

A focal length of 50mm is considered to be "normal" for the 35mm-format; due to its angle of view of 46° its rendering of perspective comes closest to that of the human eye. At the same time normal lenses are still relatively simple optically allowing fast maximum apertures without resulting in astronomically high prices. The slowest of the standard Nikkors is the 50mm,f/2. It was the first Nikkor for the Nikon F and its

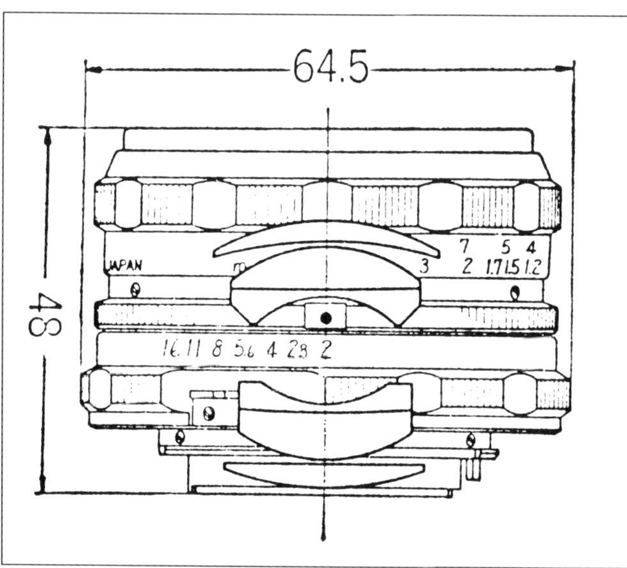

Nikon's first standard lens in cross-section, the Nikkor-H 50mm,f/2 C.

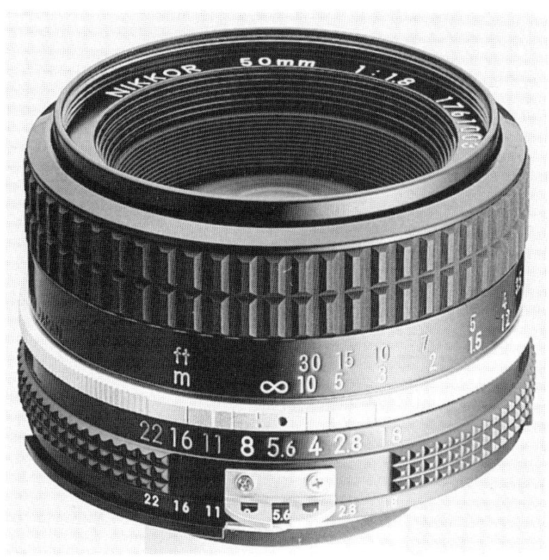

The equally compact Nikkor 50mm,f/1.8 N, immediate successor to the 50mm,f/2.

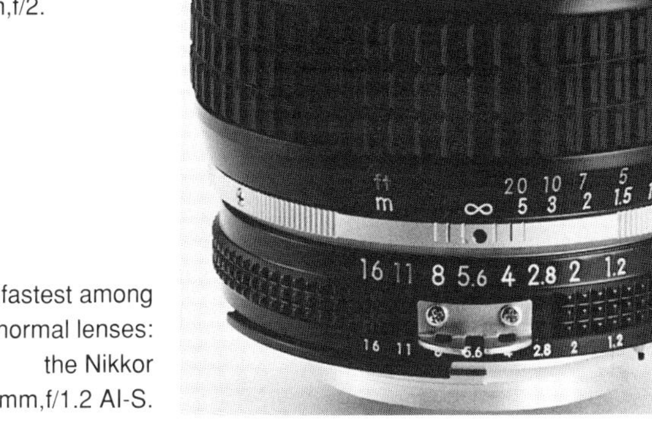

The fastest among the normal lenses: the Nikkor 58mm,f/1.2 AI-S.

basic design remained unchanged until it was discontinued in 1979. With six elements, it also performs well in close-ups thanks to its almost perfectly symmetrical layout. The restriction to a rather small maximum aperture is exactly the specification leading to the excellent image quality of this lens all the way into the corners, even at full aperture.

It was replaced by the optically only slightly modified 50mm,f/1.8 in 1978, which shows similarly fine results at a ⅓-stop larger maximum aperture. In 1985 the 50mm,f/1.8 N appeared. It had been optimized further and fitted with the E-series mechanics and as a result it was very small – just 36mm high. Unlike the 50mm,f/1.8 E, its elements are all multicoated. Together with the F-501, the 50mm,f/1.8 AF was introduced, resembling the first 50mm,f/1.8 in its proportions. As of 1989 the narrow focusing ring was widened to ensure more positive manual operation.

Shortly after the 50mm,f/2, the faster 58mm,f/1.4 was introduced for the Nikon F. A comprehensive design consisting of seven elements, but is was only produced for three years and replaced by a new one in 1962, also involving seven elements, but with considerably improved image quality. Keeping in mind its high speed, vignetting is remarkably low, and the contrast rendering is also convincing. Like most of the superfast lenses, this one is not suitable for close-ups. The N-type represents a new optical and mechanical design, somewhat more compact and 20% lighter, with equal performance. This version is still available, although in the AF- and AI-S-versions.

The 55mm,f/1.2, also a seven-element design, added yet another ½-stop of speed in 1967. It weighs in at a formidable 420g. Nobody should expect too much in terms of brilliant contrast and distortion-free images from such a lens trimmed to an extreme speed. It was simply conceived for situations in which half a stop is more important than the highest image quality. In 1978 this lens was replaced by a similar one displaying similar performance. A little known fact is that these superfast lenses are sensitive to blows from the side because their mechanics are comparatively thin so as to ensure as compact a lens as possible.

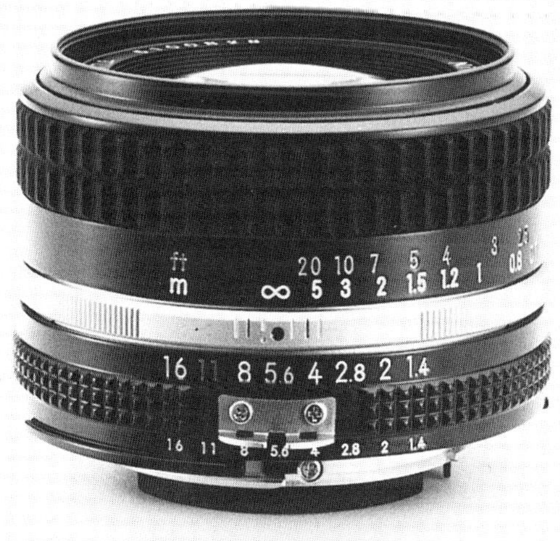

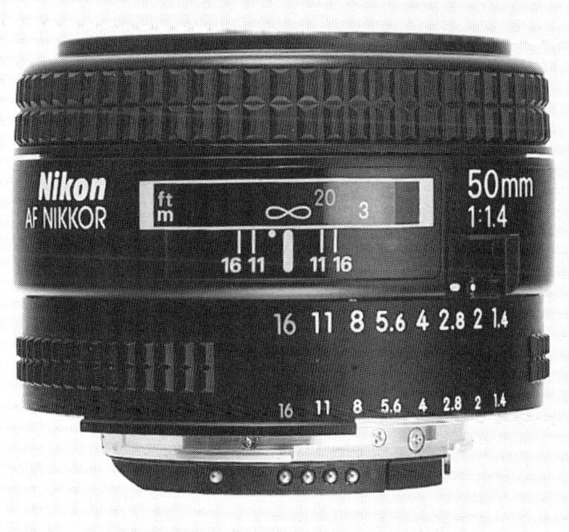

One of the most popular 50mm's, the fast 50mm,f/1.4 in the AI-S-version, left, and AF right.

Because of its universal qualities and whenever the maximum aperture is not the decisive criterion, the 55mm Micro-lens is often chosen as the normal lens.

For years now the significance of standard lenses has been diminishing, so-called standard zooms such as a 35mm to 70mm have clearly got the better of them. Although the zooms do have their indisputable benefits and have also become ever more compact – in terms of maximum aperture the normal lenses are still in the lead.

Background Information: Retrofocus design

The history of wide-angle photography began for Nikon in 1948 with the Nikkor-W 35mm,f/3.5 built for the rangefinder cameras. Five years later on their way to shorter focal lengths they had already arrived at 25mm, and in 1959 the 21mm lens appeared, with an angle of view of 92°. There is a basic problem closely related to the design of ultra-wide-angle lenses for SLR-cameras. In order to permit viewing through the lens, there must be a clearance of about 40mm between the film plane and the rear lens element so that the mirror can swing up. For wide-angle lenses from a certain focal length this distance – called back focal length (measured from the apex of the rear lens element) – can no longer be realized.

The problem was solved by adding some lens elements which increase the back focal length. This retrofocus design is normally employed nowadays and has yet another advantage: it lessens the problem of vignetting, otherwise very obvious in ultra-wide-angle lenses. Also the CRC-technique is applied in most of the modern designs to compensate image deterioration in close-up photography. Wide-angles are quite complex systems for which a designer must sometimes employ up to 16 elements in order to cope with all the problems arising.

Wideangle Lenses

A superlative right from the start, Nikon has produced – unchallenged for years now – the most extreme, practically distortion-free wide-angle lens for a 35mm SLR.

13mm Wide-angle

The Nikon compact 13mm,f/5.6 covers an angle of 118°. Every single feature of this lens, and we may as well include its price, is extraordinary. The front element has a diameter of almost 11cm, it weighs an impressive 1200 grams, and its price reaches that of a respectable small car. Anyone who has never experienced the effect of this lens by looking through the camera viewfinder should prepare himself – the impression is breathtaking. Even the slightest tilt of this gigantic wide-angle will cause the verticals in the picture to converge dramatically, an effect demonstrating dazzling sides to even the most banal subjects. Naturally, filters cannot be mounted in front of the spherical front element, instead they are attached behind the rear one. Next to the 6mm-fisheye and the 2000mm Reflex-Nikkor, the Nikkor 13mm,f/5.6 is one of the three lenses which Nikon only produce to special order. It is simply a very special lens conceived for those who really need the extreme picture angle and do not have to bother about price.

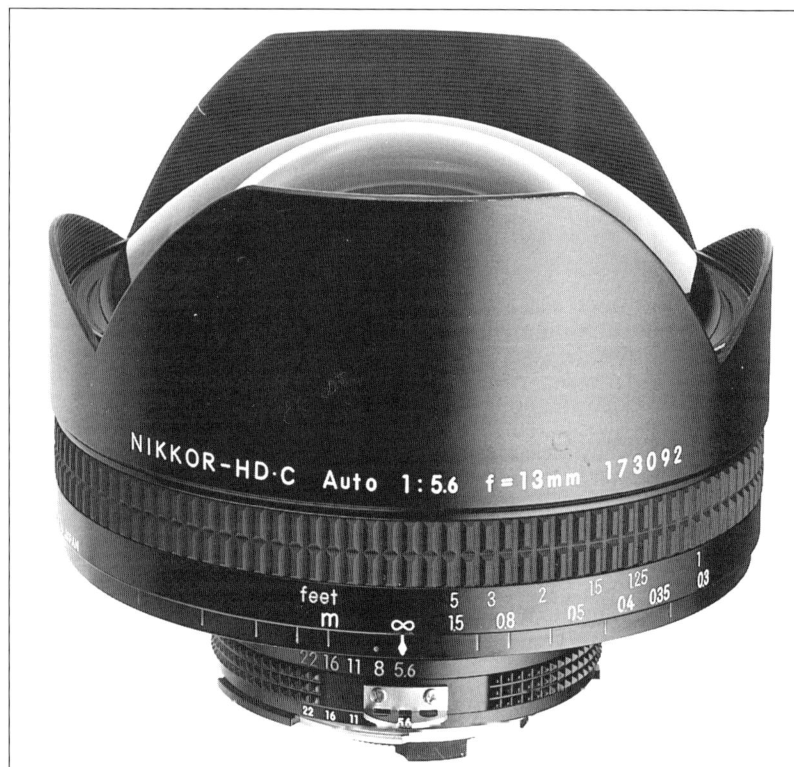

The 13mm-Nikkor, with an angle of view of 118° without any distortion, is still unequalled.

15mm-Wide-angle

The Nikkor 15mm,f/3.5 displays a similarly impressive effect with its 110° angle of view. Only 8° less, but in exchange only half as heavy and only one fifth of the price. The scalloped hood is an integral part of this lens, it serves more as a protection for the vulnerable large front element than as a hood. Filters are attached behind the rear element as with the 13mm Nikkor.

Before the 15mm,f/3.5, another version, the 15mm,f/5.6 was available from 1973 to 1978, the major difference, apart from greater bulk, being that it had a built-in filter

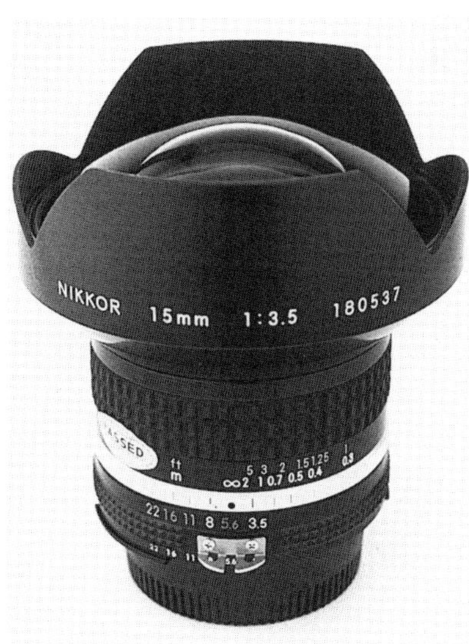

The Nikkor 15mm,f/3.5.

turret. A yellow filter Y48, an orange one O56, or a red R60 could be swung into the light path by a ring on the outside.

18mm-Wide-angle

The Nikkor 18mm,f/4 can be seen much more often than the two exotic specimens described above. With a still formidable covering power of 100° it was the favourite lens of many landscape and architectural photographers. No wonder, since its weight of a mere 315 grams makes it ideally mobile for shots on the go. This 18mm,f/4 is one of the last lenses to be designed for the use of series 9 filters mounted between the barrel and the hood. After eight years of production it was replaced by the presently still available 18mm,f/3.5 which, thanks to the use of the CRC-system, may well be the sharpest Nikon ultra-wide-angle lens of all. Its dimensions were reduced so that filters with a 72mm-thread can be attached.

20mm-Wide-angle

The latest 20mm,f/2.8 is probably the current ultra-wide-angle for the pro as well as the committed hobby photographer. It is available in the normal and autofocus versions. The most important features are its 94° angle of view, almost as compact as a fast standard lens, and the CRC-system for the best possible image quality down to the shortest focusing distance of 25cm. In terms of optical power this 12-element Nikkor is the best 20mm yet, and to top it off it gets along with 62mm filters. The fast maximum aperture of f/2.8 makes focusing a lot easier and when fully open it still produces a large depth of field – everything between 5m and infinity. Its predeccessor was the even more compact 20mm,f/3.5 with a 52mm filter thread, but because it lacked the CRC-technique you had to take the considerable vignetting towards the corners into consideration. Its predeccessor in turn, the 20mm,f/4 which also had the 52mm filter thread and was producd from 1974 to 1978, needed only 10 lens elements to achieve nearly the same image quality. During the 1976 Photokina the prototype of a 20mm,f/2.8 had been displayed but it never went into production. The very first 20mm was the Nikkor-UD 20mm,f/3.5 consisting of 11 elements and easily distinguished by its large 72mm filter

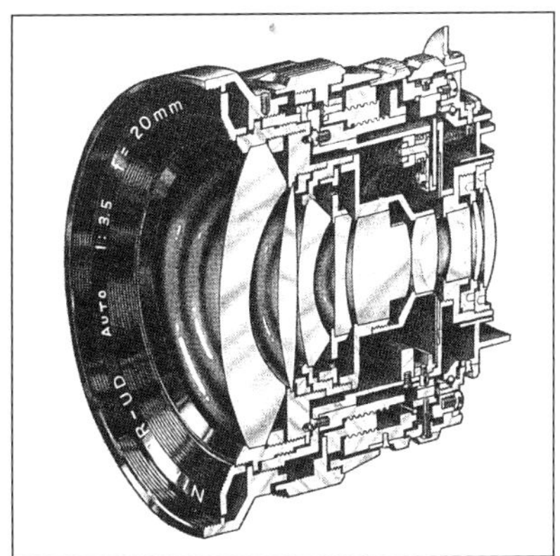

The Nikkor-UD 20mm,f/3.5 in cross-section.

thread. At the time it appeared in 1967 it was Nikon's most extreme wide-angle lens and also the first retrofocus design of this focal length. Until then, only the 21mm,f/4 conceived for the rangefinder models had been available. In order to utilize this lens, the reflex mirror had to be locked up and an external viewfinder attached above the Nikon F's rewind crank. On the other hand it only had eight lens elements and a very low weight of 135 grams.

24mm-Wide-angle

The Nikkor 24mm,f/2.8 is a favourite among photojournalists, so after its appearance in 1967 it quickly won itself a habitual place in their gadget bags. It was the first Nikon lens employing the CRC-technique, resulting in excellent image quality even in the picture corners. This nine-element lens design was up-dated in 1977, further reducing the vignetting that had been low before anyway. Today, its optical design unchanged, this lens is still available in the AF-version. The Nikkor 24mm,f/2 is a whole stop faster, but its image quality cannot quite compare to that of the 24mm,f/2.8.

28mm Wide-angle

For many amateur photographers the 28mm lens is the standard wide-angle. The first version appeared in 1960 in the form of the Nikkor 28mm,f/3.5. It had six elements,

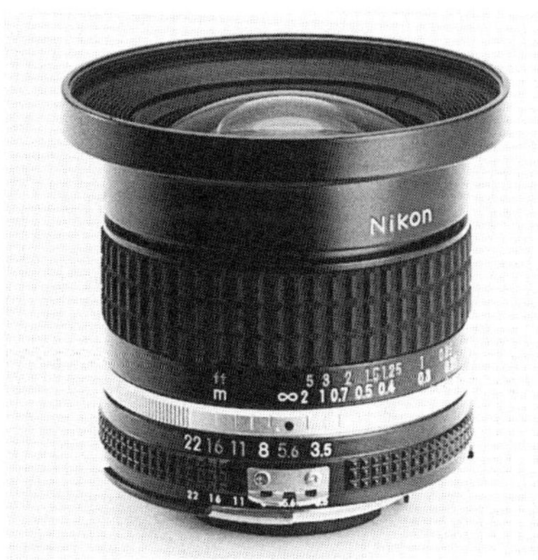

The Nikkor 18mm,f/3.5.

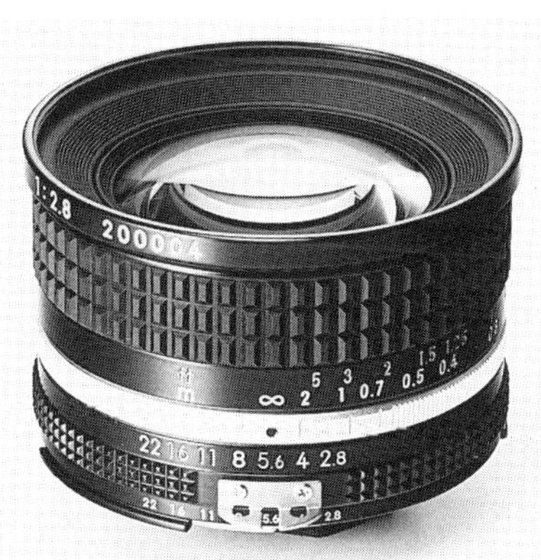
The Nikkor 20mm,f/2.8.

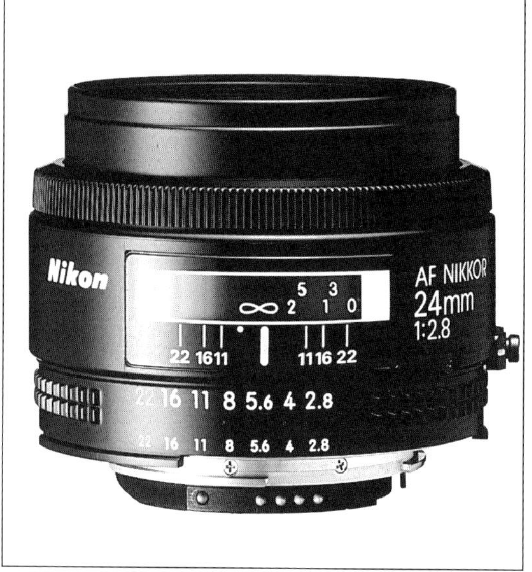

The AF-Nikkor 24mm,f/2.8. Early version left, current version with new-style focusing ring right.

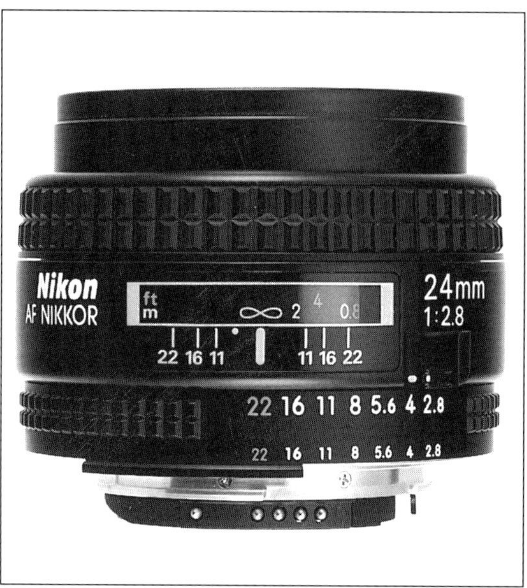

covered 74°, and, compared to today's standards, produced a rather mediocre image quality. It was the newly designed version from 1977 that offered compensation for its modest maximum aperture with visibly less vignetting. This lens is ideally suited for reproduction ratios beyond 1:1 when mounted in the retro-position on the bellows unit.

The popular lens with this focal length is the 28mm,f/2.8, which Nikon introduced in 1974. Its seven-element design did not achieve a very convincing image quality either, but its successor as of 1981 certainly did – surely one of the sharpest wide-angle lenses of all. CRC permits it to focus down to 0.2 metres where it meets the highest demands in this area too. It can rightfully be called the Micro-Nikkor for the wide-angle range.

In 1979 the 28mm from the E-series, the 28mm,f/2.8E offered an economically priced alternative. Due to its five-element design the attainable image quality is limited, but in keeping with the aim of the E-system it was a lens for the SLR-beginner who had not yet developed very high demands. The same goes for the AF 28mm,f/2.8, being identical to the 28mm E-series except for the autofocus mechanism.

Unlike these, the Nikkor 28mm, f/2 is a real treasure, convincing even at full aperture in spite of its speed. The CRC-system demonstrates its benefits quite clearly with this lens. From the very beginning this design was so well-balanced it has remained unchanged since its appearance in 1970, even in the newest outer finish. One special feature that should be mentioned is that unusually in this type of construction the CRC-system moves the front lens group independently.

A sensationally fast new lens to be introduced late in 1993 is the AF-Nikkor 28mm,f/1.4D. It incorporates

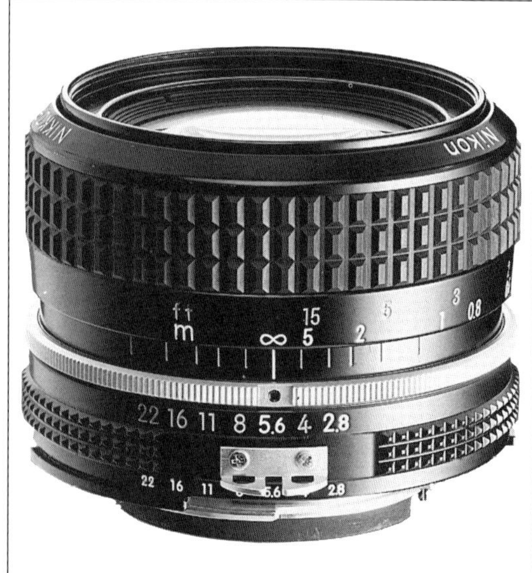

The Nikkor 28mm,f/2.8 with AF version on right.

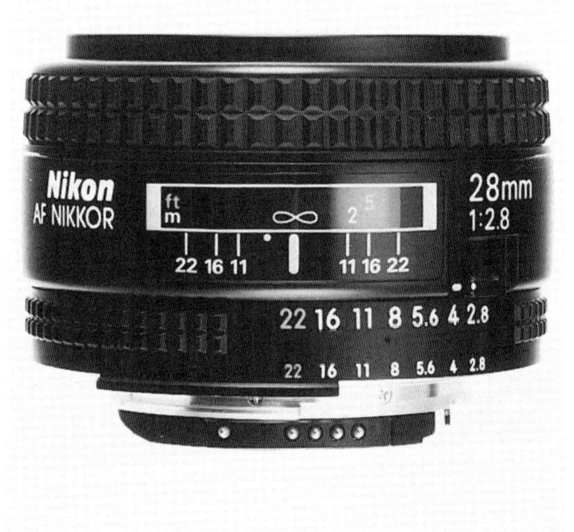

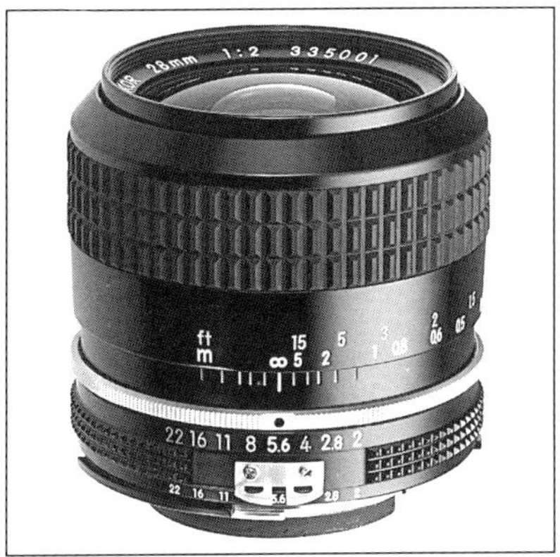

The Nikkor 28mm,f/2.

a completely new design, an aspherical element, the CRC-system, and a rear focusing system to ensure immaculate performance at any aperture and distance setting.

35mm Wide-angle

The focal length of 35mm, covering an angle of view of 62°, is a standard for many applications, especially with professional photographers. Nikon offers three different speeds within this popular focal length. The first 35mm in 1962 was the Nikkor 35mm,f/2.8 with seven elements, a featherweight of just 200g. It was recomputed in 1974 with one element less and an improved overall sharpness. As early as 1977 another new design appeared consisting of only five elements, without any visible reduction of the image quality. Just like the 28mm,f/3.5 it is also ideal for use in the retro-position when attached to the bellows unit. This lens is still

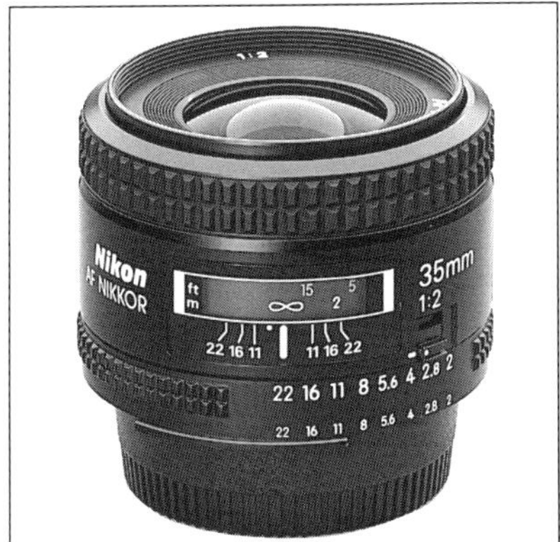

The AF-Nikkor 35mm,f/2.

available today even though the demand for a wide-angle with such a modest speed is diminishing. Thanks to its few elements the lens is ideal for shots against the light with strong contrast.

There was a 35mm in the E-series too, with a speed of f/2.5, delivering an acceptable performance at an absolutely low price. But the customer group the E-series was aimed at preferred zooms more and more so that the Nikkor 35mm,f/2.5 ended up being produced for only three years.

The unquestioned best-seller in the 35mm-class though, is the 35mm,f/2, a real classic and a well-balanced compromise between speed, sharpness, freedom of vignetting, and compact dimensions. After 13 years of production its optical layout was slightly modified in 1975, but it remained an eight-element design. The six-element AF Nikkor 35mm,f/2 represents a completely new design, equalling its non-AF partner in image quality.

In 1970 the sensational Nikkor 35mm,f/1.4 appeared – a comprehensive nine-element design including CRC. It delivers modest, but acceptable contrast at full aperture, but because of the inevitable distortion it will not be the best choice for architectural shots. This lens is also one of the few Nikkors whose optical design has remained unchanged throughout the past 20 years.

The fixed focal lengths in the wide-angle range will probably stay available for quite some time because the zooms in this area do not quite reach the current standard of the prime lenses. This is not only in terms of speed, even though the two younger AF-zooms 35-70mm,f/2.8 and 20-35mm,f/2.8 represent a new trend in this respect as well.

Telephoto Lenses

For Nikon, the telephoto range begins with the 85mm focal length. The first was the 85mm,f/2 for the rangefinder cameras. This is the lens Nikon's reputation was based upon. This is also the lens with which Nikon managed to enter the pros' world. During the Korean war the well-known American photojournalist David Douglas Duncan happened to come across this Nikon-classic and enthusiastically reported its outstanding sharpness to his colleagues.

The first 85mm for the Nikon F was the 85mm,f/1,8 introduced in 1964. A six-element design deliver-

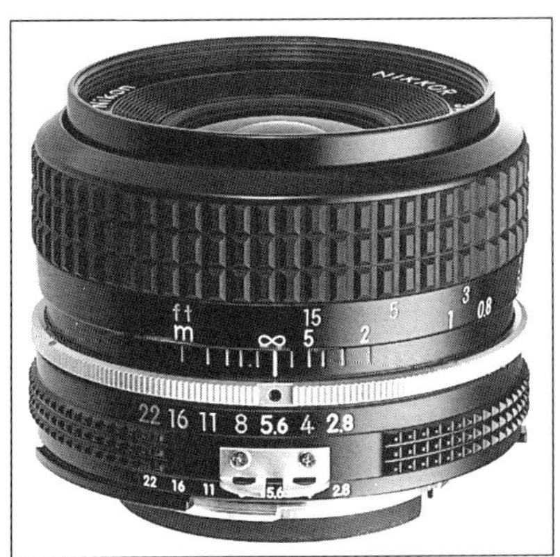

The Nikkor 35mm,f/2.8.

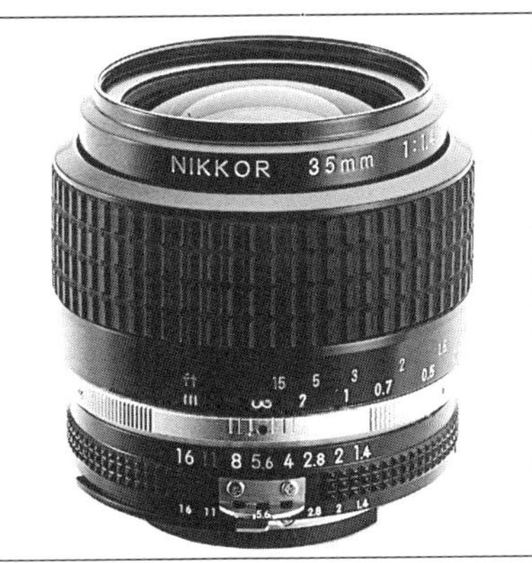

The Nikkor 35mm,f/1.4.

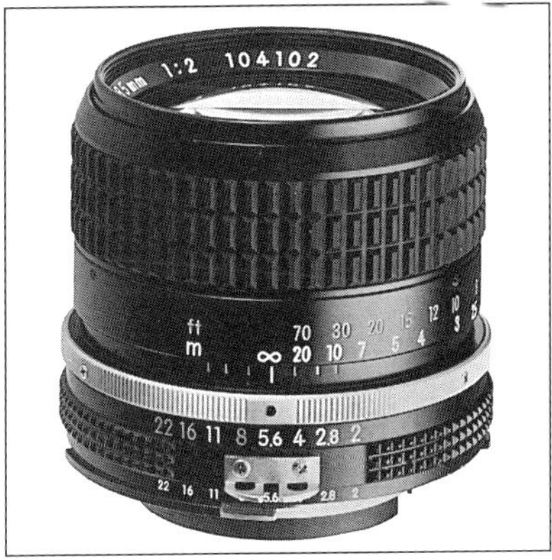

The Nikkor 85mm,f/2.

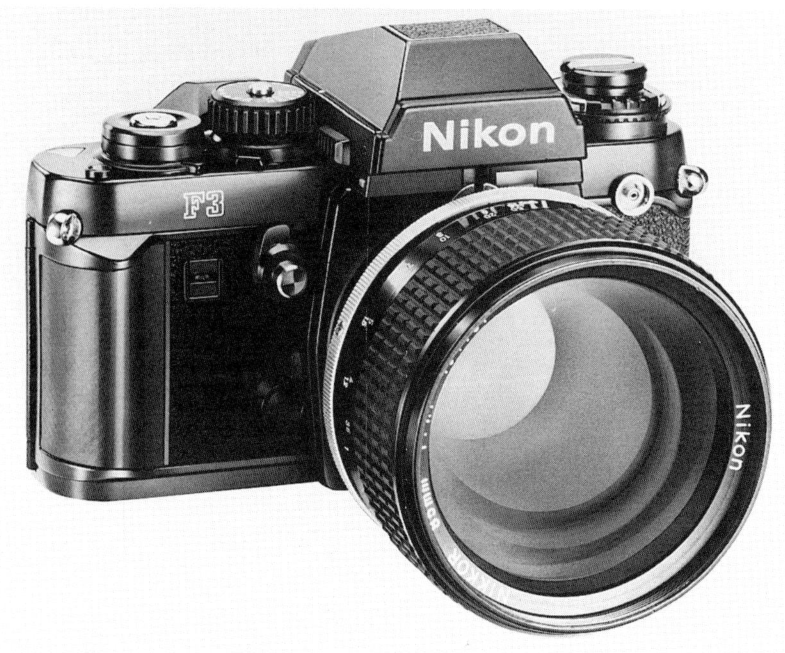

The giant front element is the predominant feature of the super-fast Nikkor 85mm,f/1.4.

ing an excellent degree of sharpness and contrast, it constituted many a photojournalist's basic equipment, together with the 35mm,f/2.

In 1977 a newly designed five-element lens with a maximum aperture of f/2 appeared as the successor – a great lens matched to the portrait photographer's demands by its intentionally reduced contrast: skin blemishes and wrinkles should not be too obvious. On the other hand this lens is not that well suited for on-the-spot photography where the full aperture is often used, as well as high-speed films delivering low contrast themselves. The desired crisp sharpness is simply missing in those shots, but together with the contrasty Kodachrome 25 it demonstrates its high resolution.

In 1981 a real on-the-spot lens finally appeared in this area, the Nikkor 85mm,f/1.4. The use of CRC made it possible to do without an expensive aspherical front element, but even so this super-fast lens delivers brilliant, contrasty negatives and slides at any aperture. Slight losses in terms of distortion and vignetting do have to be taken into consideration though, and a lens as fast as this cannot be equally well-suited for close-range shots.

In 1988 the AF-Nikkor 85mm, f/1.8, a six-element lens with a filter thread of 62mm, was introduced for the autofocus cameras. Its image quality is comparable to that of the first 85mm, that is neither too contrasty for portraits nor too soft for on the-spot-photography. A really well-balanced compromise.

The AF-Nikkor 80mm,f/2.8 conceived for the F3 AF also belongs to this category with its excellent image quality. This lens is also interesting for F-501 owners since the automatic focusing also works with this body. On the other AF-cameras it can only be used manually.

105mm Telephoto

The focal length of 100mm occurred once in Nikon's programme – in the form of the 100mm,f/2.8 E. With only four elements it delivers an acceptable performance, and its price was less than half that of a normal Nikkor in this class. Since its lens surfaces are only coated with a single layer, an NIC-coated UV or Skylight filter and the hood should always be used.

The next in the line, the Nikkor 105mm,f/2.5, can rightfully be called a Nikon legend, and many photographers consider it to be the finest lens Nikon has ever produced. The first design from 1959 was modified slightly in 1970, and the present version still belongs to the best-sellers in the Nikon programme today. With its five elements it displays a performance that places it among the top-class in terms of contrast and freedom of vignetting.

The Nikkor 105mm,f/1.8 from 1981 is a whole stop faster, and like the 85mm,f/1.4 it is virtually made for on-the-spot photography – which means high contrast even at full aperture. The combination with the Tele-

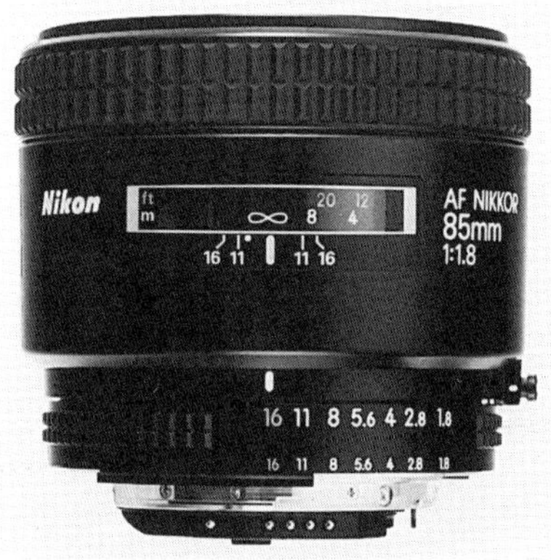

The classic and popular 85mm,f/1.8 lives as the AF-Nikkor 85mm,f/1.8.

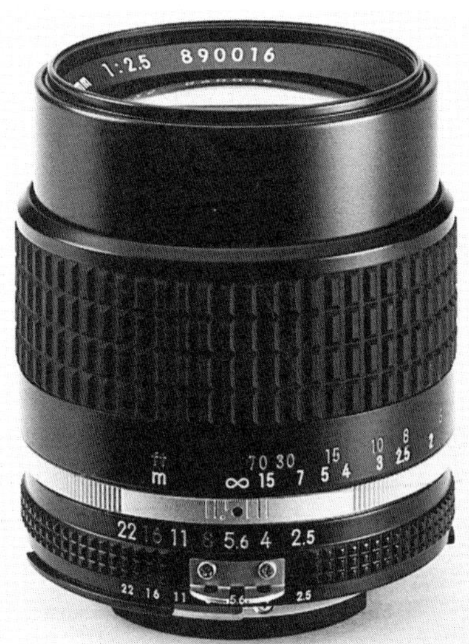

Another classic – the Nikkor 105mm,f/2.5.

converter TC-14A is also ideal, turning it into a 150mm,f/2.5.

135mm Telephoto

The 135mm lens was the classic focal length to be found in every gadget bag before the advent of the telephoto zooms. Nikon's first offer in this range was the Nikkor 135mm,f/3,5 which may have had only a modest speed but produced a respectable image quality with just four elements and was also suitable for close-ups. The modified design from 1975 is still in the Nikon list today.

A somewhat higher speed is always nice though, so that a second lens ½ stop faster was also offered. However, particularly at its maximum aperture the performance of the first Nikkor 135mm,f/2.8 can only be regarded as mediocre. So in 1976 it was replaced by a new five-element design delivering a greatly improved image quality throughout, and most of all at its maximum aperture. Together with this version another, even faster type was introduced. This was the Nikkor 135mm,f/2. This lens demonstrates the difficulty of achieving high speed without losses in performance in other ways, and it should only be recommended to those who really need that extra stop.

A 135mm,f/2.8 E also used to be available. With its four elements it achieves a respectable image quality, but without coming close to the normal Nikkor's values. It is only rarely seen since the majority of E series customers preferred a zoom.

180mm Telephoto

The Nikkor 180mm,f/2.8 created a sensation when it was introduced in 1970, and it is another one of the legendary lenses in the Nikon story. No surprise, since it contradicted the common opinion that high speed inevitably leads to a considerable reduction of image quality. That is not the case in this five-element lens,

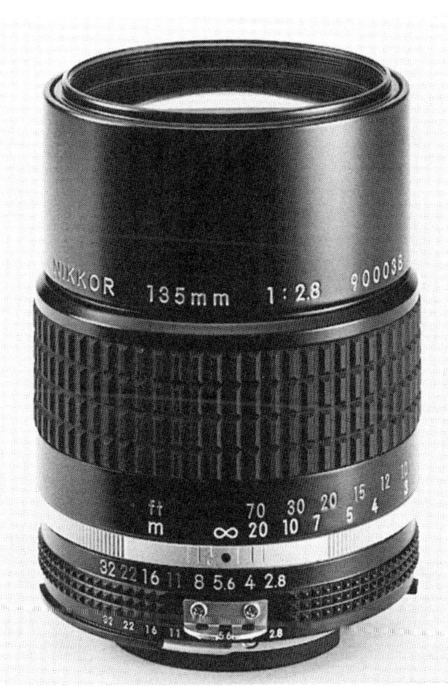

The Nikkor 135mm,f/2.8.

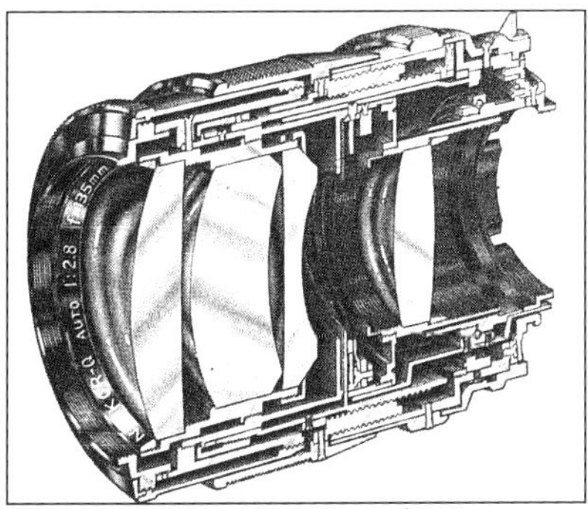

A Nikkor-C 135mm,f/2.8
in cross-section.

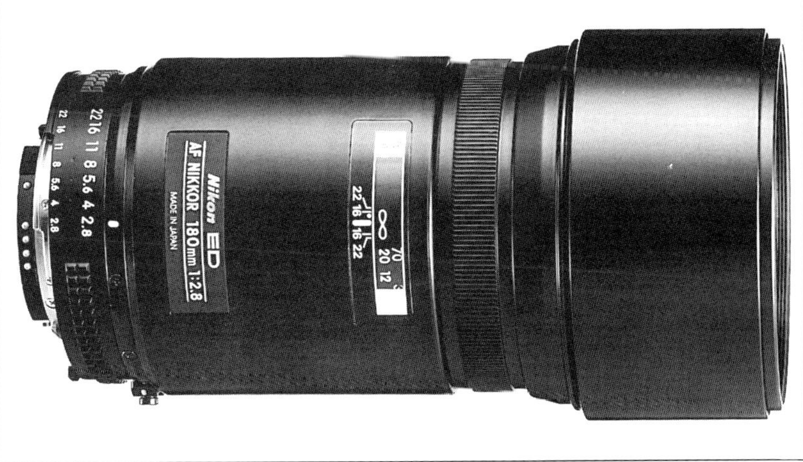

ED and autofocus: the AF-Nikkor 180mm,f/2.8 IF-ED is the present form of another classic.

Background Information: Telephoto lenses

Usually all lenses exceeding the standard 50mm are called telephoto lenses. Strictly speaking this definition is not correct. A long focal length lens can only be regarded as a telephoto if its back focal length (the distance between the film plane and the rear element) is shorter than its actual focal length. All others are simply long focal length lenses, but Nikon no longer offers any lenses of this kind. Similar to the way the retrofocus design was developed for wide-angle lenses by increasing the back focal length, additional lens elements can also shorten it – turning a long focal length into a telephoto lens of equivalent focal length. That is the reason why, for example, the 300mm,f/4.5 is only 200mm long.

For high speed in telephoto lenses it is not only a question of complex design, and hence price, but weight and size also play a much more decisive role than in the case of wide-angles. A less fast lens can be built much more compactly than a high speed one of the same focal length. In a 24mm-lens the difference between the speeds of f/2.8 and f/2 only results in an increase of just 3.5mm in the diameter of the front element, but in a 300mm tele the difference amounts to 43mm. Nikon holds the "world lens speed record" in the form of the super-tele 300mm,f/2 whose front lens diameter reaches 15 cm.

weighing only 800 grams in spite of its high speed. Along with the Nikkor 105mm,f/2.5 it belongs to the most popular Nikon telephoto lenses.

In 1981 the successor appeared. Although it had the same number of elements its front element was made of ED-glass. This increases the contrast at full aperture since ED-glass reduces chromatic aberrations, which result in low-contrast pictures and colour fringing, to a minimum. This effect only begins to become visible in longer focal lengths when the focal points of the differently coloured parts of the light diverge so strongly that it is hardly possible to achieve correct focus at the maximum aperture. In the case of this fairly short focal length the ED-glass is employed to improve the contrast.

In 1986 the 180mm appeared in the AF-version. In order to ease the job of the drive-motor the lens was given internal focusing so only the central group of lens-elements is shifted. This also permits the high quality to be maintained all the way down to the shortest focusing distance of 1.5m. Many users disliked the narrow focusing ring and the plastic coating which made a cheap impression. So two years later it was mechanically modified and fitted with a broader focusing ring. A mechanical sliding switch also allows the choice between AF and manual operation. In the AF-mode the focusing ring is blocked to ensure easy handling. Instead of the plastic barrel the lens now comes in a metal-like finish with the rippled enamel common to the long focal length IF-ED lenses.

200mm Telephoto

The next focal length, 200mm, was first available from Nikon in 1961 in the form of the Nikkor 200mm,f/4. It was a four-element design delivering only mediocre quality, and its built-in lens hood should always be used. In 1975 it was recomputed and modified into a five-element construction displaying a much better image quality throughout the whole focusing range. With its length of only 125mm it was also considerably more compact. Besides the 80mm,f/2.8, the AF-Nikkor 200mm,f/3.5 IF-ED with its integrated AF-motor was one of the two lenses available for the F3 AF. In terms of quality it can be compared to the 180mm,f/2.8 IF-ED.

The state-of-the-art and super-fast IF-ED focal lengths begin with the awe-inspiring Nikkor 200mm,f/2 IF-ED from 1977. Ten elements were necessary to secure its convincing performance even at full aperture. Thus, compared to its two-stop slower partner 200mm,f/4, it has twice as many elements, five times its weight, twice its length, and a good ten times its price. Hardly surprising with a 10cm front group, the first two elements of which are made of ED-glass. It was optimized in 1986 and fitted with a two-piece lens hood, a slip-in gelatine filter holder, and an integrated UV-filter in front of the first element. This fast telephoto lens is a favourite for sports and concert photography whenever the distances are not too great.

300mm Telephoto

The 300mm is the longest focal length still available today in the Nikon programme without the use of ED-glass (except for the mirror lenses). The Nikkor 300mm,f/4.5 appeared in 1964 as a six-element design; it provides an acceptable performance, especially when it is stopped down. Chromatic aberration

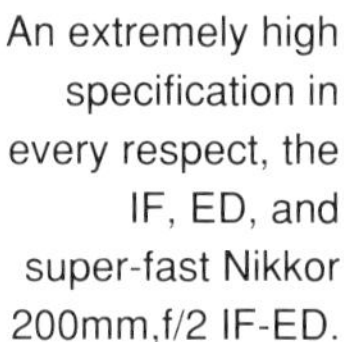

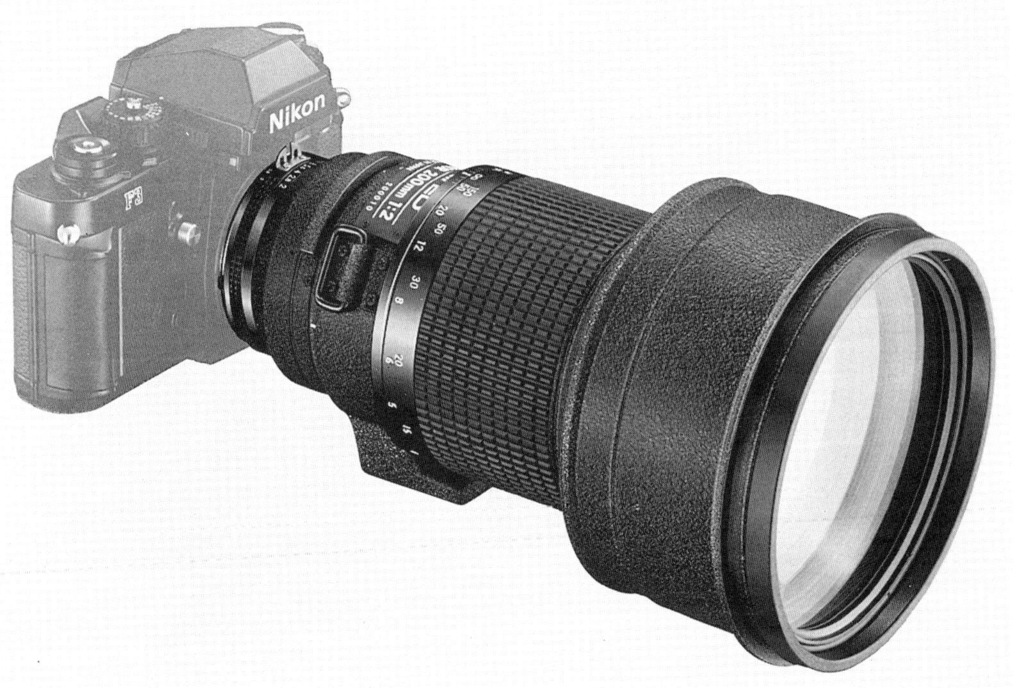

An extremely high specification in every respect, the IF, ED, and super-fast Nikkor 200mm,f/2 IF-ED.

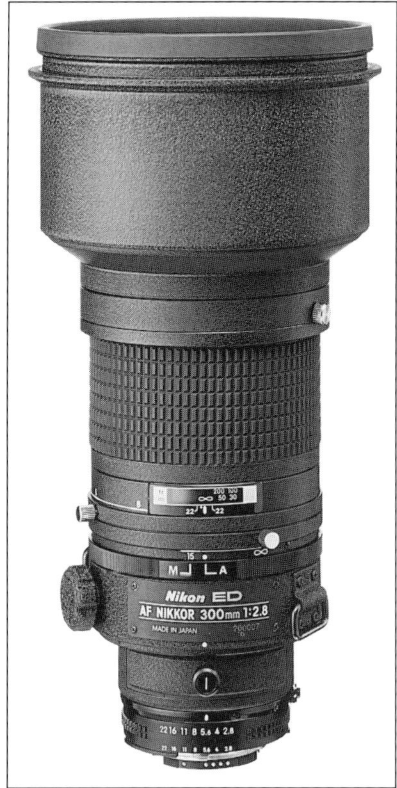

The AF-Nikkor 300mm,f/2.8 IF-ED incorporating Extra Low Dispersion glass.

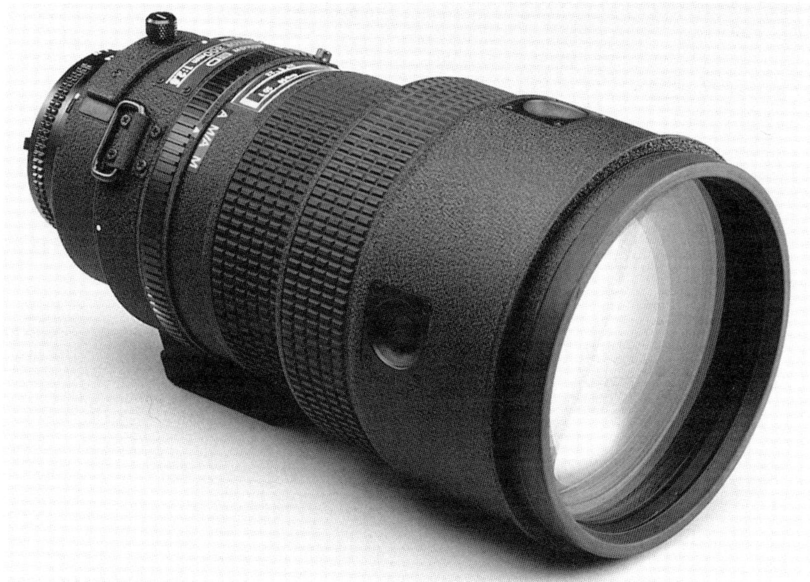

The AF-I 300mm.f/2.8 D IF-ED with its own built-in autofocus motor.

begins to become noticeable at this focal length, so that an alternative lens with ED-glass and distinctly improved optical qualities was added to the range. But it was still built with the large helices that make focusing so tedious. Just one year later it was replaced by the 300,f/4.5 IF-ED which offered quicker and more convenient focusing thanks to internal focusing. Its optical performance is beyond criticism.

In 1987 the AF-Nikkor 300mm,f/4 IF-ED appeared with internal focusing and ED-glass, and just like its counterpart without autofocus and ⅓ stop slower it delivers excellent image quality, even at its maximum aperture. Due to its increased speed it is fitted with the rare 82mm-filter thread, but this is compensated by a slip-in holder for 39mm glass or gelatine filters in the rear section of the barrel. The focusing range can be limited at the lower as well as the upper end so the motor does not always have to drive the lens all the way from 2.5m to infinity when the autofocus mode is used. A feature that improves its working speed as well as saving battery power.

The Nikkor 300mm,f/2.8 IF-ED.

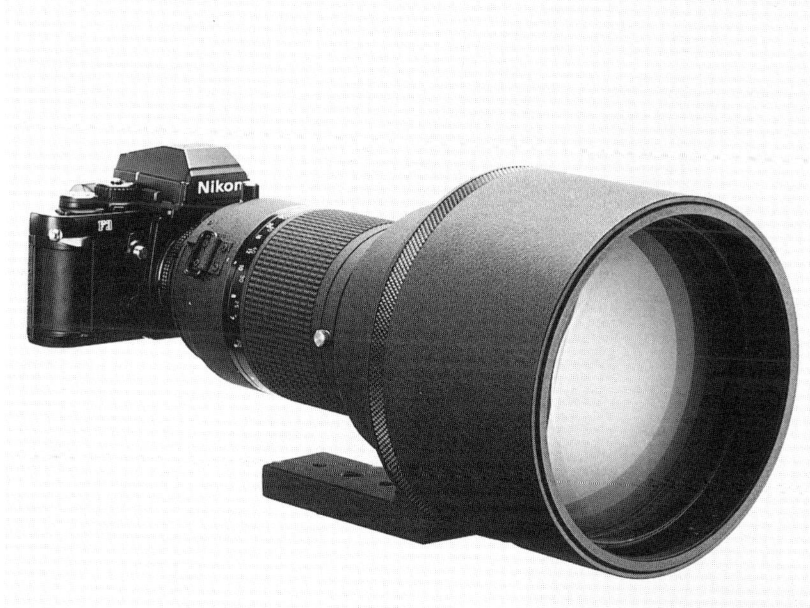

In 1971 the Nikkor 300mm,f/2.8 ED was a sensation even though it did not make use of internal focusing. One dream of a lens mainly for sports, wildlife, and fashion photographers. They can apply selective focus without any quality losses by using the largest opening to completely "dissolve" the background.

At the same time as the Nikkor 200mm,f/2 IF-ED appeared in 1977, this lens also appeared in an IF-version and quickly developed into the sports photographer's favourite telephoto lens. This version also has a 39mm filter holder and with a freely adjustable click-stop ring allows a preset distance to be found again quickly. In 1986 it was modified and also made available in an AF-version. Both have built-in UV filters and two-piece lens hoods. Some users were annoyed by play in the focusing ring of the first AF-version during manual operation caused by the autofocus drive train. Its eight-element layout was designed to produce a high degree of contrast at its largest aperture so that stopping down only increases the depth-of-field.

Early in 1992 yet another version, the AF-I Nikkor 300mm,f/2.8D IF-ED appeared. It was the first AF-lens with its own built-in autofocus drive motor making it faster and quieter. Besides being equipped with the D-type CPU for F90-standard cameras it also has a two-part focusing ring with different diameters allowing comfortable manual override with just one finger.

In 1983 Nikon presented the Nikkor 300mm,f/2 IF-ED, a giant in terms of lens speed with a 15cm front element, a weight of 7kg, and a price around that of a well-equipped small car. This lens was delivered with the specially dedicated Teleconverter TC-14C which can turn it into a 420mm,f/2.8. While all Nikkors as of 300mm are fitted with a ¼ inch tripod thread, the super-fast lenses are additionally provided with a ⅜ inch socket because the heavier pro-standard tripods usually have this stronger size. These extreme speed telephotos are often seen mounted on monopods which allow highly mobile handling.

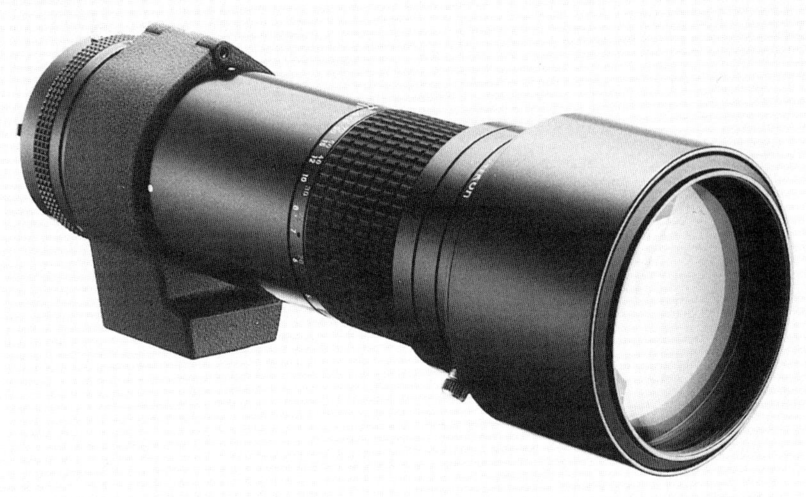
Nikon's standard unit in the 400mm-class, the Nikkor 400mm,f/5.6 IF-ED.

400mm Telephoto

From 400mm onwards the main purpose of the super-telephoto lenses is to span greater distances rather than the compression of perspective, whether it be as effective in a picture or not. In 1964 Nikon introduced a system with a separate lens head and a focusing unit, designated AU-1 in its second version. It had an automatic diaphragm but stop-down-metering was necessary. The first version, AU-1, had no distance scale. The shortest focal length head for this focusing unit was the 400mm,f/4.5, a four-element design 275mm long.

In 1973 the first complete 400mm was introduced, the Nikkor 400mm,f/5.6. It had five elements and a filter thread of 72mm. Two years later it was updated to the prevailing standard by incorporating ED-glass, and in 1978 it was followed by yet another newly designed version with seven elements and internal focusing.

Every one of the lenses described below delivers an optical performance coming close to the theoretically possible. These super-telephoto lenses were designed for the utmost speed and image quality without the slightest compromise, while their length and price were secondary considerations.

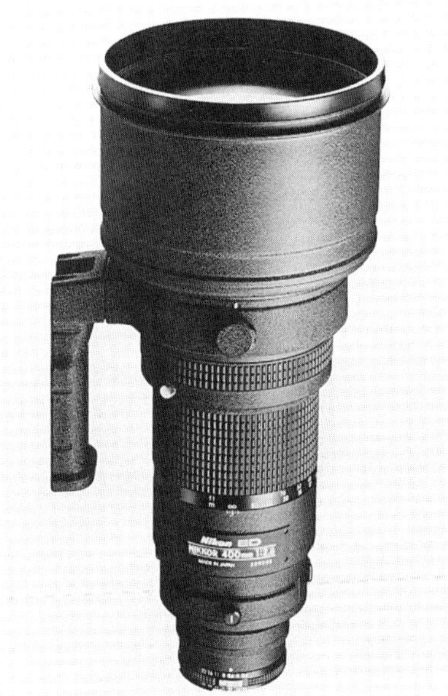
The Nikkor 400mm,f/2.8 IF-ED.

In 1976 the Nikkor 400mm,f/3.5 IF-ED appeared and then in 1985 the 400mm,f/2.8 IF-ED which remained the longest lens allowing hand-held photography until the 500mm,f/4 P IF-ED arrived.

Late in 1993 an AF-version was introduced, the AF-I Nikkor 400mm,f/2.8D IF-ED. Just like the first two AF-I D-types it has its own AF-drive motor, a D-type CPU able to relay extra distance information to the cameras' exposure control system, and an additional A-M-position on its focusing mode ring allowing manual override of autofocus operation at any time.

500mm Telephoto

The Nikkor 500mm,f/4 P IF-ED fulfilled a wish of many a sports photographer who had watched his colleagues with envy as they worked with their Canon 500mm,f/4.5 L. It was introduced in 1988, not as an autofocus version but nevertheless with an integrated CPU so it can be used together with the modern AF-cameras. It does take quite some practice to produce truly sharp hand-held pictures with this almost 40cm long eight-element lens weighing 3 kilos.

600mm Telephoto

Nikon's first 600mm unit was a f/5.6 lens head for the focusing unit AU-1. From 1975 it incorporated ED-glass, but only one year later it was replaced by the Nikkor 600mm,f/5.6 IF-ED. One general feature of all the lenses with ED-glass is that their focusing rings are not stopped at the infinity position. Depending on the outside temperature, the length of the lens changes due to the expansion or contraction of the barrel as it gets warmer or colder. We are only talking of tenths of millimetres, but even these minute differences may lead to a shift of the focal point. So, to be on the safe side, the ED-Nikkors can be focused beyond their infinity-positions.

In 1977 Nikon's fastest super-telephoto lens entered the market, the Nikkor 600mm,f/4 IF-ED. With its weight of more than 6 kilos and a length of almost 60cm it can only be employed on a tripod.

The AF-I Nikkor 600mm,f/4D IF-ED which appeared in 1992 was one of the first two lenses of a new type. Thanks to its "autonomous" AF-drive sytem, the speed and ease of autofocus operation is greatly increased when it is used in conjunction with the F4 and F90 cameras, allowing it to be used for even the fastest action shots.

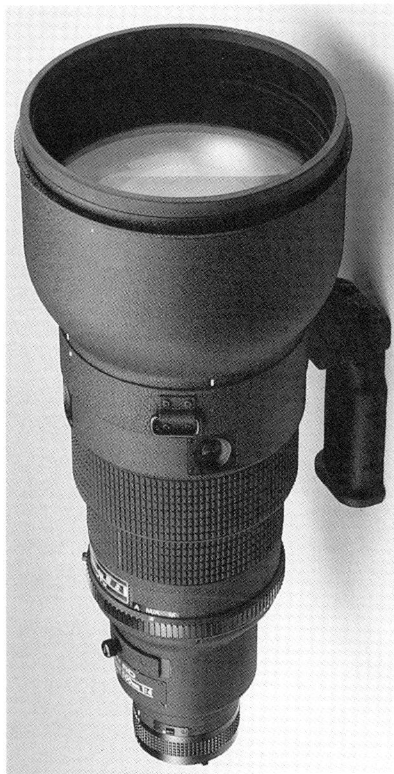

The AF-I Nikkor 600mm,f/4D IF-ED has its own built-in autofocus motor.

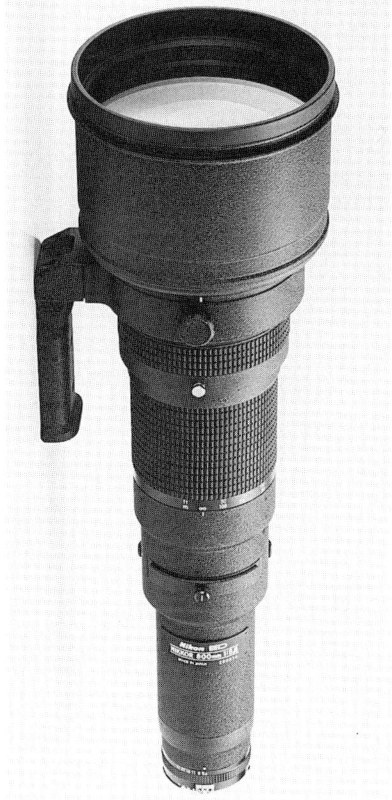

Nikon's longest telephoto, non-mirror lens: the Nikkor 800mm,f/5.6 IF-ED.

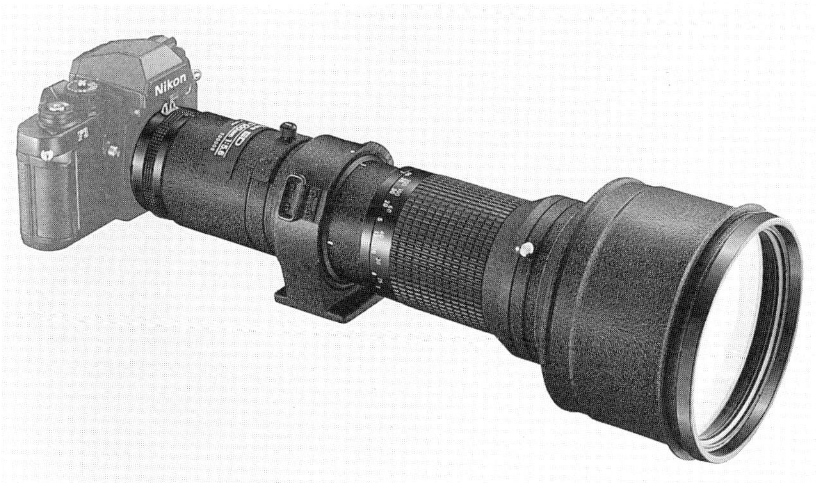

The Nikkor 600mm,f/5.6 IF-ED magnifies the image twelve times compared to a normal lens.

800mm Telephoto

A focal length of 800mm was available in 1964 in the form of a lens head with a maximum aperture of f/8 for the focusing unit AU-1. Unlike the other lens heads it had an aperture ring of its own, so when it was used the ring on the focusing unit had to be set to the smallest value. From 1975 onwards this lens was available with ED-glass, and its successor, the Nikkor 800mm,f/8 IF-ED appeared in 1978. Today it is still the longest fixed focal length (without mirrors) in the Nikon programme, but as an eight-element f/5.6 design.

1200mm Telephoto

For a time a 1200mm,f/11 lens head was available that was modified in 1975 with ED-glass and replaced in 1979 by the 1200mm,f/11 IF-ED. The demand for a super-telephoto of this calibre is very small because many would rather combine a 600mm or a 800mm with a converter. The resulting tiny production numbers lead to the almost unbelievably high price.

Mirror Lenses

Nikon's shortest focal length mirror lens is 500mm, which was first introduced in 1961 with an

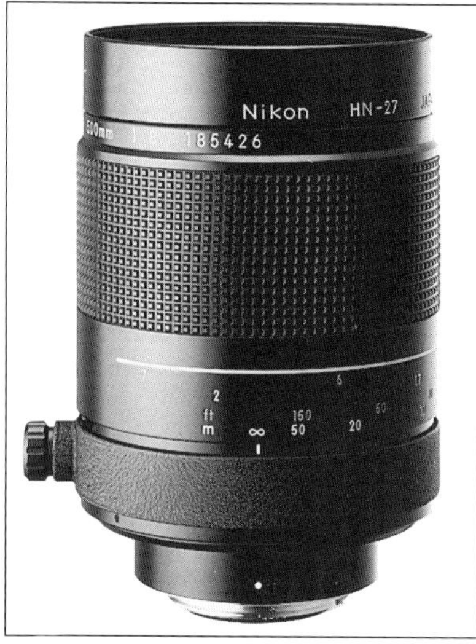

The Reflex-Nikkor 500mm, f/8 AI-S

aperture of f/5 and a front diameter of 125mm. It had to be focused with a small knob located near its bayonet, so it was difficult to produce hand-held pictures – even though its moderate weight made it seem ideal for such a purpose.

In 1968 Nikon's first Reflex-Nikkor for the SLR-models appeared, the 500mm,f/8, only 14cm long, with 5 elements – two mirrors and three lenses. It can be focused all the way down to 4m by rotating the outer part of the barrel. The lens handles so well that with a little bit of practice and luck, the occasional blur-free hand-held picture with a 1/125 sec will succeed. The bayonet mount can be rotated by 90° for vertical shots – there is no diaphragm mechanism which prevents such a construction as in the other Nikkors. The 39mm filters are screwed in behind the rear lens, in fact one must be attached at all times since it is an integral part of the optical design. In 1983 the successor appeared – it has the same specification but it was a new design consisting of six elements. Its most important new features are its considerably reduced dimensions – 114mm length – and its closest focusing distance of 1.5m. A subject area of 6x9cm can be pictured filling the complete frame. Although the theoretical speed may be f/8, compared to normal lenses with a similar maximum aperture, only about half of the light reaches the film plane.

A second lens embodying the mirror principle with 1000mm focal length was introduced in 1959 with a speed of f/6.3. It was available both with the Nikon F bayonet and also with a mirror-box for the rangefinder cameras. A diameter of 24cm and a weight of almost 10 kilos must be handled with this massive lens.

In 1965 a modified Reflex-Nikkor 1000mm,f/11 was introduced. Thanks to its reduced speed the weight could be limited to 1900g. Its closest focusing distance is 8m. Four different

Background Information: "Folded optical path"

One general problem for all long focal length lenses is their barrel length, making them rather unwieldy. By reducing the back focal length (in the telephoto design) this dimension can be reduced, in the case of the Nikkor 300mm,f/4.5 IF-ED for example this led to an overall length of only 200mm. Normal designs incorporating only lens-elements cannot be built much shorter than about 65% of their focal length. But there are systems whose unit length is less than 25% of their focal length. They are called mirror-lenses or catadioptric systems and designated Reflex-Nikkors by Nikon.

In this system the light passing through the front element is reflected back by a concave mirror near the bayonet onto a second, smaller mirror mounted immediately behind the front element. This second mirror in turn finally reflects the light back onto the film. The path of the light rays is folded, so to speak. The drawback is its fixed aperture, i.e. it is not possible to stop down. So the exposure can only be controlled by adjusting the shutter speed or by using neutral density (ND) filters. In many pictures you can tell a mirror lens has been used. Out-of-focus bright spots in the image, especially reflections from water surfaces, are not reproduced as "fuzzy" discs but as doughnut-shaped blurs. This effect is something you will have to live with since there is no way to avoid it. Some photographers make the best of it and employ the effect creatively.

In general, mirror lenses deliver an image quality inferior to normal lens-designs, but this rarely matters in practical applications when no picture at all might be the alternative. On the other hand this principle is distinguished by avoiding chromatic aberrations which take expensive ED-glass to be minimized in normal lenses. This is the reason why mirror lenses only cost a fraction of conventional designs with the same focal length.

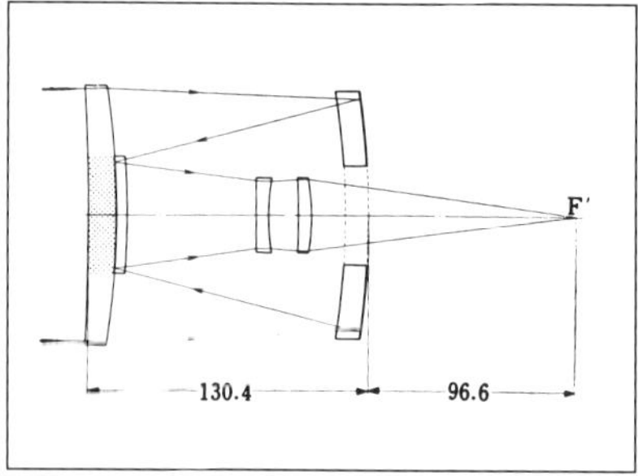

In a mirror lens the incoming light rays are reflected twice inside the body.

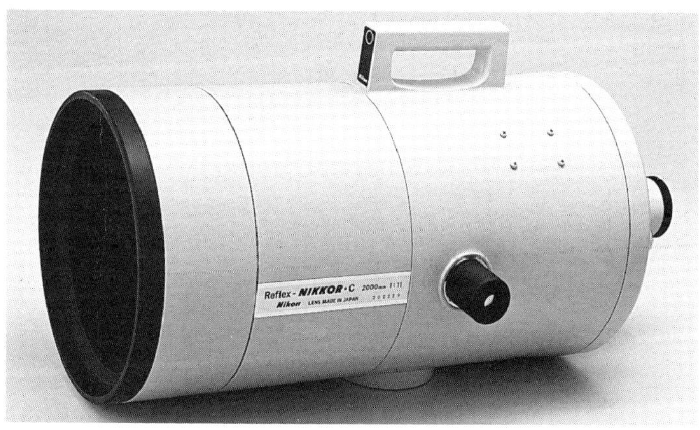

Nikon's longest focal length of all with a picture angle of just 1° 10': the Reflex-Nikkor 2000mm, f/11.

filters can be rotated into the light path with a knob.

In 1976 this lens was modified once again. The large protruding filter turret disappeared and, just as with the 500mm mirror lens, 39mm screw-in filters are used in this version. The lens hood was also built-in this time. A handle can be attached in order to ease focusing down to 8m.

The Reflex-Nikkor 2000mm,f/11 is the most expensive Nikon lens and also the one with the longest focal length. Together with the yoke mount supplied it weighs 42,5 kilos, and like the 1000mm Reflex-Nikkor it has four built-in filters. Focusing is done by a knob situated at the back, and the closest distance setting is 18m. If the extremely small picture angle of 1° 10` is still too much it can be narrowed down even further with a teleconverter.

Background Information: Zoom lenses

Zoom lenses, often also called vario lenses, have all but made fixed focal length lenses obsolete in many areas today, at least they have achieved dominance in most respects. Exceptions to the rule are extreme demands such as the utmost speed and image quality (for reproductions, for example), since only a few zooms truly match the performance of the best fixed focal lengths. The differences have long since dwindled to a minute residue, so that the statement just made must be modified. Many a high-quality zoom, designed and built with the help of the latest computer technology, equals, and sometimes even surpasses the single focal length lenses commonly used up until a few years ago. The decision on which of the two alternatives should be favoured is a purely personal one.

Generally two construction principles can be distinguished. The rarer two-ring design with separate rings for focusing and zooming and the widespread one-ring version combining both settings in one ring. The type of design has absolutely no relevance as to the image quality.

Zoom Lenses

The very first zoom lens for a 35mm-camera was the Voigtländer Zoomar 36-82mm,f/2.8 which appeared in 1955. Nikon started with the tele-zoom 85-250mm,f/4.5 in 1959, and today there are ranges available from 20mm to 1200mm.

Standard Zooms

Nikon's first zoom incorporating the normal focal length of 50mm was the Zoom-Nikkor 43-86mm,f/3.5 from 1963 which was originally developed for the Nikkorex Zoom 35. This first version of 9 elements performed rather poorly and these early zoom designs are responsible for the persistent prejudice to this very day, alleging that the image quality of zoom lenses is considerably lower than that of fixed focal length lenses.

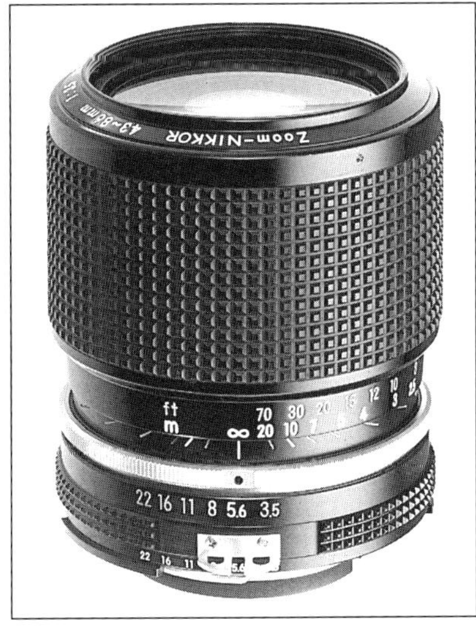
The Zoom-Nikkor 43-86mm,f/3.5

In 1975 a redesigned version with 11 elements was introduced which performed much more satisfactorily. When it is zoomed to its longest focal length the 43-86mm,f/3.5 changes its length, a feature some zooms still show today. Nikon discontinued production in 1982 because its focal range was considered to be out-of-date; the customers wanted standard zooms beginning at 35mm or even 28mm.

The first zoom displaying state-of-the-art performance in the wide-angle range was the Zoom-Nikkor 35-70mm,f/3.5 introduced in 1977. This 10-element, two-ring zoom produces excellent results, especially in terms of freedom of vignetting, a criterion zooms have particular difficulties with. The only drawbacks are its large 72mm filter thread and its modest closest focusing distance of 1m. In 1981 the successor appeared with a filter thread of only 62mm, newly designed optics, and a closest focusing distance of 35cm at the 70mm-setting. The image quality that had already been outstanding before was improved further, and in the AF

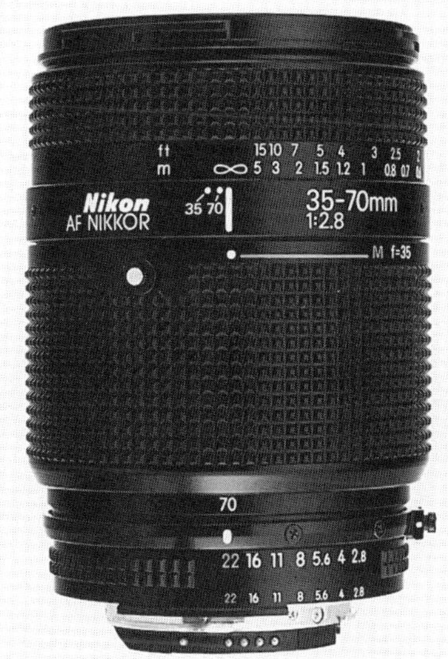

The AF Zoom-Nikkor 35-70mm,f/2.8.

Zoom-Nikkor 35-70mm,f/2.8 it has culminated in a performance level equalling that of prime lenses. It takes 15 elements to achieve such a standard in this modern one-ring zoom. It keeps up its high image quality all the way down to its so-called macro-setting, permitting a maximum reproduction ratio of 1:4. The male bayonet mount for the lens hood HB-1 outside the filter thread is a new feature.

When the F90 appeared in 1992, the AF Zoom-Nikkor 35-70mm, f/2.8D was among the first few lenses to be fitted with the new D-type CPU designed to supply the camera's "3D Matrix" automatic exposure control system with additional distance information. Otherwise, the lens remained absolutely unchanged.

In 1984 Nikon introduced the Zoom-Nikkor 35-70mm,f/3.3-4.5 in order not to leave the amateur sector of the market – where customers are sensitive to price – to "foreign" brands. It is a one-ring, eight-element design with a length of just 70mm and with a maximum aperture changing from f/3.3 at the 35mm setting to f/4.5 at its longest focal length. The effective aperture for the respective focal length can be identified with the help of two differently coloured marks on the appropriate ring. In practice the varying speed only has to be taken into consideration in flash photography without TTL-control where the aperture may have to be adjusted. Naturally, when TTL-Flash control is used, and of course during normal daylight TTL-metering, the changing aperture is automatically compensated. Since nowadays every zoom is expected to have a macro-setting, Nikon also designates the distance range from 50cm to 35cm as "Macro".

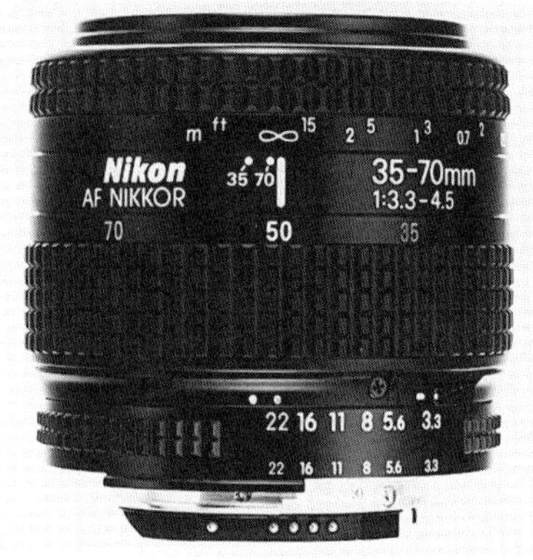

The AF Zoom-Nikkor 35-70mm,f/3.3-4.5.

As of 1986 Nikon has also offered this lens in an AF-version fitted with an extremely narrow focusing ring in case someone actually had the intention of working an AF lens manually. A modified barrel did away with this inconvenience in 1990.

The predecessor of this standard zoom for the mass-market was the Nikon Zoom 36-72mm,f/3.5 E, an eight-element design from 1981. This one-ring zoom delivered an average image quality whereas vignetting and light fall-off were unacceptable. Probably this was the main reason why the lens was discontinued after just two years.

The direct successor of the 43-86mm,f/3.5, the Zoom-Nikkor 35-105mm,f/3.5-4.5 was a major success. It is a one-ring, 16-element design displaying a respectable contrast, and is fitted with a 52mm filter thread and is quite compact. At its closest focusing distance of only 1.4m light fall-off towards the corners becomes clearly visible. The macro-range is accessible by unlocking and turning the appropriate ring on the lens barrel which results in both the distance apart of the lens groups and the focal length changing until 1:4 is reached at the 35mm-setting. In the AF-version it turns out as a two-ring zoom with the same performance while its macro-range is extended even further to 1:3.5.

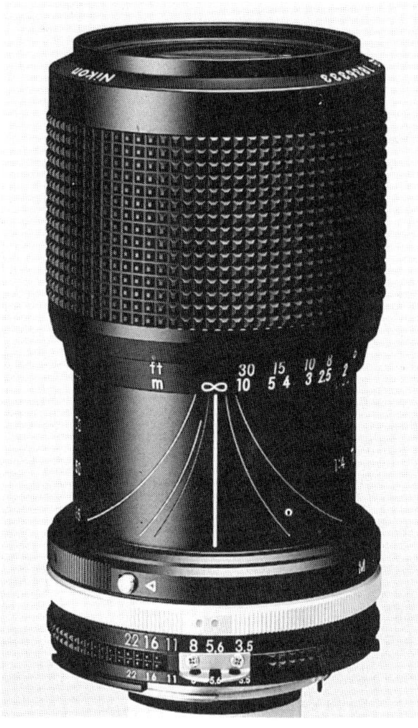

The Zoom-Nikkor 35-105mm,f/3.5-4.5.

In 1984 a sister-model with a slightly longer telephoto range was introduced, the Zoom-Nikkor 35-135mm,f/3.5-4.5 consisting of 15

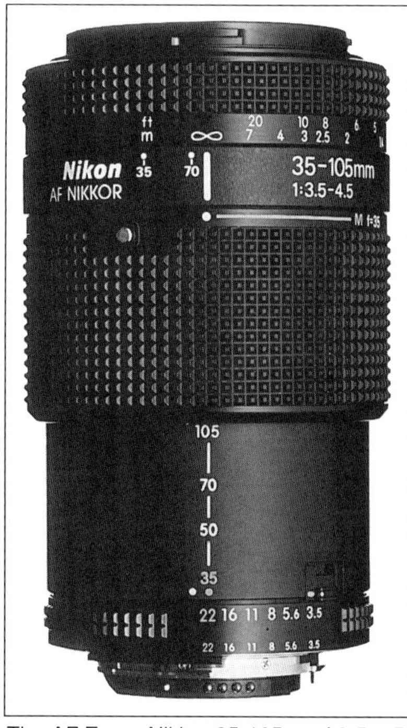

The AF Zoom-Nikkor 35-105mm,f/3.5-4.5.

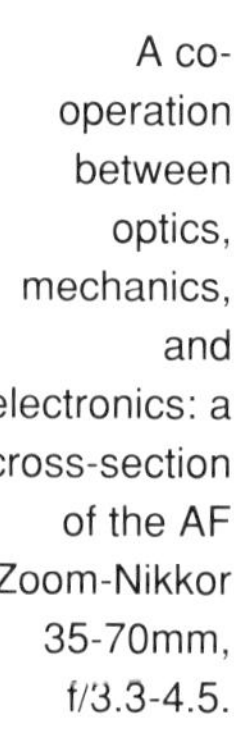

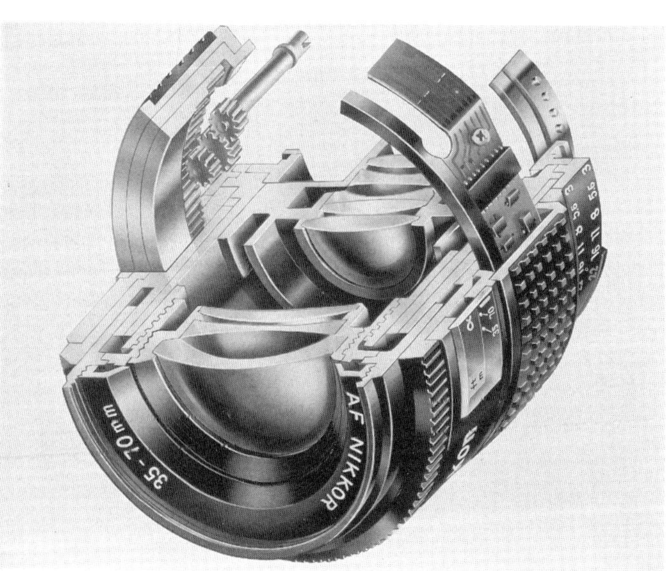

A co-operation between optics, mechanics, and electronics: a cross-section of the AF Zoom-Nikkor 35-70mm, f/3.3-4.5.

elements and fitted with a 62mm filter thread.

It is just under 2cm longer than a fixed focal length 135mm. The main difference from the 35-105mm,f/3.5-4.5 described above is a big advantage in practical use: the 35-135mm-zoom achieves its largest magnification rate of 1:3.8 at 135mm focal length and a distance from the subject of 40cm. The AF-version from 1986 was an optically and mechanically modified, two-ring design with the same specifications as its non-AF partner. In 1989 another rearrangement of the mechanics turned it back into a one-ring zoom, but with a separate focusing ring as in all the new AF-zooms.

In 1985 the last unit in this group followed, the Zoom-Nikkor 35-200mm,f/3.5-4.5. It weighs 740g and is nearly 13cm long. This 17-element design features a zoom range of almost 6x for all those who wish to be able to cover every situation with only one lens. Such a zoom range was only available from independent makers before. Restrictions as to the performance of such a "jack of all trades" must be taken into account, especially since it covers both the wide-angle and the telephoto ranges.

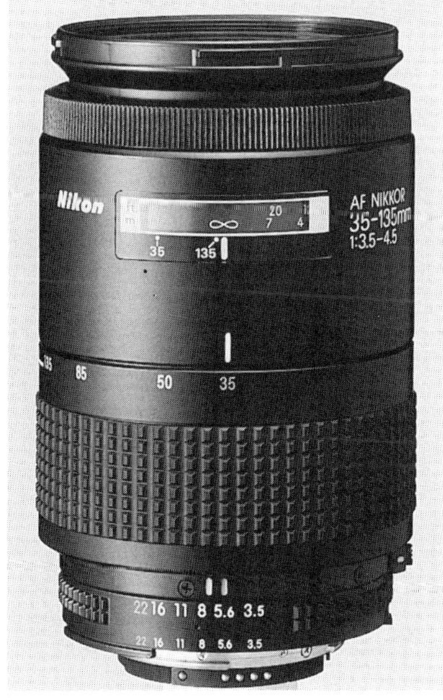

The AF Zoom-Nikkor 35-135mm,f/3.5-4.5 in its first version.

Wide-angle Zooms

The development of fixed focal length wide-angle lenses give their designers the most headaches, and creating a zoom operating within this range is a very critical and tricky task indeed. Limiting distortion to a tolerable degree is the most difficult part of all. Nikon's debut in wide-angle zooms was marked by the Zoom-Nikkor 28-45mm,f/4.5 which appeared in 1975. In addition it was the first zoom employing the retro-focus design. Its 1.6x-range does not make it very flexible and its rather low speed of 1:4.5 does not exactly make focusing easy either. On the other hand, this two-ring, 11-element lens offers an image quality allowing quite respectable pictures. The front lens does not rotate during focusing, permitting convenient handling of polarizing filters.

In 1979 the Zoom-Nikkor 25-50mm,f/4 replaced the first model. It also is an 11-element design, but with a more complex lens-moving mechanism. Distortion particularly was reduced.

It was another ten years before Nikon introduced a second representative in this range, the AF Zoom-Nikkor 24-50mm,f/3.3-4.5. Its relatively high speed in the wide-angle setting is worth pointing out, even though it will probably be used most often in the autofocus mode. This versatile lens, with 9 elements, is very compact, weighs only 375 grams, and performs surprisingly well, coming close to the standard of the 24mm fixed focal length Nikkors. Its quality is particularly obvious in terms of low distortion and vignetting. The "macro" setting must be considered to be more the marketing department's idea. While the normal focusing range ends at 0.6 metres, the additional macro setting only extends it to 0.5 metres.

A further wide-angle zoom, the Zoom-Nikkor 28-50mm,f/3.5 which was introduced in 1984, did not receive very much attention. Its relatively high speed for this interesting range, just one half stop less than that of comparable fixed focal lengths really should have attracted more photographers. This compact 9-element, one-ring zoom performed well and had a special design feature: its hood zooms along automatically whenever the focal setting is

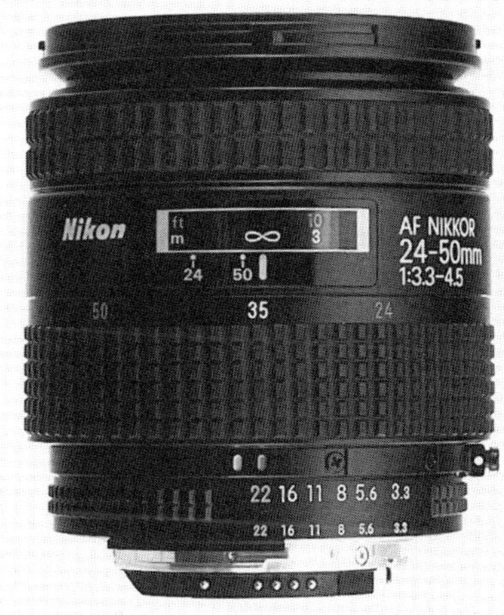

The AF Zoom-Nikkor 24-50mm,f/3.3-4.5.

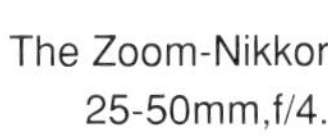
The Zoom-Nikkor 25-50mm,f/4.

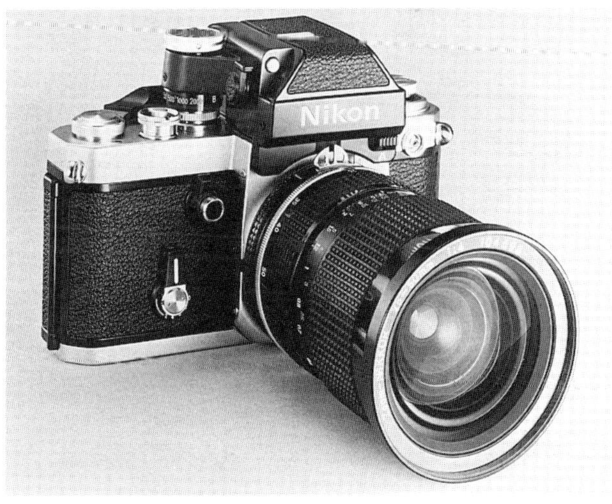

changed, securing optimum effectiveness at all times. Normally hoods for zooms are matched to the largest picture angle at their shortest focal length.

The Zoom-Nikkor 28-85mm,f/3.5-4.5 is a very popular lens in this area – not surprising since the 15-element construction has a 3x-coverage. Due to its many elements and its front element placed at the very front of the barrel it is rather sensitive to stray light which results in low-contrast if the hood is not used properly. When the lens is set to 28mm and maximum aperture one should be prepared for visible vignetting. Whereas in the non-AF version the macro-setting is obtained by unlocking an additional ring beneath the zoom ring, it is integrated in the latter in the AF-version.

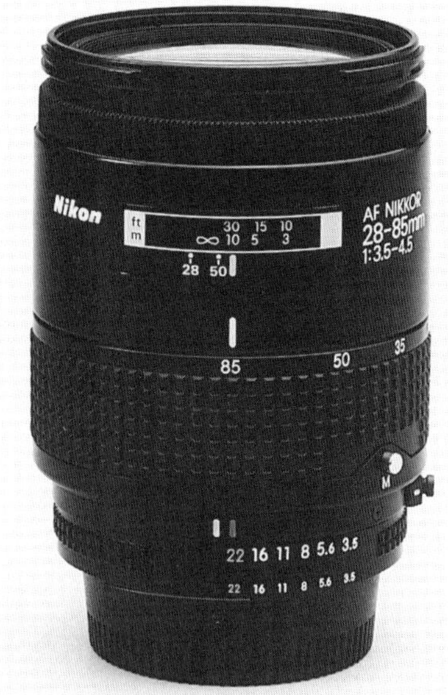

The AF Zoom-Nikkor 28-85mm,f/3.5-4.5 in the original version.

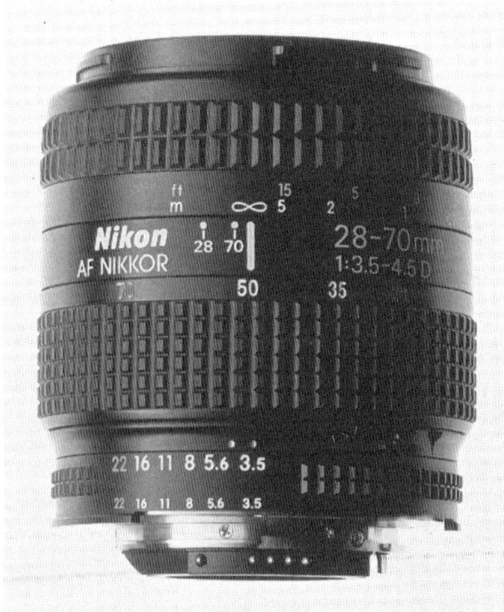

The AF Zoom-Nikkor 28-70mm,f/3.5-4.5, light-weight and economical.

In 1992 the AF Zoom-Nikkor 28-70mm,f/3.5-4.5 was marketed, an astonishingly compact, lightweight, and economical unit. With only eight elements it delivers a very respectable performance even in the difficult wide-angle range. All this was achieved through a completely new type of "compound" aspherical element. Instead of going through the trouble of grinding and polishing a glass blank exactly to the computed aspherical surface, a costly process, Nikon developed a much simpler production method. The glass element is only finished to much less stringent tolerances, then an optical plastic is applied in an ultra-thin layer, differing in thickness from the centre to the edges. This secures a surface profile with the necessary precision as well as the expected image quality while being much less expensive to manufacture. The modification of the integrated CPU turning this zoom into a D-type lens for the F90-standard cameras in 1992 did not involve any other part of its design.

Ever since the existence of a 20-35mm zoom lens, Nikon-photographers had craved for one they could attach to their cameras. When professionals started to use the two fast AF-Nikkors, 35-70mm,f/2.8 and 80-200mm,f/2.8, just as naturally as they had rejected any zoom before, they of course included a maximum aperture of f/2.8 on their list of wants.

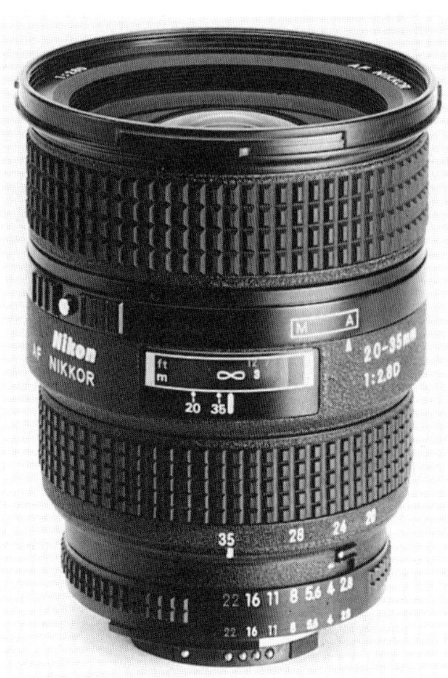

The AF Zoom-Nikkor 20-35mm,f/2.8D has an aspherical element.

Over a year and a half after a similar lens was introduced for the new underwater camera Nikonos RS, the AF Zoom-Nikkor 20-35mm,f/2.8D finally appeared on the scene in 1993. A spectacular lens with an aspherical element to reduce aberrations to a minimum, even at its full aperture which is effective throughout its focal range. The internal zooming and focusing system ensures a constant length as well as durable construction. In spite of its rather high price it will no doubt find its way into many gadget bags.

Telephoto Zooms

As mentioned above, zoom lenses are particularly difficult to design in the wide-angle range. This is one of the reasons why the first zooms were

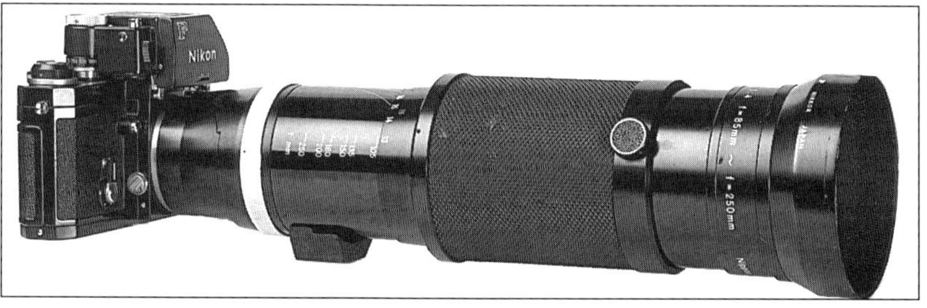

Nikon's first telephoto zoom from 1959, the Zoom-Nikkor 85-250mm,f/4-4.5, mounted on a Nikon F.

telephotos. Today, these lenses have reached an image quality that can be compared to fixed focal lengths in every respect. Nikon's first zoom appeared the same year the F was introduced, in 1959. It was a 30cm lens with a focal range from 85-250mm and a speed of f/4-4.5. The designers needed 16 elements to secure an acceptable performance. Except for a somewhat lower contrast it can well stand comparison with the 135mm and 200mm designs of the time. When NIC-coating was added in 1969 its performance in respect to contrast was improved further. The first series was a strange type of two-ring design – its focal length was changed by push/pull movement of the rear ring – and is a rarity much sought after by collectors today. From 1960 the one-ring version was available, fitted with a button to secure the focal length setting against any accidental movement. A close-up lens came with the lens, reducing the closest focusing distance from 4m to 2.5m. In the NIC-version from 1969 the maximum aperture remained the same throughout its focal range. Nikon's best-known and also extremely popular telephoto zoom lens is the 80-200mm,f/4.5. It was introduced in 1969 and soon took over from the 85-250mm as first choice, being just half as long and weighing less than half as much. The first version with 15 elements was produced until 1977 and delivered an outstanding performance compared to the standard of the time, but the successor version with its 12 elements was even better. Many users were annoyed because the zoom ring of this lens often operates all too smoothly. A short visit in a Nikon service facility could always quickly restore satisfaction. There is no need to worry about mechanical noises caused by the use of the focus ring, they are because the mechanics are hardly greased at all. Even if it rattles slightly when shaken this does not mean an element has come loose but is simply due to the system's necessary mechanical play. The 15 and 12 element versions of the lenses can easily be distinguished by the rectangular blind behind the latter's rear element.

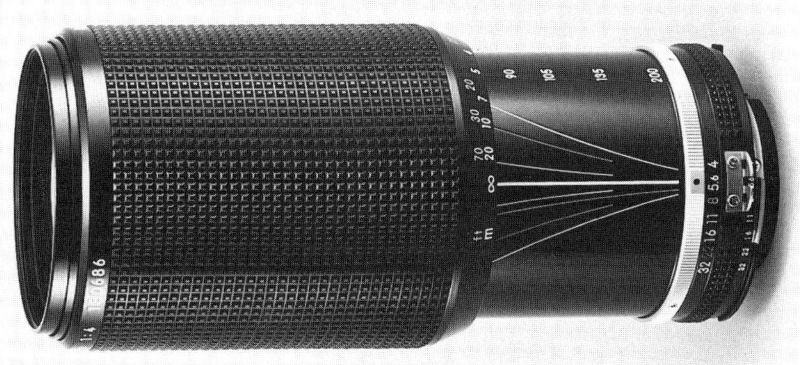
The Zoom-Nikkor 80-200mm,f/4.

The better is always the enemy of the good, and so in 1981 the successor of this Nikon classic was introduced, the Zoom-Nikkor 80-200mm, f/4. This version is readily identified by its 62mm filter thread. Sharpness and contrast can hardly be improved further and the vignetting at the 200mm setting was also all but eliminated. Without having an extra macro range the lens can be focused all the way down to 1.2m throughout its complete range, resulting in a reproduction ratio of 1:4.4. Together with the close-up lens 6T it is possible to come close to 1:1. Thanks to its excellent performance the lens is well suited to be combined with a teleconverter without having to take into account any visible deterioration of image quality.

On the occasion of the 1978 Photokina a prototype of a compact 80-200mm,f/2.8 ED two-ring zoom was displayed but it was never put into production. Instead a different 80-200mm,f/2.8 ED was introduced in 1982 that displayed a fantastic performance throughout the whole focal length range. The reasons why it did not develop into a best-seller were its very large size and its very high price. Compared to the slower 80-200mm,f/4 it was 50% longer, more than twice as heavy, and four times the cost.

In 1988 the successor with AF-technology arrived, doing away with all these drawbacks. This intriguing lens is hardly larger and heavier than the manual focusing 80-200mm,f/4, and not much more expensive either. So it comes as no surprise that even Nikon photographers who had no use for the AF-facility took a liking to this lens, and for two years Nikon could not keep pace with demand. It is a 16-element, one-ring zoom performing almost as well as its predecessor. The combined zoom and

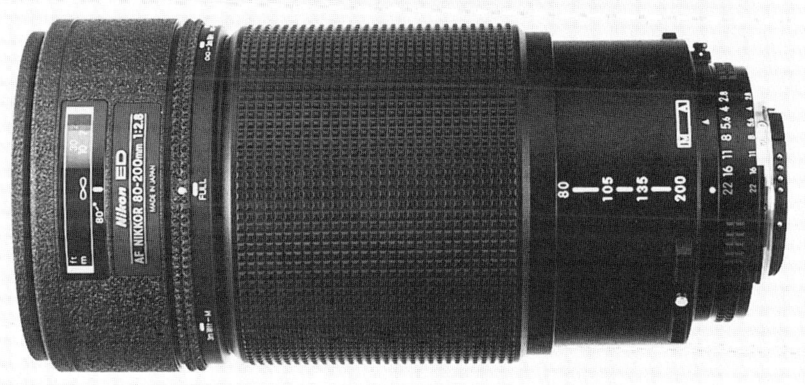

A favourite of even those Nikon photographers working without autofocus – the top-of-the-line AF Zoom-Nikkor 80-200mm,f/2.8 ED in its first version.

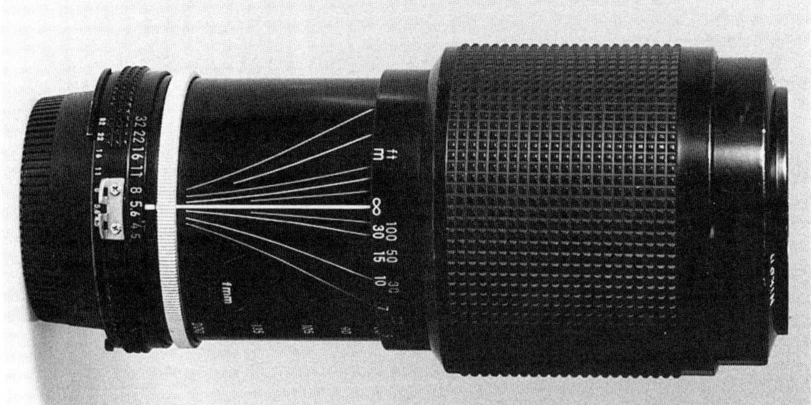

An absolute telephoto-zoom classic is the Zoom-Nikkor 80-200mm,f/4.5.

focusing ring handles very well manually too. An additional ring permits the focusing range to be limited in order to enhance the AF-working speed. The only note of discord is the 77mm filter thread unusual with Nikon. Well, maybe not really the only point of criticism: among Nikon AF-lenses it was admittedly one of the slowest, large and heavy parts of its optical system had to be shifted for focusing. The professionals who had acquired this lens because of its superior optical performance and speed were particularly annoyed about this. So in 1992 when its CPU was modified to meet the requirements of the new F90, its mechanical construction was completely redesigned. The new version, the AF Zoom-Nikkor 80-200mm,f/2.8D ED proves that focusing speed is not a question of lens-integrated motors. The improvement is impressive, it operates much more smoothly, quietly, and very much faster. Mechanical play which had been irritating before, even though not impairing its operation, was decisively reduced as well. The front barrel of the new lens does not rotate during focusing (the front element still does though), making polarizing and other filters very much easier to handle – at the cost of having to use a new lens hood. The switch limiting the focusing range which replaced the ring on the former version is more convenient to operate, too.

A small telephoto zoom was available for the EM, the one-ring 75-150mm,f/3.5 E, a 12-element design just 12cm long. The image quality of this NIC-coated lens is so good that it would have fitted perfectly into the Nikkor programme. But the market called for a focal range up to 200mm, and so it was discontinued in 1983.

A 70-210mm,f/4 E with a 13-element design appeared as an inexpensive alternative to the 80-200mm, f/4 in 1981. Its performance must be regarded as inferior to that of the 80-200mm,f/4, but only due to a slightly less contrasty rendition. The lower price was made possible by employing simpler mechanics so that it was not recommended for a pro's demanding daily work. On the other hand it only cost about 50% of the comparable Nikkor-zoom.

In 1986 this lens appeared in an AF-version, this time as a two-ring zoom. Its macro-range, which used to be accessible down to 56cm at the 70mm-setting, was altered to 1.1m throughout the complete focal length range. The newly designed AF Zoom-Nikkor 70-210mm,f/4-5.6 with its 12 elements is a good 5cm shorter. The decreasing speed towards its longer focal lengths does not result in improved performance but just helps keep the lens nice and compact, a trend that was becoming ever more important in the mass-market. If a telephoto-zoom with a longest focal length of 200mm was still not sufficient, a customer could find a Zoom-Nikkor 100-300mm,f/5.6 in the programme as of 1984. Due to its moderate speed this 14-element design delivers a fine performance even at its largest opening, and its length of just 20cm allows safe hand-held operation.

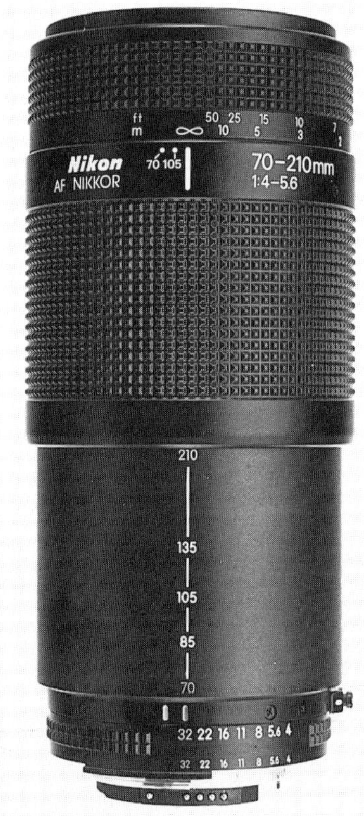

The AF Zoom-Nikkor 70-210mm,f/4-5.6.

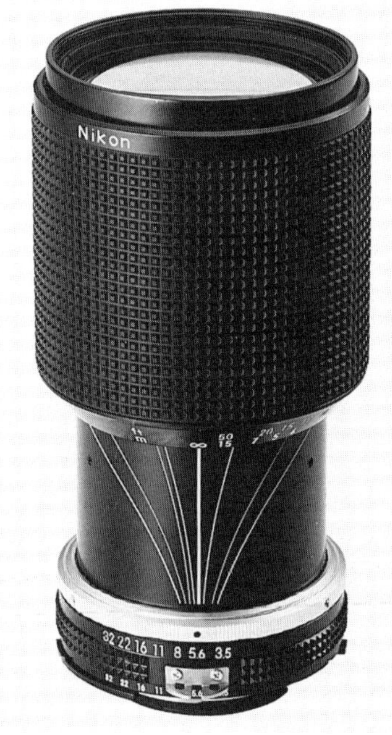

The Zoom-Nikkor 50-135mm,f/3.5.

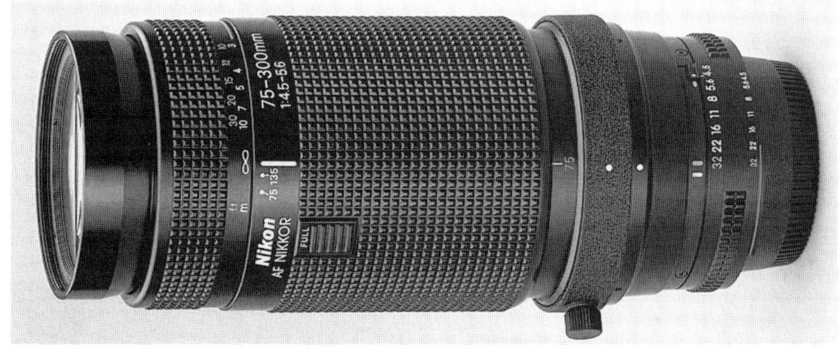

The AF Zoom-Nikkor 75-300mm,f/4.5-5.6.

This lens was replaced by the AF Zoom-Nikkor 75-300mm,f/4.5-5.6 in 1989, a 13-element design only 17cm long, the higher speed permitting more positive manual focusing, especially at the shorter focal lengths, goes with a slight reduction in image quality compared to the non-AF version. A switch on the focusing ring can limit the distance range to 3m to infinity, in the "Full"-position the closest focusing distance is 1.5m even at the 300mm-setting, leading to a reproduction ratio of 1:3.8 – ideal for close-ups of insects.

The Zoom-Nikkor 50-135mm, f/3.5 was an attempt to offer photojournalists a fast, compact, high-performance zoom including a short telephoto range with the standard focal length. The image quality of this 16-element design can be compared to that of prime lenses. It never made very many friends among the pros though. Perhaps this was because of the moderate speed of f/3.5, or the closest focusing distance of only 1.3m. It is Nikon's only one-ring zoom whose front element does not rotate during focusing.

Nikon had already surprised the experts in 1967 with the Zoom-Nikkor 50-300mm,f/4.5. A range of this extent had previously only been known in cine cameras. This lens employed 20 elements in a 30cm long barrel which extended a further 10cm at the 300mm-setting. The early ones without NIC-coating could be criticised concerning contrast. This zoom was used particularly in situations not requiring later enlargements, for dramatic zoom blurs in advertisement shots or for photographic observation. In 1977 it was redesigned, 15 elements including ED-glass yielded contrast similar to that of other telephoto-zooms. At the same time its length and weight were reduced, allowing the occasional successful hand-held shot. The Zoom-Nikkor 50-300mm,f/4.5 ED is a two-ring design with a closest focusing distance of 2.5m.

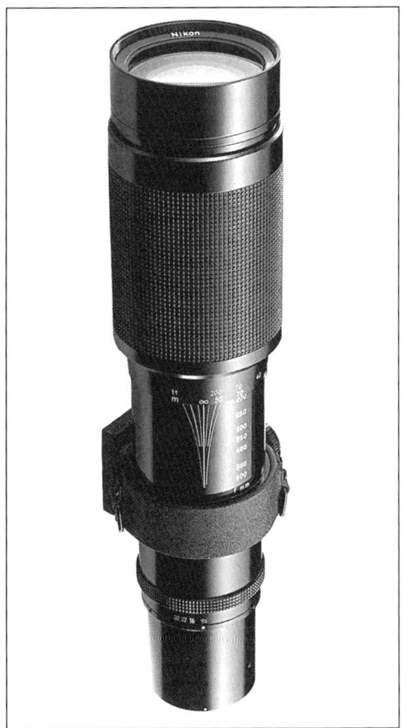

Nikon's second telephoto-zoom was the Zoom-Nikkor 200-600mm,f/9.5.

The second telephoto-zoom produced by Nikon was the 200-600mm,f/9.5, which had been introduced back in 1961. This one ring zoom is made of 19 elements, and it looks like a larger version of the 85-250mm. As of 1971, when NIC-coating was added, its image quality could be considered to be acceptable, and its price placed it within reach of non-pros too. Just as in the case of the 85-250mm zoom, a close-up lens came with the lens, reducing the closest focusing distance from 4m to 2.3m. In the first series the maximum aperture dropped from f/9.5 at 200mm to f/10.5 at 600mm; the following versions had a fixed value. It was only

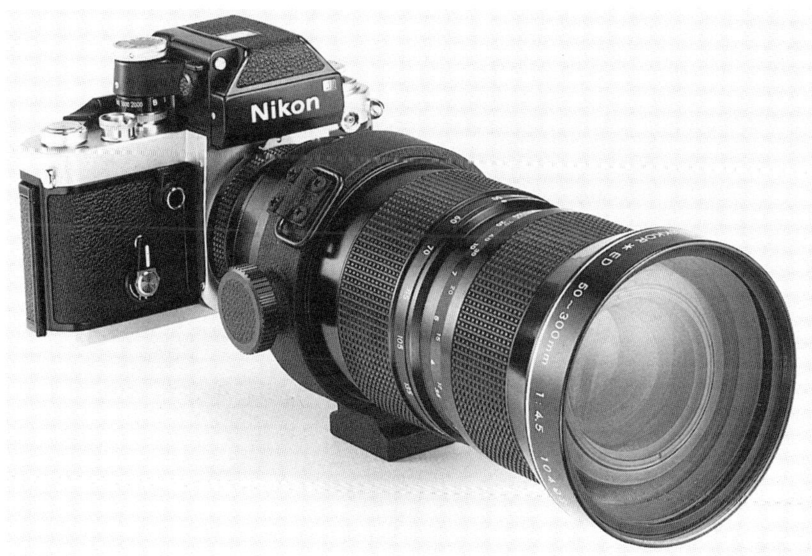

The combination of a 6x zoom range and ED-quality: the Zoom-Nikkor 50-300mm,f/4.5 ED in an earlier version.

the AI-S version from 1982 that coupled automatically with the camera's metering system, before that one used stop-down metering.

The Zoom-Nikkor 200-400mm,f/4 ED Nikon introduced in 1983 was meant for wildlife photographers. The maximum aperture of this outstanding 15-element design is remarkable, especially since it can be employed without any limitations in terms of image quality. But this attempt to convince the pros also failed, maybe because of its weight of 3.5 kilos. The tripod mounting collar was definitely annoying as it had to be rotated out of the way to permit focusing.

1975 was the year of the extremely long telephoto-zooms for Nikon. First came the Zoom-Nikkor 180-600mm,f/8 ED, and after that the Zoom-Nikkor 360-1200mm,f/11 ED. Both one-ring zooms with 18 and 20 elements respectively, were intended solely for tripod operation due to their enormous weight of 3.4 and 7.9 kilos. With the AI-S versions connection to the camera's metering system was added.

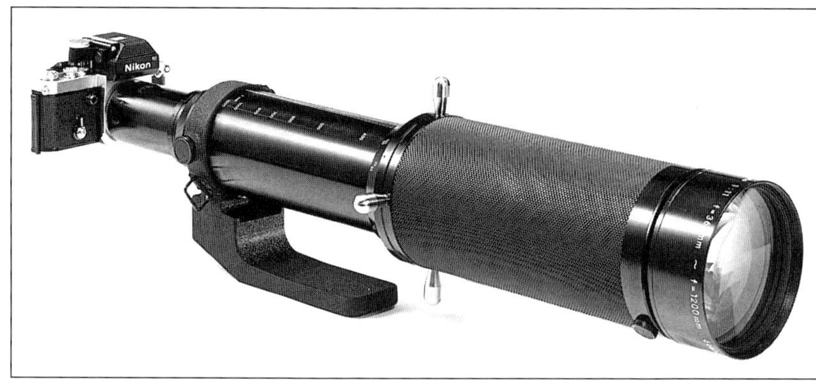

Nikon's super-zoom containing 20 elements, the Zoom-Nikkor 360-1200mm,f/11 ED.

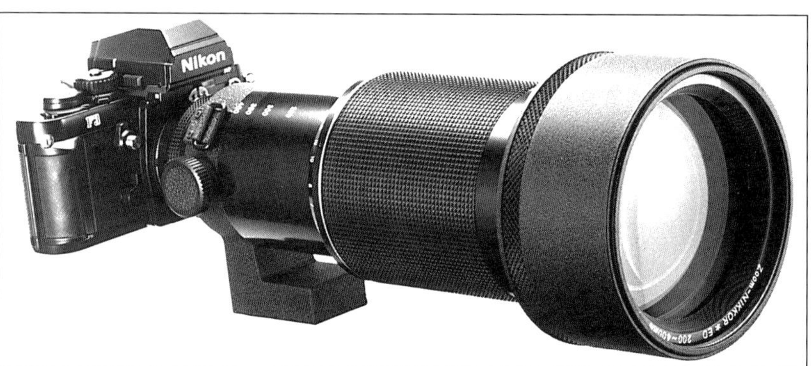

The Zoom-Nikkor 200-400mm,f/4 ED delivers a high speed and excellent image quality thanks to ED-glass.

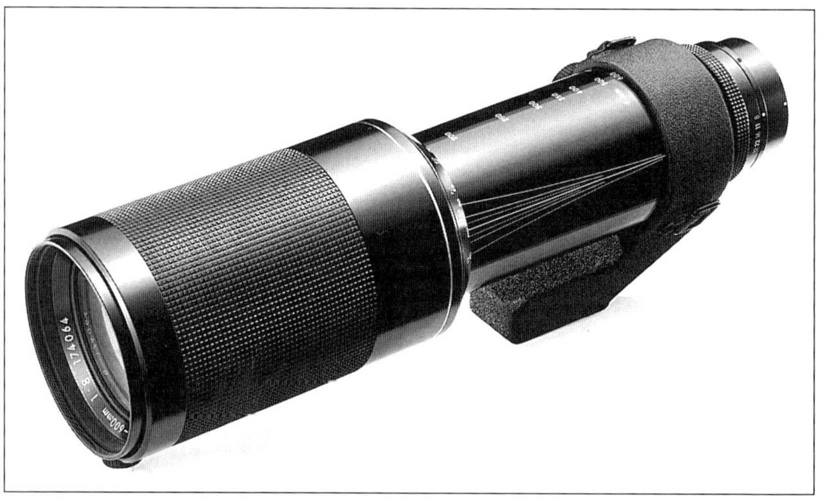

The Zoom-Nikkor 180-600mm,f/8 in the version with ED-glass.

Special Purpose Lenses

Generally all lenses have the job of conveying the information within the subject to the film with as little loss as possible. There are certain applications which would be asking too much of conventional lenses, and where only specialist lenses optimized for very special photographic task can solve the problem. Traditionally Nikon has always offered quite a number of such lenses, allowing even the most unusual or exotic problems to be solved.

Fisheye Lenses

Fisheye lenses with their extreme picture angles between 170° to 220° were originally developed for scientific applications in meteorology and astronomy, such as the observation of cloud formations and movements or the determination of azimuth and zenith angles of stars. Another use is in the observation of extremely restricted spaces such as combustion chambers, boilers, or pipelines. In normal photography these lenses are employed to achieve dramatic effects due to their "unreal" distortion.

The first representative of this type was the Fisheye-Nikkor 8mm,f/8 from 1962, with nine elements and an enormous angle of view of 180°, creating a circular image 24mm in diameter on the film. This lens is not a retrofocus construction; before mounting it on the camera the mirror has to be locked up because the rear element comes less than 1cm from the shutter. The separate viewfinder DF-1 only covers an angle of 160°. Focusing is not necessary with a depth-of-field from

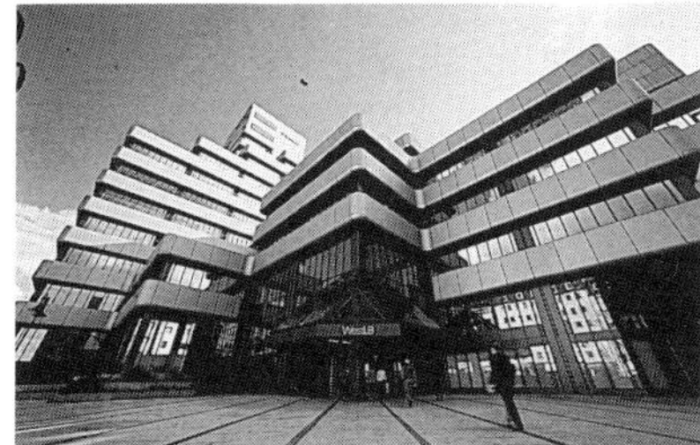

Dynamically exaggerated converging verticals: a picture made with the Nikkor 13mm,f/5.6.

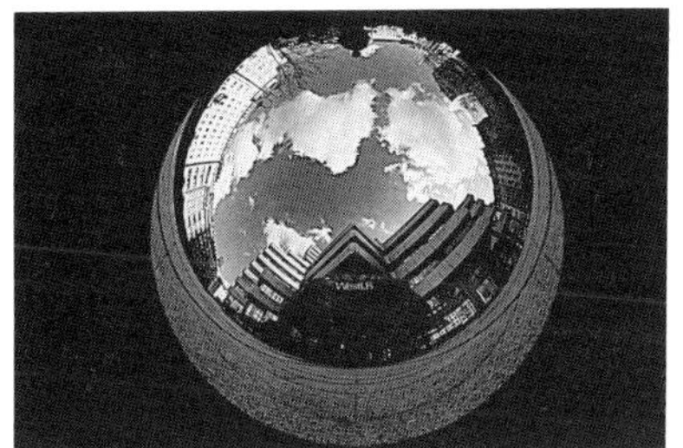

The same view, but this time resulting in a circular image, made with the Fisheye-Nikkor 6mm,f/2.8.

0.5m to infinity at full aperture. Six filters are built-in and can be rotated into the light path. The successor to this lens was the Fisheye-Nikkor 7.5mm,f/5.6 with almost identical specification and features except for its one stop faster speed.

In 1968 a very special fisheye was introduced, the Fisheye-Nikkor 10m/,f5.6 OP, designed for scientific applications. OP stands for "orthographic projection" which permits the exact measurement of brightness distribution. This lens shows no light fall-off towards the corners and is

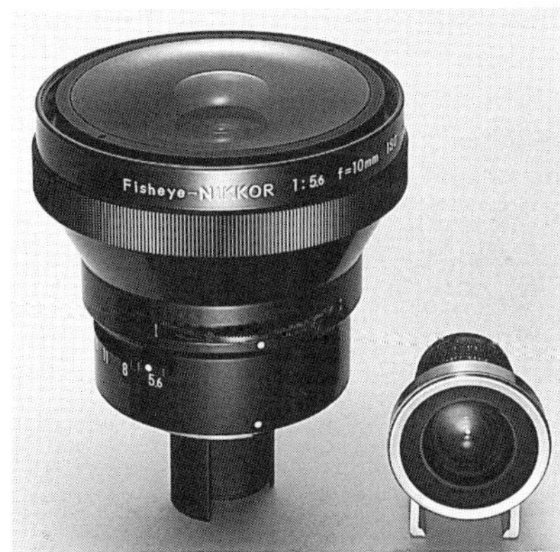

The Fisheye-Nikkor 10mm,f/5.6 OP.

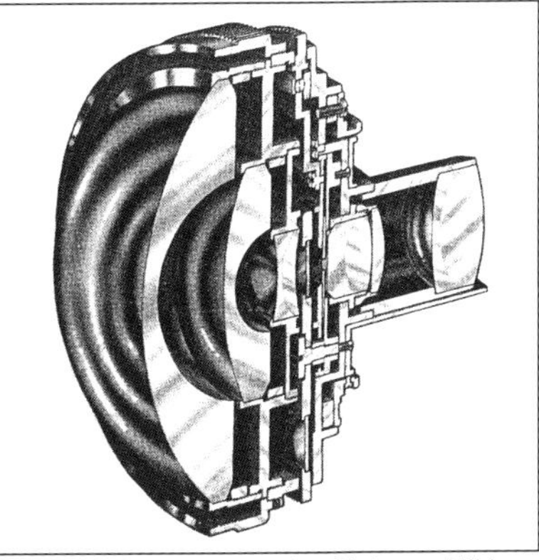

220° in cross-section, the Fisheye-Nikkor 6mm,f/5.6.

still Nikon's only lens incorporating a plastic element.

In 1969 Nikon's next fisheye followed in the form of the Fisheye-Nikkor 6mm,f/5.6, displaying an almost unbelievable picture angle of 220°. This results in parts of the photographer's surroundings that are situated laterally behind him being included in the image. Space is so restricted behind the huge front of the lens that the aperture has to be set by a lever.

In 1970 the Fisheye-Nikkor 8mm,f/2.8 was introduced, the first such lens in a retrofocus design. This allows normal viewing on the focusing screen in spite of the angle of view of 180°. Thanks to its relatively light weight of 1100g photographers who don't get dizzy easily can even risk hand-held shots.

The Fisheye-Nikkor 6mm,f/2.8 represents an awe-inspiring masterpiece of optical design, impressive with its gigantic 20cm front element. In its centre this element is just 7mm thick, growing to 60mm at the edges, and the circular image on the film is 23mm in diameter. This retrofocus construction weighs more than 5 kilos and can be focused down to 25 cm. When it is stopped-down to f/22 the depth-of-field is from 17cm to infinity.

Unlike the fisheye lenses described up to now which produce a circular image, the so-called full-frame fisheyes fill the complete 24x36mm, although they still render straight lines not passing through the lens axis as curved and to an increasing degree the further from the axis

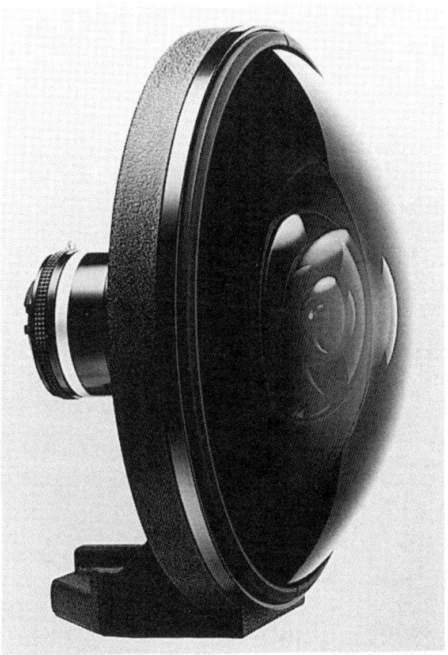

A lens that can look behind: the Fisheye-Nikkor 6mm,f/2.8 with a picture angle of 220°.

they are. This type of lens constitutes an alternative to the distortion-free wide-angles, and the first Nikon representative was the Fisheye-Nikkor 16mm,f/3.5 of 1973. The retrofocus design has resulted in compact dimensions, no more than a 50mm lens. Focusing is possible down to 30 cm, and the four most commonly needed filters are built-in.

Two years later its successor was introduced, the Fisheye-Nikkor 16mm,f/2.8, with an increased angle of view to 180° as opposed to the earlier 170°. The filters are attached behind the rear element as with the 13mm and 15mm super-wide-angles. In 1993 the AF-version of this lens was introduced. While the AF Fisheye-Nikkor 16mm,f/2.8D optical

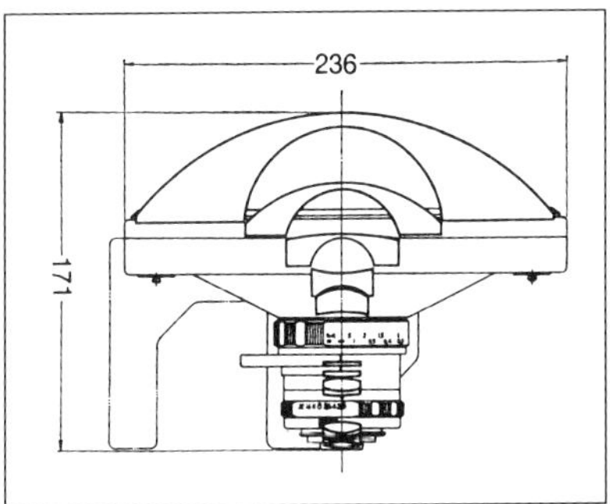

A diagram of a record wide-angle, the Fisheye-Nikkor 6mm,f/2.8.

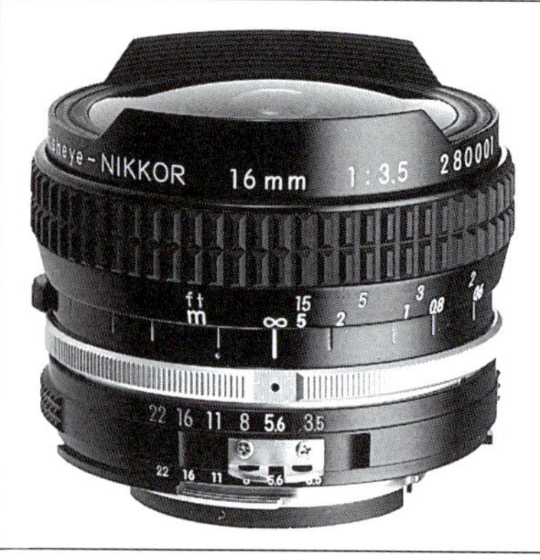

The first version of a full-frame fisheye, the Fisheye-Nikkor 16mm,f/3.5.

Background Information: Converging lines

Some large-format cameras offer the important possibility of shifting the lens laterally, or tilting it, relative to the film, in order to alter the perspective. Users of ordinary cameras are aware of the problem which arises when, for example they photograph buildings. If the camera is tilted upwards in order to include the whole building in the picture, the result will be a kind of image distortion. The normally parallel lines of the building converge towards the top of the picture, the building seems to topple over backwards. This effect is due to the rules of projection and has nothing to do with optical distortion. The phenomenon of converging verticals can be avoided by keeping the film plane exactly parallel to the subject plane. Shift lenses offer this possibility, their optical systems can be shifted out of the bayonet axis so that the camera need not be tilted but the complete subject will still be included.

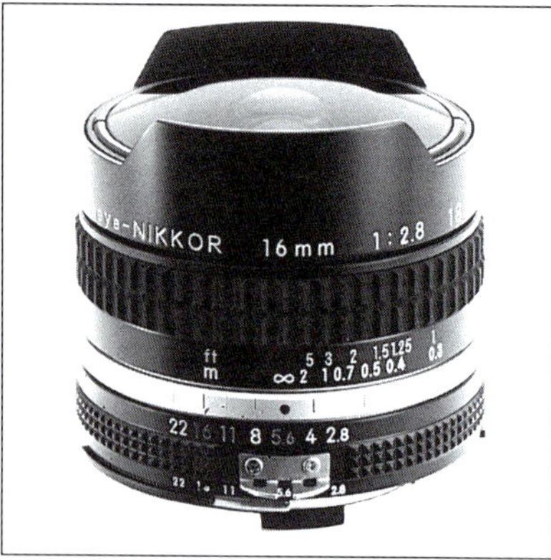

The Fisheye-Nikkor 16mm,f/2.8.

design remained unchanged, it was matched to the new F90-type cameras, i.e. the CPU relays additional distance data to the camera exposure control system.

All Nikon fisheye lenses deliver excellent sharpness and contrast. NIC-coating prevents anything more than relatively slight ghost images even when the sun shines directly onto the front element. But light sources should still be kept as close to the optical axis as possible since no effective lenshoods are available for these immense picture angles.

Shift Lenses

In 1965 Nikon introduced the first ever shift lens. The front section of the barrel can be shifted up to 11mm off-axis on a dovetail slide. The lens can be rotated a full 360° with click-stops every 30° so that shifting is possible vertically, horizontally, and diagonally. The latter direction only permits a shift of 7mm in order to prevent vignetting. These lenses cannot be fitted with automatic diaphragms or couplings for the metering system, but this is less of a problem because they will be used on a tripod. The desired aperture is chosen with a preset ring built around the filter thread and actually stopped-down to this preset value with the second ring immediately before the shutter is released. It is important to perform TTL-metering before the lens is shifted, otherwise the meter reading may be false. When the lens is shifted as far as possible the mirror is partly shaded since it is not near enough to the rear element to receive all the incoming light.

PC-lenses (PC stands for perspective control) are not just suited for architectural photography, but also for panoramic pictures. This is done by first shifting the lens as far as it will go to one side, exposing the first shot, and then rotating the lens 180° so that it points in the other direction and exposing the second – the result will be two overlapping pictures with a horizontal picture angle of 88° (4° more than a 24mm-lens).

The first 35mm,f/3,5 PC-Nikkor was a six-element design with mediocre sharpness and contrast, and it did not have NIC-coating. The

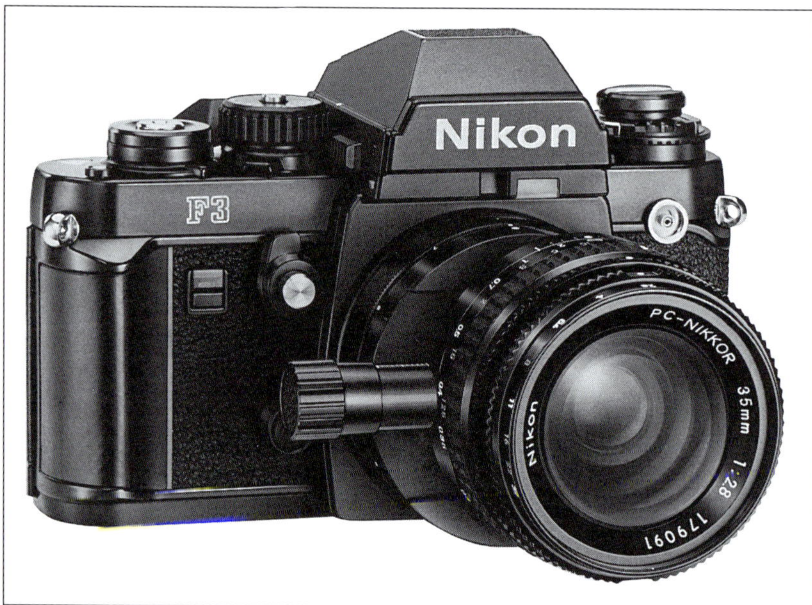

A moderate wide-angle designed to avoid converging verticals, the PC-Nikkor 35mm,f/2,8.

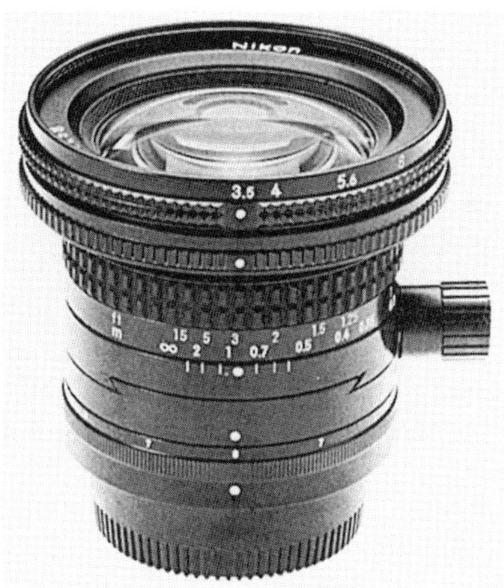

The PC-Nikkor 28mm,f/3.5 offers a larger angle of view as well as a higher speed.

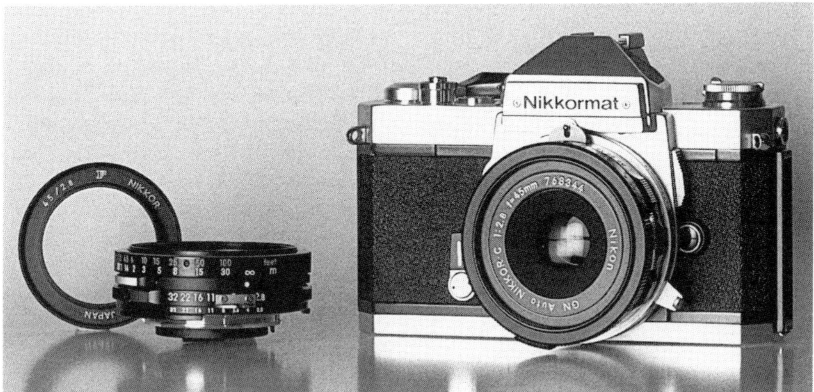

The GN-Nikkor 45mm,f/2.8 can substitute for an automatic flash unit.

35mm,f/2.8 version with eight elements introduced three years later had a visibly improved image quality. In 1980 the presently still available version appeared, distinguished by the cover protecting the spindle from getting soiled.

In 1975 Nikon answered the demand for a larger angle of view with the PC-Nikkor 28mm,f/4, a 10-element design. It can be shifted up to 11mm and produces a stronger perspective effect due to its shorter focal length. In 1980 it was replaced by the 9-element PC-Nikkor 28mm,f/3,5 displaying an improved sharpness at the edges, particularly when shifted all the way. The PC-lenses are almost completely free of distortion and only show a minimal amount of vignetting towards the corners.

GN-Nikkor

One exotic specimen in the Nikon programme designed specially for flash photography protrudes just 2cm from the camera body. This is the GN-Nikkor 45mm,f/2.8 which was introduced in 1968. Before the advent of "computer-controlled" automatic flash units it was the normal procedure to calculate the aperture by dividing the guide number by the measured distance. This method demands a new calculation every time the distance is changed, so a way was found to link the two parameters mechanically. In the GN-Nikkor the aperture ring can be connected to the focusing ring by setting the guide number of the flash unit in use on a scale on the focusing ring, ranging between 10 and 80 at ISO 100/21°. When the focusing ring is then set to a shorter distance the aperture is automatically closed too. As a result the shortest focusing distance of 0.8m may not be accessible, for example when the smallest aperture setting of f/32 is reached first, and vice-versa at the infinity end. The GN-Nikkor is the only Nikon lens in which the helix rotates counter-clockwise and with a variable pitch. This is the reason why focusing is not as smooth as with the normal Nikkors. In order to ensure a gradual change between the sharp and unsharp areas in front of as well as behind the focused plane, the GN-Nikkor has a seven-blade diaphragm that forms an almost perfect circle at the most frequently used aperture of f/8. The image quality is average by Nikon-standards, but its rather low contrast is ideal for the high degree of subject contrast encountered with direct flash.

Noct-Nikkor

An aperture of 1:1.2 has been available in the Nikon range since 1967, and as of 1978 there have been two lenses with this speed to choose from, the normal Nikkor 50mm,f/1.2 and the Noct-Nikkor 58mm,f/1.2. In the latter coma was all but eliminated. Coma is caused by rays coming from points of light passing through the lens off axis, especially at full aperture, to produce unsymmetrical blurring of the image. This becomes particularly obvious in night-time shots due to the usually numerous bright light sources when points of light become comet shaped. The high degree of correction for coma was achieved by utilizing an aspherical front element. All other image quality parameters are similar to those of the normal 50mm,f/1.2. The Noct-Nikkor is a dream-lens for available-light photography, a dream that has to be paid for with about three times the price of the non-aspherical equivalent.

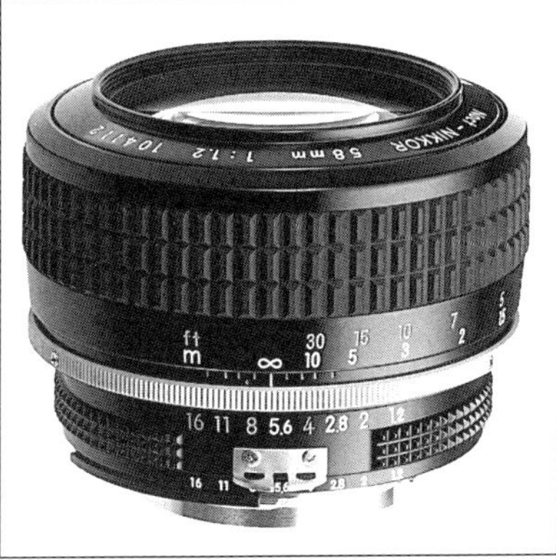

A state-of-the-art lens: the Noct-Nikkor 58mm,f/1.2.

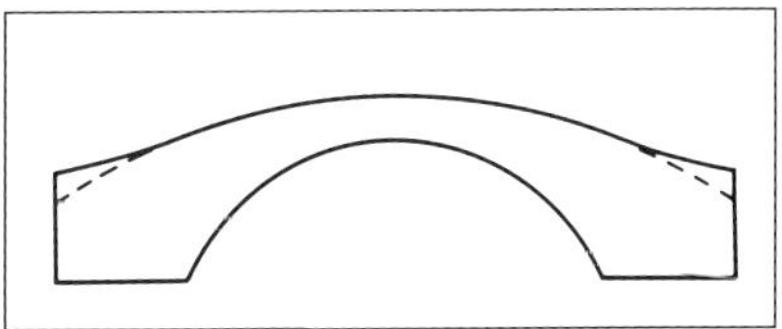

Outline of the front element of the Noct-Nikkor.

DC-Nikkors

In 1990 a completely new type of lens was added to the Nikon list: the AF DC-Nikkor 135mm,f/2.0. It has a special Defocus Control ring which shifts certain elements within the lens independently, thus directly influencing curvature of field. As a result the photographer can intentionally change the area covered by depth-of-field and also make out-of-focus blurs of points of light look somewhat like those created by mirror-lenses. Apparently the first DC-type lens had been successful enough to be followed by another late in 1993, the AF DC-Nikkor 105mm,f/2D. An interesting combination of medium focal length and wide aperture allowing the natural perspective and the shallow depth-of-field so very favourable in portrait photography. Besides the secondary ring mentioned above, it also has the D-type AF-CPU.

Both DC-models stand out from the rest of AF-Nikkors since they are the only ones with the good old silver ring on their barrels which had been so typical for the early manual focusing Nikon lenses. Perhaps Nikon thought this was necessary to secure positive handling because the three rotatable rings leave little space to grip the fixed part of the lens.

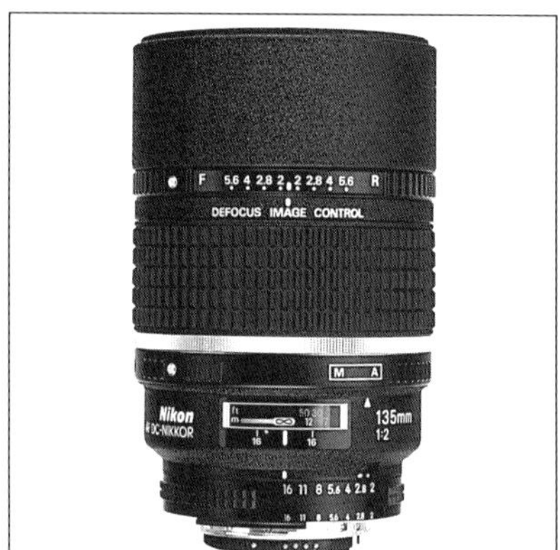

The AF DC-Nikkor 135mm,f/2 came as a surprise at the 1990 Photokina.

Micro-Nikkors

Normal Nikkors offer reproduction ratios between 1:10 and 1:7 at their closest focusing distances. The use of extension rings or close-up lenses provides higher ratios but at the cost of more or less clearly visible deterioration in image quality. Almost all lenses are corrected for distant subjects (for infinity) and deliver their best performance in this area. A correction specifically designed for short distances ensures the outstanding performance of the Micro-Nikkors at close ranges. A more fitting name would be Macro-Nikkor since the ratios from 1:10 to 1:1 are usually regarded as the macro range. Nikon's first representative of this type was introduced in 1956 for the rangefinder cameras. It was a five-element design with a focal length of 55mm, a maximum aperture of f/3.5, and a closest focusing distance of 45cm. In 1961 this design was taken over for the Micro-Nikkor 55mm,f/3.5 which then had an extended helix allowing a closest focusing distance of 24cm. The achievable reproduction ratios between 1:10 and 1:2 were noted on a second scale above the distance values. The adjacent range up to 1:1 was obtained with the extension ring M2 which used to be supplied with the lens. This lens was optimized for a reproduction ratio of 1:10, but it performed so well throughout the whole distance range that many photographers used it as their standard lens as long as a high speed was not required. The sharpness and contrast of the Micro-Nikkor and contrast were so excellent that they exceeded that of most films by far. Vignetting and distortion were also so minute they can only be established with the help of extremely sensitive measuring equipment. In 1975 the 55mm Micro-Nikkor was modified mechanically and delivered with the automatic extension ring PK-3 (PK-13 in the AI-version).

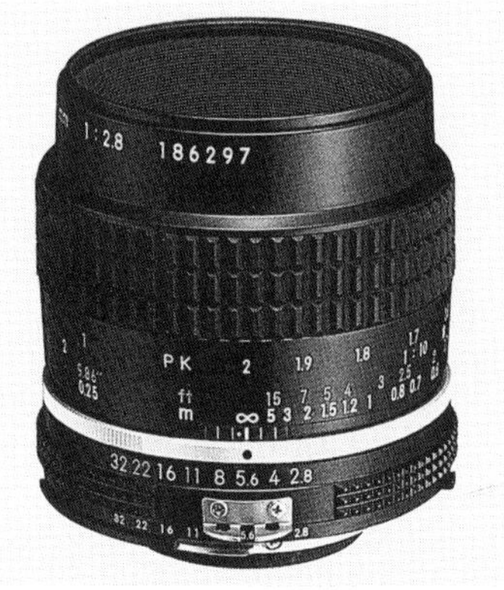

A macro-specialist: the Micro-Nikkor 55mm,f/2.8 AI-S.

The slightly faster successor, the Micro-Nikkor 55mm,f/2.8 was introduced in 1979. CRC allowed the half-stop larger aperture without any sacrifice in performance, but its image quality in the infinity range could even be improved. In this six-element design the CRC mechanics move the central lens group. The 55mm Micro-Nikkor does not necessarily call for the use of its hood since the front lens is recessed far into the barrel. In 1987 the autofocus version

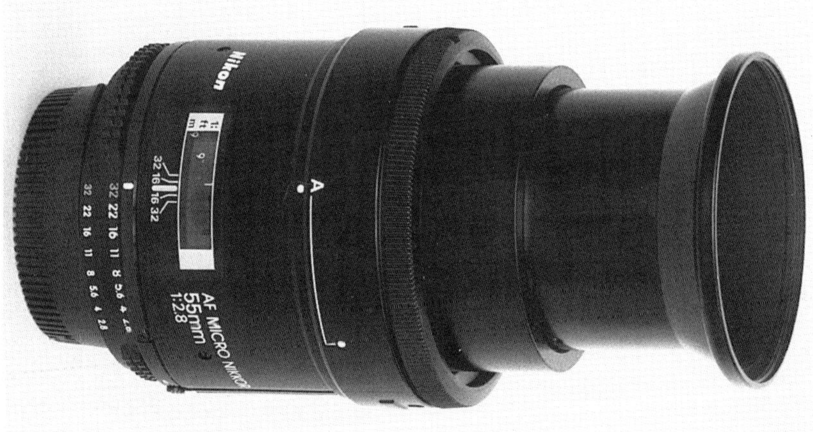

Infinitely variable reproduction ratios without an extension ring all the way down to 1:1: The AF Micro-Nikkor 55mm / 2,8.

appeared which could be focused down to 23cm, thus covering the complete range between infinity and 1:1 steplessly and without having to use an additional extension ring. This capability did increase the diameter and length by around one centimetre, and the filter thread changed to 62mm. A second ring marked with an "A" and a dot is situated beneath the narrow focusing ring so typical for the first AF-lenses. The dot-setting must be chosen if the lens is to be focused manually. This increases the friction of the focusing ring and if the lens is mounted on a reproduction stand for example, it prevents the setting from changing by itself.

In 1989, just two years later, this Micro-Nikkor was improved once again and the 60mm,f/2,8 was introduced. The main reason for this short production time will have been the unacceptable narrow focusing ring that hampered manual operation and the mechanical construction. Even when shaken just slightly the noises coming from inside sounded as if every single element was loose, although it was actually only the play in the cam system used in the AF-lenses. The present 60mm macro lens offers excellent manual as well as AF-handling. The focusing range can be restricted in three settings in order to facilitate even faster AF-operation, 0.3m to infinity, 30cm to 22cm, and "Full", meaning infinity to 22cm. Its image quality is comparable to its 55mm predecessors.

The 55mm and 60mm focal lengths have one drawback in that their working distances to the subject are too short in certain situations. At 1:1 there are just 8cm between the subject and the front of the lens. This means the photographer may obstruct his own light or has to get too close to timid creatures. The only remedy for such problems is a lens with a longer focal length. Nikon's first version was a 135mm,f/4 lens head without a focusing mount. It came from the rangefinder camera programme and had to be turned into an F-lens with the help of the BR-1 ring. Together with the bellows units PB-2 or PB-3 it allowed reproduction ratios from infinity to 1:1. In 1969 this lens head was succeeded by the Bellows-Nikkor 105mm,f/4, still depending on a bellows but with an F-bayonet. This lens does not have an automatic diaphragm (which is only possible with a double cable release with the newer bellows units) but its aperture values can be set in 1/3-stops.

In 1975 the five-element design was incorporated into the Micro-Nikkor 105mm,f/4 which now had a mount permitting focusing down to 47cm resulting in a reproduction ratio of 1:2. The PN-1 extension ring, which was turned into the PN-11 in the AI-version, extended this to 1:1. It had a pull-out lenshood. During reproduction work problems sometimes arose because the lighting often softened the lubricant in the focusing mount so that the lens would change its focus setting itself. In 1981 it received a new mount, including a small locking screw which presses a felt pad against the inside tube,

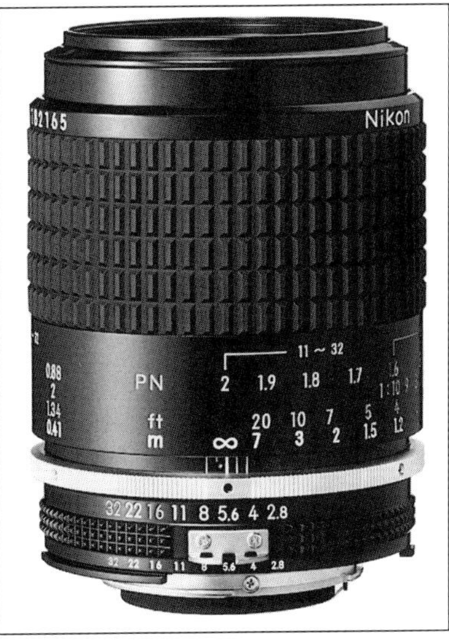

A fast long focal length macro lens: the Micro-Nikkor 105mm,f/2.8.

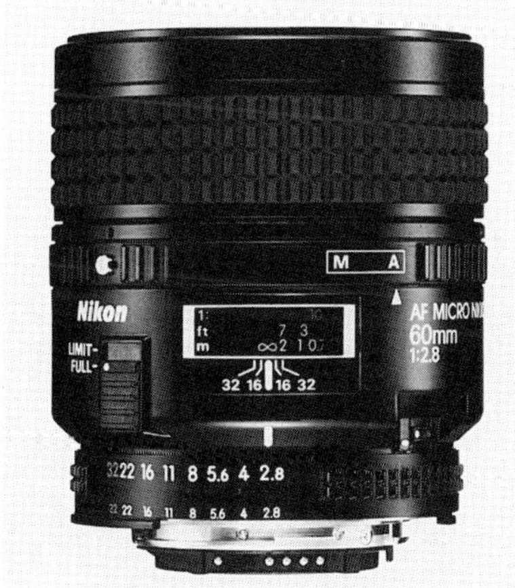

The improved version, especially for manual focusing, the AF Micro-Nikkor 60mm,f/2.8.

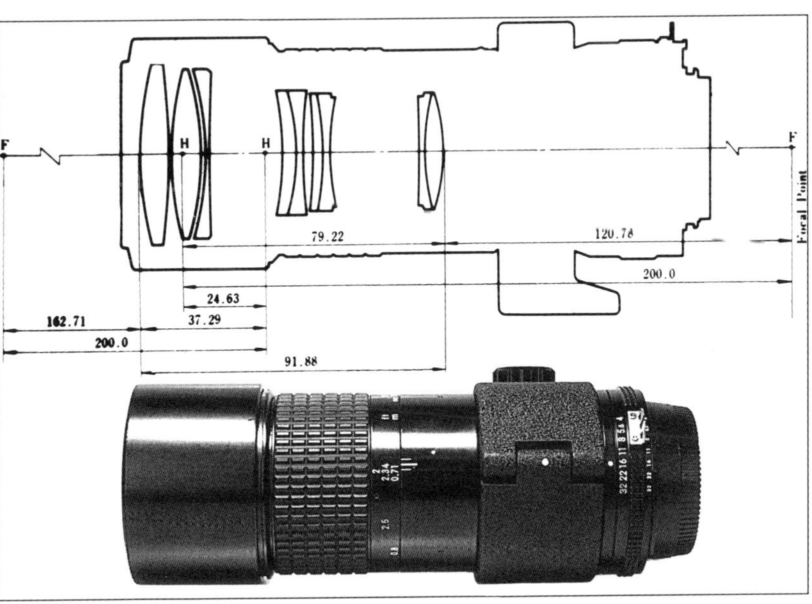

The Micro-Nikkor 200mm,f/2 IF offers a reproduction ratio of 1:2 from a distance of 71cm.

thus securing the focus-setting. Just like the 55mm, this lens is without a flaw.

In 1983 the Micro-Nikkor 105mm,f/2.8 with CRC appeared, a full stop faster than its predecessor. Ten elements were necessary and it is just in terms of contrast that this lens is inferior to the former model, but this never shows unless the hood provided with it is not mounted. When the PN-11 ring is used, ratios beyond 1:1 up to 1:0.88 become accessible.

In 1990 the AF Micro-Nikkor 105mm,f/2.8 appeared. The new nine-element design can be focused to 0.31m, resulting in a ratio of 1:1. Just like the Micro-Nikkor 60mm,f/2.8 its focusing range can be restricted if desired.

The longest Micro-Nikkor is the 200mm,f/4 which achieves its largest reproduction ratio of 1:2 at a working distance of 0.71m. This nine-element design with internal focusing appeared in 1978, and is very good for long distances too. It is fitted with a rotatable tripod mount collar that also provides balanced handling. A reproduction ratio of 1:1 can be achieved in two ways: either in combination with two PN-11 extension rings, or with a 2x teleconverter. The model TC-300/301 is recommended because it is the better combination optically. But this converter is almost as expensive as the lens itself and not as universal in use as the TC-200/201 because it was designed for focal lengths of 300mm upwards. The TC-200/201 can also be used, but vignetting towards the corners at full aperture is a bit more obvious, caused by the greater distance between the rear lens element and the converter's front element.

A teleconverter can be used with the other Micro-Nikkors as well. In the case of the 55mm and 105mm lenses there will be slight reductions in contrast and sharpness, but in practical use this is tolerable since the lens image quality is of such a high standard in the first place.

Background Information: UV-light

Lenses and especially their coatings are designed to let only those wavelengths of light pass through that the human eye can register. This part of the spectrum ranges from around 400 to 750 nanometres (nm). The infrared range begins at 750nm and turns into pure heat radiation beyond 1400nm. The ultraviolet range is from 100 to 380 nm. In normal photography this radiation is usually eliminated by the lens coating and/or UV-filters, which should actually be called UV-blocking filters. These uv-rays are the cause of bluish tints in shots made on the beach or in the mountains since they are rather intense, and many films react quite strongly. On the other hand there are certain proceedings and special situations in the areas of medicine, science, and technology that can only be made visible in uv or infrared light. This calls for lenses with the appropriate features.

UV-Nikkors

In 1964 Nikon introduced a UV 55mm,f/4 with an especially high transmission rate for wavelengths between 300nm and 400nm within the spectral range. It was a three-element design allowing a closest focusing distance of 36cm thanks to the Micro-Nikkor's mechanics. In 1985 the present UV-Nikkor 105mm,f/4.5 appeared, which is optimized for wavelengths from 220nm to 1100nm with the help of lens elements made of quartz and fluorite glass. Its image quality comes close to the theoretically possible throughout the focusing range.

Ultraviolet rays and the visible parts of the spectrum converge at the same focal point, but settings made by sight will have to be adjusted when working with infrared sources. The six-element design has the Micro-Nikkor 105mm,f/4 focusing mount, which means it allows reproduction ratios to 1:2. A special UV-filter and the matching holder UR-2 are delivered with the lens. Unlike usual UV-filters (they should strictly be called UV-blocking filters) this one is designed to permit only ultra-

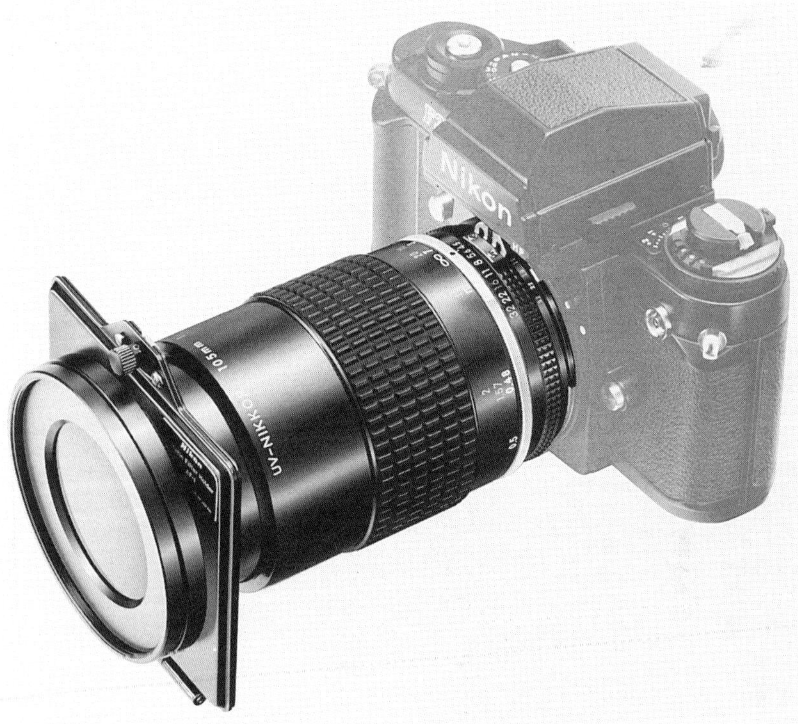

Designed for special applications and delivering an outstanding performance: the UV-Nikkor 105mm,f/4.5.

violet light from 250nm to 380nm to pass through and keep out the rest of the spectrum. In UV-photography it must be kept in mind that no coated lens accessory can be employed such as filters, close-up lenses, and tele-converters. One year later a special flash unit, the SB-140, was introduced for this lens. It is capable of emitting just ultraviolet or infrared light with the help of appropriate filters. At the 1988 Photokina a prototype of a second UV-lens was displayed, the UV-Nikkor 50mm, f/4.5, but so far it has not been put into production.

Medical-Nikkors

During the course of time there have been two models. The "Medical" actually combines a macro-lens and a ring-light flash unit. It was developed for the photographic documentation of medical and dental operations, treatments, or diagnoses. The first Medical-Nikkor 200mm, f/5.6 was introduced in 1962. It consists of four elements and is fixed at a focusing distance of 3.35m (a reproduction ratio of 1:15). The six supplementary lenses, some of which can be combined with each other, enable this to be increased to 3:1. Due to its layout the lens can only be used with the built-in flash unit, this is why there are no couplings for the camera metering system. The film speed is set on the lens barrel, and depending on the focused distance the correct aperture is automatically set between f/5.6 and f/45. If desired, numerals from 1 to 38 or the reproduction ratio can be imprinted directly onto the picture. The Medical-Nikkor has an automatic diaphragm and a focusing lamp in the flash tube to improve handling. The power is supplied by the AC-unit LA-1 or the battery compartment LD-1, which can also be employed for the ringlights SR-2/SM-2. They permit the output to be reduced by two EV-steps to 1/4.

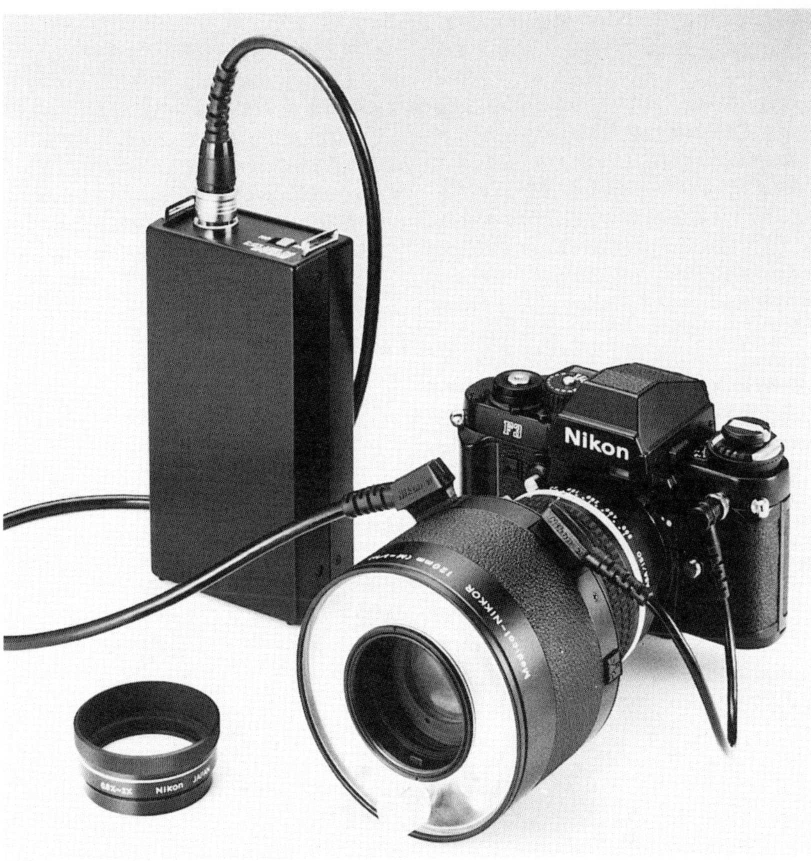

Equipped with internal focusing and a larger ringlight: the Medical-Nikkor 120mm,f/4 IF.

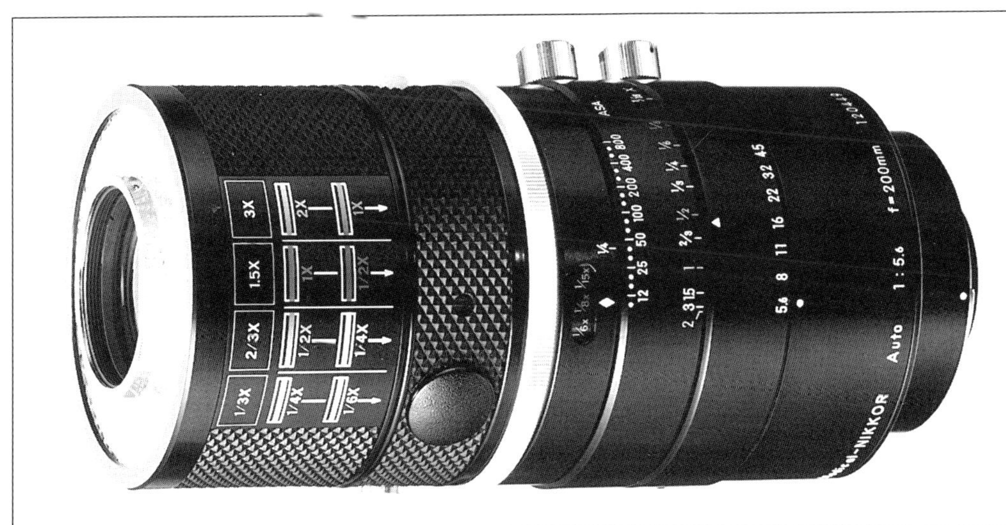

The first and only one of its kind: the Medical-Nikkor 200mm,f/5.6 with its built-in ringlight.

In 1974 a mechanically modified version appeared which looked almost identical to the original. It can easily be distinguished though by its three-pin terminal as opposed to the older four-pin version. The image quality of the Medical-Nikkor cannot compare to that of the Micro-Nikkor. The built-in ringlight has a guide number of just 7.5, but this is quite sufficient for the short distances involved.

The new Medical-Nikkor 120mm, f/4 IF introduced in 1981 offers much more convenient handling. The most conspicuous difference is the much easier focusing which is effected directly with the IF-system. It allows focusing from 1.6m to 0.35m, and the dedicated close-up lens adds the range from 1:1 to 2:1. The larger ringlight softens the illumination while the flash exposure is controlled by setting the film speed on the lens. The correct aperture is then automatically set by focusing. Either the AC-unit LA-2 or the battery compartment LD-2 can be used as power supplies for both this lens and the SB-21 macroflash-unit. When desired the reproduction ratio can be imprinted onto the picture. A small lamp in the reflector lights up for 16 seconds when the button is pressed to support focusing. If the focal length of 120mm is not sufficient it can be extended by a factor of 1.4 with the Teleconverter TC-14A/B, turning it into a 170mm. A loss of one stop must be considered when the film speed is set on the lens.

Background Information: Teleconverters

Teleconverters, also called extenders, are optical systems capable of increasing the focal length of a lens. They are mounted between lens and camera and enlarge the image the lens would normally create in the film plane, i.e. they create a cropped part of the image in the film plane. In the case of a 2x-converter it will be 50% of the original, a 1,4x will result in around 70%. In the process there is a loss of light, two stops with a 2x and one with a 1.4x. This fact prevents the construction of a faster converter, for example a 2x-model with a loss of less than two stops. The additional loss due to reduced transmission rate and internal reflection is negligible.

In the early days teleconverters were available only from independent lens manufacturers. Compared to the image quality of the prime lens a considerably reduced performance had to be accepted due to the relatively simple design and construction of these early converters. This reduction is not a general feature of all teleconverters though, carefully manufactured designs to match specific lenses have minimal influence on their quality, hardly visible in everyday shots. But not all lenses are equally suited for the use with teleconverters. The lens itself should display excellent contrast since every additional element inevitably leads to some deterioration.

The deterioration of contrast is one factor to be aware of when employing a converter. Normally a 400mm lens will always deliver a more brilliant image than the combination of a 200mm lens and a 2x-converter. On the other hand, light fall-off towards the corners may even be improved, i.e.reduced since the final picture is the result of only the central part of the original image so that only the converter's vignetting will come into effect.

In terms of distortion things can improve as well as deteriorate since the rendering of the lens and the converter may either be additive or cancel each other out.

The depth-of-field of the lens on its own is halved, corresponding to that of the focal length of the combination. It is important to keep in mind that the resulting effective aperture will be the preset value plus one or two stops. So, if f5.6 is set on the aperture ring, the combination with the TC-201 will be f/11, while the TC-14 will turn it into f/8. One of a converter's big advantages is the fact that it leaves the shortest focusing distance of the lens unchanged, thus enhancing the close-up abilities of the combination. For example, when a 2x-converter is used, the reproduction ratio is doubled.

Teleconverters

Nikon's first teleconverter was introduced in 1976, it was called TC-1 and designed for focal lengths up to 200mm, including the zooms in this range as well as the Reflex-Nikkor 500mm,f/8. It consisted of a seven-element optical system with NIC-coating and was suitable for lens speeds of f/2 and less.

The TC-1 was sold for just one year and replaced in 1977 by the TC-200 with the AI-aperture coupling system. Its optical system remained unchanged. The same goes for the TC-201 which appeared in 1983 and also conveys the lens speed and lens type information with the pin and notch system. So in this respect it is comparable to an AI-S standard lens.

The TC-2 was introduced together with the TC-1, it was also a 2x-converter but because its optical system was optimized for telephoto lenses of 300mm upwards, it protruded about 23mm from its front bayonet flange. It was a five-element design, usable for lens speeds up to f/2.8. Besides longer focal lengths beyond 300mm, shorter ones can also be attached as long as their rear elements are located far enough inside the barrel. The TC-2 was modified to become the TC-300 and again in 1983 to finally turn out as the present TC-301.

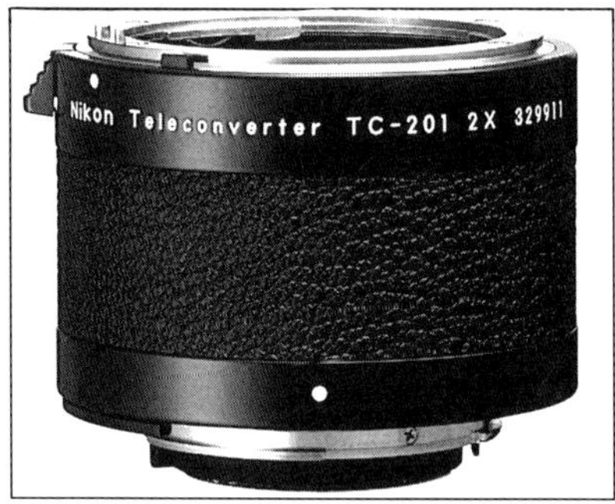

A very popular 2x-converter for focal lengths up to 200mm: the TC-201.

The reason for differentiating between converters for focal lengths up to 200mm and from 300mm onwards is that if the TC-200/201 were to be used with lenses which call for the TC-300/301 the result

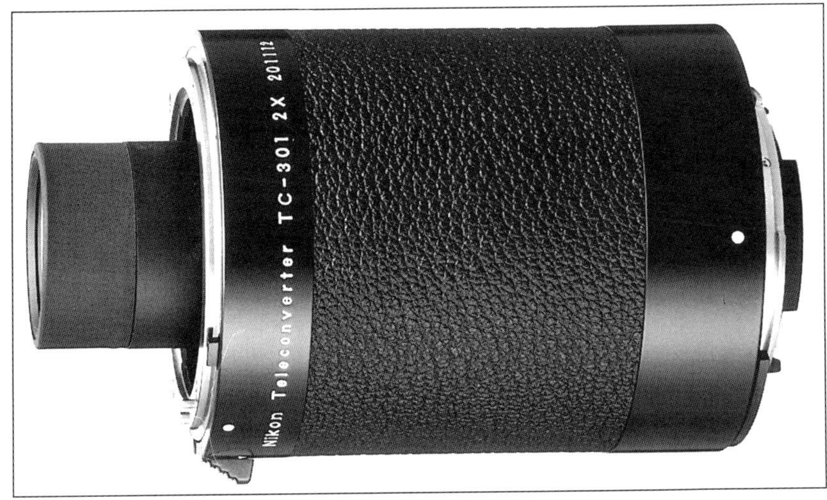

The model for focal lengths beyond 300mm: the TC-301.

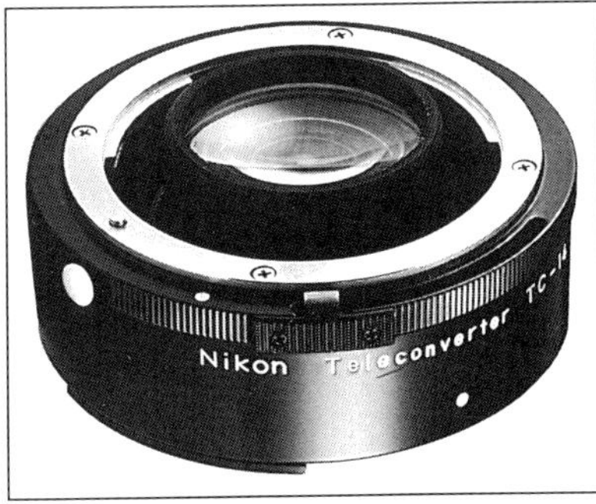

The TC-14 extends the focal length of an attached lens by a factor of 1.4 and therefore only causes a loss of one stop.

would be drastic light fall-off in some combinations.

In 1977 another converter was added to the range, the TC-14. This model extends the lens focal length by a factor of 1.4, but on the other hand the combination's maximum aperture is only reduced by one stop. It too is made of five elements and designed for focal lengths of 300mm and longer even though its optical system protrudes only slightly beyond the bayonet flange. As a result the TC-14 can not only be used with the two longer Micro-Nikkors but also with the 200mm,f/2 IF-ED and the 135mm,f/3.5. It operates with apertures of f/2 and smaller and thus, for example, turns the Nikkor 200mm,f/2 IF-ED into a 280mm,f/2.8. In the AI-S version it mutated into the TC-14B. Another model designated TC-14C was developed especially for the extremely fast Nikkor 300mm,f/2.8 IF-ED. It was delivered along with the lens. Its performance is comparable to that of the TC-14B.

A 1.4x-converter can also be an interesting addition to shorter telephoto lenses, and so in 1983 the TC-14A for focal lengths up to 200mm was introduced. It too is a five-element design, but usable for maximum apertures of f/1.8 and smaller. In this case a 105mm,f/1.8, for example, would be converted to a 150mm,f/2.5 or a 180mm,f/2.8 into a 250mm,f/4.

AF-Teleconverters

In the age of autofocus teleconverters have an additional task. In combination with an AF-camera body the TC-16 permits automatic focusing even with non-AF lenses. To facilitate this the camera's AF-motor focuses the converter's movable optical system. This is just possible within a limited range since the optical system can only be shifted 5mm. In the case of a 35mm lens that is sufficient to focus between infinity and 60cm, but with a 180mm lens the focusing range will be restricted to infinity to 13m – when the lens in use is set to infinity manually. It will work just as well though to roughly preset the distance and leave the remaining precise focusing to the AF-converter, especially since this method will increase the accessible range.

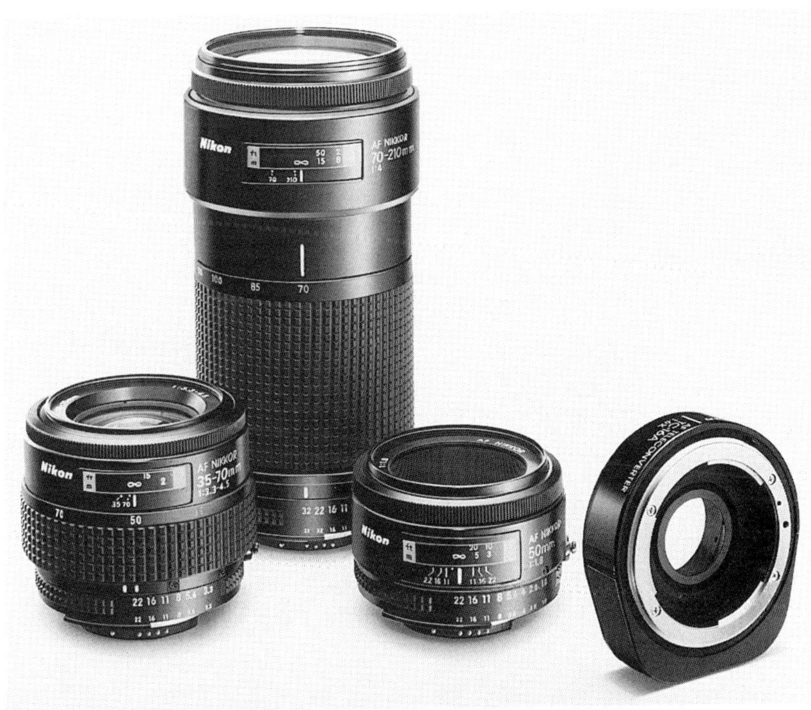

The 1,6x Autofocus Converter TC-16A along with three AF-lenses.

Nikon Teleconverters												
Designation	Type	Period in production	Extension factor	Light loss (EV)	Elements/ groups	Usable lens speeds	Effective aperture	Hard case	Soft pouch	Weight	Dimensions (mm)	Special features
TC-1	K	06/76 - 06/77	x2	2 EV	7/5	2.0-32	4.0-64	CL-30 S	61	230g	51.5 x 64.5	
TC-200	N	08/77 - 09/83	x2	2 EV	7/5	2.0-32	4.0-64	CL-30 S	61	230g	51.5 x 64.5	
TC-201	Ai-S	from 10/83	x2	2 EV	7/5	2.0-32	4.0-64	CL-30 S	61	230g	51.5 x 64.5	
TC-2	K	06/76 - 06/77	x2	2 EV	5/5	2.8-32	5.6-64	CL-33 S	62	280g	115.0 x 64.5	
TC-300	N	08/77 - 09/83	x2	2 EV	5/5	2.8-32	5.6-64	CL-33 S	62	280g	115.0 x 64.5	
TC-301	Ai-S	from 10/83	x2	2 EV	5/5	2.8-32	5.6-64	CL-33 S	62	280g	115.0 x 64.5	
TC-14	N	08/77 - 10/83	x1.4	1 EV	5/5	2.0-32	2.8-45	CL-30 S	61	170g	33.5 x 64.5	
TC-14B	Ai-S	from 10/83	x1.4	1 EV	5/5	2.0-32	2.8-45	CL-30 S	61	165g	33.5 x 64.5	
TC-14C	Ai-S	from 06/83	x1.4	1 EV	5/5	2.0-16	2.8-22	CL-30 S	61	200g	35.5 x 64.5	special for 300/2.0 IF-ED
TC-14A	Ai-S	from 10/83	x1.4	1 EV	5/5	1.8-32	2.8-45	CL-30S	61	145g	25.5 x 64.5	
TC-16	AF	05/84 - 01/86	x1.6	1 1/3 EV	5/5	1.8-32	2.8-51	—	61	285g	44.0 x 88.0	for F3 AF only
TC-16A	AF	from 03/86	x1.6	1 1/3 EV	5/5	1.8-32	2.8-51	CL-30 S	61	150g	30.0 x 69.0	for F-501/801/ 801s/F-90/F4
TC-14E	AF	from 03/93	x1.4	1 EV	5/5	2.0-32	2.8-45	CL-30 S	61	200g	24.5 x 65.0	only for AF-I 300/2.8 and 600/4
TC-20E	AF	from 03/93	x2	2 EV	7/6	2.0-32	4-64	CL-31 S	62	340g	55.0 x 65.0	only for AF-I 300/2.8 and 400/2.8

The TC-16 extends the focal length of the attached lens by a factor of 1.6 while it causes a loss of 1 1/3 stops. The maximum usable speed of the mounted lens is f/1.8. The first model appeared with the F3 AF and can only be employed with this body. It has its own integrated AF-drive motor. The TC-16A was introduced with the F-501 and can also be used with the F4, F-801 and F-801s, and the F90.

The advent of the AF-I type Nikkors with their built-in AF-motor drive systems called for converters that are able to relay the necessary focusing information back and forth between the body and the attached lenses. So it came as no surprise that two such models appeared early in 1993 soon after the mentioned lenses had been introduced: the AF-I Teleconverters TC-14E and TC-20E. Except for their electrical connections they remained unchanged, i.e. their optical design is exactly that of the performance-proven TC-201/301. Since they neither have motor drives of their own nor an AF-coupling like the TC-16A, they cannot serve as AF-converters for any other than AF-I type lenses though.

Filters and Lens Accessories

Filters are designed to prevent certain of the visible wavelengths of light from passing through and exposing the film. As a rule, the filters employed in black-and-white photography increase contrast by darkening the impression of the complementary colours of the filter, i.e.lightening up objects of its own colour. Filters for black-and-white photography are used to influence the spectral sensitivity of the film while those employed with colour films are supposed to eliminate colour casts.

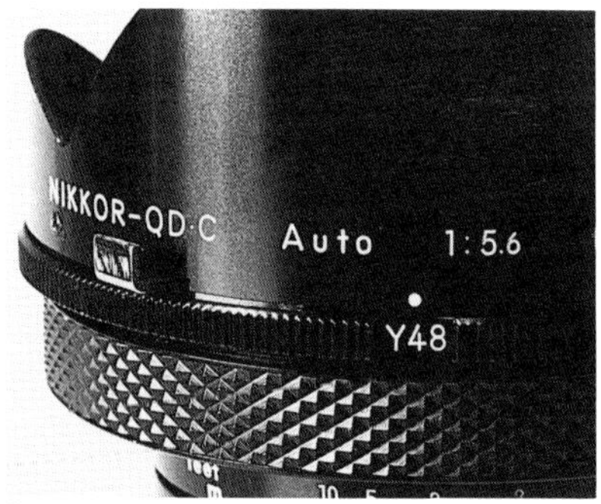

Some of the older Nikon super-wide-angle lenses have integrated filter turrets allowing the desired filter to be rotated into the light path.

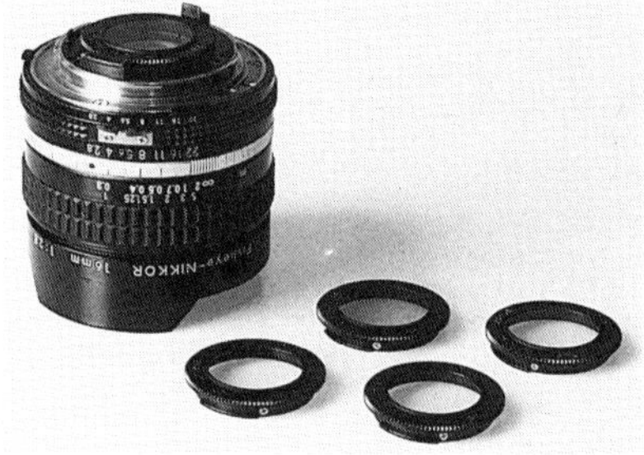

The bayonet filter mount of the Fisheye Nikkor 16mm,f/2.8.

Naturally the optical qualities of filters should not be any lower than those of the lens, otherwise they will cause a deterioration in performance. Nikon filters are made of high-quality optical glass and precision ground to absolute flatness. In order to prevent any ghost images or flare they are NIC-multicoated just like the lenses. Nikon is also very particular about the filter rings. They are solidly made of metal, but at the same time so thin they will not cause any vignetting, even when mounted on an extreme wide-angle lens such as the Nikkor 18mm,f/3.5 with its 100° angle of view.

Lens/Camera Combinations

Type of lens or bayonet	Cameras models to 1976	F2 A/AS; EL-2; FT-3; FM; FE; F3	EM; FG-20	FG	FM-2; FE-2	FA	F3 AF	F-301; F-501	F-401; F-401 S	F-601; F-801	F4
Non-AI Nikkors	+	1	–	–	–	–	1	–	–	–	1; 5; 6; 9; 14
Nikkors modified to AI	+	+	2	4	+	4; 6; 7; 8	+	4; 7; 12	X 13	5; 6; 8; 9	5; 6; 9
Original AI-Nikkors	+	+	+	+	+	7	+	7; 12	X 13	5; 6; 8; 9	5; 9
AI-S Nikkor	+	+	+	+	+	+	+	+	X 13	5; 6; 8; 9	5; 9
E-Series	1	+	+	+	+	+	+	+	X 13	5; 6; 8; 9	5; 9
AF-Nikkors for F3 AF	+	+	+	+	+	+	+	+	X 13	5; 6; 8; 9; 15	5; 9
AF-Nikkors	1	+	+	+	+	+	10; 15	+	+	+	+
AF-I Nikkors	1	+	+	+	+	+	10; 15	+	+	+18	+
AF P-Nikkor (500mm, f/4 IF-ED)	1	+	+	+	+	+	10; 15	+	+	+	+
Medical-Nikkor 120mm,f/4 IF	1	1	3	3	1	1; 5; 6; 9	1	3	–	3	1; 5; 6; 9; 14
Mirror and PC-Nikkors	1	1	1	1; 5	1	1; 5; 6; 9	1	1; 5;	X 13	1; 5; 6; 8; 9	1; 5; 6; 9; 14
Bellows units	1	1	1	1; 5	1	1; 5; 6; 9	1	1; 5	X 13	1; 5; 6; 8; 9	1; 5; 6; 9
PK-1/2/3 and PN-1	+	1	–	–	–	–	1	–	–	–	1; 5; 6; 9
PK-11/12/13 and PN-11	1	+	2	4	+	4; 6; 7; 8	11	4; 12; 11 with F-501	X 11; 13	5; 6; 8; 9; 11	5; 6; 9; 11
Extension ring set K	1	1	1	1; 5	1	1; 5; 6; 9	1	1; 5	X 13	1; 5; 6; 9	1; 5; 6; 9
TC-14; TC-200; TC-300	1	+	2	4	+	4; 6; 7; 8	+	4; 7; 12	X 13	5; 6; 8; 9	5; 6; 9; 14
TC-14A/B/C; TC-201/301	1	+	+	+	+	+	+	+	X 13	5; 6; 8; 9	5; 9
TC-14E/20E	1	+	+	+16	+	+17	+15	+15	X 13	5; 6; 8; 9; 18	5; 9
TC-16 AF (for F3 AF)	–	–	–	–	–	–	+	–	–	–	–
TC-16A	–	–	–	–	–	–	–	with F-501	–	5; 6; 8; 9	5; 9

+= usable without restriction
X= attachable, but hardly sensible due to major restrictions
–= not usable
1= only stop-down metering possible
2= just one automatic aperture accessible with SB-E and SB-19
3= usable only for flast operation
4= displayed shutter speed in viewfinder may differ from effective value in P-mode
5= programmed automatic exposure not accessible
6= AMP or Matrix metering not accessible
7= no automatic switchover to High-Speed program in P-dual mode
8= aperture value not displayed in viewfinder
9= shutter speed priority automatic exposure mode not accessible
10= only attachable when the DX-1 finder is not loaded with batteries
11= Pk-11 not usable – use Pk-11A instead; BR-2 not usable – use BR-2A instead
12= programmed automatic flash exposure mode not accessible
13= exposure metering not accessible — just focus-assist displays
14= spot-metering not accessible
15= autofocus operation not accessible
16= With FG and F-301 use only aperture priority or manual exposure modes
17= With FA do not use matrix metering or programmed exposure modes
18= With F90 out of focus possible; others manual

Nikon provides filters with diameters from 39mm to 160mm, and bayonet versions for the Nikkors 13mm,f/5.6, 15mm,f/3.5, and 16mm,f/2.8. Their wide angles of view permit the use of filters only behind their rear elements.

Filters for black-and-white photography

Eight different types of filter are available for black-and-white photography. The UV-filter L39 which can be used as a lens protector cuts ultraviolet light up to 390nm. There are three kinds of yellow filter: the pale yellow Y44, the medium Y48, and the strong Y52. They absorb blue light more or less completely, thus rendering the colours tonally correct on the negative. The orange filter O56 additionally absorbs green so that a blue sky and green meadow are both reproduced darker. The red filter R60 has even more dramatic effects since it renders a blue sky almost black, making the scene appear to be a night-time shot with moonlight as the only source of illumination.

The light losses caused by the use of filters are automatically compensated by the metering system in the camera – except in the case of red filters. Even so, test exposures should be made to determine the exact amount of necessary compensation. The AF-system in the AF-cameras may also be hampered or disabled by the use of the orange O56 or the red R60 filter so that it is advisable to focus manually.

Just like the yellow filters, the light green filter XO serves to reproduce the subject colours tonally correct in black-and-white negatives.

The denser green filter X1 is employed to reduce the effect of red light in the case of portraits shot in available light.

Filters for colour photography

In colour photography it is advisable to use the L37C filter to screen out UV-radiation below 370nm which can lend a blue cast in shots made in mountains or at the seaside. All the other wavelengths can pass freely. Neutral filters such as this are always left attached to the lens as a protection for the front element. Today this is probably its main task since modern NIC-coated lenses only permit a very small portion of UV-radiation to pass through. The extremely pale pink Skylight filter L1BC is also quite popular for this purpose. People photographed with this filter in bright sunlight are rendered with a more a pleasing complexion.

The effect is even stronger with the amber coloured A2-filter. This version is advisable for overcast weather when the UV-portion of the light tends to be particularly high.

The colour-conversion filter A12 is used when the existing light and the films colour balance have to be matched, in this case when a tungsten-type film is to be employed in normal daylight. The blue filters B2, B8, and B12 work the other way round, i.e. to counteract too warm existing light. The colour-conversion filter B12 matches artificial light to a normal daylight film.

The polarizing filters are very special. They can reduce or even eliminate reflections from non-metallic surfaces such as glass or water, thus improving their "transparency". At the same time, depending on the sun's angle to the optical axis, colour saturation can be improved considerably which becomes particularly apparent in the darker rendering of blue skies. The front ring of a polarizing filter can be rotated in its mount to vary the strength of the effect.

Restrictions with special lenses

Lens	Serial numbers	not usable with
PC 28mm/4.0*	under 180 901	EM; FM-2; FG; FE-2; FA; FG-20; F-301/501/401/801
PC 35mm/2.8*	-906 201 and from 851 000	—
1000mm/11.0*	under 143 002	—
2000mm/11.0*	under 200 311	—
220-600mm/9.5*	under 300 491	—
180-600mm/8.0*	under 174 167	—
360-1200mm/11.0*	under 174 088	—
Focusing mount AU-1	all versions	—
28mm/3.5 also AI converted	625 611-999 999	EM; FG; FG-20; FA; F-301/501; F4
35mm/1/4 also AI converted	385 001-400 000	—
55mm/1.2 also AI converted	184 711-400 000	—
28mm/2.0	under 540 021	TC-16 A
28mm/2.8	under 5 000 001	TC-16 A
35mm/1.4	AI and AI converted	TC-16 A
35mm/2.0	under 931 001	TC-16 A
35mm/2.8	under 880 001	TC-16 A
50mm/1.4	under 3 980 001	TC-16 A
50mm/2.0	under 3 640 001	TC-16 A
16mm/3.5	272 281-290 000	F4
8mm/8.0	All types	F4

* Nikon service agents will advise whether or not modification is possible

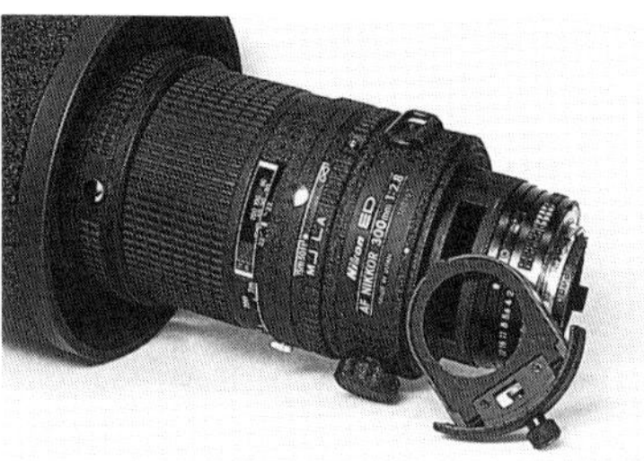
The slip-in type filter clips used in the longer telephoto lenses.

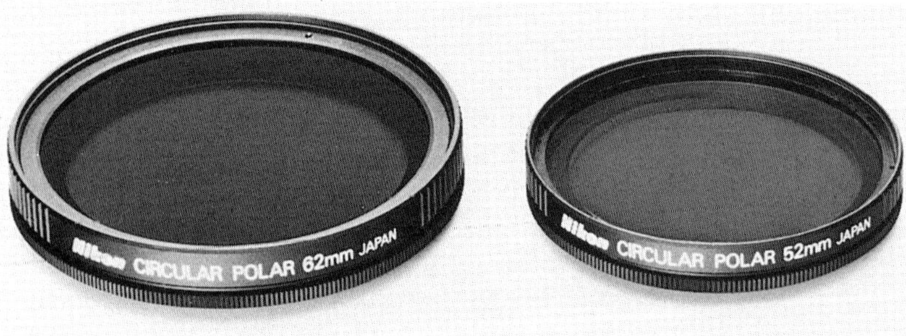

High-quality filters for high-class lenses: original Nikon polarizing filters.

There are two types of polarizing filters. The lower priced linear and the more expensive circular versions. Today Nikon only offers the circular version which is mandatory for AF-cameras anyway. All the other Nikon cameras can be used with the former normal linear versions. One of the specialities of Nikon polarizing filters is their larger front thread diameter compared to that of the lenses they are mounted on. This makes special lenshoods necessary. With 52mm lenses the two-part model HN-12 is available for focal lengths of 35mm and more, the 62mm models take the HN-26 which can also be used on lenses as of 35mm. In the case of 72mm filter threads and the focal lengths of 180mm and more the HN-13 is necessary.

Special purpose filters

Neutral density, or grey filters which reduce the amount of light passing through, can be used with

Nikon Filters															
Designation	Bayonet	39mm Ø	52mm Ø	62mm Ø	72mm Ø	77mm Ø	82mm Ø	95mm Ø	122mm Ø	160mm Ø	Series 9	Kodak designation	Insert filter for AF-2	Filter factor for daylight(EV)	Filter factor for artificial light(EV)
L1BC	+	+	+	+	+	–	–	–	–	–	–	1A	–	–	–
L37C	–	+	+	+	+	+	+	+	+	+	–	–	–	–	–
L39	–	–	+	–	+	–	–	+	+	–	+	2B	–	–	–
Y44	–	–	+	–	+	–	–	–	–	–	+	3	–	–1/2	–
Y48	+	+	+	+	+	–	–	+	+	–	+	9	–	–2/3	–1/4
Y52	–	+	+	–	–	–	–	–	–	–	+	15	–	–1	–1/2
O56	+	+	+	+	+	–	–	+	+	–	+	22	–	–1 2/3	–1
R60	+	+	+	+	+	–	–	+	+	–	+	25	–	–3	–2 1/4
X0	–	–	+	–	–	–	–	–	–	–	–	11	–	–1	–2/3
X1	–	–	+	–	–	–	–	–	–	–	–	58	–	–2 1/4	–1 2/3
A2	+	+	+	+	+	–	–	–	–	–	–	81A	–	–1/4	–1/4
A12	–	+	1	+	–	–	–	–	–	–	–	85	–	–1	–1
B2	+	+	+	+	+	–	–	–	–	–	–	82A	–	–1/4	–1/4
B8	–	+	+	–	–	–	–	–	–	–	–	80C	–	–2/3	–2/3
B12	–	+	+	+	–	–	–	–	–	–	–	80B	–	–1	–1
ND2	–	+	–	–	–	–	–	–	–	–	–	ND 0.3	–	–1	–1
ND4	–	+	+	–	+	–	–	–	–	–	–	ND 0.6	–	–2	–2
ND8	–	+	+	–	–	–	–	–	–	–	–	ND 0.9	–	–3	–3
ND-400	–	–	+	–	–	–	–	–	–	–	–	–	–	–8.5	–8.5
Pola linear	–	–	1)	1)	+	–	–	–	–	–	–	–	–	–1.2	–1.2
Pola circular	–	–	+	+	–	+	–	–	–	–	–	–	–	–1.2	–1.2
L37	–	–	+	–	+	–	–	–	–	–	–	–	+	–	–
No. 1	–	–	+	+	+	–	–	–	–	–	–	–	–	–	–
No. 2	–	–	+	+	+	–	–	–	–	–	–	–	–	–	–

1 = no longer available

both black-and-white- and colour films. The designation of the filter includes the necessary compensation factor. The ND-2 version cuts brightness by 1EV, the ND-4 by 2EV, the ND-8 by 3EV, and the ND-400 by 8.5 EV. These filters are used, for example, when a shot is purposely to be made with the largest aperture but even the fastest shutter speed will not deliver a correct exposure, or if a long exposure is to be made in bright daylight.

Nikon offers two holders for 7.5x7.5 gelatine filters. These are the AF-1 for 52mm-mounts, and the AF-2 for 72mm-mounts. When a lens-hood proves necessary, the versions for the polarizing filters can be used with these holders.

If the exceptional sharpness of a Nikkor is to be reduced deliberately this can be done with the Nikon Soft-Focus filters. One of their surface coatings includes a minute amount of silver resulting in an even softening effect at all apertures. No.1 is ideal for portraits while No.2 can create a slightly foggy impression in landscapes, for example.

In order to attach the 72mm filters to the ever increasing number of Nikon lenses with 62mm threads Nikon offers the adaptor ring UR-1.

Lens Hoods

An effective lenshood is a must for every lens, since they help to maintain the high contrast even when light sources are situated near the edges of the frame. Their task is to prevent unnecessary and therefore undesirable light from outside the picture area from entering the optical system. This is only possible when lens and hood are perfectly matched. Zoom and telephoto lenses are particularly sensitive to such stray light.

Nikon's fixed focal lengths up to 18mm and from 85mm upwards have built-in lenshoods or are at least supplied with them. Apart from their allocation to certain lens models five different versions can be distinguished. All the non-collapsible metal screw-in types are designated HN-xx, while HS-xx indicates the snap-on type otherwise identical to the first. The HK-versions are non-collapsible slip-on types, HB-xx stands for plastic hoods with a bayonet mount for the AF-zoom lenses, HR-xx is what the rubber versions are called, and HE-xx marks the extension units for the fast telephoto lenses with integrated hoods of their own.

Miscellaneous lens accessories

Nikon's Lens Scope Converter, also called a telescope converter, is an eyepiece which can be attached to a lens to form a telescope. It will give a magnification 1/10 of the focal length of the lens, so a 50mm lens will result in a 5x-magnification. Its exit pupil is just 2.5mm in diameter so it only makes sense to use it as long as the subject is brightly lit. When the lens is set to its 1:1-position it results in a 25x-magnification. The correction facility can be adjusted between -5 and +3 dioptres.

A C-mount adaptor is available for the use of Nikkor lenses on 16mm

Nikon Large-format Lenses

Lens	Type	Angular field at maximum aperture	Angular field at f/22	Format	Optimum focusing range	Shutter size	Filter thread (mm)	Diameter of rear element mount	Mount size (mm)	Overall length	Weight (g)
65mm/4.0	SW	80°/110mmø	105°/170mmø	4x5"	∞-1;5	0	67x0.75	54	71	67	370
75mm/4.5	SW	80°/126mmø	106°/200mmø	4x5"	∞-1:5	0	67x0.75	60	81	73.5	420
90mm/4.5	SW	80°/154mmø	105°/235mmø	5x7"	∞-1:5	0	82x0.75	70	97	86	600
90mm/8.0	SW	80°/154mmø	105°/235mmø	5x7"	∞-1:5	0	67x0.75	60	97	71	360
120mm/8.0	SW	80°/200mmø	105°/312mmø	8x10"	∞-1:5	0	77x0.75	80	131	92.5	610
150mm/5.6	SW	80°/253mmø	106°/400mmø	10x12"	∞-1:5	1	95x1	100	166	115.5	950
105mm/5.6	W	60°/121mmø	73°/155mmø	4x5"	∞-1:3	0	52x0.75	42	103	44	185
135mm/5.6	W	60°/156mmø	73°/200mmø	4x5"	∞-1:3	0	52x0.75	42	134	46	200
150mm/5.6	W	60°/174mmø	70°/210mmø	5x7"	∞-1:3	0	52x0.75	42	149	50	230
180mm/5.6	W	60°/208mmø	70°/253mmø	5x7"	∞-1:3	1	67x0.75	54	179	60	380
210mm/5.6	W	60°/243mmø	70°/295mmø	5x7"	∞-1:3	1	67x0.75	60	209	69	460
240mm/5.6	W	60°/278mmø	70°/333mmø	8x10"	∞-1:3	3	82xx0.75	60	227	77	820
300mm/5.6	W	60°/346mmø	70°/420mmø	10x12"	∞-1:3	3	95x1	80	287	94.5	1250
360mm/6.5	W	60°/415mmø	69°/494mmø	11x14"	∞-1:3	3	95x1	80	346	107	1420
105mm/3.5	M	51°/100mm∞	53°/110mmø	6x9 cm	∞-1:1	0	40.5x0.5	31.5	96.5	35.5	170
200mm/8.0	M	45°/166mmø	55°/210mmø	5x7"	∞-1:1	0	52x0.75	31.5	193	43	180
300mm/9.0	M	55°/312mmø	57°/325mmø	8x10"	∞-1:1	1	52x0.75	42	294	43	290
450mm/9.0	M	50°/420mmø	52°/440mmø	10x12"	∞-1:1	3	67x0.75	60	436	55	640
270mm/6.3	T-ED	21°/100mmø	31°/154mmø	4x5"	∞-1:5	1	67x0.75	42	182	98	400
360mm/8.0	T-ED	24°/154mmø	32°/205mmø	5x7"	∞-1:5	1	67x0.75	60	260	124	450
500mm/11.0	T-ED	17°/154mmø	24°/210mmø	5x7"	∞-1:5	1	67x0.75	54	350	130	760
720mm/16.0	T-ED	12°/154mmø	17°/210mmø	5x7"	∞-1:5	1	67x0.75	54	470	124	780
600mm/9.0	T-ED	19°/200mmø	29°/310mmø	8x10"	∞-1:5	3	86x1	80	410	175	1550
800mm/12.0	T-ED	14°/200mmø	22°/310mmø	8x10"	∞-1:5	3	86x1	70	528	176	1500
1200mm/18.0	T-ED	10°/200mmø	15°/310mmø	8x10"	∞-1:5	3	86x1	60	755	179	1480
120mm/5.6	AM	47°/210mmø	55°/255mmø	5x7"	1:5-5:1	0	52x0.75	42	116	64	295
210mm/5.6	AM	41°/310mmø	51°/400mmø	10x12"	1:5-5:1	1	67x0.75	70	203	104	850

1 Lens type
SW = Super-wide-angle
W = Wide-angle
T-ED = Tele construction with ED glass
AM = Apochromatic macro lens
M = Normal lens

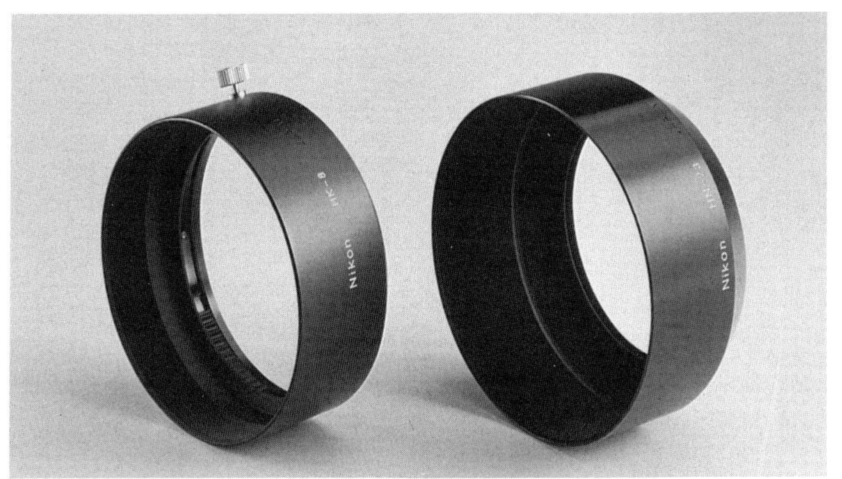

Two of the many sturdy metal lens hoods in the snap-on version.

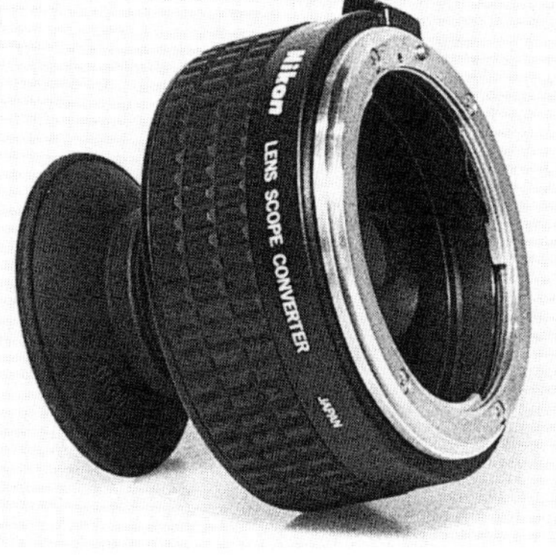

The Lens Scope Converter, also called telescope converter, turns lenses into monocular telescopes.

and video cameras. A cable release can be attached to operate the automatic diaphragm.

An array of cases is available for storage and protected transport of Nikkor-lenses. The CL versions are hard while soft leather pouches are also available for focal lengths up to 180mm. Strong, large box-type cases designated CT-xx are delivered with the fast telephoto lenses from 200mm to 800mm.

The cover for the bayonet mount of the camera was called BF-1 before the advent of autofocus, AF-bodies should only be covered with the newer BF-1A version, to prevent damage to the AF-contacts. The cover for the lens bayonet is LF-1.

Other Nikon Lenses

For the sake of completeness, tables have been included here listing Nikon enlarging lenses and also Nikon large-format lenses which will be of great interest to Nikon enthusiasts who want to explore medium and larger format formats.

Nikon Enlarging Lenses

Lens	Elements/Groups	Angle of view	Maximum negative size	Image circle (Ø mm)	Optimum degree of enlargement	Practicable enlarging range	Aperture range	Illuminated aperture scale	Filter thread	Mounting thread	Dimensions (mm)	Weight (g)	Minimum extension
40mm/4.0	6/4	52°	24x36	40.5	10x	5-30x	4.0-22	+	40.5x0.5	39x1/26	52x39	100	44
50mm/2.0	6/4	46°	24x36	43.2	8x	2-20x	2.8-16	+	40.5x0.5	39x1/26	51x39	105	44
50mm/4.0	4/3	46°	24x36	43.2	8x	2-20x	4.0-22	+	40.5x0.5	39x1/26	51x33	85	44
63mm/3.5	6/4	46°	24x36	56	8x	2-20x	3.5-16	–	40.5x0.5	39x1/26	47x44	130	55
63mm/2.8	6/4	46°	24x36	55.2	8x	2-20x	2.8-16	+	40.5x0.5	39x1/26	51x42	120	55
75mm/4.0	4/3	52°	6x6	80	5x	2-10x	4.0-22	+	40.5x0.5	39x1/26	51x33	90	63
80mm/5.6	6/4	56°	6x7	95	5x	2-15x	5.6-22	+	40.5x0.5	39x1/26	51x38	100	70
105mm/5.6	6/4	51°	6x9	120	5x	2-10x	5.6-22	+	40.5x0.5	39x1/26	51x40	110	90
135mm/5.6	6/4	54°	4x5"	160	5x	2-10x	5.6-45	–	52x0.75	39x1/26	56x47	190	123
150mm/5.6	6/4	51°	4x5"	180	4x	2-8x	5.6-45	–	52x0.75	39x1/26	56x50	210	130
180mm/5.6	6/4	54°	5x7"	230	4x	2-8x	5.6-45	–	67x0.75	72x1	77x62	455	158
210mm/5.6	6/4	54°	5x7"	270	4x	2-8x	5.6-45	–	72x1	72x1	77x62	600	181
240mm/5.6	6/4	54°	8x10"	330	3x	1-6x	5.6-45	–	77x0.75	82x1	96x82	910	211
300mm/5.6	6/4	57°	10x12"	410	4x	1-8x	5.6-45	–	86x1	90x1	97X94	1190	267
360mm/5.6	6/4	52°	11x14"	500	2x	1-4x	5.6-45	–	120x1	130x1.5	143x119	2700	326

CHAPTER 10

The Nikonos Programme

For many years now underwater photography has been a subject of special interest within the Nikon programme. As a result the Nikonos system has been totally unique from the very beginning. The Nikonos models represent the only professional camera systems that can be used under water without any restriction or the need for further equipment. This is by no means as simple as it may seem. In underwater photography both photographer and his equipment must meet the highest demands. It is a commonplace that the photographer makes the picture and not the camera, but with respect to underwater-photography this embraces even more. Just as the successful bird photographer must also be an ornithologist, underwater work not only calls for the appropriate equipment but also for diving skills. Experience and practice are absolutely obligatory because the unique and dangerous conditions have to be taken into account as well as the equipment.

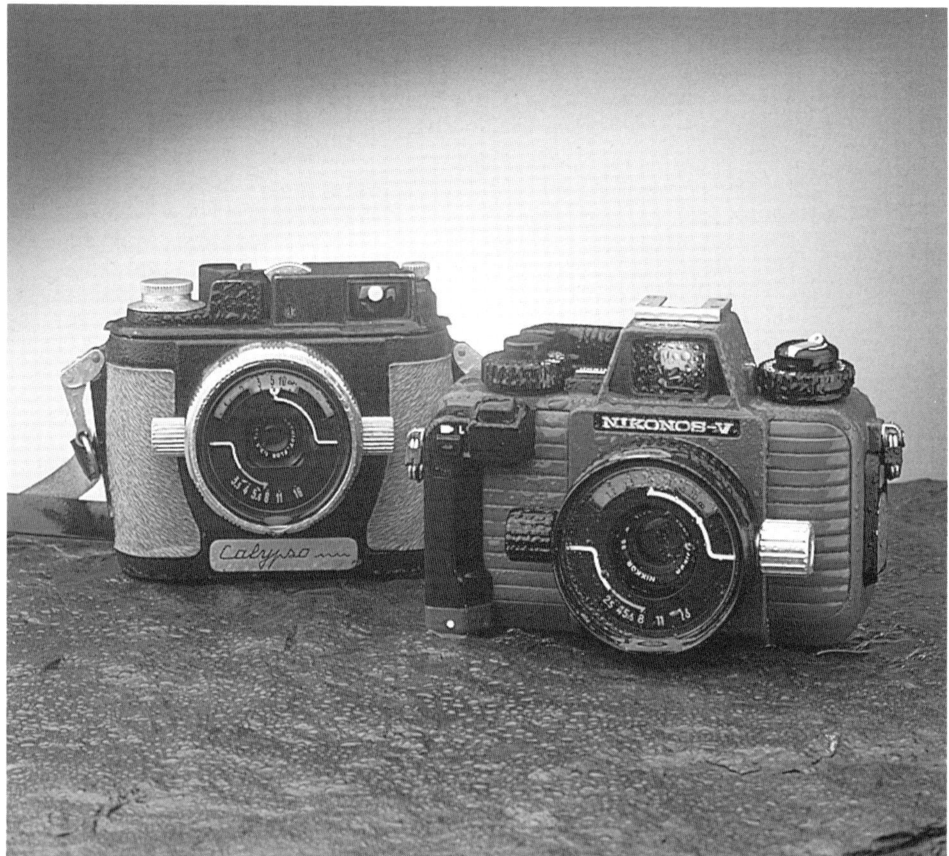

Two generations of Nikon for underwater photography: the original Nikonos "Calypso" and the Nikonos V.

Water is much more dense than air, this has consequences not just for fish and divers but also for light. Water has a different refractive index from air, making everything under water appear to be about 30% larger than at the same distance on land. Since none of the Nikonos viewfinder models have a rangefinder, this must be considered when distances are estimated. Only an SLR can fill the need for accurate focusing, but with any other camera than the Nikonos RS this makes an additional – and usually extremely expensive – watertight housing necessary. The reduced angle of view is another characteristic feature encountered under water – a 35mm lens will only show the view of a 50mm. Finally, today's water round industrial countries is rarely clear enough to allow large distances between subject and camera. This explains why wide-angle lenses are used almost exclusively under water, except for close-ups.

Yet another problem is posed by the tendency of water to absorb parts of the visible spectrum. At a depth of three metres the red portion of the light has already been filtered out almost completely, followed by yellow after five metres at the most. What is left is blue. To stress the point: the distances of three and five metres are likely to be those between surface and subject or subject and camera. All in all it is clear that underwater photography is hardly feasible without special flash units since filters cannot solve the problems. Two further factors are the angle at which the light enters the water and the texture of its surface.

These special and unique conditions illustrate why underwater photography is an exotic and intriguing hobby. Nikon's first efforts concerning underwater photography began during the reign of the rangefinder cameras, when they introduced an underwater housing for the S2, S3, and SP. It was designed for depths down to 50m and could accommodate the camera with one of the following Nikkor lenses attached: 28mm,f/3.5; 35mm,f/1.8; 35mm,f/2.5. Film transport as well as distance and aperture setting facilities were accessible from the outside, and a flash unit and an action finder could be attached to the housing.

From the Calypso to the Nikonos RS

At the beginning of the 1960's the Belgian camera designer Jean de Wouters, in collaboration with the French maritime scientist Jacques Yves Cousteau, developed a 35mm model capable of withstanding water pressure down to 50m. This was the legendary Calypso, named after Cousteau's exploration ship. The three-part camera design consists of the watertight outer housing, an interior body incorporating the film transport mechanism, shutter and controls, and finally the lens as the third part. The resulting double-walled construction permits comfortable handling on land as well as under water. Every single joint is sealed perfectly with the help of 14 greased O-rings.

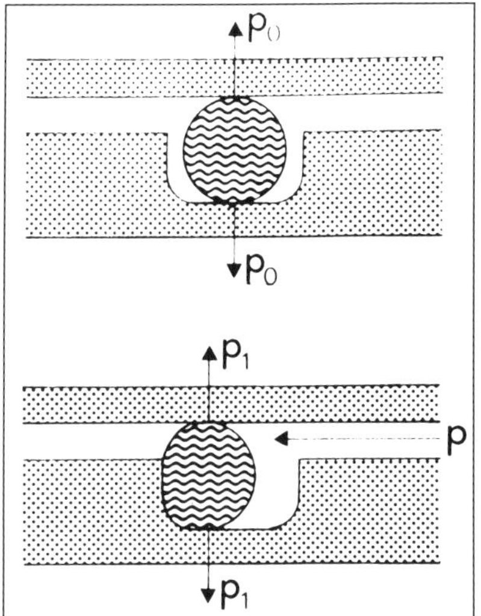

The enormous pressure at depths of up to 50m demands waterproofing with O-rings. The intentional deformation under pressure (below) increases their effectiveness as seals.

The original lens was the French Som-Berthiot 35mm,f/3.5. Distance and aperture are set with two rotating knobs to the left and right of the lens barrel. The film is transported and the shutter cocked with one lever which also incorporates the release function. This lever springs back to its ready-position after every shot and cocks the shutter when pressed inwards towards the camera body. This unusual solution ensures positive handling even with thick gloves. Shutter speeds are from 1/1000 to 1/20 sec. as well as a B-position. The bright frame in the viewfinder is matched to the 35mm-lens. The body was trimmed with sealskin – something that not only Greenpeace members would object to today. Nikon immediately realized how ingenious the concept was and acquired the licences to produce it in Japan.

In 1963 the result of their own manufacture appeared, the Nikonos I. The most significant modification was its Nikkor-W 35mm,f/2.5, a design revitalized from earlier rangefinder days. The sealskin was replaced by a plastic coating producing a more positive grip. The first lens designed specifically for underwater use, the UW-Nikkor 28mm, f/3.5 was introduced the next year. It was a six-element design corrected

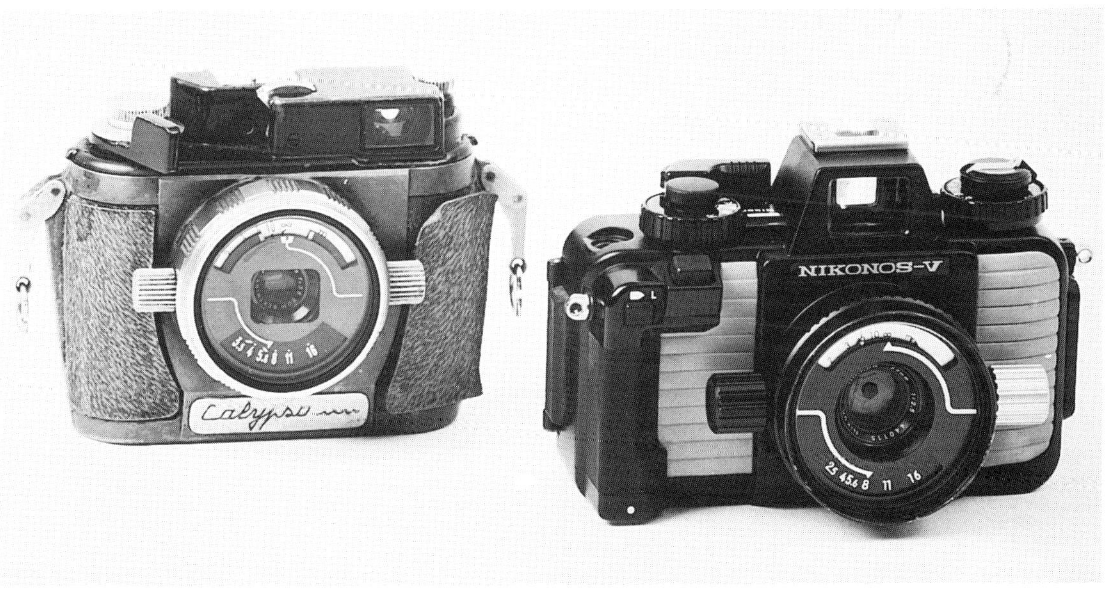

Two concepts, one common feature: the Calypso and the Nikonos V designed for diving depths up to 50m.

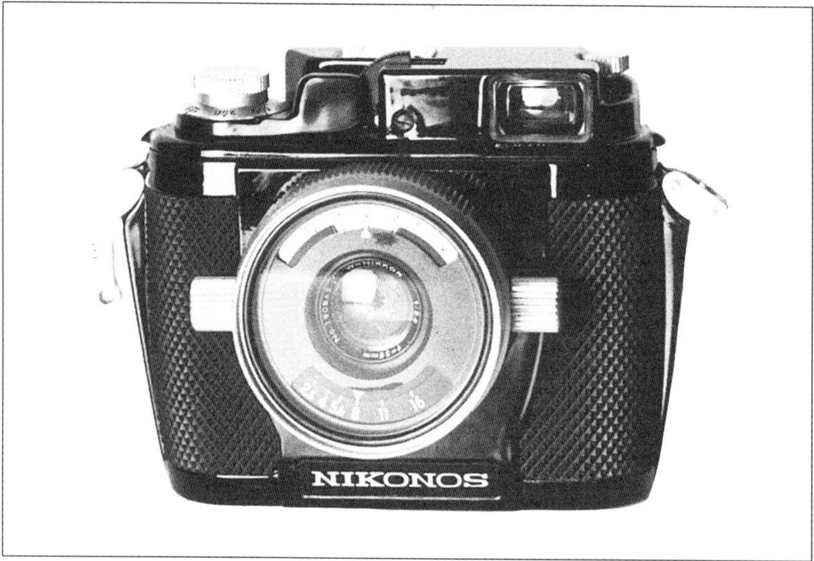

The first Nikonos built by Nikon fitted with the UW-Nikkor 35mm,f/2.5.

for the refractive index of water and thanks to this performs visibly better than the first 35mm,f/2.5. Since this lens can only be used under water, its distance scale is marked with the apparent values when submerged.

In 1968 the Nikonos II appeared. Its rewind crank which replaced the cumbersome knob was the most obvious distinguishing feature. The film transport mechanism was also modified: as well as the shutter speeds from 1/500 to 1/30 sec. and B, the scale includes the position "R" which must be set when the film is to be rewound. The Nikonos II permits underwater flash units to be triggered at speeds of 1/60 and 1/30 sec. The depth-of-field indicator and the markings on the lens scales were enlarged to improve their legibility.

The slowly growing family was supplemented by a third lens, the Nikkor-W 80mm,f/4, a four-element design that can be employed both above and below the water surface. This lens is particularly interesting under water in combination with the close-up outfit. This consists of a two-element achromat for the lens, and an almost 24cm-long supporting rod which takes up one of the three available field frames depending on the lens in use. The following reproduction ratios are possible under water: 1:6 with the 28mm,f/3.5, 1:4.5 with the 35mm,f/2.5, and 1:2.2 with the 80mm,f/4.0. Unlike the extension rings which were already available from independent manufacturers at that early date, this kit has the advantage of being attachable both above and under water.

When the lenshoods and a watertight case for the Sekonic exposure meter Auto-Lumi L-86 were added, a serious system was gradually coming into existence around the Nikonos. Above all, this included the sensational UW-Nikkor 15mm, f/2.8 made exclusively for use submerged with its underwater angle of view of 94°. Many underwater photographers consider this eight-element design to be the best UW-lens ever manufactured. Its specially dedicated optical viewfinder can be attached to the camera's accessory shoe and allows comfortable composition. Later, an optical viewfinder for the 28mm-lens was introduced which could be masked in order to be used with the standard 35mm lens too. A very comprehensive accessory, because the camera's viewfinder cannot be completely overseen with a diving mask on. This would be asking too much of even the F3's HP-finder. Two convenient frame finders, one for the 28mm lens and one suitable for both the 35mm and 80mm lenses further enhanced the Nikonos accessory program.

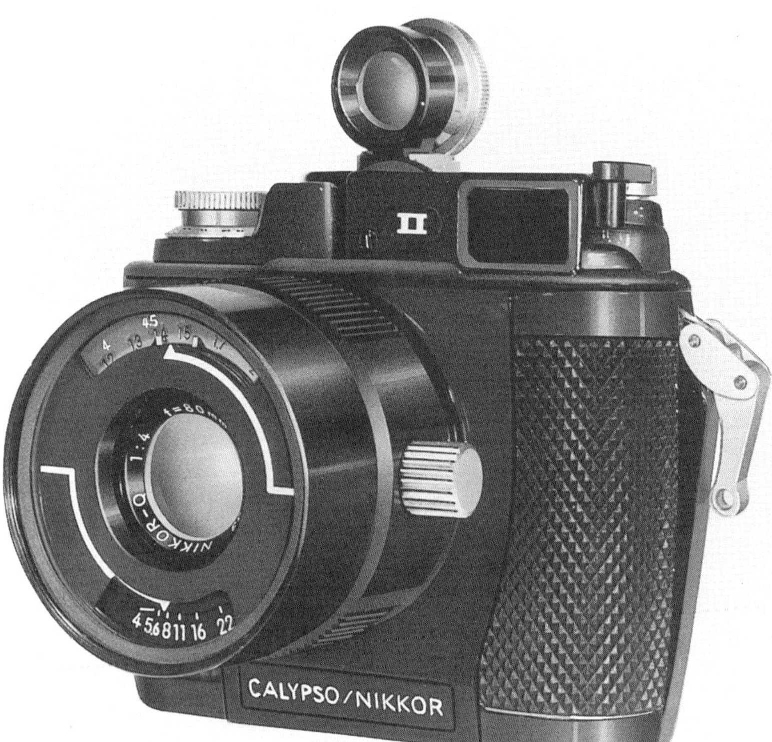

The Nikonos II with its more convenient rewind crank and the W-Nikkor 80mm,f/4.

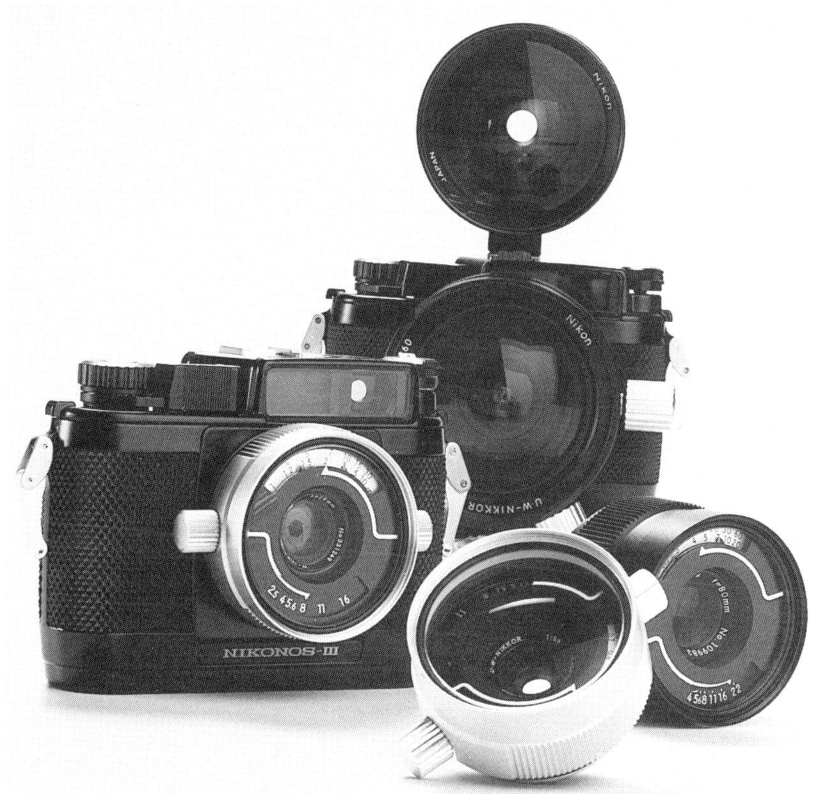

The Nikonos classic for many years: the model III with four of the then available lenses.

The last model in the Calypso design

In 1975 the Nikonos III appeared with a new outer casing but still resembling its predecessor. The controls were enlarged to improve handling and bright frames for both 35mm and 80mm lenses were visible in the viewfinder, as well as parallax-marks for distances below 80cm. The frame counter could finally be viewed from above and the watertight flash terminal was modified to the three-pin version still prevailing today. The lens setting knobs were enlarged and unmistakeably marked: black for the aperture and silver for the distance. But even so, many photographers prefer to mount the lens upside down on the body so they can read the scales easier from above.

The film transport mechanism was improved further so that the lever can be operated in several short strokes and the advance is much more precise. The body bayonet is made of stainless steel and no longer a part of the housing itself. On land the Nikonos III weighs 620g along with the 35mm lens, but just 300g under water.

Nikonos IV-A – a new concept

In 1980 the Nikonos III was replaced by the Nikonos IV-A, a design which represented a completely new concept. It has no more in common with the previous models than the name and the bayonet mount. The Nikonos IV-A is designed like a normal SLR with a one-piece body with a hinged back. It is the first Nikonos with an integrated TTL-metering and exposure control system. It was adapted from the EM, which meant exclusively aperture priority mode with speeds from 1/1000 to 1/30 sec. A red LED indicates when the speed chosen by the camera is within this range, a blinking LED indicates under- or overexposure. Contrary to Nikon's official information though, it is usually no problem to ignore the warning against underexposure: the electronics proved to operate sufficiently precisely even below 1/30 sec. and up to several seconds. The light is measured through the lens: the SPD-cell located beneath the viewfinder

The TTL-exposure metering and control system with the aperture priority mode of the Nikonos IV-A were adapted from the EM.

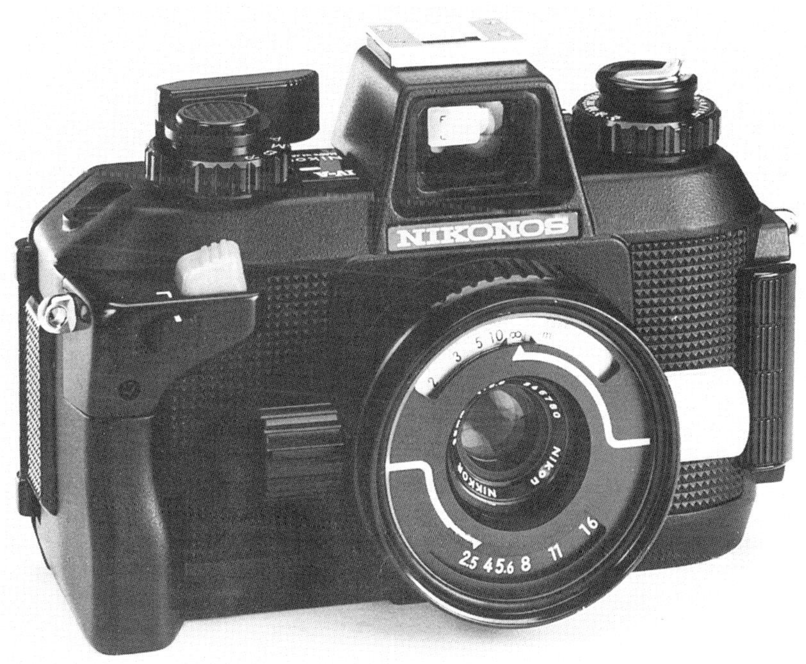

meters the light coming from an additional grey reflector in front of the shutter blinds. The two mechanically controlled shutter settings, 1/90 sec. and B, are available besides the aperture-priority mode, and the position "R" unlocks the transport system in order to rewind the film. Film speeds from ISO 25/15° to 1600/33° can be set. The ISO-value can be changed under water too, for example to compensate for backlit situations – especially important since the Nikonos IV-A is neither equipped with a manual compensation facility nor a memory-lock function. The new bright-frame finder was developed to show the complete frame from a distance of 40mm, with a diving mask on. The frame for the 35mm lens is visible in the viewfinder as well as the red exposure LED and the flash-ready signal. It is matched to the dedicated flash unit SB-101 that switches the camera to its sync-speed of 1/90 sec. automatically when both are connected. The one-piece outer body is waterproofed by twelve O-rings and a flat seal in the back. The film pressure-plate is hinged to the internal body and not the back in order to secure optimum flatness on land and under water, where a pressure of up to 5 kilograms per cm² at a depth of 50m is exerted on the body.

Thanks to its versatility the Nikonos IV-A is not just an underwater specialist but is also suited for many applications in extreme conditions on land where other cameras would fail. For example in rain and snow, in sandy or dusty surroundings, and even in operating theatres where, thoroughly sterilized, it can serve for documentation purposes. However, the target group the Nikonos IV-A was originally aimed at was not completely satisfied by this model. For example, they considered its sync-speed of 1/90 sec. to be too fast in underwater flash situations to be able to use the available light for a balanced exposure. A slower speed cannot be set though. The flat seal in the back was the second drawback. Even the tiniest grain of sand on the gasket was enough to cause a leak. So scrupulous care must be taken to keep the Nikonos IV-A back and O-ring perfectly clean. The third point of criticism was that the UW-Nikkor 15mm,f/2.8 could not be used because its rear protrudes so far into the camera body that the metering cell is partly shaded. This problem was solved in 1982 with a newly designed lens built as a retrofocus design with 12 elements, but it cannot quite match its predecessor's performance. A newly designed optical finder, the DF-11, went with it.

Another optical viewfinder, designated DF-10, was available for the 80mm-telephoto lens. It was conceived for use on land only though, and is fitted with a ring permitting parallax-compensation between infinity and 1m. In 1983 a new lens, the LW-Nikkor 28mm,f/2.8 was added to the range. Although it was not designed for underwater applications it is water-resistant. It resembles the 28mm,f/2.8 E-series lens and has the normal aperture and distance rings. A matched viewfinder is not available. As a makeshift solution the complete finder area can be employed. Its filter attachment has the dimension typical for Nikon while the 28mm, 35mm, and 80mm UW-Nikkors have a 58mm thread. But beware, if a filter is to be used under water, the rigid lens hood which has a 52mm thread must be

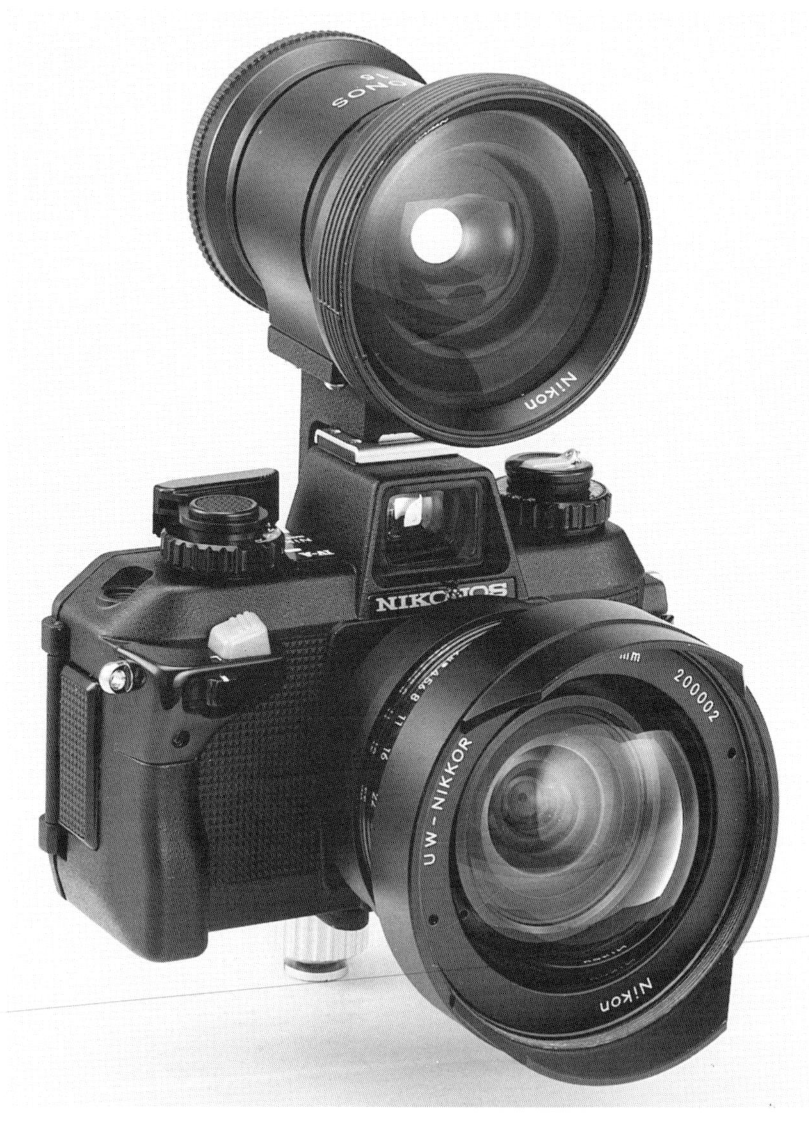

The most extreme and highly acclaimed Nikonos wide-angle, the UW-Nikkor 15mm,f/2.8.

attached. When a 58mm filter is mounted directly it is in danger of being crushed by the pressure under water.

Problems solved, the Nikonos V

In 1984 the Nikonos V appeared, a model that had taken into account the criticisms expressed about the Nikonos IV-A. The first and most conspicuous change was that the body was available with either an olive or an orange coloured plastic surface material. The technical advances were far more significant of course, and very useful at that. In addition to the aperture priority mode, shutter speeds can be set manually between 1/1000 and 1/30 sec. and are displayed in the viewfinder too.

Other important features and improvements are the TTL-controlled flash exposure system with the dedicated flash units SB-102 and SB-103 and the modified camera back-lock system. The back is once again sealed by a proven O-ring which automatically pushes away any particles clinging to it from the vital surfaces of its channel when

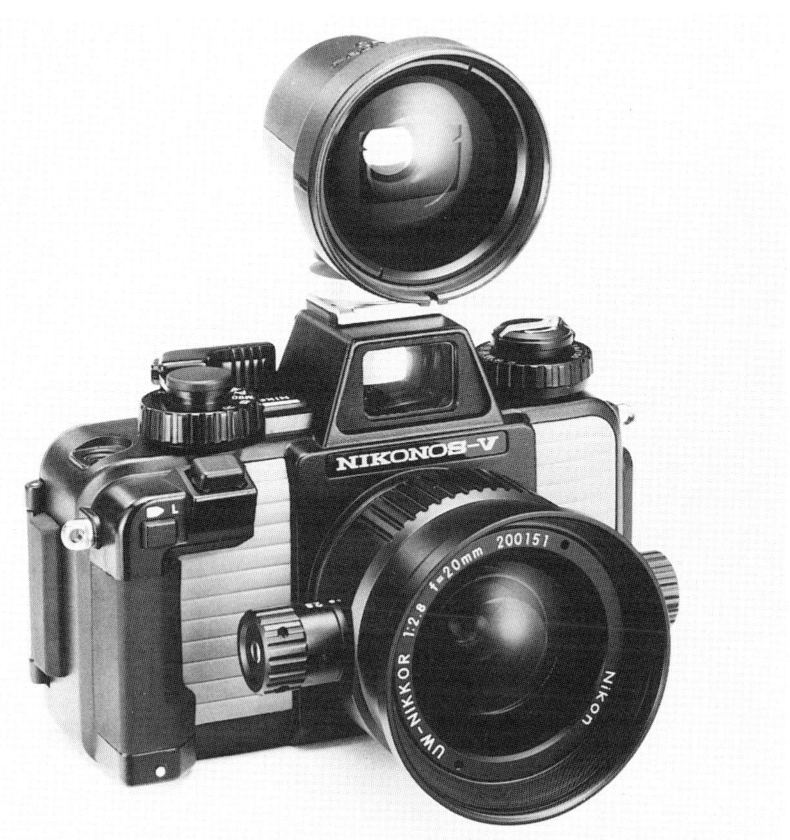

The UW-Nikkor 20mm,f/2.8 is an attractive alternative to the 15mm,f/2.8, also in cost.

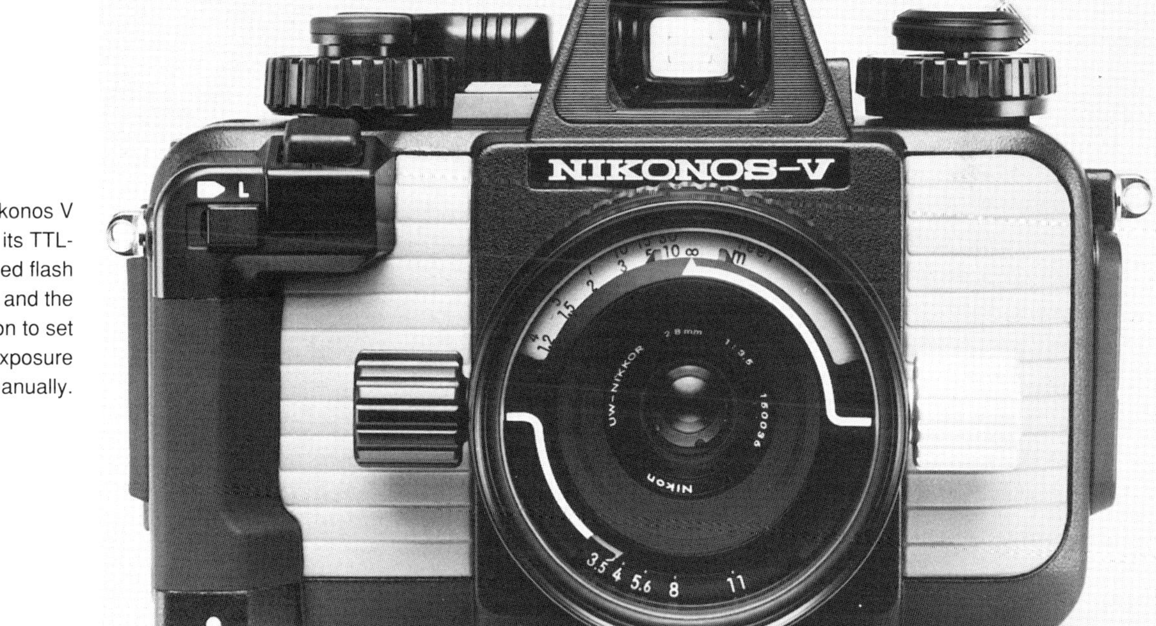

The Nikonos V with its TTL-controlled flash system and the option to set the exposure manually.

Technical data on Nikonos cameras

Camera	Shutter speeds	Shutter control	Exposure control	Film speed range	Viewfinder displays	Shutter speeds	Synch. terminal	TTL flash	Weight with 35mm f/2/5[1]	Dimensions (mm)
Calypso/ Nikonos I	1/20-1/1000 B	m	M	–	–	M=1/20-1/1000 X=1/20-1/60	Nik. II	–	720 (255)g	100x130x45
Nikonos II	1/20-1/500; B	m	M	–	–	M=1/30-1/500; X=1/30-1/60	Nik. II	–	700 (250) g	100x130x45
Nikonos III	1/30-1/1000; B	m	M	–	–	M=1/30-1/500; X=1/30-1/60	Nik. III	–	780 (270)g	99x144x47
Nikonos IV A	1/30-1/1000; B	e	A; M90	25/15°- 1600/33°	Exp. R	X=1/90	Nik. III	–	800 (280)g	99x149x58
Nikonos V	1/30-1/1000; B	e	A; M	25/15°- 1600/33°	Exp. R, S	X=1/30-1/90	Nik. III[2]	+	860 (300)g	99x146x58
Nikonos RS[5]	1-1/2000;	e	A; M	25/40°- -5000/38° DX 6/4°- 6400/39° Manual	Exp. R; S; AV; AF; Exp. comp.; Exp. mode; ISO film speed	1-1/250	Nik. III[3]	+[4]	2060 (920)g	196x151x85

1 on land (under water
2 plus TTL-contacts
3 Slightly different dimensions with TTL contacts
4 Including Matrix-Balanced Fill Flash
5 Autofocus, Matrix and Centre-Weighted Metering

m= mechanical; e= electrical
M= Manual; A= automatic (aperture priority)
Exp.= Exposure; R= Flash-ready symbol; S= Shutter speeds

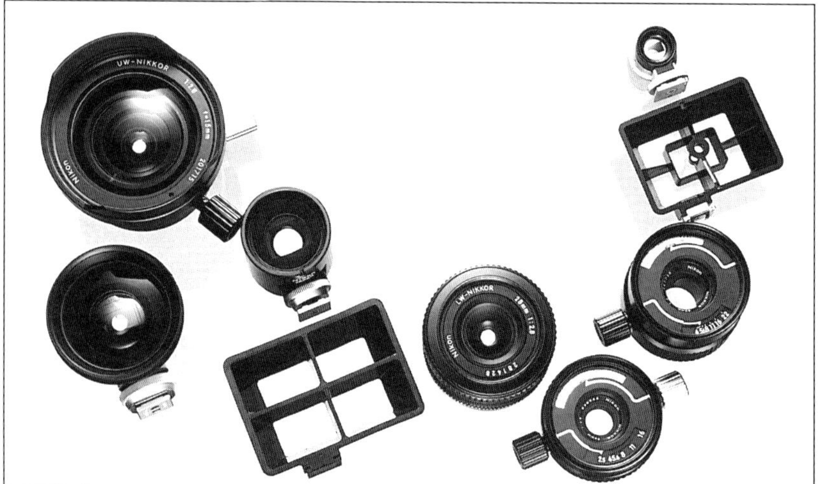

Parts of an incomparable system: lenses and viewfinders for the first five Nikonos-models.

under pressure. The sync-terminal, which had remained unchanged since the Nikonos III, was fitted with two additional contacts for the TTL-control circuitry. The whole sealing system was optimized in details, satisfying criticisms from divers. In 1986 the lens range was completed by a very interesting wide-angle lens, the UW-Nikkor 20mm,f2.8 which only costs about half the price of the 15mm,f/2.8. The nine-element design has an angle of view of 78° and can be focused down to 0.4m. A fitting optical finder, the DF-12 is available for this lens. It can also be used for the 28mm,f/3.5 by including a mask.

Underwater SLR, the Nikonos-RS

All the time the different Nikonos generations were being perfected, ambitious divers and amateur underwater photographers regularly asked Nikon when they could expect an underwater SLR. The fact that Nikon was asked was both flattering and logical, for who else had the know-how and had cared for them in the past? Bearing in mind how expensive such a camera would have to be – an SLR calls for a completely new set of lenses, for example – and how small the target group for such an instrument must be, nobody really expected one. So when Nikon announced the world's first fully-fledged UW-SLR system early in 1992 the surprise – and the suspense – was great. When it was finally unveiled, the astonishment and the respect was even greater. The Nikonos-RS combines most of the desired features of the proven Nikonos viewfinder models as well as the latest technology appreciated in cameras such as the F-601!

But what an amazing piece of machinery it is, watertight down to an almost unbelievable 100m, autofocus operation including focus tracking and freeze-focus functions (only available in other Nikon cameras with an additional multi-function-back), Matrix metering

Technical data on Nikonos lenses

Lens	Angle of view[1]	Angle of view[2]	Elements/groups	Closest focusing distance	Smallest aperture	Filter thread	Case	Max repro ratio[3]	Max. repro ratio[4]	Weight (on land)	Optical viewfinder	Dimensions (diam./length)
UW 15mm/2.8	94°	–	9/5	0.3m	22	–	–	–	–	310 g	–	90x80mm
UW 15mm/2.8N	94°	–	12/9	0.3m	22	–	–	–	–	665 g	DF-11	93x90mm
UW 20mm/2.8	78°	–	9/7	0.4m	22	67mm	–	–	–	350 g	DF-12	70x74mm
LW 28mm/2.8	–	74°	5/5	0.5m	22	52mm	CL-51	–	–	240 g	–	68x57mm
UW 28mm/3.5	59°	–	6/5	0.6m	22	58mm[5]	CL-50	1:6.0	–	175 g	DF-12	62x44mm
W 35mm/2.5	43°	62°	7/5	0.8m	22	58mm[5]	CL-50	1:4.5	1:6.5	160 g	–	62x40mm
80mm/4.0	22°	30°	5/5	1.0m	22	58mm[5]	CL-51	1:2.2	1:3.0	275 g	DF-10	62x66mm
R-UW AF Nikkor 28mm/2.8	59.8°	—	6/6	0.26m	22	88mm	—	1:6	—	550 g	—	99x85mm
R-UW AF Zoom Nikkor 20-35mm/2.8	79°-51°	—	10/9	0.38m	22	148mm	—	1:10	—	1750 g	—	162x129 mm
R-UW AF Micro-Nikkor 50mm/2.8	35°	—	10/9	0.167m	22	88mm	—	1:1	—	1100 g	—	103x126 mm

1 underwater
2 on land
3 with close-up attachment; underwater
4 with ckise-up attachment, on land
5 underwater use a 52mm filter with rigid lens hood

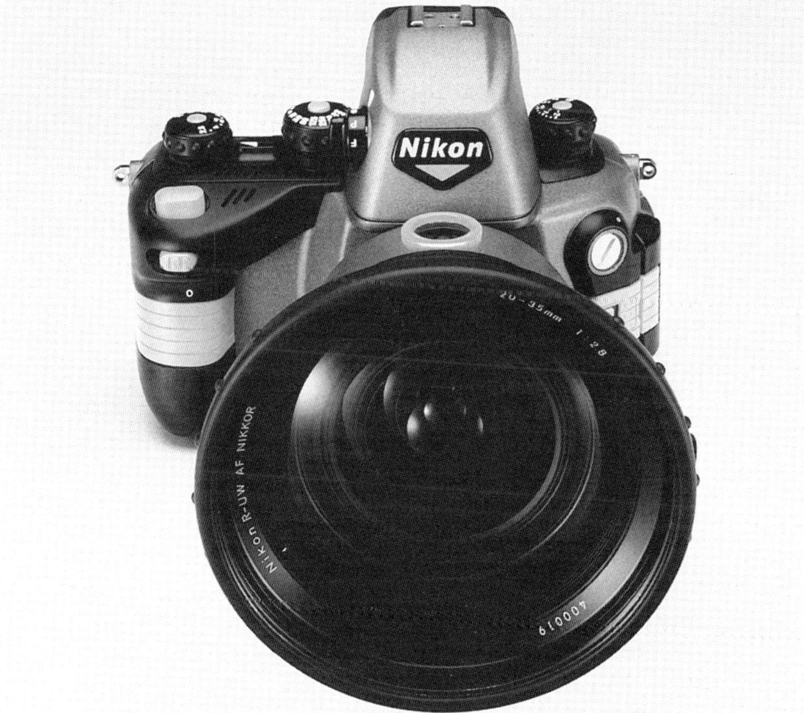

The world's first fully-fledged underwater, autofocus SLR, the Nikonos-RS, with the R-UW AF Nikkor 20-35mm,f/2.8.

including Matrix balanced fill-flash control, aperture priority automatic exposure mode or manual operation with 75/25% centre-weighted metering, shutter speeds from 1/2000 to 1 sec. and B with sync-speeds up to 1/125 sec. including the choice between front or rear blind sync modes, completely automatic film handling with integrated motors including automatic DX-coding from ISO 25/15° to 5000/38°, and a large action-type viewfinder including all the necessary indications with illuminated LCDs.

Out of breath? You will be if you have to carry the camera around – the body alone weighs 2.06 kilos while under water it is 920g. It is so large people are always asking how long Nikon have been producing a medium-format camera. But when you take a look at the bayonet it seems very familiar. Except for two details it is exactly like that of other Nikon SLR's. The claws are not situated at the same angles and there are actually two bayonets. The

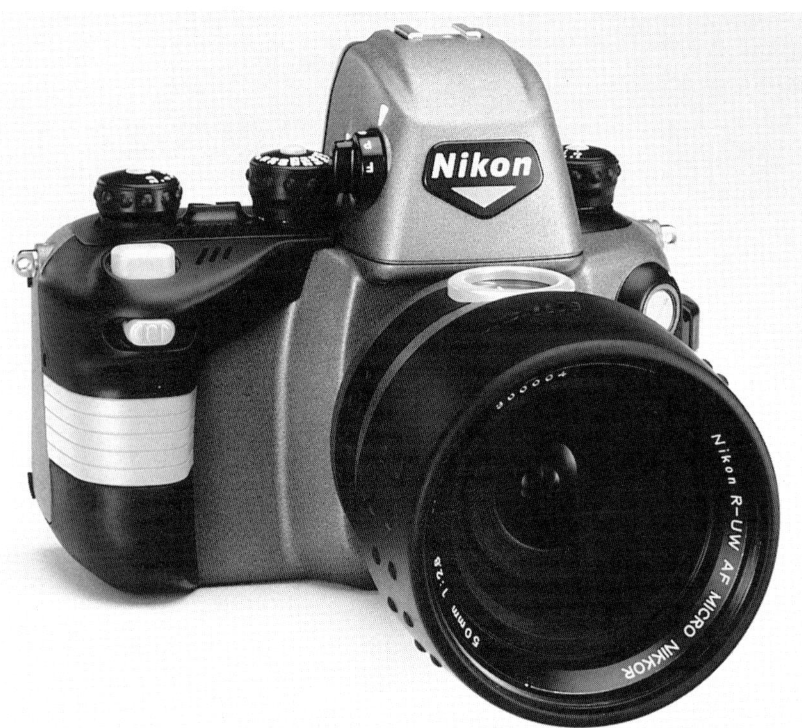

The R-UW AF Micro-Nikkor 50mm,f/2.8, which allows reproduction ratios continuously down to 1:1, is one of the three new lenses specially developed for the Nikonos-RS.

second, larger one fastened to the outer body of the camera helps to secure the equally weighty lenses by their metal barrels.

Which brings us to the three completely new lenses. The R-UW AF-Nikkor 28mm,f/2.8 will most likely develop into the standard focal length since it is the lightest of the trio at 550 grams and has a universally usable picture angle of 60° under water. Its six independent elements indicate a modern construction and of course its distance scale is illuminated. The next in line is a specialist, the R-UW AF Micro-Nikkor 50mm,f/2.8 which permits reproduction ratios to 1:1 continuously without additional accessories and including automatic focusing. Although all three presently available lenses have been designed for underwater use, this unit will produce pictures of acceptable quality with only slight colour fringes out of water. The image the other two produce in the viewfinder out of water is best described by a slightly annoyed Nikon demonstrator's outburst after being constantly questioned on the last day of Photokina: "As you can see, there is nothing to be seen." But a blur, we should add. Which is particularly sad because it means the enjoyment of the world's first underwater zoom lens will remain confined to those who can experience it under water. The R-UW AF Zoom-Nikkor 20-35mm,f/2.8 offers spectacular angles of view, continuously from 51° to 80°, with a design incorporating just 10 independent elements. Only now do we know what we have missed in the past.

Nikonos Speedlights

As mentioned at the beginning of this chapter, underwater photography is closely linked to the subject of flash exposure. Only artificial light sources allow us to reproduce the submerged world in all its colour and splendour.

The first flash unit appeared during the early 70's for the Nikonos II. It was a reflector mounted on an extension rod. The flash bulbs were triggered by a 22.5v battery hidden in the grip section. This model was available later with the appropriate connection for the Nikonos III sync-terminal. The first electronic flash

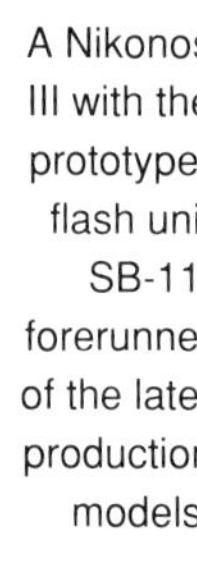

A Nikonos III with the prototype-flash unit SB-11, forerunner of the later production models.

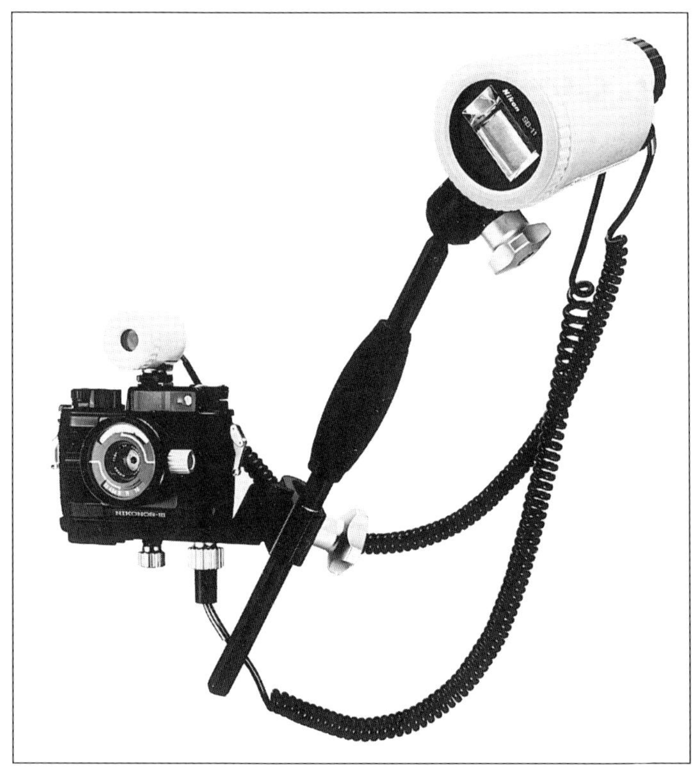

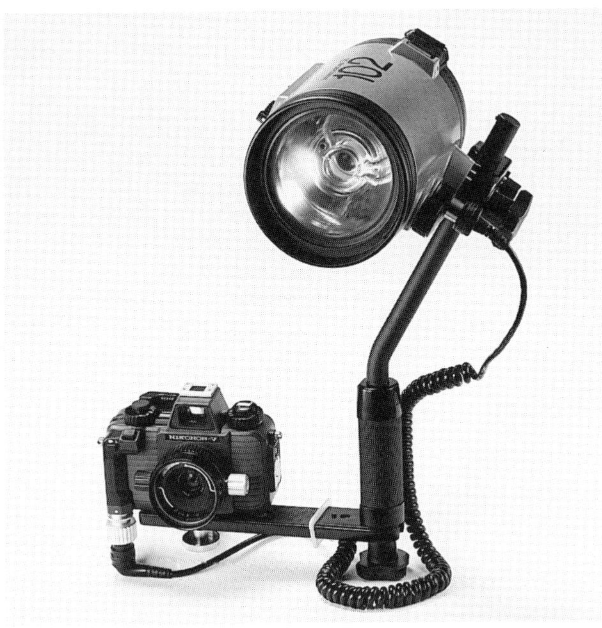

An impressive appearance due to its giant reflector, the TTL-controlled SB-102.

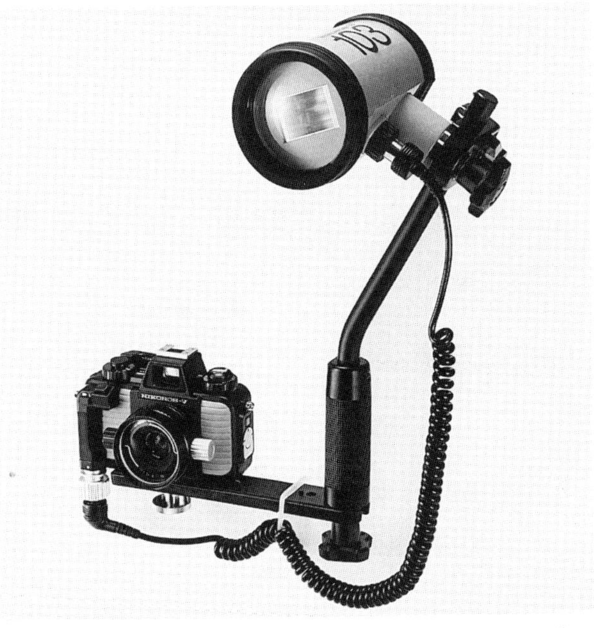

A smaller flash unit without automatic settings of its own, a pilot light, or an integrated slave-cell, the SB-103.

unit was introduced as a prototype in 1978 but never manufactured. It was computer controlled with a guide number of 28 and one automatic setting of f/5.6. Its illumination angle covered that of a 28mm lens. The first production electronic flash unit was called SB-101 and designed for the Nikonos IV-A.

At this point it may be helpful to discuss some technical aspects of underwater flash operation. Depending on the water's condition, the guide number is reduced by 50 to 70% compared to operation on land. This is less critical than it may seem though, since even a guide number of 10 would be sufficient for the usual short distances used under water. It is vital to place the reflector as far away from the optical axis as possible so that the ever-present suspended particles cannot reflect the light from the flash back to the lens to cause reduced contrast and hazy pictures. This is why only grip-type flash units are used in underwater photography.

The SB-101 has a guide number of 32 on land at ISO 100/21° and illuminated the picture angle of a 35mm lens completely. The diffuser SW-101 was available for a focal length of 28mm. Besides full and 1/4 manual output, the automatic mode can also be selected. To use this mode the external sensor SU-101 must be attached to the camera's accessory shoe. It provides the two automatic settings f/4 and f/8 at ISO 100/21°. The reflector head can be tilted and rotated freely on its ball-head. Eight AA-size batteries in the grip section give a recycling time of

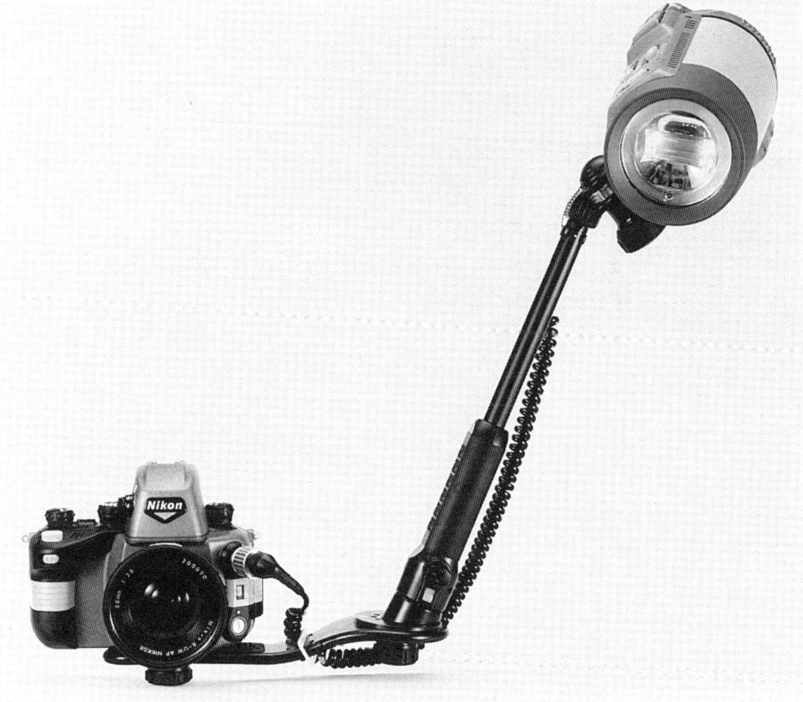

The Nikonos-RS required a new flash unit, the SB-104, capable of accompanying it down to its incredible maximum depth of 100m.

Technical data on Nikonos flash units														
Flash Unit	Guide number at ISO 100/21° on land	Guide number at ISO 100/21° under water	Focal length covered by illumination angle	Focal length covered with diffuser	Guide number with diffuser on land	Guide number with diffuser under water	TTL flash exposure control	Automatic aperture with Sensor SU-101 at ISO 100/21°	Flash duration at full output (sec.)	Flash duration at 1/4 output (sec.)	Flash duration at 1/16 output (sec.)	Recycling time at full output with batteries	No. of flashes per set batteries at full output	Dimensions (mm)	Weight (g)
SB-101	32	10/16	35mm	SW-101/28	22	8/11	–	4+8	1/800	1/3000	—	8	150	403x93x157	2000
SB-102	32	10/16	28mm	SW-102/15	22	8/11	+	4+8	1/500	1/1400	1/5500	14	120	152x139x212	1670
SB-103	20	7/10	28mm	SW-103/15	11	5/7	+	—	1/1500	1/5000	1/16000	9	130	130x175x99	780
SB-104	32	16	14mm	—	—	—	+	—	1/1000	1/1800	1/7000	3	120	124øx222	1990

8 sec. at full output. The elegant carrying case SS-101 is delivered with the flash unit.

The SB-102, introduced for the Nikonos V, is a TTL-controlled unit with a guide number of 32 and an illumination angle sufficient for 28mm focal length. Together with the diffuser SW-102, the picture angle of the 15mm lens can be covered.

The six C-size cells serving as its power source are situated in the reflector head which is fitted with a pilot-lamp, making it easier to aim the unit precisely. In spite of the big batteries the resulting recycling time is 15 seconds at full output. Besides the TTL-controlled operation available with the Nikonos V, the unit can also be set to manual full, ¼, and 1/16 output, and together with the external sensor SU-101 two automatic positions can be chosen, for example for the Nikonos III or IV-A. The integrated slave sensor is a further feature, permitting the SB-102 to be triggered by any other flash unit without a cord connection. The sync-cord is detachable since tough, everyday use may well cause contact difficulties. A double bracket is available for ambitious UW-photographers as well as a multiflash sync-cord allowing two flash units SB-102/103 to be operated simultaneously in TTL-mode. Furthermore, an extension arm is available with which the distance between the reflector and the optical axis can be increased.

In 1986 the SB-103 with a guide number of 20 at ISO 100/21° was introduced as the "little brother". It covers a 28mm picture angle, and a 20mm angle with the diffuser SW-103. The automatic settings, the pilot light, and the slave sensor were omitted in favour of a moderate price. Four AA-size batteries in the reflector head serve as the power source, and so this compact flash unit weighs just 780g.

Of course Nikon also guarantees a maximum operating depth of 50m for these flash-models. But even that would not be enough for the Nikonos-RS. So, a dedicated UW-flash unit tested to 100m, the SB-104, appeared together with the camera. Resembling the SB-102 in size, weight, and guide number, it differs in some decisive features. It is powered exclusively by the special NC-battery SN-104, allowing around 120 full-output flashes before it has to be replenished by the recharging unit SH-104. It satisfies all the camera's comprehensive flash modes including rear blind sync. It is equipped with slave-sensor circuitry which can release the camera in addition to the flash itself. The bracket/extension rod system was modified to improve its handling.

Normal flash units can be employed on all Nikonos models on land with the help of either a TTL-cord or a terminal adaptor. The TTL-cord is equipped with an ISO-type hot-shoe that can be attached to the camera's accessory shoe and even has TTL-terminals of its own for multiflash operation while the adaptor is fitted with the well-known PC-type sync-cord socket.

APPENDIX

Nikon Camera Guides, Lenses at a Glance, Battery Requirements, Product Codes and Index

The following pages contain comprehensive technical specifications on Nikon cameras and lenses, including battery requirement charts, as well as a guide to Nikon product codes, followed by an Index for easy referencing of specific items of interest.

Model	Type of bayonet	Shutter blind travel direction	Shutter construction	Shutter speeds	Shutter control	Exposure control	Metering cell	Metering range	Metering patterns	ISO Film speed range	Exposure compensation	Auto exp. ock	change viewfinder	Viewfinder displays [10]	Exp. meter display	Focusing screen provided/optional	Viewfinder image coverage	Viewfinder illum.
F	Non-Ai	H	Titan blades	1/1000-1 Sec.; B; T	mechan.	M	–	–	–	–	–	–	+	–	–	A/ B-R	100%	—
F Photomic (D3)	Non-Ai	H	Titan blades	1/1000-1 Sec.; B; T	mechan.	M	CdS	EV 3-17	integ.	25/15°-6400/39°	–	–	+	F; T; meter	needle	A/ B-R	100%	-
F Photomic T (D4)	Non-Ai	H	Titan blades	1/1000-1 Sec.; B; T	mechan.	M	CdS	EV 2-17	integ.	25/15°-6400/36°	–	–	+	F; T; meter	needle	A/ B-R	100%	-
F Photomic TN (D5)	Non-Ai	H	Titan blades	1/1000-1 Sec. B; T	mechan.	M	CdS	EV 2-17	60:40%	25/15°-6400/39°	–	–	+	F; T; meter	needle	A/ B-R	100%	-
F Photomic FTN (D9)	Non-Ai	H	Titan blades	1/1000-1 Sec.; B; BT	mechan.	M	CdS	EV 2-17	60:40%	6/3°-6400/39°	+2/ -1/2	–	+	F; T; meter	needle	A/ B-R	100%	(DL-1)
F2	Non-Ai	H	Titan blades	1/2000-10 Sec.; B; T; X 1/80	mechan.	M	CdS	–	–	–	–	–	+	R	–	A/ B-R	100%	–
F2 Photomic (DP-1)	Non-Ai	H	Titan blades	1/2000-10 Sec.; B T; X 1/80	mechan.	M	CdS	EV 1-17	60:40%	6/3°-6400/39°	+2/ -1/2	–	+	F; T; meter; R	needle	A/ B-R	100%	(DL-1)
F2 S Photomic (DP-2)	Non-Ai	H	Titan blades	1/2000-10 Sec.; B; T; X 1/80	mechan.	M	CdS	EV -2-17	60:40%	12/12°-6400/39°	+2/ -1/2	–	+	F; T; meter; R	LED	A/ B-R	100%	-
F2 SB Photomic (DP-3)	Non-Ai	H	Titan blades	1/2000-10 Sec.; B; T; X 1/80	mechan.	M	SPD	EV -2-17	60:40%	12/12°-6400/39°	+2/ -1/2	–	+	F; T; meter; R	LED	K/ B-R	100%	-
F2 A Photomic (DP-11)	Ai	H	Titan blades	1/2000-10 Sec.; B; T; X 1/80	mechan.	M	CdS	EV 1-17	60:40%	6/3°-6400/39°	+2/ –1/2	–	+	F; T; meter; R	needle	K/ B-R	100%	(DL-1)
F2 AS Photomic (DP-12)	Ai	H	Titan blades	1/2000-10 Sec.: B; T; X 1/80	mechan.	M	SPD	EV -2-17	60:40%	12/12°-6400/39°	+2/ -1/2	_	+	F; T; meter; R	LED	K/ B-R	100%	_
F2 H	Non-Ai	H	Titan blades	1/1000-1 Sec.	mechan.	M	SPD	EV 2-17	60:40%	–	–	–	+	R	–	B/ A-R	100%	-
F3; F3 HP; F3T	Ai	H	Titan blades	1/2000-8 Sec.; B; T; X 1/80	quartz	A; M	SPD	EV 1-18	80:20%	12/12°-6400/39°	+/-2	+	+	F; T; meter; R	LCD	K/ A-U	100%	+
F3 P	Ai	H	Titan blades	1/2000-8 Sec.; B; T; X 1/80	quartz	A; M	SPD	EV 1-18	80:20%	12/12°-6400/39°	+/-2	+	+	F; T; meter; R	LCD	B/ A-U	100%	+
F3 AF	Ai 1)	H	Titan blades	1/2000-8 Sec.; B; T; X 1/80	quartz	A; M	SPD	EV 1-18	80:20%	12/12°6400/39°	+/-2	+	+	T; meter; R; AF	LCD	-/ A-U	100%	+
F4/F4 S/F4 E	AF	V	2 x 4 Alu- & plastic-blades	1/8000-4 (30)Sec.: B; T; X	quartz	P; PH; A; S; M	2x3 SPDs	EV 2-21	Matrix 60:40%; Spot	25/15°-5000/38° 6/9°-6400/39° DX	+/-2	+	+	T; F; meter; R; C; AF; FC	LED + LCD	B/ A-U	100%	+
Nikkormat FS	Non-Ai	V	Metal blades	1/1000-1 Sec.; B	mechan.	M	–	–	–	–	–	–	–	–	–	J	92%	–
Nikkormat FT	Non-Ai	V	Metal blades	1/1000-1 Sec.: B	mechan.	M	CdS	EV	60:40% 3-17	12/12°-1600/33°	–	–	–	meter	needle	J	92%	_
Nikkormat FTN	Non-Ai	V	Metal blades	1/1000-1 Sec.: B	mechan.	M	CdS	EV 3-17	60:40%	12/12°-1600/33°	–	–	–	T; Beli	needle	A or J	92%	–
Nikkormat FT2	Non-Ai	V	Metal blades	1/1000-1 Sec.; B	mechan.	M	CdS	EV 3-17	60:40%	12/12°-1600/33°	–	–	–	T; meter	needle	K	92%	_
Nikkormat FT3	Ai	V	Metal blades	1/1000-1 Sec.; B	mechan.	M	CdS	EV 3-17	60:40%	12/12°-1600/33°	–	–	–	T; meter	needle	K	92%	–
Nikkormat EL	Non-Ai	V	Metal-blades	1/1000 - 4 Sec.; B;	electron.	A; M	CdS	EV 1-18	60:40%	25/15°-1600/33°	—	+	–	T; meter	needle	A; J K	92%	—
Nikkormat EEV	Non-Ai	V	Metal-blades	1/1000 - 4 Sec.; B;	electron.	A; M	CdS	EV 1-18	60:40%	25/15°-1600/33°	—	+	–	T; meter	needle	K	92%	—

Eyepiece shutter	Synch. speed	Synch. contacts	Synch. cord terminal	Accessory shoe	Flash-ready signal in viewfinder	ISO-range for TTL-flash control	Programmed TTL flash control	Mirror lock-up	Depth of field preview	Self-timer	Cable release terminal	Multiple exposure facility	Rewind	Camera back interchangeable	Motor drive	AF operating range	Min. lens speed for AF operation	Autofocus sensor	Focus priority	Focus tracking	AF-Tele. TC-16A; TC-14E; TC-201E usable	Weight (g)	Dimensions (HxWxD in mm)
—	1/60	X; M	+	F Type	–	–	–	+	+	mechan.	Leica bell	–	crank	+	F-36	–	–	–	–	–	–	685	98.0 x 147.0 x 56.0
—	1/60	X; M	+	F Type	–	–	–	+	+	mechan.	Leica bell	–	crank	+	F-36	–	–	–	–	–	–	830	102.0 x 147.0 x 67.0
—	1/60	X; M	+	F Type	–	–	–	+	+	mechan.	Leica bell	–	crank	+	F-36	–	–	–	–	–	–	830	102.0 x 147.0 x 67.0
—	1/60	X; M	+	F Type	–	–	–	+	+	mechan.	Leica bell	–	crank	+	F-36	–	–	–	–	–	–	830	102.0 x 147.0 x 67.0
—	1/60	X; M	+	F Type	–	–	–	+	+	mechan.	Leica bell	–	crank	+	F-36	–	–	–	–	–	–	860	102.0 x 147.0 x 66.0
—	1/80	X; M	+	F Type	+ 3)	–	–	+	+	mechan.	Leica bell	–	crank 5)	+	MD-1/2/3	–	–	–	–	–	–	730	98.0 x 152.0 x 65.0
—	1/80	X; M	+	F Type	+ 3)	–	–	+	+	mechan.	Leica bell	–	crank 5)	+	MD-1/2/3	–	–	–	–	–	–	810	98.0 x 152.0 x 65.0
—	1/80	X; M	+	F Type	+ 3)	–	–	+	+	mechan.	Leica bell	+	crank 5)	+	MD-1/2/3	–	–	–	–	–	–	880	110.0 x 152.0 x 65.0
—	1/80	X; M	+	F Type	+ 3)	–	–	+	+	mechan.	Leica bell	–	crank 5)	+	MD-1/2/3	–	–	–	–	–	–	850	102.0 x 152.0 x 66.0
—	1/80	X; M	+	F Type	+ 3)	–	–	+	+	mechan.	Leica bell	–	crank 5)	+	MD-1/2/3	–	–	–	–	–	–	820	102.0 x 152.0 x 65.0
—	1/80	X; M	+	F Type	+ 3)	–	–	+	+	mechan.	Leica bell	–	crank 5)	+	MD-1/2/3	–	–	–	–	–	–	840	102.0 x 152.0 x 65.0
—	1/80	X; M	+	F Type	+ 3)	–	–	– 2)	+ 4)	mechan.	Leica bell	–	crank 5)	+	MD-100	–	–	–	–	–	–	700	98.0 x 152.0 x 56.0
+	1/80	X	+	F3 Type	+	25/15° 400/27°	–	+	+	electron.	ISO	+	crank 6)	+	MD-4	–	–	–	–	–	–	700/ 745	96.5x 101.0 x 69.0
+	1/80	X; M	+	F3 Type	+	25/15° 400/27°	–	+	+	electron.	ISO	–	crank 6)	+	MD-4	–	–	–	–	–	–	745	105.0 x 148.0 x 69.0
+	1/80	X; 8)	+	F3 Type	+	25/15° 400/27°	–	+	+	electron.	ISO	+	crank	+	MD-4	4-20	1:3.5	2 SPD	–	+	– 7)	950	115.0 x 148.0 x 90.0
+	1/250	X; 8)	+	ISO	+	25/15° 1000/31°	+	+	+	electron.	+	+	motor & manual	+	built-in	-1-18	1:5.6	200 CCD	+	+ 12)	+ 13)	1090	117.0 x 168.5 x 76.6
—	1/125	X; M	+	–	–	–	–	+	+	mechan.	ISO	–	crank	–	–	–	–	–	–	–	–	740	95.0 x 146.0 x 54.0
—	1/125	X; M	+	–	–	–	–	+	+	mechan.	ISO	–	crank	–	–	–	–	–	–	–	–	745	95.0 x 146.0 x 54.0
—	1/125	X; M	+	–	–	–	–	+	+	mechan.	ISO	–	crank	–	–	–	–	–	–	–	–	765	95.0 x 148.0 x 54.0
—	1/125	X; M	+	ISO	–	–	–	+	+	mechan.	Leica bell ISO	–	crank	–	–	–	–	–	–	–	–	770	96.0 x 148.0 x 54.0
—	1/125	X; M	+	–	–	–	–	+	+	mechan.	Leica bell ISO	–	Kurbel	–	–	–	–	–	–	–	–	750	96.0 x 148.0 x 54.0
–	1/125	X; M	+	ISO	–	–	–	+	+	mechan.	Leica bell ISO	–	Kurbel	–	–	–	–	–	–	–	–	780	93.0 x 145.0 x 54.0
–	1/125	X; M	+	ISO	–	–	–	+	+	mechan.	Leica bell ISO	–	Kurbel	–	AW-1	–	–	–	–	–	–	790	93.0 x 145.0 x 54.0

Model	Type of bayonet	Shutter blind travel direction	Shutter construction	Shutter speeds	Shutter control	Exposure control	Metering cell	Metering range	Metering patterns	ISO Film speed range	Exposure compensation	Auto exp. ock	change viewfinder	Viewfinder displays [10]	Exp. meter display	Focusing screen provided/optional	Viewfinder image coverage	Viewfinder illum.
Nikon EL-2	Ai	V	Metal-	1/1000 - 8 sec.; B;	electron.	A; M	2CdS/ SPD/ GAs	EV 1-18	60:40%	12/12°-3200/36°	+2/ -1	+	–	T; meter	needle	K	92%	—
Nikon FM	Ai	V	Metal-	1/1000 - 1 sec.; B;	mechan.	M	2CdS/ SPD/ GAs	EV 1-18	60:40%	12/12°-6400/34°	—	–	–	T; F; meter	LED	K	43%	—
Nikon FM-2	Ai	V	Titan.	1/4000 - 1 sec.; B; X 1/200	mechan.	M	2CdS/ SPD/ GAs	EV 1-18	60:40%	12/12°-400/27°	—	–	–	T; F; meter R	LED	K/ B; E	43%	—
Nikon FM-2N	Ai	V	Titan.	1/4000 - 1 sec.; B	mechan.	M	2CdS/ SPD/ GAs	EV 1-18	60:40%	12/12°-4000/37°	—	–	–	T; F; meter R	LED	K2/ B2; E2	93%	—
Nikon FE	Ai	V	Metal	1/1000 - 8 sec.; B; M 1/90	electron.	A; M	2CdS/ SPD/ GAs	EV 1-18	60:40%	25/15°-1600/33°	+/-2	–	–	T; F; meter R	needle	K/ B; E	93%	
Nikon FE-2	Ai	V	Titan.	1/4000 - 8 sec.; B; M 1/250	quarz	A; M	2CdS/ SPD/ GAs	EV 1-18	60:40%	12/12°-400/27°	+/-2	+	–	T; F; meter; R; C	needle	K2/ B2; E2	93%	—
Nikon FA	Ai-S	V	Titan.	1/4000 - 1 sec.; B; M 1/250	quarz	P; S; A; M	2x3 SPD	EV 1-18	AMP 40:60%	12/12°-4000/37°	+/-2	–	–	T; meter; R	LED	K2/ B2; E2	93%	—
Nikon EM	Ai	V	Metal-	1/1000 - 1 sec.; B; M 1/90	electron.	A	SPD	EV 1-16.3/ 1-20	AMP 60/40%	25/15°-3200/36°	+2	–	–	T; meter; R	needle	K	92%	—
Nikon FG	Ai	V	Metal-	1/1000 - 1 sec.; B; M 1/90	quarz	P; A; M	SPD	EV 1-18	40:60%	12/12°-3200/36° 25/15°-5000/38° DX	+/-2	–	–	T; meter; R	LCD	K	92%	—
Nikon FG-20	Ai	V	Metal-	1/1000 - 1 sec. B; M 1/90	electron.	A; M	SPD	EV 1-18	40:60%	12/12°-3200/36°	—	–	–	T; meter; R	needle	K	92%	—
Nikon F-301	Ai-S	V	Alumin.	1/2000 - 1 sec.; B	quarz	P; PH; A; M	SPD	EV 1-18	40:60%	25/15°-3200/36°	—	–	–	meter; R; AF;	LED	K	92%	—
Nikon F-401	AF	V	Alumin.	1/2000 - 1 sec.; B	quarz	P; S; A; M	3 seg SPD	EV 1-19	IMC; 60:40%	25/15°-5000/38° DX	+/-2	+	–	meter; R; AF;	LED	B	92%	—
Nikon F-401S	AF	V	Alumin.	1/2000 - 1 sec.; B	quarz	S; A; M	3 seg SPD	EV 1-19	IMC; 60:40%	25/15°-5000/38° DX	+/-5	+	–	T; meter; R; AF	LED	B	92%	—
Nikon 401 X	AF	V	Alumin.	1/2000- 30 sec.; T	quarz	S; A' M	5 seg. SPD	EV 1-19	Matrix 60:40%	25/15°-5000/38° DX	+/-5	+	–	T; meter R; Af	LED	B	92%	—
Nikon F-501	AF	V	Alumin.	1/2000 - 1 sec.; B	quarz	P; PH; A; M	SPD	EV 1-19	40:60%	12/12°-3200/36°; 25/15°-5000/38° DX	+/-5	+	–	T; F; meter; Li; R; C	LED	B/ E; J	92%	—
Nikon F-601	AF	V	Alumin.	1/2000 - 30 sec.; B	quarz	P; M; PM; S; A	6 seg SPD	EV 0-19 4-19 9)	Matrix; 75:25% Spot	6/9°-6400/39: 25/15°-5000/37° DX	+/-5	+	–	T; F; meter; Li; R; C	LCD	B	92%	+
Nikon F-601 M	Ai-S	V	Alumin.	1/2000 - 30 sec.; B	quarz	P; M; PM: S; A	5 seg SPD	EV 0-19	Matrix; 75:25%	6/9°-6400/39: 25/15°-5000/37° DX	+/-5	+	–	T; F; meter; Li; R; C	LCD	K	92%	+
Nikon F-801	AF	V	Alumin.	1/8000 - 30 sec.; B	quarz	P; PH; S; A; M	5 seg SPD	EV 0-21	Matrix; 75:25%	6/9°–6400/39°; 25/15°-5000/37° DX	+/-5	+	–	T; meter	LCD	B/ E; J	92%	+
Nikon 801 S	AF	V	Alumin.	1/8000- 30 sec.; B	quarz	P; PH; S; A; M	6 seg SPD	EV 0-21 4-21 9)	Matrix 75:25% Spot	6/9°–6400/39°; 25/15°-5000/37° DX	+/-5	+	–	T; meter	LCD	B/ E; J	92%	+
Nikon F90	AF	V	Alumin.	1/8000- 30 sec.; B	quarz	P; PV; S; A; M	8 seg SPD	EV- -1-21 3-21 9)	3D Matrix 75:25% Spot	6/9°–6400/39°; 25/15°-5000/37° DX	+/-5	+	–	T; meter FC	LCD	B/E	92%	+

1 AF-operation only with F3AF-lenses
2 Fixed and partly transparent mirror
3 Only with F2 – dedicated flash units
4 Lens is permanently stopped down
5 Automatically with Motor-Drive MD-1 and MD-2
6 Automatically with Motor-Drive MD-4
7 Only TC-16 usable
8 Rear blind synch. possible
9 With spot-metering mode
10 T = shutter speed; F = aperture; meter = metering indication; C = exposure compensation; R = flash-ready signal; AF = Autofocus
11 Aluminium as of
12 Focus Tracking automatically activated
13 TC 14E/20E also usable for AF-operation with AF-I lenses
14 Also FP – high speed synch. up to 1/4000 sec.
15 With MF-25 or electronic organiser
16 Spot and wide-field AF-operation available
17 Weight F4S – 1280g; F4E – 1400g.
18 Dimensions F4S – 138 x 169 x 77m; F4E – 157 x 169 x 77g.

Eyepiece shutter	Synch. speed	Synch. contacts	Synch. cord terminal	Accessory shoe	Flash-ready signal in viewfinder	ISO-range for TTL-flash control	Programmed TTL flash control	Mirror lock-up	Depth of field preview	Self-timer	Cable release terminal	Multiple exposure facility	Rewind	Camera back interchangeable	Motor drive	AF operating range	Min. lens speed for AF operation	Autofocus sensor	Focus priority	Focus tracking	AF-Tele. TC-16A; TC-14E; TC-201E usable	Weight (g)	Dimensions (HxWxD in mm)
–	1/125	X	+	ISO	–	–	–	+	+	mechan.	Glocke/ ISO	–	crank	–	AW-1	–	–	–	–	–	–	780	93.0 x 145.0 x 54.0
–	1/125	X	+	ISO	–	–	–	–	+	mechan.	Glocke/ ISO	+	crank	+	MD-11/12	–	–	–	–	–	–	590	90.0 x 142.0 x 60.0
–	1/200	X	+	ISO	+	–	–	–	+	mechan.	ISO	+	crank	+	MD-11/12	–	–	–	–	–	–	540	90.0 x 142.0 x 60.0
–	1/250	X	+	ISO	+	–	–	–	+	mechan.	ISO	+	crank	+	MD-11/12	–	–	–	–	–	–	550	90.0 x 142.0 x 60.0
–	1/125	X	+	ISO	+	–	–	–	+	mechan.	Glocke/ ISO	+	crank	+	MD-11/12	–	–	–	–	–	–	590	90.0 x 142.0 x 57.0
–	1/250	X	+	ISO	+	25/15° 400/27°	–	–	+	mechan.	ISO	+	crank	+	MD-11/12	–	–	–	–	–	–	550	90.0 x 142.0 x 57.0
+	1/250	X	+	ISO	+	25/15° 400/27°	–	–	+	mechan.	ISO	+	crank	+	MD-11/12/ 15	–	–	–	–		–	625	92.0 x 142.0 x 64.0
(DK -5)	1/90	X	(AS-15)	ISO	+	– –	–	–	–	mechan.	ISO	–	crank	–	MD-E/ MD-14	–	–	–	–	–	–	460	86.0 x 135.0 x 54.0
(DK -5)	1/90	X	(AS-15)	ISO	+	25/15°-400/27°	–	–	–	mechan.	ISO	–	crank	+	MD-E/ MD-14	–	–	–	–	–	–	490	87.0 x 136.0 x 54.0
(DK -5)	1/90	X	(AS-15)	ISO	+	25/15°-400/27°	–	–	–	mechan.	ISO	–	crank	–	MD-E/ MD-14	–	–	–	–	–	–	440	88.0 x 136.0 x 54.0
(DK -5)	1/125	X	(AS-15)	ISO	+	25/15°-1000/31°	+	–	–	electron.	AR-3/ ISO	–	crank	+	built-in	–	–	–	–	–	–	570	97.0 x 148.0 x 51.0
(DK -5)	1/100	X	(AS-15)	ISO	+	25/15°-400/27°	+	–	–	electron.	–	–	motor	+	built-in	2-18	1:5.6	200 CCD	+	–	–	650	102.0 x 154.0 x 65.0
(DK -5)	1/100	X	(AS-15)	ISO	+	25/15°-400/27°	+	–	–	electron.	–	–	motor	+	built-in	-1-17	1:5.6	200 CCD	+	–	–	655	102.0 x 154.0 x 65.5
(DK-5)	1/125	X	(AS 15)	ISO	+	25/15°-800/30°	+	–	–	electron.	–	–	motor	+	built-in	-1-19	1:5.6	200 CCD	+ 12)	–	–	647	102.0 x 154 x 65.0
(DK -5)	1/125	X	(AS-15)	ISO	+	25/15°-1000/31°	+	–	–	electron.	AR-3/ ISO	–	crank	+	built-in	4-17	1:4.5	96 CCD	+	+	+	610	97.0 x 148.0 x 54.0
(DK -5)	1/125	X 8)	(AS-15)	ISO	+	25/15° 1000/31°	+	–	–	electron.	ISO	–	motor	–	built-in	-1-19	1:5.6	200 CCD	+ 12)	+ 12)	+	650	100.0 x 155.0 x 66.0
(DK -5)	1/125	X	(AS-15)	ISO	+	25/15°-1000/31°	+	–	–	electron.	ISO	–	motor	–	built-in	-1-19	1:5.6	200 CCD	–	–	–	565	96.0 x 155.0 x 66.0
(DK -5)	1/250	X 8)	(AS-15)	ISO	+	25/15°-1000/31°	+	–	+	electron.	AR-3/ ISO	+	motor	+	built-in	-1-19	1:5.6	200 CCD	+	+	+	695	102.0 x 153.0 x 67.0
(DK -5)	1/250	X 8)	(AS-15)	ISO	+	25/15°-1000/31°	+	–	+	electron.	AR-3/ ISO	+	motor	+	built-in	-1-19	1:5.6	200 CCD	+ 12)	+ 12)	+	695	102.0 x 153.0 x 67.0
+	1/250	X 8) 14)	+	ISO	+	25/15°-1000/31°	+	–	+	electron.	AR-3/ MC-25/ ISO	+ 15)	motor	+	built-in	-1-19	1:5.6	246 CCD 16)	+ 12) 14)	+ 12) 14)	+ 13)	755	106.0 x 154.0 x 69.0

All Nikon Lenses at a Glance

Lens	Type of bayonet	Serial numbers	Period of production	Angle of view	Elements/groups	Smallest aperture	Closest focusing distance	Filter size	Lens hood	Hard case	Soft pouch	Weight (g)	Dimensions (diam x length in mm)	Usable teleconverters	Special features
6mm/5.6	A	656001-660102	01/69-03/78	220°	9/6	22	Fixed focus	built-in Filter	–	–	–	430	92.0 x 81	–	Image diam.: 21.6mm Necessary finder: DF-1
6mm/2.8	C	628001-628028	03/72-09/81	220°	12/9	22	0.25	built-in Filter	–	Holskof-fer	–	5200	236.0 x 171	A; D; F	Image diam.: 23mm Necessary finder: DF-1
6mm/2.8	Ai-S	629001-	03/82-	220°	12/9	22	0.25	built-in Filter	–	Holzkof-fer	–	5200	236.0 x 171	A; D;	Image diam.: 23mm
7.5mm/5.6	A	750011-752222	10/65-02/70	180°	9/6	22	Fixed focus	built-in Filter	–	–	–	315	82.0 x 80	–	Image diam.: 23mm Necessary finder: DF-1
8mm/8.0	A	–	07/62 04/65	180°	9/5	22	Fixed focus	built-in Filter	–	–	–	300	89.0 x 80	–	Image diam.: 24mm Necessary finder: DF-1
8mm/2.8	C	88010-88388; 230011-243000	03/70-02/82	180°	10/8	22	0.30	built-in Filter	-	CL-11	–	1000	123.0 x 140	A; D; F	Image diam.: 23mm
8mm/2.8	Ai-S	243001-	12/81-	180°	10/8	22	0.30	built-in Filter	–	CL-11	–	1000	123.0 x 140	A; D	Image diam.: 23mm
10mm/5.6 OP	A	180011-190168	07/68-08/76	180°	9/6	22	Fixed focus	built-in Filter	–	CL-4	–	400	84.0 x 105	–	Image diam.: 20mm
16mm/3.5	C	272281-275988	02/73-03/76	170°	8/5	22	0.30	built-in Filter	built-in	CL-31	61	330	68.0 x 60.5	A; D	Full-format fisheye
16mm/3.5	K	280001-	12/75-05/79	170°	8/5	22	0.30	built-in Filter	built-in	CL-31	61	330	68.0 x 60.5	A; D	Full-format fisheye
16mm/2.8	N	178051-	07/79-02/82	180°	8/5	22	0.30	Bayonet	built-in	CL-30 S	61	310	63.5 x 62.5	A; D; F	Full-format fisheye
16mm/2.8	Ai-S	185001-	12/81-	180°	8/5	22	0.30	Bayonet	built-in	CL-30 S	61	310	63.5 x 62.5	A; D; F	Full-format fisheye
13mm/5.6	K	175021-	12/75-10/81	118°	16/12	22	0.30	Bayonet	built-in	CL-14	–	1200	115.0 x 88.5	A; D	CRC=Close range correction
13mm/5.6	Ai-S	175901-	10/81-	118°	16/12	22	0.30	Bayonet	built-in	CL-14	–	1200	115.0 x 88.5	A; D	CRC
15mm/5.6	C	321001-	06/73-08/76	110°	15/12	22	0.30	built-in Filter	built-in	CL-26	–	560	82.0 x 85.5	A; D	
15mm/5.6	K	340001-	07/76-07/78	110°	15/12	22	0.30	built-in Filter	built-in	CL-26	–	560	82.0 x 85.5 A; D		
15mm/3.5	N	177051-	08/78-12/81	110°	14/11	22	0.30	Bayonet	built-in	CL-17	–	630	90.0 x 94	A; D	CRC
15mm/3.5	Ai-S	180001-	12/81-	110°	14/11	22	0.30	Bayonet	built-in	CL-17	–	630	90.0 x 94	A; D	CRC
16mm/2.8 D-AF	Ai-S	—	9/93	180°	8/5	22	0.25	Bayonet	built-in	CL-30S	61	325	63.0 x 54.8	A; D; F	Full-format fisheye
18mm/4.0	K	173111-190001(Ai)	11/74-03/82	100°	13/9	22	0.30	Series 9 86mm	HN-15	CL-28	–	390	89.0 x 58.5	A; D	
18mm/3.5	Ai-S	180051-	12/81-	100°	11/10	22	0.25	72mm	HK-9	CL-37	–	350	75.0 x 72	A; D	CRC
20mm/3.5	C	421241-480633	11/67-04/74	94°	11/9	22	0.30	72mm	HN-9	CL-34	51	390	75.0 x 69	A; D	
20mm/4.0	K	103001-130001(Ai)	08/74-01/78	94°	10/8	22	0.30	52mm	HN-14	CL-31	61	210	63.5 x 47	A; D	
20mm/3.5	N	176121-	12/77-12/81	94°	11/8	22	0.30	52mm	HK-6	CL-30 S	61	235	63.5 x 50.5	A; D	
20mm/3.5	Ai-S	210001-	10/81-12/84	94°	11/8	22	0.30	52mm	HK-6	CL-30 S	61	235	63.5 x 50.5	A; D	
20mm/2.8	Ai-S		10/84-	94°	12/9	22	0.,25	62mm	HK-14	CL-30 S	61	260	65.0 x 64	A; D	CRC
20mm/2.8 AF	Ai-S	–	2/89-	94°	12/9	22	0.25	62mm	HB-4	CL-30 S	61	260	69.0 x 54	A; D; F	CRC
21mm/4.0	A	220111-227163	10/59-09/67	92°	8/4	16	0.90	52mm	HN-14	CL-30 S	61	135	63.5 x 50	–	Special viewfinder necessary

Lens	Type of bayonet	Serial numbers	Period of production	Angle of view	Elements/groups	Smallest aperture	Closest focusing distance	Filter size	Lens hood	Hard case	Soft pouch	Weight (g)	Dimensions (diam x length in mm)	Usable teleconverters	Special features
24mm/2.0	N	176021-	08/77- 11/82	84°	11/10	22	0.30	52mm	HK-2	CL-30 S	61	305	63.0 x 61	A; D	CRC
24mm/2.0	Ai-S	200001-	10/81-	84°	11/10	22	0.30	52mm	HK-2	CL-30 S	61	305	63.0 x 61	A; D	CRC
24mm/2.8	C	242821- 434287	06/87- 03/75	84°	9/7	16	0.30	52mm	HN-1	CL-31	61	290	64.5 x 59	A; D; E; F	CRC
24mm/2.8	K	450001-	01/75- 03/77	84°	9/7	22	0.30	52mm	HN-1	CL-31	61	280	63.5 x 59	A; D; E; F	CRC
24mm/2.8	N	525001-	01/77- 09/81	84°	9/9	22	0.30	52mm	HN-1	CL-31	61	280	63.5 x 59	A; D; F	CRC
24mm/2.8	Ai-S	700001-	08/81-	84°	9/9	22	0.30	52mm	HN-1	CL-31	61	250	63.0 x 57	A; D; F	CRC
24mm/2.8 AF	Ai-S	–	10/86- 6/91	84°	9/9	22	0.30	52mm	HN-1	CL-31	61	260	65.0 x 55	A; D; F	CRC
24mm/2.8 AF N	Ai-S	–	6/91	84°	9/9	22	0.30	52mm	HN-1	CL-31	61	260	65.0 x 55	A; D	CRC
28mm/4.0 PC	K	174041-	06/75- 09/83	74° (92°)	10/8	22	0.30	72mm	HN-9	CL-34 A	61	410	78.0 x 67.5	A; D	max. shift 11mm off axis
28mm/3.5 PC	Ai-S	179121-	10/80-	74° (92°)	9/8	22	0.30	72mm	HN-9	CL-34 A	61	380	78.0 x 69	A; D	max. shift 11mm off axis
28mm/3.5	A	301011- 355242; 625611- 792167	03/60 03/67; 01/65- 10/73	74°	6/6	16	0.60	52mm	HN-2	CL-31	61	215	62.5 x 54	A; D	
28mm/3.5	C	850001- 898367	06/73- 03/75	74°	6/6	16	0.60	52mm	HN-2	CL-31	61	215	62.5 x 54	A; D	
28mm/3.5	K	195531- 301010	02/75- 03/77	74°	6/6	22	0.30	52mm	HN-2	CL-31	61	230	63.5 x 54	A; D	
28mm/3.5	N	1760201-	01/77- 09/81	74°	6/6	22	0.30	52mm	HN-2	CL-31	61	230	63.5 x 54	A; D	
28mm/3.5	Ai-S	2100001-	07/81-	74°	6/6	22	0.30	52mm	HN-2	CL-30 S	61	220	63.0 x 54	A; D	
28mm/2.8	K	382011-	08/74- 09/81	74°	7/7	22	0.30	52mm	HN-2	CL-30 S	61	240	63.0 x 54	A; D; F	
28mm/2.8	Ai-S	635001-	08/81-	74°	8/8	22	0.20	52mm	HN-2	CL-30 S	61	250	63.0 x 59	A; D; F	CRC
28mm/2.8 E	Ai-S	1790601-	11/79-	74°	5/5	22	0.30	52mm	HR-6	CL-30 S	61	150	62.5 x 44.5	A; D; F	
28mm/2.8 AF	Ai-S	–	09/86-	74°	5/5	22	0.30	52mm	HN-2	CL-30 S	61	195	65.0 x 48.7	A; D; F	
28mm/2.8 AF N	Ai-S	–	6/91	74°	5/5	22	0.30	52mm	HN-2	CL-30S	61	195	65.0 x 48.7	A; D	
28mm/2.0	C	280001- 327984	08/70- 12/75	74°	9/8	22	0.30	52mm	HN-1	CL-31	61	345	64.5 x 70	A; D	CRC
28mm/2.0	K	335001-	11/75- 11/81	74°	9/8	22	0.30	52mm	HN-1	CL-31	61	355	64.5 x 68.5	A; D; E; F	CRC
28mm/2.0	Ai-S	575001-	09/81-	74°	9/8	22	0.25	52mm	HN-1	CL-31	61	360	63.0 x 68.5	A; D; E; F	CRC
28mm/1.4 D AF	Ai-S	–	9/93	74°	11/8	16	0.35	72mm	HK-7	CL-32S	62	565	75.0 x 77.5	A; D; E; F	aspherical element; CRC rear focusing
35mm/3.5 PC	A	102105-	11/65- 04/68	62° (76°)	6/6	32	0.30	52mm	HN-1	CL-34	61	290	73.0 x 55	A; D	Shift up to 11mm off axis
35mm/2.8 PC	C	851001- 886420	01/68- 12/75	62° (76°)	8/7	32	0.30	52mm	HN-1	CL-34	61	335	70.0 x 66.5	A; D	Shift up to 11mm off axis
35mm/2.8 PC	K	900001-	10/75- 05/80	62° (76°)	8/7	32	0.30	52mm	HN-1	CL-34	61	330	66.5 x 66	A; D	Shift up to 11mm off axis
35mm/2.8 PC	Ai-S	179091-	06/80-	62° (76°)	7/7	32	0.30	52mm	HN-1	CL-34	61	320	62.0 x 66	A; D	Shift up to 11mm off axis
35mm/2.8	A	225311- 920110	02/62- 08/74	62°	7/6	16	0.30	52mm	HN-3	CL-31	61	200	62.5 x 57	A; D	
35mm/2.8	K	773111-	06/74- 01/81	62°	6/6	22	0.30	52mm	HN-3	CL-31	61	240	63.5 x 54	A; D; F	
35mm/2.8	N	350001-	11/77- 09/81	62°	5/5	22	0.30	52mm	HN-3	CL-31	61	240	63.5 x 54	A; D; F	

All Nikon Lenses at a Glance (continued)

Lens	Type of bayonet	Serial numbers	Period of production	Angle of view	Elements/groups	Smallest aperture	Closest focusing distance	Filter size	Lens hood	Hard case	Soft pouch	Weight (g)	Dimensions (diam x length in mm)	Usable teleconverters	Special features
35mm/2.8	Ai-S	521001-	08/81-	62°	5/5	22	0.30	52mm	HN-3	CL-30 S	61	240	63.5 x 54.5	A; D; F	
35mm/2.5 E	Ai-S	1780801-	03/79- 10/82	62°	5/5	22	0.30	52mm	HR-4	CL-30 S	61	150	63.5 x 44.5	A; D; F	
35mm/2.0	A	102105- 110999	08/62- 03/67	62°	8/6	22	0.30	52mm	HN-3	CL-31	61	285	63.5 x 61	A; D	
35mm/2.0	C	690101- 871141	11/67- 04/75	62°	8/6	22	0.30	52mm	HN-3	CL-31	61	285	63.5 x 61	A; D;	
35mm/2.0	K	880001-	03/75- 08/81	62°	8/6	22	0.30	52mm	HN-3	CL-31	61	280	63.5 x 61	A; D; E; F	
35mm/2.0	Ai-S	210001-	06/81-	62°	8/6	22	0.30	52mm	HN-3	CL-31	61	280	63.5 x 59.5	A; D; E; F	
35mm/2.0 AF	AI-S	–	3/89-	62°	6/5	22	0.25	52mm	HN-3	CL-31	61	215	63.0 x 53	A; D; E; F	
35mm/1.4	C	350001- 377067	05/70- 01/76	62°	9/7	22	0.30	52mm	HN-3	CL-32	62	415	66.5 x 74.5	A; D	CRC
35mm/1.4	K	385001-	12/75- 11/81	62°	9/7	16/ 22	0.30	52mm	HN-3	CL-32	62	410	67.5 x 74	A; D; E; F	CRC
35mm/1.4	Ai-S	430001-	12/81	82°	9/7	16	0.30	52mm	HN-3	CL-31S	61	400	67.5x74	A; D; E; F	CRC
45mm/2.8 GN	C	710101-	08/68- 03/77	50°	4/3	32	0.80	52mm	HN-4	CL-30 S	61	155	64.0 x 32	A; D	Automatic flash exposure by coupling aperture and dist. ring
50mm/2.0	A	520102- 636021	02/59- 06/67	46°	6/4	16	0.60	52mm	HN-5	CL-34	61	205	64.0 x 48	A; D	
50mm/2.0	C	742111- 2329000	05/67- 08/74	46°	6/4	16	0.60	52mm	HS-2	CL-34	61	205	64.0 x 50.5	A; D	
50mm/2.0	K	3100001-	06/74- 01/79	46°	6/4	16	0.60	52 mm	HS-6	CL-34	61	205	64.0 x 53	A; D	
50mm/1.8	N	1760801-	01/78- 10/82	46°	6/5	22	0.45	52mm	HS-6	CL-30 S	61	220	63.5 x 48	A; D; E; F	
50mm/1.8	Ai-S	3135001-	07/81- 09/85	46°	6/5	22	0.45	52mm	HS-6	CL-30 S	61	220	63.5 x 48	A; D; E; F	
50mm/1.8 N	Ai-S	–	08/85-	46°	6/5	22	0.60	52mm	HR-4	CL-30 S	61	145	63.5 x 48	A; D; E; F	
50mm/1.8 E	Ai-S	1055001-	12/78- 07/85	46°	6/5	22	0.60	52mm	HR-4	CL-30 S	61	135	63.5 x 33	A; D; E; F	
50mm/1.8 AF	Ai-S	–	04/86-	46°	6/5	22	0.45	52mm	HR-2	CL-30 S	61	210	65.0 x 48	A; D; E; F	
50mm/1.8 AF N	Ai-S	–	1/90-	46°	6/5	22	0.45	52mm	HR-2	CL-30 S	61	155	65.0 x 43	A; D; E; F	
50mm/1.4	A	314101- 910215	01/62- 06/72	46°	7/5	16	0.60	52mm	HS-1	CL-34	61	325	67.0 x 56.5	A; D	
50mm/1.4	C	1280001- 1613735	11/70- 06/74	46°	7/5	16	0.60	52mm	HN-5	CL-34	61	325	67.0 x 56.5	A; D	
50mm/1.4	K	2797021- 3004000	08/74- 06/76	46°	7/5	16	0.45	52mm	HN-5	CL-34	61	325	67.0 x 56.5	A; D	
50mm/1.4	N	3750401-	01/76- 06/81	46°	7/6	16	0.45	52mm	HR-1	CL-34	61	260	64.0 x 49	A; D; E; F	
50mm/1.4	Ai-S	5100001-	07/81-	46°	7/6	16	0.45	52mm	HS-9	CL-34	61	250	63.0 x 50	A; D; E; F	
50mm/1.4 AF	Ai-S	–	09/86-	46°	7/6	16	0.45	52mm	HS-7	CL-30 S	61	255	65.0 x 52	A; D; E; F	
50mm/1.4 AF N	Ai-S	–	6/91	46°	7/6	16	0.45	52mm	HS-7	CL-30 S	61	255	65.0x52	A; D	
50mm/1.2	N	177051-	03/78- 06/81	46°	7/6	16	0.50	52mm	HS-12	CL-31 S	61	390	70.0 x 59	A; D; E; F	

Lens	Type of bayonet	Serial numbers	Period of production	Angle of view	Elements/groups	Smallest aperture	Closest focusing distance	Filter size	Lens hood	Hard case	Soft pouch	Weight (g)	Dimensions (diam x length in mm)	Usable teleconverters	Special features
50mm/1.2	Ai-S	250001-	06/81-	46°	7/6	16	0.50	52mm	HR-2	CL-31 S	61	390	70.0 x 59	A; D; E; F	
55mm/4.0 UV	A	–	–	43°	3/3	32	0.36	52mm	HN-3	CL-33	62	230	66.0 x 66	–	
55mm/3.5 Micro	A	171513-273153	08/61-06/70	43°	5/4	32	0.24	52mm	HN-3	CL-33	62	235	66.5 x 64.5	A; D	
55mm/3.5 Micro	C	600001-811928	04/70-03/75	43°	5/4	32	0.24	52mm	HN-3	CL-33	62	235	65.5 x 64.5	A; D	
55mm/3.5 Micro	K	850001-	04/75-10/79	43°	5/4	32	0.24	52mm	HN-3	CL-33	62	245	66.0 x 64.5	A; D	
55mm/2.8 Micro	Ai-S	179041-	12/79-	43°	6/5	32	0.25	52mm	HN-3	CL-31 S	62	290	63.5 x 70	A; D; F	CRC
55mm/2.8 Micro AF	Ai-S	–	4/86-11/89	43°	6/5	32	0.23	62mm	HN-22	CL-32 S	62	420	74.0 x 82	A; D; F	CRC
55mm/1.2	C	184711 970110; 250001-300556	11/67-12/74	43°	7/5	16	0.60	52mm	HR-2	CL-34	62	420	73.5 x 58.5	A; D	
55mm/1.2	K	350011-400001(Ai)	11/74 04/78	43°	7/5	16	0.50	52mm	HS-7	CL-34	61	410	72.0 x 58.5	A; D; E; F	
58mm/1.2 Noct	N	172011-	02/77-11/81	40°50'	7/6	16	0.50	52mm	HR-2	CL-31 S	61	485	74.0 x 63	A; D	aspherical front element
58mm/1.2 Noct	Ai-S	185001-	11/81	40°50'/	7/6	16	0.50	52mm	HS-7	CL-31S	61	465	74.0 x 63	A; D; E; F	aspherical front element
58mm/1.4	A	140051-179051	10/59-01/62	40°50'	7/6	16	0.60	52mm	HS-7	CL-31 S	61	365	69.0 x 63	A; D; E; F	
60mm/2.8 Micro AF	Ai-S	–	11/89-	39°40'	8/7	32	0.22	62mm	HN-22	CL-32 S	62	455	70.0 X 74.5	A; D	
80mm/2.8 AF	Ai-S	–	01/83-	30°20'	6/4	32	1.00	52mm	HS-7	CL-32 S	62	390	69.0 x 78	A; D; F	for F3 AF
85mm/2.0	N	175111-	04/77-09/81	28°30'	5/5	22	0.85	52mm	HS-10	CL-31 S	61	310	63.5 x 61	A; D; E; F	
85mm/2.0	Ai-S	270001-	08/81-	28°31'	5/5	22	0.85	52mm	HS-10	CL-31 S	61	310	63.5 x 61	A; D; E; F	
85mm/1.8	C	188011-284661	05/64-04/75	28°30'	6/4	22	1.00	52mm	HN-7	CL-32	62	420	72.0 x 70	A; D	
85mm/1.8	K	410001-	03/75-02/77	28°30'	6/4	22	0.45	52mm	HN-7	CL-32	62	430	70.0 x 70	A; D	
85mm/1.8 AF	AI-S	179091-	03/88-	28°30'	6/6	22	0.85	62mm	HN-23	CL-15 S	62	415	71.0 x 78.5	A; D; E; F	focused by rear
85mm/1.4	Ai-S	179091-	03/81-	28°30'	7/5	16	0.85	72mm	HN-20	CL 17	62	620	80.0 x 72	A; D; E; F	CRC
100mm/2.8 E	Ai-S	178701-	03/79-	24°30'	4/4	22	1.00	52mm	HR-5	CL-30 S	61	215	63.0 x 58	A; D; E; F	
105mm/4.5 UV	Ai-S	–	04/85-	23°20'	6/6	32	0.45	52mm	built-in	CL-33 S	62	525	69.0 x 116	A; C;	Fluorite and Quartz
105mm/4.0	A	910001-	10/69-	23°20'	5/3	32	–	52mm	HN-8	CL-31	61	230	64.0 x 55	–	Lens head only for bellows
105mm/4.0 Micro	K	174001-	05/75-	23°20'	5/3	32	0.47	52mm	built-in	CL-35 A	63	500	74.5 x 104	A; B; C; D;	
105mm/4.0 Micro	Ai-S	232001-	09/81-03/83	23°20'	5/3	32	0.47	52mm	built-in	CL-33	63	500	68.5 x 104	A; B: C; D; F	
105mm/2.8 Mlcro	Ai-S	–	03/83-	23°20'	10/9	32	0.41	52mm	HS-10	CL-33 S	63	515	66.5 x 91.5	A; D; F	CRC
105mm/2.8 Micro AF	Ai-S	–	6/90-	23°20'	9/8	32	0.314	52mm	HS-7	CL-15 S	63	555	75.0 x 104.5	A; D	CRC
105mm/2.5	A	120102-253907	02/59-03/71	23°20'	5/3	22	1.20	52mm	HS-4	CL-32	62	435	66.0 x 78	A; D	
105mm/2.5	C	407301-571564	12/70-03/75	23°20'	5/4	32	1.00	52mm	HS-8	CL-32	62	435	66.0 x 78	A; D	

All Nikon Lenses at a Glance (continued)

Lens	Type of bayonet	Serial numbers	Period of production	Angle of view	Elements/groups	Smallest aperture	Closest focusing distance	Filter size	Lens hood	Hard case	Soft pouch	Weight (g)	Dimensions (diam x length in mm)	Usable teleconverters	Special features
105mm/2.5	K	673101-	09/74- 09/81	23°20'	5/4	22	1.00	52mm	HS-8	CL-32	62	435	66.0 x 78	A; D; F	
105mm/2.5	Ai-S	890001-	08/81-	23°20'	5/4	22	1.00	52mm	built-in	CL-32	62	435	64.0 x 77.5	A; D; F	
105mm/2.0 D AF DC	Ai-S	—	09/93	20°20'	6/6	16	0.9	72mm	built-in	CL-38	63	640	79.0 x 111	A; D; E; F	rear focusing
105mm/1.8	Ai-S	179091-	03/81-	23°20'	5/5	22	1.00	62mm	built-in	CL-15 S	62	580	78.5 x 88.5	A; D; E; F	
120mm/4.0 Medical	Ai-S	180041-	02/81-	18°50'	9/6	32	1.60- 1.33	49mm	–	box	–	890	98.0 x 105	C; D	built-in ring flash
135mm/4.0	A	–	06/59-	18°	4/3	22	–	43mm	–	–	–	250	57.0 x 94	–	lens head only for bellows
135mm/3.5	A	720101- 865100	02/59- 05/69	18°	4/3	32	1.50	52mm	HS-4	CL-33	62	460	66.0 x 93.5	A; C; D	
135mm/3.5	C	865101- 141500	05/69- 06/75	18°	4/3	32	1.50	52mm	HS-8	CL-33	62	460	66.0 x 93.5	A; C D	
135mm/3.5	K	158101- 193500	05/75- 03/77	18°	4/3	32	1.50	52mm	built-in-	CL-33	62	400	65.0 x 98.5	A; C; D	
135mm/3.5	N	193501-	03/77- 09/81	18°	4/4	32	1.30	52mm	built-in-	CL-32 S	62	400	65.0 x 98.5	A; C; D	
135mm/3.5	Ai-S	290001-	09/81- 03/83	18°	4/4	32	1.30	52mm	built-in-	CL-32 S	62	400	65.0 x 98.5	A; C: D	
135mm/2.8	C	1350010 421067	11/65- 03/75	18°	4/4	22	1.50	52mm	built-in-	CL-33	62	620	72.0 x 104	A; D	
135mm/2.8	K	430001- 465000	06/75- 03/76	18°	4/4	22	1.50	52mm	built-in-	CL-33	62	620	72.0 x 104	A; D	
135mm/2.8	N	730000-1 900000	01/76- 09/81	18°	5/4	32	1.30	52mm	built-in-	CL-32 S	62	430	64.5 x 91	A; D; F	
135mm/2.8	Ai-S	900001-	09/81-	18°	5/4	32	1.30	52mm	built-in-	CL-32 S	62	430	64.5 X 91	A; D; F	
135mm/2.8 E	Ai-S	180031-	03/81- 02/83	18°	4/4	32	1.50	52mm	built-in-	CL-32 S	62	395	88.5 x 62.5	A; D; F	
135mm/2.0	K	175011- 201000	12/75- 12/81	18°	6/4	22	1.30	72mm	built-in-	CL-15 S	62	860	81.0 x 103	A; D; E; F	
135mm/2.0	Ai-S	201001-	12/81-	18°	6/4	22	1.30	72mm	built-in-	CL-15 S	62	860	81.0 x 103	A; D; E; F	
135mm/2.0 AF-DC	Ai-S	–	10/90-	18°	7/6	16	1.10	72mm	built-in-	CL-38	63	870	79.0 x 120	A; D; E; F	Optical flat front element; degree of soft-focus adjustable
180mm/2.8	C	312011- 336108	06/70- 01/74	13°40'	5/4	32	1.80	72mm	built-in-	CL-35	63	830	81.0 x 141	A; D	
180mm/2.8	K	350001- 380000	06/75- 10/81	13°40'	5/4	32	1.80	72mm	built-in-	CL-35	63	830	81.0 x 141	A; D; F	
180mm/2.8 ED	Ai-S	380001-	03/81-	13°40'	5/5	32	1.80	72mm	built-in-	CL-35	63	800	78.5 x 138	A; D; F	
180mm/2.8	Ai-S	–	09/86-	13°40'	8/6	22	1.50	72mm	built-in-	CL-38	63	750	78.5 x 144	A; D; F	black barrel
180mm/2.8	Ai-S	–	11/88-	13°40'	8/6	22	1.50	72mm	built-in-	CL-38	63	750	78.5 x 153	A; D; F	grey barrel
200mm/5.6 Medical	A	104011- 113011	11/62- 03/72	12°20'	4/4	45	3.35	38mm	–	box	–	670	80.0 x 176	–	built-in ring-flash 4-pin terminal
200mm/5.6 Medical	C	120011-	06/74- 12/79	12°20'	4/4	45	3.35	38mm	–	box	–	670	80.0 x 176	–	Sx Terminal ring flash
200mm/4.0 Micro	N	178021-	08/78- 03/82	12°20'	9/6	32	0.71	52mm	built-in-	CL-36	63	740	180.0 x 76	A; R; C; D	
200mm/4.0 Micro	Ai-S	200001-	02/82-	12°20'	9/6	32	0.71	52mm	built-in-	CL-36	63	800	180.0 x 76	A; B; C; D	
200mm/4.0	A	169211- 319959	10/61- 04/69	12°20'	4/4	32	2.00	52mm	built-in-	CL-35	63	630	163.0 x 72	A; D	
200mm/4.0	C	420001- 640000	04/69- 01/76	12°20'	4/4	32	2.00	52mm	built-in-	CL-35	63	630	163.0 x 72	A; D	

Lens	Type of bayonet	Serial numbers	Period of production	Angle of view	Elements/groups	Smallest aperture	Closest focusing distance	Filter size	Lens hood	Hard case	Soft pouch	Weight (g)	Dimensions (diam x length in mm)	Usable teleconverters	Special features
200mm/4.0	K	670003-900000	08/75-10/81	12°20'	5/5	32	2.00	52mm	built-in-	CL-13	63	530	126.0 x 68	A; D	
200mm/4.0	Ai-S	900001-	11/81-	12°20'	5/5	32	2.00	52mm	built in	CL-13	63	510	124.0 x 65	A; D	
200mm/3.5 IF-ED AF	Ai-S	–	01/83-	12°20'	8/6	32	2.00	62mm	built in	CL-35A	–	870	80.0 x 157.0	A; B; C; D	for F3 AF
200mm/2.0 IF-ED	N	176111-178500	04/77-02/82	12°20'	10/8	22	2.50	122mm	built in	CL-63	57	2300	128.0 x 214	A; C; D; E; F	
200mm/2.0 IF-ED	Ai-S	178501-	01/82-	12°20'	10/8	22	2.50	122mm	built in	Cl-63	57	2300	138.0 x 222	A; C; D; E; F	
200mm/2.0 IF-ED	Ai-S	–	03/86-	12°20'	10/8	22	2.50	filter slot	HE-4	CT-200	58	2550	132.0 x 233.5	A; C; D; E; F	
300mm/4.5	C	304501-466702	06/64-12/74	8°10'	6/5	22	4.00	72mm	built in	CL-20	–	1100	80.0 x 203	A; B; C	
300mm/4.5	K	480001-	01/75-12/81	8°10'	6/5	22	4.00	72mm	built in	CL-20 A	–	1140	78.0 x 203	A; B; C	
300mm/4.5	Ai-S	–	11/81-	8°10'	6/5	32	3.50	72mm	built in	CL-20 A	–	1200	78.0 x 203	A; B; C	
300mm/4.5 ED	K	190001-	03/77-01/79	8°10'	6/4	22	4.00	72mm	built in	CL-20 A	–	1100	78.0 x 203	A; B; C	
300mm/4.5 IF-ED	N	200001-	08/78-12/81	8°10'	7/6	32	2.50	72mm	built in	CL-36	–	990	80.0 x 200	B; C	
300mm/4.5 IF-ED	Ai-S	210001-	12/81	8°10'	7/6	32	2.50	72mm	built in	CL-36	–	990	80.0 x 200	B; C	
300mm/4.0 IF-ED	Ai-S	–	06/87-	8°10'	8/6	32	2.50	39/82 mm	built in	CL-42	–	1330	89.0 x 219	B; C	
300mm/2.8	C	603011-605100	11/71-05/76	8°10'	6/5	32	4.00	122mm	built in	–	–	2600	125.0 x 251	B; C; F	
300mm/2.8 IF-ED	N	605101-609000	11/77-01/82	8°10'	8/6	22	4.00	39/122 mm	built in	CL-63	57	2500	138.0 x 249	B; C; F	
300mm/2.8 IF-ED	Ai-S	609001-	01/82-	8°10'	8/6	22	4.00	39/122 mm	built in	CL-63	57	2500	138.0 x 249	B; C; F	
300mm/2.8 IF-ED	Ai-S	–	03/86-05/90	8°10'	8/6	22	3.00	39mm	HE-4	CT-302	58	2400	132.0 x 263	B; C; F	
300mm/2.8 IF-ED AF	Ai-S	–	11/86-11/88	8°10'	8/6	22	3.00	39mm	HE-6	CT-303	58	2700	133.0 x 263	B; C; F	
300mm/2.0 IF-ED	Ai-S	–	06/83-	8°10'	11/8	16	4.00	52mm	HE-1	CT-300	–	7100	183.0 x 339	A; B; C; E; F	Teleconverter TC-14C included
300mm/2.8 IF-ED N AF	Ai-S	–	11/88	8°10'	8/6	22	3.00	39mm	HE-6	CT-303	58	2700	133.0 x 263	B; C	
300mm/2.8 IF-ED DAF-1	Ai-S	–	09/92	8°10'	11/9	22	2.50	39mm	HK-19	CT-303	–	2900	124.0 x 241	B; C; F; G; H	
400mm/5.6	C	256031-257440	02/73-09/75	6°10'	5/3	32	5.00	72mm	built in	CL-27	57	1400	85.0 x 262	B; C	
400mm/5.6 ED	K	260001-280000	09/75-06/83	6°10'	5/3	32	5.00	72mm	built in	CL-27	57	1400	85.0 x 262	B; C	
400mm/5.6 IF-ED	N	280001-287600	08/78-01/82	6°10'	7/6	32	4.00	72mm	built in	CL-27	57	1200	85.0 x 262	B; C	
400mm/5.6 IF-ED	Ai-S	287601-	12/81-	6°10'	7/6	32	4.00	72mm	built in	CL-27	57	1200	85.0 x 262	B; C	
400mm/4.5	C	400111-	08/64-06/75	6°10'	4/4	22	5.00	52/122 mm	built in	CE-8	–	3100	135.0 x 471	–	usable only with focusing mount AU-1
400mm/4.5 IF-ED	N	175121-181500	04/76-02/82	6°10'	8/6	22	4.50	39/122 mm	built in	CL-61 A	57	2800	134.0 x 304	B; C	
400mm/3.5 IF-ED	Ai-S	181501-	01/82-	6°10'	8/6	22	4.50	39/122 mm	built in	CL-61 A	57	2800	134.0 x 304	B; C	
400mm/2.8 IF-ED	Ai-S	–	12/85-	6°10'	8/6	22	4.00	52mm	HE-3	CT-400	59	5150	172.0 x 432	B; C	

All Nikon Lenses at a Glance (continued)

Lens	Type of bayonet	Serial numbers	Period of production	Angle of view	Elements/groups	Smallest aperture	Closest focusing distance	Filter size	Lens hood	Hard case	Soft pouch	Weight (g)	Dimensions (diam x length in mm)	Usable teleconverters	Special features
400mm/2.8 IF-ED DAF-1	Ai-S	–	10/93	6°10'	10/7	22	3.30	52mm	HK-20	CT-401	–	3300	158.0 x 374	B; C; F; H	
500mm/8.0 Reflex	C	501001-	12/68-10/83	5'	5/3	8	400	39/87 mm	+	CI-23	–	1000	93.0 x 142	A; C; D	
500mm/8.0 Reflex	Ai-S	–	10/83-	5'	6/6	8	1.50	39/82 mm	HN-27	CL-39	–	840	89.0 x 116	A; C; D	
500mm/5.0 Reflex	A	171011-183318	08/61-12/70	5'	5/4	5	15.00	39mm	+	–	–	1600	125.0 x 197	B; C	
500mm/4.0 P IF-ED	Ai-S	–	04/88-	5'	8/6	22	5.00	39mm	HK-17	CT-500	59	2950	138.0 x 387	B; C	integrated CPU
600mm/5.6	C	600111-611258	08/64-01/78	4°10'	5	22	11.00/8.00	52/122 mm	built in	CE-5	–	3600	135.0 x 516	–	usable only with focusing mount AU-1
600mm/5.6 ED	K	650001	04/75-09/77	4°10'	5/4	22	11.00/8.00	52/122 mm	built in	CE-5	–	3600	135.0 x 516	–	usable only with focusing mount AU-1
600mm/5.6 IF-ED	N	176011-	04/76-04/82	4°10'	7/6	32	5.50	39/122 mm	built in	CL-62	57	2700	134.0 x 382	B; C	
600mm/5.6 IF-ED	Ai-S	178501-	03/82-	4°10'	7/6	32	5.50	39/122 mm	built in	CL-62	57	2700	134.0 x 382	B; C	
600mm/5.6 IF-ED	Ai-S	–	03/86-	4°10'	7/6	32	5.00	39mm	HE-4	CT-603	–	2800	132.0 x 395	B; C	
600mm/4.0 IF-ED	N	176121-178000	06/77-05/82	4°10'	8/6	22	6.50	39/160 mm	built in	CT-601	–	6300	177.0 x 460	B; C	Teleconverter TC-14 included
600mm/4.0 IF-ED	Ai-S	178001-	04/82-	4°10'	8/6	22	6.50	39/160 mm	built in	CT-601	–	6300	177.0 x 460	B; C	
600mm/4.0 IF-ED	Ai-S	–	03/86-	4°10'	8/6	22	6.50	39mm	HE-5	CT-602	–	5650	173.0 x 473	B; C	
600mm/4.0 IF-ED DAF-1	Ai-S	–	09/92-	4°10'	9/7	22	6.00	39mm	HK-18	CT-604	–	6050	166.0 x 417	B; C; G	
800mm/8.0	C	800111-810763	08/64-11/77	3°	5/5	22	19.00/14.00	52/122 mm	built in	CE-6	–	3500	135.0 x 711	–	usable only with focusing mount AU-1
800mm/8.0 ED	K	850001-	05/75-03/77	3°	5/5	22	19.00/14.00	52/122 mm	built in	CE-6	–	3500	135.0 x 711		usable only with focusing mount AU-1
800mm/8.0 IF-ED	N	178041-	12/78-12/81	3°	9/7	22	10.00	39/122 mm	built in	CT-1203	–	3300	134.0 x 460	B; C	
800mm/8.0 IF-ED	Ai-S	179001-	12/81-	3°	9/7	32	10.00	39/122 mm	built in	CT-1203	–	3300	134.0 x 460	B; C	
800mm/5.6 IF-ED	Ai-S	–	09/86-	3°	8/6	32	8.00	52mm	HE-3	CT-800	–	5450	163.0 x 554	B; C	
1000mm/6.3 Reflex	A	–	06/59-09/65	2°30'	3/2	6.3	30.00	built-in filter	–	–	–	9900	238.0 x 500	B; C	
1000mm/11.0 Reflex	C	111001-130886	10/65-06/76	2°30'	5/5	11	8.00	built-in filter	+	CL-24	–	1900	117.0 x 238	B; C	
1000mm/11.0 Reflex	K	142301-	06/76-	2°30'	5/5	11	8.00	39/108 mm	built in	CL-29	–	1900	119.0 x 241	B; C	
1200mm/11.0	C	120011-150000	08/64-11/77	2°	5/5	64	43.00/31.00	52/122 mm	eingep in	CE-7	–	4300	135.0 x 922	–	usable only with focusing mount AU-1
1200mm/11.0 ED	K	150001-	06/75-12/77	2°	5/5	64	43.00/31.00	52/122 mm	built in	CE-7	–	4300	135.0 x 922	–	usable only with focusing mount AU-1
1200mm/11.0 IF-ED	N	178051-	01/79-05/82	2°	9/8	32	14.00	39/122 mm	built in	CT-1203	–	3900	134.0 x 577	B; C	
1200mm/11.0 IF-ED	Ai-S	179001-	02/82-	2°	9/8	32	14.00	39/122 mm	built in	CT-1203	–	3900	134.0 x 577	B; C	
2000mm/11.0 Reflex	C	20011-	11/71	1°10'	5/5	11	18.00	built-in filter	built in	box	–	7500	262.0 x 600	B; C	
20-35mm/2.8 DAF	Ai-S	–	09/93-	94°-64°	14/11	22	0.50	77mm	HB-8	CL-38	63	585	82.0 x 94	A; D; F	aspherical element, internal focusing and zooming
24-50mm/3.3-4.5 AF	Ai-S	–	02/88-	84°-46°	9/9	22	0.50	62mm	HB-3	CL-32 S	62	375	70.5 x 75.5	A; D	Macro-focusing to 1:8 5

Lens	Type of bayonet	Serial numbers	Period of production	Angle of view	Elements/groups	Smallest aperture	Closest focusing distance	Filter size	Lens hood	Hard case	Soft pouch	Weight (g)	Dimensions (diam x length in mm)	Usable teleconverters	Special features
25-50mm/4.0	N	178041-	04/79-12/81	80°-48°	11/10	22	0.60	72mm	HK-7	CL-15 S	62	600	75.0 x 112	A; D	
25-50mm/4.0	Ai-S	201001-	11/81-03/83	80°-48°	11/10	22	0.60	72mm	HK-7	CL-15 S	62	600	75.0 x 112	A; D	
28-45mm/4.5	K	174011-	04/75-08/78	74°-50°	11/7	22	0.60	72mm	HK-1	CL-35 A	62	440	75.0 x 91	A; D	
28-50mm/3.5	Ai-S	–	01/84-	74°-46°	9/7	22	0.60	52mm	HK-12	Cl-34 A	61	395	68.5 x 75.0	A; D	Macro-focusing to 1:5 1
28-70mm/3.5-4.5 AF	Ai-S	–	06/91–09/92	74°-34°20'	8/7	22	0.39	52mm	HB-6	CL-32 S	62	350	67.5 x 71.0	A; D	aspherical glass/plastic compund element
28-70mm/3.5-4.5 DAF	Ai-S	–	09/92-	74°-34°20'	8/7	22	0.39	52mm	HB-6	CL-32 S	62	355	67.5 x 71.0	A; D	aspherical glass/plastic compund element
28-85mm/ 3.5-4.5	Ai-S	–	12/85-	74°-28°30'	15/11	22	0.80	62mm	HK-16	CL-33 S	62	510	67.0 x 97.5	A; D	Macro-focusing to 1:3.4
28-85mm/ 3.3-4.5 AF	Ai-S	–	09/86-08/90	74°-28°30'	15/11	22	0.80	62mm	HB-1	CL-33 S	62	540	71.0 x 97.5	A; D	Macro-focusing to 1:3.4
28-85mm/ 3.5/4.5 AF-N	Ai-S	–	09/90-	74°-28°30'	15/11	22	0.80	62mm	HB-1	CL-33 S	62	540	71.0 x 89.5	A; D	Macro-focusing to 1:3.4
35-70mm/3.5	N	760701-	09/77-10/81	62°-34°20'	10/9	22	1.00	72mm	HK-4	CL-33 S	62	550	75.0 x 101	A; D	
35-70mm/3.5	Ai-S	821001-	09/81-10/87	62°-34°20'	10/9	22	0.70	62mm	HN-22	CL-33 S	62	550	66.0 x 105	A; D	Macro-focusing to 1:3.9
36-72mm/3.5 E	Ai-S	1800701-	09/81-03/83	62°-33°30'	8/8	22	1.20	52mm	HK-8	CL-32 S	62	380	67.0 x 71	A; D	
35-70mm/3.3-4.5	Ai-S	–	10/84-	62°-34°20'	8/7	22	0.35	52mm	HN-2	CL-31 S	61	255	63.0 x 69	A; D	Macro-focusing to 1:4.4
35-70mm/ 3.3-4.5 AF	Ai-S	–	03/86-	62°-34°20'	8/7	22	0.35	52mm	HN-2	CL-32 S	62	275	69.0 x 70	A; D	Macro-focusing to 1:4.4
35-70mm/ 3.3-4.5 AF N	Ai-S	–	10/89-	62°-34°20'	8/7	22	0.35	52mm	HN-2	CL-32 S	62	240	66.5 x 65.5	A; D	
35-70mm/ 2.8 AF	Ai-S	–	02/88 09/92	62°-34°20'	15/12	22	0.60	62mm	HB-1	CL-33 S	62	665	72.0 x 95.0	A; D	Macro-focusing to 1:4.0
35-70mm/ 2.8 DAF	Ai-S	–	09/92	62°-34°20'	8/7	22	0.60	62mm	HB-1	CL-33 S	62	675	74.5 x 44.5	A; D; F	
35-105mm/ 3.5-4.5	Ai-S	–	01/83-	62°-23°20'	16/12	22	1.40	52mm	HK-11	CL-33 S	62	510	64.0 x 95.0	A; D	Macro-focusing to 1:4.0
35-105mm/ 3.5-4.5 AF	Ai-S	–	09/86-	62°-23°20'	16/12	22	1.40	52mm	HB-2	CL-33 S	62	460	69.0 x 95.5	A; D	Macro-focusing to 1:3.5
35-105mm/ 3.5-4.5 AF-N	Ai-S	–	06/91-	62°-23°20'	16/12	22	1.40	52mm	HB-2	CL-33 S	62	510	70.0 x 87	A; D	Push/pull type zoom
35-135mm/ 3.5-4.5	Ai-S	–	10/84-	62°-18°	15/14	22	1.50	62mm	HN-22	CL-41 S	62	600	68.0 x 112	A; D	Macro-focusing to 1:3.5
35-135mm/ 3.5-4.5 AF	Ai-S	–	09/86-09/88	62°-18°	15/12	22	1.50	62mm	HB-1	CL 41 S	62	630	72.0 x 117	A; D	Macro-focusing to 1:3.5
35-135mm/ 3.5-4.5 AF-N	Ai-S	–	09/88-	62°-18°	15/12	22	1.50	62mm	HB-1	CL-41 S	62	685	72.5 x 109	A; D	Push/pull-type zoom
35-200mm/ 3.5-4.5	Ai-S	–	12/85-	62°-12°20'	17/13	22	1.30	62mm	HK-15	CL-13 A	63	740	70.0 x 128	A; D	Macro-focusing to 1:4.0
43-86mm/3.5	C	438611-613210	02/63-03/76	53°-38°20'	9/7	22	1.20	52 mm	HN-3	CL-32	62	410	65.0 x 78	A; D	
43-86mm/3.5	K	774071-	11/75-03/82	53°-38°20'	11/8	22	1.20	52mm	HN-3	CL-32	62	450	66.0 x 81.5	A; D	
50-135mm/ 3.5	Ai-S	–	04/82-	46°-18°	16/13	32	1.30	62mm	HK-10	CL-38	63	700	71.0 x 133	A; D	Macro-focusing to 1:9.3
50-300mm/ 4.5	C	740101-765700	09/68-10/75	46°-8°10'	20/13	22	2.50	95mm	HN-11	CE-2	–	2300	98.0 x 292	A; D	
50-300mm/ 4.5	K	770401-	06/75-03/79	46°-8°10'	20/13	22	2.50	95mm	HN-11	CE 2	–	2300	98.0 x 292	A; D	
50-300mm/ 4.5 ED	N	175111-	06/77-02/82	46°-8°10'	15/11	32	2.50	95mm	HK-5	CL-64	–	2200	98.0 x 247	A; D	
50-300mm/ 4.5 ED	Ai-S	183001-	02/82-	46°-8°10'	15/11	32	2.50	95mm	HK-5	Cl-64	–	1950	98.0 x 247	A; D	

All Nikon Lenses at a Glance (continued)

Lens	Type of bayonet	Serial numbers	Period of production	Angle of view	Elements/groups	Smallest aperture	Closest focusing distance	Filter size	Lens hood	Hard case	Soft pouch	Weight (g)	Dimensions (diam x length in mm)	Usable teleconverters	Special features
70-210mm/ 4.0 E	Ai-S	–	12/81-	34°- 12°	13/9	32	1.50	62mm	HN-24	Cl-35 A	63	730	72.5 x 156	A; D	Macro-focusing to 1:5.5
70-210mm/ 4.0 AF	Ai-S	–	03/86- 09/87	34°- 12°	13/9	32	1.10	62mm	HN-24	CL-35 A	63	760	76.5 x 156	A; D	Macro-focusing to 1:3.9
70-210mm/ 4.0-5.6 AF	Ai-S	–	09/87-	34°- 12°	12/9	32	1.20	62mm	HN-24	CL-15 S	63	590	73.5 x 108	A; D	Macro-focusing to 1:4.3
75-150mm/ 3.5 E	Ai-S	1790801-	02/79- 02/83	31°40' 17°	12/9	32	1.0	62mm	HN-21	CL-15 S	63	520	65.0 x 125	A; D	
75-300mm/ 4.5-5.6 AF	Ai-S	–	02/89-	31°10°- 8°10°	13/11	32	1.50	62mm	HN-24	CL-36	–	860	72.0 x 166	A; D	Macro-focusing to 1:3.8
80-200mm/ 4.5	A/C	101911- 192626	12/69- 03/75	30°- 12°	15/10	32	1.80	52mm	HN-7	CL-35 A	63	830	74.5 x 162	A; D	
80-200mm/ 4.5	K	210001-	02/75- 08/77	30°- 12°	15/10	32	1.80	52mm	HN-7	CL-35 A	63	830	74.5 x 162	A; D	
80-200mm/ 4.5	N	760801-	07/77- 12/81	30°- 12°	12/9	32	1.80	52mm	HN-7	CL-35 A	63	750	73.0 x 162	A; D	
80-200mm/ 4.0	Ai-S	180081-	08/81-	30°- 12°	13/9	32	1.20	62mm	HN-23	CL-35 A	63	810	73.0 x 162	A; D	
80-200mm/ 2.8 ED	Ai-S	–	08/82-	30°- 12°	15/11	32	2.50	95mm	HN-25	CL-66	57	1900	99.0 X 231	A; D; F	
80-200mm/ 2.8 ED AF	Ai-S	–	02/88- 09/92	30°- 12°	16/11	32	1.50	77mm	HN-28	CL-43	–	1280	85.5 x 176	A; D	Macro-focusing to 1:5.9
80-200mm/2.8 DAF-ED	Ai-S	–	09/92-	30°- 12°	16/11	22	1.80	77mm	HB-7	CL-43 A	–	1300	87 x 187	A; D; F	New mechanical design, faster AF-operation; non-rotating filter mount
85-250mm/ 4.0-4.5	A	–	11/59- 04/61	28°30'- 10°	16/9	16	2.20* 4.00	82mm (Series 9)	+	–	–	2010	89.0 x 305	B; C	Two-ring zoom *= with close-up lens
85-250mm/ 4.0-4.5	A	157911- 174661	12/59- 04/69	28°30'- 10°	16/9	16	2.00* 4.00	82mm (Series 9)	+	–	–	2000	89.0 x 305	B; C	*= with close-up lens
85-250mm/ 4.0	C	184711- 186262	04/69- 01/73	28°30'- 10°	16/9	16	2.00* 4.00	82mm (Series 9)	+	–	–	1900	89.0 x 305	B; C	*= with close-up lens
100-300mm/ 5.6	Ai-S	–	01/84-	24°-8°	14/10	32	2.00	62mm	HN-24	CL-40	–	930	74.0 x 199	A; C; D	Macro-focusing to 1:4.4
180-600mm/ 8.0 ED	K	174041- 174700	09/75- 01/82	13°40'- 4°10'	18/11	32	2.50	95mm	HN-16	CZ-1860	–	3400	105.0 x 403	B; C	
180-600mm/ 8.0 ED	Ai-S	174701-	03/82-	13°40'- 4°10'	18/11	32	2.50	95mm	HN-16	CZ-1860	–	3600	105.0 X 403	B; C	
200-400mm/ 4.0 ED	Ai-S	–	06/83-	12°-6°	15/10	32	4.00	122mm	HE-2	–	58	3650	144.0 x 338	B: C	Slip-in filter holder
200-600mm/ 9.5-10.5	A	170111- 171709	09/61- 10/70	12°-4°	19/12	32	2.30* 4.00	82mm (Series 9)	HN-10	CE-3	–	2300	89.0 x 382	B; C	*= with close-up lens
200-600mm/ 9.5	C	290001- 290830	06/71- 10/75	12°-4°	19/12	32	2.30* 4.00	82mm (Series 9)	HN-10	CE-3	–	2300	89.0 x 382	B; C	*= with close-up lens
200-600mm/ 9.5	K	300001-	11/75- 06/81	12°-4°	19/12	32	2.30* 4.00	82mm (Series 9)	HN-10	CE-5	–	2400	89.0 x 382	B; C	*= with close-up lens
200-600mm/ 9.5	Ai-S	305001-	04/82- 03/83	12°-4°	19/12	32	2.30* 4.00	82mm (Series 9)	HN-10	CL-65	–	2500	89.0 x 382	B; C	*= with close-up lens
360-1200mm/ 11.0 ED	K	174031-	11/75- 01/81	6°50'- 2°	20/12	32	6.00	122mm	HN-17	CZ-3612	–	7100	125.0 x 704	B; C	
360-1200mm/ 11.0 ED	Ai-S	174701-	03/82-	6°50'- 2°	20/12	32	6.00	122mm	HN-17	CZ-3612	–	7900	125.0 x 704	B; C	

NOTES ON LENS TABLES

- New D-type AF lenses are equipped with modified CPU for F-90-standard cameras.
- New I-type AF lenses are equipped with built-in AF-motor for F4 and F-90-standard cameras.
- Teleconverter codes: A=TC-201; B=TC-301; C=TC-14B; D=TC-14A; E=TC-16AF[1]; F=TC-16A[2]; G=TC-14E; H=TC-20E,
  [1] Autofocus possible with F3AF (with finder DX-1), certain batches of the noted lenses not usable.
  [2] Autofocus possible with F-501/801(S)/F90/F4(S)(E); certain batches of the noted lenses not usable.

Battery requirements

Unit	Number	Duracell	Ucar	Varta	Panasonic	Seiko	Maxell	Remarks
F Photomic T; TN; FTN	2	PX-625	EPX-625	V 625 PX				
F2 Photomic; S; SB; A; AS	1	DL 1/3 N	2 L 76	CR 1/3 N				
	2	10 L 14	EPX-76	V 76 PX				
F3	1	DL 1/3 N	2 L 76	CR 1/3 N				
	2	10 L 14	EPX-76	V 76 PX				
F3 AF	1	DL 1/3 N	2 L 76	CR 1/3 N				
	2 + 2	10 L 14 + MN 2400	EPX-76 + E 92	V 76 PX + V 2400 PX				
F4	4	MN 1500	E 91	V 1500 PX				
F4 S; F4E	6	MN 1500	E 91	V 1500 PX				
Nikkormat FT; FTN	1	10 L 14	EPX-625	V 76 PX				
Nikkormat FT-2; FT-3	1	10 L 14	EPX-76	V 76 PX				
Nikkormat EL; ELW; EL-2	1	PX-28 (or Lith.)	544	V 28 PX				
FM; FM-2; FE; FE-2; FA	2	10 L 14	EPX-76	V 76 PX				
	1	DL 1/3 N	2 L 76	CR 1/3 N				
EM; FG; FG-20	2	10 L 14	EPX-76	V 76 PX				
	1	DL 1/3 N	2 L 76	CR 1/3 N				
F-301; F-501	4	MN 2400	E 92	V 2400 PX				
F-301; F-501 with MB-3	4	MN 1500	E 91	V 1500 PX				
F-401; F-401 S; F 401 X	4	MN 1500	E 91	V 1500 PX				
F-401 QD; F-401 S QD F-401 X QD	4 + 1	MN 1500 + CR 2025	E 91 + CR 2025	V 1500 PX + CR 2025				
F-601; F-601 M	1	DL-223 A			CR-P2			
F-601 Quartz-Date	1 + 1	DL 223 A + CR 2025	CR 2025	CR 2025	CR-P2 + CR 2025			
F-801 F-801 S	4	MN 1500	E 91	V 1500 PX				
F90	4	MN 1500	E 91	V 1500 PX				

Unit	Number	Duracell	Ucar	Varta	Panasonic	Seiko	Maxell	Remarks
Nikonos IV A and V	2	10 L 14	EPX-76	V 76 PX				
	1	DL 1/3 N	2 L 76	CR 1/3 N				
Nikonos RS	1	DL-223A			CR-P2			
AW-1	6	MN-1500	E 91	V 1500 PX				
DB-1	4	MN 1400	E 93	4014				
DB-2	2	MN 1500	E 91	V 1500 PX				
DB-3; DB-4	2	MN 2400	E 92	V 2400 PX				
DB-5	1 + 1	MN 1500 + CR 2025			BR-P 2/6 V			
DB-6	6	MN-1300	E 95	4020				
DL-1	1	PX-625	EPX-625	V 625 PX				
DX-1	2	MN 2400	E 92	V 2400 PX				
F-36 cordless	8	MN 1500	E 91	V 1500 PX				
F-36 External battery pack	8	MN 1400	E 93	4014				
LD-1	8	MN 1300	E 95	4020				*
LD-2	8	MN 1500	E 91	V 1500 PX				
MB-1	10	MN 1500	E 91	V 1500 PX				
MB-2	8	MN 1500	E 91	V 1500 PX				
MB-3	4	MN 1500	E 91	V 1500 PX				
MB-4	4	MN 2400	E 92	V 2400 PX				
MB-20	4	MN 1500	E 91	V 1500 PX				
MB-21; MB-23	6	MN 1500	E 91	V 1500 PX				
MB-100	20	MN 1500	E 91	V 1500 PX				
MC-20	1	CR 2032						
MD-4; MD-11 MD-12; MD-14 MD-15	8	MN 1500	E 91	V 1500 PX				
MD-E	6	MN 2400	E 92	V 2400 PX				
MF-10	2	MN 1500	E 91	V 1500 PX				
MF-11	4	MN 1500	E 91	V 1500 PX				
MF-12/14/15/16/18/19	2	10 L 14	EPX-76	V 76 PX				
MF-20; MF-22; MF-25	1	CR 2025	CR 2025	CR 2025				

Battery requirements (continued)

Unit	Number	Duracell	Ucar	Varta	Panasonic	Seiko	Maxell	Remarks
MF-21;- MF23; MF-24 MF-26	2	CR 2025	CR 2025	CR 2025				
MF-17	4	MN 1500	E 91	V 1500 PX				
MF-17	1					T2 726 SW	SR 726 SW	
ML-1 Sender	4	MN 1500	E 91	V 1500 PX				
ML-1 Receiver	1	MN 1604	522	4022				
ML-2 Set	4 each	MN 1500	E 91	V 1500 PX				
ML-3 Sender	2	MN 2400	E 92	V 2400 PX				
MT-1/2	4	MN 1500	E 91	V 1500 PX				
MW-1 Sender/ Receiver	je 8	MN 1500	E 91	V 1500 PX				
MW-2 Sender/ Receiver	je 4	MN 1500	E 91	V 1500 PX				
R8	6 + 2	MN 1500 + PX-625	E 91 + EPX-625	V 1500 PX + V 625 PX				
R10	6	MN 1500	E 91	V 1500 PX				
SB-2/3	4	MN 1500	E 91	V 1500 PX				
SB-4	2	MN 1500	E 91	V 1500 PX				
SB-7/8	4	MN 1500	E 91	V 1500 PX				
SB-9	2	MN 1500	E 91	V 1500 PX				
SB-10	4	MN 1500	E 91	V 1500 PX				
SB-11	8	MN 1500	E 91	V 1500 PX				

Unit	Number	Duracell	Ucar	Varta	Panasonic	Seiko	Maxell	Remarks
SB-12/15/16/ 17/18/19/20/ 21/22/23/ 24/25	4	MN 1500	E 91	V 1500 PX				
SB-101	8	MN 1500	E 91	V 1500 PX				
SB-102	6	MN 1400	E 93	4014				
SB-103	4	MN 1500	E 91	V 1500 PX				
SB-E	4	MN 2400	E 92	V 2400 PX				
SD-2	6	MN 1300	E 95	4020				
SD-3	1						510 Volt	
SD-4	2						240 Volt	
SD-6	1						315 Volt	
	6	MN 1500	E 91	V 1500 PX				
SD-7	6	MN 1400	E 93	4014				
SD-8	6	MN 1500	E 91	V 1500 PX				

*Rechargeable batteries cannot be used

Nikon Product Codes

A

A Extension ring 5.8mm
A2 Filter for colour photography
A12 Filter for colour photography
AC-1E Data-link card for electronic organizer
ACT Camera case for Nikon F with attached Action Finder and 50mm lens
AF-Nikkor Autofocus lens
AF-1 Gelatine filter holder 52mm diam.
AF-2 Gelatine filter holder 72mm diam.
AH-1 Grip-strap for F2 + MD-2
AH-2 Tripod adapter for MD-4/11/12/14/15
AH-3 Tripod adapter for MD-4/11/12/14/15, F-301/501
AH-4 Grip strap for F4/401/s/x/601/QD/M/801/s/90/d/s
AI Automatic indexing - standard of lens mount
AI-S Automatic indexing plus linear diaphragm operation - standard of lens mount
AM-1 Film cassette for F2 (for 36 exposures)
AN-1 Neckstrap, leather
AN-2 Neckstrap, leather
AN-3 Neckstrap, leather
AN-4B Neckstrap, leather
AN-4Y Neckstrap, nylon, black
AN-5W Neckstrap, nylon, yellow
AN-5Y Neckstrap, nylon, red
AN-6W Neckstrap, nylon, yellow
AN-6Y Neckstrap, nylon, red
AN-7 Neckstrap, nylon, black
AN-10 Neckstrap, nylon, brown-beige
AN-11 Neckstrap, nylon
AN-12 Neckstrap, nylon
AP-2 Panorama head
AR-1 Soft shutter-release button for Leica-type threading
AR-2 Cable release for Leica-type threading
AR-3 Cable release for ISO-type threading
AR-4 Double cable release for ISO/Leica type threading
AR-5 Cable release for pistol grip/Leica-typ threading
AR-6 Cable release for ISO-type threading
AR-7 Double cable release for ISI/ISO-type threading
AR-8 Adapter Leica-/ISO-type threading
AR-9 Soft shutter-release button for ISO-type threading
AR-10 Double cable release for ISO-type threading/F4-type electrical terminal
AS-1 Flash adapter ISO/F and F2
AS-2 Flash adapter SB-2/SB-7E - ISO
AS-3 Flash adapter SB2/SB-7E - F3
AS-4 Flash adapter ISO - F3
AS-5 Flash adapter SB-12/17/16A/21A - F2
AS-6 Flash adapter SB-12/17/16A/21A - ISO
AS-7 Flash adapter ISO - SB-12/17/16A/21A
AS-8 F3-type adapter for SB-16
AS-9 ISO-type adapter for SB-16
AS-10 ISO-type multiflash connector
AS-11 F3-type multiflash connector
AS-12 F3-type controller and battery compartment for SB-21
AS-14 ISO-type controller and battery compartment for SB-21
AS-15 ISO-type adapter for PC-type sync-cords
AU-1 Focusing unit for lens heads from 400mm to 1200mm
AW-1 Winder for Nikkormat ELW and EL-2
AY-1 Yoke mount for Reflex-Nikkor 2000mm/11

B

B1 Extension ring 5mm
B2 Extension ring 5.8mm
B2 Filter for colour photography
B8 Filter for colour photography
B12 Filter for colour photography
BC-6 ISO-type bulb flash unit
BC-7 F2-type bulb flash unit
BCT Blimp case for Nikon F
BD-1 Case for BC-7
BD-2 Sync-cord for BC-7
BF-1 Body cap (except for AF-bodies)
BF-1A Body cap
BF-2 Front cap for TC-300/301
BF-3 Front cap for TC-14/14B/14C
BR-1 Adapter ring for 135mm/4.0 on PB-type bellows units
BR-2 Retro-ring 52mm diam. (except for AF-SLRs)
BR-2A Retro-ring 52mm diam.
BR-3 Bayonet adapter ring 52mm diam.
BR-4 Automatic diaphragm adapter for retro-mounted lenses (except AF SLRs)
BR-5 Adapter ring 52mm - 62mm diam. for BR-2A
BR-6 Automatic diaphragm adapter for retro-mounted lenses

C

C Extension ring 10mm
CA-1 Filter case for 6 x 52mm
CA-2 Filter case for 6 x 39mm
Calypso Nikonos-model; underwater camera
CB-1 Shoulder case red-blue
CB-2 Shoulder case green
CB 3 Shoulder case beige
CE-2 Lens case for 50-300/4.5 plus body
CE-3 Lens case for 200-600/9.5 plus body
CE-5 Lens case for lens head 600mm/5.6
CE-6 Lens case for lens head 800mm/8
CE-7 Lens case for lens head 1200mm/11
CE-8 Lens case for lens head 400mm/4.5
CF-1 Camera case, semi-soft, for F2 + 50mm
CF-2 Camera case, semi-soft, for F2 + 105/2.5
CF-4 Camera case, semi-soft, for FTN - FT-3 + 50mm
CF-5 Camera case, semi-soft, for FT-3 + 105/2.5
CF-6 Action case, semi-soft, new version CF-34
CF-7 Camera case, semi soft, for FM/FE + 50mm
CF-8 Camera case, semi soft, for FM/FE + 105mm
CF-8A Front part CF-8 for 35-70/3.5
CF-9 Camera case, semi soft, for FM/FE + MD + 50mm

CF-11 Camera case, semi soft, for EM + 50mm
CF-12 Camera case, semi soft, for EM + 100mm E
CF-14 Camera case, semi soft, for EM + 36-72mm E
CF-15D Camera case rear part for FM/2/FE/2 with MD-11/12
CF-16 Camera case, semi soft, for EM + MD-E + 36-72mm E
CF-17 Camera case, semi soft, for FG + 50mm
CF-18 Camera case, semi soft, for FG + 36-72mm E
CF-18A Front part CF-18 for 35-70/3.5
CF-19D Camera case rear part for FG + MF-15
CF-20 Camera case, semi soft, for F3 + 50mm
CF-21 Camera case, semi soft, for F3 + 35-105mm
CF-21A Front part CF-21 for 35-70mm
CF-22 Camera case, semi soft, for F3 HP + 50mm
CF-23D Camera case rear part for F3 + MF-14
CF-24 Camera case, semi soft, for F3 AF + 80/2.8
CF-27 Camera case, semi soft, for FM/FE-2 + 50mm
CF-27D Camera case rear part for FM/FE-2 + MF
CF-28 Camera case, semi soft, for FM/FE-2 + 35-70/3.3-4.5
CF-28D Front part CF-27 for 35-200mm
CF-29 Camera case, semi soft, for FM/FE-2 + MD + 50mm
CF-30 Camera case, semi soft, for FA + 50mm
CF-30D Camera case rear part for FA + MF
CF-31 Camera case, semi soft, for FA + 35-70/3.5
CF-32 Camera case, semi soft, for FG-20 + 50mm
CF-33 Camera case, semi soft, for FG-20 + 35-70/3.3-4.5
CF-34 Action case, semi-soft, for SLR + 80-200mm
CF-35 Camera case, semi soft, for F-301/501 + 35-70/3.3-4.5
CF-35D Camera case rear part for F-301/501 + MF
CF-36 Camera case, semi soft, for F-301/501 + 35-70/2.8
CF-36A Front part CF-35 for 35-105mm
CF-37 Camera case, semi soft, for F-401 + 35-70/3.3-4.5
CF-37 QD Camera case, semi soft, for F-401QD + 35-70/3.3-4.5
CF-38A Front part CF-37 for 35-105mm
CF-39 Camera case, semi soft, for F-801 + 50mm
CF-39D Camera case rear part for F-801 + MF
CF-40 Camera case, semi soft, for F-801 + 35-135 AF
CF-41 Camera case, semi soft, for F4 + 35-70/3.3-4.5 AF
CF-42 Camera case, semi soft, for F4S + 135mm
CF-43 Camera case, semi soft, for F4S + 35-70/3.3-4.5
CF-100 Camera case, semi soft, for F3 + MD-4 + 35-70/3.5
CH-1 Camera case, hard, for F2 + 50mm
CH-2 Camera case, hard, for F2 + 105/2.5
CH-3 Camera case, hard, for EL + 50mm
CH-4 Camera case, hard, for F2 + 50mm
CH-5 Camera case, hard, for F2 + 105/2.5
CH-6 Camera case, hard, for Nikkormat FTN-FT3 + 50mm
CH-7 Camera case, hard, for Nikkormat FTN-FT3 + 43-86mm
CH-8 Camera case, hard, for Nikkormat EL2 + 50mm
CH-9 Camera case, hard, for Nikkormat EL2 + AW-1 + 50mm
CH-10 Camera case, hard, for Nikkormat EL2 + AW-1 +105.2.5
CH-11 Camera case, hard, for F2 + DS + 105/2.5
CK-1 Case for HK-1
CL-4 Leather lens case for 10/5.6 OP
CL-11 Leather lens case for 8/2.8
CL-12 Leather lens case for 180/2.8
CL-13 Leather lens case for 200/4
CL-14 Leather lens case for 13/5.6
CL-15 Leather lens case for 135/2
CL-15S Leather lens case for 70-210 AF
CL-17 Leather lens case for 15/3.5 & 85/1.4
CL-20 Leather lens case for 300/4.5
CL-23 Leather lens case for 500/8 C
CL-24 Leather lens case for 1000/11 C
CL-26 Leather lens case for 15/5.6
CL-27 Leather lens case for 400/5.6
CL-28 Leather lens case for 18/4
CL-29 Leather lens case for 1000/11 K
CL-30 Leather lens case for 50/1.4 & TC-201
CL-31 Leather lens case for 58/1.2 & 55/2.8
CL-31S Leather lens case for 50/1.2
CL-32 Leather lens case for 135/2.8
CL-33 Leather lens case for 35-135 + TC-301
CL-33S Leather lens case for 35-105 AF
CL-34 Leather lens case for 28 PC
CL-35 Leather lens case for 80-200/4
CL-36 Leather lens case for 300/4.5 IF-ED
CL-37 Leather lens case for 18/3.5
CL-38 Leather lens case for 180/2.8 AF
CL-39 Leather lens case for 500/8
CL-40 Leather lens case for 100-300/5.6
CL-41 Leather lens case for 35-135 AF
CL-42 Leather lens case for 300/4 AF
CL-43 Leather lens case for 80-200/2.8 AF
CL-43A Leather lens case for 80-200 AF-D
CL-50 Leather lens case for 28/3.5 & 35/2.5 UW
CL-51 Leather lens case for 80/4 UW
CL-61 Leather lens case for 400/3.5 IF-ED
CL-62 Leather lens case for 600/5.6 IF-ED
CL-63 Leather lens case for 300/2.8 IF-ED
CL-64 Leather lens case for 50-300/4.5 ED
CL-65 Leather lens case for 200-600/9.5
CL-66 Leather lens case for 80-200/2.8
COM-Nikkor Special lens
CP-1 Plastic lens case for 85/1.8
CP-2 Plastic lens case for 135/2.8
CP-3 Plastic case for 52mm filter
CP-4 Plastic case for 52mm polarizing filter
CP-5 Plastic case for 72mm filter
CP-6 Plastic case for 62mm filter
CP-7 Plastic case for AM-1
CP-8 Plastic case for 85/2
CP-9 Plastic case for 135/2.8
CRT-Nikkor Special lens
CS-F1 Soft camera case for F + 50mm
CS-F2 Soft camera case for F + 135mm
CS-F3 Soft camera case for F + 200mm
CS-4 Soft camera case for F2 + 50mm
CS-5 Soft camera case for F2 + 135/2.8
CS-6 Soft camera case for F2 + 200/4
CS-7 Soft camera case for SLR + 50mm
CS-8 Soft camera case for SLR + 55/1.2

CS-9 Soft camera case for SLR + 135/2.8

CS-10 Soft camera case for SLR + 80-200/4

CS-11 Soft camera case for EL + 50mm

CS-12 Soft camera case for F2 + 50mm

CS-13 Blimp case

CS-15 Soft camera case for F3 + 50mm

CS-16 Soft camera case for FM/FA + 35-70/3.3-4.5

CT-200 Aluminium lens case for 200/2

CT-300 Aluminium lens case for 300/2

CT-302 Aluminium lens case for 300/2.8

CT-303 Aluminium lens case for 300/2.8 AF

CT-400 Aluminium lens case for 400/2.8

CT-500 Aluminium lens case for 500/4 P

CT-601 Aluminium lens case for 600/4 (old)

CT-602 Aluminium lens case for 600/4 (new)

CT-603 Aluminium lens case for 600/5.6

CT-604 Aluminium lens case for AF 600/4I IF-ED

CT-800 Aluminium lens case for 800/5.6

CT-1203 Aluminium lens case for 800/8 and 1200/11

CTM-2 Hard camera case for FTN + 50mm

CT-MZ Hard camera case for FTN + 43-86mm

CT Hard camera case for F + 50mm

CTTZ Hard camera case for F Photomic with lenses up to 135/3.5

CTZ Hard camera case for F + 105/2.5

CZ-1860 Aluminium case for 180-600/8

CZ-3612 Aluminium case for 360-1200/11

D

D Extension ring 20mm

DA-1 Action finder for F2

DA-2 Action finder for F3

DA-20 Action finder for F4/S/E

DB-1 External battery compartment for DS-units

DB-2 External battery compartment for SLRs from EM to F3

DB-3 External battery compartment for MF-12

DB-4 External battery compartment for DX-1

DB-5 External battery compartment for F-801

DB-6 External battery compartment for F4 (with MC-28) and F90 (with MC-29)

DE-1 Prism finder for F2

DE-2 Prism finder for F3

DE-3 Prism finder for F3 HP

DE-4 Prism finder for F3 T

DE-5 Prism finder for F3 P

DF-1 Fisheye finder for 6/5.6 & 10/5.6 OP

DF-10 Finder for UW 80/4

DF-11 Finder for UW 15/2.8

DF-12 Finder for UW 20/2.8

DG-2 Viewfinder magnifier

DH-1 Charging unit for DN-1

DK-1 Eyepiece adapter HP-type finders - normal diameter accessories

DK-2 Eyecup for F3 HP/F4

DK-3 Eyecup for SLRs from FM to FA

DK-4 Eyecup for F2 and F3

DK-5 Eyepiece cover for SLRs from EM to F-601/QD/M

DK-6 Eyecup for F-801/s/F90

DK-7 Eyepiece adapter for F-801/s/F90/F4

DK-8 Eyepiece cover for F-801/s

DL-1 Illuminator for DP-1/DP-11/Photomic FTN

DM-1 Connecting cord MA-4 to DS-units

DN-1 NC-type rechargeable battery for DS-units

DP-1 Metering finder for F2 Photomic

DP-2 Metering finder for F2 S

DP-3 Metering finder for F2 SB

DP-11 Metering finder for F2 A

DP-12 Metering finder for F2 AS

DP-20 Metering finder for F4

DR-2 Right-angle finder attachment

DR-3 Right-angle finder attachment

DS-1 Automatic aperture control unit for F2

DS-1H Case for DS unit

DS-2 Automatic aperture control unit for F2

DS-12 Automatic aperture control unit for F2 (AI-version)

DW-1 Waist-level finder for F2

DW-2 6x Magnification finder for F2

DW-3 Waist-level finder for F3

DW-4 6x Magnification finder for F3

DW-20 Waist-level finder for F4

DW-21 6x Magnification finder for F4

DX-1 Autofocus viewfinder for F3 AF

E

E-Series Group of economically priced lenses

E-2 Extension ring 14mm

ED-Nikkor Lenses with elements made of special optical glass

EL SLR camera

EL-2 SLR camera

ELW SLR camera

EM SLR camera

ES-1 Slide-copying adapter for 55mm Micro-Nikkor

F

F SLR camera

F Photomic SLR camera with metering finder (also F Photomic T/TN/FTN

F-36 Motor-drive for Nikon F

F-250 Bulk-film magazine with motor-drive for Nikon F

F2 SLR camera

F2 Photomic SLR camera with DP-1

F2 S SLR camera with DP-2

F2 SB SLR camera with DP-3

F2 A SLR camera with DP-11

F2 AS SLR camera with DP-12

F2 H High-speed version of Nikon F2

F2 T Titanium version of Nikon F2

F3 SLR camera

F3 HP High-eyepoint version of Nikon F3

F3 T Titanium version of Nikon F3

F3 AF AF version of Nikon F3

F3 P Limited edition prof/press version of F3

F4 AF-SLR camera

F4S AF-SLR camera

F4E AF-SLR camera

F-301 SLR camera

F-401 AF-SLR camera

F-401 QD F-401 data version

F-401s AF-SLR camera

F-401s QD F-401s data version

F-401x AF-SLR camera

F-401x QD F-401x data version

F-501 AF-SLR camera

F-601 AF-SLR camera

F-601M SLR camera

F-601 QD F-601 data version

F-801 AF-SLR camera
F-801s AF-SLR camera
F90 AF-SLR camera
F90d F90 data version
F90s F90 with multifunction back
FA SLR camera
FB-3 Compartment case
FB-4 Compartment case
FB-5 Compartment case
FB-6 Compartment case
FB-7 Compartment case
FB-8A Compartment case
FB-9 Compartment case
FB-10 Compartment case
FB-11A Compartment case
FB-12 Compartment case
FB-13 Compartment case
FB-14 Compartment case
FB-15 Compartment case
FB-16 Compartment case
FB-17 Compartment case
FB-E Compartment case for E-system
FE SLR camera
FE-2 SLR camera
FG SLR camera
FG-20 SLR camera
FM SLR camera
FM-2 SLR camera
FM-2n SLR camera
FS SLR camera
FT SLR camera
FT-2 SLR camera
FT-3 SLR camera
FTN SLR camera

G

GN-Nikkor Special lens with guide number coupling

H

HB-1 Lenshood for AF 28-85 & AF 35-135
HB-2 Lenshood for AF 35-105
HB-3 Lenshood for AF 24-50
HB-4 Lenshood for AF 20/2.8
HE-1 Lenshood extension for 300/2
HE-2 Lenshood extension for 200-400/4
HE-3 Lenshood extension for 400/2.8 & 800/5.6
HE-4 Lenshood extension for 200/2, 300/2.8 & 600/5.6
HE-5 Lenshood extension for 600/4
HE-6 Lenshood extension for AF 300/2.8
HK-1 Lenshood for 28-45/4.5
HK-2 Lenshood for 24.2
HK-3 Lenshood for 20/4
HK-4 Lenshood for 35-70 (72mm diam.)
HK-5 Lenshood for 50-300mm ED
HK-6 Lenshood for 20/3.5 (52mm diam.)
HK-7 Lenshood for 25-50/4
HK-8 Lenshood for 36-72mm E
HK-9 Lenshood for 18/3.5
HK-10 Lenshood for 50-135/3.5
HK-11 Lenshood for 35-105/3.5-4.5
HK-12 Lenshood for 28-50/3.5
HK-14 Lenshood for 20/2.8
HK-15 Lenshood for 35-200/3.5-4.5
HK-16 Lenshood for 28-85/3.5-4.5
HK-17 Lenshood for 500/4 P
HK-18 Lenshood for AF-I 600/4D
HK-19 Lenshood for AF-I 300/2.8D
HK-20 Lenshood for AF-I 400/2.8D
HN-1 Lenshood for 24/2.8 & 35 PC
HN-2 Lenshood for 28/2.8 & 35-70/3.3-4.5
HN-3 Lenshood for 35/1.4, 35/2, 35/2.8 & 55/2.8
HN-4 Lenshood for 45/2.8 GN
HN-5 Lenshood for 50/1.4
HN-6 Lenshood for 55/1.2
HN-7 Lenshood for 85/1.8 & 80-200/4.5
HN-8 Lenshood for 105/2.5
HN-9 Lenshood for 28/3.5 PC
HN-10 Lenshood for 200-600/9.5
HN-11 Lenshood for 50-300/4.5
HN-12 Lenshood for 52mm polarizing filter
HN-13 Lenshood for 72mm polarizing filter
HN-14 Lenshood for 20/4
HN-15 Lenshood for 18/4
HN-16 Lenshood for 180-600/8
HN-17 Lenshood for 360-1200/11
HN-20 Lenshood for 85/1.4
HN-21 Lenshood for 75-150 E
HN-22 Lenshood for 35-135 & 55/2.8 AF
HN-23 Lenshood for 80-200/4 & 85/1.8 AF
HN-24 Lenshood for 70-210 AF & E and 100-300/5.6
HN-25 Lenshood for 80-200/2.8 ED
HN-26 Lenshood for 62mm polarizing filter
HN-27 Lenshood for 500/8
HN-28 Lenshood for 80-200/2.8 AF
HN-29 Lenshood for 77mm polarizing filter
HP High Eyepoint F3
HR-1 Lenshood for 50/1.4 & 1.8
HR-4 Lenshood for 35mm & 50mm Series-E
HR-5 Lenshood for 100/2.8 E
HR-6 Lenshood for 28/2.8
HS-1 Lenshood for 50/1.4 C
HS-2 Lenshood for 50/2 C
HS-3 Lenshood for 55/1.2
HS-4 Lenshood for 105/2.5 C
HS-5 Lenshood for 50/1.4 K
HS-6 Lenshood for 50/1.8 & 50/2 Ai
HS-7 Lenshood for 50/1.4 AF
HS-8 Lenshood for 105/2.5 & 135/3.5 C
HS-9 Lenshood for 50/1.4 AI-S
HS-10 Lenshood for 85/2
HS-11 Lenshood for 50/1.8
HS-12 Lenshood for 50/1.2
HS-14 Lenshood for 105/2.8 Micro

K

K1 K-series extension ring No.1
K2 K-series extension ring No.2
K3 K-series extension ring No.3
K4 K-series extension ring No.4
K5 K-series extension ring No.5

L

L1A Skylight filter
L1BC Skylight filter
LA-1 AC/DC-unit for Medical-Nikkor 200/5.6 & SM-2/SR-2
LA-2 AC/DC-unit for Medical-Nikkor 120/4 & SB-21
LD-1 Battery case for Medical-Nikkor 200/5.6 & SM-2/SR-2

LD-2 Battery case for Medical-Nikkor 120/4 & SB-21
LF-1 Rear lens cap
LF-2 Rear lens cap for 6/5.6 & 10/5.5
LW-Nikkor Nikonos lens

M

M Rangefinder camera
M2 Extension ring 27.5mm
MA-1 AC/DC-unit for F-36 motor
MA-2 AC/DC-unit for MD-1/2/3 motor
MA-3 Blimp case for MB-1
MA-4 AC/DC-unit for MD-1/2/3/4 & DS automatic aperture control unit
MB-1 Battery compartment for MD-1/2/3 (15v)
MB-2 Battery compartment for MD-1/2/3 (12v)
MB-3 Battery compartment for F-301/501 (AA)
MB-4 Battery compartment for F-301/501 (AAA)
MB-20 Battery compartment for F4
MB-21 Battery compartment for F4S
MB-22 Battery compartment for external power supply for F4/F4S
MB-23 Battery compartment for F4S/MF-24
MB-100 Battery compartment for MD-100 (30v)
MC-1 Remote control cord for MD-1/2
MC-2 Connecting cord MA-2/4 MD-1/2/3
MC-3 Connecting cord Pistol grip II MD-1/2/4/11/12/15
MC-3A Connecting cord Pistol grip II F-301/501/801/s/F4S/E
MC-4 Connecting cord with banana plugs MD-1/2/3/4/11/12/15
MC-4A Connecting cord with banana plugs F-301/501/801/F4S
MC-5 Connecting cord MT-1 MD-1/2/3/4/11/12
MC-6 Triggering cord for MF-10/11
MC-7 Connecting cord MD-1/2/3 MB-1/2
MC-8 Connecting cord ML-1 MD-1/2/3/4/11/12
MC-8A Connecting cord ML-1 F-301/501/801/F4S
MC-9 Connecting cord SB-6 F-36
MC-10 Remote control cord for MD-3/11/12
MC-11 Connecting cord MA-4 MD-4
MC-11A Connecting cord MA-4 MD-4
MC-12 Remote control cord for MD 3/4/11/12/15 & F-301/501/801/F4S
MC-12A Remote control cord for MD-3/4/11/12/15 & F-301/501/801/F4S
MC-14 Triggering cord for MF-4
MC-15 Connecting cord external power supply MF-17
MC-16 Connecting cord MT-2 MD-1/2/3/4/11/12/15
MC-16A Connecting cord MT-2 F-301/501/801/F4
MC-17 Connecting cord for simultaneous release 3m MD-4 MD-3/4/11/12/15; F-301/501/801/F4S
MC-17S Connecting cord for simultaneous release 0.3m MD-4 MD-3/4/11/12/15; F-301/501/801/F4S
MD-1 Motor-drive for F2
MD-2 Motor-drive for F2
MD-3 Motor-drive for F2
MD-4 Motor-drive for F3
MD-11 Motor-drive for FM, FE, FA
MD-12 Motor-drive for FM, FE, FA
MD-14 Motor-drive for EM, FG-20, FG
MD-15 Motor-drive for FA
MD-100 Motor-drive for F2 High Speed
MD-E Motor-drive for EM, FG-20, FG
Medical-Nikkor Macro lens with built-in ring-flash
MF-1 Bulk-film magazine (250 expos.) for F2
MF-2 Bulk-film magazine (750 expos.) for F2
MF-3 Rewind stop-back for MD-2
MF-4 Bulk-film magazine (250 expos.) for F3
MF-6 Rewind stop-back for MD-4
MF-6B Rewind stop-back for MD-4
MF-10 Data-back for F2 Data
MF-11 Bulk-film and data-back for F2
MF-12 Data-back for FM/FE
MF-14 Data-back for F3
MF-15 Data-back for FG
MF-16 Data-back for FM-2, FE-2, FA
MF-17 Bulk-film and data-back for F3
MF-18 Data-back for F3 with MD-4
MF-19 Multi-function back for F-301/501
MF-20 Data-back for F-801/s
MF-21 Multi-function back for F-801/s
MF-22 Data-back for F4/S/H
MF-23 Multi-function back for F4/S/H
MF-24 Bulk-film and data-back for F4
MH-1 Recharging unit for 2 x MN-1
MH-2 Recharging unit for 1 x MN-2
MH-20 Recharging unit for 1 x MN-20
MH-100 Recharging unit for 4 x MN-1
Micro-Nikkor Special lens for close-ups
MK-1 Firing rate converter for MD-4
ML-1 Wireless remote control unit
MN-1 NC-battery unit for MB-1/2
MN-2 NC-battery unit for MD-4
MN-20 NC-battery unit for MB-23
MR-1 Terminal release (Leica-type thread)
MR-2 Terminal release (Leica-type thread)
MR-3 Terminal release (ISO)
MS-1 Battery clip for MB-1
MS-2 Battery clip for MB-2, SB-2/3/7/8/10
MS-3 Battery clip for MD-4
MS-4 Battery clip for MD-14/15
MS-5 Battery clip for SB-16/103
MS-6 Battery clip for SB-15/17
MS-7 Battery clip for F-801
MS-8 Battery clip for F90/d/s
MS-21 Battery clip for MB-21
MS-23 Battery clip for MB-23
MT-1 Intervalometer for motor-drives (except MD-E/14) and F-301/501/801/s, F90 (with MC-25), F4S/E
MT-2 as MT-1
MW-1 Wireless remote control unit for MD-SLR (except MD-E/14)
MW-2 as MW-1
MZ-1 10.5m Film cassette for MF-1/4/11/17/24
MZ-2 30m Film cassette for MF-1/4/11/17/24

N

N2000 F-301 in N. America
N2020 F-501 in N. America
N4004 F-401 in N. America

N4004s	F-401s in N. America
N5005	F-401x in N. America
N6000	F-601 in N. America
N6006	F-601M in N. America
N8008	F-801 in N. America
N8008s	F-801s in N. America
N90	F90 in U.S.A.
ND2	Neutral density filter - 1EV
ND4	Neutral density filter - 2EV
ND8	Neutral density filter - 3EV
ND400	Neutral density filter - 10EV
N-F-Adapter	Adapter rangefinder lenses to F-bayonet
Nikkor	Nikon brand name for lenses
Nikkormat	SLR camera, models EL, EL-2, ELW, FS, FT, FT-2, FT-3, FTN
Nikonos	Nikon brand name for underwater cameras, models II, III, IVA, V, RS
No.0	Close-up lens +0.7 dpt. 52mm
No.1	Close-up lens 1.5 dpt. 52mm
No.2	Close-up lens 3.0 dpt. 52mm
No.3T	Close-up lens 1.5 dpt. 52mm
No.4T	Close-up lens 2.9 dpt. 52mm
No.5T	Close-up lens 1.5 dpt. 62mm
No.6T	Close-up lens 2.9 dpt. 62mm
No.51	Soft lens pouch for up to 55/1.2
No.52	Soft lens pouch for up to 135/2.8
No.53	Soft lens pouch for up to 200/4
No.54	Soft lens pouch for up to 55/1.2
No.55	Soft lens pouch for up to 135/2.8
No.57	Front lens cap 300/2.8 - 600/5.6
No.58	Front lens cap 200 - 400/4
No.59	Front lens cap 400/2.8
No.61	Soft lens pouch for 85/2 or TC-201
No.62	Soft lens pouch for 35-70/3.6 or TC-301
No.63	Soft lens pouch for 80-200/4
Noct-Nikkor	Special lens for available-light photography

O

O56	Orange filter
OM-9	Compartment case
OM-10	Compartment case
OP-Nikkor	Fisheye lens 10/5.6

P

PA-1	Wooden case for reproduction unit PF-2
PA-2	Baseboard for PF-2
PA-3	Table clamp for PF-2
PA-4	Camera adapter for F-801 and PF-4
PB-1	Bellows unit
PB-2	Bellows unit
PB-3	Bellows unit
PB-4	Bellows unit
PB-5	Bellows unit
PB-6	Bellows unit
PB-6D	Bellows spacer
PB-6E	Bellows extension unit
PB-6M	Macro copy stand
PC-3	Table clamp for PF-3/4
PC-Nikkor	Shift lens for perspective control
PF-1	Reproduction stand
PF-2	Reproduction stand
PF-3	Reproduction stand
PF-4	Reproduction stand
PG-1	Focusing stage
PG-2	Focusing stage
PH-3	Camera cradle for PF-3
PH-4	Camera cradle for PF-3/4
PK-1	Automatic extension ring 8mm
PK-2	Automatic extension ring 14mm
PK-3	Automatic extension ring 27.5mm
PK-11	Automatic extension ring (AI) 8mm
PK-11A	Automatic extension ring (AI) 8mm for AF-SLR
PK-12	Automatic extension ring (AI) 14mm
PK-13	Automatic extension ring (AI) 27.5mm
PL-3	Illumination unit for PF-3/4
PL-3A	Attachment adapter for PL-3
PN-1	Automatic extension ring 52.5mm
PN-11	Automatic extension ring (AI) 52.5mm
PS-4	Slide copying adapter for PB-4/5
PS-5	Slide copying adapter for PB-5
PS-6	Slide copying adapter for PB-6

R

R60	Red filter

S

SA-1	AC/DC-unit for SB-1
SA-2	AC/DC-unit for SB-2/3
SA-3	AC/DC-unit for SB-6
SB-1	Grip-type flash unit GN36, cord connected
SB-2	Flash unit, GN25, for F/F2
SB-3	Flash unit, GN25, ISO-type mount
SB-4	Flash unit, GN16, ISO-type mount
SB-5	Grip-type flash unit, GN32, cord connected
SB-6	Stroboscopic flash unit, GN45, cord connected
SB-7E	Flash unit, GN25, for F/F2
SB-8E	Flash unit, GN25, ISO-type mount
SB-9	Flash unit, GN14, ISO-type mount
SB-10	Flash unit, GN25, ISO-type mount
SB-11	TTL flash unit, GN36, cord connected
SB-12	TTL flash unit, GN25, for F3
SB-14	TTL flash unit, GN32, cord connected
SB-15	TTL flash unit, GN25, ISO-type mount
SB-16A	TTL flash unit, GN32, for F3
SB-16B	TTL flash unit, GN32, ISO-type mount
SB-17	TTL flash unit, GN25, for F3
SB-18	TTL flash unit, GN20, ISO-type mount
SB-19	Flash unit, GN20, ISO-type mount
SB-20	AF-TTL flash unit, GN30, ISO-type mount
SB-21A	TTL-Macro-flash unit, GN16, for F3
SB-21B	TTL-Macro-flash unit, GN16, ISO-type mount
SB-22	AF-TTL flash unit, GN25, ISO-type mount
SB-23	AF-TTL flash unit, GN20, ISO-type mount
SB-24	AF-TTL flash unit, GN36, ISO-type mount
SB-25	AF-TTL flash unit, GN36, ISO-type mount
SB-101	UW-flash unit, GN32, for Nikonos III, IVa
SB-102	TTL-UW-flash unit, GN32, for Nikonos III, IVa, V
SB-103	TTL-UW-flash unit, GN20, for Nikonos V
SB-104	TTL-UW-flash unit, GN32, for Nikonos RS
SB-140	UV/IR-flash unit, GN30, cord connected
SB-E	Flash unit, GN17, ISO-type mount
SC-2	Release button for MD-1/2
SC-3	Release button for MD-1/2
SC-4	Flash-ready light adapter for F2 Photomic - SB-2/3
SC-5	Synchro-cord SB-2/3/5/6, 15cm

SC-6	Synchro-cord 1m
SC-7	Adapter cord SB-2/3/5/6 - 25cm
SC-8	Adapter cord SB-4 cord
SC-9	Extension cord for SU-1
SC-10	Adapter cord SB FT/FTN
SC-11	Synchro-cord 30cm
SC-12	TTL-connecting cord SB-11/14/140 F3
SC-13	Extension cord SU-2/3
SC-14	TTL-extension cord for F3
SC-15	Synchro-cord 1m
SC-16	Sync-connecting cord 1m
SC-17	Multiflash connecting cord 1m, with ISO-type shoe and foot
SC-18	Multiflash connecting cord 1,5m
SC-19	Multiflash connecting cord 3m
SC-20	Sync-connecting cord for Medical 120/4
SC-21	Power supply cord for Medical and SB-21 - LA-2/LD-2
SC-22	Sync-connecting cord Medical 120/4 ISO-type mount
SC-23	TTL-sync cord with ISO-type foot for SB-11/14/140
SC-24	TTL-sync connecting cord for DW-20/21 - TTL-flash units
SC-100	Double TTL-sync cord for SB-102/103/104
SCT	Camera case for F plus 50mm
SD-2	Battery pack for SB-1
SD-3	Battery for SB-1
SD-4	Battery for SB-5
SD-5	Compartment for rechargeable battery for SB-6
SD-6	Battery for SB-11/14/140
SD-7	Battery pack for SB-11/14/20/22/24/140
SD-8	Battery pack for SB-20/21/22/24/25
SE-2	Extension cord for SB-1/2/3/7.8, 5m
SF-1	Flash-ready light for SB-1/2/3/5/6/7/8, SR-1/2
SH-1	Charging unit for SN-1
SH-2	Charging unit for SN-2
SH-3	Charging unit for SN-3
SH-104	Charging unit for SN-104
SK-2	Bracket for SB-1
SK-3	Bracket for SB-5
SK-4	Bracket for SB-11
SK-5	Bracket for SB-14/140
SK-101	Bracket for SB-101
SK-104	Bracket set for SB-104
SK-104A	Flash-head mounting arm for SB-104
SK-104B	Bracket for SB-104
SK-104C	Flash-head mounting arm for SB-102/103
SK-104E	Extension arm for SB-104
SK-104W	Double bracket for SB-104
SL-1	Focus-stop ring for AF-lenses 52mm diam.
SL-2	Focus-stop ring for AF-lenses 62mm diam.
SM-1	Ringlight for retro-mounted lenses, cord connected
SM-2	Ringlight for retro-mounted lenses, cord connected
SN-1	Rechargeable NC-battery for SB-1
SN-2	Rechargeable NC-battery for SB-5
SN-3	Rechargeable NC-battery for SD-5
SN-104	Rechargeable NC-battery for SH-104
SR-1	Ringlight, GN16, cord connected
SR-2	Ringlight, GN16, cord connected
SS-1	Soft case for SB-1
SS-2	Soft case for SB-2/3
SS-3	Soft case for SB-4
SS-7	Soft case for SB-7/8
SS-9	Soft case for SB-9
SS-15	Soft case for SB-15
SS-16	Soft case for SB-16 A/B
SS-17	Soft case for SB-17/AS-12/14
SS-18	Soft case for SB-18/19
SS-20	Soft case for SB-20
SS-21	Soft case for SB-21
SS-22	Soft case for SB-22
SS-23	Soft case for SB-23
SS-24	Soft case for SB-24
SS-101	Soft case for SB-101/102/103
SU-1	External sensor for SB-5/6
SU-2	External sensor for SB-11/14
SU-3	External sensor for SB-11/14/140
SU-101	External sensor for SB-101/102
SW-1	Wide adapter for SB-2/3
SW-2	Wide adapter for SB-7/8E/10
SW-3	Wide adapter for SB-11
SW-4	Wide adapter for SB-12
SW-5	Wide adapter for SB-14
SW-6	Wide adapter for SB-15/17
SW-7	Wide adapter for SB-16A/B
SW-8	Wide adapter for SB-21A/B
SW-101	Wide adapter for SB-101
SW-102	Wide adapter for SB-102
SW-103	Wide adapter for SB-103

T

TC-1	2x-Converter
TC-2	2x-Converter
TC-14	1.4x-Converter
TC-14A	1.4x-Converter
TC-14B	1.4x-Converter
TC-14C	1.4x-Converter
TC-14E	1.4x-AF-Converter
TC-16	1.6x-Converter
TC-16A	1.6x-Converter
TC-20E	2x-Converter
TC-200	2x-Converter
TC-201	2x-Converter
TC-300	2x-Converter
TC-301	2x-Converter

U

UR-1	Filter adapter 72-62mm
UR-2	Filter adapter for UV-Nikkor 105/4.5
UR-3	Adapter ring SB-21 - 60/2.8 AF
UV-Nikkor	Special lens for UV- and IR-photography
UW-Nikkor	Underwater lens

X

X0	Light green filter
X1	Dark green filter

Y

Y44	Light yellow filter
Y48	Medium yellow filter
Y52	Dark yellow filter

Index

Notes